Long-Term Care around the World

NBER
NATIONAL BUREAU *of* ECONOMIC RESEARCH

National Bureau of Economic Research
Conference Report

NBER

NATIONAL BUREAU *of* ECONOMIC RESEARCH

Long-Term Care around the World

Edited by **Jonathan Gruber and Kathleen McGarry**

The University of Chicago Press

Chicago and London

The University of Chicago Press, Chicago 60637
The University of Chicago Press, Ltd., London

Published 2025
Printed in the United States of America

34 33 32 31 30 29 28 27 26 25   1 2 3 4 5

ISBN-13: 978-0-226-83843-4 (cloth)
ISBN-13: 978-0-226-84039-0 (e-book)

DOI: https://doi.org/10.7208/chicago/9780226840390.001.0001

Library of Congress Cataloging-in-Publication Data

Names: Gruber, Jonathan, editor. | McGarry, Kathleen, editor.
Title: Long-term care around the world / edited by Jonathan Gruber and Kathleen McGarry.
Other titles: National Bureau of Economic Research conference report.
Description: Chicago : The University of Chicago Press, 2025. | Series: National Bureau of Economic Research conference report | Includes bibliographical references and index.
Identifiers: LCCN 2024039584 | ISBN 9780226838434 (cloth) | ISBN 9780226840390 (ebook)
Subjects: LCSH: Older people—Long-term care—Developed countries—Longitudinal studies. | Long-term care of the sick—eveloped countries—Longitudinal studies. | Older people—Long-term care—Developed countries—Costs—Longitudinal studies. | Long-term care of the sick—Developed countries—Costs—Longitudinal studies.
Classification: LCC HV1451 .L66 2025 | DDC 362.609172/4—dc23/eng/20241015
LC record available at https://lccn.loc.gov/2024039584

♾ This paper meets the requirements of ANSI/NISO Z39.48-1992 (Permanence of Paper).

National Bureau of Economic Research

Relation of the Directors to the Work and Publications of the NBER

1. The object of the NBER is to ascertain and present to the economics profession, and to the public more generally, important economic facts and their interpretation in a scientific manner without policy recommendations. The Board of Directors is charged with the responsibility of ensuring that the work of the NBER is carried on in strict conformity with this object.

2. The President shall establish an internal review process to ensure that book manuscripts proposed for publication DO NOT contain policy recommendations. This shall apply both to the proceedings of conferences and to manuscripts by a single author or by one or more co-authors but shall not apply to authors of comments at NBER conferences who are not NBER affiliates.

3. No book manuscript reporting research shall be published by the NBER until the President has sent to each member of the Board a notice that a manuscript is recommended for publication and that in the President's opinion it is suitable for publication in accordance with the above principles of the NBER. Such notification will include a table of contents and an abstract or summary of the manuscript's content, a list of contributors if applicable, and a response form for use by Directors who desire a copy of the manuscript for review. Each manuscript shall contain a summary drawing attention to the nature and treatment of the problem studied and the main conclusions reached.

4. No volume shall be published until forty-five days have elapsed from the above notification of intention to publish it. During this period a copy shall be sent to any Director requesting it, and if any Director objects to publication on the grounds that the manuscript contains policy recommendations, the objection will be presented to the author(s) or editor(s). In case of dispute, all members of the Board shall be notified, and the President shall appoint an ad hoc committee of the Board to decide the matter; thirty days additional shall be granted for this purpose.

5. The President shall present annually to the Board a report describing the internal manuscript review process, any objections made by Directors before publication or by anyone after publication, any disputes about such matters, and how they were handled.

6. Publications of the NBER issued for informational purposes concerning the work of the Bureau, or issued to inform the public of the activities at the Bureau, including but not limited to the NBER Digest and Reporter, shall be consistent with the object stated in paragraph 1. They shall contain a specific disclaimer noting that they have not passed through the review procedures required in this resolution. The Executive Committee of the Board is charged with the review of all such publications from time to time.

7. NBER working papers and manuscripts distributed on the Bureau's web site are not deemed to be publications for the purpose of this resolution, but they shall be consistent with the object stated in paragraph 1. Working papers shall contain a specific disclaimer noting that they have not passed through the review procedures required in this resolution. The NBER's web site shall contain a similar disclaimer. The President shall establish an internal review process to ensure that the working papers and the web site do not contain policy recommendations, and shall report annually to the Board on this process and any concerns raised in connection with it.

8. Unless otherwise determined by the Board or exempted by the terms of paragraphs 6 and 7, a copy of this resolution shall be printed in each NBER publication as described in paragraph 2 above.

Contents

Acknowledgments

We are grateful to all project participants for their comments and assistance. Please see individual country chapters for important notes on data access and funding sources. We also gratefully acknowledge support for this research from the National Institute on Aging of the National Institutes of Health under grant number P30-AG012810 for support with the overall project.

Introduction

Jonathan Gruber, Kathleen McGarry,
and Charles Hanzel

The developed world is in the midst of an enormous demographic transition, with life expectancy increasing and fertility falling, leading to a rapid aging of the population. This transition has a wide variety of implications for all nations in a variety of areas. Health care costs rise with age and thus with the aging of the population, and are becoming the leading source of spending for governments around the world. Pension funding typically depends on the ratio of workers to the retired, a ratio that is shrinking rapidly. And the aging of the population threatens the supply of an adequate workforce to meet the needs of society. Chief among the numerous important issues arising from the aging of the population is the increase in demand for long-term care services for the growing population of the elderly.

There is substantial variation across countries in how long-term care services are provided and paid for. But while considerable attention has been paid to cross-country differences in the provision of acute health care

Jonathan Gruber is the Ford Professor of Economics and head of the Economics Department at the Massachusetts Institute of Technology, and a research associate of the National Bureau of Economic Research.

Kathleen McGarry is a professor in and chair of the Department of Economics at Stony Brook University, a professor of economics at the University of California, Los Angeles, and a research associate of the National Bureau of Economic Research.

Charles Hanzel is a PhD student in economics at Northwestern University.

This paper summarizes lessons from the 10 individual chapters in the volume *Long-Term Care around the World*. We are grateful to all project participants for their comments and assistance. Please see individual country chapters for important notes on data access and funding sources. We also gratefully acknowledge support for this research from the National Institute on Aging of the National Institutes of Health under grant number P30-AG012810 for support with the overall project. For acknowledgments, sources of research support, and disclosure of the authors' material financial relationships, if any, please see https://www.nber.org/books-and-chapters/long-term-care-around-world/introduction-long-term-care-around-world.

and pensions, there has been far less attention paid to the heterogeneity in the nature of long-term care. This omission is unfortunate because countries are at very different points in their demographic trajectories and have approached the financing of long-term care in very different ways—for example in terms of the use of formal versus informal care, and the use of home care versus nursing homes. These different systems may perform very differently in terms of how effectively long-term care is provided and how well it meets the needs of the aging population. It ought therefore to be possible to learn much about how best to provide this care through international comparisons.

This volume and the work that underlies it aim to fill that void in providing a summary of long-term care programs across a set of 10 nations, highlighting the similarities and differences, and aiding in our understanding of how to provide care for our elderly populations.

We view this volume as exceptionally timely in that countries are nearly all considering changes in their long-term care systems yet lack information on how well various policies serve the needs of their populations.

The volume is the work of a group of experts on long-term care drawn from 10 countries: Canada, Denmark, England, Germany, Italy, Japan, the Netherlands, Singapore, Spain, and the United States. This set of countries represents developed economies of varying sizes, geographic locations, and industrial mixes, and with very different structures for dealing with current long-term care as well as other health needs. Yet despite these differences, they all face the common issue of rapidly aging populations and a growing need to care for those populations. These scholars worked together over the course of two years to compile comparable statistics across countries, each focusing on their home populations. In undertaking these activities these researchers drew on original analyses of survey data, published studies, and government statistics. This book includes 10 chapters, which represent the significant efforts of each of the 10 teams to document the long-term care systems in their countries.

In this introductory chapter we summarize the key lessons learned from the comparisons, drawing on the excellent work in each country chapter. We make every effort to acknowledge when the information is comparable across countries and where data limitations make such comparability inexact. Our summary analysis is not a substitute for the richer picture painted in each country-specific chapter but provides an overview to set the stage for a study of the remaining chapters.

The highlights of our comparison can be summarized as follows:

1. The population is aging rapidly in each of these countries, with particularly rapid growth in the "oldest old" (those age 85 or older). This rapid aging is reflected in statistics regarding formal long-term care spending, which currently comprises 2.1 percent of GDP on average, and which has grown by 60 percent as a share of GDP from 2000 to 2019. Furthermore,

this growth is likely to continue to accelerate as numbers of the oldest old continue to grow.

2. The need for long-term care rises rapidly with age and with disability, while measures of well-being such as depression worsen.

3. Only a minority of those elderly receiving assistance rely solely on formal care (i.e., care in an institution or through paid home care) while informal care from family or other unpaid caregivers comprises the majority of care. This fact illustrates the importance of including the implicit costs of informal care when assessing the economic burden of long-term care.

4. Women provide the vast majority of formal care in all these countries, but there is a somewhat more equal distribution of care across genders in the provision of informal rather than formal care. Even here, however, women continue to dominate with respect to the provision of personal care—care which may have less flexibility in scheduling and thus place greater demands on the provider.

5. Highly skilled formal caregivers in all countries are fairly well compensated, usually at or above the average economy-wide wage, but there is substantial variation across countries in the compensation of low-skilled caregivers, with wages ranging from less than one-half of the average wage in the United States to more than three-quarters of the average in Denmark and Japan.

6. Without public support, the cost of long-term care would be beyond the financial means of a large fraction of the elderly in each country. Moreover, the relationship between health and economic well-being in most countries means that those who are most likely to need long-term care are the least likely to be able to afford it.

7. Perhaps because of this difficulty in affording care, the public sector bears most of the cost of formal long-term care. Even in the United States, which lacks public long-term care insurance, the public sector pays well over two-thirds of the cost. Despite the similarity across countries in this respect, there is substantial variation in the share of costs borne by the public sector, as well as a strong positive correlation between the public share and total long-term care spending as a share of GDP.

8. Countries vary substantially in their use of formal home care versus institutional care, with the share of spending on home care varying from 23 percent in Spain to 63 percent in Japan. Strikingly, there is no correlation between the share of spending on home care and total long-term care spending—that is, countries which appear to favor formal home care do not appear to spend less than those emphasizing nursing home care. We note, however, that the two countries with the largest fraction of spending devoted to home care—Japan and Germany—are also two of the oldest countries in our sample.

9. Informal care comprises a substantial portion of total long-term care, and the cost of this informal care, in terms of forgone wages and other costs, should be included in any measure of the true cost of long-term care

although it is missing from official tallies. In the chapters, we discuss alternative methods for valuing this informal care and argue in favor of a measure that reflects the total value of the caregivers' time including the loss of leisure. Using this measure, informal care comprises at least one-third of all long-term care spending for all nations, with an average portion of nearly 50 percent. Interestingly, the reliance of countries on informal care does not appear correlated with the amount of formal care spending.

Our chapter proceeds as follows. In Part I we present some statistics highlighting the growing need for long-term care and the increasing share of resources devoted to this sector. Part II then describes how care is currently provided in an international context. Part III focuses on the types of care and financing arrangements that exist across countries and then delves into the key differences that mark these international comparisons. Part IV incorporates the underlying costs of informal care with the more typical measures examining just formal care, to create a new internationally comparable measure of the cost of care that provides a more accurate representation of the true cost. The final section concludes.

I. The Growing Need for Long-Term Care around the World

The dramatic aging of the world's population is illustrated in figure I.1, which shows the fraction of the population ages 65 or older (Panel A) and the fraction of the population 85 or older (Panel B). While there is a steady rise in the share of each nation's population over age 65, there is a particularly sharp projected rise in the oldest old. Most notable among the countries in our sample is the extremely high fraction of the population ages 85 or older in Japan—forecasted to rise to over 9 percent by 2050, less than 30 years from now. Also of note is the lower initial percentage, but rapid increase in that share in Singapore. Singapore began this period with the smallest percentage among the oldest old but has by far the most rapid growth and is forecast to surpass all countries except Italy and Japan by 2050.

Table I.1 breaks down these increases into what occurred in roughly the past 30 years (the rise from 1990 to 2020) and what is anticipated going forward (2020 to 2050). It is clear from these numbers that the most rapid increases are yet to come. In 7 of the 10 countries at least 70 percent of the increase is in the coming decades, and for Singapore, as illustrated in figure I.1, nearly 90 percent of the increase is in the years ahead. In fact, for all countries, including Japan, more than one-half of the increase in the oldest old comes in the latter half of the period. Thus, as pressing as the demand for long-term care is now among these countries, the situation is likely to deteriorate substantially in the coming years, and each country faces substantial increases in the share of the population that is in the age range associated with most needing care.

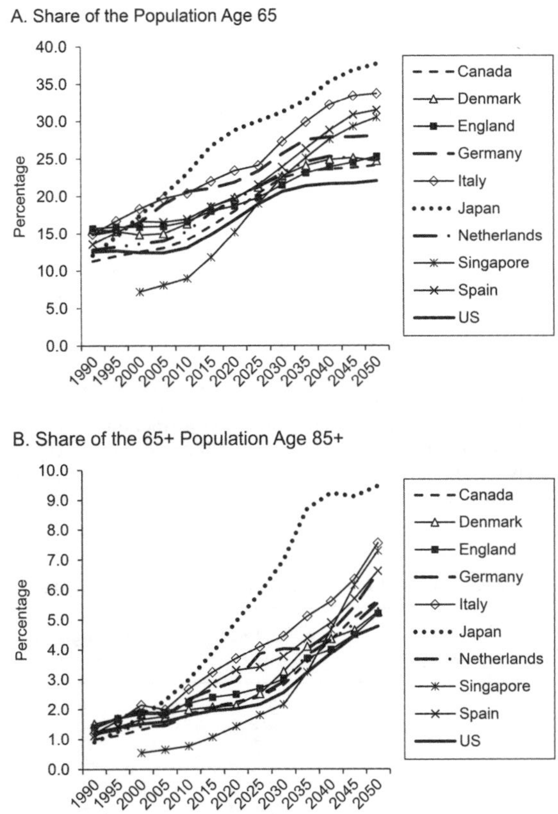

Fig. I.1 An saging global population

Notes: Each figure displays the corresponding fraction of the population per country in 5-year intervals. Data were not available in Singapore until 2000.

Table I.2 highlights the current cost of formal long-term care and the sharp rise in the recent past. The table reports the share of GDP devoted to formal long-term care in each of our sample countries in 2000 and in 2019. Two facts are immediately clear. First, long-term care is an important component of spending in nearly every country. Setting Singapore aside due to its considerably younger population, the share of GDP devoted to long-term care varies from 0.9 percent of GDP in Spain to more than 4 percent in the Netherlands. On average, in our sample, it amounted to 1.9 percent of GDP in 2019. For comparison purposes, the 1.3 percent of GDP devoted to long-term care in the US may be relatively low on the list, but it is larger than the share of US GDP attributable to agriculture or auto manufacturing.

The second fact illustrated in the table is the rapid growth in LTC spending obligations over time. LTC spending has grown as a share of GDP in

Table I.1 Decomposing the change in the age 85+ population share

	Total Change	1990–2020 Change	2020–2050 Change	2020–2050 Share
Canada	4.6	1.3	3.4	0.73
Denmark	3.7	0.6	3.1	0.83
England	3.8	1.1	2.7	0.71
Germany	5.2	1.5	3.6	0.70
Italy	6.4	2.5	3.9	0.61
Japan	8.6	4.0	4.5	0.53
Netherlands	4.4	1.0	3.3	0.76
Singapore	6.7	0.9	5.9	0.87
Spain	5.5	2.2	3.3	0.60
US	3.5	0.8	2.8	0.78

Notes: Column 1 shows the percentage point change in the fraction of the population aged 85 or older between 1990 and 2050. Columns 2 and 3 split this change into pre- and post-2020 changes, respectively. Column 4 reports the share of the change that is accounted for by the change from 1990 to 2020. Due to data limitations, the base year for Singapore is 2000 rather than 1990.

Table I.2 Share of GDP spent on formal long-term care over time

Country	Share GDP 2000 or Nearest	Share GDP 2019	Change: 2000 to 2019	Percentage Change
Canada	1.3	2.1	0.8	61%
Denmark	1.9	2.1	0.2	11%
England	—	2.3	—	—
Germany	1.4	2.2	0.8	55%
Italy	1.6	1.8	0.2	13%
Japan	0.7	2.1	1.4	212%
Netherlands	2.7	4.1	1.4	50%
Spain	0.5	0.9	0.3	62%
US	1.1	1.3	0.2	17%
Mean	1.4	2.1	0.7	60%

Notes: The reported fractions of GDP are for all formal LTC expenditures, regardless of the age of the care recipient. As a result, the estimates do not align perfectly with those reported in later tables. Because of data availability limitations, Spain's estimates are for 2003 and 2019, while Italy's are for 2004 and 2019. England cannot obtain data from before 2013.

every country, in many cases quite rapidly. Japan, whose population is currently the oldest and aging the most rapidly, has seen the share of its GDP attributable to formal long-term care increase by 200 percent between 2000 and 2019, while Spain's and Canada's have risen by over 60 percent. On the lower end, the US share has risen by a far smaller amount, approximately 20 percent from 2000 to 2019, while Italy's and Denmark's have increased by 13 and 11 percent (although it is worth noting that even with this small increase, Denmark remains among the top tier of countries in terms of absolute spending as a fraction of GDP).

II. Long-Term Care Provision in International Context

Long-term care (LTC) is a somewhat ambiguous term that can cover a wide variety of different types of spending. In this section we highlight some of the similarities and differences that exist across countries in the nature of LTC.

To measure the need for LTC services, we focus on limitations in Activities of Daily Living (ADLs) and Instrumental Activities of Daily Living (IADLs). Limitations in the measures provide consensus indicators for the need for assistance of elders with their functioning. The standard ADL limitations used in the literature and which we adopt here are dressing, bathing, eating, getting in and out of bed, walking across a room, and using a toilet. The IADL are cooking, shopping for groceries, using a telephone, managing money, and taking medications as prescribed. In most countries, these limitations are measured in the primary data sources employ, although occasionally questions vary slightly. In two cases—Japan and the Netherlands—a separate set of limitations is measured, but the comparability of these measures was validated using other data sources. In Singapore, the same limitations are used but the questions ask about activities where the respondents need help, as opposed to those with which they have difficulty. While there are no data sources in Canada that contain a comparable set of limitations and meet our other requirements (e.g., nationally representative samples), there do exist measures of care needs that shed light upon disability levels among the elderly Canadian population, and we rely on those for comparison.[1]

Data

This project benefits enormously from a massive investment that has been made in most of these nations in creating comprehensive, longitudinal data sets for their elderly population. Many of these efforts were modeled after the Health and Retirement Study (HRS) in the United States, including the Survey of Health, Ageing and Retirement in Europe (SHARE), the English Longitudinal Study of Ageing (ELSA), and the Japanese Study of Aging and Retirement (JSTAR).[2]

These studies each consist of lengthy surveys of nationally representative samples of thousands of adults typically over the age of 50. Following the HRS model, the studies elicit detailed information about respondents' health, finances, demographics, family structure, and long-term care receipt. Because these surveys are designed with comparability in mind, they elicit the same set of ADL and IADL limitations and measure a similar set of

1. The individual chapters contain detail on the measurement of these items.

2. See Health and Retirement Study description of international family surveys, https://hrs.isr.umich.edu/about/international-family-studies

care-related outcomes. Because our focus is on the effects of population aging, we follow the standard definition of elderly and restrict analyses to those aged 65 or older whenever possible.

In some cases, HRS-style data are not available, or those data are insufficient to address all the topics we explore. To address these shortcomings, additional data sources have been used to supplement or replace these surveys. For example, the last set of interviews for JSTAR was conducted in 2013 and was not nationally representative. As a result, most analyses in Japan are performed using the Comprehensive Survey of Living Conditions (CSLC), which collects much of the information needed for our comparisons. In Canada, where no HRS-style survey has been fielded, several labor force and health surveys are used to compile the necessary information for comparisons. And in the Netherlands, the National Health Survey is used rather than SHARE because of the much larger sample size and respondent links to administrative registers.

A common limitation of the data used across countries is a lack of information on nursing home residents. The initial rounds of HRS, ELSA, and SHARE did not sample individuals living in institutional settings, so the early rounds of the survey do not have population representative samples of nursing home residents. However, because respondents continue to be followed if they *enter* a nursing home, the sample becomes more representative over time. However, both access restrictions and high rates of sample attrition mean that despite the sampling frame, these surveys all tend to under-sample nursing home residents. In the HRS, separate weights are provided for nursing home residents so that the sample of institutional residents matches the characteristics of the national nursing home population. In most other countries where there exist administrative data on the age and gender distribution of nursing home residents (e.g., Denmark, England, and the Netherlands), we adjust sample weights of respondents to approximate this distribution.

Unfortunately, no such corrections can be made for Japan, Canada, and Singapore because micro-data on nursing home residents are unavailable. When possible, the teams employ aggregate data on nursing home resident characteristics to supplement results from survey data. However, in some cases the analyses must be restricted to the community-dwelling population.

An additional challenge with using data on nursing home care is that nursing homes can serve very different roles across countries. In the United States, for example, a large share of nursing home residents are those who are receiving short-term post-acute care (e.g., recovering from surgery) and not long-term care. This is less true in most other nations. Ideally, our measures for institutional care would be able to define exactly what type of care is being received, but that is not possible given the available data.[3]

An additional difficulty in comparing across countries is that subtle dif-

3. Note that where possible, we limit our US sample to individuals with nursing home stays of more than 100 days.

ferences in the way in which measures of long-term care are collected can have substantial implications. In the HRS and ELSA, for example, measures of formal and informal home care from all sources have a *one month* look-back period. Meanwhile, SHARE asks about all sources of home care over the last *twelve months*. Given the substantially longer period of time over which care is reported, it is unsurprising that the fraction of the elderly reporting any form of home care is generally higher in SHARE countries than in the HRS or ELSA. There is no clear method to adjust the reporting period. There are also differences in the wording of questions for different types of care: In SHARE, for example, informal care received from people outside the household is reported regardless of the frequency with which it was received, while care from people within the household must be provided daily or almost daily if it is to be reported.

One way to circumvent these limitations is by focusing on cost estimates that are generally less susceptible to the issues arising from variation in survey measures, because the estimates are for a common time frame (one year) and the overwhelming majority of costs are concentrated among people receiving higher-frequency care.

In all countries, the micro-level data have been supplemented with data from other sources. For instance, OECD population data are used to measure past and projected population aging across countries. Labor force and population surveys are used to present information on formal care worker characteristics and when conducting our valuation of informal care. And aggregate data on spending and formal care provision is incorporated into the analysis of the formal long-term care sector. Furthermore, we rely upon aggregate information about the age composition of formal care recipients to impute the amount of long-term care spending that goes toward the elderly. The efforts made in this regard have been great. Across the 10 countries, nearly 100 different data sources have been used to provide a comprehensive look at long-term care systems around the world.

Finally, it is important to note that our use of aggregate statistics across countries can mask important differences driven by the age composition of the population. Ideally, all facts below would be age adjusted within each country, but we were unable to do so. Instead, when we return to the facts on total LTC spending, we will use a crude cross-country age comparison.

Division by Age

Because of our interest in assessing the effects of population aging on long-term care, we limit our analyses to long-term care for the population ages 65 or older.[4] However, it is important to note that LTC is not solely for the elderly. Indeed, for many of the nations in our sample, a large share of

4. For some statistics in some countries, we will necessarily have a broader sample. However, when conducting survey analysis we restrict to the 65 and older population, and where possible, we perform a basic imputation of aggregate spending devoted to the elderly by adjusting by the share of recipients who are aged 65+.

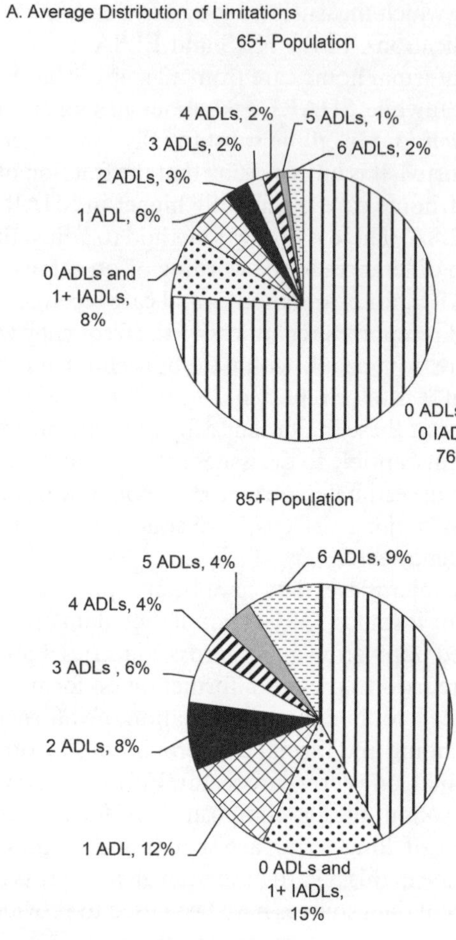

Fig. I.2 Distribution of limitations by age

Notes: Each figure shows the fraction of individuals with ADL/IADL limitations by age group in each country. The figures are generally comparable, although the question structure differs somewhat in Singapore, asking about activities with which an individual needs help rather than those with which they have difficulty.

LTC is devoted to those below age 65. For example, in the United States, approximately 17–18 percent of nursing home residents and home health care recipients are under the age of 65. This figure is higher in some countries, with 20 percent of LTC users in Germany and nearly one-third of institutional residents in the Netherlands under age 65.

Within the population of elderly, the need for LTC also rises rapidly with age. We illustrate this pattern in figure I.2, which shows the average across countries in the share of the population with different degrees of limitations for all elderly and for the oldest old. On average, 76 percent of the population

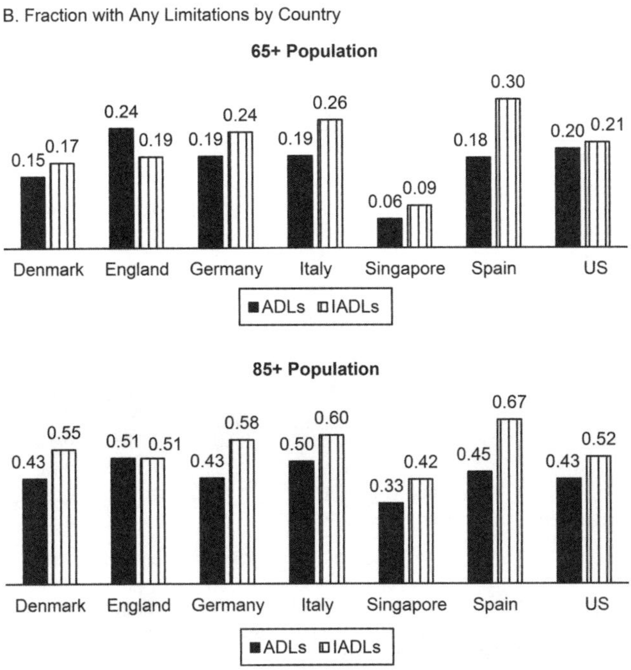

Fig. I.2 (cont.)

ages 65 or over have no ADL or IADL limitations. Another 8 percent have only IADL limitations, while 16 percent have at least one ADL limitation. Among those ages 85 or older, however, the share with no limitations falls to 42 percent. While the share of those with only IADL limitations rises to 15 percent for this age group, the share with at least one ADL limitation more than doubles to 43 percent. Because the population of individuals ages 85 or older is rising more quickly than the share 65 or older, the prevalence of limitations and the need for long-term care is expected to rise rapidly in the coming years.

Across countries, there is notable variation in the share of the population reporting limitations (Panel B of figure I.2). To some extent, this variation may be driven by the specific wording of the questions. In Singapore, for example, respondents are asked whether they need help with ADLs or IADLs, while other surveys ask whether respondents have difficulty with these activities. It is also likely, however, that a mix of cultural differences in reporting disabilities, the underlying age distribution of the elderly population (e.g., a larger fraction of the elderly population in Japan is over the age of 85 than in other countries), and general population health drive some of the variation. Notably, after restricting the samples to a smaller age band (those age 85 or older), the variation in ADL limitations across countries

Table I.3 **Prevalence of specific activity limitations**

Share	Denmark	England	Germany	Italy	Singapore	Spain	US
			Panel 1- IADLs				
IADL—Use a Phone	0.36	0.37	0.20	0.25	0.37	0.25	0.29
IADL—Manage Money	0.79	0.45	0.41	0.36	0.68	0.40	0.51
IADL—Take Meds as Prescr.	0.57	0.38	0.32	0.28	0.46	0.25	0.21
IADL—Shop for Groceries	0.87	0.80	0.80	0.52	0.35	0.47	0.62
IADL—Prepare a Meal	0.78	0.52	0.47	0.34	0.34	0.40	0.54
Observations	244	747	494	667	521	992	2,195
			Panel 2- ADLs				
ADL—Use the Toilet	0.45	0.30	0.24	0.33	0.54	0.44	0.36
ADL—Get Dressed	0.87	0.75	0.72	0.70	0.67	0.70	0.58
ADL—Take a Bath	0.87	0.58	0.60	0.74	0.71	0.77	0.47
ADL—Walk Across a Room	0.53	0.29	0.19	0.33	0.71	0.35	0.47
ADL—Eat	0.36	0.20	0.22	0.27	0.37	0.27	0.24
ADL—Get In/Out of Bed	0.52	0.39	0.26	0.44	0.51	0.51	0.38
Observations	208	1,051	707	467	347	599	2,033

Notes: Each cell in panel 1 shows the fraction of people aged 65+ by country with any IADL limitation who have difficulty with the given activity, while the rows in panel 2 report the fraction of those with any ADL limitation who have difficulty with the activity.

becomes smaller, suggesting that distribution of age may play an important role.

Which specific limitations create the largest demand for long-term care? We explore this question in table I.3. Across countries, the most prevalent IADL is grocery shopping, typically followed by cooking a meal and managing money. Meanwhile, among ADLs, getting dressed and taking a bath were the most commonly reported limitations.

The relationship between age and disability and the need for LTC is further illustrated by the deterioration in other measures of elderly well-being. Although comparable measures of subjective and emotional well-being do not exist across our sample of countries, in table I.4 we select a set of well-being measures for all those 65 or older and for those with ADL or IADL limitations, and similarly for the oldest old. Panel 1 shows a set of measures positively related to well-being, while panel 2 shows a set of negative depression-related measures. Importantly, in every country within our sample, measures of depression and of life or retirement satisfaction are worse among those with ADL or IADL limitations than without and similarly worse for those ages 85 or older relative to younger elderly. The negative effects on these well-being measures are particularly pronounced for being disabled; in the United States, for example, those 65-year-olds who have 3+ ADLs are three times as likely to be depressed as the average 65-year-old. While these comparisons are interesting, they are of course limited by the

Table I.4 **Well-being measures by age and limitation**

Country	Question	65+	65+, 3+ Limitations	85+	85+ 3+ Limitations
	Panel 1: Positive Well-Being Measures				
Denmark	Good life satisfaction for those retired	0.85	0.63	0.80	0.70
England	Satisfied with life	0.66	0.38	0.61	0.40
Germany	Life satisfaction (0–10)	7.83	6.94	7.71	7.31
US	Very satisfied with retirement	0.55	0.33	0.55	0.43
	Panel 2: Negative Well-Being Measures				
Italy	Depressed in the last month	0.38	0.78	0.55	0.75
Japan	Kessler 6 Scores (0–24)	2.97	6.12	3.89	6.03
Netherlands	Depression score: moderate or high	0.43	0.88	0.67	0.88
Singapore	Self-Report Depression	0.03	0.08	0.06	0.08
Spain	Depressed much of the Time	0.29	0.35	0.35	0.35
US	Depressed much of Time	0.10	0.29	0.12	0.19

Notes: Limitations are defined broadly to include both ADL and IADL limitations. Details of specific measures (such as the Kessler score) can be found in specific chapters. Panel 1 includes measures for which a higher fraction or value indicates higher well-being, while panel 2 is for measures where higher values indicate worse well-being.

different meanings of terms such as depression in different international contexts.

What Is Long-Term Care?

The international context allows us to assess differences in how countries target resources employed under the general heading of long-term care. We focus our analysis on three specific types of LTC.

The first type on which we focus is institutional care, which we refer to as *nursing home care*. We focus here on full-service institutional care, which includes housing, food, medical services, and supports with activities of daily living. There are several subtleties involved in defining this category. First, many elders live in congregate housing, but only some of them receive help with medical care and activities of daily living. In most countries, there is a relatively clear distinction between assisted living facilities, which do not include skilled nursing services, and nursing homes, which do. This distinction is often important in determining public support, as nursing home care is covered to at least some degree by the government in all countries in our sample, whereas assisted living is typically not; the two exceptions being the Netherlands and England.

Unfortunately, in the survey data used for many analyses, institutional residents are often identified without distinguishing whether skilled nursing services are received. Because survey weights are adjusted to reflect the aggregate population in nursing homes specifically, this limitation does not alter estimates of the overall prevalence of nursing home care. However, because at least some of the respondents included in the nursing home population may actually be living in assisted living facilities, we generally place less weight on comparisons of nursing home population characteristics coming from survey data.

The second type of care on which we focus is care from paid caregivers in the elder's home, termed "formal home care." This care can include anything from help with ADLs, to skilled nursing care at home, or to housekeeping assistance that enables the individual to remain in the community. In all countries, the government pays for most formal home care, though the degree of coverage varies substantially. In the United States, for instance, roughly one-quarter of formal home care is paid for by private insurance or out of pocket, while in Denmark, public home care is provided with no cost-sharing requirement, so almost none of it is paid for privately (although some individuals do choose to purchase private care outside of the public system). Because formal home care can include a broad range of activities, including administering medications and delivering meals, the source of financing often varies across activities. For instance, in the Netherlands, public health insurance covers home health care and personal care with ADLs, while a separate program, the Social Support Act, provides supports such as housekeeping services and even pays for equipment such as mobility scooters and stair lifts. This situation also exists in the United States, with Medicaid waiver programs providing many ancillary services.

The third type of care on which we focus is informal (generally unpaid) care delivered in the home. This care consists primarily of unpaid care provided by relatives or other community members, though we also include care from relatives in cases in which the relative receives compensation.[5] This informal care can be particularly important for those elderly who are ineligible for publicly financed care and as such is quite prevalent, but often excluded from estimates of the total cost of long-term care. This exclusion is unfortunate because this informal care can imply significant financial cost to the caregiver in terms of forgone wages as well as to the economy as a whole in terms of productivity and economic growth due to the lost workers. As such, we place particular emphasis on measuring the provision of this form of care and quantifying its costs.

With both formal and informal home care, there is a challenge in defining exactly what we mean by long-term care and other services, like general cleaning, that do not depend on health. This distinction is particularly problematic in countries such as Singapore, where a sizeable portion of home services is provided by foreign nationals who provide both general home

5. In some countries, such as the Netherlands and Germany, care-needy people can receive vouchers/allowances to compensate informal caregivers. Moreover, individuals may choose to compensate family members directly from personal resources.

Table I.5 **Composition of long-term care types across countries**

Country	Home Care: Only Formal	Home Care: Only Informal	Home Care: Both	Nursing Home
Panel 1: 65+				
Canada	8	35	40	17
Denmark	4	78	8	10
England	6	70	11	14
Germany	15	54	24	7
Italy	21	55	15	8
Japan	17	21	46	16
Netherlands	29	19	23	29
Singapore	18	66	18	—
Spain	27	49	10	14
US	5	69	13	13
Panel 2: 85+				
Canada	5	27	41	28
Denmark	5	57	12	27
England	5	58	11	25
Germany	20	21	42	17
Italy	24	47	21	9
Japan	16	15	48	22
Netherlands	22	8	24	45
Spain	19	51	14	16
Singapore	22	47	32	—
US	5	57	20	18

Notes: Each cell shows the portion of people receiving any LTC who receive each mode of care. Singapore lacks survey data on nursing home residents and cannot obtain aggregate statistics on the age distribution of residents.

management and housekeeping services as well as long-term care. For most of the countries in our sample, survey data specifically measure care received due to a health or aging condition that is expected to last more than three months. Moreover, even help received with finances or other housekeeping activities can be critical for seniors if they are to remain in the community. Thus, we generally do not restrict home care by the type of care received, examining the prevalence of care with both ADLs and IADLs in addition to nursing care and other community support programs, although we caution that the availability of such care through government programs differs across countries.

The degree of reliance on each of these three types of long-term care in each country is summarized in table I.5. Each column reports the fraction of the elderly (both for those aged 65+ and 85+) who receive only formal home care, only informal home care, and both types of home care, as well as the fraction living in a nursing home. Denmark, England, and the United

States rely to a large degree on informal care, while formal care (both institutional and at home) plays a much larger role in the Netherlands. Across all countries, reliance upon formal care increases with age. This pattern is likely due to both the reduction in the availability of informal care provided by spouses for older widows, as well as the increased intensity of care needs that accompany aging. Consistent with the latter explanation, there is also an increasing reliance upon formal care as the number of ADL limitations rises.

Importantly, though, comparisons drawn directly from survey data are sensitive to differences in measurement as well as actual differences in the reliance on types of care. Some data sources, such as SHARE, ask respondents about broad categories of care received (e.g., personal care, household help), while other sources, such as the HRS, ask about care received for a specific list of activities (e.g., bathing, grocery shopping). Furthermore, as discussed earlier, variation in how different types of care is measured may affect the estimates, particularly for SHARE countries where the threshold for reporting within-household informal care is greater than that for informal and formal care provided by those outside the household. The estimates in table I.5 should therefore be interpreted with caution, as greater harmonization of survey measures is needed across countries.

Who Provides Home Care?

The increasing demand for long-term care associated with population aging creates not just fiscal challenges but also an increase in demand for caregivers. With fewer workers relative to elderly people as the population ages, countries are struggling to find an adequate number of caregivers, with many turning to immigration. The difficulty in the case of the availability of informal caregivers is further exacerbated by the rise in labor force participation among women. Each chapter in this volume includes details on the demographic makeup of the caregiving population. While details vary, it is generally true that the providers of formal home care are among the least skilled workers in the economy, while providers of informal care more closely match population characteristics.

One striking feature evident across countries is the gender composition of caregivers shown in figure I.3. Formal caregiving is dominated by women across all countries, with an average of 87 percent of formal caregivers being women. Informal care is more balanced across genders, with the share of informal caregivers who are men being several times larger than formal caregivers, though it remains provided primarily by women. Notably, caregivers providing help with personal care or ADLs are, in most countries, more likely to be women than those providing household help or assistance with IADLs.

Table I.6 shows who is providing this informal care. Across countries, spouses and children are consistently the primary informal caregivers. Moreover, daughters consistently provide more care than sons, though care from

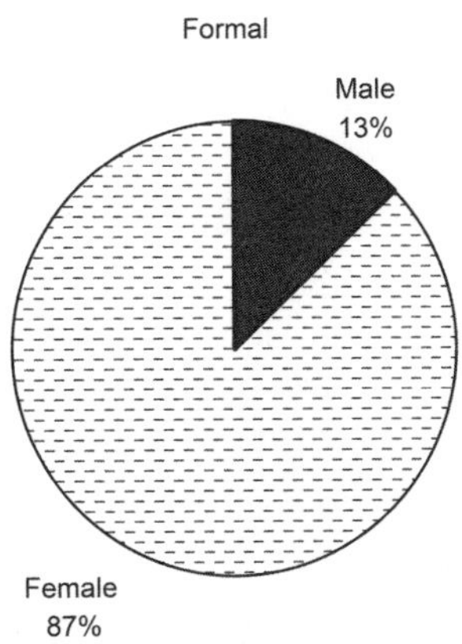

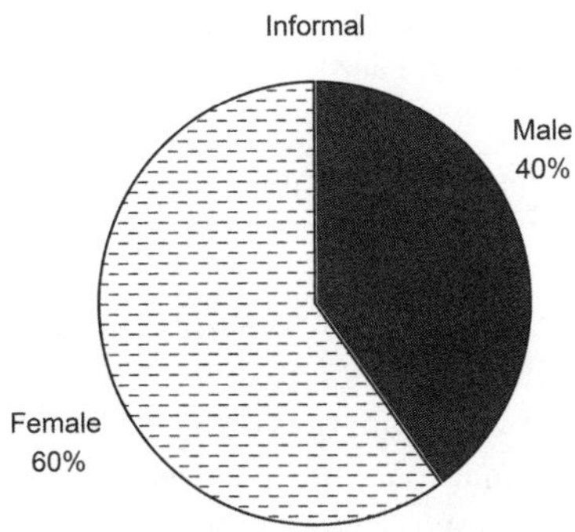

Fig. I.3 Average gender mix of formal and informal caregivers
Notes: The fractions reported are the average across countries in the sample.

Table I.6 Informal caregivers by relationship to care recipient

Country	Spouse	Son	Daughter	Child	Son-/ Daughter-in-Law	Grandchild	Other Rel.	Unpaid Non-Rel.
Canada	36	15	31	46	3	—	7	8
Denmark	5	—	—	38	5	3	15	35
England	35	15	25	40	—	8	5	11
Germany	11	—	—	41	5	—	14	28
Italy	21	10	19	30	7	—	27	16
Japan	32	17	21	39	14	—	16	—
Netherlands	13	—	—	41	—	—	25	21
Singapore	24	18	48	66	6	—	4	
Spain	30	19	40	59	—	—	11	
US	32	13	27	40	6	8	7	7

Notes: Each cell reports the fraction of informal caregivers by relationship category in the given country. Missing categories are those not reported in the individual chapter. Other relative and unpaid non-relative categories are combined for Singapore and Spain.

Table I.7 **Ratio of average wages for long-term care workers to the average wage of all workers**

	Nursing Home Industry			Home Care Industry			Both Industries	
	Higher Skill	Lower Skill	All	Higher Skill	Lower Skill	All	Higher Skill	Lower Skill
Canada							1.57	0.86
Denmark	0.96	0.78		0.93	0.73			
England	0.94	0.50		0.96	0.52			
Germany	0.86	0.74		0.82	0.62			
Italy			0.75			0.72		
Japan	1.13	0.79		1.13	0.78			
Netherlands							0.99	0.78
Singapore	1.01	0.57		1.03	0.54			
Spain			0.97			0.101		
US	1.00	0.47		1.02	0.43			

Notes: *Higher skill* refers to registered nurses or the country-specific equivalent, while *lower skill* refers to nursing assistants/home health aides or the country-specific equivalent. More details on the specific definitions for each worker type can be found in the specific country chapters. Canada's ratio is the median occupation-specific wage compared to the median economy-wide wage.

children is more evenly balanced across gender in Japan than in other countries, likely arising from the strong patrilinear traditions. It is important to note that the manner in which surveys treat informal care from inside and outside the household can impact the distribution of care across sources—in Europe, the lower fraction of caregivers who are spouses may be driven by how informal care is measured, wherein, as discussed earlier, there is a greater threshold for reporting care provided by those within the household.

Countries also differ in the training requirements for formal caregivers and in their wages. Table I.7 reports the wages of both high- and low-skilled long-term care workers by sector, measured relative to the economy-wide average wage of all workers. Due to data limitations, Italy and Spain are separated only by sector, while Canada and the Netherlands are separated only by skill level. Notably, in all countries except Canada,[6] higher-skilled care workers (roughly akin to registered nurses in the United States) receive similar compensation to the average worker. However, there is considerable variation in pay for less-skilled caregivers (generally nursing assistants and home health aides). In the United States, England, and Singapore, the least-skilled workers are paid approximately one-half as much as the average worker, while in Japan and Denmark, their wages are at approximately the 75th percentile. This pay differential likely reflects differences in training requirements and thus in the definitions of low- and high-skilled categories. For example, a nursing assistant in Denmark must complete over two years

6. The data from Canada is for all nurses, though, rather than only those in the long-term care sector.

of schooling/training, whereas in most states in the United States, nursing assistants are required to have only 75 hours of training. In general, there are only limited differences between nursing home and home care workers at the same skill level.

These pay differences may have very important implications for the quality of care that is delivered and likely to the availability of care. Higher pay will make it easier for this sector to attract workers and to attract higher-quality workers. This raises the key issue of the need to assess the quality of care and differences in quality across countries, an issue which we cannot address directly here, but to which we return in the conclusion.

Varying Supply of Long-Term Care

One area with significant variation across countries is the nursing home sector, both in terms of utilization and staffing. We illustrate these differences by showing the ratio of nursing home residents to the population over age 65 and the ratio of nursing home employees to residents in figure I.4.

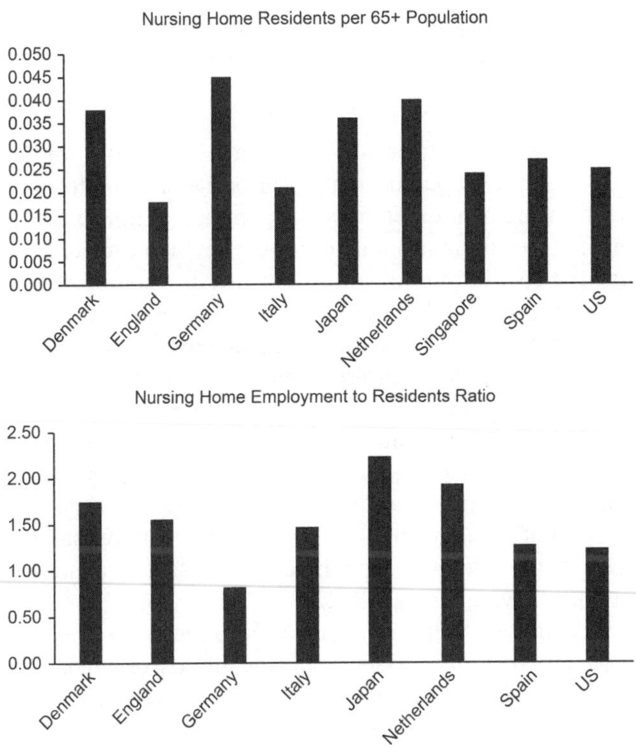

Fig. I.4 Variation in nursing home supply, staffing, and availability

Notes: The residents-to-population ratio uses the total number of residents, because in many cases the total number of residents over age 65 is not available. The number of residents is also based upon point-in-time estimates. Nursing home employment includes all employees, regardless of occupation.

Denmark, Japan, and the Netherlands have roughly 3.5–4 nursing home residents per 100 people ages 65 or older, while England and Italy have only 2. Strikingly, Germany has a very high 4.5 nursing home residents per 100 elderly individuals.

A key measure of supply is the availability of staff. In fact, there is also sizeable variation in the ratio of nursing home workers to residents. Japan and the Netherlands have approximately two nursing home employees per resident, while Germany and the United States are around 1.[7] Importantly, these results are sensitive to how the nursing home industry is defined as well as the fraction working full-time. The correlation between the two panels in figure I.4 is fairly high,[8] with Germany being a notable outlier of high nursing home residency rates and low staffing rates.

III. The Financing of Long-Term Care

Long-term care is costly—particularly relative to the resources available to the elderly. In this section, we discuss the financial burden imposed by long-term care spending in an international context. We then discuss the different routes that nations take in meeting that financing burden.

The Financial Burden of Long-Term Care

Table I.8 shows the distribution of income and wealth for the elderly across countries in 2019 purchasing power parity (PPP)-adjusted dollars.[9] Because of measurement differences, the goal here is not to use these data to compare income distributions across countries but rather to make a common point: the cost burden of long-term care is outsized relative to the financial resources of the elderly.

In the United States, the median private nursing home room costs over $100,000 per year, greater than the income of over 90 percent of the elderly (Genworth 2019). When considering all financial resources at their disposal, the median elderly person would need to exhaust nearly all of their wealth to pay for just two years in a nursing home. (This result holds true even when including less-liquid forms of wealth such as housing.) In England, the corresponding cost of a nursing home is $75,000, again more than the income of 90 percent of the elderly, though this cost represents a somewhat smaller share of wealth (Paying for Care 2022).

In countries with public insurance, it is more difficult to measure the counterfactual scenario in which residents paid the full cost of nursing home care. For comparison, table I.9 reports a back-of-the-envelope estimate of the

7. Our measures of workers include all those working in a nursing home regardless of occupational title.

8. The correlation coefficient is roughly 0.6 and rises to almost 0.7 when Germany is excluded.

9. Purchasing power parity attempts to control for differences across countries in the true cost of living or the amount of "purchasing power" of a unit of currency.

Table I.8 **Elderly income and wealth by country (PPP-adjusted 2019 $)**

	Income				Wealth			
Country	10th Percentile	50th Percentile	90th Percentile	Mean	10th Percentile	50th Percentile	90th Percentile	Mean
Canada	16,000	26,000	51,000	31,000	7,000	309,000	1,244,000	515,000
Denmark	23,000	31,000	57,000	39,000	–2,000	108,000	684,000	291,000
England	14,000	26,000	53,000	32,000	8,000	357,000	1,072,000	510,000
Germany	16,000	29,000	53,000	33,000	0	96,000	490,000	220,000
Italy	5,000	18,000	34,000	19,000	3,000	166,000	479,000	225,000
Japan	11,000	30,000	72,000	39,000	0	49,000	306,000	116,000
Netherlands	20,000	29,000	49,000	33,000	1,000	112,000	521,000	253,000
Spain	8,000	24,000	62,000	34,000	13,000	179,000	772,000	332,000
US	13,000	35,000	93,000	52,000	2,000	217,000	1,345,000	612,000

Notes: All values are normalized by the OECD equivalence scale and adjusted to be in 2019 PPP-adjusted dollars.

Table I.9 **Spending per nursing home resident (PPP-adjusted 2019 $)**

Country	Nursing Home Spending per Resident
Canada	118,000
Denmark	101,000
England	49,000
Germany	59,000
Italy	35,000
Japan	25,000
Netherlands	81,000
Singapore	66,000
Spain	48,000
US	108,000

Notes: Nursing home spending per resident is defined as the spending on nursing homes divided by the number of residents. It is likely an underestimate in many cases as the numerator excludes those under age 65 while the denominator often does not. All values are in 2019 PPP-adjusted dollars.

per person annual cost of a nursing home across countries. To arrive at this estimate, we divide total spending on nursing homes from table I.12 by the number of nursing home residents, as reported in the individual chapters. While our cost estimates are generally restricted to the 65 or older population, the number of nursing home residents reported is often unrestricted by age, likely producing an underestimate. Nonetheless, even with estimates that are likely to be biased downward, the imputed cost of a nursing home is greater than the income of at least 90 percent of the elderly population in all countries except Germany and Japan (notably two of the oldest countries in our sample and countries with national long-term care insurance programs).

Although it is more expensive than institutional care on a per hour basis,

Table I.10 **Distribution of income and wealth by limitations**

Country	% Median HH Income/ Wealth	Income: 0 ADLs and 0 IADLs	Income: 1 ADL	Income: 3+ ADLs	Wealth: 0 ADLs and 0 IADLs	Wealth: 1 ADL	Wealth: 3+ ADLs
England	Share < 50	0.07	0.10	0.07	0.21	0.35	0.44
	Share 200+	0.12	0.06	0.06	0.25	0.15	0.09
Germany	Share < 50	0.07	0.12	0.23	—	—	—
	Share 200+	0.08	0.04	0.02	—	—	—
Italy	Share < 50	0.15	0.28	0.23	0.21	0.39	0.47
	Share 200+	0.11	0.04	0.05	0.22	0.17	0.13
Japan	Share < 50	0.17	0.24	0.19	0.36	0.42	0.35
	Share 200+	0.16	0.15	0.14	0.38	0.31	0.38
Netherlands	Share < 50	0.01	0.01	0.01	0.30	0.53	0.53
	Share 200+	0.07	0.02	0.02	0.38	0.24	0.25
Singapore	Share < 50	0.33	0.41	0.44	0.21	0.39	0.34
	Share 200+	0.25	0.16	0.13	0.24	0.10	0.14
Spain	Share < 50	0.05	0.05	0.22	0.21	0.26	0.30
	Share 200+	0.15	0.10	0.08	0.25	0.19	0.09
US	Share < 50	0.14	0.26	0.40	0.29	0.46	0.63
	Share 200+	0.21	0.09	0.07	0.39	0.21	0.17

Notes: Each cell conditions on the column—in other words, it is the fraction of people in the limitation category (column) that fall in each income and wealth category. The full tables in the chapters also include columns for 1+ IADLs and no ADLs and for 2 ADLs, as well as rows for 50–100 percent, 100–150 percent, and 150–200 percent of median income and wealth. In these tables, the columns sum to 1.

formal home care is generally less intensive and in turn a less costly form of formal care. Nonetheless, the costs can be substantial—in the United States, the median hourly cost of a home health aide is over $20 per hour, so hiring an aide for 40 hours per week for a single year would cost almost $45,000, more than the income of a majority of elderly. Cost data are more difficult to obtain in other countries, particularly those with publicly supplied home care, but even the annual cost of paying the full-time wages of home health aides from table I.6, without considering any overhead costs, is more than the income of most elders in nearly all countries.

Importantly, the need for care is primarily concentrated among those with the most limited ability to pay. Table I.10 shows the distribution of income and wealth by ADL limitations across countries. The numbers in the columns show the fraction of elderly with no limitations, some limitations (1 ADL) and severe limitations (3+ ADLs). We also show the shares with income below 50 percent of the median, and for those above 200 percent of the median, of either income or wealth. For example, in the United States, 14 percent of those with no ADL or IADL limitations have an income below 50 percent of the elderly median income, while 40 percent of those with 3+ ADL limitations have incomes below 50 percent of the median.

Two striking conclusions can be drawn from this table. First, in most countries, the share of people with the lowest income and wealth levels is increasing with the number of limitations, suggesting that those with the greatest care needs have the least ability to pay. Second, there are striking differences across countries in the strength of this relationship. In Japan, for example, the income distribution shows very little difference by limitation, while in the United States and Germany, the share in the lowest income category is nearly three times larger for those with 3+ ADL limitations relative to those with no ADL or IADL limitations. While the pattern is obvious, we note that relationship could stem in part from those who have the greatest needs having spent much of their wealth to purchase care.

The Financing of Long-Term Care

Given the substantial costs of long-term care and the generally negative relationship between ability to pay and need for care, it is unsurprising that public support for long-term care is widespread. In all the countries in our study, the majority of formal long-term care costs are paid for by the government. When care is not paid for through public programs, individuals and their families shoulder much of the burden through out-of-pocket expenditure (only the United States, and to a lesser extent Germany, have a meaningful share of expenses covered by private insurance).

Details of the division of payments are provided in table I.11. In every country except Singapore, the public sector pays for at least 70 percent of formal long-term care costs, but there is also sizeable variation. Only 6–10 percent of costs are paid for privately in Denmark, the Netherlands and Japan, while in the United States, England, Germany, and Italy, private sources pay for at least 25 percent of costs.

There is a strong positive correlation between the public sector share and

Table I.11 **Financing of long-term care by source**

Country	Public	Out-of-Pocket	Private Insurance
Canada	78	18	3
Denmark	90	10	0
England	74	26	0
Germany	70	24	6
Italy	75	25	<1
Japan	92	8	0
Netherlands	94	6	0
Singapore	51	40	0
Spain	79	21	0
US	71	19	10

Notes: These figures are for all formal long-term care spending, regardless of the age of the care recipient. Additionally, 9 percent of spending in Singapore is attributed to charitable donations, which is why the totals do not sum to 100.

Table I.12 Formal long-term care spending by sector per 65+ (PPP-adjusted 2019 $)

Country	Total Spending			Share Accruing to	
	All	Nursing Home	Home Care	Nursing Home	Home Care
Canada	4.8	3.2	1.6	0.67	0.33
Denmark	5.1	3.6	1.5	0.71	0.29
England	2.5	1.7	0.9	0.66	0.34
Germany	4.5	2.3	2.2	0.51	0.49
Italy	1.3	0.8	0.5	0.60	0.40
Japan	2.5	0.9	1.6	0.37	0.63
Netherlands	7.7	5.1	2.6	0.66	0.34
Singapore	2.6	1.6	1.0	0.60	0.40
Spain	1.6	1.3	0.4	0.77	0.23
US	4.4	2.7	1.7	0.61	0.39

Notes: Spending is for formal care only and restricted to (or imputed) spending on the elderly. It is expressed per person age 65+ in the population, in units of $1,000.

total formal spending on long-term care (shown in table I.2). Denmark, the Netherlands, and Japan are three of the top four spenders on long-term care within our sample, while the United States, England, and Italy are three of the bottom four. Interestingly, Germany is an outlier here, with both a high private share of spending and a high level of spending as a share of GDP (recall also the higher fraction of elderly in nursing homes in Germany show in figure I.4.) In countries with public insurance, coverage of room and board appears to be an important driver of cross-country differences. Public systems in the Netherlands and Japan pay for room and board for all nursing home residents (at least those in public facilities), while in Germany they do not, though there exist means tested social assistance programs to aid those who cannot afford the out-of-pocket expenses.

There are also important differences across countries in the degree to which they rely on nursing home versus formal care and in the amount spent on these services (table I.12). Japan spends very little on nursing home care relative to other countries, with just over one-third of its long-term care spending used to pay for institutional care; it is also the lowest in terms of spending per elderly individual, this despite an age distribution that skews far older than other countries. In contrast, Spain devotes 77 percent of its long-term care spending to nursing home care and has the second lowest per capita amount. As these differences illustrate, it is not just the type of care but the use of formal care at all that drives much of the differences across countries. We revisit this point below when we consider the value of informal care.

The heterogeneity in spending is often a product of the unique aspects of the long-term care systems in each country. Many countries with high out-of-pocket spending—the United States, Canada, England, and Italy—have both need-based and means-based systems, determining public eligibility by both the level of disability and by the availability of the financial resources to meet that need. In contrast, the Netherlands, Denmark, and Japan have universal systems, with eligibility for public support based upon care needs alone (though co-payments are still means tested in these countries). Others, such as Germany and Singapore, have public long-term care systems but rely upon substantial cost-sharing, resulting in a significant private share of spending.

Meanwhile, the relative reliance on institutional versus home-based care at times reflects the emphasis of each system. In the Netherlands, for example, public benefits can be directed toward assisted living communities as well as to more intensive forms of institutional care. This flexibility results in a high level of institutional spending. In contrast, as was apparent in table I.12, Japan has made a concerted increase in the use of home care relative to institutional care, an emphasis that has led to greater formal home care spending. The United States differs from other countries in relying on nursing homes to provide post-acute care in an effort to reduce hospital stays, while other countries reserve the use of nursing homes for those needing long-term around-the-clock care.

There is also heterogeneity in the degree of centralization of policies within countries. Some countries, such as the Netherlands, Singapore, and Spain, have strong centralized systems. Others rely upon a mix of local and central government administration. For example, in Japan and Denmark the administration of a universal system is at the municipal level, while in the United States, long-term care systems differ across states in eligibility and types of support. Italy also displays substantial variation in eligibility for public support across regions. Lastly, in Canada, formal long-term care systems are largely decentralized, with large differences across provinces in the mix of private and public care, the level of cost-sharing, and the universality of public support.

IV. The Full Costs of Long-Term Care

Importantly, focusing only on formal care spending ignores the critical role played by informal home care across countries. Countries that lack a universal public long-term care insurance system, such as the United States and England, may in turn rely more heavily on informal care. If the measurement of costs was confined solely to formal spending, we would underestimate the true cost of long-term care in each country and would miss important differences in patterns of long-term care use.

To address the importance of informal care, we provide estimates of the total cost of informal care across countries using a novel approach that relies on estimates of the opportunity cost of caregiver time in terms of both forgone wages and forgone leisure. In most past work, the cost of informal caregiving has been estimated by valuing hours of care either at the average (or median) wage rate for formal home caregivers, or at the opportunity cost of informal caregivers, defined as the wage a caregiver would earn if caregiving hours were spent working (Hurd et al. 2013; Meijer et al. 2022). There is some appeal to these approaches, which we refer to as the "proxy good" and "forgone wage" methods, as these represent what a potential caregiver would need to pay to hire either a formal caregiver or the amount of earnings the caregiver could obtain were every caregiving hour spent in the labor market at their current (or imputed) wage rate.

In theory, the true opportunity cost of each hour of informal care provided is the potential wage that could be earned during that hour of work. In practice, proxying this by actual wages earned raises a host of problems. For example, caregivers may have moved to a job with a lower wage in exchange for more flexibility in their schedule or to move to part-time employment. Alternatively, caregivers may face hours limitations at their jobs, such that all those caregiving hours could not be gainfully employed at the current wage. Moreover, for many caregivers a current wage is not observable because they have left the workforce completely to provide care, while others may have previously retired of their own accord so they would not be working even if not providing care (this would be particularly true for older spouses who themselves are past typical retirement ages when a partner needs care).

To address these concerns, we proceed in two steps. First, rather than using actual wages which may be biased through caregiving or unobserved, we use predicted wages. Specifically, we use country-specific labor market data to predict the wage rate for informal caregivers based upon their observable characteristics including age, education, and gender. We also use the same model to predict the probability that caregivers are working to account for the fact that many caregivers (particularly spouses) would not be working even if not caregiving. We then construct a forgone wage measure as predicted probability of work multiplied by the predicted wage.

However, this approach ignores completely the value of leisure time (or time spent on other activities such as caring for one's own children). As a second step, we therefore combine the "forgone wage" method with the "proxy good" method, valuing non-work hours at wage of a home care worker (or more specifically multiplying the wage of a home health aide by the probability of *not* working). Our "combined" valuation method therefore reflects the weighted average of each caregiver's valuation under the forgone wage and the proxy good methods. In the country chapters, we also offer a second alternative as a lower bound, where we value the forgone leisure hours at zero.

To see how this methodology works in practice, consider a 55-year-old caring for their aging parent. Because most people at this age are working and are at the peak of their earnings trajectories, the unconditional predicted wage of this caregiver will be quite high, as would be the probability of

Table I.13 **Informal care cost as a fraction of formal spending**

Country	Informal to Formal Care Ratio
Canada	0.72
Denmark	0.53
England	1.56
Germany	0.70
Italy	2.03
Japan	0.75
Netherlands	0.52
Singapore	0.53
Spain	1.21
US	0.65

Notes: Informal care estimates are for the combined valuation approach and are for the 65+ population, as are the formal care spending totals.

working. The forgone wage component would thus itself be high. However, because the probability that this person is not working is relatively low, the predicted proxy good cost will also be low, and most of the valuation of their caregiving time will be driven by the predicted forgone wage. In contrast, consider a 75-year-old caring for their spouse. At this age, most people do not work, so the probability of working and thus the forgone wage component will be relatively low, and predicted proxy good component will comprise the majority of the imputed value of care.

Table I.13 reports the ratio of our informal care cost estimates to the total cost of formal long-term care in each country. The first feature to note is that in every country, there is meaningful spending on informal care relative to formal care; informal care cannot be ignored as a cost of long-term care. But it is also important to note that these ratios vary dramatically, ranging from around 0.5 in the Netherlands, Denmark, and Singapore to 2.03 in Italy.

In table I.14, we then report our estimates of the total cost of long-term care across countries as a fraction of GDP, reporting the division between private versus public financing, institutional versus at-home settings, and formal versus informal provision of care.

In each country, informal care plays a substantial role. As a result, including the cost of informal care reduces the relative reliance of each country on publicly provided care. However, even with these informal care costs included as part of the privately borne costs, the Netherlands, Denmark, and Japan rely more on public than private care. Canada, the United States, and Germany share these costs more evenly divided between public and private sources, though private costs remain greater in all three. And finally, in England, Italy, Spain, and Singapore, public costs are strictly dominated by private costs.

The importance of including the cost of informal care is also clear when drawing comparisons in the reliance of each country on home versus insti-

Table I.14 **Total costs of long-term care across countries**

Care Type	Source	Canada	Denmark	England	Germany	Italy	Japan	Netherlands	Singapore	Spain	US
Nursing Home	Public	0.9%	1.1%	0.4%	0.5%	0.3%	0.5%	1.6%	0.1%	0.3%	0.5%
	Private	0.4%	0.1%	0.2%	0.4%	0.1%	0.1%	0.2%	0.1%	0.3%	0.2%
	All	1.2%	1.2%	0.6%	0.9%	0.4%	0.6%	1.8%	0.2%	0.6%	0.7%
Home Care	Public	0.4%	0.4%	0.3%	0.7%	0.2%	1.0%	0.9%	0.1%	0.1%	0.3%
	Private	0.2%	0.1%	<0.1%	0.2%	<0.1%	0.1%	<0.1%	0.1%	<0.1%	0.1%
	All	0.6%	0.5%	0.3%	0.9%	0.3%	1.0%	0.9%	0.2%	0.2%	0.4%
Informal Care	Private	1.3%	0.9%	1.4%	1.2%	1.4%	1.2%	1.4%	0.2%	0.9%	0.7%
Total	Public	1.3%	1.5%	0.6%	1.3%	0.5%	1.5%	2.5%	0.1%	0.5%	0.8%
	Private	1.8%	1.1%	1.7%	1.8%	1.5%	1.3%	1.6%	0.4%	1.2%	1.0%
	All	3.1%	2.7%	2.3%	3.0%	2.1%	2.8%	4.1%	0.5%	1.7%	1.8%
Age-Adjusted Total		3.3%	2.7%	2.4%	2.9%	1.7%	2.0%	4.2%	1.0%	1.8%	2.1%

Notes: Each cell reports the fraction of GDP spent by each country (column) on the specific category of care (row). In the total section, informal care costs are included as private costs. The age adjusted total is computed by regressing total care costs in our sample on the fraction of the population over age 65, then adding the residuals back to the predicted cost for the average fraction aged 65+.

tutional care settings. Whereas most countries spend more on formal nursing home care than formal home care, home care costs are unsurprisingly higher than nursing home costs when the cost of informal care is included. However, the degree to which this is the case varies, with home care costs more than twice the cost of nursing home costs in Japan, England, Italy, and Germany, but only about 25 percent greater in Denmark.

Perhaps the most substantial differences lie in the relative reliance on care from formal versus informal sources. On one hand, formal sources of care are dominant in the Netherlands, with formal costs approximately twice those of informal care. Formal costs are also larger than informal costs in the United States, Japan, Denmark, Canada, Germany, and Singapore. In contrast, informal costs in Spain, Italy, and England are larger than formal costs, with each country relying upon family and friends to care for their aging populations.

In making these tabulations, countries intentionally excluded the cost of programs designed to compensate informal caregivers directly, because doing so would result in a double-counting of those costs—the value of an informal caregiver's time would be included in both the publicly paid component and in the estimate of the cost of informal care. However, it is notable that in every country with programs that compensate informal caregivers, the costs of these programs are still far below our estimates of the true informal care costs. For example, in Germany, the total spending for compensating informal caregivers was approximately one-third of our imputed value of that informal care. (The estimate of the publicly paid compensation for caregivers is biased upward because the allowances can be used to purchase private formal care rather than to compensate caregivers.)

A similar issue exists in Italy wherein public support for home care is provided primarily through cash payments that can be spent on either purchasing formal care or compensating informal caregivers. The amount of this support is equivalent to approximately 0.6 percent of GDP. By excluding this spending from the formal home care category, the results shown here underestimate the extent of formal home care, because at least some of the cash support is spent on formal care. However, it is also important to note that the cost of informal care in Italy remains well over twice the amount spent on these cash payments. Finally, in England, spending on the "Carer's Allowance" to compensate informal caregivers is equivalent to only 10 percent of the imputed cost of informal care.

An important factor driving differences across countries in these costs is the difference in the degree of population aging. In Japan the age 65 or older population comprises nearly 30 percent of its population, while in Singapore the share is less than 15 percent. To demonstrate the importance of the age distribution in driving our results, we regress total LTC spending (formal and informal) as a fraction of GDP on the fraction of the population over age 65. We then add the fitted values from this regression to the residual from

Table I.15 Categorization of long-term care systems

		Formal Setting		Cost Burden		Provision	
County	Eligibility	Nursing Home	Home Care	Public	Private	Formal	Informal
Canada	Means Tested	1.2%	0.6%	1.3%	1.8%	1.8%	1.3%
Denmark	Universal	1.2%	0.5%	1.5%	1.1%	1.8%	0.9%
England	Means Tested	0.6%	0.3%	0.6%	1.7%	0.9%	1.4%
Germany	Universal	0.9%	0.9%	1.3%	1.8%	1.8%	1.2%
Italy	Means Tested	0.4%	0.3%	0.5%	1.5%	0.7%	1.4%
Japan	Universal	0.6%	1.0%	1.5%	1.3%	1.6%	1.2%
Netherlands	Universal	1.8%	0.9%	2.5%	1.6%	2.7%	1.4%
Singapore	Universal	0.2%	0.2%	0.1%	0.4%	0.3%	0.2%
Spain	Universal	0.6%	0.2%	0.5%	1.2%	0.8%	0.9%
US	Means Tested	0.7%	0.4%	0.8%	1.0%	1.1%	0.7%

Notes: Column 1 shows if eligibility (but not necessarily cost sharing) is universal or means tested. Columns 2–3 are based upon formal care only, while columns 4–7 use the combined cost totals that include both formal and informal care costs. Columns 2–7 are derived from table I.13. The percentages reported in the table express costs as a fraction of GDP.

each country to produce age-adjusted cost estimates. These are reported in the last row of table I.14. As noted earlier, this is a crude adjustment, but it allows for a sense of the importance of age differences for our results.

In many cases, the effect of this exercise is relatively minor. However, for a handful of countries at either extreme of population aging—Japan and Italy as the oldest and the United States and Singapore as the youngest—the adjusted estimates are notably different. In both Japan and Italy, the overall percentage of GDP from LTC costs after adjustment falls from 2.8 and 2.1 percent to 2.0 and 1.7 percent; in Singapore and the United States, the percentages rise from 0.5 and 1.8 percent to 1.0 and 2.1 percent.

Based upon our analyses, we propose categorizing long-term care systems on four dimensions: eligibility (need versus means based); setting (institutional versus home); cost burden (public versus private); and provision (formal versus informal). To be clear, this is a subset of the potentially interesting dimensions of heterogeneity across these national systems. But given our limited set of countries we have decided to create a broad classification for illustration and then to provide more specific details below.

We illustrate the results of this exercise in table I.15. Column 1 of the table classifies systems by eligibility, while columns 2–7 report the relevant fractions of GDP based on the estimates in table I.13. We summarize these dimensions below:

1. While Germany, Denmark, Japan, Spain, and the Netherlands have universal public systems that focus primarily on care needs (though often determine co-payments based upon means), the United States, England, Canada, and Italy base eligibility for support on both needs and financial

means. It should be noted, however, that Spain's universal care system is geared toward home care rather than nursing homes, which remain means tested, and that Singapore's system is designed as a compulsory savings program, the deposits to which can be spent on long-term care in the future.

2. In the formal care sector, only Japan spends more on home care than nursing homes, while Singapore and Germany devote a similar fraction of GDP to each. Most countries devote substantially higher shares to nursing homes, with the Netherlands, Denmark, Canada, England, and Spain spending more than twice as much on nursing homes.

3. In Japan, the Netherlands, and Denmark, the majority of long-term care costs are borne by the public sector, while over two-thirds of the cost are borne by private sources in Italy, England, Spain, and Singapore.

4. In all countries, regardless of the generosity of their public systems, informal care plays an important role, with wider variation in the amount of formal care spending than informal care.

Notably, the universality of coverage is not necessarily a good proxy for the generosity of LTC systems as measured by the distribution of public versus private costs, and there appears to be little relationship between the generosity of formal care systems and the costs borne by informal sources.

It is important to recognize that there is a wide range of factors that impact differences between countries in cost estimates, even beyond differences in the long-term care systems of each country. We have already illustrated the importance of the fraction of the population over age 65 in the fraction of GDP countries spend—this is particularly the case in Japan, where we estimate a 40 percent increase in relative costs due to population aging, and in Singapore, where we estimate that the younger population reduces costs by 50 percent.

Of course, this broad summary misses important country-specific context. In the United States the patchwork public support system means that obtaining a perfect estimate of long-term care costs on the elderly is impossible—much nursing home spending is actually spending on post-acute care through Medicare (included in cost totals) rather than on what is traditionally considered long-term care, and much of the spending through home and community-based services (excluded from cost totals) goes toward people under age 65.

In contrast, in England, the reported total cost of care includes all residential care, in facilities both with and without nursing care, both of which receive some public support. And in Japan, per person nursing home costs are far lower than elsewhere, in part due to a stronger reliance on unskilled aides rather than more skilled nurses.

In several countries, the variation in wages drives differences in cost. Denmark has some of the highest wages for home care aides relative to the average wage within the country, although the effect on costs is somewhat mitigated by a relatively high reliance on aides rather than nurses. Italy, in contrast, has both a relatively low fraction of the population living in nursing homes as well as relatively low pay in the nursing home sector compared to the average wages.

Relatedly, differences in the composition of caregivers can drive differences in the predicted conditional or unconditional wages of informal caregivers, which in turn can yield higher estimates of the value of informal care. In Canada, the predicted wage conditional on working is quite high compared to the average wage, while in the Netherlands, the caregiving population is on average younger than elsewhere, also resulting in a high predicted unconditional wage.

Utilization is also an important factor. Germany has the highest ratio of nursing home residents to its elderly population, over twice the rate of some countries in our sample, while Spain's administrative statistics indicate a strikingly low ratio (roughly 3 percent) of home care recipients to the elderly population.

The age distribution of those over the age of 65 is also an important factor driving cost differences. For example, Singapore has a far younger elderly population as measured by the fraction of the elderly who are over age 85. In turn, its elderly population appears considerably healthier as measured by limitations with daily activities.

Finally, one striking feature should be noted about the United States relative to other countries. While the United States has lower total long-term care spending, spending on formal long-term care, and public long-term care spending, are at about the median of our sample. The United States is actually a particular outlier in terms of low private long-term care spending, and in terms of low informal care. This is inconsistent with the view of the United States as having a more privately financed system than other countries.

V. Conclusion

As this introduction clearly demonstrates, the provision of long-term care is a key issue around the world. While countries differ in their spending and modes of long-term care delivery, every country is facing a rapid rise in the oldest old population and the associated need for long-term care services. To facilitate thinking about this issue in a global perspective, the project brings together the foremost experts in the economics of long-term care, for 10 of developed nations, to understand the approaches that different countries take to the issue of long-term care and the resulting costs.

We outline here the current trends and policies existing in each country. In future work we will delve into more detail on various topics under the umbrella of long-term care, examining types of care, forecasts of coming needs, and potential solutions for this growing worldwide problem.

Key topics going forward will be an examination of long-term care needs for those with Alzheimer's disease and related dementias, the impact of caregiving on the financial and emotional well-being of informal caregivers, how we might improve the provision of formal care, attract more workers to this sector and improve their training and support, and the potential for technological and medical advances to alleviate some of the caregiving burden.

We hope this current volume and any subsequent studies will fill an important void in the literature on caregiving by providing cross-country comparisons, highlighting similarities and differences, and learning what policies and practices are most effective. Each of the chapters is organized in a parallel structure with tables being largely comparable across countries and arranged in a similar order. In structuring the chapters this way, we hope it will be relatively easy for the interested reader to move back and forth across chapters to compare the various statistics. While we have highlighted here what we think are some of the most striking patterns, we encourage readers to explore the individual chapters in depth to understand the full richness and complexities of the various systems.

We note that this work only begins to scratch the surface of what is a wide variety of important economic and policy issues surrounding long-term care and related government policies and programs and how countries will deal with these issues and others in the face of rapidly aging societies. Complicating the issues is the fact that changes in one program or policy will likely impact other programs. Consider for example, changes designed to increase the normal retirement age or make early retirement less affordable. Changes along these lines will increase the cost to potential caregivers of leaving the labor force and perhaps reduce the availability of informal care.

On a more optimistic note, there may be labor saving technological advances (such as the use of robots as discussed in the Japan chapter) that reduce the demand for labor, freeing up workers for other jobs in a society facing a declining workforce due to population aging.

Immigration, a highly controversial topic around the world, will likely play an important role as many countries have become dependent on immigrants to provide long-term care. Other policies such as increases in wage rates, as well as improvements in training and working conditions, may make employment in the long-term care sector more attractive.

Perhaps most importantly, medical advances can dramatically change the landscape. A cure or treatment for Alzheimer's disease may greatly reduce the need for care, while other advances may lengthen life and lead to more care albeit at older ages.

The chapters in this volume also raise important questions about the governance of long-term care. In many countries, the responsibility for the organization and financing of long-term care resides with local governments, rather than existing at a central level. While this policy may align with local political preferences, given geographic differences in the demographic characteristics of the population (difference in the age structure, wealth, and family structure), there may be a need for more cost-sharing at a national level.

An important issue that we do not address is the quality of care provided and what governments can do to measure and ensure high-quality care. One of the most significant weaknesses of our cross-country comparisons is that we have no means of comparing quality or intensity of care beyond a measure of hours, nor can we accurately measure the severity of need. An important goal for future work in this area should be to develop internationally comparable measures of quality to assess how the long-term care strategies of different nations are reflected in the quality of care received. This is a difficult task, as even families which care greatly about the well-being of a family member have difficulty in assessing care received and elderly individuals, particularly those with cognitive impairments, may be unable to provide input in this regard.

Finally, this volume has had relatively little to say regarding the role of private insurance markets in addressing these issues in the long run. Private long-term care insurance currently plays a minor role around the world, and future work could examine the barriers to the development of these markets and how they might evolve given the growing need in our aging world. Other solutions to providing for care include the assets elders have tied up in housing or life insurance. Programs allowing the elderly to access these funds to finance long-term care needs could provide relief for many.

References

Genworth (2019). Cost of Care Survey. https://www.genworth.com/aging-and-you/finances/cost-of-care.

Hurd, Michael, Paco Martorell, Adeline Delavande, Kathleen J. Mullen, and Kenneth M. Langa. 2013. "Monetary Costs of Dementia in the United States." *New England Journal of Medicine* 368: 1326–1334. DOI: 10.1056/NEJMsa1204629.

Meijer, Erik, Maria Casanova, Hyewon Kim, Ana Llena-Nozal, and Jinkook Lee. 2022. "Economic Costs of Dementia in 11 Countries in Europe: Estimates from Nationally Representative Cohorts of a Panel Study." *Lancet Regional Health-Europe* 20: 100445. June 24. DOI: 10.1016/j.lanepe.2022.100445.

Paying for Care. 2022. https://www.payingforcare.org/how-much-does-care-cost/.

1

The Economics of Long-Term Care in Canada

Kevin Milligan and Tammy Schirle

1.1 Introduction

The COVID-19 pandemic brought the current state of long-term care into broad public focus as many people in Canada and other countries wondered about the available quality of care. Going forward, these concerns about the quality of long-term care will grow more acute with the aging of the population. The first Canadians born in the baby boom generation are now approaching their eighties, an age range where the use of long-term care grows rapidly. So, with increased demand for higher-quality care and an increase in the demographic demand for care, the pressures on the long-term care sector are set to increase.

This paper contributes a broad overview of the Canadian long-term care system. Taking an economist's viewpoint, we bring together supply and demand factors to provide an economic analysis of the current and future path for long-term care. Canada's situation shares similarities with other countries but also embodies unique structural characteristics.

The two key similarities of the Canadian situation with most other OECD

Kevin Milligan is a professor of economics at the Vancouver School of Economics at the University of British Columbia, and a research associate of the National Bureau of Economic Research.

Tammy Schirle is a professor of economics at Wilfrid Laurier University.

This paper is written for the NBER international comparison project on long-term care. We thank the organizers and other participants in the project for helpful suggestions, and Moyosoreoluwa Sogaolu for research assistance. Some of the research was conducted at the SWORD Research Data Centre under contract 21-MAPA-SWO-7104. Statistics Canada is not responsible for the results presented in this paper. For acknowledgments, sources of research support, and disclosure of the authors' material financial relationships, if any, please see https://www.nber.org/books-and-chapters/long-term-care-around-world/economics-long-term-care-canada.

countries are the demographic pressures and the focus on residential care. Because of the aging of the baby boom population, the share of Canadians over age 65 will more than double from 11 percent of the population in 1990 to a forecast of 24 percent in 2050. For those over age 85, the population share is projected to go from 1 percent in 1990 to over 5 percent by 2050. These trends are broadly aligned with other OECD countries. The other main similarity is the focus of the system on residential care. While there has been increasing attention paid to home and community non-residential care, the majority of public expenditures still goes to residential care in nursing homes.

The main difference of the Canadian case with other OECD countries is the mix of public and private care. There is large variance across countries in the public share of long-term care spending, and Canada is overall in the middle of the pack. The Canadian private long-term care insurance market is small, and shrinking further in recent years. The biggest difference from other countries is the dispersion of the public-private mix within Canada, as other countries have more uniform country-wide systems. Long-term care in Canada is regulated provincially, and the public systems are designed and funded provincially. The result is that different provinces have very different systems. Quebec's long-term care is largely in a unified public system, while New Brunswick's system is dominated by private not-for-profits, and Ontario's has a majority of private for-profit facilities.

The analysis below aims to provide an introduction to, and overview of, the economics of long-term care in Canada in the context of international comparison. We are somewhat constrained in this comparison by lack of a large survey like the Health and Retirement Study in the United States, or the SHARE data in many European countries. For this reason, we lack data on some key metrics used to compare across countries, such as standardized measures of activities of daily living. In addition, there is not one national system to describe but instead a plethora of subnational systems, each with its own administrative information and design features.

This paper begins with background information on the demographics, well-being, health, and living arrangements of Canadian seniors. We then provide information on caregiving, focusing both on the receivers and givers of care in institutional settings, as well as formal and informal home-based settings. We then describe the structure of the long-term care system in Canada, including public and private components. Finally, we offer calculations estimating the total cost of long-term care of the elderly in Canada, including implicit costs for informal home care.

1.2 Demographics, Well-Being, Health, and Living Arrangements

This section provides background context to the discussion of caregiving for Canadian seniors. We begin with statistics on demographic trends. We

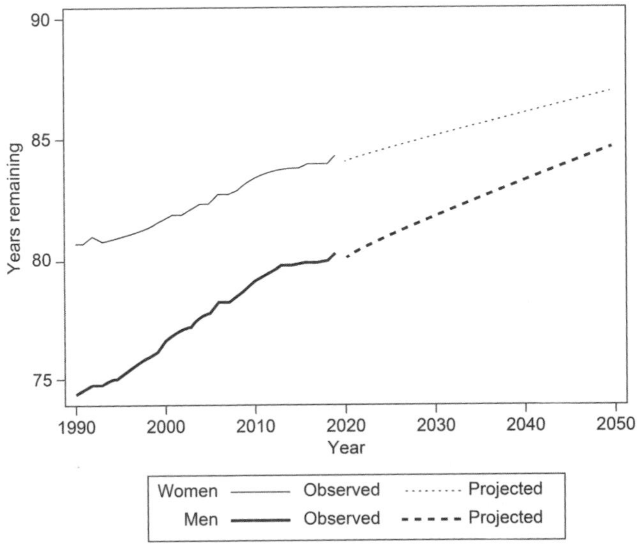

Fig. 1.1 Life expectancy at birth
Source: Authors' tabulations using Canadian Human Mortality Database (2022) mortality rates. Our projections are based on Lee-Carter methods.

then provide an overview of the health of Canadian seniors, their economic well-being, and their living arrangements.

1.2.1 Demographic Facts and Trends

The Canadian population is aging and is expected to age further over the next few decades. The figures discussed in this section illustrate this trend. For women, life expectancy at birth (figure 1.1) increased from 80.6 years in 1990 to 84.3 years in 2019. Our projections suggest women's life expectancy will increase further, reaching 87 years by 2050.[1] For men, life expectancy at birth was 74.3 years in 1990, increasing to 80.2 by 2019 and expected to increase to 84.7 by 2050. Life expectancy at age 65 shows similar trends (figure 1.2). In 1990, women aged 65 could expect to live an additional 19.4 years and are projected to see that increase to 24 years by 2050. Men have seen greater improvements in old-age mortality, as men in 1990s expected to live another 15.4 years after age 65, while men are projected to live another 22.2 years after age 65 in the year 2050.

1. We use a simple Lee-Carter method for projecting mortality rates, estimating Canada-wide mortality separately for men and women, using single-age mortality rates from 1981–2019 to form projections. We made use of the leecarter command in Stata in developing these estimates, and the general time trend component is projected as a random walk with drift process (using ARIMA in Stata). Projections are sensitive to the time period used in estimates and these projections appear to underestimate life expectancy. See Bohnert et al. (2015) for information on the methods used by Statistics Canada, which are more involved than what is used here.

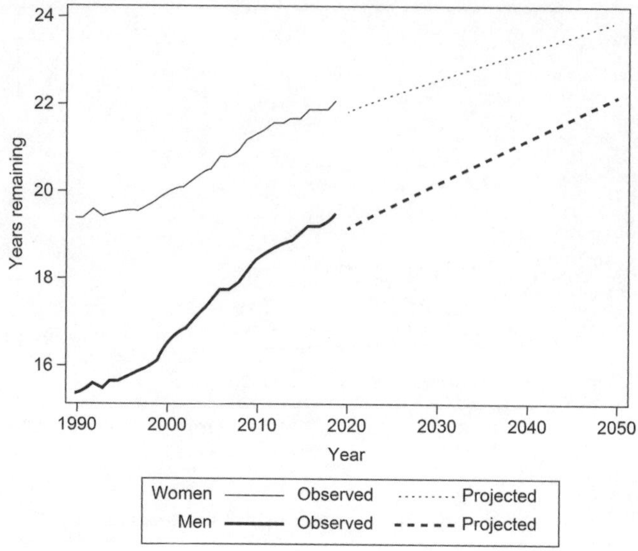

Fig. 1.2 Life expectancy at age 65

Source: Authors' tabulations using Canadian Human Mortality Database (2022) mortality rates. Our projections are based on Lee-Carter methods.

Overall, these projections indicate a large and sustained increase in lifespans, on average. In Milligan and Schirle (2021) these average lifespan changes are disaggregated by splitting people into quantile groups using earnings from ages 50–54. That paper finds that longevity is greater for high earners than low earners, but that the gains in longevity over time have been almost uniform across the earnings distribution.

Alongside general reductions in fertility rates in Canada, the increase in life expectancy is a key reason why older individuals now represent a larger share of the population. The share of the population that is over the age of 65 (figure 1.3) rose from 11 percent in 1990 to nearly 18 percent in 2019. The trend is expected to slow after 2030 as the baby boom generation ages, with the share age 65 and over reaching 24 percent by 2050.

For the population share age 85 or older, the baby boom generation again dominates the trends. In figure 1.4, the rapid increase in the population age 85 and older begins around 2030, 85 years after the war's end in 1945. The 85 and older population share will go from about 1 percent in 1990 to almost 6 percent by 2050. Correspondingly, those over 85 represent an increasingly larger share of the older population after 2030 (figure 1.5). So, the elderly population will grow to have a much heavier share of the oldest old. These demographic trends underlie projections for the increase and timing of an upswing in the demand for long-term care in the coming decades.

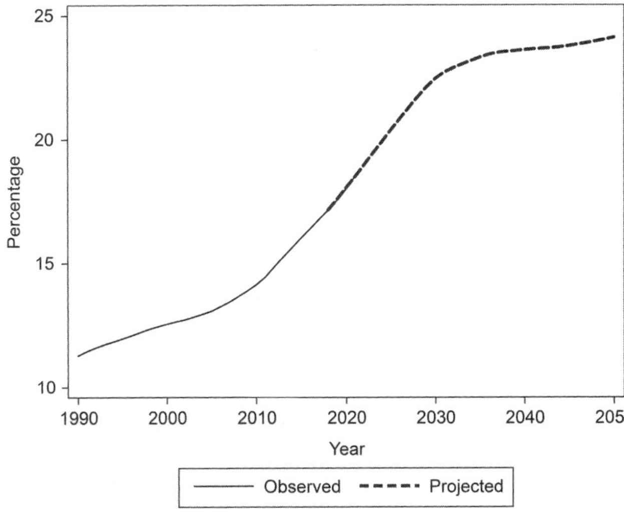

Fig. 1.3 Population over age 65
Source: Authors' tabulations based on Statistics Canada Tables 1700005 and 1700057

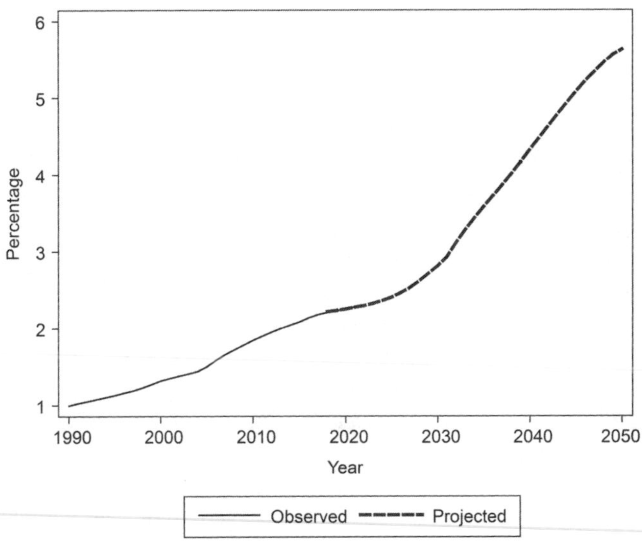

Fig. 1.4 Population over age 85
Source: Authors' tabulations based on Statistics Canada Tables 1700005 and 1700057

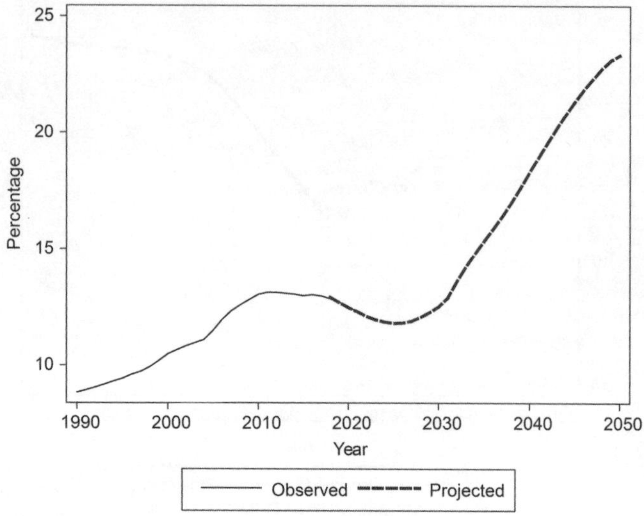

Fig. 1.5 Share of age 65+ population age 85+
Source: Authors' tabulations based on Statistics Canada Tables 1700005 and 1700057

1.2.2 Health Measures

In Canada, we do not have the standard Activities of Daily Life (ADL) measure available in the data sets we use for this paper. Instead, we focus on questions that report whether the respondent needs "help" with an activity. Needing help is potentially a distinct concept from having a limitation. When comparing our results to other countries, this difference should be kept in mind.

From pooling years in the Canadian Community Health Survey for those living in private homes, we find that 22 percent of the population aged 65 or older, and 59 percent of the population aged 85 or older, report requiring help with at least one daily activity due to a long-term health condition or aging.[2] In table 1.1 we present both the types of help needed and the count for the number of items with which help is needed, for the 65 and older and 85 and older populations.

It appears common for people to need support with tasks required for independent living (as 48 percent of seniors aged 85 or over need help running errands). However, a significant portion also requires help with basic activities of daily living: 6 percent of those 65 and older, and 20 percent of those 85 and older, required help with personal care (which includes washing, dressing, eating, or taking medications). The increase in need between the 65 and older and 85 and older population is striking. For many categories

2. This number can be inferred from table 1.1; by taking one minus the proportion needing help with zero activities in the right-hand panel.

Table 1.1 **Proportion of older population needing help with activity**

Activity	65+	85+	Total	65+	85+
Meals	0.080	0.261	0	0.777	0.408
Errands	0.156	0.481	1	0.086	0.159
Housework	0.157	0.423	2	0.046	0.119
Finances	0.083	0.291	3	0.033	0.107
Basic			4	0.021	0.070
Personal care	0.057	0.201	5	0.019	0.075
Moving	0.033	0.093	6	0.019	0.063

Note: Canadian Community Health Survey master file tabulations, years 2009, 2010, 2013, and 2014. Individuals report whether they require help with each activity. Total indicates how many of these activities an individual has reported needing help with.

Table 1.2 **Health and well-being of individuals**

	18–64	65+		85+	
	All	All	Personal care	All	Personal care
Good health	0.904	0.773	0.364	0.666	0.419
Good mental health	0.940	0.944	0.810	0.916	0.831
Satisfied	0.908	0.820	0.419	0.651	0.372

Note: Canadian Community Health Survey master file tabulations, years 2009, 2010, 2013, and 2014. Personal care refers to anyone who reports needing help with personal care needs due to a long-term health condition or aging. Good health indicates good, very good or excellent self-reported health. Satisfied indicates that on a scale of 1 to 10 the respondent rates satisfaction with life as 6 or higher.

in table 1.1 the need increases by a factor of more than three between the two age categories. This finding emphasizes the very steep gradient of need for help with the activities of life as Canadians age.

The greater need for help with daily activities seen above reflects a general deterioration in health. In table 1.2, we see older individuals are less likely to report good (or better) health than younger individuals aged 18–64. Among older individuals, however, there is a large gap between those who report needing help with personal care and the general elderly population. For example, while 77 percent of those 65 and older report good health, only 36 percent of those 65 and older who require help with personal care also report good health. Those requiring personal care are also less likely to report good mental health, although the gap between them and the general population is not as large (81 percent vs. 94 percent among those 65 and older). Life satisfaction, however, appears to decline with age and is quite low among those requiring help with personal care. For those aged 65 and older who require help, 42 percent are satisfied with life. For ages 85 and older, this proportion drops slightly to 37 percent.

In table 1.3, we describe the income position of seniors who require help with personal care or housework. We split the population of seniors by

Table 1.3 **Distribution of household income**

	All 65+	Personal care	No Personal Care	
			Housework	No Housework
<50% median	0.295	0.364	0.334	0.285
50–100% median	0.305	0.256	0.293	0.310
100–150% median	0.122	0.096	0.097	0.128
150–200% median	0.045	0.027	0.032	0.048
200% + median	0.232	0.258	0.241	0.229

Note: Canadian Community Health Survey master file tabulations, years 2009, 2010, 2013, and 2014. Household income (normalized for family size) is compared to the median (normalized) household income for respondents age 18 and over. The second column restricts the sample to those reporting need for help with personal care.

their position relative to the median income, where the median income line is drawn using the incomes of all families with main income earner age 18 and older. From our tabulations here, we find nearly 30 percent of people aged 65 and over have a household income that is less than half the median income of the broader population. When restricted to the subset of seniors requiring help with personal care or housework, there are fewer seniors in the middle-income groups, and more in the lowest-income groups. Among those needing help with personal care, 36.4 percent have less than half the median income, a higher share than for the full age 65 and older population.

1.2.3 Economic Well-Being

We now describe the financial situation of Canadian seniors as context to the affordability of care among older Canadians. The surveys we use here for assessing the economic well-being of Canadians exclude from the sampling frame those who live in congregate living facilities. So, the results are representative only for those who live in private dwellings. We return to this discussion when assessing living arrangements below.

In table 1.4, we report the income distribution of older families (age 65 and over) relative to the income distribution of younger families (aged 18–64). To account for differences between the two groups in terms of average family size, the lower panel (B) in table 1.4 offers estimates based on normalized income. When considering the incomes of those 65 and older against those age 18–64, the high ratio at the fifth percentile of each distribution clearly stands out: the fifth percentile of after-tax normalized income among older families and individuals is 1.65 times the income of younger families. This largely reflects the relative generosity of Canada's retirement income system in the supports available to the non-elderly at the lowest part of the income distribution (where child benefits are relatively generous but minimal supports are available to childless non-elderly families).

Table 1.4 **Income distribution**

	After-tax income			Before-tax income		
	18–64	65+	Ratio	18–64	65+	Ratio
			A. Total			
5th	14319	20696	1.45	14477	20798	1.44
10th	23703	21970	0.93	24544	22046	0.90
25th	45857	31834	0.69	50286	32649	0.65
50th	79016	48431	0.61	90786	51612	0.57
75th	121350	73490	0.61	145787	82655	0.57
90th	169658	104498	0.62	209811	124480	0.59
95th	208547	132187	0.63	265705	162991	0.61
Mean	91302	59293	0.65	109814	67660	0.62
			B. Normalized			
5th	11291	18606	1.65	11469	18831	1.64
10th	15901	20330	1.28	16162	20492	1.27
25th	25332	23313	0.92	27118	23478	0.87
50th	38501	32246	0.84	44220	34378	0.78
75th	54592	46254	0.85	65898	53058	0.81
90th	74224	64024	0.86	92750	77481	0.84
95th	90160	79196	0.88	116184	98814	0.85
Mean	43151	39081	0.91	51844	44552	0.86

Note: Incomes presented in 2019 Canadian dollars, using the 2018 Canadian Income Survey, representing income of a census family, authors' tabulations. For the bottom panel, income is "normalized" using the OECD equivalence scale to account for the number and age of census family members.

For middle- and higher-income seniors, the numbers reported in table 1.4 suggest seniors have incomes that are lower than among younger families. Seniors at the 75th percentile of the normalized after-tax income distribution have incomes that are 85 percent of the incomes of younger families at the 75th percentile. It is worth noting that the ratio of normalized before tax incomes among seniors to younger families is similar in magnitude to the earnings replacement rates of retired couples in the upper half of the income distribution described in Ostrovsky and Schellenberg (2010). The overall picture that emerges is a more compressed income distribution for seniors than for younger Canadians. This finding is consistent with more detailed (but earlier) research in Baker and Milligan (2009).

As older individuals may use their assets to finance consumption in retirement, we also consider the wealth available to older and younger families (table 1.5). We categorize families by the age of the major income earner within the family. At the 10th percentile, the net worth of seniors is more than eight times that of younger families (18–64). At the median, however, this ratio falls to just over two. Both groups' distributions are highly skewed,

Table 1.5 **Wealth distribution**

Percentile	18–64	65+	Ratio
10th	1075	9000	8.37
25th	25950	103075	3.97
50th	192000	385000	2.01
75th	573350	850000	1.48
90th	1177005	1551050	1.32
95th	1812505	2147500	1.18
Mean	445891	642207	1.44

Note: Canadian dollars, 2019, Survey of Financial Security. Net worth of an economic family excluding employer pensions.

Table 1.6 **Consumption distribution**

	A. Total			B. Normalized		
	18–64	65+	Ratio	18–64	65+	Ratio
5th	13186	10432	0.79	8929	8159	0.91
10th	17941	12477	0.70	11418	9733	0.85
25th	28021	17889	0.64	16122	12860	0.80
50th	45051	28298	0.63	23644	18834	0.80
75th	68289	45776	0.67	34970	28316	0.81
90th	96514	68738	0.71	49690	41673	0.84
95th	121288	87047	0.72	62922	53115	0.84
Mean	53002	35925	0.68	28192	23084	0.82

Note: Canadian 2019 dollars, using the 2017 Survey of Household Spending. Total consumption of a household is presented here. Normalized amount adjusts household spending to account for the number of household members and whether members are adults or children using available information about household size and type and the OECD equivalence scales.

with seniors at the 95th percentile holding 1.18 times the assets of younger families at the 95th percentile (worth C$1.8 million in 2019 for younger families and C$2.1 million for senior families).

Tables 1.4 and 1.5 then suggest the flow of income may be most important for judging the financial well-being of lower-income seniors while net worth is more important for seniors in the middle or upper end of the distribution. In table 1.6 we consider the distribution of consumption expenditures more directly. Across the distributions, the ratio of expenditures among seniors is lower than among younger households. The normalized income estimates are important to highlight—consumption at the lowest end of the distribution is nearly identical among seniors (65+) and younger households (18–64), with a ratio of 0.91 at the fifth percentile.

Note the middle of these normalized expenditure distributions is where there appears the greatest difference (0.80), however this is a much larger ratio than what was observed in table 1.4 with respect to income measures. This suggests that consumption of seniors is more similar to younger fami-

Table 1.7 **Dwelling type by age group, 2021**

	All ages		Age 65+		Age 85+	
	(1000s)	(%)	(1000s)	(%)	(1000s)	(%)
All	36986	100%	7021	100%	861	100%
Private dwellings:						
Single detached	21496	58.12%	3948	56.23%	322	37.39%
Other	14832	40.10%	2639	37.58%	301	35.00%
Collective dwellings:						
Health care facility	485	1.31%	408	5.82%	233	27.07%
Hospitals	11	0.03%	8	0.11%	4	0.44%
Nursing homes	185	0.50%	172	2.45%	100	11.62%
Seniors' residence	160	0.43%	151	2.15%	89	10.33%
Nursing+res.	68	0.18%	65	0.92%	38	4.46%
Other	234	0.63%	39	0.56%	7	0.76%

Source: Tabulations based on 2021 Census tables 98100046 and 98100045

lies than is income. The difference is explained by more seniors having the ability to draw down savings to fund current expenditures. These differences in younger and older family consumption patterns are explored in detail in Milligan (2008).

1.2.4 Living Arrangements

The well-being of individuals also depends on their living arrangements. Living with others is an important determinant of opportunities to share income or receive care from family or friends.

In table 1.7 we provide counts of Canadians in 2021 by the type of dwelling they lived in. The vast majority of Canadians aged 65 or older (94 percent) live in private dwellings (whether owned or rented). The remaining 6 percent of Canadians aged 65 or older live in "collective" dwellings, which for the most part are the long-term care facilities—nursing homes and seniors' residences—that provide care. A larger portion of those aged 85 and older (27 percent) live in these collective dwellings. Later in the paper (section 1.3) we return to discussing the situation of seniors in long-term care facilities.

As mentioned earlier, survey-based data on income, consumption, and wealth are limited by the sampling frame which includes only those in private dwellings. This means that for the older (85 and older) population, the 27 percent in nursing homes and seniors' residences are not included in those data.

The types of family Canadians live in change over a person's life cycle. In figure 1.6 we consider the living arrangements of individuals in private dwellings in 2016 using the Census. The figure describes the likelihood of couples or single individuals to live independently (without others).

We see that at ages 65–74 and over age 75, most people are living inde-

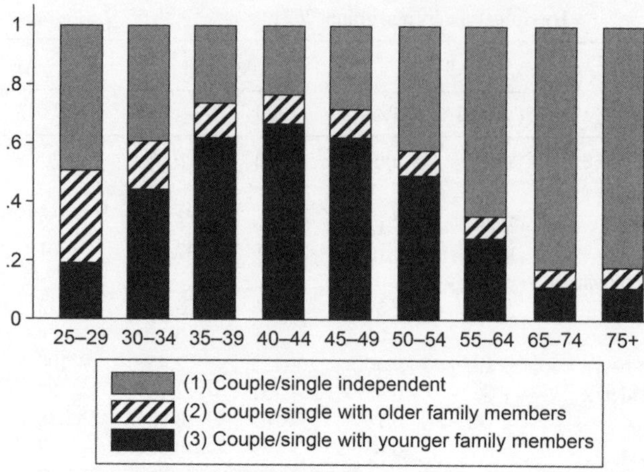

Fig. 1.6 Living arrangements of individuals in private dwellings

Note: Economic family considered. Age group is the age of the single individual or oldest in the couple. Category (3) implies individual or spouse is oldest family member.

Source: Authors' tabulations using Census 2016 PUMF

Table 1.8 Living arrangements of older individuals in private dwellings

	65+		85+	
	All	Personal care	All	Personal care
Living arrangements				
With spouse	0.587	0.447	0.313	0.260
With child	0.085	0.130	0.118	0.164
Alone	0.286	0.264	0.469	0.317
Other	0.092	0.199	0.124	0.274
Homeowner	0.779	0.692	0.654	0.655

Note: Canadian Community Health Survey master file tabulations, years 2009, 2010, 2013, and 2014. Personal care refers to anyone who reports needing help with personal care needs due to a long-term health condition or aging.

pendently (82 and 81 percent, respectively). A small share has older family members in their household (6 percent and 7 percent respectively) but are less likely than younger individuals to have older family living with them. A slightly larger share of seniors over 65 are the oldest members of their household, with younger family present (11 percent).

In order to understand how living arrangements vary by health status, we turn back to a pooled sample from the Canadian Community Health Survey. Tabulations presented in table 1.8 indicate that the seniors living with younger members may be able to rely on those younger members for some care. The seniors (65 and older) needing help with personal care appear more likely to live with one of their children (13 percent) than the broader sample of seniors (8.5 percent). Those needing care are also slightly less likely to live alone.

The analysis in this section shows that contemporary Canadian seniors are, overall, in a solid economic situation, with higher wealth and less low-income incidence than younger Canadians. Most live in a home they own with their spouse. However, when looking at the age 85 and older compared to the age 65 and older group, more live with their child or alone, and fewer live in their own house. These patterns are driven in part by deteriorating health at older ages, with incidence of the need for help more than triple in the 85 and older population what is seen in the age 65 and older population. Because the age 85 and older population is set to grow substantially, the patterns among the older seniors we document in this section should attract particular attention by policymakers.

1.3 Receipt and Provision of Care

After the broad overview of the demographic and economic situation of Canadian seniors in the previous section, we now turn to the use and provision of care for Canadian seniors. We begin with the receipt of care, looking at how institutional residential care and home-based care are provided. We then focus on the labor market for caregivers, with analysis of the number of workers and their wages.

1.3.1 Receipt of Care

In Canada, the vast majority of individuals over age 65 live in private dwellings—either independently or with extended family, as described earlier in section 1.2.4. As individuals age and require more care, they are more likely to rely on institutional care—in nursing homes, residential care facilities, or facilities that combine the two (see table 1.7 in the previous section). In this section, we describe the extent to which elderly Canadians are receiving care in each setting and the types of care they receive.

1.3.1.1 Institutional Care

In 2021, there were 408 thousand individuals aged 65 or older living in seniors' homes, nursing homes, and health care facilities according to the Census (see table 1.7 in the previous section). According to an institutional accounting provided by the Canadian Institute for Health Information that we analyze in this section, the number of formal long-term care beds is just under 200,000. This is consistent with the Census count if one considers that many of those who identify as living in a "seniors' home" may live in a facility that does not meet the technical definition for a "long-term care bed."

The Canadian Institute for Health Information assembles the National Health Expenditure Database, part of which focuses on long-term care. The database is assembled from the national income and product accounts,

Table 1.9 Number of beds and facilities

Jurisdiction	Beds: Number of LTC beds	Beds: Beds per 1000 persons age 65+	Facilities: Number of LTC homes	Facilities: Share Public	Facilities: Share private / for profit	Facilities: Share private / NFP
Newfoundland and Labrador	3014	26	40	98%	2%	0%
Prince Edward Island	1244	39	19	47%	47%	6%
Nova Scotia	6842	33	84	14%	44%	42%
New Brunswick	4925	29	70	0%	14%	86%
Quebec	40823	24	440	88%	12%	0%
Ontario	78902	30	627	16%	57%	27%
Manitoba	9765	44	125	57%	14%	29%
Saskatchewan	8924	47	161	74%	5%	21%
Alberta	15762	26	186	46%	27%	27%
British Columbia	27478	28	308	35%	37%	28%
Yukon	312	56	4	100%	0%	0%
Northwest Territories	201	51	9	100%	0%	0%
Nunavut	28	18	3	100%	0%	0%
Canada total	198220	29	2076	46%	31%	23%

Source: National Health Expenditure Database, Canadian Institute for Health Information, 2021

provincial administrative records, and a number of different surveys.[3] We use these data to report the overall counts of beds and facilities, along with the breakdown by who owns the facility—publicly owned, owned by private for-profit organizations, or owned by private not-for-profit organizations.

The first column of table 1.9 shows the number of beds in each province and territory, and the second column normalizes the beds by the population age 65 and older. There is a large spread in the number of beds per capita, ranging from 18 per 1,000 in Nunavut Territory to 56 per 1,000 in Yukon Territory. The patterns defy easy description, with different mixes of political culture, rural-urban differences, and incomes being contributing factors.

The right-hand panel of table 1.9 shows facilities counts and how they break down into the share owned by public, private for-profit, and private not-for-profit organizations. There is a wide range. The systems in the territories are fully public, and Quebec is almost fully public. On the other end, New Brunswick has no publicly owned homes, but an 86 percent share for private not-for-profit. Ontario has the largest for-profit share, at 57 percent. British Columbia has an even mix of the three types.

The main explanation for this cross-provincial difference is the constitutional assignment of responsibilities to federal and provincial governments. Long-term care facilities are regulated provincially. As facilities-based long-term care is not publicly insured as part of federal-provincial agreements,

3. See Canadian Institute for Health Information (2021). See also Grignon and Spencer (2018) for refinements and criticisms of the measures used in the database.

standards of care and staffing are set by provincial governments under provincial statutes and regulations. For example, Ontario's (recently rewritten) legislation is called the Fixing Long-Term Care Homes Act, 2021 (Statutes of Ontario Chapter 39). To be granted a license, there must be an infection prevention and control program, a policy to prevent abuse and neglect, and a procedure for reporting and complaints, among other rules. For staffing, the regulations require that personal support workers complete a program that meets established standards, including 600 hours of class time and practical time. Other provinces have similar types of legislation and regulations, but the scope and level of regulation varies across provinces.

1.3.1.2 Noninstitutional Care

In 2021, there were 6.6 million Canadians aged 65 or older living outside of institutions, often independently but also in private homes with other family members (see table 1.7 and figure 1.6 in the previous section). A substantial portion of this group requires help with personal care and other daily activities in their own homes.

In figure 1.7 we describe how often older individuals (65 or older and 85 or older) indicate receiving help, and whether they paid for the help they received. Among those aged 85 or older, 56 percent did not receive any care or help. Only 3 percent relied exclusively on paid help, 16 percent relied exclusively on unpaid help, and a larger group (25 percent) relied on both paid and unpaid help.

We can also examine the intensity of care by looking at the number of hours of care received. Table 1.10 reports the distribution of hours of care received of both unpaid and paid types. There is stronger reliance on unpaid care than paid care. Comparing the medians to the means, it appears the distribution of hours is highly skewed. The mean of unpaid hours at age 65

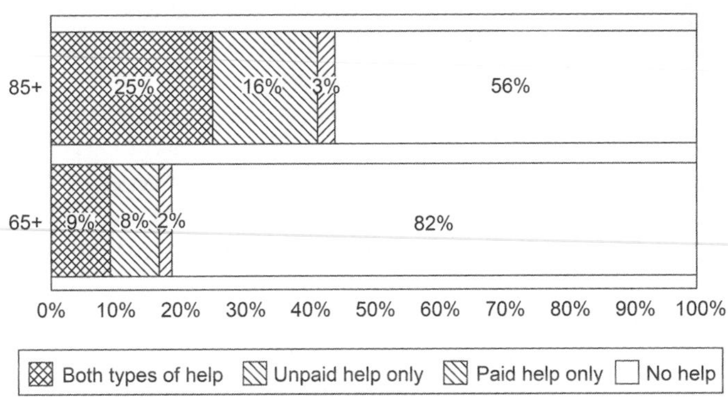

Fig. 1.7 Older individuals receiving help, paid and unpaid

Source: GSS Cycles 32 (2018) and 26 (2012) tabulations by authors. Respondents are asked about the hours of care or help received in an average week.

Table 1.10 Hours of care received by older individuals

	65+		85+	
	Unpaid	Paid	Unpaid	Paid
Average	22	8	26	13
25th percentile	2	1	3	1
Median	7	2	10	3
75th percentile	21	6	24	8

Source: GSS Cycles 32 (2018) and 26 (2012) tabulations by authors. Respondents are asked about the hours of care or help received in an average week.

Table 1.11 Use of paid home care services, by type of service

	Portion who report use	
Type of home care used	65+	85+
Nursing care	0.038	0.114
Other health care	0.015	0.038
Medical equipment and supplies	0.019	0.050
Personal or home support	0.055	0.234
Other services	0.013	0.051
Any care	0.092	0.313

Source: CCHS tabulations, years 2015, 2016, 2018, 2019

and older, for example, is 22 hours but the median is only 7 hours, and the 75th percentile only reaches 21 hours. The average number of hours rises with age, but only by 30 percent on average across the two age groups shown. This contrasts with the extensive margin (any care being received) in figure 1.7, which showed the proportion using any care at all more than doubled from ages 65 and older to ages 85 and older. So while there are age gradients in both the intensive margin (table 1.10) and the extensive margin (figure 1.7), it is the extensive margin that shows the stronger age gradient as more seniors find they need at least some care at older ages.

1.3.1.3 Reliance on Paid Home Care Services

In table 1.11 we provide further information on the types of home care services individuals receive. (We note that figure 1.7 and table 1.11 are based on different sources and that the former suggests only a slightly different percentage of seniors relying on paid care.) Among the services people pay for, it is most common for the elderly to require nursing care (11 percent of those age 85 or over) and personal or home support (23 percent of those age 85 or over). Both of these categories also exhibit very strong growth from the younger (age 65 and older) to the older (age 85 and older) groups.

In table 1.12, we describe the length of time people over age 65 have used

Table 1.12 **Duration of home care services used, by type of service (age 65+)**

Duration of Care	Nursing	Other health	Med. Equip	Support	Other
Less than 1 month	0.203	0.233	0.125	0.076	0.115
1-less than 3 months	0.152	0.199	0.167	0.076	0.094
3-less than 6 months	0.089	0.098	0.118	0.067	0.078
6 months—less than 1 year	0.135	0.141	0.114	0.110	0.133
1–3 years	0.220	0.168	0.224	0.311	0.285
More than 3 years	0.202	0.161	0.252	0.361	0.296

Source: CCHS tabulations, years 2015, 2016, 2018, 2019. Each column sums to 1.

different types of home care services. It appears most types of home supports reflect a need for longer-term care: 42 percent of those using nursing care have been receiving help for more than one year, and 67 percent of those receiving personal and home supports have received the help for more than one year. Reliance on other health care services appears a bit more short term, which includes services such as physiotherapy. This pattern of shorter-term care may arise from recovery from specific acute health events like a broken bone or a heart attack.

When home care services are paid, it is not necessarily the care recipients paying for these services directly. Similar to facilities-based long-term care, home care services are not publicly insured as part of federal-provincial agreements. As such, the standards for assessing home care needs and the out-of-pocket costs to recipients vary by province. For example, in Quebec a needs assessment determines whether individuals qualify for home care services (such as nursing or personal support) and if approved there is no payment required by individuals. For domestic help services (such as housekeeping) in Quebec, those needing assistance can receive a subsidy (up to C$18.65 per hour) depending on age, income, and family situation. In British Columbia, a needs assessment also determines eligibility for home care services, but payment for services depends on income. BC individuals with low income (e.g., such as those receiving the Guaranteed Income Supplement) are not required to pay anything, but those with a modest income will be charged up to C$300 per month for support.[4]

Overall, a large part of home care services is paid for by provincial governments (as discussed in more detail in the next section). In table 1.13 we see that most people receiving nursing care services did not typically pay anything at all (as 87 percent of those aged 65 and over who used nursing services report spending C$0). Only 6 percent of seniors who use nursing services paid C$200 or more in a typical month for the help received. People

4. A measure of annual income is multiplied by 0.00138889 to define a daily rate.

Table 1.13 Amounts paid for home care services used, by type of service (age 65+)

Amount paid (typical month)	Nursing	Other health	Med. Equip	Support	Other
$0	0.87	0.83	0.66	0.51	0.35
$1-less than $50	0.04	0.05	0.08	0.11	0.22
$50-less than $100	0.02	0.03	0.05	0.11	0.17
$100-less than $200	0.01	0.03	0.06	0.10	0.10
$200 or more	0.06	0.06	0.14	0.18	0.16

Source: CCHS tabulations, years 2015, 2016, 2018, 2019. Each column sums to 1.

are more likely to pay for personal and home support (which includes things like housekeeping) and other supports (such as meal delivery). In a typical month, 18 percent of those relying on personal and home supports spend C$200 or more.

1.3.1.4 Reliance on Informal or Unpaid Care

Our tabulations presented earlier in figure 1.7 and table 1.11 suggest 17 percent of individuals aged 65 or older, and 41 percent of individuals aged 85 or older, rely heavily on unpaid care or help. We provide more granular detail on informal care provision at the end of the next subsection.

1.3.1.5 Total Use of Care

Combining our information on help received at home in figure 1.7 with the information on the proportion of people living in collective dwellings in table 1.7 allows some insight into the overall distribution of types of care. In figure 1.8 we combine these data for those using care (either at home or because they live in a nursing home or hospital) into one chart for each of the two age groups.[5] These data come from different sources but are useful to gain a rough sense of how the types of care are distributed. Among those using some type of care, the share in a nursing home or hospital rises from 17 percent in the age 65 and older population to 28 percent in the age 85 and older population. A smaller proportion uses only unpaid help at age 85 and older than at younger ages. The pattern here can be characterized as showing an increase in the use of professional care types at older ges.

1.3.2 Care Providers

The care sector is labor intensive, but the labor is employed through various occupations spread across multiple sectors. There is also paid and

5. For this calculation, we exclude the residents of "seniors' residences" reported in table 1.7, since these are not care facilities. We do include the category of facilities that combine seniors' residence and nursing home services, since those facilities do provide care.

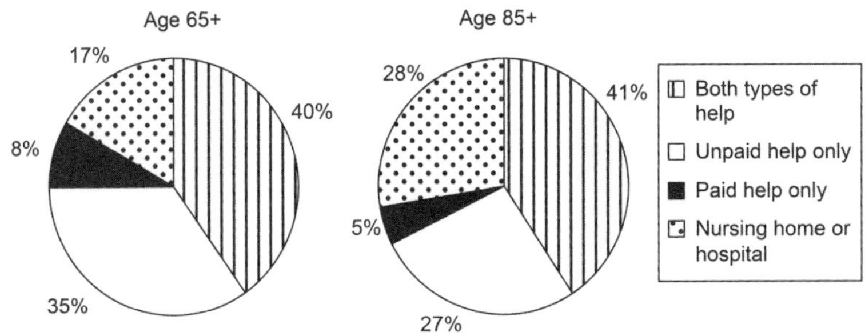

Fig. 1.8 Distribution of types of care

Source: Combined data from figure 1.7 and table 1.7; see the sources indicated there. Each pie segment shows the proportion needing the indicated care type, among the population using any type of care for each age group.

Table 1.14 Individuals working in nursing homes and residential care, 2016

Occupations	NOCs (4-digit)	Number	Female (%)	Canadian born (%)
Registered nurses, Supervisors	3011–3012	32,240	92.3	64.1
Licensed nurses	3233	23,095	91.2	64.4
Nurses' aides, orderlies	3413	131,030	90.3	62.5
Total	NA	186,375	90.7	63.0

Source: Tabulations using Census 2016 master files. Sample of individuals working in NAICS 6230.

unpaid work performed in this sector, with various degrees of skill, both with and without formal training. This subsection looks at the types and characteristics of the workers providing the care, then moves onto wages and understanding those who work without pay.

1.3.2.1 Institutional Care Workers

A wide range of occupations is involved in providing care to elderly individuals in institutions. We describe those care workers who report working in the "nursing and residential care facilities" industry (NAICS code 6230) in table 1.14 and figure 1.9.

From Census data in table 1.14, we see that in 2016 there were more than 186 thousand people working in institutional care as care workers. Nurse aides and orderlies were the most common occupation in this industry (131 thousand workers), and 55 thousand licensed and registered nurses worked in these facilities. These jobs are predominantly filled by women (90.7 percent overall). We note that while nursing occupations are more than 90 percent female, management positions (not listed here) are more likely filled by men than other occupations (being 71 percent female). The

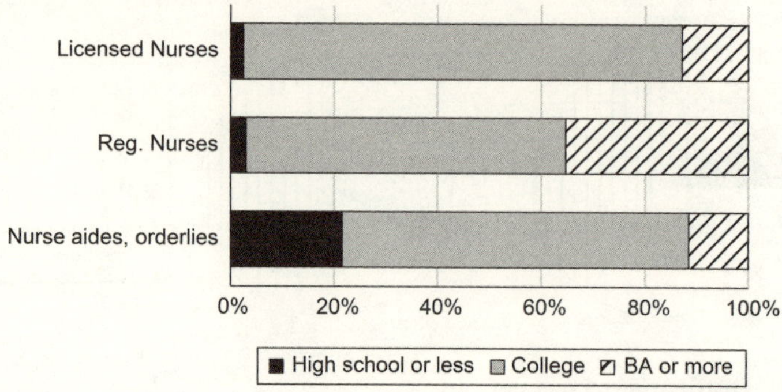

Fig. 1.9 Education of workers in nursing homes and residential care, 2016
Source: Tabulations using Census 2016 master files. Sample of individuals working in NAICS 6230 within select occupations. See table 1.14 for occupation classifications.

Table 1.15 Number of home care workers in Canada by NAICS

Home Care Workers (NOC 4412) NAICS:	Number of workers	Portion
Home health care (6216)	18490	0.19
Nursing homes and res. care (6230)	10190	0.11
Individual and family services (6241)	28630	0.30
Private households (8141)	15050	0.16
All other NAICS	23650	0.25
Total	96010	1

Source: Census 2016 tabulations

industry also tends to have fewer Canadian-born workers than the broader labor force.[6] This is particularly true among those working as nurses' aides and orderlies, where only 62.5 percent of workers are Canadian born.

Looking at education levels, there are very few nurses who have only completed high school, as most positions require formal training in a college or university program.[7] Education standards are part of regulations for long-term care facilities, and the precise details of the standards vary across provinces. Those working as nurse aides and orderlies are more likely to have lower levels of education, while 78 percent have completed college or university.

6. Using Statistics Canada Table 14–10–0085–01, Canadian-born individuals represented 76 percent of the labor force in 2016.

7. Given the small sample sizes within some professions at the lowest education levels, we have grouped high school graduates with those having less than high school to meet confidentiality requirements associated with using the Census master files.

Table 1.16 **Select characteristics of home care workers**

	Portion
Female	0.894
Canadian born	0.634
Education	
Less than high school	0.128
High school	0.247
College	0.482
University (BA+)	0.144

Source: Census 2016 tabulations

Table 1.17 **Usual hourly wages of workers in select occupations, April 2019**

		April 2019 wages		Relative to Median Wages of	
	NOC	Average	Median	All workers	High School or less
Nurse supervisors	3011	40.27	43.00	1.68	2.39
Registered nurses	3012	37.63	39.00	1.57	2.17
Aides, orderlies	3413	20.76	20.35	0.86	1.13
Home care support	4412	18.45	17.00	0.77	0.94

Source: Average and median wages by NOC are provided by the Labour Market Information Council, using LFS master files. The median wage of all workers (C$26.92) and those whose highest degree is high school or less (C$20) is found using the LFS April 2019 PUMF. All dollar amounts are in nominal terms.

1.3.2.2 Formal Home Care Workers

In table 1.15 and table 1.16 we describe individuals who report working as home care workers (NOC 4412) in 2016. These data are also drawn from the Census.

In table 1.15 we see these workers describe themselves as working in a range of industries—including home health care, nursing homes, individual and family services and private households. Like nurses and nurses' aides in institutional care, home care workers (in table 1.16) are predominantly female (89 percent) and less likely than the broader labor force to be Canadian born (63 percent). Home care workers are also less educated, on average, than those working in institutional care, with 37 percent having completed high school or less.

1.3.2.3 Wages of Paid Care Workers

For many individuals providing paid care, occupation-specific skills are transferable between industries. As such, we consider the usual hourly wages with select occupations without restricting to specific industries. These wage data are presented in table 1.17 (for April 2019), and broader trends in nominal wages are presented in figure 1.10.

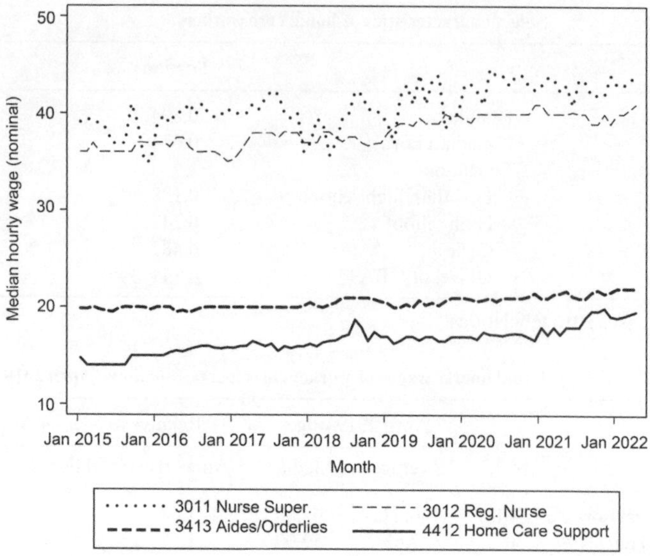

Fig. 1.10 Wages of care workers

Source: Custom tabulations provided by the Labour Market Information Council, using LFS master files

Given the higher education requirements for nurses, it is not surprising that their average and median wages are relatively high. In table 1.17, we see that the median wage of registered nurses is 1.57 times the median wage of all workers. Aides and orderlies, who are less educated than nurses (figure 1.10), are paid roughly half as much as nurses and are paid slightly more than the average worker with high school or less. Home care support workers are paid less than aides and orderlies, with wages more in line with other workers with high school or less.

In figure 1.10 we see that wages of home care support workers have been catching up to those of nurses' aides and orderlies. Some of these workers are covered by centralized bargaining and union contracts in some provinces. For example, Ontario nurses have contracts with hospitals and nursing homes, using templates that are then tailored to specific workplaces.

1.3.2.4 Unpaid Caregivers

As shown in figure 1.7, many seniors rely on unpaid care and help. In figure 1.11, we describe the portion of individuals (by age group) who report providing informal unpaid care to someone because of a long-term health condition or aging. We see that a significant portion of the population provides such care, with the largest share among those aged 50–59 (37 percent). We also see that older individuals are more likely to be the caregivers of elderly recipients compared to a broader sample of all caregivers.

The characteristics of caregivers are reported in table 1.18. We see that

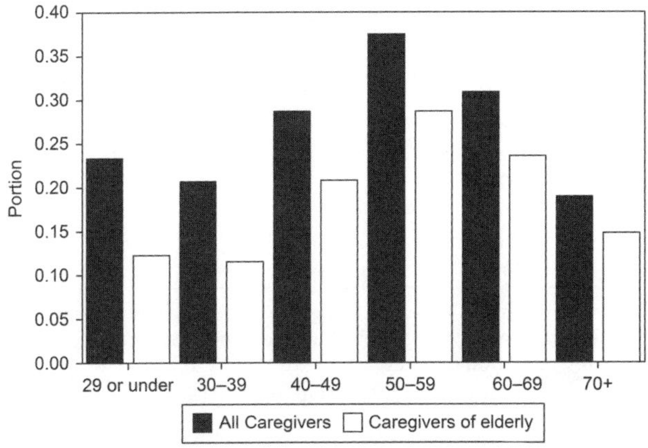

Fig. 1.11 Provision of care by age

Source: GSS Cycles 32 (2018) and 26 (2012) tabulations by authors. All caregivers represent individuals who indicate they provide care to someone because of a long-term health condition or aging. Caregivers of the elderly represent the subset of individuals who provide care to at least one person age 65 or older.

Table 1.18 Characteristics of informal care providers

	All caregivers	Care for elderly person
Age group		
29 or under	0.205	0.158
30–39	0.128	0.105
40–49	0.176	0.188
50–59	0.243	0.272
60–69	0.159	0.177
70+	0.089	0.101
Female	0.540	0.540
Education		
Less than high school	0.129	0.113
High school grad.	0.268	0.256
Trades/College	0.334	0.339
BA+	0.270	0.291

Notes: Sample of individuals who report being caregivers, providing care to family or friends due to a long-term health condition or aging. Caregivers for an elderly person are the subset of caregivers who provide care to at least one person age 65 or older.

Source: GSS Cycles 32 (2018) and 26 (2012) tabulations by authors

caregivers are distributed across all age groups, although those caring for at least one elderly person (age 65 or older) are more likely from older age groups themselves. Caregivers are slightly more likely to be female (54 percent), and their education levels closely resemble those of the broader population.[8]

8. The education levels presented in table 1.18 are similar to 2018 levels found using LFS PUMFs, where for example 26 percent of all individuals have a BA or more and 15 percent have less than high school.

Table 1.19 Primary caregiver relationship to elderly recipients

Relationship to care recipient	Portion
Spouse	0.357
Son	0.153
Daughter	0.305
Son-/daughter-in-law	0.034
Other relatives	0.073
Non-relative	0.079

Notes: Sample represents individuals aged 65 or older who receive informal care; relationship characterizes who their primary caregiver is. Caregivers provide care to family or friends due to a long-term health condition or aging.

Source: GSS Cycles 32 (2018) and 26 (2012) tabulations by authors

Table 1.20 Hours of informal care provided per week

Hours of care	All caregivers	Care for elderly person
Mean	12	11
25th percentile	2	1
Median	4	3
75th percentile	10	10

Notes: Caregivers provide care to family or friends due to a long-term health condition or aging. Caregivers for an elderly person are the subset of caregivers who provide care to at least one person age 65 or older.

Source: GSS Cycles 32 (2018) and 26 (2012) tabulations by authors

We now turn to the question of who is providing informal care. In table 1.19, the data show that spouses provide a lot of informal care, as 35.7 percent of care recipients reported their spouse as the primary caregiver.[9] As one might expect given the age distribution of caregivers in table 1.18, the elderly often rely on their children for care. Daughters are commonly a person's primary caregiver (30.5 percent), while sons and in-laws are less likely to be the primary caregiver (15.3 percent and 3.4 percent respectively).

The elderly will also rely on relatives other than their children and spouses. We also see in table 1.19 that 7 percent of elderly care recipients report their primary caregiver is another relative—such as an aunt or cousin. A sizeable group of elderly individuals rely on caregivers who are not their relatives.

Finally, we turn to the hours of care provided by informal caregivers, in table 1.20. Many individuals provide care (as in figure 1.11), but most provide only a few hours of care every week. Typically, caregivers who provide care to at least one elderly person are providing only three hours of care

9. We note that when caregivers are asked who their primary care recipient is, only 8 percent of those caring for at least one elderly person reports their spouse as the primary recipient. This suggests many caregivers are many individuals' primary caregiver.

every week (median). The distribution of hours of care, however, is clearly skewed, with an average hours of care that is higher than the 75th percentile. Worth noting, the hours of care among caregivers of the elderly is not higher than the hours of care among all caregivers.

1.4 Canada's Long-Term Care System

Long-term care in Canada is financed by public and private sources. In this section, we describe the general structure of the public funding programs and the features of the private long-term care insurance market. We close the section with a summary of the shares of spending from different sources.

1.4.1 Public Systems

Each province and territory operates its own long-term care system. There are publicly owned long-term care homes and also public subsidies for lower-income people. In many provinces the public subsidies can be used at private facilities. Access to public facilities is by application, with the criteria generally including citizenship, residency, age, and health. For example, in British Columbia an applicant needs to be a Canadian citizen or permanent resident, have lived in British Columbia for at least three months, be 19 years of age or older, and "be unable to function independently because of chronic, health-related problems . . ."[10] Needs are assessed, and the appropriate care facility type is offered.

For public subsidies, each province has its own formula.[11] Typically, there is a minimum contribution required, which is generally aligned closely with the value of federal Old Age Security and Guaranteed Income Supplement payments (designed to set a minimum personal allowance for the person receiving care). For income higher than these federal pensions, the provincial subsidy is typically clawed back. There are also asset tests in Quebec and in Newfoundland and Labrador.

The public subsidy formula's minimum personal allowance (or minimum contribution) and clawback rates differ across provinces. For example, in Quebec (in 2022) the personal allowance was set at C$290 per month. Every dollar of income over that allowance is clawed back to pay for the individual's long-term care fees (at C$2,019 per month). In British Columbia, a minimum allowance of C$325 is set aside, and 80 percent of additional income is clawed back (with a maximum rate of C$3,847.20 in 2023). In Saskatchewan, the personal allowance (for 2023) was set at C$466 per month

10. See "Are You Eligible?" on the website of the government of British Columbia, https://www2.gov.bc.ca/gov/content/health/accessing-health-care/home-community-care/are-you-eligible.

11. See Blomqvist and Busby (2012) for a description of the system and details on each province. Library of Parliament (2020) provides an update.

Table 1.21 Features of long-term care insurance market

Age	Has LTCI	Average Premium	Average Benefit
50–54	0.154	83	2307
55–59	0.113	173	1693
60–64	0.089	117	2310
65–70	0.054	120	2155

Source: Retirement Savings Institute, HEC Montreal survey RSI-01. See Boyer et al. (2020)

(as the difference between their minimum fee and a first income threshold defined at C$1,759), and income is then clawed back at a rate of 57.5 percent (with a maximum rate of C$3,218).

1.4.2 Private Long-Term Care Insurance

Health insurance in Canada is dominated by provincial public health insurance programs that list a wide range of insurable services. Many employers offer supplemental health insurance to cover services not insured by the public plans, most notably pharmaceuticals, dental, and vision care. Those on public income assistance have access to public coverage for these supplemental needs, but some Canadians have no supplemental health coverage. For long-term care insurance, few employer-sponsored supplemental plans cover long-term care risks.

Beyond the group insurance market, there is a small and shrinking market for individual private long-term care insurance. The available policies typically require two or more ADLs to trigger a payment under the policy. The policies are priced by age and sex. These long-term care insurance policies are not often bundled with other insurance products on the private market, but instead sold as a standalone product (Boyer et al. 2020, 139). This might make these products more difficult to sell because of the increased marketing costs. Several providers have fallen out of the market, with few options left on the market.[12]

A 2016 survey of Quebec and Ontario residents ages 50–70 found that 10.5 percent had purchased a long-term care insurance policy. The average premium was C$116, and the average insured benefit was C$2,467.[13] The age pattern of these characteristics is shown in table 1.21. There is a clear downward gradient in long-term care insurance uptake from 15.4 percent at ages 50–54 to 5.4 percent at ages 65–70. The premium and the benefit,

12. For example, in 2021 SunLife (a major insurer) raised their long-term care insurance policy premiums for existing customers and closed the product to new sales. SunLife now offers a new product that requires a one- to two-year waiting period for any benefit. See "Important information for Clarica and Sun Long Term Care Insurance policy owners," https://www.sunlife.ca/en/health/long-term-care-insurance/clarica-and-sun-long-term-care-insurance-policyowners/.

13. See Boyer et al. (2020) for details.

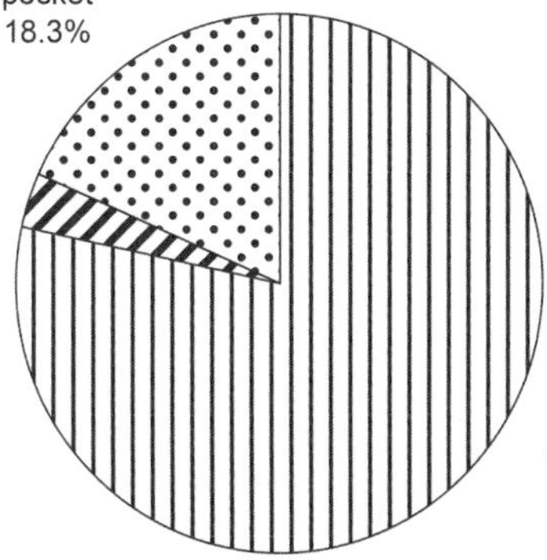

Fig. 1.12 Long-term care financing by source
Source: OECD Health Expenditure and Financing database

however, do not have clear trends across ages. As the number of firms offering such insurance has continued to shrink since 2016, the proportions with a policy are likely even lower today.

1.4.3 Summary of Financing Shares

Taking the different financing sources together, we can depict the different financing shares as a percent of the total. The data from the OECD used here include all types of long-term care (institutional, community care, and home care) for care recipients of any age. Later in the paper, we focus more closely on those age 65 and older. Figure 1.12 shows that public financing represents 78.4 percent of spending, with private spending making up the residual 21.6 percent. The strong majority of the private financing comes from out-of-pocket spending, with insurance payments making up only 3.3 percent of the total.

1.4.4. Long-Term Care as Share of Economy

In figure 1.13 we put these costs in context by comparing them to GDP. This comparison is useful both to understand the impact of the long-term care system on the Canadian economy and also to facilitate international comparisons. Again, we use the OECD data that include spending on all types of long-term care and at all ages. Over the 31 years from 1990 to 2021, the share of GDP going to long-term care rose from under 1 percent of GDP in 1990 to more than 2 percent by 2021. In constant 2019 Canadian dollars, this represents an increase from C$11 billion in 1990 to C$52 billion in 2021.[14] The nominal value in current dollars for 2021 is C$54 billion.

14. See Grignon and Spencer (2018) for a discussion of the shortcomings of the OECD long-term care estimates.

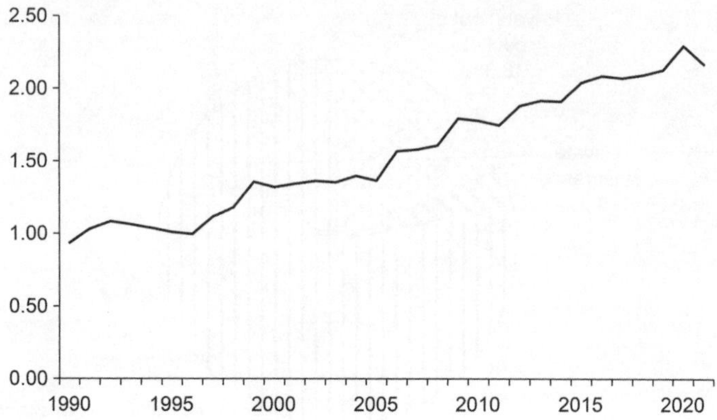

Fig. 1.13 Share of GDP spent on long-term care
Source: OECD Health Expenditure and Financing database

1.5 Total Cost of Long-Term Care

In this section we bring together elements of the data presented in this paper to produce an estimate of the total cost of care. We now narrow our focus to those age 65 and older. We aim our calculations for 2019, reported in 2019 Canadian dollars. For each of three line items (residential long-term care, home care, informal care) we present an estimate of the number of users and total spending. We then calculate a cost per user for each of the three line items. We begin by going through the source of each element of the calculation for each line item, then bring it together in a final calculation at the end of the section.

1.5.1 Residential Long-Term Care

We have different sources to draw on for the total number of people in care and the total cost. We describe the sources and our choices for the total cost calculation here.

For the count of people, our Census counts reported in table 1.7 show 172,000 in nursing homes, 151,000 in seniors' residence, and another 65,000 in combined nursing homes and seniors' residences. So, a narrow definition of just "nursing homes" would yield 237,000 people. In table 1.9, we report the National Health Expenditure Database count of beds in long-term care residences, which is 198,220. For the total cost calculation, we use the Census count of nursing homes: 237,000 people.

For costs, we rely primarily on data from the OECD Health Statistics Database OECD (2022), supplemented with information from the National Health Expenditure Database (Canadian Institute for Health Information 2021). The differences between these data sources are documented and explored in Grignon and Spencer (2018), who find the OECD measures too broad in most cases compared to their preferred measure. For residential long-term care, we begin with the OECD estimates for "in-patient long-term care." This includes individuals of any age. To produce an estimate for ages 65 and older, we use the age-based breakdown from the National Health Expenditures Database, which finds for 2019 that those age 65 and older represent 78.7 percent of total residential long-term care expenditures.[15]

Our estimate for residential long-term care expenditures using this method is C$27.9 billion for 2019. This is split between C$19.6 billion in public spending and C$8.3 billion in private spending, for roughly a 70/30 percent public/private split. Our estimates are in line with other estimates, including the results presented in National Institute on Ageing (2019).

1.5.2 Paid Home Care

We now turn to formal, paid home care. In table 1.11 we use the Canadian Community Health Survey and find that for those age 65 and older, the proportion who report paid care is 9.2 percent. In Figure 1.7 we employ the General Social Survey, where the percent who report using any paid care is 11 percent. For our calculations, we use the number from the GSS: 11 percent. There were 6.6 million Canadians ages 65 and older in 2019, so we estimate 726,000 are users of formal paid home care.

For costs, we again rely on data from the OECD Health Statistics database (OECD 2022), which provides a total cost of home care for the public sector. Grignon and Spencer (2018) note that the OECD does not provide estimates for private home care but instead allocates those expenditures elsewhere in its health accounts. Alternatively, Grignon and Spencer (2018) present a method to estimate private expenditures, finding for the period up to 2014 the average share of private spending is about 28 percent. We use this number to interpolate a private expenditure for home care, by applying the 28 percent share to the dollar value provided by the OECD.

The OECD public home care estimate (across all ages) is C$11.5 billion. To adjust for the proportion of these expenditures associated with those age 65 or higher, we draw on a data source from the Canadian Institute for Health Information, which reports the age splits for clients in a subset of provinces.[16] This source has 87 percent of clients age 65+. Of course, the services provided across ages may differ, so this division is perhaps rough. We apply this 87 percent then multiply by (0.28/0.72 = 0.3888) to find the associated private sector home care spending amount. We arrive at an estimate of C$10 billion for public home care and C$3.9 billion for private home care. This is larger than found by National Institute on Ageing (2019), which reports only C$4 billion in public and C$2 billion in home care expenditures.

15. We use Series E3, Table E.3.24.1. The category "other institutions" is mainly residential long-term care facilities.

16. We use tables from the 2021 Home Care Reporting System data provided by the Canadian Institute for Health Information.

However, our public home care estimate is in line with the National Health Expenditures Database reported total for 2019 of C$10.2 billion for the public sector across all ages.

1.5.3 Unpaid Home Care

To estimate the cost of unpaid home care, we first derive an estimate for the number of hours of care that is used by recipients. Since those hours of care are not contracted in a market, there is no wage to observe. The person providing the care does have a value for their time, either because those hours could potentially be sold to the market (if the caregiving person is working) or because those hours must come out of leisure time that could otherwise be maintained by paying for care. Below, we explain two different methods of valuing these hours provided to caregiving that incorporate these opportunity costs of time in different ways.

For someone who has a job, hours spent caregiving might come out of hours that could be sold to their employer. If the labor market is competitive and flexible, then we can value that time at the observed market wage for those individuals. We do so by taking the average hourly wages in the 2019 Labour Force Survey by age-gender-education group. Then, we use the age-gender-education information in table 1.18 to develop a composite wage that corresponds to the typical demographics of caregivers. The average wage calculated in this way for 2019 is C$27.34/hour. This estimate of a caregiver's opportunity cost is how we value forgone potential work hours that are devoted to informal caregiving. Below, we refer to this as $wage_{employed}$.

For someone without a job, the hours spent caregiving can be valued in different ways, depending on how we think about leisure. At one extreme, hours taken out of leisure could be valued at zero. At the other extreme, the hours could be valued at the potential cost of market care—the observed hourly wage of home care workers. Our estimate for this wage comes from table 1.17. For home care support workers, the average hourly wage is C$18.45/hour. Below we refer to this as $wage_{caregiver}$.

We combine this information into a single estimate by using the composite wage for workers to value time for those who have a job, and two different estimates (C$0 and C$18.45) for valuing the time of those without a job. Using the comparable age-education-gender groups in the Labour Force Survey, we find the proportion of people in each group who are working and use this proportion and the implicit wage information to form the estimate. The proportion working using this cell-average strategy in 2019 is 0.584.

The "low" valuation assigns no value to leisure:

$$prob(employed) \times wage_{employed} + [1 - prob(employed)] \times 0.$$

The "high" valuation incorporates the value of leisure at the cost of hiring a paid caregiver:

Table 1.22 **Valuation of informal care**

	Low	High
Valuation (billions)	20.5	30.4
Total hours unpaid work (millions)	1,284	1,284
Prob (employed)	0.584	0.584
Wages/hour if employed	\$27.34	\$27.34
Wages/hour of caregiver	0	\$18.45
Valuation per hour	\$15.97	\$23.64

Source: Authors' calculations, as described in the text. Dollar values are in 2019 Canadian dollars.

$$prob(employed) \times wage_{employed} + [1 - prob(employed)] \times wage_{caregiver}.$$

In each valuation case, we multiply the resulting implicit cost by the total number of hours of unpaid caregiving in Canada. To find this number, we start with table 1.10, where we report that the average number of hours per week of informal care, among those receiving care, is 22. Figure 1.7, using data from the Canadian Community Health Survey, finds that the proportion using any unpaid help is 17 percent. With 6.6 million Canadians ages 65 and older, that is 1,122,000 recipients of unpaid help. At an average of 22 hours per week and 1,144 hours per year, the total number of hours per year comes to 1,284 million hours.

We summarize these valuation calculations in table 1.22 below. The left column shows the "low" valuation described above, while the right column shows the "high" valuation.

1.5.4 Total Cost of Care

We aggregate the estimates discussed above for residential long-term care, formal home care, and informal care in table 1.23 below. The first two columns are drawn directly from the discussion above. The third column provides a comparison in terms of GDP, and the last column shows a per capita amount for each category. These estimates are for Canadians ages 65 and older, and the estimates are centered around 2019 so we report in 2019 Canadian dollars. We provide both public and private sector estimates for residential long-term care and formal home care, along with a total. The informal care cost considers the two cases with the low valuation (zero value of leisure) and the high valuation (leisure funded by paying for market-wage home care).

Summed across these three types, the total cost of care is C\$62.3 billion for the low valuation, and C\$72.2 billion for the high valuation. Nominal GDP in 2019 for Canada was C\$2.31 trillion, so in the second last column we restate all the total cost information as a share of GDP to provide better context for the overall fiscal bite and for international comparisons. Using the low valuation, long-term care costs 2.69 percent of 2019 GDP; using the

Table 1.23 **Estimates of total cost of care**

	Number of users	Total spending (billions)	GDP share	Spending per user
Residential long-term care				
Public		19.6	0.85%	
Private		8.3	0.36%	
Total	**237,000**	**27.9**	**1.21%**	**$117,865**
Formal home care				
Public		10.0	0.43%	
Private		3.9	0.17%	
Total	**726,000**	**13.9**	**0.60%**	**$19,150**
Informal care				
Low valuation	**1,122,000**	**20.5**	**0.89%**	**$18,270**
High valuation	**1,122,000**	**30.4**	**1.31%**	**$27,000**
Total (low valuation)		**62.3**	**2.69%**	
Total (high valuation)		**72.2**	**3.12%**	

Source: Authors' calculations, as described in the text. Dollar values are in 2019 Canadian dollars; shares are the share of 2019 GDP.

high valuation, it is 3.12 percent. Finally, in the last column we express the cost per user. Residential long-term care is much more expensive, at nearly $118,000 per year per resident. Formal home care is about $19,000 per year on average, with informal care in the range of $18,000 to $27,000.

1.6 Conclusions

This paper has provided a broad overview of long-term care for older Canadians, looking at the economics of both the demand and supply sides of caregiving. Like other OECD countries, the coming demographic wave of older baby boomers will put tremendous stress on the existing financial, organizational, and physical structures of the long-term care system. Unlike other OECD countries, Canada's system is organized almost entirely at the subnational level, with provinces and territories having by far the largest role in financing and regulating long-term care.

The unique federal structure of long-term care in Canada presents challenges and opportunities. The greater ease of the federal government to tax and borrow could provide extra revenue to fund necessary investments in brick-and-mortar infrastructure or in ongoing annual expenditures. However, whatever financial role the federal government may play, the opportunity of decentralized experimentation (in the "federalism as a laboratory" spirit of Justice Brandeis) should not be dismissed.[17] Innovations on regula-

17. In the well-known case of *New State Ice Co. V. Liebman* 285 US 262 (1932), Justice Brandeis wrote, "It is one of the happy incidents of the federal system that a single courageous

tions, training, and financing may arise from provinces pursuing different models. Even here, the federal government can contribute by encouraging learning and cooperation through federal benchmarks as well as convening national dialogue.

References

Baker, Michael, and Kevin Milligan. 2009. "Government and Retirement Incomes in Canada." Report prepared for the Council of Federal, Provincial, and Territorial Finance Ministers.

Blomqvist, Ake, and Colin Busby. 2012. "Long-Term Care for the Elderly: Challenges and Policy Options." C.D. Howe Institute Commentary No. 367.

Bohnert, Nora, Jonathan Chagnon, Simon Coulombe, Patrice Dion, and Laurent Martel. 2015. Population Projections for Canada (2013 to 2063), Provinces and Territories (2013 to 2038): Technical Report on Methodology and Assumptions. Statistics Canada, Catalogue No. 91–620-X. https://www150.statcan.gc.ca/n1/en/pub/91–620-x/91–620-x2014001-eng.pdf?st=UxgEwf70.

Boyer, M. Martin, Philippe De Donder, Claude Fluet, Marie-Louise Leroux, and Pierre-Carl Michaud. 2020. "Long-Term Care Insurance: Information Frictions and Selection." *American Economic Journal: Economic Policy* 12 (3): 134–69.

Canadian Human Mortality Database. 2022. Department of Demography, Université de Montréal (Canada). Data downloaded April 5, 2022. http://www.bdlc.umontreal.ca/CHMD/.

Canadian Institute for Health Information. 2021. National Health Expenditure Trends, 2021—Methodology Notes. Ottawa, ON: CIHI.

Grignon, Michel, and Byron G. Spencer. 2018. "The Funding of Long-Term Care in Canada: What Do We Know, What Should We Know?" *Canadian Journal on Aging* 37 (2): 110–20.

Library of Parliament. 2020. "Long-Term Care Homes in Canada—How are They Funded and Regulated?" Hillnotes online publication. https://hillnotes.ca/2020/10/22/long-term-care-homes-in-canada-how-are-they-funded-and-regulated/.

Milligan, Kevin. 2008. "The Evolution of Elderly Poverty in Canada." *Canadian Public Policy* 34 (4): s79–s94.

Milligan, Kevin, and Tammy Schirle. 2021. "The Evolution of Longevity: Evidence from Canada." *Canadian Journal of Economics* 54 (1): 164–92.

National Institute on Ageing. 2019. *Enabling the Future Provision of Long-Term Care in Canada*. Toronto, ON: National Institute on Ageing White Paper.

Organisation for Economic Cooperation and Development. 2022. OECD Health Statistics 2022. Online database, https://www.oecd.org/els/health-systems/health-data.htm.

Ostrovsky, Yuri, and Grant Schellenberg. 2010. "Pension Coverage and Earnings Replacement among Canadian Couples." Statistics Canada Analytical Branch Studies Working Paper No. 327, Catalogue no. 11F0019M.

state may, if its citizens choose, serve as a laboratory; and try novel social and economic experiments without risk to the rest of the country."

2

Long-Term Care in Denmark

Mette Gørtz, Bent Jesper Christensen,
and Nabanita Datta Gupta

In Denmark, life expectancy at birth is projected to increase from 83 to 87 for women over the next 30 years, and from just below 80 to almost 85 for men. This development follows up on a substantial increase in life expectancy since the 1950s. At the same time, fertility rates have been declining since the 1960s, with the largest dip in the 1980s, when the total fertility rate (TFR) was around 1.4. Since the early 1990s, TFR has been relatively stable, at about 1.7–1.8, below the required level for securing a constant population size. The upshot is that the population is aging in Denmark, as in many other countries, with increasing life expectancy and low TFR together implying an increasing share of elderly in the total population. This is potentially putting the Danish welfare state under pressure, particularly the pension and health care sectors, including long-term care (LTC) for the elderly.

Figures 2.1 and 2.2 illustrate trends in life expectancy and aging of the Danish population. The analysis here and throughout the paper considers two broad age groups, namely, those aged 65 and above, and 85 and above. Figure 2.1 shows that the share of the population above 65 years of age

Mette Gørtz is a professor in the Department of Economics at the University of Copenhagen and a member of the Centre for Economic Behavior and Inequality.

Bent Jesper Christensen is a professor in the Department of Economics and Business Economics at Aarhus University.

Nabanita Datta Gupta is a professor in the Department of Economics and Business Economics at Aarhus University.

We thank the Novo Nordisk Foundation (grant no. NNF17OC0026542), and the Danish National Research Foundation for funding through its grant (DNRF-134) to Center of Economic Behavior and Inequality (CEBI). We are grateful to Julie Uldum Lyhr and Astrid Louise Waltenburg for excellent research assistance. For acknowledgements, sources of research support, and disclosure of the authors' material financial relationships, if any, please see https://www.nber.org/books-and-chapters/long-term-care-around-world/long-term-care-denmark.

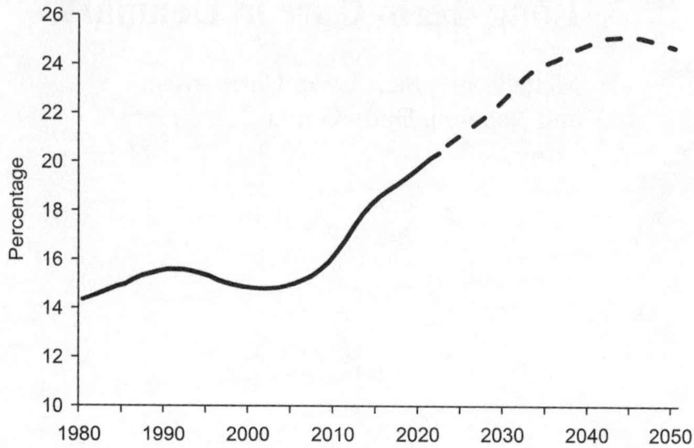

Fig. 2.1 Percentage of population aged 65 or older, Denmark, 1980–2050
Source: Statistics Denmark. Historical data (1980–2022) table FOLK2 (https://www.statistikbanken.dk/FOLK2) and forecast (2023–2050) table FRDK120 (https://www.statistikbanken.dk/FRDK120)

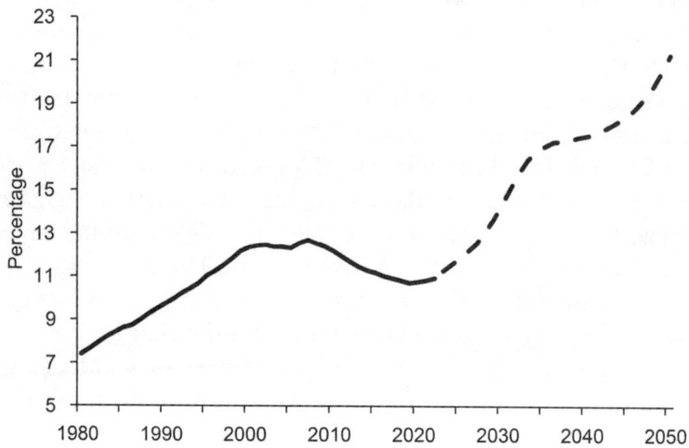

Fig. 2.2 Percentage of 65+ population that is aged 85 or older, Denmark, 1980–2050
Source: Statistics Denmark. Historical data (1980–2022) table FOLK2 (https://www.statistikbanken.dk/FOLK2) and forecast (2023–2050) table FRDK120 (https://www.statistikbanken.dk/FRDK120)

has risen from 14 percent in 1980 to 20 percent today. Projections indicate that the share of individuals aged 65+ will rise to around one-quarter by 2040–2050. Moreover, population forecasts suggest that life expectancy at 65 has risen significantly, especially since the early 2000s, and more than one in five people can at the age of 65 expect to live beyond the age of 85 by the middle of the century. From figure 2.2, it is expected that by 2050, more than one in five among the elderly population (65+) will be older than 85. Forecasts suggest that relative to the full population, the proportion aged 85 or older will be rising from around 2 percent in 2020 to more than 5 percent by 2050. These trends may challenge the long-term care system in Denmark if the rising proportion of elderly 85+ is leading to an increasing number of elderly requiring assistance, and relatively fewer working people to finance these expenditures in the coming years.

Much of the public debate in recent years in Denmark has revolved around the pension system. The increasing share of elderly in the total population is more of a challenge to public finances if it implies an increasing ratio of the number of non-working elderly to the total working population. Although projections show that the (absolute) labor force size will keep increasing throughout the century, from currently 3 million persons in 2020 to slightly above 3.6 million by 2100, the labor force as a percentage of the population is expected to decline in the coming years, from its current level of almost 53 percent to under 50 percent in 2040. This has led to several reforms of the Danish pension system. First, there is a trend toward later retirement, resulting from various retirement reforms enabled by the Welfare Agreement from 2006 and the Retirement Reform from 2011 and enacted since 2014. The reforms have raised the early and normal retirement ages and starting from 2030 will index them to increases in life expectancy (The Danish Economic Council 2021). As a result, the labor force is expected to start rising again. This labor force pattern, referred to as the demographic "hammock," is a result of smaller working cohorts replacing larger retiring cohorts in the coming years, until the reversal of the "U" secured by later retirement in the future. By the end of the century, the labor force will constitute about 52.5 percent of the population again, despite a smaller "hammock" that will follow through 2060–2080.

The indexation of retirement age to life expectancy is targeting an expected retirement period of 14.5 years for all cohorts. A second measure is the introduction of mandatory employer-administered defined contribution plans that are intended to supplement public pensions and will surpass the latter in financial importance by 2040, starting from amounting to less than 10 percent of public pension expenditures in 1980. Together, later retirement and the partial privatization of the pension system have helped secure a surplus on projected government budgets through the end of the century. At the same time, later retirement implies fewer opportunities for older workers to provide informal care to the oldest old. For example, if an individual aged 65 is working instead of retiring, there is less time to care for a 90-year-old parent, say, so more formal care may be required, again putting public finances under pressure.

The projections of government budgets rely on a number of assumptions regarding the use of the health care system, and budgets will be challenged if health care expenditures grow faster than expected. The growth of health care expenditures is affected by growing life expectancy and the generational effect of the baby boomers, healthy aging, and "steepening" of health expenditures due to an increased chronic diseases burden, or greater demand for health care as incomes of the elderly increase and they make up a larger fraction of the voting population and the market. Healthy aging works in the opposite direction and, at every age, will exert a downward pressure on health expenditures. Health expenditures can grow faster than predicted due to increased availability of new and costly technologies combined with difficulties in prioritizing, lack of productivity growth in the health care sector, and a shortage of personnel, leading to wage increases, increased demand for quality in health care, increases in the share of elderly in the population and their use of the health care system, and later retirement of children who could otherwise provide informal care. These issues have played an increasing role in the public debate in Denmark in recent years. One challenge is that there is not a single, simple rule, such as the indexation of retirement age to life expectancy in the pension case that could apply throughout the health sector, so the search for adequate policy measures for controlling expenditures is ongoing.

While total government expenditures in Denmark have constituted a constant share of GDP since the 1980s, at about 25 percent, the health expenditure share has been rising, from 6 percent of GDP in 1995 to 7 percent in 2019. Indeed, health expenditures have grown more than what demographic changes and an affluence adjustment would require, while other public expenditures have grown less. The main increase in health expenditures took place in the first decade of the 2000s (see Christensen et al, 2016), while there has been a slight fall over the last 10 years. This is mainly the result of a 2010 law on better control over public finances and the establishment of expenditure ceilings at the municipal, regional, and national level (*Genopretningsaftale* 2010). However, the changes in demography, technology, and demand for educated personnel and quality care make adherence to expenditure ceilings a challenge going forward. While existing prognoses for government expenditures indicate that they will decline as share of GDP, to about 22 percent in 2100, if the current trend of 1995–2019 is to continue, health expenditures are expected to increase, to about 8–10 percent of GDP by 2100. This is sustainable as long as retirement ages keep increasing over time, in line with the retirement reforms, but not if health expenditures increase more than expected. Kollerup et al. (2022) document steepening of health care expenditures in Denmark, in that the increase in per capita health care expenditures with age is rising over time, and advocate that the phenomenon should be added to future health care expenditure forecasts. Their analysis leaves out the LTC component of expenditures, suggesting that the steepening problem may be even more severe with LTC expenditures included. Indeed, other analyses have indicated that the steep age profile in total health expenditures is driven in particular by LTC expenditures, in a manner consistent with the hypothesis that proximity to death rather than age is the main determinant of expenditures (see The Danish Economic Council 2020). Thus, further attention to LTC expenditures is called for. The present paper offers one step in this direction.

In recent years, recruitment of personnel for the health care sector, especially for the LTC sector, has proven increasingly difficult. LTC institutions suffer from a high rate of personnel turnover, and currently policies to improve working conditions and salaries are on the political agenda. A report from Local Government Denmark (KL, an interest organization for the 98 Danish municipalities) from 2021 shows that by 2030, the demand for social and health care helpers (nursing assistants) will exceed the supply by 16,000 persons if current enrollment levels persist. This is expected to occur even when accounting for healthy aging in the health cost projections via a time-to-death correction. This suggests that there may be high returns not only to boosting enrollment but also to recruiting and retaining students in the education programs for health care personnel. Non-completion rates from social and health care helper educations were found to be 36 percent among students who enrolled in the program within a nine-year window after graduating from high school in 2002 or 2003, representing 16 percent who were still enrolled (censored observations), and 20 percent who were no longer enrolled (Stratton et al. 2018). The present government has accordingly announced a plan to increase the practical training wage for social and health care helpers who are enrolled in the program by between 5,942 and 7,213 DKK (US$780–950) monthly, a 50 percent increase on average, depending on the age and experience levels of the students at the time of entering the educational program. Similar challenges, and planned policy measures, relate to social and health care assistants (licensed practical nurses) and registered nurses.

Further, while these steps are aimed at maintaining current standards, the public debate has revealed increasing attention toward the quality of care provided. A recent Danish survey shows that people are willing to make additional out-of-pocket payments to supplement the care provided for free by the municipality (see Amilon et al. 2022). Presumably, an increase in quality of care will require both an increase in the education level of caregivers and a further increase in wages and salaries. These effects could well contribute to faster long-term care expenditure growth than so far projected.

This paper discusses the demographic and socioeconomic situation of the elderly in Denmark. The focus is on the health status and financial situation of the elderly, and on long-term care in particular. We rely on a combination of survey data, mainly from the Survey of Health, Ageing and Retirement in Europe (SHARE) and high-quality register data covering the entire Danish population. SHARE is a national representative biennial survey that is now collected in 28 European countries and Israel. We focus on SHARE wave 6 from 2015 and wave 7 from 2017. The wave 6 data have been merged to register data at the individual level, allowing us to use information on income, wealth, and other socioeconomic information based on administrative records rather than self-reported information.

We find that a large fraction of the elderly is in a fairly favorable health situation, but that those in the older age group, 85+, face considerably more functional limitations in daily living. The younger group, 65+, enjoys higher incomes than the older, presumably due both to higher labor market participation and the reforms of the pension system, as well as higher median wealth, excluding pension wealth, possibly because older individuals have spent down more of their initial wealth. However, the younger group faces more wealth inequality, too, which may be related to outstanding mortgage debt. We document that higher income and higher wealth are associated with fewer limitations and better health. Self-reported well-being is relatively high, although less so for the 85+ group than the 65+ group, and for those with functional limitations.

Regarding long-term care, expenditures increased as share of GDP until 2010, and has remained relatively stable since then. One in three of the elderly and more than half the 85+ group receive some form of long-term care. Of those with two or more functional limitations, 70 percent receive LTC, and nearly 90 percent of the 85+ year olds. Some of this care is provided in nursing homes and residential care facilities, which are in effect end stations in Denmark, with long, terminal stays, more than two years at the median.[1] About 3.6 percent of the elderly live in nursing homes, and 17 percent of the older subgroup. The availability of beds/slots varies considerably across the municipalities offering formal care, between 1 and 22 beds per 100 elderly. The older group receives more formal care than the younger. Home care is both formal, largely publicly provided, and informal, provided by relatives, friends, etc. The institutional share of care, relative to home care, has increased from 54 percent in 2010 to 57 percent in 2019. Both publicly provided home-based care and nursing homes involve an out-of-pocket (OOP) element, of about 10 percent of expenses. Less than 1 percent of the elderly have private LTC insurance. Individuals receiving home care typically receive only a few hours of care per week, about three hours at the median, and 4.5 hours for the 85+ year olds, but more than 25 hours per week at the 95th percentile for both age groups. Individuals with up to two functional limitations in most cases rely on informal care only. The relatively low number of hours of help received by a large portion of the elderly is consistent with their relatively favorable overall health condition. The relatively low number of hours of informal care offered in many cases is consistent with the labor market situation in Denmark, with high female participation rates, and many workers retiring late, especially follow-

1. Bom et al. (2023) compare the drivers of nursing home admissions across Denmark, the Netherlands, and the United States.

ing the pension reforms, i.e., there is simply less time left for care of older relatives.

Regarding employees in the long-term care sector, about 40 percent hold a formal education targeting this. Registered nurses earn annual wages comparable to the median across all workers in all industries but clearly fall short of those with college education. Earnings of licensed practical nurses and nursing assistants are at the level of workers without a high school degree. These formal care workers, including registered nurses, are primarily women. In contrast, informal care providers are both women and men, typically slightly older, and most often a child or an unpaid friend or neighbor of the care recipient. The relatively low wages and unattractive working conditions in the formal long-term care sector contributes to the recruiting problems and upward pressure on wages, both for attracting and retaining workers. It has been suggested that immigrants could fill some of the positions in the sector. However, language is a barrier because these jobs involve a high degree of personal contact, and many of the elderly care recipients have poor foreign language skills. Further, to the extent that other OECD countries face similar problems as Denmark, attracting the required number of qualified immigrants to this sector is not automatic. The Danish labor market model requires that immigrants be offered the same wages and working conditions as domestic workers, implying that there are no easy cost reductions along this route. In addition, the long-term care sector has been one of relatively low productivity growth, and automatization can be expected largely to be supplementing rather than saving on labor over the foreseeable future. Together, these challenges add up to an increased risk of faster growth in long-term care expenditures than projected.

Informal care in recipients' homes, provided by family, friends, neighbors, etc., is offered voluntarily, and generally unpaid. Nevertheless, informal care represents an opportunity cost to society, as time spent providing it could have been spent on other (productive) activities, or in leisure. Therefore, we finally undertake a calculation of the full cost of long-term care in Denmark, including an imputed value of informal care. Given the measurement problems associated with calculating hours of informal care provided, as well as valuing time spent on informal care activities, we emphasize that the imputation lies within a fairly broad band. However, we find that the value of informal care is of an order of magnitude comparable to that of formal home care, between one-quarter and one-third of total costs of long-term care.

The remainder of the paper is laid out as follows. In section 2.1, we investigate the interaction between functional limitations and the financial situation and well-being of the elderly. Limitations studied include Activities of Daily Living (ADLs) and Instrumental Activities of Daily Living (IADLs). In section 2.2, we discuss the organization of long-term care in Denmark, including the division between institutionalized care and home care, and the combination of formal and informal provision of home care, and we offer evidence on the workforce in the long-term care sector. Section 2.3 discusses costs of long-term care, including the imputed value of informal care. Section 2.4 concludes.

2.1 Aging, Functional Limitations, and Well-Being

This section discusses the socioeconomic and health situation of the elderly in Denmark.

2.1.1 Sample and Definitions

The data used in this paper come from the Survey of Health, Ageing and Retirement in Europe (SHARE) for Denmark, from wave 6 of 2015 and wave 7 of 2017. SHARE has been collected since 2004 (wave 1), with Denmark participating in all waves. SHARE is collected for a population of individuals aged 50 and older. We focus in our analyses on individuals who were 65 years or older in 2015. For more information on SHARE, we refer to a general/common SHARE description in the other chapters of this volume.

Wave 6 of the SHARE survey data for Denmark have been linked to Danish administrative register data at the individual level for the majority of individuals in SHARE. Danish register data is a longitudinal data set for the entire Danish population. It includes all Danes from birth until death, and it allows for family links through the general population register. This means that we can identify children and grandchildren of our population and find information, e.g., on education and employment of offspring.[2] Information on income and wealth reported in this paper are from tax registers. The advantage of this is that the information is not self-reported but usually reported by employers, pension funds, public authorities, etc. The registers also contain information on health care and use of long-term care reported by the health care sector and public authorities providing formal long-term care. The register data furthermore allow us to document socioeconomic as well as educational background and wages for employees in the long-term care sector.

We mainly base our analysis of health in this paper on functional limitations, a self-reported measure included in SHARE.[3] The limitations include Activities of Daily Living (ADLs) and Instrumental Activities of Daily Living (IADLs). ADLs capture self-reported difficulties carrying out the fol-

2. Family links are not complete for individuals born before 1935.

3. Our linked survey-register data will allow us to compare self-reported measures in SHARE with more objective measures of health care use from the register data. For example, a frailty index based on ADLs and IADLs (such as in The Danish Economic Council, Autumn 2021) can be compared to an index of diagnoses based on register data. Population data will also allow exploring heterogeneity with respect to gender, education, etc. We leave these analyses for future studies.

Table 2.1 **Share with ADLs by age, Denmark, 2015/201**

	65+	85+
0 ADLs & 0 iADLs	0.780	0.408
0 ADLs & 1+ iADLs	0.0751	0.164
1 ADL	0.0562	0.112
2 ADLs	0.0276	0.0512
3 ADLs	0.0206	0.104
4 ADLs	0.00655	0.0198
5 ADLs	0.0138	0.0264
6 ADLs	0.0202	0.115
Any ADLs	0.145	0.428
Any iADLs	0.173	0.546
Observations	3395	303

Note: ADLs include walking across a room, dressing, bathing, eating, going to bed, and using the toilet. IADLs include using a telephone, managing money, taking medications as prescribed, shopping for groceries, and cooking a hot meal. Respondents were asked to exclude any difficulties they expect to last less than three months.

Source: SHARE (waves 6 & 7). SHARE population weights are used, and nursing home residents are weighted to match population in nursing homes.

lowing six activities: using the toilet, getting dressed, taking a bath, walking across a room, eating, and getting in/out of bed. IADLs are self-reported measures of difficulties related to using a phone, managing money, taking medicine as prescribed, shopping for groceries, preparing a meal, and reading a map. Respondents were asked to exclude any difficulties they expected to last for less than three months.

Population shares with different numbers of limitations with respect to activities of daily living (ADLs and IADLs) are shown in table 2.1, for each of the two age groups considered. From the table, there are considerable differences between the distributions of limitations for people aged 65+ and 85+. For the 65+ population, about four in five have zero ADLs and zero IADLs, and 91 percent have at most one limitation, while 9 percent have two or more ADLS. For the 85+ population, only half the fraction, two in five, have zero ADLs and IADLs, while about one in three (32 percent) reports difficulties carrying out two or more everyday activities. Our findings are consistent with frailty studies finding that health deteriorates by 2–5 percent per year for individuals in Western countries (for Europe, see Abeliansky and Strulik 2018). For Denmark, the rates of aging based on a health deficit index measure including ADLs and IADLs from SHARE data have been found to be 3.2 percent per year for men and 3 percent for women (The Danish Economic Council 2021). It should be noted that the response rate for the 85+ population is fairly low. Only 302 individuals above 85 years of age have responded in SHARE, and it is highly likely that there is somewhat higher

Table 2.2 **Distribution of limitations with specific ADLs/iADLs, Denmark, 2015/2017**

	65+	65+ Conditional	85+	85+ Conditional
	Panel 1: IADLs			
IADL—Use a Phone	0.0412	0.364	0.255	0.608
IADL—Manage Money	0.0948	0.785	0.389	0.864
IADL—Take Meds as Prescr.	0.0622	0.565	0.265	0.635
IADL—Shop for Groceries	0.117	0.866	0.454	0.946
IADL—Prepare a Meal	0.0927	0.775	0.362	0.856
IADL—Read a Map	0.0902	0.699	0.352	0.798
Observations	3395	244	303	87
	Panel 2: ADLs			
ADL—Use the Toilet	0.0420	0.445	0.160	0.495
ADL—Get Dressed	0.115	0.868	0.360	0.943
ADL—Take a Bath	0.0895	0.870	0.338	0.952
ADL—Walk Across a Room	0.0500	0.529	0.175	0.529
ADL—Eat	0.0334	0.359	0.196	0.610
ADL—Get In/Out of Bed	0.0492	0.520	0.172	0.521
Observations	3,395	208	303	55

Note: Column 1 shows the share of the sample that reports having difficulties with each activity, while column 2 shows the share of the sample with at least one iADL (panel 1) or at least one ADL (panel 2) who report having difficulty with each activity. Respondents were asked to exclude any difficulties they expect to last less than three months.

Source: SHARE (waves 6 & 7). SHARE population weights are used, and nursing home residents are weighted to match population in nursing homes.

attrition among those with more limitations. Therefore, population weights have been used on SHARE data in tables 2.1, 2.2, and 2.3.[4] Furthermore, nursing home residents have been weighted to match population shares.

Table 2.2 provides more details on which activities the elderly find most difficult. The results suggest that among IADLs, the most prevalent difficulties are related to managing money and shopping for groceries, but also preparing meals and reading a map. Among ADLs, the dominant difficulties are related to taking a bath and getting dressed, but also functional limitations, such as getting in/out of bed, and walking across a room. In all cases, prevalence is at least three times higher in the 85+ group, compared to the 65+ group, and in some cases much more.

Table 2.3 shows well-being for the elderly using SHARE data, waves 6 and 7. Nursing home residents are included and weighted to match population shares. We find that almost three in four of the 65+ group self-report that their health is good or very good, while only just above half of the 85+

4. Adding SHARE population weights, however, did not change the results much.

Table 2.3 **Well-being for those aged 65+ and 85+ by ADL limitations, Denmark, 2015/2017**

	65+	65+ with 3+ Limits	85+	85+with 3+ Limits
Reports good or better health status	0.713	0.243	0.515	0.250
Good life satisfaction for those retired	0.850	0.629	0.801	0.701
Depressed or sad within the last month	0.223	0.253	0.208	0.143
Observations	3,408	267	305	84

Note: Our limitations index runs from 0–12 and is the number of ADLs/IADLs that are either difficult or not done from eating, bathing, dressing, using the toilet, walking across a room, and getting in/out of bed (ADLs) + using a telephone, managing money, taking medications as prescribed, shopping for groceries, and cooking a hot meal (IADLs). Life satisfaction is reported on a scale from 0 to 10, where 0 means completely dissatisfied and 10 means completely satisfied. Life satisfaction is assumed to be good if the respondent reported 8 or higher. The means for life satisfaction only include people who are retired. The survey asks whether respondents have felt sad or depressed in the last month.

Source: SHARE (wave 6 & 7). SHARE population weights are used, and nursing home residents are weighted, to match general population in nursing homes.

group self-report such good health levels. However, there is considerable heterogeneity among the elderly, as persons with 3+ ADLs are substantially less likely to report that their health is good or very good. Similarly, life satisfaction in retirement is fairly high, but less so for elderly with 3+ ADLs. More than one in five individuals in the 65+ group report having been sad or depressed within the last month, and this is more than one-quarter in the 65+ group with 3+ ADLs.[5] Overall, the level of well-being is relatively high, based on self-reported health status, but less so for the 85+ group than the 65+ group, for those with functional limitations, or when focusing on sadness and depression.

Overall, the results show that a large fraction of the elderly is in a fairly favorable health situation, although individuals in the older age group face considerably more functional limitations in daily living.

2.1.2 Financial Well-Being

We next investigate the financial well-being of the elderly. Table 2.4 shows the distributions of income and wealth for the 65+ and 85+ year olds, respectively. These results are based on register data for the entire population of elderly. Income here is disposable income, including transfers and net of taxes, measured as equivalent household income using the OECD scale. The income distributions in the two left columns show that income at all percentiles is considerably lower for the 85+ than the 65+ year olds, reflecting not only that some fraction of those aged 65+ are still working, but also that

5. The combination of linked SHARE survey and register data will allow us in future studies to compare self-reported depression with detailed information in registers about diagnoses and who is receiving medication or other treatment for depression.

Table 2.4 **Income and wealth distribution, Denmark, 2019**

	Income		Wealth	
	65+	85+	65+	85+
5th percentile	136,332	72,479	−259,335	0
10th percentile	154,558	123,597	−12,009	0
25th percentile	176,706	157,443	62,357	64,844
50th percentile	212,198	181,343	736,346	550,363
75th percentile	283,897	221,445	2,258,542	2,300,295
90th percentile	384,192	286,862	4,645,813	5,010,299
95th percentile	478,319	347,719	7,080,999	7,564,922
Mean	261,918	207,393	1,974,627	2,074,350
Observations	1,136,044	121,656	1,136,044	121,656

Note: Household income/wealth data are at the individual level and include only respondents' and spouses' income/wealth. Income and wealth are at the household level (summed over spouses in the household). Income is disposable income (income net taxes and including transfers). Percentiles are pseudo percentiles defined as the mean five observations around each percentile. Values are in 2019 DKK.

Source: Danish Administrative Data

private pension schemes are more prevalent among the younger cohorts of elderly, while a relatively larger share of the 85+ year olds rely exclusively on public pensions (ATP 2019). We also observe a greater dispersion in income among the older group of 85+ than among the younger, with income at the fifth percentile for the older group barely half of that for the younger, reflecting perhaps the more widespread employer-administered pension schemes across the entire labor market since the late 1980s. More information about public and private pension schemes is provided in section 2.2.

Table 2.4, right columns, shows the distributions of net wealth in 2015, which includes financial assets and housing wealth minus liabilities/debt, but not pension wealth.[6] The table reveals an unequal distribution in net wealth, with negative wealth in the lowest deciles of the group of 65+, but not for the 85+ year olds. First of all, renters may incur debt without having positive assets. Moreover, housing wealth is by far the largest source of assets in Denmark, and largely financed by mortgage debt. After the financial crisis, housing values went down, and some households experienced negative net wealth. This affects the 65+ group, whereas the 85+ group tends to have paid off their mortgage debt. Further, median wealth for the 85+ group is only three-quarters that of the 65+ group, consistent with the older group having run down some of their wealth over time, possibly due to their less attractive pension plans.

6. Net wealth is defined as the sum of financial assets (bank accounts, stocks, and bonds) plus housing wealth minus liabilities/debt. Housing wealth is measured using the tax-assessed value of people's home, scaled with the average ratio between market values of traded houses and the tax-assessed value of these, see Browning et al. 2013. Pension wealth is not included.

Table 2.5 **Income and wealth distribution by limitations for 65+ population, Denmark, 2015**

	0 ADLs & 0 iADLs	0 ADLs & 1+ iADLs	1 ADL	2+ ADLs	Total
	Panel 1: Income				
<100% Median HH income	0,448	0,678	0,603	0,800	0,500
100–150% Median HH income	0,324	0,253	0,270	0,122	0,301
150+% Median HH income	0,228	0,069	0,127	0,078	0,199
Total	0,797	0,074	0,053	0,076	
Observations	940	87	63	90	1180
	Panel 2: Wealth				
<100% Median HH wealth	0,465	0,602	0,619	0,711	0,500
100–150% Median HH wealth	0,094	.	0,095	0,067	0,085
150+% Median HH wealth	0,441	0,398	0,286	0,222	0,412
Total	0,797	0,070	0,053	0,076	
Observations	940	83	63	90	1,180

Note: Household income data are at the individual level and include only respondent and spouse income. Our ADL index runs from 0–6 and is the number of ADLs that are difficult. ADLs include eating, bathing, getting dressed, using the toilet, walking across a room, and getting in/out of bed. IADLs include using a telephone, managing money, taking medications as prescribed, shopping for groceries, cooking a hot meal, and reading a map. Each cell reports the share of respondents in the respective ADL category who are in that row's income group, such that each column (excluding horizontal totals) sum to one. In panel (1) the median* disposable HH income is 203,058 DKK per year and in panel (2) the median wealth is 882,670 DKK per year. Columns for 3+ ADLs are not included due to data restrictions caused by too few observations. The number of observations differs between panels (1) and (2) due to this data restriction. Medians are pseudo medians defined as the mean of five observations around the median. Numbers in some cells marked with "." are not shown due to limited sample size.

Source: SHARE (wave 6) linked to Danish administrative data

Table 2.5 shows the income and wealth distributions for individuals reporting zero, one, and two+ ADLs, respectively. For individuals with two+ ADLS, the likelihood of being in a lower-income and lower-wealth group is much higher than for the group reporting zero ADLs. This indicates that people with higher income and wealth are generally in better shape. Similarly, individuals with fewer ADLs and IADLs are more likely to be in the groups having 150+ percent of median income, or 150+ percent of median wealth. These results surely in part reflect an age profile, as older individuals are likely to have spent down more of their wealth (see table 2.4), and have more limitations (tables 2.1 and 2.2).

All in all, the results indicate fairly high levels of both objective financial and self-reported levels of well-being, although lower in the older subgroup, and for those in poorer health. Furthermore, the results are consistent with the pension reforms, with more widespread employer-administered schemes, having had a real impact on society, in our data benefitting the 65+ group, not the 85+ group.

2.2 Long-Term Care System in Denmark

Long-term care is either provided as informal care, by family and friends, or as formal care, which is for the main part provided and financed by the municipalities. Care can be provided in the recipient's own home, or in a nursing home, or residential care facility. Home care can take the form of either personal care or practical help.

2.2.1 Public Insurance

Some form of publicly subsidized long-term care has been in place in Denmark for more than 125 years. Before that time period, in early- and mid-19th-century Denmark, impoverished elderly who did not have the means to finance their own care were relegated to poorhouses (*fattiggården),* where they were given room and board in exchange for their (often very hard) labor, and where their free mobility and other rights were restricted, i.e., almost prison-like conditions.[7] For the wealthy, private foundations ran old-age homes even at that time. However, in April 1891, the watershed Law on Old Age Support (*Alderdomsunderstøttelse*) guaranteed the right of public support to elderly over 60 with care needs who in the last 10 years had not received any form of poverty assistance. In 1933, a large social reform strengthened the principles of individual rights to receiving aid.[8]

In the years that followed, the sector flourished, and about 500 municipality-run old age homes were established, increasing to about 1,000 municipal homes and 400 private homes in 1970 (Rasmussen 2012). In 1988, legislation was passed to put a stop to the building of any new municipality nursing homes or residential care facilities (protected housing) and instead to promote the building of elderly apartments, emphasizing the living needs of the elderly rather than health needs and equating the elderly's housing needs to that of any other group in society. Thus, the policy is to keep the elderly in their own homes for as long as possible, perhaps in housing for the elderly, if necessary with home care. Consequently, since the 1970s, the number of nursing home slots and institutions has experienced a decline. In 2007, 78,553 persons above the age of 60 were registered as residing in nursing homes, protected housing, sheltered housing units, or co-housing schemes. In 2022, that number was 66,976, i.e., a 15 percent decline over 15

7. See Wikipedia (in Danish) on Fattighus, https://da.wikipedia.org/wiki/Fattighus. See also "Fattiggårdens historie" ("The History of the Workhouse") on the web site of the Danmark Forsorgsmuseum, Denmark's Welfare Museum, https://www.svendborgmuseum.dk/om-museet/fattiggardens-historie.

8. See the Danish Social History web site for more on the social reform of 1933, http://www.socialhistorie.dk/socialreformen-1933.php.

years.[9] This decline has occurred in the face of rising life expectancy over the same period. Both men and women in Denmark have gained three years more in average life expectancy between 2007 and 2022, 76 to 79 for men and 80 to 83 for women.[10]

Long-term care in Denmark is mainly provided by the public sector, and more specifically by the municipalities (of which there are 98 across the country). Around 950 municipality nursing homes and 75 approved private nursing homes serve the needs of the elderly requiring institutional care. Core LTC activities are provided by the municipalities, which are responsible for taking care of patients after hospital stays (training and rehabilitation activities), for nursing homes, and for home care, home nursing, etc.

By far the majority of all costs of LTC in Denmark are covered by public finance (general taxes). While the elderly who move into a nursing home or residential care facility need to pay a price corresponding to the value of the housing and meals provided (this fee is means-tested and thus varies across the elderly), the municipalities offer a substantial subsidy to nursing homes and residential care and are responsible for financing health services and care. The charge for room and board before subsidization is around 10,000 DKK per month, to which a means-tested subsidy applies (*boligstøtte*).

Municipalities are responsible for allocating slots in nursing homes and residential care facilities based on a waiting list and a needs assessment system. According to the Social Service Law (*Lov om social service, Bekendtgørelse om plejehjem og beskyttede boliger*), all elderly residents who are no longer able to live independently in their own homes are eligible for a slot in either a public nursing home, protected housing, sheltered housing unit, or co-housing scheme. Eligibility is determined after visitation in the individual's municipality of residence, initiated either by the individual themselves or by the municipality. Once eligibility is established, the municipality council is required by law to offer a slot within a period of two months.

Moreover, municipalities are obliged to subsidize (finance) and supply formal home care to the elderly. This care consists of a combination of personal care and practical help (cleaning, shopping, and preparing a light meal). The elderly can choose a municipal supplier or a supplier from a private firm. In the latter case, the municipality subsidizes the care provided by the private firm.

All individuals in Denmark are eligible for old-age pension from a certain age, irrespective of possible private pension schemes.[11] Moreover, everyone

9. See Statistics Denmark (www.statistikbanken.dk) for Indskrevne i pleje- og ældreboliger efter område, alder og foranstaltningsart—Statistikbanken—data og tal.

10. See life expectancy data from Statistics Denmark: https://www.dst.dk/da/Statistik/emner/borgere/befolkning/middellevetid.

11. In 2022, the public old-age pension was 10,347 DKK per month (US$1,480) for individuals living in marriage or cohabitation, and 14,019 DKK per month (US$2,000) for singles. People on old-age pension are allowed to work, but deductions in pension are made if earnings exceed a certain level. From July 2022, individuals born after 1955 can receive public

Table 2.6 Population with LTC insurance, Denmark, 2015/2017

	65+
Population with LTC Insurance	13,875
Share of 65+ Population	0.009
Observations	2,630

Note: Long-term care (LTC) insurance covers only private insurance.
Source: SHARE (wave 6 & 7) and www.statistikbanken.dk/FOLK1A

has access to free publicly provided health care. User costs in health care constitute a small part of individual health care expenditures, the only exceptions being prescription medicine (which is subsidized, but with a partial out-of-pocket payment by the patient), dentist expenditures (partly subsidized), and psychotherapy.

2.2.2 Private Insurance

While private health insurance historically has played a very limited role, the proportion of Danes having additional private health insurance has been rising steeply over the last two decades. Thus, while only 4 percent of the population had a private health insurance plan in 2003, this number had risen to almost 40 percent by 2020.

However, private insurance for long-term care is still very rare, and information about such schemes is limited.[12] According to information from SHARE, waves 6 and 7, shown in table 2.6, 0.9 percent of the 65+ population responded that they have private insurance for long-term care.[13] This is based on 24 responses out of 2,630 and should thus be interpreted with care. Due to the very limited sample in SHARE reporting having private insurance for LTC, the information about socioeconomic background for this group is limited. A comparison of respondents with and without private

old-age pension from the age of 67, while individuals born from 1967 and onwards can retire and receive old-age pension from age 69. Sources: Danish Ministry of Employment, National Pension at https://bm.dk/satser/satser-for-2022/folkepension/, and the Ældresagen web site on jobs and disability at https://www.aeldresagen.dk/viden-og-raadgivning/vaerd-at-vide/f/folkepension-og-foertidspension/folkepension/ansoegning.

12. Recently, Tryg, the largest non-life insurer in Scandinavia, has issued a new "care insurance" product with a premium level of 190 DKK per month, marketed toward mainly the adult children of individuals over 70. This insurance covers extra expenditures related to illness, hospitalization, or diagnoses.

13. The question used for this analysis is based on a question in SHARE corresponding to the variable HC116_LongTermCareInsurance. SHARE asks the following question: "Do you have any of the following public or private long-term care insurances?" and explains that "Long-term care insurance helps cover the cost of long-term care. It generally covers home care, assisted living, adult daycare, respite care, hospice care, and stays in nursing homes or residential care facilities. Some of the long-term care services might be covered by your health insurance." We count people who respond that they have this type of insurance as a private voluntary/supplementary insurance.

LTC insurance (unreported) suggests that it is to a greater extent those with higher income and wealth and receiving formal and/or informal care who have private LTC insurance, consistent with the notion that self-insurance of expenses not covered by the public sector is more likely adopted by individuals in worse financial situations or in less need of care.

2.2.3 Key Reforms and Policy Questions

Here, we briefly touch upon the key reforms that have been enacted in the LTC area over the last 50 years, and point out some of the pressing policy issues that are currently being discussed.

In the decades after the Second World War, the Nordic countries led the world in expanding tax-funded universal public LTC. In the 1970s and 1980s, the responsibility of LTC was moved from the regions to the municipalities. Faced with a growing number of elderly putting pressure on pay-as-you-go systems, the general trend since the 1990s in most of the Nordic welfare states has been on increasing efficiency in elder care via various New Public Management (NPM) style reforms and initiatives (Vabø et al. 2022). The main focus has been on decentralization of management practices and some elements of wage bargaining, enhancing cost-effectiveness in LTC provision, requiring involvement of family and volunteer organizations in sharing care responsibilities, and facilitating increased cooperation and coordination with the health care system.

In Denmark, despite the fact that the number of municipalities was reduced with the 2007 Structural Reform, from 271 to the current 98, the focus has been on moving the care administration even more to the local levels, through a series of recent reforms in the Social Service Act, intended to strengthen the elderly's own role and participation in their care management, and to enhance rehabilitation. This points to a new era emerging within LTC, of new public governance (NPG), based on collaboration across sectors.

Another new development since 2007 is that private nursing homes and elderly housing are now allowed to operate in Denmark (*Friplejeboligloven*) for the purpose of giving the elderly more choice in terms of their living arrangements. A report from VIVE based on a 2015 questionnaire to nursing home directors combined with scores from 2014–2016 audit reports found little difference between public and private nursing home care quality, measured according to both structural and process quality parameters (Hjelmar et al. 2016).

KL, Local Government Denmark, the interest organization of the 98 municipalities, in a recent white paper (KL November 2021) points to a number of areas where the quality of LTC in Denmark can be further enhanced and made sustainable for the long term. Some points that particularly relate to our analysis are those of increasing recruitment and retention of qualified personnel, strengthening the collaboration with the health care sector, and increasing cooperation and participation of family members, which is part of informal care. Additional recommendations include ensuring continuity of care through self-organized teams, simplifying the quality assurance system, reducing documentation requirements, increasing qualified management at local levels and lifelong learning opportunities, and employing assistive technologies and digital solutions for enhancing quality of life and independence of the elderly, and enabling a better and more effective working environment for the employed in the sector. The latter should support recruitment and retention in the sector, as well.

Overall, increased reliance on informal care, based on collaboration and participation, holds a promise of contributing to keeping costs down, but feasibility is challenged by the high female labor force participation rate and later retirement, and cost increases stemming from wage and quality demands in the formal sector threaten to become major issues going forward.

2.2.4 Expenditures on Long-Term Care

As evidenced by figure 2.3, expenditures for long-term care have been rising from a level just above 1 percent of GDP in the late 1990s to above 2 percent of GDP by 2010, then remained approximately constant at this level since 2010, according to data from OECD and Statistics Denmark that are comparable across countries. These data include expenditure on home-based care, nursing homes, and residential care facilities with nursing.

Figure 2.4 shows that 90 percent of the costs of long-term care are financed via public expenditures, while households finance the remaining 10 percent. Figure 2.5 shows a rising role for institutional care over the last decade, rela-

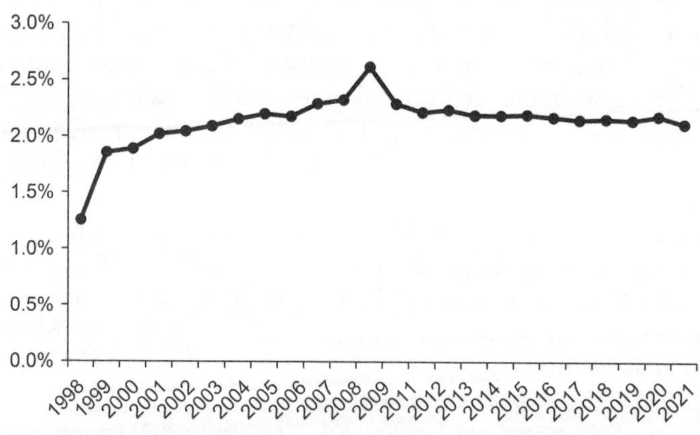

Fig. 2.3 Share of GDP spent on long-term care, Denmark, 1988–2019

Source: Statistics Denmark table NAN1 and SHA1 and OECD SHA. Note: Expenditure from 1998—2009 is from OECD, where room and board are excluded, however spending on residences for mentally ill and drug abusers is included. Expenditure from 2010–2021 is from Statistics Denmark, room and board is included, and spending on residences for mentally ill and drug abusers is excluded.

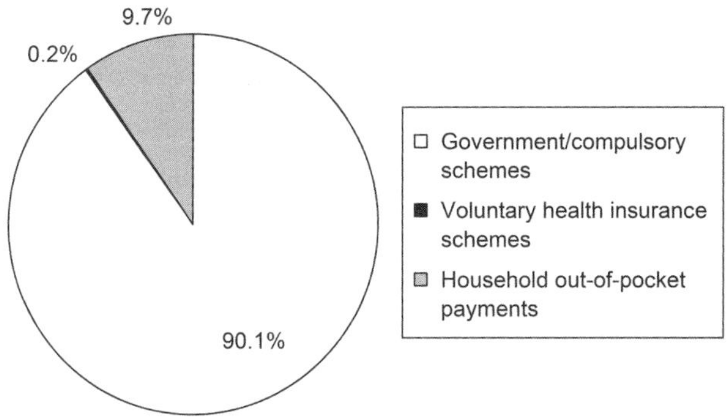

Fig. 2.4 Share of LTC financing by source, Denmark, 2019

Note: Room and board is included for residents in nursing homes. Long-term care spending data are adjusted with the proportion of residents in nursing homes and home care above 65 to approximately reflect the proportion of LTC costs spent on the elderly. Spending on residences for mentally ill and drug abusers is excluded.

Source: Statistics Denmark, www.statistikbanken.dk, tables SHA, AED022, AED06 and RESI

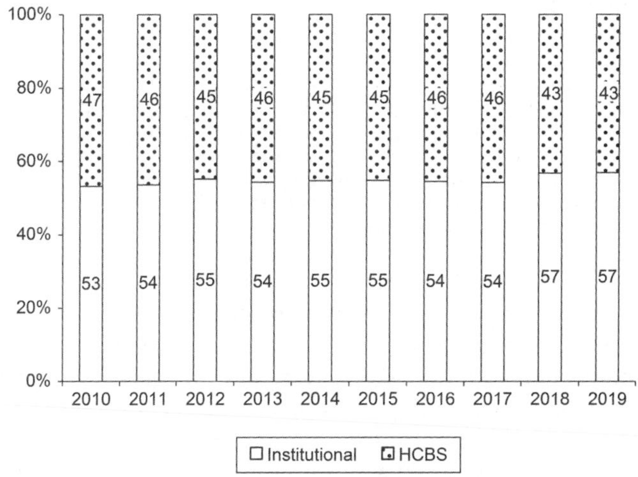

Fig. 2.5 Spending on institutional care versus home-based care, Denmark, 2010–2019

Note: Room and board is included for residents in nursing homes. Long-term care spending data in SHA1 includes spending on people below the age of 65 requiring care. Long term care spending data are adjusted with the proportion of residents in nursing homes and home care above 65 to approximately reflect the proportion of LTC costs spent on the elderly. Spending on residences for mentally ill and drug abusers is excluded.

Source: Statistics Denmark,www.statistikbanken.dk, tables SHA1, AED022, AED06 and RESI. Total long-term care expenditures in year, subdivided by inpatient long-term care (institution) and home-based long-term care (HCBS).

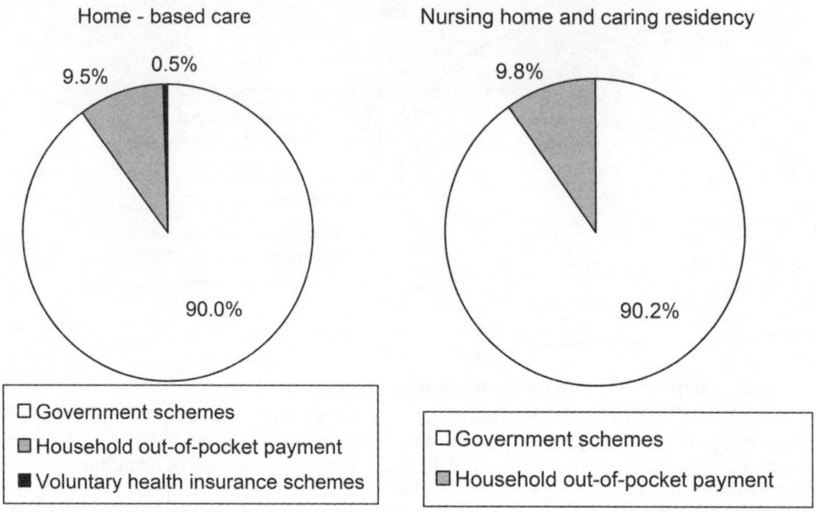

Fig. 2.6 Percentage spent on home-based care and nursing care facilities, by source of funds, Denmark, 2019

Source: Eurostat/SHA. Note: Home-based care is defined as the medical, ancillary, and nursing services that are consumed by patients at their home and involve the providers' physical presence. Nursing home and caring residency means the treatment and/or care provided in a health care facility to patients formally admitted and requiring an overnight stay. Room and board is included for residents in nursing homes. Long-term care spending data in SHA1 include spending on people below the age of 65 requiring care. Long-term care spending data are adjusted with the proportion of residents in nursing homes and home care above 65 to approximately reflect the proportion of LTC costs spent on the elderly. Spending on residences for mentally ill and drug abusers is excluded.

tive to home-based public care, with 57 percent of total public care costs stemming from institutional care by 2019. Figure 2.6 shows that both home care and nursing home and residential care stays are partly financed by out-of-pocket payments, accounting for around 10 percent of total costs in both cases. Room and board is included for nursing homes and residential care facilities. The results indicate that the policy of keeping people in their own home for as long as possible, if necessary with home care, is under challenge.

2.2.5 Long-Term Care Receipt

Informal care is reported in SHARE, where respondents were asked if they receive help from family or friends, who provided help, and how often. SHARE wave 6 does not report number of hours. Instead, respondents report how often they received help. Categories are daily, weekly, monthly, and less often. These questions were asked for up to three helpers. We impute average hours of informal care for each frequency using information on hours provided in SHARE waves 1 and 2.[14]

14. See the appendix for details. A related approach was adopted by Meijer et al. (2022).

Table 2.7 **Distribution of hours of help received per week, Denmark, 2015**

	65+	85+
5th percentile	0.9	0.6
10th percentile	1.1	0.9
25th percentile	1.1	2.3
50th percentile	3.1	4.5
75th percentile	6.1	9.0
90th percentile	12.9	24.0
95th percentile	26.1	29.5
Mean	5.9	8.4
1 hour per day or less	0.79	0.61
5 hours per day or more	0.02	–
Observations	449	71

Note: The hours are imputed using SHARE wave 1 and 2. Nursing home residents are excluded from all calculations. The table only includes people with a number of hours helped pr. week larger than zero. Percentiles are pseudo percentiles defined as the mean five observations around each percentile. Hours include both formal and informal care. Data on formal care come from Danish administrative data and include both personal and practical help. Data on informal care come from SHARE, where respondents reported the number of times getting help over the past 12 months. Categories were About daily (assumed 200 times), About every week (assumed 40 times), About every month (assumed 10 times) and Less often (assumed 5 times). Respondents answered the question for up to three different helpers, and the number of days with informal help is calculated as the sum over the different helpers.

Source: SHARE (wave 6) and Danish administrative data

Formal home care is in general provided and financed by the municipalities. The number of hours of formal care provided is decided by municipal administrators based on an assessment of the needs of the elderly person. Information on home care received is found in the register data, which have information at the individual level about hours delivered to each person, both in the form of personal care and practical help. The elderly may supplement care supplied by the municipalities with private services, e.g., private cleaning, or gardening. We do not include such private services below, as we assume that they will typically not be related to needs stemming from functional limitations as measured through ADLs or IADLs.

Table 2.7 shows the distribution of hours of help received in total, i.e., the sum of formal and informal care as defined as above, for the 65+ and 85+ age groups, respectively. According to SHARE, around one-third of the elderly aged 65+ received a positive number of hours of informal care from either members of the household or people from outside the household (adult children, relatives, friends, neighbors). Table 2.7 only includes hours for individuals with a positive number of care hours received. Conditional on receiving care, we observe that the median number of weekly hours of care is around 3 hours for the 65+ and 4.5 hours for the 85+ year olds. Moreover, the table suggests that there is great dispersion in number of care hours received, with the bottom quartile receiving very limited care, and a

Table 2.8 Distribution of nursing home stay lengths, Denmark, 2016

Average # Days since entry	961
Median # Days since entry	791
10th Percentile # Days since entry	189
90th Percentile # Days since entry	2,057
Share in NH –2 Years	0.77
Observations	29,488

Note: The table includes people who moved into the nursing home or residential care facility in 2008 or later and were living there on January 1, 2016. The median and percentiles are pseudo percentiles defined as the mean of five observations around each percentile.
Source: Danish Administrative Data

large number of hours for the top receivers, more than 25 hours per week at the 95th percentile for both age groups.

For individuals needing intensive care beyond what can be provided in their home, nursing homes and residential care provide alternatives.[15] Over the last decades, the number of traditional nursing home beds has declined, and alternatives such as residential care, which offer more independent housing but still provide some care, have increased in importance. Stays at such facilities are publicly subsidized, with some private costs related to the rent paid and meals received.

Table 2.8 gives details about stays in nursing homes and residential care facilities. Information about nursing home stays is found in register data from Statistics Denmark. These nursing home stays are of a rather permanent nature, where the individual has changed address permanently to the care facility. Thus, short-term stays in facilities for recreation, training, and rehabilitation, e.g., after a hospital stay, are not recorded in the registers on stays in nursing homes and residential care facilities. According to table 2.8, the median duration of a stay is around 790 days, more than two years, and the average stay is around 960 days. In total, almost 30,000 individuals aged 65+ were living in a nursing home or residential care facility in 2016.

The results are consistent with the relatively good health condition of a large share of the elderly in Denmark, in combination with a labor market situation where female participation rates are high, and many workers retire late. Accordingly, many elderly only require relatively few hours of help per week, given their favorable health condition and level of well-being, and relatively few hours of informal help are offered by children who are still active on the labor market. Older individuals, and those in poor health, do require help, and some of this is publicly provided formal help, with fairly long, terminal stays in nursing homes for some.

15. Residential care includes independent protected housing for the elderly with additional long-term care supplied (*Beskyttet bolig* and similar facilities). Nursing home and residential care facility residents are excluded from table 2.7.

Table 2.9 Any care by age and ADL. Denmark, 2015/2017

	65+	85+
Full sample	0.335	0.625
0 ADLs 1+ IADL	0.576	0.592
1 ADL	0.524	0.710
2 ADLs	0.748	0.877
3+ ADLs	0.765	0.887
Observations	3,408	305

Note: The care variable is defined as either being in a nursing home or having received formal or informal home help. For informal help from outside household, SHARE also includes practical help. For help inside the household, SHARE asks if respondents have received help regularly over a longer period within last 12 months.

Source: SHARE (wave 6 & 7). SHARE population weights are used, and nursing home residents are weighted, to match population in nursing homes.

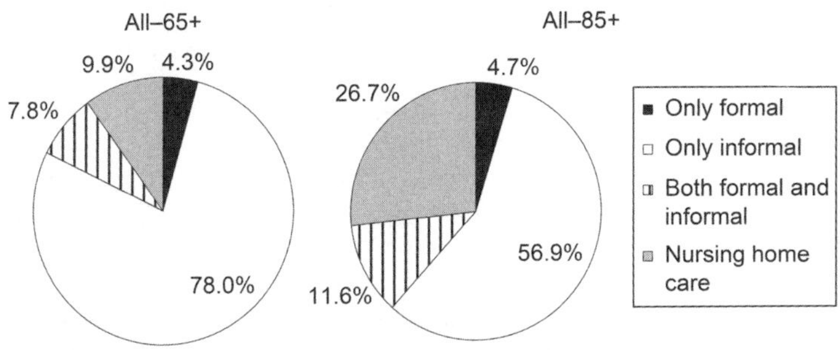

Fig. 2.7 Type of care received, by age, Denmark, 2015/2017

Notes: The care variable is defined as either living in a nursing home or care residency or having received formal or informal home care. For informal care from outside the household, practical help is included. For care from within the household, only personal care is included, and consists of those having received help approximately daily for a longer period within the last 12 months.

Source: SHARE (waves 6 & 7). SHARE population weights are used, and nursing home residents are weighted to match population in nursing homes.

From table 2.9, around one-third of the 65+ year olds receive some kind of long-term care, i.e., either living in a nursing home, or receiving formal or informal help in the home. This proportion rises to almost two-thirds of the 85+ year olds. Care received is increasing in number of ADLs, with more than three-quarters of the 65+ and nearly 90 percent of the 85+ group with 3+ ADLs receiving LTC. Furthermore, SHARE data suggests that around 31 percent of the 65+ receive informal care, mainly for practical tasks. SHARE data thus shows that less than 3 percent of the elderly receive informal care in the form of personal care.

For those receiving long-term care, figure 2.7 shows the distribution across formal and informal care. The shares of elderly living in a nursing home or

Table 2.10 **Distribution of hours of help received per week, Denmark, 2015**

	65+		85+	
	Formal	Informal	Formal	Informal
5th percentile	0.2	1.1	0.3	1.1
10th percentile	0.3	1.1	0.3	1.7
25th percentile	0.5	1.1	0.5	2.7
50th percentile	1.2	3.1	1.5	4.4
75th percentile	4.0	5.3	4.8	7.7
90th percentile	8.9	11.8	10.0	22.9
95th percentile	13.7	25.0	14.7	26.0
Mean	3.4	5.5	3.7	7.5
Observations	141,662	396	49,332	55

Note: See note to table 2.6. Data on formal care come from Danish administrative data and include both personal and practical help. The table only includes people with a number of hours helped pr. week larger than zero. Percentiles are pseudo percentiles defined as the mean five observations around each percentile. Data on formal care come from Danish administrative data and include both personal and practical help. Data on informal care come from SHARE, where respondents reported the number of times getting help over the past 12 months.
Source: SHARE (wave 6) and Danish administrative data.

receiving both formal and informal care are higher for the 85+ year olds than for the 65+ year olds, reflecting that they need more intensive care. One in ten of the 65+ year olds receiving care is in a nursing home, and one-quarter of the 85+ group. The figure furthermore shows that more than three-quarters of the 65+ year olds receiving long-term care, and more than half of the 85+ group, rely solely on informal care, suggesting that they do not have access to formal care.

Despite the widespread use of home care, the majority of the elderly receive only a few hours a week of formal home care. This is illustrated in table 2.10, which shows the number of hours of both formal home care (subsidized by the municipalities) and informal home care. The table shows that most individuals receive only very few hours of formal care over a week, less than two hours at the median for both the 65+ and the 85+ group. The top 10 percent receive close to 10 hours or more of formal care per week, with the 85+ group receiving slightly more than the 65+ group. The reported numbers for informal help are considerably higher, especially for the 85+ group, with four hours of informal care at the median, and for the high end of the 65+ distribution. At the 90th percentile, the 65+ year olds receive about 12 hours of informal care per week, and the 85+ year olds about 23 hours. Calculations are based on the number of times of getting help as reported in SHARE, combined with an imputed number of hours per visit (see the appendix for details).

Figure 2.8 shows the type of care by number of limitations for each age group. Those with up to two ADLs rely primarily on informal care, only.

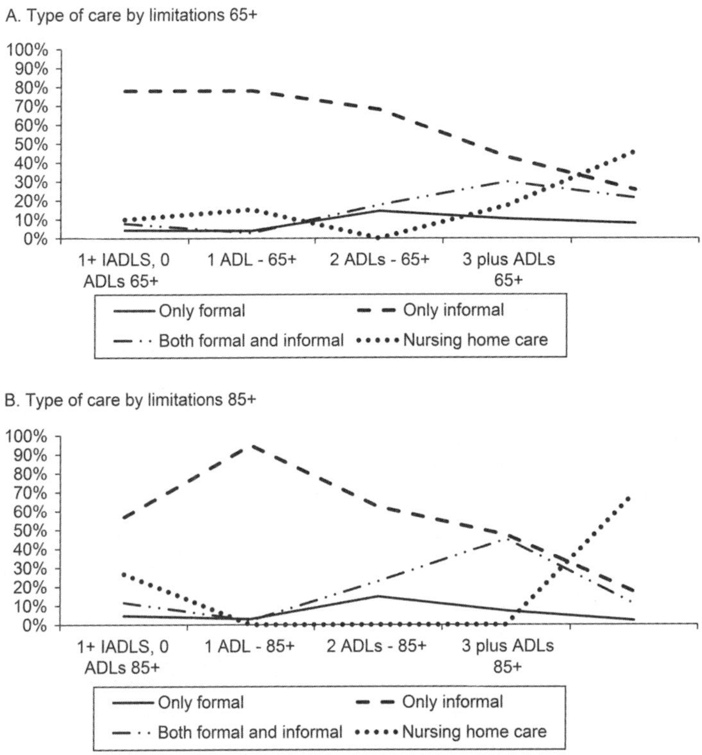

Fig. 2.8 Type of care received, by age and limitations, Denmark, 2015/2017

Notes: The care variable is defined as either living in a nursing home or having received formal or informal home care. For informal care from outside the household, practical help is included. For care from within the household, only personal care is included, and consists of those having received help approximately daily for a longer period within the last 12 months.

Source: SHARE (waves 6 & 7). SHARE population weights are used, and nursing home residents are weighted to match population in nursing homes.

For two and more ADLs, other types of care start increasing in number of ADLs, particularly the shares in nursing homes and residential care or receiving both formal and informal care. The pattern across number of ADLs is similar for both age groups, except that the shares of elderly with three+ ADLs and receiving both formal and informal care or living in a nursing home or residential care facility are higher in the older group.

Table 2.11 provides information on the availability of nursing homes for the elderly. There are nearly 1,000 nursing homes and residential care facilities in Denmark, with more than 40 beds per home on average, of which 92 percent are occupied. About 1 in 10 of 65+ year olds are in the 85+ group, with about 4 percent of 65+ year olds in nursing homes, rising to 17 percent among the 85+ group.

Table 2.12 shows the availability of beds/slots in nursing homes and resi-

Table 2.11 **Absolute number of beds and occupancy rate in nursing homes and residential care facilities, Denmark, 2019**

	2019
Nursing homes and caring residency	950
Beds, all age groups	46,499
Nursing home residents, all age groups	42,886
Occupancy rate, all	92.2%
Nursing home residents, 65+	40,474
Population aged 65+	1,136,063
Nursing home residents per population 65+	3.6%
Nursing home residents, 85+	20,618
Population aged 85+	121,658
Nursing home and caring residency employees	75,001
Protected caring residency employees	544
Nursing home employment as proportion of public employees	7.88%
Nursing home employment as proportion of total employment	2.42%
Protected caring residency employment as proportion of public employees	0.06%
Protected caring residency employment as proportion of total employment	0.02%

Source: Data on number of nursing homes from www.seniorhaandbogen.dk, data on number of beds and nursing home residents, figure table RESP01 (https://www.statistikbanken.dk/RESP01) and RESI01 (https://www.statistikbanken.dk/RESI01). Categories included are nursing homes and protected caring residency (residential care facility) for the elderly. Population data, Statistics Denmark table FOLK2 (https://www.statistikbanken.dk/FOLK2). Data on employment from Statistics Denmark table KAS309 (https://www.statistikbanken.dk/KAS309) and KAS311 (https://www.statistikbanken.dk/KAS311).

Table 2.12 **Distribution of occupation rate and beds across municipalities for nursing homes and residential care facilities, Denmark, 2019**

Percentile	Occupation rate (percent)	Beds per one hundred 65+
5th percentile	81.6	1.26
10th percentile	83.9	1.85
20th percentile	85.0	2.40
30th percentile	87.7	2.75
40th percentile	88.9	3.04
50th percentile	89.9	3.55
60th percentile	91.2	4.10
70th percentile	92.8	5.17
80th percentile	95.4	6.63
90th percentile	97.6	11.18
95th percentile	100.8	21.85
Min	76.5	0.18
Max	114.1	57.31

Source: Data on the number of beds and nursing home residents from Statistics Denmark, www.statistikbanken.dk, table RESP01 and RESI01. The population data on municipal level are from Statistic Denmark table BY2. Categories included are nursing homes and protected residential housing (residential care facilities) with care for the elderly. A number of municipalities have an occupation rate above 100 percent. This is possible as municipalities have the opportunity to use nursing homes in other municipalities.

dential care facilities, and the corresponding occupancy rates, across the 98 municipalities in Denmark. According to Piil Damm et al. (2022), the elderly are distributed increasingly unevenly across the municipalities. While the 65+ share has been relatively constant in the cities (Copenhagen, or municipalities with more than 45,000 inhabitants), at around 16 percent, from 1985 to 2019, the share in remote municipalities (where the median inhabitant has more than half an hour's drive to the center of a city of 45,000) has increased, from 16 percent in 1985 (the same as in the cities) to 24 percent in 2019. Table 2.12 reveals substantial heterogeneity in the availability of beds across municipalities, ranging from 1.3 beds/slots per 100 65+ year olds at the 5th percentile to 22 beds/slots at the 95th, but also a fairly low overall coverage, with only 3.6 beds/slots per 100 elderly at the median. This reflects the Danish policy of staying in one's own home for as long as possible, with extensive home care if needed. This policy may be challenged as retirement ages increase, leaving less opportunity to provide informal care.

Overall, the results show that a large fraction of the elderly receive relatively few hours of care per week, consistent with their fairly favorable health situation and the labor market situation in Denmark. Older individuals, and those in poorer health, receive more care. Formal care is primarily for those in worse health. Institutional care is already increasing as share of total public LTC costs, relative to home-based public care, and this trend could be strengthened as retirement ages rise, leaving the provision of informal care and thus the elderly's staying in their own home more difficult.

2.2.6 Workforce in LTC Sector

Next, we consider the workforce in the formal long-term care sector. According to figure 2.9, about 40 percent of the employees in long-term care have an education as either nurse or social and health care assistant or helper. The remaining employees have other education, including no education beyond primary school. The share with relevant education is slightly higher in nursing homes and residential care facilities than in home care services.

Table 2.13 provides an overview of the level and content of education and training of employees in long-term care. Before 1990, home care workers did not require specific education. After 1990, home care workers are recruited among social and health care helpers (*SOSU or social- og sundhedshjælper*). This education takes two years and two months. The education is a combination of schooling and practical training. Practical training takes place in home care and nursing homes. The admission criterion is to have passed primary school examinations. Another important group of employees in home care are social and health care assistants (*social- og sundhedsassistent*). This education takes three years, nine months, and three weeks. The education is partly school based, partly practical training in home care, nursing

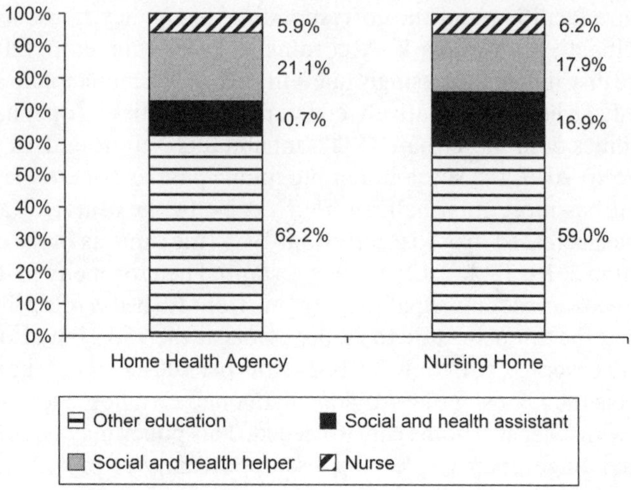

Fig. 2.9 Percent distribution of nurses, and social and health care assistants and helpers, at care facilities, Denmark, 2019

Source: Danish administrative data. The variable is the highest achieved education of the workers. The large other education category particularly consists of workers whose highest education is secondary school or high school, and those educated as pedagogue or social worker. The group also includes smaller numbers of nursing assistants, nursing home assistants, physiotherapists, occupational therapists, and workers with office training.

Table 2.13 Training requirements for formal home care workers, Denmark

	Admission criteria	Duration	Type of training
Nursing assistants *(Social and health care helpers)*	Passed primary school exams (skills in Danish at D level and science at E level)	2 years and 2 months	School and practical training in home care and nursing homes
Licensed practical nurses *(Social and health care assistants)*	Passed criteria as for social and health care helpers plus competencies in first aid, fire extinction	3 years, 9 months, 3 weeks	School based with practical training in home care, nursing homes, residential care facilities, hospitals, and psychiatric units
Registered nurses	High school (gymnasium) or equivalent	3½ years	School based courses and clinical training

Notes: For nursing assistants, the education for home care worker was in 1990 replaced by the education for social and health care helper. For licensed practical nurse, the education for nursing home assistant was in 1990 replaced by the education for social and health care assistant.

Source: Uddannelsen til social- og sundhedshjælper | FOA Social-Sundhed; https://www.foa.dk/raad-regler/uddannelse/i-gang-med-uddannelse/social-og-sundhedsassistent.

homes, residential care facilities, hospitals, and psychiatric units. Registered nurses receive the most advanced course based and clinical training among the groups considered.

Table 2.14 shows hourly and annual wages for professionals working in long-term care. Licensed practical nurses correspond to the Danish social

Table 2.14 **Pay for full-time care workers at nursing facility and in home health care, Denmark, 2019**

	Mean hourly wage	Median hourly wage	Annual mean wage	Annual median wage
Panel 1: Nursing Home Industry				
Nursing Assistants	201	192	343,236	330,163
Licensed Practical Nurses	212	201	373,797	358,789
Registered Nurses	247	230	445,621	426,789
Panel 2: Home Health Care Industry				
Nursing Assistants	188	179	336,013	321,234
Licensed Practical Nurses	211	197	381,246	361,456
Registered Nurses	241	222	446,887	422,684
Panel 3: All Industries				
All Workers	258	228	494,570	433,205
No High School Degree	201	190	378,215	355,600
No College Degree	244	210	470,416	400,752
College Degree or More	267	235	513,623	447,139
Poverty Line for a family of 4	–	–	265,728	–

Note: Nursing Assistants correspond to the Danish social and health care helpers; Licensed Practical Nurses correspond to social and health care assistants, see table 2.13 for training requirements. Median wages are calculated as the average of five observations around the median. The sample is restricted to those working full-time in 2019. The poverty line is defined as 50 percent of the median wage in 2019 for a family of two parents and two children (statistikbanken.dk, table IFOR10).

Source: Danish Administrative Data, www.statistikbanken.dk/IFOR10

and health care assistants, and nursing assistants to the Danish social and health care helpers. The latter receive the lowest wages of the three groups of professional workers. The third group, registered nurses, receive the highest wages of the three, almost on par with the annual median wage across all workers in all industries, but clearly falling short of those with at least a college degree. Licensed practical nurses receive annual wages roughly at the level of the group without a high school degree, and nursing assistants fall short of this. Nursing assistants earn slightly more in nursing homes than in the home health care industry, whereas registered nurses and licensed practical nurses earn about the same in both cases. The annual income of a nursing assistant would put a family of four above the poverty line, although not by a wide margin.

The relatively low levels of compensation in the long-term care sector, combined with demanding working conditions, have contributed to the difficulties in recruiting and retaining employees in the sector. This may lead to increasing wages in the future, and the demand for an increase in quality of care and the increased availability of new and expensive technology only reinforce that expenditures could grow faster than projected.

Table 2.15 **Home care provision—population estimates, Denmark, 2017**

	65+	85+
Formal helpers	41,383	8,756
Relative to elderly population	(0.038)	(0.073)
Relative to 18 to 65 population	(0.012)	(0.003)
Informal helpers	84.527	40,070
Relative to elderly population	(0.077)	(0.335)
Relative to 18 to 65 population	(0.024)	(0.011)
All helpers	125,910	48,826
Relative to elderly population	(0.115)	(0.408)
Relative to 18 to 65 population	(0.036)	(0.014)
Observations (SHARE population)	1,661	157
Observations (population 65+/85+)	1,095,172	119,594
Population 18 to 64	3,485,374	3,485,374

Note: The number of informal helpers is calculated by calculating the fraction of SHARE respondents who receive informal care by age group and the average number of helpers from SHARE data. Multiplying this with entire population in the given age group from administrative data gives us an estimate of the total number of informal helpers. SHARE is asking about help received, and as it is not possible to report more than three helpers, the measure of informal helpers is imprecise. The number of formal helpers is calculated by finding the fraction of home care receivers who are 65 + and 85 + respectively and multiplying with total home care workers.

Source: SHARE (wave 7), Danish administrative data, and www.statistikbanken.dk, tables AED06 and RAS309

2.2.7 Who Are the Caregivers?

As previously discussed, home care for the elderly is provided through formal as well as informal care, often in combination. Table 2.15 shows statistics on the population of caregivers at the national level for both formal and informal caregivers. There are about 40,000 workers employed in formal home care and providing care for the 65+ group. This corresponds to 4 percent of this group, and 1 percent of the working (18 to 65) population. On top of this, there is more than twice the number, almost 85,000 full-time equivalents of people providing informal care. Similarly, nearly 9,000 workers provide formal care for the 85+ group, corresponding to 7 percent of this group receiving formal care from 0.3 percent of the working population. For the 85+ group, informal care is relatively more important, with 40,000 full-time equivalent workers, corresponding to one-third of the 85+ population.

Figure 2.10 shows the demographic composition of employees in the formal home care in the left-hand side of the figure, while figures on the right-hand side show the demographic composition of informal care providers. Formal care employees are predominantly women (87 percent), and more than half have some college education (this includes the specific educations for the sector), while 15 percent have completed college or beyond. Moreover, around 13 percent are immigrants or descendants. The age distribution is

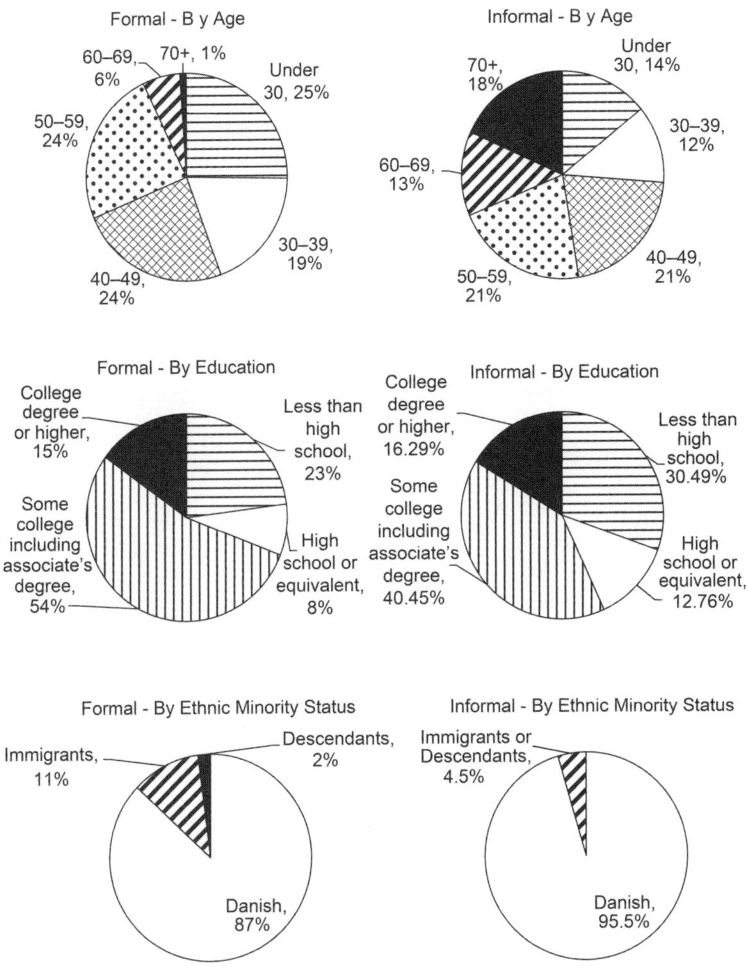

Fig. 2.10 Demographic composition of formal and informal care workers, Denmark, 2013/2015

Note: Data do not include information on citizenship, but instead by immigration status. Descendants are people born to immigrant parents. For informal care, age is provided for children and spouses and is estimated. Immigration status is only provided for spouse and children, where immigrant and descendant are merged into one category due to data restrictions. Education is provided for spouses, children, and grandchildren. Children's education is taken as the lowest education of the care receiver's children, and similarly for grandchildren. Data for informal care are from 2015 (SHARE, wave 6). Data for formal helpers are from 2013 and include both practical help and personal care. Both care inside and outside household is included for informal care, although care from inside the household represents a very small fraction of the sample. For informal care, SHARE population weights are used.

Source: SHARE and Danish administrative data

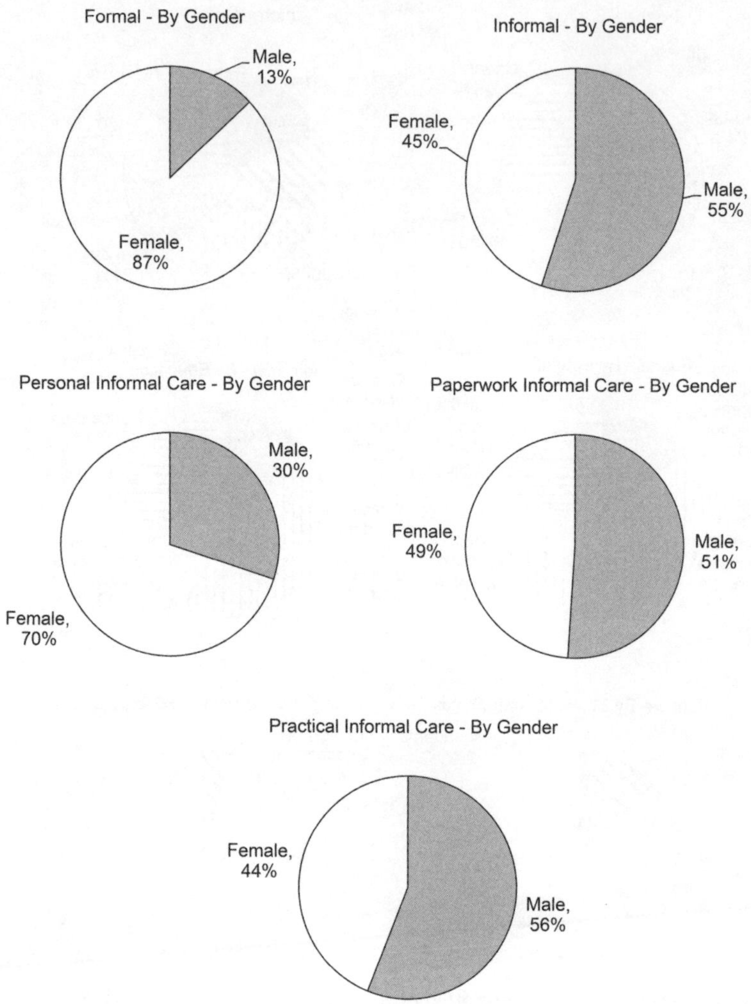

Fig. 2.10 (cont.)

relatively even, with roughly equally many workers in each of the age groups below 30, 30–39, 40–49, and 50–59, but few workers aged 60+, presumably due to early retirement, and virtually no one aged 70+. In contrast, informal care providers are both men and women. Surprisingly perhaps, informal care in general is more often performed by men than women. When zooming in on the informal care activities performed by men and women, in the bottom of figure 2.10, we observe that when it comes to personal informal care, around 70 percent is provided by female carers, while the informal care activities dominated by male carers is related to help with paperwork and practical care. Moreover, informal care is to a much larger degree offered

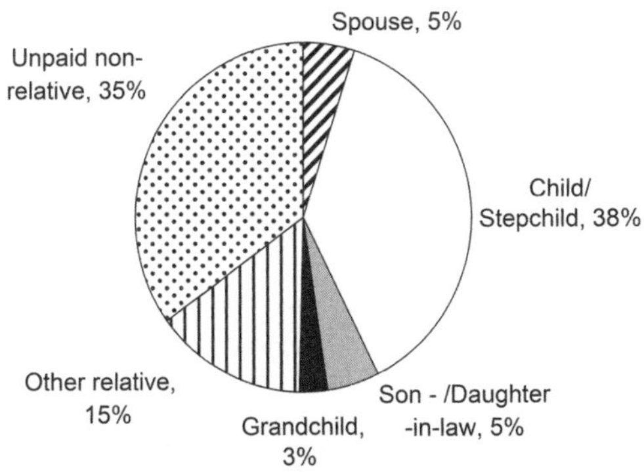

Fig. 2.11 Informal caregivers by relationship to care recipient, Denmark, 2015
Note: Informal care includes both practical help and personal care. Both care inside and outside household is included, although care from inside the household represents a very small fraction of the sample. SHARE population weights are used.

by older individuals, including retirees, with nearly one in three helpers aged 60+, suggesting that these people have time to offer informal care, and spouses, relatives and friends etc. who need this. For example, if alive, the parents of a person in the 60+ group are likely to belong to the 85+ group, and thus more likely to require help than, say, the parents of a person in the group aged 49 and below. We furthermore examined the educational background of informal caregivers by using information about education of spouses and children providing informal care. As SHARE reported up to three informal caregivers, and since for care provided by children we do not know the educational background for most of these children from the survey, we use educational background of the children from the registers. If several children provided care, we choose the educational background of the child with least education. This implies that we may underestimate the educational background of caregivers. Still, we find that more than half of all informal care is provided by individuals with some college and above.

As shown in figure 2.11, more than one-third of informal care is provided by a child of the care recipient, and more than one-third by unpaid non-relatives, including friends, neighbors, etc. Other caregivers are less common, e.g., spouse, grandchildren, and so on. Care includes both practical help and personal care.

The results indicate a dilemma in terms of policy decisions. Informal care is primarily offered by older individuals, including retirees. With the pension reforms, and the trend toward later retirement, access to informal care may be reduced, thus leading to increased pressure on the formal public care sector. In a sense, there is a trade-off between pensions and formal care, in terms of public finance. Thus, with the aging population, the pressure on the welfare state is still on.

Table 2.16 **Formal care costs, annual, Denmark, 2019**

Types	Number of users 65+	Total spending 65+ (billion DKK)
Nursing home and residential care	40,474	28.04
Home care	125,579	11.56

Source: Statistics Denmark, www.statistikbanken.dk, tables REGK31, AED06, SHA1 and note from KL—Local Government Denmark. Expenditure on nursing home and residential care include room and board. Private costs are imputed from Statistikbanken, SHA1.

2.3 Costs of Long-Term Care

Expenditures on long-term care comprise a sizeable share of total health care spending in Denmark. Table 2.16 reviews the public expenditures related to nursing homes, residential care, and home care for the 65+ year olds. In 2019, total public spending for residents in nursing homes and residential care (protected housing for the elderly) was 25 billion DKK, when adjusted to include only the 65+ age group.[16] Spending on formal home care was nearly half of the public expenditure on nursing home and residential care.

As shown in sections 2.1 and 2.2, a substantial part of care in people's home is provided in the form of informal care by family, friends, neighbors, etc. Such care is usually provided voluntarily, unpaid, and as part of general care toward each other in the family, or among friends. Still, the time spent providing informal care represents a cost to society, as this time could have been spent on other (productive) activities, or in leisure. The valuation of the opportunity cost of informal caregivers hinges on numerous assumptions. These are discussed at some length in other chapters of this volume, but we will nevertheless provide a short discussion of the issues involved here, as well.

In principle, assuming perfectly competitive labor markets and market wages equal to the value of leisure, we may value the time spent in informal care by the forgone wage. In this case, the opportunity cost of time is equal to the individual wage, even if the individual does not participate in the labor market, e.g., due to being retired. Table 2.17 presents two alternatives for valuing hours of informal care. In both cases, if informal care is delivered by those who are working, the care is valued at their predicted wage, based on gender, age, and education. In the same way, we predict employment by gender, age, and education of people providing informal care on the basis of administrative register data for a similar population. For the case considered in column 1, time for those not working is valued at zero ("low valuation").

16. This figure includes the privately financed fee paid for room and board in nursing homes and residential care, amounting to about one-fifth of total expenditure, with the remainder publicly financed.

Table 2.17 **Informal care valuation, Denmark, 2019**

	I	II
Valuation (billion DKK)	14.06	21.71
Total hours informal help (billion)	0.102	0.102
Probability of working	0.5788	0.5788
Probability of working * Predicted wage if working	138	138
(1 – Probability of working) * Wage of home care worker	75	75
Hours of working caregiver	0.059	0.059
Hours of non-working caregiver	0.043	0.043
Predicted wage if working	239	239
Wage of home care worker	179	179
Observations	3,408	3,408

Note: Total annual hours of informal help are estimated using information on average hours of informal care if receiving care (5.5 hours per week) from table 2.10, scaled by the proportion that receive informal care (31.4 percent of the 65+) as reported in SHARE, and scaled to the total population of 65+ year olds in 2019 (1,136,045 individuals). Employment probabilities of informal carers, E(Work), are predicted for each type of caregiver (by caregiver's gender, age, and education) based on an estimation of being employed by gender, age, and education, using administrative register data for the population. These are weighted by number of informal hours provided by each informal carer as reported in SHARE. Average wages for informal care providers working are based on predicted wages by gender, age and education for similar individuals in population. Valuation of shadow wage for non-working individuals providing informal care is based on wage of nursing assistants, as given in table 2.14.

Source: SHARE and Danish administrative register data from Statistics Denmark

For the case considered in column 2 ("high valuation"), we value informal care time of those who are not working at the replacement cost of home care (the average cost of a home care worker in 2019). We assume that productivity in privately provided long-term care is constant across individuals. Our valuation ranges from $14 billion DKK (low valuation) to 22 billion DKK (high valuation). It should be stressed that this valuation hinges on a number of sensitive assumptions, is primarily thought of as an illustration of the order of magnitude of the value of informal care, and thus the results should be interpreted with care.

Table 2.18 combines these findings with the previous data on long-term care spending across public and private sources. Most of the costs relating to nursing homes, residential care, and formal home care are publicly financed. The privately financed component corresponds to payments by residents for room and board (meals) in nursing homes and residential care facilities, and OOP payments for additional help (both personal care and practical help) beyond what is publicly covered in home care, whereas the full cost of informal care is privately financed by its providers. From the table, the largest portion of long-term care expenditures consists of public spending on formal care, but with informal care representing a considerable cost to society, too, both according to the conservative valuation method (low valuation), and the method that relies on the higher valuation of informal care (high

Table 2.18 **Total costs by type of care and source, Denmark, 2019**

Care Type	Source	Cost I	Cost II	Cost I–Share of GDP	Cost II–Share of GDP
Nursing home and residential care	Public	25.29	25.29	1.1%	1.1%
	Private	2.75	2.75	0.1%	0.1%
	All	28.04	28.04	1.2%	1.2%
Home care	Public	10.27	10.27	0.4%	0.4%
	Private	1.29	1.29	0.1%	0.1%
	All	11.56	11.56	0.5%	0.5%
Informal care	Private	14.06	21.71	0.6%	0.9%
Total	Public	35.56	35.56	1.5%	1.5%
	Private	18.09	25.75	0.8%	1.1%
	All	53.65	61.31	2.3%	2.7%

Note: Numbers in this table are based on tables 2.16 and 2.17. Numbers for GDP are from Statistics Denmark, www.statistikbanken.dk/NAN1.

valuation). Imputations from the two methods put the share of informal care between one-quarter and one-third of total costs of long-term care.

2.4 Conclusions

As in many other Western countries, the Danish economy faces important challenges as a consequence of an aging population. Over the next three decades, elderly individuals aged 65+ will constitute an increasing proportion of the Danish population, and this is expected to generate an elevated demand for long-term care.

This paper provides evidence on the health state of the elderly, assessed by a number of health measures, but with an emphasis on the ability of the elderly to perform everyday activities. ADL and IADL measures generally point to fairly high functioning levels, but also to a negative association between income and wealth on the one side, and ADL/IADL levels on the other side.

Using a combination of survey data from SHARE and administrative register data, we document the extent of care provided for the elderly. These data show that around one in three of the elderly aged 65+ receive some form of care, with three-quarters of these relying solely on informal care from friends or family, while the majority of the elderly are self-reliant, consistent with their relatively good health condition.

Most formal long-term services are provided free of charge by the Danish public sector. Such services constitute a substantial part of the economy. Total costs of care, including nursing homes, residential care, and home-based care, have increased from just above 1 percent of GDP in 1998 to above 2 percent of GDP in recent years. Further, the public debate has recently shown increasing attention toward the quality of care provided. At the same time, the sectors providing health care and long-term care are increasingly facing recruitment problems, and higher salaries are currently debated politically as a means to address these problems. Going forward, these tendencies could lead to costs of long-term care growing faster than currently projected.

Finally, we impute the total costs of informal care. Despite controversy related to the valuation of the time spent providing informal care to family and friends, we provide evidence of substantial costs to society in terms of potentially lost income and reduced welfare of caregivers, with estimated costs of informal care amounting to between one-quarter and one-third of total costs of long-term care. In the future, pension reforms that are intended to expand the labor force and keep the elderly working for an extended period of time until they are in their early seventies are likely to put pressure on the provision of informal caregiving. This could challenge the Danish policy of keeping the elderly in their own homes for as long as possible. The share of institutional care in total costs of public long-term care is already rising. Policymakers will thus increasingly have to consider the balance between, on the one side, securing a large labor supply, also among individuals in their late sixties and early seventies and, on the other side, meeting increasing demands for long-term care with a higher reliance on informal caregiving.

References

Abeliansky, Ana Lucia, and Holger Strulik. 2018. "How We Fall Apart: Similarities of Human Aging in 10 European Countries." *Demography* 55 (1): 341–59.

Amilon, Anna, Agnete Aslaug Kjær, Jacob Ladenburg, and Anu Siren. 2022. "Trust in the Publicly Financed Care System and Willingness to Pay for Long-term Care: A Discrete Choice Experiment in Denmark." *Social Science & Medicine* 311.

ATP. 2019. "Offentlige Pensioner Får Større Betydning med Alderen." ("Public Pensions Gain Significance with Age"). *Faktum*, November.

Bom, Judith, Pieter Bakx, Eddy Van Doorslaer, Mette Gørtz, and Jonathan Skinner. 2023. "What Explains Different Rates of Nursing Home Admissions? Comparing the United States to Denmark and the Netherlands." *The Journal of the Economics of Ageing* 25: 100456.

Browning, Martin, Mette Gørtz, and Søren Leth-Petersen. 2013. "Housing Wealth and Consumption: A Micro Panel Study." *Economic Journal* 123 (568): 401–28.

Christensen, Bent Jesper, Mette Gørtz, and Malene Kallestrup-Lamb. 2016. "Medical Spending in Denmark." *Fiscal Studies* 37: 461–97.

Danish Economic Council. 2019. Dansk Økonomi Autumn 2019. Copenhagen.

Hjelmar, Ulf, Yosef Bhatti, Tine Rostgaard, Ole Helby Petersen, Karsten Vrangbæk, Patricia Thor Larsen, and Lily Michelle Molsbergen Jacobsen. 2016. "Kvalitet på offentlige og private plejecentre i Danmark." VIVE Forskningsprojektet"dokume ntation af effekter ved konkurrenceudsættelse af offentlige opgaver," Del-rapport 6 (Quality of Public and Private Care Centers in Denmark, VIVE Research Project "Documentation of Effects of Exposure to Competition of Public Tasks," Sub-report 6).

Kollerup, Anna, Jakob Kjellberg, and Rikke Ibsen. 2022 "Ageing and Health Care Expenditures: The Importance of Age per se, Steepening of the Individual-level Expenditure Curve, and the Role of Morbidity." *European Journal of Health Economics* 23: 1121–149.

Law on Old Age Support. 1891. April 9. (*Lov om Alderdomsunderstøttelse, 9. april 1891*).

Local Government Denmark (KL). 2021. "KL's Perspektiver på Fremtidens Ældrepleje." November. Holdningspapir ("Perspectives on Future Elder Care," November 2021, Opinion Paper).

Local Government Denmark (KL). 2021. Udbud og Efterspørgsel efter Udvalgte Velfærdsuddannelser—2021 (Supply and Demand of Selected Welfare Sector Educations—2021).

Piil Damm, Anna, Ahmad Hassani, Torben Tranæs, Marie Louise Schultz-Nielsen. 2022. *Bosætning i Danmark—i et 35-årigt perspektiv* (*Settlement in Denmark—in a 35-year perspective*). Odense: University of Southern Denmark University Press.

Meijer, Erik, Maria Casanova, Hyewon Kim, Ana Llena-Nozal, Jinkook Lee. 2022. "Economic Costs of Dementia in 11 Countries in Europe: Estimates from Nationally Representative Cohorts of a Panel Study." *Lancet Regional Health*—Europe, Volume 20.

Rasmussen, Jacob Knage. 2012. Plejehjemmenes kulturhistorie skal sikres og bevares. (The Cultural History of Nursing Homes Must Be Secured and Preserved.) *Kristeligt Dagblad*, August 8. https://www.kristeligt-dagblad.dk/kronik/plejehjemmenes-kulturhistorie-skal-sikres-og-bevares.

Stratton, Leslie S., Nabanita Datta Gupta, David Reimer, and Anders Holm. 2018. "Modeling Completion of Vocational Education: The Role of Cognitive and Noncognitive Skills by Program Type." *B.E. Journal of Economic Analysis & Policy* 18 (4): 1–17.

The Danish Economic Council. 2020. *Dansk Økonomi* (*The Danish Economy*), Autumn 2020, Report.

The Danish Economic Council. 2021. *Dansk Økonomi* (*The Danish Economy*), Autumn 2021, Report.

Vabø, Mia, Minna Zechner, Anneli Stranz, Lea Graff, and Sigurveig H. Sigurðardóttir. 2022. "Is Nordic Elder Care Facing a (New) Collaborative Turn?" *Social Policy & Administration* 56 (4): 549–62.

3 Long-Term Care in England

James Banks, Jeremy McCauley, and Eric French

3.1 Introduction

This chapter describes the state of long-term care (LTC) in England. LTC, which is generally referred to in England as adult social care, supports activities of daily living for older and disabled individuals to improve their quality of life. This includes stays in nursing homes as well as home-based help with tasks such as washing, dressing, and feeding.

England's LTC system is facing increasing strain due to population aging. Longer lives, combined with fertility rates below replacement rates, means that an increasingly large share of the English population is aged

James Banks is professor of economics at the University of Manchester and senior research fellow at the Institute for Fiscal Studies.

Jeremy McCauley is a senior lecturer in economics at the University of Bristol and a research associate of the Institute for Fiscal Studies.

Eric French is the Montague Burton Professor of Industrial Relations and Labour Economics at the University of Cambridge, and a codirector of ESRC Centre for the Microeconomic Analysis of Public Policy at the Institute for Fiscal Studies.

Thanks are due to Carl Emmerson and Polly Simpson for allowing us to use some of the background material from an unpublished IFS briefing paper, "Adult social care in England." We are grateful to the Economic and Social Research Council for funding through the ESRC Institute for the Microeconomic Analysis of Public Policy at IFS (grant reference ES/T014334/1) and ESRC grant "Inequality and the insurance value of transfers across the life cycle" (ES/P001831/1)). The ELSA data used here were made available through the UK Data Archive (UKDA) and developed by a team of researchers based at University College London, the Institute for Fiscal Studies and the National Centre for Social Research with funding provided by the National Institute of Aging in the United States, and a consortium of UK government departments coordinated by the National Institute for Health and Care Research. The developers and funders of ELSA and the UK Data Archive bear no responsibility for the analyses or interpretations presented here. For acknowledgments, sources of research support, and disclosure of the authors' material financial relationships, if any, please see https://www.nber.org/books-and-chapters/long-term-care-around-world/long-term-care-england.

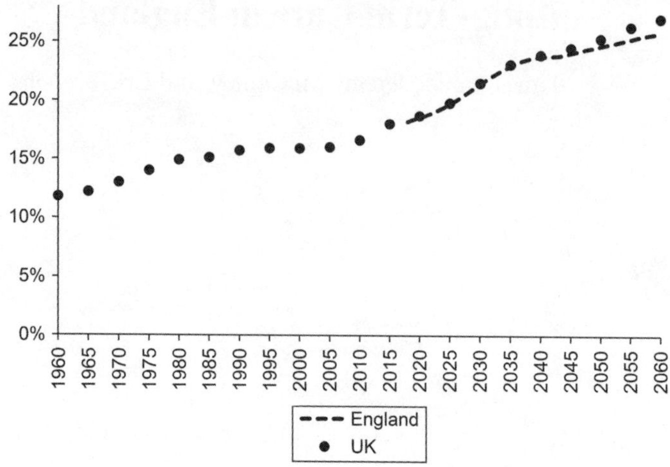

Fig. 3.1 Percentage of population ages 65 or older, England and UK, 1960–2060
Source: UK Data (Historic and projected) from World Population Prospects (2019) (https://data.un.org/Data.aspx?d=PopDiv&f=variableID%3A66). England data projections from ONS Population Projections, https://www.ons.gov.uk/peoplepopulationandcommunity/populationandmigration/populationprojections/bulletins/nationalpopulationprojections/2018based.

65 or older. Figure 3.1 shows that the share of the population that is aged 65+ has approximately doubled over the last 60 years. It currently stands at 20 percent of the population and is projected to continue growing over time. Importantly, figure 3.2 shows that the oldest old, i.e., those aged 85+, are forecast to grow especially rapidly as a share of the population over the next 20 years from 2030 onwards. Because LTC needs grow with age, and particularly after age 85, expenditure on formal LTC services will most likely need to rise. In addition, population aging will also increase the already significant burden of informal care faced by families. In this paper we estimate the value of informal care provided to the age 65+ population in England in 2018 to be between 0.7 percent and 2.5 percent of GDP, i.e., around one to three times the size of formal LTC costs.[1]

While the National Health Service (NHS) provides free public medical care, it does not provide LTC. Instead, local authorities pay for most public

1. Where possible in this paper we present all statistics and analysis for the English population, since that is the jurisdiction that corresponds most closely to our microdata. In certain instances, however, typically when drawing from National Accounts type analysis which are computed at the UK level, England specific statistics are not available. Hence we occasionally use UK statistics and explicitly label them as such. The English population makes up the large majority of the UK population and the demographics across England and the other UK nations are similar; the English population is slightly richer and healthier on average but experiences a slightly less generous LTC care system. So one might expect English statistics to be similar to the UK statistic were they to be available.

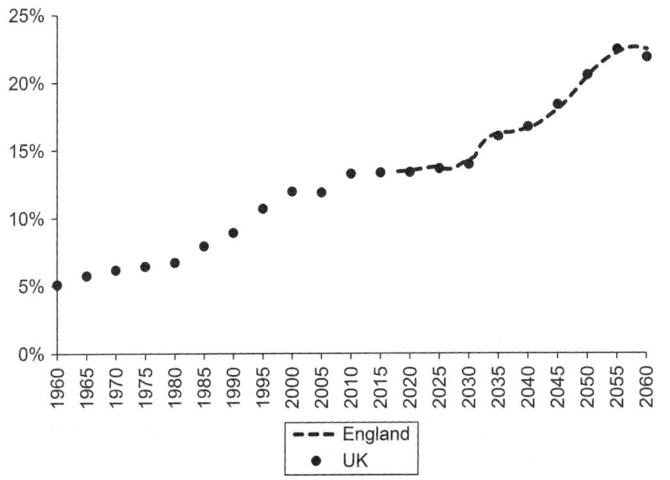

Fig. 3.2 Percentage of 65+ population that is age 85 or older, England, 1960–2060
Source: UK Data (Historic and projected) from World Population Prospects (2019) (https://data.un.org/Data.aspx?d=PopDiv&f=variableID%3A66). England data projections from ONS Population Projections, https://www.ons.gov.uk/peoplepopulationandcommunity/populationandmigration/populationprojections/bulletins/nationalpopulationprojections/2018based.

LTC and have considerable flexibility to organize and provide that care as they see fit. Eligibility for care depends on both a needs test and a means test. Depending on their current income, those receiving means-tested care are expected to contribute to the cost. Around 65 percent of the cost of formal LTC is financed by local authorities and other public providers.

England has seen multiple reforms to LTC funding policy in recent years. These reforms have given families more choice in how care is received. For example, there has been a push in recent years for older people to receive care in their own home—60 percent of recipients of public social care currently receive care at home. There has also been a move toward "personal budgets" and "direct payments," which allow recipients to choose how their allocated money is spent and can enable them to choose their own care worker. Perhaps more radically, there have been plans to address the often high out-of-pocket cost of care. In 2021 the government legislated certain recommendations of the Dilnot Commission (2011), including a fixed lifetime cap on LTC charges and a more generous means test. The current policy, to take effect from October 2025, is for a lifetime out-of-pocket spending cap of £86,000 and an increase in the asset limit, above which individuals are not eligible for support, from £23,250 to £100,000 to help insure against the risk of catastrophic costs.

This paper pieces together microeconomic and aggregate data in order to give an overview of the demand and supply of LTC in England in a way that facilitates comparisons with other countries, and briefly discusses current LTC policy and recent reforms. The analysis in this paper proceeds in three sections. The first part of our analysis looks at the demand for care. First, we explore the association between functional limitations on the financial well-being of the age 65+ population. We focus on the well-known measures of limitations with respect to activities of daily living (ADLs, or activities such as toileting and bathing) as well as limitations with respect to instrumental activities of daily living (IADLs, or activities such as cooking or shopping). We show that those who are older and in worse health have fewer financial resources as measured in several dimensions. In the second part of our analysis we consider the supply side and discuss how LTC is provided in England. We document the division in financing between public and private sources. We then show the distribution of care across types by age and degree of limitation, highlighting the growing use of both formal home care and nursing homes as individuals age and become more disabled. We discuss the workforce engaged in LTC, focusing on their low level of pay. Finally, in the third part of our analysis, we undertake a full calculation of the cost of LTC in England—including the costs of informal care. This paper is designed to also be a useful first step in highlighting the data available for microeconomic research on LTC in England. However, we also note that one might argue that there is not enough systematically harmonized information available on the way in which each local authority provides, organizes, and funds its LTC, to carry out a meaningful microeconomic analysis of such a question in England or the UK.

3.2 The Demand for Care: Aging, Disability, and Well-Being of the Older Population

The primary data for our analyses come from the English Longitudinal Study of Aging (ELSA). The design of ELSA was broadly modeled on the US Health and Retirement Survey (HRS), with biennial measurement of health, functional capabilities demographics, employment, wealth, and information on health conditions and long-term care needs. If a sample member was unable to respond in person, a proxy respondent was asked questions in their place.

We use data from the 2018/19 survey (wave 9) and focus on those aged 65 and older, for which there is a sample size of 4,947 individuals. We use cross-sectional survey weights throughout to correct for systematic nonresponse to the ELSA survey. Such cross-sectional weights are designed to make the ELSA sample representative of the English non-institutionalized population aged 50 and over in the survey year, but not the total population, which includes those in nursing homes and other (communal) institutions. While respondents are still members of the ELSA sample if they become institutionalized, ELSA under-represents this population due to high rates

Table 3.1 **Share with ADLs/IADLs by age, England, 2018**

	65+	85+
0 ADLs & 0 IADLs	0.712	0.385
0 ADLs & 1+ IADLs	0.045	0.105
1 ADL	0.102	0.140
2 ADLs	0.047	0.096
3 ADLs	0.031	0.081
4 ADLs	0.021	0.048
5 ADLs	0.018	0.045
6 ADLs	0.025	0.101
Any ADLs	0.243	0.511
Any IADLs	0.185	0.510
Any ADLS or IADLs	0.288	0.615
Observations	*4,947*	*540*

Source: Data are from ELSA Wave 9 (2018). Weights are used so that the proportion of individuals in nursing homes match national aggregates (see appendix). ADLs include walking across room, dressing, bathing, eating, going to bed, and using the toilet. IADLs include using a telephone, managing money, taking medications as prescribed, shopping for groceries, and cooking a hot meal.

of attrition when entering nursing homes.[2] To account for this problem we use the reweighting procedure described in the appendix. The reweighted ELSA sample matches the share of the age 65+ population that is institutionalized in nursing and/or residential homes.

As is conventional in the literature, the key measures of functioning we use as indicators of the demand for LTC are self-reported limitations in activities of daily living (ADLs) and in instrumental activities of daily living (IADLs). We use six ADL measures: walking across the room, dressing, bathing, eating, getting in and out of bed, and using the toilet. In addition, we use five IADLs measures: preparing a hot meal, shopping for groceries, making telephone calls, taking medications, and managing money. As shown in table 3.1, about 14 percent of those age 65+ have difficulties with two or more ADLs, and about 9 percent have difficulties with at least three. The number of limitations grows with age. For those 85+ almost 37 percent have difficulty with at least two and 28 percent at least three ADLs. Table 3.2 shows the distribution of specific ADLs and IADLS. The most common limitation to IADLs is shopping for groceries (15 percent report this limitation) and the most common limitation to ADLs is getting dressed (18 percent report this limitation). Table 3.3 reports the relationship between limitations and

2. In 2018, for example, individuals in nursing homes represented 1.3 percent of the over 65 sample in ELSA, whereas recent estimates (for early 2020) from the Office for National Statistics put this fraction at 3.3 percent. This estimate was calculated by combining information from the 2011 census and the 2016-based population projections for communal establishments. See ONS (2020a) for more details.

Table 3.2 **Distribution of limitations with specific ADLs/IADLs, England, 2018**

	65+ All	65+ Conditional	85+ All	85+ Conditional
i) IADLs:				
IADL—Use a Phone	0.068	0.370	0.250	0.488
IADL—Manage Money	0.083	0.446	0.309	0.605
IADL—Take Meds as Prescr.	0.071	0.382	0.249	0.486
IADL—Shop for Groceries	0.148	0.799	0.435	0.850
IADL—Prepare a Meal	0.097	0.522	0.316	0.618
Observations	4,943	747	538	237
ii) ADLs:				
ADL—Use the Toilet	0.072	0.295	0.205	0.401
ADL—Get Dressed	0.182	0.749	0.404	0.789
ADL—Take a Bath	0.141	0.579	0.389	0.759
ADL—Walk Across a Room	0.070	0.286	0.225	0.440
ADL—Eat	0.049	0.203	0.148	0.289
ADL—Get In/Out of Bed	0.095	0.392	0.231	0.450
Observations	4,943	1,051	538	242

Source: Data are from ELSA Wave 9 (2018). Weights are used so that the proportion of individuals in nursing homes match national aggregates (see appendix). Column 1 shows the share of the sample that report having difficulty with each activity, while column 2 shows the share of people with at least 1 IADL (panel i) or at least 1 ADL (panel ii) who report having difficulty with each activity.

Table 3.3 **Well-being for those 65+ and 85+ by ADL limitations, England, 2018**

	65+	65+ with 3+ Limitations	85+	85+ with 3+ Limitations
Reports good or better health status	0.703	0.225	0.582	0.310
Satisfied with life	0.659	0.376	0.608	0.398
Very satisfied with life	0.161	0.086	0.144	0.093
Depressed much of time	0.118	0.301	0.176	0.241
Observations	4,708	429	473	121

Source: Data are from ELSA Wave 9 (2018). Weights are used so that the proportion of individuals in nursing homes match national aggregates (see appendix). This table is directly comparable to US table 10.3, however as ELSA does not contain a question about retirement satisfaction, instead we report "life satisfaction."

several self-reported measures of subjective well-being. Cells in the table are split by age of the respondent and number of ADL limitations. All indicators of subjective well-being are negatively correlated with the number of limitations. On average, well-being declines after age 85, although this is largely due to the greater number of limitations they face.

We now turn to the question of how these limitations, and hence potential care needs, vary across the distribution of income and wealth. Table 3.4 reports the distribution of household income and wealth for those

Table 3.4 **Income and wealth distribution, England, 2018**

	Income		Wealth		Wealth (Excl. Housing)	
	65+	85+	65+	85+	65+	85+
5th Percentile	8,360	7,328	559	1,524	0	136
10th Percentile	9,727	8,620	5,390	7,119	814	1,302
25th Percentile	13,039	11,419	113,563	58,019	7,051	7,119
50th Percentile	17,860	15,253	246,109	201,362	37,222	20,340
75th Percentile	25,716	20,752	436,285	358,701	132,208	71,189
90th Percentile	36,268	29,213	738,328	553,611	347,292	187,045
95th Percentile	44,729	35,772	1,019,107	777,991	558,662	358,701
Mean	22,089	18,422	351,463	265,257	139,594	87,198
Observations	4,907	539	4,907	539	4,907	539

Source: Data are from ELSA Wave 9 (2018). Weights are used so that the proportion of individuals in nursing homes match national aggregates (see appendix). Income is net of taxes. Wealth is total net (non-pension) wealth and includes housing. All amounts are normalized using the OECD-modified equivalence scale and reported in 2019 GBPs.

65 and older, and those 85 and older. Both income and wealth are normalized using the OECD-modified equivalence scale, and we present values in 2019 GBPs. Older individuals on average have lower income than those nearing retirement age, although the UK basic state pension (which has increased in generosity in comparison to average earnings in recent years) means that very few retirees live in extreme poverty. Current retired and soon-to-be retiring generations still receive some means-tested public pension income from the State Earnings Related Pension Scheme. In addition, a large fraction of individuals have private pension income—80 percent of all those between aged 50 and the State Pension Age in 2018/19 had some (current or past) private pension entitlements or were already receiving income from such a pension (Banks et al. 2019, table E5a, 168). Home ownership rates are also relatively high in England, and in 2018/2019 primary housing wealth accounted for 59.6 percent of the total non-pension wealth of the over 65s (authors' calculations from table E3 of Banks et al. 2019).

Table 3.5 shows how the distribution of household income and wealth varies according to the number of reported ADLs. In keeping with the extensive other evidence on the socioeconomic gradient in health, the table shows that those with more ADLs and IADLs usually have lower income and wealth. Each cell in the table reports the share of respondents in an ADL category who are in that row's income or wealth group. For example, of those with zero ADLs and zero IADLs, 6.5 percent have less than half of median income, whereas 11.3 percent of those with two ADLs have less than half of median income. Only 7.3 percent of the overall sample have less than half of median income since the UK's state pension benefit creates a very

Table 3.5 **Income and wealth distribution by limitations for 65+ population, England, 2018**

	0 ADLs & 0 IADLs	0 ADLs & 1+ IADLs	1 ADL	2 ADLs	3+ ADLs	Total
		Panel 1: Income				
<50% Median HH Income	0.065	0.118	0.101	0.113	0.069	0.073
50–100% Median HH Income	0.393	0.520	0.492	0.495	0.527	0.426
100–150% Median HH Income	0.285	0.252	0.252	0.278	0.228	0.274
150–200% Median HH Income	0.135	0.064	0.092	0.071	0.111	0.122
200%+ Median HH Income	0.123	0.045	0.064	0.042	0.064	0.104
		Panel 2: Wealth				
<50% Median HH Wealth	0.207	0.393	0.347	0.492	0.444	0.265
50–100% Median HH Wealth	0.230	0.273	0.228	0.234	0.257	0.234
100–150% Median HH Wealth	0.189	0.183	0.171	0.159	0.157	0.183
150–200% Median HH Wealth	0.124	0.063	0.102	0.030	0.051	0.107
200%+ Median HH Wealth	0.251	0.088	0.153	0.086	0.091	0.211
Total	0.712	0.045	0.102	0.047	0.095	
Observations	3,665	203	488	212	339	4,907

Source: Data are from ELSA Wave 9 (2018). Weights are used so that the proportion of individuals in nursing homes match national aggregates (see appendix). ADLs include walking across room, dressing, bathing, eating, going to bed, and using the toilet. IADLs include using a telephone, managing money, taking medications as prescribed, shopping for groceries, and cooking a hot meal. Each cell reports the share of respondents in the respective ADL category who are in that row's income group. The median household income and wealth are for the 65+ population, calculated in the ELSA. If individuals did not have their income/wealth reported in wave 9, their last reported values were used. The median, normalized using the OECD-modified equivalence scale and reported in 2019 GBPs, is roughly £17,900 per year for income and £246,000 for wealth.

flat lower half of the income distribution after retirement, and those with the very lowest household incomes may well be experiencing transitory short-term fluctuations while not being particularly disadvantaged. So the "lowest" income group is both small and rather unusual. From 50 percent of median income and above, the gradient is systematic and large, with those between 50 and 100 percent of the median being increasingly overrepresented in the more disabled groups, and the reverse being true as the income groups get higher. When considering patterns by wealth, which, for this age group, varies more systemically in a way that is related to permanent lifetime income, the socioeconomic gradients are more uniformly evident across the whole distribution. For example, among those 65+, 20.7 percent of those with no ADLs and no IADLs have wealth below half of the median HH wealth—but that rises to 49.2 percent of those with two ADLs.

In the next sections we discuss the care system that individuals with ADL limitations have access to, and the hours (and costs) of the care that they receive.

3.3 The Long-Term Care System in England

Figure 3.3 shows that in 2018, LTC spending was 1.8 percent of GDP according to the UK Health Accounts 2018 (ONS, 2020b), and this has been broadly constant over the previous five years. This spending measure includes care for younger disabled people as well as for older people with disabilities and functional limitations. Of this amount, most (1.1 percent of GDP) was spent on residential long-term care facilities (i.e., nursing and care homes), and 0.5 percent was spent on home health services. The right panel of figure 3.3 shows that if we expand our definition of LTC to include "social care" for IADLs (care such as help with cooking and cleaning), then LTC comprised 2.2 percent of GDP. We should note that this is only for paid care: we discuss informal care in detail later.

In contrast to the National Health Service (NHS), which provides universal health care free at the point of use in England, publicly funded LTC services in England are provided through 152 local authorities, each with their own funding formulas. Individuals who do not qualify for this support must rely on self-funded formal or informal care services. Overall, the public provision of LTC is like the one used in the United States. Those with (non-pension) wealth of more than £23,250 are ineligible for local authority funded care, and those with wealth between £14,250 and £23,250 must pay for at least part of their care. Housing wealth is not exempt for those in residential homes (e.g., nursing homes), although it is exempt for the means

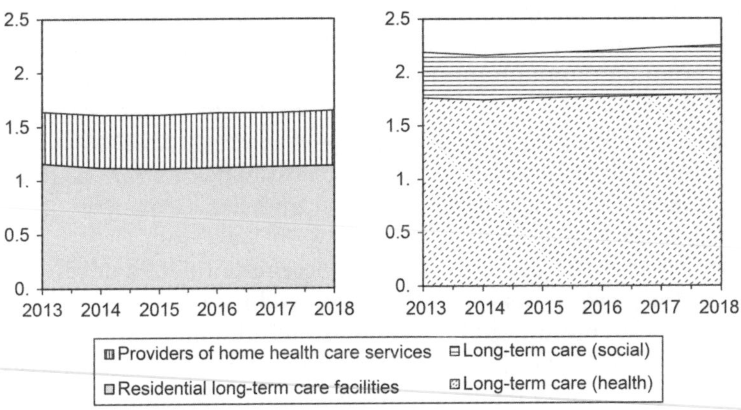

Fig. 3.3 Share of GDP spent on long-term care, UK, 2013–2018

Source: Eurostat. Statistics are for whole of UK and include all ages, not just those age 65+. Residential long-term facilities are categorized as health care providers under code HP2. Providers of home health care services are categorized as health care providers under code HP35. Health-related LTC (HC3) relates to services where care ordinarily includes help with activities such as bathing, dressing, and walking. Social LTC (HCR1) refers to assistance-based services, such as shopping, cooking, and managing finances.

test for care received at home. Recipients of care are usually charged co-payments based on income with local authorities setting their own charging policy. Most services are supplied by private providers, paid for by the local authority, with recent reforms giving more control to the individual for how and where the budget is spent. Each recipient receives a needs assessment, in which their local authority will create a "personal budget," which explicitly states the amount of money the local authority will pay toward any care. The recipient can then opt to have this personal budget paid directly to them in the form of a "direct payment." This allows a recipient to choose how their allocated money is spent, instead of receiving the care from the local authority's chosen provider. This has allowed recipients to choose their own care worker (paid through the direct payment), which can often be a family member.

The needs-based criteria determining eligibility for LTC are set out in the Care Act 2014, which established a national approach to assessing care needs and eligibility requirements for care (subject to the local authority specific financial means test). These standards state that an individual has an eligible LTC need if they have care and support needs as a result of a physical or mental condition and because of those needs (i) they cannot achieve two or more of a number of outcomes related to daily living, such as dressing or feeding themselves appropriately, keeping themselves safe, maintaining personal relationships, etc. and (ii) their well-being is significantly adversely affected (for more details see the Care and Support (Eligibility Criteria) Regulations, 2015). The somewhat subjective nature of these criteria means that, in practice, different local authorities may interpret and implement the centrally determined rules in somewhat different ways, in addition to having different funding and co-payment rules. They can also apply more generous rules if they so wish. This creates substantial variation across local authorities in availability and quality of care. However, very little substantive data exist on these differences and as such, the possibilities for serious research on the funding of LTC at the national level, and detailed analyses of policy reforms, are limited.

While most public LTC is provided by local authorities, some care is provided by the central government. Firstly, individuals whose care needs arise from a "primary health need" may have their health and social care arranged and fully funded by the NHS through the Continuing Healthcare program. Unlike local authority funding, it is not means tested, and is reserved for individuals with particularly severe, complex, or unpredictable care needs. There is no formal legal definition for eligibility; entitlement is subject to an assessment of whether "having taken account of all their needs [. . .], it can be said that the main aspects or majority part of the care they require is focused on addressing and/or preventing health needs" (Department of Health and Social Care 2018). These individuals tend to be less healthy than those receiving care through the local authority. Second, those with daily care and/or mobility needs and their carers may receive cash benefits from the central government budget. The most important benefit for those age 65+ is the Attendance Allowance, where claimants need to be of pension age and entitlement is based on an assessment of the assistance required to undertake various activities of daily living (with higher-assessed needs resulting in a larger entitlement). In contrast to local authority funded care, eligibility for Attendance Allowance is not means tested, nor does an individual actually need to be receiving care to claim it—assessment is purely based on care needs, not care receipt. While Attendance Allowance is the main benefit for new claimants in the over 65 population with care needs, many still have continuing claims for the other government disability-related benefits if they began claiming before reaching pension age. In 2018, 12 percent of those above State Pension Age in the UK were claiming Attendance Allowance, and a further 8.4 percent were claiming either Disability Living Allowance or Personal Independence Payments, with average weekly payments of around £86 (OBR, 2019). Additionally, the Carer's Allowance provides a cash payment payable to adults who have low (less than £120 per week) earnings, are not in full-time education, and spend at least 35 hours a week caring for a person who receives disability benefits.

Individuals who do not qualify for local authority (or NHS) funded LTC must either receive care informally or pay out of pocket for that care. Furthermore, higher-income people receiving local authority funded care often must make co-payments. As discussed previously, and shown in table 3.3, most individuals have a significant proportion of their wealth tied up in the value of their home. If this wealth is needed to fund care costs, this can involve selling the property. To help households keep their homes while still alive, a Deferred Payment Agreement can allow a user of local authority co-funded care to delay payment for the cost of their care until a later date (including the option of waiting until death) so that they can avoid selling their home in the meantime. Deferred Payment Agreements are only available to those receiving local authority funded care, but similar "equity release" products are available through private sector organizations; however, not much is known about how many individuals use equity release products to fund care.

Using evidence from the Personal Social Services Research Unit's CARESIM model, the Dilnot Commission (2011) estimates that the mean expected future lifetime cost of care for someone age 65 in 2011 is £25,000 for a man and £44,000 for a woman (in 2011 GBPs). However, they also estimate that around a quarter of those adults aged 65 in 2011 will face no significant care costs during the remainder of their life, but around 1 in 20 face costs of more than £150,000. For these individuals, even those with the median level of wealth could use 60–80 percent of their wealth to pay for these costs. Despite this risk, few individuals have private long-term care insurance, with only approximately 5,000 LTC insurance policies in

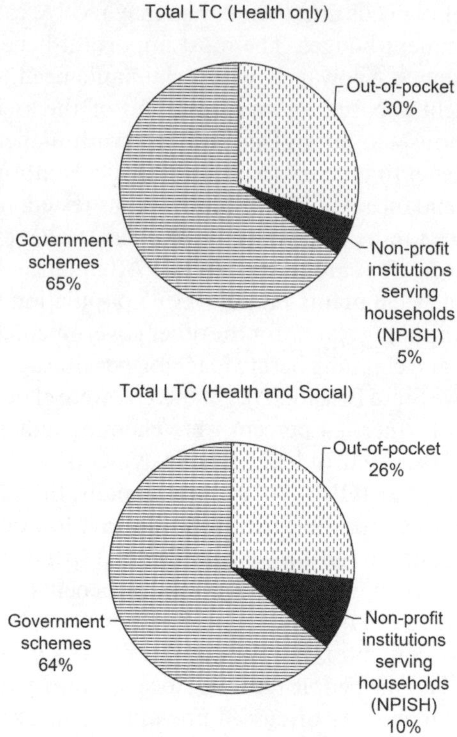

Fig. 3.4 Percent of LTC financing by source, UK, 2018

Notes: UK Health Accounts, 2018. Statistics are for whole of UK and include all ages, not just those age 65+. Health-related LTC (HC3) relates to services where care ordinarily includes help with ADLs such as bathing, dressing, and walking. Social LTC (HCR1) refers to assistance-based services for IADLS, such as shopping, cooking, and managing finances. Non-profit institutions serving households (NPISH) includes grants from government health bodies and local governments.

force in the entire UK. Still, much of the cost of LTC is borne by government programs. Figure 3.4 shows how this expense is shared across various financing sources. Even without the existence of a true national long-term care insurance program, the public sector is the primary payer for long-term care. Figure 3.4 reports that the largest source of long-term care financing is the government, accounting for 65 percent of total spending, with most of the remainder (30 percent) (of care expenses) being paid out of pocket. Charities also contribute 5 percent to LTC, although this share is larger when the definition of care is expanded to include care for IADLs (social care).

Figure 3.5 reports the percentage of spending on home health care and residential LTC facilities (e.g., nursing homes) by source. Despite LTC being means tested, the vast majority (83 percent) of formal home health care in England is financed by government sources (i.e., through local authorities or

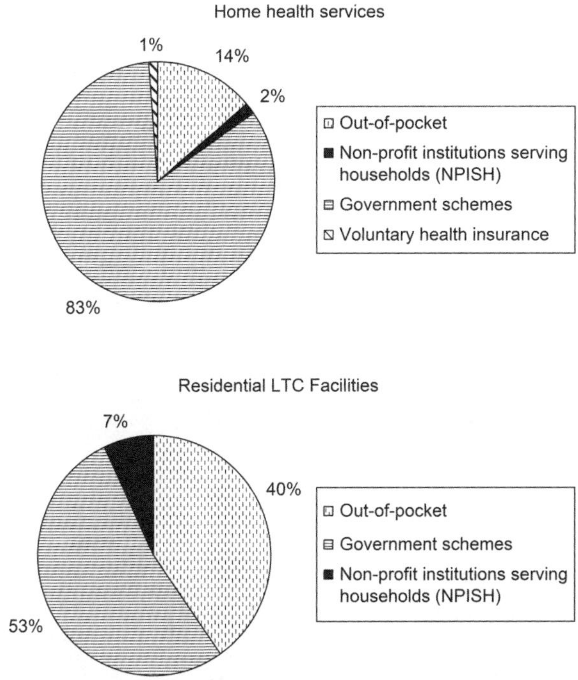

Fig. 3.5 Percent spent on home health care and nursing care facilities, by source of funds, England, 2018

Note: Data are for the year 2018. Health Care Accounts Data (https://www.cms.gov/Research-Statistics-Data-and-Systems/Statistics-Trends-and-Reports/NationalHealthExpendData/NationalHealthAccountsHistorical). Non-profit institutions serving households (NPISH) includes grants from government health bodies and local governments. Residential long-term facilities are categorized as health care providers under code HP2. Providers of home health care services are categorized as health care providers under code HP35. This figure is directly comparable to US figure 6.

the NHS Continuing Healthcare program). The same is true for residential care, but to a lesser extent, with the government paying for 53 percent of the care. Note that for residential care almost 40 percent is paid out of pocket, which means many households face significant financial risk.

Long-term care can be provided either at home or in institutional settings. Table 3.6 shows the share of people who receive any care either in a nursing home or at home in the form of formal or informal help. Overall, roughly 24 percent of people ages 65 or over receive some form of LTC, a fraction that rises to 59 percent of those 85+. Unsurprisingly, the likelihood of care rises in the number of limitations to ADLs and IADLs.

Figure 3.6 illustrates the breakdown of care type among those receiving care. It shows that for over 65s receiving some form of care, most individuals receive informal home care. Very few (6 percent) only receive formal home

Table 3.6 **Any care by age and ADL, England, 2018**

	65+	85+
Full Sample	0.24	0.59
0 ADLs, 1+ IADL	0.67	0.82
1 ADL	0.48	0.71
2 ADL	0.67	0.78
3+ ADL	0.89	0.94
Observations	*4,947*	*540*

Source: Data are from ELSA Wave 9 (2018). Weights are used so that individuals in nursing homes match national aggregates. The care variable is defined as either being in a nursing home or having received either formal or informal home help. Respondents in ELSA are asked the number of hours of help in the past month they required due to any physical, mental, emotional or memory problems. Sample includes only respondents who reported receiving help. This table is directly comparable to US table 10.10.

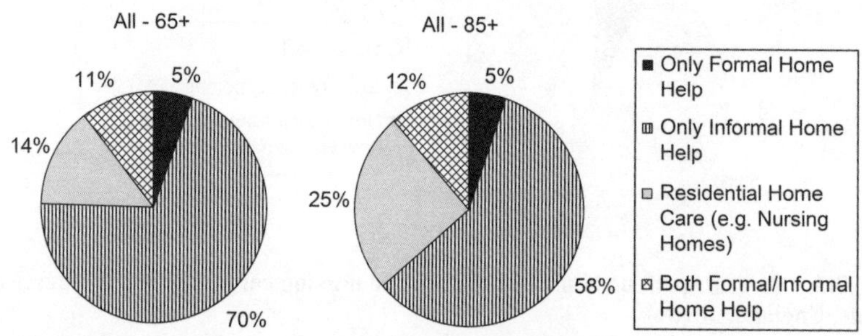

Fig. 3.6 Type of care received by age, England, 2018

Source: Data are from ELSA Wave 9 (2018). Weights are used so that individuals in nursing homes match national aggregates. Sample is restricted to respondents in a nursing home or having received either formal or informal home help. Respondents in ELSA are asked the number of hours of help in the past month they required due to any physical, mental, emotional or memory problems. Sample includes only respondents who reported receiving help. This figure is directly comparable to US figure 7.

help. Figure 3.7 shows how the type of care received varies by the number of ADL-limitations. The number of ADLs strongly predicts the type of care received. Among those receiving care with two or fewer ADLs, over 80 percent receive only informal care. However, the fraction in residential care (e.g., nursing homes) increases sharply for those with 3+ ADLs. In fact, for those who are 85+ year olds with 3+ ADLs, residential care is the most common type of care receipt.

Figures 3.6 and 3.7 show that the most used type of LTC is home care whether formal or informal (or both). There has been a push in recent years for older people to receive care in their own home; in 2018, 61 percent of age 65+ recipients of public LTC received this form of care (NHS Digital 2019). Respondents in ELSA are asked whether they required any help in the past

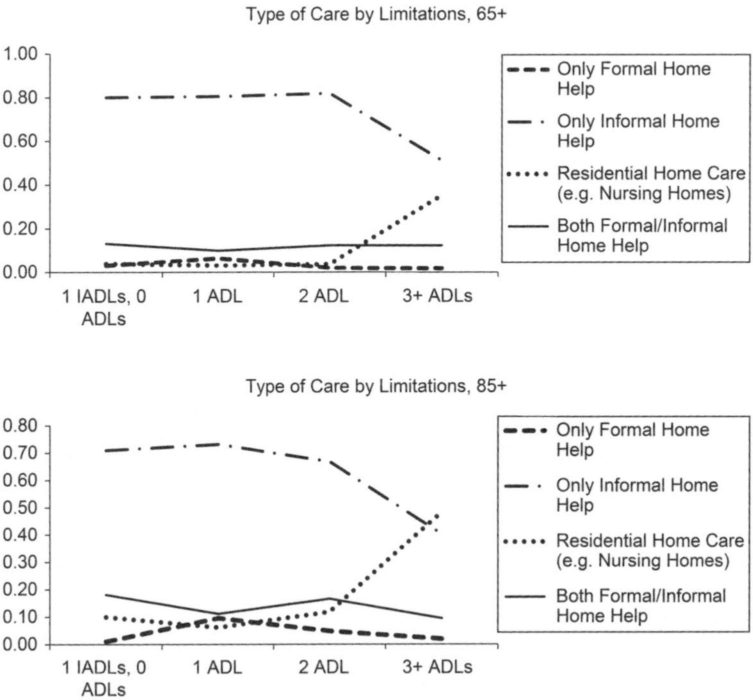

Fig. 3.7 Type of Care Received by Age and Limitations, England, 2018

Source: Data are from ELSA Wave 9 (2018). Nursing home care refers to any residential care homes. Weights are used so that individuals in nursing homes match national aggregates. Sample is restricted to respondents in a nursing home or having received either formal or informal home help. Respondents in ELSA are asked the number of hours of help in the past month they required due to any physical, mental, emotional or memory problems. Sample includes only respondents who reported receiving help. This figure is directly comparable to US figure 8.

month because of any physical, mental, emotional or memory problems. If so, respondents are asked to list up to 35 "informal" (e.g., spouse, daughter) and "formal" helpers (e.g., home care worker, cleaner). Then for each helper, respondents list the number of hours of help provided each week in bands (e.g. "1–4 hours") up to a maximum of "100 hours or more." We take the midpoint of each time band (e.g., 2.5 hours for "1–4 hours") and cap the maximum numbers of hours of help of an individual helper at 100 hours per week. Table 3.7 shows the distribution of weekly hours of care received (by all helpers) for both formal and informal care, conditional on receiving help. The distribution of care received is skewed. The median number of hours of care received is 7, but the mean is 25 hours and 10 percent of this group receives over 92 hours. Care needs are only somewhat higher for the oldest old. The median number of hours of care for this group is 8, the mean is

Table 3.7 **Distribution of weekly hours of home help received by type, England, 2018**

	65+			85+		
	Any	Formal	Informal	Any	Formal	Informal
5th Percentile	1	1	1	1	1	1
10th Percentile	1	1	1	1	1	3
25th Percentile	3	1	3	3	1	3
50th Percentile	7	3	7	8	3	7
75th Percentile	27	15	27	36	17	30
90th Percentile	92	42	82	100	42	100
95th Percentile	103	75	100	113	75	105
Mean	25	13	24	29	15	27
% with:						
1 Hour per Day or Less	0.54	0.70	0.55	0.48	0.64	0.51
5 Hour per Day or More	0.22	0.07	0.20	0.25	0.09	0.19
Observations	*962*	*205*	*882*	*243*	*66*	*219*

Source: Data are from ELSA Wave 9 (2018). Sample is restricted to respondents who received either formal or informal home help. Respondents in ELSA are asked the number of hours of help in the past month they required due to any physical, mental, emotional or memory problems. This table is directly comparable to US tables 10.6 and 10.11.

29, and the top 10 percent of the distribution receives 100 or more hours of care. Most of the elderly receiving assistance rely, at least in part, on some form of informal care. Not only are the elderly much more likely to receive informal than formal care (as indicated by our discussion of the previous figures and by the sample sizes in table 3.7) but those receiving informal care receive more total hours of care. For individuals 65 and over, those receiving formal care on average receive 13 hours per week, and half receive 3 or fewer hours per week, but for those receiving informal care these numbers are 24 hours and 7 hours, respectively.

The evidence in this section makes it clear that although most care recipients receive their care at home, most of the (formal) costs are incurred by those in residential LTC facilities. In the remainder of this section, we document residential LTC services and costs in more detail, before turning to issues of labor costs and labor market issues for care workers whether in the nursing home or formal home care sector.

Table 3.8 shows the number of nursing homes (i.e. residential homes with nursing facilities), beds, and residents relative to the overall elderly population in England. Roughly 85% of available beds are occupied at any point in time. England has 0.021 beds per 65+ population, but 0.157 beds per 85+. However, these are not beds exclusively for the aged, and some will be used by the disabled under 65s. Table 3.9 compares the size of this nursing home sector to residential homes without nursing facilities. Although spending on residential LTC facilities comprises a large share of GDP, most LTC

Table 3.8 **Number of nursing homes, beds, and occupancy rate, England, 2020**

	England, 2020
Residential homes with nursing facilities	4,393
Beds	222,959
Pop 65+	10,505,000
Beds per pop 65+	0.021
Pop 85+	1,417,000
Beds per pop 85+	0.157
Nursing home residents	189,054
Occupancy rate	85%

Source: Population data from ONS. Number of residents from ONS, Care homes and estimating the self-funding population, England: 2019 to 2020, Table 11. Number of beds from Public Health England, https://fingertips.phe.org.uk/profile/end-of-life/data. Additional data from Skills for Care adult social care workforce estimates 2020/21. Estimates of beds and residents are pre-COVID. Number nursing homes is from CQC directory (February 26, 2020), with nursing homes being counted as having the service type "Nursing Home". This table is directly comparable to US table 10.12.

Table 3.9 **Residential care, England, 2020**

	England, 2020
Residential homes with nursing facilities	
Number	4,393
Beds	222,959
Residents	189,054
% Self-funded residents	35.9
% State-funded residents	64.1
Residential homes without nursing facilities	
Number	11,140
Beds	234,336
Residents	202,873
% Self-funded residents	37.4
% State-funded residents	62.6
Workforce size	
Residential homes with nursing facilities	295,000
Residential homes without nursing facilities	305,000
All residential	675,000
% Direct care	68
% Regulated profession (e.g., nurses)	6
% Managerial / supervisory	7
% Other	19

Note: State funded means that some of the cost is paid by the state, but the resident may still have to make contributions. Estimates of beds and residents are pre-COVID. Number of care and nursing homes is from CQC directory (February 26, 2020), with nursing homes being counted as having the service type "Nursing Home" and care homes having the service type "Residential Home". Workforce size estimates are for 2018/19 and come from Skills for Care's adult social care workforce estimates 2018/19, Tables 2 and 3.1. Total job numbers in each column have been rounded to the nearest thousand. "All residential" includes adult placement homes; care homes with nursing; care homes without nursing; sheltered housing; and other adult residential care services. In 2019 the size of total workforce aged 16 and over in England is estimated at 27.9 million based on LFS data.

Source: Number of residents from ONS, Care homes and estimating the self-funding population, England: 2019 to 2020, Table 11. Number of beds from Public Health England, https://fingertips.phe.org.uk/profile/end-of-life/data. Additional data from Skills for Care adult social care workforce estimates 2020/21.

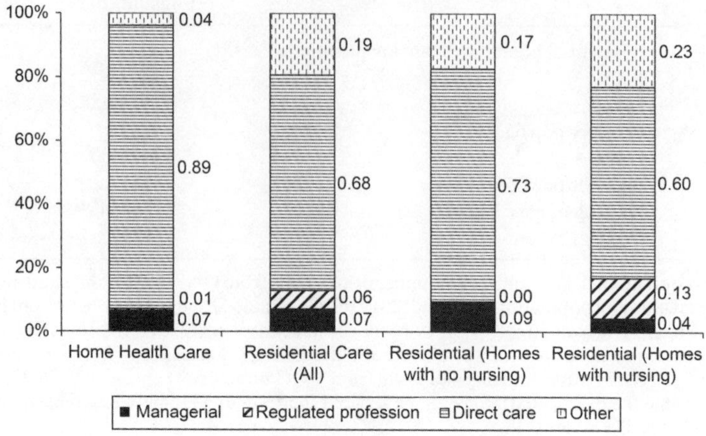

Fig. 3.8 Distribution of staff types at facilities, England, 2019

Notes: Managerial: middle- and first-line managers, registered managers, supervisors and managers and staff in care-related but not care-providing roles. Regulated professions: social workers, occupational therapists, registered nurses, allied health professionals and other regulated professions. Direct care: senior care workers, care workers, community support and support/outreach workers and other care providers. Other roles: administrative or office staff not care-providing, ancillary staff not care-providing and other non-care-providing job roles. This figure is directly comparable to US figure 9.

facilities, housing half of all LTC residents, have no nursing facilities. In many dimensions (beds, residents, percentage of self- versus state-funded residents, and size of workforce) the two sectors are similar, although residential homes without nursing facilities are smaller on average.

Figure 3.8 shows the types of staff for various types of care. In (formal) home care most workers are involved in direct care (e.g., a care worker) and almost none of these workers (1 percent) are in a regulated profession (e.g., nurses, social workers). The fraction of workers who are in a regulated profession is higher in residential care. However, they still only account for 6 percent of employment at these care homes, and almost all of these are employed in residential homes with nursing facilities (where they represent 13 percent of employees).

The labor force providing LTC tends to be low skill and tends to receive low pay, although wages in the English labor market are all subject to the UK National Minimum Wage, which is high relative to the minimum wage in most European and North American economies (see Giupponi and Machin 2021, Appendix C1). Unlike in many European and North American countries there are no compulsory registration or qualifications for social care workers[3] although there are voluntary sets of standards (e.g. the Care

3. The Care Quality Commission (CQC) is the independent regulator of all health and social care services in England. It monitors, inspects, and regulates care homes.

Certificate launched by the Skills for Care charity in 2015). The UK has a points-based immigration system, which has a "Skilled Workers" route for occupations listed on a Shortage Occupation List. Currently, social workers, registered nurses, and occupational therapists are listed as skilled workers; however, "care workers" more generally are not designated as such and are hence not eligible for the skilled workers route.

Table 3.10, which uses data collected by the Skills for Care charity, shows the distribution of skills and formal qualifications across the sector as a whole, split by provider type (panel i) and split by the location of care (panel ii). Almost half of workers in the sector have no formal qualifications, although this fraction is substantially lower in the (very small) part of the sector where care is delivered by a public sector provider. Table 3.11 shows the earnings of full-time workers in the LTC sector. In keeping with the low skills and qualifications of workers in the sector, the average direct care worker in residential care earns £8.52 per hour, which is only slightly more than the adult minimum wage (£8.21) and about half the economy-wide average wage (£16.99). Once again, consistent with the skills data in table 3.10, employees working for public providers have considerably higher pay for all roles.

Table 3.10 **Qualifications held in social care by sector**

		i) by provider type			ii) by location of care:		
	All	Public	Private	Direct payment recipients	Residential	Home Help	Other
Total jobs	1,515,000	112,000	1,260,000	145,000	675,000	685,000	151,000
Care certificate status							
Achieved	19%	4%	19%	30%	13%	27%	12%
In progress	19%	7%	21%	5%	20%	20%	9%
Not started	62%	89%	59%	65%	67%	53%	80%
Highest relevant qualification:							
None	49%	33%	49%	61%	48%	52%	43%
Entry or level 1	1%	1%	1%	1%	1%	2%	1%
Level 2	21%	20%	23%	11%	22%	22%	15%
Level 3	18%	16%	19%	16%	20%	17%	17%
Level 4 or above	10%	29%	8%	10%	9%	7%	24%

Notes: There are no mandatory qualifications to work in the social care sector in England. Data from Skills for Care's adult social care workforce estimates 2018/19, tables 7.1 and 7.2. Total job numbers in each column have been rounded to the nearest thousand. The Care Certificate is an agreed set of standards that define the knowledge, skills, and behaviors expected of specific job roles in the health and social care sectors. Beyond the Care Certificate there are six qualifications for adult social care, ranging from Level 1 to Level 5. The information in the table refers to the adult social care sector as those 1.52 million jobs in local authorities, the private/independent sector and jobs working for direct payment recipients. The "Other" column in the location of care includes some forms of day care and other community-based services. Those working in the NHS are not included in these workforce estimates.

Table 3.11 Pay for full-time care workers at nursing facilities and in home health care, England, 2018/19

	Mean hourly wage		
Occupation titles	Private	Public	All
i) Residential homes (with or without nursing)			
Managerial	13.97	16.37	14.06
Regulated profession	15.95	19.10	15.98
Direct care	8.47	10.22	8.52
Other	8.69	9.55	8.71
ii) Home Health Care Industry			
Managerial	13.48	16.65	13.63
Regulated profession	15.66	18.82	16.34
Direct care	8.74	10.36	8.80
Direct payment recipients	—	*9.43*	*9.43*
Other	9.55	11.44	9.66
iii) All care sector, by role:			
Senior management	17.53	42.24	18.60
Registered manager	16.15	20.57	16.31
Social worker	10.30	18.82	18.37
Occupational therapist	16.41	18.59	18.19
Registered nurse	16.07	18.90	16.09
Senior care worker	9.32	12.54	9.42
Care worker	8.55	10.30	8.62
Support and outreach	8.93	12.30	9.70
iv) All industries			
All employees	16.61	18.13	16.99
Men	17.95	20.42	18.39
Women	14.25	16.81	15.21
Minimum Wage (Age 25+)	8.21	8.21	8.21
Minimum Wage (Age 21–25)	7.70	7.70	7.70
Minimum Wage (Age 18–20)	6.15	6.15	6.15

Source: Hourly pay data for panels (i)-(iii) are from Skills for Care's weighted workforce estimates, 2018/19, table 6.2. The "All" column for these panels has been calculated as a weighted average of the hourly pay and number of jobs in each row. Direct payments are cash transfers from the local authority to the recipient of care, allowing them to choose and pay a carer directly. Data for hourly pay (gross) for all industries (panel iv) is from ASHE (2018) tables 14.5a and 13.5a. The Minimum Wage is from April 2019. Amounts are all in 2019 GBPs. Managerial: middle- and first-line managers, registered managers, supervisors and managers and staff in care-related but not care-providing roles. Regulated professions: social workers, occupational therapists, registered nurses, allied health professionals, and other regulated professions. Direct care: senior care workers, care workers, community support and support/outreach workers and other care-providers. Other roles: administrative or office staff not care-providing, ancillary staff not care-providing and other non-care-providing job roles. This table is directly comparable to US table 10.15.

Turning to the informal care "workforce," table 3.12 presents estimates of the total number of individuals providing help to elderly individuals each month at a national level, along with the number of such carers relative to the elderly population and to the population ages 18–64. We derive these measures from self-reports given by older recipients of care. Respondents in

Table 3.12 Home care provision—population estimates, England, 2018

	65 Plus	85 Plus
Formal Helpers—ADL/IADLs	973,216	408,562
Relative to 65+/85+ Population	0.10	0.34
Relative to 18–64 Population	0.03	0.01
Informal Helpers—ADL/IADLs	3,153,206	932,492
Relative to 65+/85+ Population	0.31	0.77
Relative to 18–64 Population	0.09	0.03
All Helpers—ADL/IADLs	4,126,422	1,341,054
Relative to 65+/85+ Population	0.41	1.11
Relative to 18–64 Population	0.12	0.04
Observations	4,895	501

Notes: Authors' calculations based on data are from ELSA Wave 9 (2018). Respondent weights are used for all calculations. Respondents in ELSA are asked the number of hours of help in the past month they required due to any physical, mental, emotional or memory problems. The estimates in this table are calculated by multiplying the mean number of helpers in each group by the population size from the ONS (i.e., the size of the non-care home for the 65+ and 85+ populations are 10,178,394 and 1,210,416, respectively). The 16–64 non-care home population is 35,149,297. This table is directly comparable to US table 10.16.

ELSA are asked about who provides care for the individual receiving care, and are also asked to report the age of the carer. Using the sample weights in ELSA, we can use this to calculate the number of elderly carers in the aggregate. We estimate that over four million individuals in England provide care to the 65+ population, which is equal to 12 percent of the population ages 18–64. Around 76 percent of those helping someone over age 65 were informal caregivers, with the remainder being formal (paid) carers. The fraction of formal carers is higher when focusing on care to those 85 years old or older.

There are important differences between the set of formal carers and the set of informal carers, which are illustrated in figure 3.9. The predominance of women among caregivers is particularly dramatic for formal care workers, with 83 percent of formal home care workers being female in comparison to 58 percent of informal carers. Formal carers are predominantly working age, whereas informal carers much more likely to be older. The proportion of non-white minority ethnic groups employed in the formal care sector is three and a half times higher than that providing informal care. Many of these differences are a natural consequence of the informal care sector being provided within a family and even within a household context as opposed to in the paid labor market. Figure 3.10 shows the relationships between informal caregivers and care recipients and highlights that spouses are the most common informal carer, accounting for 35 percent, followed by daughters, who make up 25 percent of informal carers. Unsurprisingly, spouses or children account for three-quarters of informal caregivers for older care recipients.

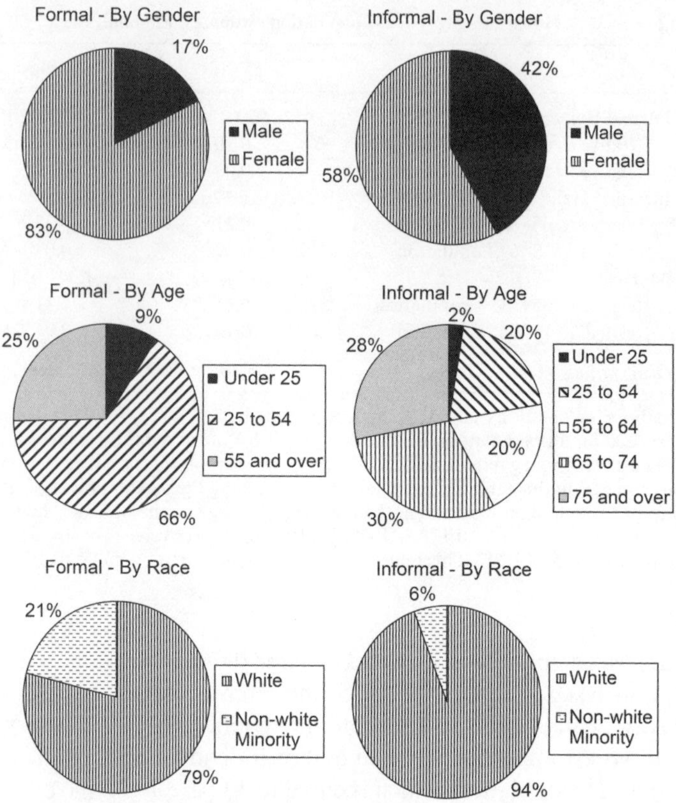

Fig. 3.9 Demographic composition comparison of formal and informal caregivers, England, 2018

Notes: Data on formal caregivers are from Skills for Care's weighted workforce estimates, 2019. Informal care data come from ELSA Wave 9 (2018). Respondent weights are used for all calculations, with respondent weights for the person being helped used in all calculations. Respondents are asked about their relationship to the helper, however most other demographic information is not known about the helper unless they live in the same household as the respondent. As such, if the demographic information is unknown, we make various assumptions. For age, we assume that spouses, siblings, friends, and neighbors are the same age as the respondent, and that children are 25 years younger, and grandchildren 50 years younger. For race we assume that siblings and children are the same race as the respondent. The total sample size of informal helpers is 1,306. Due to missing demographic information, the gender figure has a sample of 1,285, the age band has a sample of 1,299, and race has a sample of 1,112. This figure is directly comparable to US figure 10.

3.4 The Cost of Providing Long-Term Care

In this section, we calculate the total cost of providing long-term care for the age 65+ population in England, pulling together various pieces of evidence on formal care spending (both at home and in institutional settings) and combining it with a measure of the opportunity cost of informal care

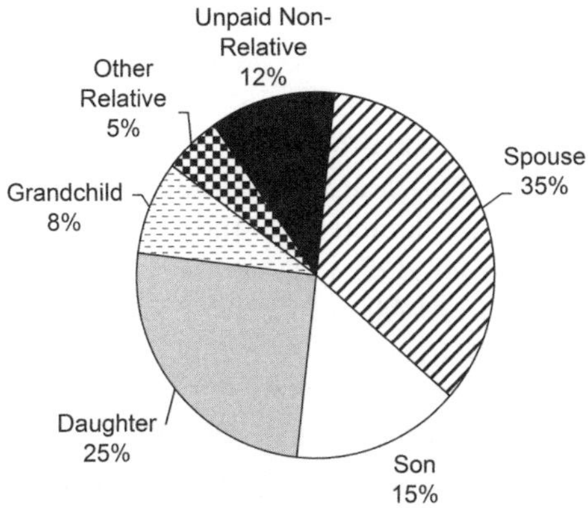

Fig. 3.10 Informal caregivers by relationship to care recipient, England, 2018

Notes: Informal care data come from ELSA Wave 9 (2018). Respondent weights are used for all calculations, with respondent weights for the person being helped used in all calculations. Respondents are asked about their relationship to the helper. The total sample size of informal helpers is 1,306. This figure is directly comparable to US figure 11.

Table 3.13 Formal care costs, annual, England, 2018

	Age 65+ Population, England			All ages, UK
	Number of users	Weekly Cost (£)	Total (£ bn)	Total Cost (£ bn)
Residential care (Nursing homes)	348,832	661	12.0	24.9
Home health services (Formal)	406,904	291	6.2	11.1

Notes: Weekly cost of £661 for residential care taken from NHS Digital (2018). The number of over 65s in residential care is taken from aggregate statistics. Weekly costs of home health are calculated as £22.37 multiplied by an average of 13 hours help per week taken from ELSA. The number of users of formal home help is estimated from ELSA. Total Cost for all ages in the UK comes from the Health Accounts 2018. All amounts have been inflated from 2018 GBPs to 2019 GBPs. This table is directly comparable to US table 10.17.

provision. We are not the first to have done this for England, but our choices of measurement and methodology differ from previous studies, since we set out to be internationally comparable with the other papers in this volume.

Table 3.13 displays the cost of formal care. Multiplying the number of users by the average yearly cost of that form of care reveals that residential care costs £12 billion and formal home health services cost £6.2 billion each year for the 65+ population in England. These amounts are lower than those reported in the UK Health Accounts (presented in the final column of the table) for two reasons. Firstly, the Health Accounts are for the whole of the UK, not just England. England's population is around 84 percent of the UK, and the age demographics are similar throughout the UK. Secondly, and much more importantly, the amount in the Health Accounts includes the disabled under 65s, who account for around 40 percent of all LTC spending. Taking these two factors into account, our estimates for 65+ spending on formal care in England match the Health Accounts well. To put the £12 billion and £6.2 billion numbers into context, summing the two and comparing to an estimate of GDP for England (see footnote 5) suggests that this formal care costs around 0.9% of GDP. This number omits certain government payments such as the Carer's Allowance, which amounts to approximately 0.1 percent of GDP, and Attendance Allowance, which amounts to around 0.3 percent of GDP.[4]

Next, we estimate the cost of informal care. We do this in three different ways. The first approach values the time spent caregiving using the wage that the worker could have earned were they engaged in market activity. This approach requires that we have information on hourly wages of all caregivers, yet many caregivers in our survey data are not employed. Additionally, the set of caregivers who are also in paid work is a non-random set, and furthermore, their jobs and wages will presumably be affected, either directly or indirectly, by the constraints associated with, and consequences of, their caregiving. We therefore construct an imputed measure of wages for all informal caregivers. We use employment data from the 2018 Annual Survey of Household Earnings (ASHE) to calculate the probability that an individual is working and, if they are working, the expected wage, conditional on an individual's age (band) and sex. Thus, we estimate the probability that a person works and their wage were they to work for each age-sex cell. We can use these probabilities and predicted wages to impute the (typical) labor market earnings that are being given up when a carer chooses to supply an hour of informal care. Note that implicitly this method will take account of the likelihood that the individual would have been working had they not been caring, as well as the earnings that they might have accrued if they had worked. Using this approach, an hour of informal care from an older retired individual will have a low "cost," since the likelihood that they would have been working would have been low, even if their predicted wage was quite high. This has a substantive impact on our calculations, since many of those providing informal care are retired (figure 3.9 shows that 58 percent of informal carers are 65+). In this sense, by assuming that the only cost or "value" of care is in market earnings forgone, our measure may understate the true cost or value of care received, and therefore should be seen as a lower bound.

In a second strategy we add some value to the hours of informal care where the carer is predicted not to have been working. Here we assume that carers get paid their expected wage for the predicted hours they would work

4. In February 2019 there were 868,000 recipients of Carer's Allowance in Great Britain, and the total expenditure in 2019–20 was forecast to be £2.98 billion (Kennedy and Gheera 2020). In 2018/19 the UK government expenditure on Attendance Allowance was £5.7 billion (OBR 2019).

Table 3.14 **Informal care valuation, England, 2018**

	I	II	III
Valuation (billions, £)	13.37	27.00	48.73
Total Hours Informal Help (billions)	2.49	2.49	2.49
Probability of Working	0.37	0.37	0.37
Predicted Wage × Probability of Working (£)	5.37	5.37	5.37
Predicted Wage if Working (£)	15.79	15.79	15.79
Care Worker Hourly Pay (£)		8.62	
Care Worker Cost (£)			22.37
Observations	1,285	1,285	1,285

Notes: Total hours of informal help are calculated as the average number of informal hours of help per week for 65+ population from ELSA multiplied by the number of over 65 year olds (10.18million). Column I values predicted working hours using predicted wages and hours worked, given individuals' age and sex, and values non-working hours at £0. Column II is as column I, and values predicted working hours at the predicted wage, but values predicted non-working hours at the average care worker hourly pay of £8.62 (see table 3.11). Column III is as column II but instead of care worker hourly pay it uses the care worker hourly cost of £22.37 (from the Unit Costs of Health and Social Care 2018, by PSSRU). This is made up of an average salary, salary oncosts, direct overheads, and indirect overheads. Predicted wage if working is weighted by hours of informal care. Amounts have been adjusted to 2019 GBPs. This table is directly comparable to US table 10.18.

(as in the first strategy) and get paid the average formal home care market wage for the hours of care that we predict they would not be working in. The average care worker hourly pay is £8.62, which is only half of the expected pay of the carers (£15.79).

Finally, in a third strategy we make the same assumptions as the second strategy, but instead of assigning a value of the average care worker hourly pay we assign the cost that the recipient would need to pay to buy an hour of care in the paid formal home care market. This cost has been estimated by Curtis and Burns (2018) to be £22.37 per hour (in 2019 GBPs). Note this full economic cost is much larger than the mean wage for workers in this sector (£8.62), since the cost of providing care takes into account paid vacation and sick leave, as well as other costs such as administration overheads, travel costs, payroll taxes, and pension contributions. It is not obvious whether the wage or the full cost is the best measure to use for capturing the economic cost to families. Some of these costs, such as vacation and pension contributions, show that the true compensation paid to care workers is greater than the mean wage paid to these workers. Other costs, such as taxes and administration, represent transaction costs that need not be paid if provided by a family member.

The results of these three methods are illustrated in table 3.14. We calculate that in 2018 a total of 2.49 billion hours of informal care were provided. The total cost of this informal care in 2018 is estimated to be between £13.4 billion and £48.7 billion, depending on the valuation method used. To put

Table 3.15 Total costs by type of care and source, England, 2018

		Cost I		Cost II		Cost III	
Care Type	Source	£ bn	% GDP	£ bn	% GDP	£ bn	% GDP
Residential Care	Public	7.2	0.4%	7.2	0.4%	7.2	0.4%
	Private	4.8	0.2%	4.8	0.2%	4.8	0.2%
	All	12	0.6%	12	0.6%	12	0.6%
Formal Home Care	Public	5.4	0.3%	5.4	0.3%	5.4	0.3%
	Private	0.8	0.0%	0.8	0.0%	0.8	0.0%
	All	6.2	0.3%	6.2	0.3%	6.2	0.3%
Informal Care	Private	13.4	0.7%	27.0	1.4%	48.7	2.5%
Total	Public	12.5	0.6%	12.5	0.6%	12.5	0.6%
	Private	19.0	1.0%	32.7	1.7%	54.4	2.8%
	All	**31.6**	**1.6%**	**45.2**	**2.3%**	**66.9**	**3.5%**

Notes: The costs for residential and formal home care come from table 3.13. Informal care costs come from table 3.14. We use the percentage of spending that is private or public from the Health Accounts (2018), which is for the whole of the UK and includes the under 65s, so may overstate the percentage that is Public. We also include spending by charities in Public. Cost I values informal care at the predicted wages of the informal carers multiplied by the predicted hours they would have worked, and values predicted non-working hours at zero. Cost II is as Cost I, and values predicted working hours at the predicted wage, but values predicted non-working hours at the average care worker hourly pay. Cost III is as Cost II but instead of care worker hourly pay it uses the care worker hourly cost. GDP for England in 2018 is estimated at £1.9 trillion (see footnote 5). Amounts in the table have been adjusted to 2019 GBPs. This table is directly comparable to US table 10.19.

these sums into context they equate to an estimate that informal care for the elderly cost the English economy a sum equivalent to between 0.7 percent and 2.5 percent of English GDP.[5]

Table 3.15 aggregates the estimates from the previous two tables—expenditures on formal care and implicit expenditures on informal care—to provide a national estimate of total long-term care spending, and provides an additional breakdown by public and private. Our estimates of the total cost of care for English adults aged 65 and over in 2018 range between £32 billion and £67 billion, which is a sum equivalent to between 1.6 percent and 3.5 percent of English GDP. Within this total, the costs and value of informal care are at least equal to the costs and value of formal care provided, and potentially up to much larger—making up between 42 percent and 73 percent of the total, depending on which basis is used.

Our strategy costs out all care provided for the 65+ population. How-

5. The Office for National Statistics does not produce GDP data broken down by nations within the UK, so English GDP data are not available. ONS statistics on Gross Value Added suggest that 86 percent of UK Gross Value Added in 2018 is produced in England (see ONS 2022), so we estimate English GDP by applying this ratio to UK GDP data for 2018 (£2,218 billion) prior to converting to 2019 GBPs.

ever, we should note that there is some ambiguity in the distinction between public and private care. We have categorized all informal care as private care, but some of this care is publicly subsidized through the Carer's Allowance. Expenditure from the government benefit Carer's Allowance, which compensates informal carers and amounts to £2.98 billion per annum, is not included in this table. In this table, hours of those providing informal care and receiving the Carer's Allowance are valued using the three different approaches listed in the table. That care is counted as private informal care. Since their hours (and the implicit value of that care) are captured in the table, we do not include the Carer's Allowance so as to not double count these informal care hours. This means that the "private" component of costs might be overstated, although even in our most conservative estimate of informal care Carer's Allowance would account for only a modest proportion of the cost. The broad message, however, is not dependent on this assumption. Once one includes informal care in the total costs of calculations, it becomes clear that by far the lion's share of the costs of care—between 60 percent and 81 percent of the total—are borne by private individuals as opposed to by government.

3.5 Conclusions

This paper brings together evidence on the current state of demand and supply of LTC in England using both new and existing data sources. We show that ADLs and IADLs measures, which capture the need for care, are decreasing in wealth and increasing in age, and conditional on ADLs and IADLs the demand for, and use of LTC, is increasing in age. On the supply side the formal system (taking residential and formal home care together) is organized locally, supplied by private providers but with a mix of roughly two-thirds public funding and one-third private funding. The overall size of the formal care sector for those aged 65+ (at around 1 percent of GDP) is small compared to the implicit size of the informal care services which are provided by (predominantly) families to help meet the care needs of their elderly and more dependent members, which we estimate to be between 0.7 percent and 2.5 percent of GDP.

In many ways England is similar to most other developed economies in Europe and Northern America. And as such the underlying policy pressures and policy debates are also similar. There are three particular issues driving policy debates in England about LTC. The first is the affordability of even the current system in the face of demographic trends. This has been exacerbated in recent years by the decade of low economic growth and fiscal austerity from 2010 through to the start of the COVID-19 pandemic, which saw cuts in LTC care spending, with real spending lower in 2019 than in 2011. This fiscal austerity led to reductions in the fees paid by local authorities to providers and falling number residential home beds per older person in the population, with supply struggling to match the growing needs of the population over the past decade. Looking forward, the increasing size of the 65+ population is well known, and we are already well into the period where these numbers are increasing. What hasn't happened yet, but is approaching rapidly, is the rapidly increasing numbers of 85+ individuals that is forecast to occur from 2030 to 2050, which, given our data on the age profile of ADL limitations, will have acute effects on the demand for LTC.

The second issue is the fact that, as quantified by our estimates in section 3.4 of this paper, the current system already places a high (and often unmeasured) burden of informal care on many families and/or exposes individuals to potentially very high out-of-pocket LTC costs. This burden will only rise rapidly with the ongoing aging of the population and forecast increase in the fraction in the 85+ groups going forwards, and particularly so if the formal LTC system is not reformed to allow it to keep up with increasing demographic needs.

The third issue in the policy debate relates more to distributional issues, as opposed to the aggregate issues which have been the focus of most of the discussion in this paper. The current system offers limited protection to anyone other than the least wealthy in society. While the wealthiest in society may be able to provide privately for any formal LTC needs, the large and uncertain costs associated with potentially long stays in nursing homes mean that this care may be financially well beyond those in the middle of the wealth distribution.

Given the funding of LTC, individuals must exhaust their personal savings (and other assets) before they receive much in the way of public assistance. Economists generally see it as socially optimal to pool financial risk to insure those who face the risk of costs. The current system pools risk but provides incentives to run down their wealth, which economists do not see as socially optimal. Evidence from the United States looking at Medicaid, which has many similarities to the LTC system in the England, shows that most individuals (even the wealthy) value these systems more than they cost due to the risk pooling that is provided (De Nardi et al 2016). However, there currently is little systematic analysis of all the possible funding options.

In England, as in the United States, the market for private LTC insurance is tiny. There is an active literature that attempts to disentangle the reasons for the small LTC market (Braun et al. 2019). Some have argued that the presence of public insurance may crowd out the private insurance market—as those who may have otherwise got private insurance instead opt for the public insurance (Brown and Finkelstein 2006) and because of the difficulties of operating private insurance markets in situations with the possibility of catastrophic costs.

Better insurance against catastrophic costs is not the only rationale advanced by advocates of reform. They also argue that a more generous

LTC system may reduce health care costs for the NHS.[6] This is because when LTC is lacking, it can result in more frequent, and potentially longer, hospital visits. And the burden of informal care, which has to substitute for the lack of formal care, tends to fall disproportionately on women, which has distributional and welfare implications, as well as potentially resulting in aggregate productivity losses through the misallocation of talent and skills in the economy.

For all the above reasons there has been much debate around reforms of LTC in England over previous decades, but little action until recently. The main proposals stem from the 2011 Dilnot Commission (Dilnot Commission 2013), which recommended a fixed lifetime cap on social care charges and a more generous means test. The current proposal, initially planned to take effect from October 2023,[7] is for a lifetime cap of £86,000 and an increase in the upper asset limit above which individuals are not eligible for local authority support toward their care costs (the means test) from £23,250 to £100,000. This reform will help to insure against the risk of catastrophic costs and, it is hoped, will create the right conditions for a private LTC insurance market to exist (to insure costs below the cap). But the proposed changes will not fully insure against catastrophic costs as "hotel costs" (for example, food and accommodation) of nursing and other residential homes—which tend to be very large—are not included in the cap. Furthermore, by reducing the effective cost of residential home care, it may increase use of that care, further increasing the cost of the program (although then potentially reducing the costs, and burden, of informal care).

The full medium- and long-run fiscal implications of this need to be worked through, but even then, the current fragmented nature of LTC on the supply side due to variation across local authorities, coupled with the lack of any systematic national-level data on the various local authorities' specific arrangements for eligibility, pricing, and means testing, presents difficult challenges for those wanting to undertake any detailed analysis of the aggregate or distributional consequences of this (or any other LTC) reform. There would be high returns to the assembly and release of better data on geographical differences in the funding and supply of formal LTC, such that any analysis of future reform options can be as informed as is possible in other areas of equal economic importance, such as pensions and health care. At present the microeconomics and macroeconomics of LTC in

6. Evidence on this is mixed. For example, Crawford et al. (2021) estimate the impacts of cuts to LTC spending in England, and find only modest impacts on NHS hospital spending. However, Martin et al. (2021) find evidence of impacts on mortality.

7. This was to be funded by an additional Health and Social Care levy of 1.25 percent on National Insurance contributions, which the Conservative government briefly led by Liz Truss subsequently announced would be repealed. The levy was projected to raise £12 billion, and the consequences of its repeal was that in the Autumn Statement of November 2022 the next Conservative government, led by Rishi Sunak, postponed the implementation of the Dilnot review proposals for a further two years until October 2025.

England are relatively understudied in any detailed granular way, and this is going to become an increasingly significant gap in the evidence base as the importance of LTC provision grows.

Appendix

Reweighting the ELSA Data to Make It Representative of the Full 65+ Population

In this appendix we describe our weighting scheme to address attrition problems that arise when individuals enter nursing or care homes. ELSA has high-quality information on the non-institutionalized population (e.g., those outside of a nursing or care home) and is representative of this population in a number of dimensions. While attrition exists in ELSA, there is no statistically significant correlation between attrition and prior health or the SES indicators such as education, income, and wealth (Banks et al. 2011). However, ELSA is not fully representative of the nursing and care home population. Individuals who enter these homes are often missed in the survey. For example, in ELSA we calculate the probability of being in a nursing or care home conditional on being age 65+ is 0.013, whereas the probability of being in a nursing or care home in the full population is estimated by the Office for National Statistics (based on the 2011 Census and other administrative data) is 0.033. Furthermore, ELSA does not create sample weights for those in nursing or care homes.

To address the under-sampling of the nursing home population we use the following procedure: For the non-institutionalized population, we use the wave 9 cross-sectional weight. For institutionalized individuals (e.g., those in nursing/care homes) we use the cross-sectional weight from the last wave in which they were observed in the household sample. We recalibrate these weights to ensure the reweighted sample composition matches the institutionalized/non-institutionalized percentages from the full population based on age and gender. Implicitly, we are assuming that the probability of attrition from ELSA is a function of nursing home status, gender, and age, but nothing else.[8] That is, we assume the probability of attrition is independent of all variables once we have conditioned on age, gender, and nursing/care home status.

Define the variables age, gender, and nursing home/care home status

8. Barczyk and Kredler (2019) make a similar assumption and estimate selection models to address the attrition problem. Instead, we use weighting, which is another popular approach to addressing this problem. See Solon et al. (2015) and Valliant and Dever (2018) for recent surveys on weighting.

Table 3A.1

	Men 65–74	Men 75–84	Men 85+	Women 65–74	Women 75–84	Women 85+	Total
Pr(NH=1)	0.0015	0.0034	0.0047	0.0016	0.0066	0.0153	0.0331
Pr(NH=1) if observed in ELSA	0.0005	0.0004	0.0028	0.0004	0.0013	0.0074	0.0128
Pr(NH=0)	0.2552	0.1478	0.0461	0.2752	0.1737	0.0689	0.9669
Pr(NH=0) if observed in ELSA	0.2610	0.1430	0.0472	0.2827	0.1743	0.0790	0.9872

Notes: *NH* is being in a nursing/care home. Individual cells in this table gives the joint probability of a given nursing home status and set of covariates, both in the population and in the ELSA data.

as z. We then calculate the objects: Pr(z), Pr(z | Observed in ELSA). We then calculate the relative probability of an individual in group z (i.e., whether in a nursing home or not and of a given age and gender) relative to being observed in ELSA: p(z)= Pr(z)/ Pr(z| Observed in ELSA). We then reweight the data when presenting statistics in the main text, and thus for any variable (gender, income, age, etc.), we multiply the observed number of people in cell z by p(z). We have three age groups (65–74, 75–84, 85+), for both men and women, and show the probabilities for each group that we use to construct p(z). Consistent with previous findings, ELSA appears representative of the full population not in a nursing home by age and gender, but significantly understates the share in a nursing home for men and women of all age groups.

References

Banks, James, James Nazroo, Andrew Steptoe, and Paola Zaninotto, eds. 2019. *The Dynamics of Aging: Evidence from the English Longitudinal Study of Ageing 2002–2019*. London: Institute for Fiscal Studies. https://www.elsa-project.ac.uk/_files/ugd/540eba_a521228fef944892b2942d6135be6734.pdf.

Banks, J., A. Muriel, J. P. Smith. 2011. "Attrition and Health in Ageing Studies: Evidence from ELSA and HRS." *Longitudinal and Life Course Studies* 2: 101–26.

Barczyk, Daniel, and Matthias Kredler. 2019. "Long-Term Care across Europe and the United States: The Role of Informal and Formal Care." *Fiscal Studies* 40 (3): 329–73.

Braun, R. Anton, Karen A. Kopecky, and Tatyana Koreshkova. 2019. "Old, Frail, and Uninsured: Accounting for Features of the US Long-Term Care Insurance Market." *Econometrica* 87 (3): 981–1019.

Brown, Jeffrey R., Norma B. Coe, and Amy Finkelstein. 2006. "Medicaid Crowd-Out of Private Long-Term Care Insurance Demand: Evidence from the Health and Retirement Survey." NBER Working Paper 12536. Cambridge, MA: National Bureau of Economic Research.

Brown, Jeffrey R., and Amy Finkelstein. 2008. "The Interaction of Public and Private

Insurance: Medicaid and the Long-Term Care Insurance Market." *American Economic Review* 98 (3): 1083–1102.

Care and Support (Eligibility Criteria) Regulations. 2015. (SI 2015/313). www.legislation.gov.uk/uksi/2015/313/pdfs/uksi_20150313_en.pdf.

Crawford, Rowena, George Stoye, and Ben Zaranko. 2021. "Long-Term Care Spending and Hospital Use among the Older Population in England." *Journal of Health Economics* 78: 102477, July.

Curtis, Lesley A., and Amanda Burns. 2018. "Unit Costs of Health and Social Care 2018." Project report, University of Kent. https://doi.org/10.22024/UniKent/01.02.70995.

De Nardi, Mariacristina, Eric French, and John Bailey Jones. 2016. "Medicaid Insurance in Old Age." *American Economic Review* 106 (11): 3480–3520.

Department of Health and Social Care. 2018. National Framework for NHS Continuing Healthcare and NHS-Funded Nursing Care. https://www.gov.uk/government/publications/national-framework-for-nhs-continuing-healthcare-and-nhs-funded-nursing-care.

Dilnot Commission. 2011. Fairer Care Funding: The Report of the Commission on Funding of Care and Support. https://webarchive.nationalarchives.gov.uk/20130221121529/https://www.wp.dh.gov.uk/carecommission/files/2011/07/Fairer-Care-Funding-Report.pdf.

Dilnot Commission. 2013. Commission on Funding of Care and Support. Archived February 21, 2013. https://webarchive.nationalarchives.gov.uk/ukgwa/20130221121534/http:/www.dilnotcommission.dh.gov.uk/our-report/.

Emmerson, Carl, and Polly Simpson. 2018. "Adult Social Care in England." Unpublished briefing paper. London: Institute for Fiscal Studies.

Giupponi, Giulia, and Steve Machin. 2021. "Labour Market Inequality." *IFS Deaton Review of Inequalities*.

Kennedy, S., and M. Gheera. 2020. "Carer's Allowance." House of Commons Library briefing paper: Number 00846. January 9. Accessed September 28, 2022. https://researchbriefings.files.parliament.uk/documents/SN00846/SN00846.pdf.

Martin, Stephen, Francesco Longo, James Lomas, and Karl Claxton. 2021. "Causal Impact of Social Care, Public Health and Healthcare Expenditure on Mortality in England: Cross-Sectional Evidence for 2013/2014." *BMJ Open* 2021; 11:e046417. https://bmjopen.bmj.com/content/11/10/e046417.

NHS Digital. 2019. "Adult Social Care Activity and Finance Report, England-2018–19." Accessed September 28, 2022. https://digital.nhs.uk/data-and-information/publications/statistical/adult-social-care-activity-and-finance-report/2018–19.

Office for Budget Responsibility (OBR). 2019. "Welfare Trends Report January 2019." Office for Budget Responsibility. Accessed February 1, 2023. https://obr.uk/wtr/welfare-trends-report-january-2019/.

Office for National Statistics (ONS). 2020a. "Care Home and Non-care Home Populations Used in the Deaths Involving COVID-19 in the Care Sector Article, England and Wales." *Statistical Bulletin*. Accessed September 28, 2022. https://www.ons.gov.uk/peoplepopulationandcommunity/birthsdeathsandmarriages/deaths/adhocs/12215carehomeandnoncarehomepopulationsusedinthedeathsinvolvingcovid19inthecaresectorarticleenglandandwales.

Office for National Statistics (ONS). 2020b. "UK Health Accounts: 2018." *Statistical Bulletin*. Accessed September 28, 2022. https://www.ons.gov.uk/peoplepopulationandcommunity/healthandsocialcare/healthcaresystem/bulletins/ukhealthaccounts/2018/pdf.

Office for National Statistics (ONS). 2022. "Regional Gross Value Added (Balanced) by Industry: All ITL Regions." *Statistical Bulletin*. Accessed September 28, 2022.

https://www.ons.gov.uk/economy/grossvalueaddedgva/datasets/nominalandrealregionalgrossvalueaddedbalancedbyindustry.

Solon, Gary, Steven J. Haider, and Jeffrey M. Wooldridge. 2015. "What Are We Weighting For?" *Journal of Human Resources* 50 (2): 301–16.

Valliant, Richard, and Jill A. Dever. 2018. *Survey Weights: A Step-by-Step Guide to Calculation*. College Station, TX: Stata Press.

4 Long-Term Care in Germany

Johannes Geyer, Axel Börsch-Supan, Peter Haan, and Elsa Perdrix

4.1 Introduction

A constant increase in life expectancy and persistent low fertility rates since the 1970s explain why the population in Germany is among the oldest in the world. Germany will continue to see a strong increase in the share of people aged 65 and older (figure 4.1); among them, the increase of the share of those aged 85 or older is even more dramatic (figure 4.2). In the international context, these numbers are striking. For example, the share of population older than 65 is predicted to be close to 30 percent in Germany by 2060, while the comparable number for the United States is less than 25 percent. The difference between the two countries is similar for the group of individuals aged 85 and older.

The aging of the society challenges the organization of the welfare state. Among others it has important consequences for the financing and the pro-

Johannes Geyer is deputy head of the Public Economics Department at DIW Berlin.

Axel Börsch-Supan is director of the Munich Research Institute for the Economics of Aging and SHARE Analyses (MEA), director emeritus of the Max Planck Institute for Social Law and Social Policy, and a research associate of the National Bureau of Economic Research.

Peter Haan is head of the Public Economics Department at DIW Berlin and a professor of economics at FU Berlin.

Elsa Perdrix is an associate professor of economics at Paris Dauphine University-PSL and a researcher at the Laboratoire d'Économie de Dauphine (LEDa).

We are grateful for excellent research support by Lars Felder and Pablo Neitzsch. We also thank Adam Lederer. Funding by the Joint Policy Initiative—More Years Better Lives (JPI-MYBL) through the project "Unequal ageing: life-expectancy, care needs and reforms to the welfare state" (PENSINEQ) is gratefully acknowledged. For acknowledgments, sources of research support, and disclosure of the authors' material financial relationships, if any, please see https://www.nber.org/books-and-chapters/long-term-care-around-world/long-term-care-germany.

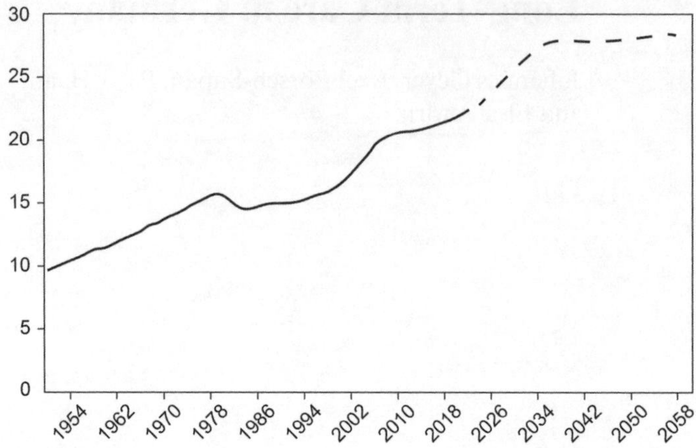

Fig. 4.1 Percentage of population aged 65 or older (1950–2060), 2020
Source: OECD Stat. https://stats.oecd.org/Index.aspx?DataSetCode=POPPROJ#

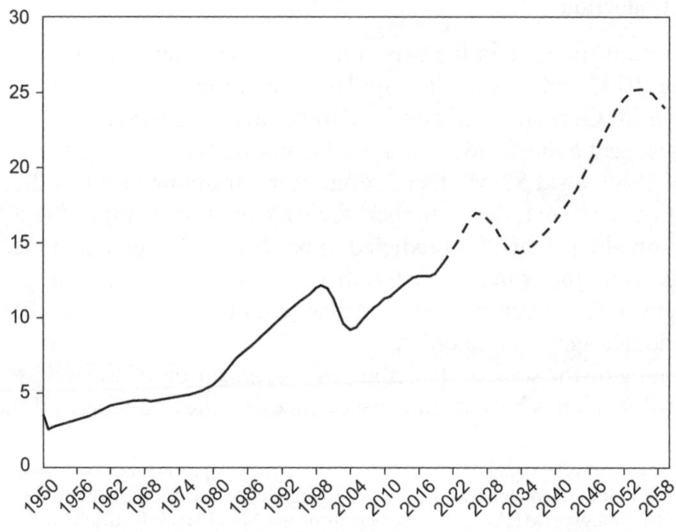

Fig. 4.2 Percentage of 65+ population aged 85 or older, 1960–2060
Source: OECD Stat. https://stats.oecd.org/Index.aspx?DataSetCode=POPPROJ#

vision of long-term care. The demand for care provision is strongly increasing with age. This is documented in table 4.1, which shows the increasing age pattern of the share of individuals with at least one limitation in activities of daily living. Additionally, the data show that the number of limitations is strongly determined by age. Thus, demand for long-term care is increas-

Table 4.1 **Share with ADLs or IADLs by age, 2015/17**

# of limitations in ADL	65+	85+
0 ADLs & 0 IADLs	0.721	0.397
0 ADLs & 1+ IADLs	0.094	0.180
1 ADL	0.087	0.127
2 ADLs	0.040	0.134
3 ADLs	0.023	0.054
4 ADLs	0.012	0.014
5 ADLs	0.010	0.028
6 ADLs	0.014	0.066
Any ADL	0.186	0.430
Any IADL	0.235	0.584

Note: Pooled data from SHARE waves 6 & 7. Weighted data. ADLs include walking across room, dressing, bathing, eating, going to bed, and using the toilet. ADLs include using a map to figure out how to get around in a strange place, preparing a hot meal, shopping for groceries, making telephone calls, taking medications, doing work around the house or garden, managing money, such as paying bills, keeping track of expenses, leaving the house independently and accessing transportation services, and doing personal laundry.

Source: SHARE (doi: 10.6103/SHARE.w6.800 & doi:10.6103/SHARE.w7.800)

ing. At the same time the working population is declining. This has severe consequences for the supply of long-term care at home and in nursing homes as well as for ambulatory care alongside the supply for informal care by family members and friends. Increasing employment rates and a later retirement age crowd out informal care provision, since it is difficult to reconcile employment and long-term care provision. For Germany, a reduction in the supply of informal care provision has important implications for overall care provision, as informal care provision is the most common care mode and the most popular care mode.

To better understand the challenges of an ageing society for the long-term care system in the next decades, this chapter provides an overview about the current state of long-term care and the long-term care system in Germany. The main empirical data sources for our analysis are the Survey of Health and Retirement (SHARE) and the Socio-Economic Panel Study (SOEP); both provide representative household data with relevant demographic and socio-economic information. In the first part, we provide a distributional analysis and show how income and wealth vary with the limitations of daily activities and well-being. In the second part, we present the institutional framework of long-term care and how long-term care is organized in Germany. Finally, we turn to the financial implications of long-term care. Importantly, in this analysis, we not only consider the direct financial costs of formal care provision but also the sizable indirect costs of informal care provision by applying different approaches to value the opportunity costs of informal care and the time spent in informal care.

4.2 Care Needs, Well-Being, and Cost of Care

4.2.1 Sample and Definitions

The main empirical data sources for our analysis are the Survey of Health and Retirement (SHARE) (Börsch-Supan et al. 2013) and the Socio-Economic Panel Study (SOEP) (Goebel et al. 2019), which are both representative household data with relevant demographic and socio-economic information.

SHARE is a cross-national longitudinal panel data set with information covering 28 European countries as well as Israel. The data include information about individuals aged 50 or older and their spouses of any age. In Germany, the sample frame of SHARE covers private households and individuals living in institutions if they are registered at the address of such institutions. Moreover, SHARE follows respondents who have been sampled in the community when they move to retirement and nursing homes. If not otherwise stated, these individuals are included in the calculations. SHARE data collection started with wave 1 in 2004, followed up by panel waves every second year. Fieldwork for wave 8 in 2020 was disrupted due to the COVID-19 pandemic with a corresponding delay in the publication of the latest survey wave, which was released in 2022 together with two telephone-administered waves mainly focused on the effects of the pandemic. Fieldwork for wave 9 was finished in September 2022. Currently eight panel waves of SHARE plus two telephone waves are available. The following analysis mainly uses pooled data from SHARE waves 6 and 7 corresponding to interview years 2015 and 2017, respectively. In addition, we use information from the first and second waves of SHARE, which includes information on how many hours of formal and informal care were received.

The health of individuals is defined by information about limitations related to six activities of daily living (ADLs) and nine instrumental activities of daily living (IADLs). ADLs are defined as: dressing, bathing, eating, toileting, getting in and out of bed, and walking across a room. IADLs include: using a map to figure out how to get around in a strange place, preparing a hot meal, shopping for groceries, making telephone calls, taking medications, doing work around the house or garden, managing money, such as paying bills, keeping track of expenses, leaving the house independently and accessing transportation services, and doing personal laundry. Survey respondents report which of the listed ADLs and IADLs they have difficulties with. SHARE then asks if respondents receive care for: "personal care, i.e. dressing, including putting on shoes and socks; bathing or showering; eating, e.g. cutting up your food; getting in or out of bed; using the toilet, including getting up or down; or practical household help, e.g. with home repairs, gardening, transportation, shopping, household chores; or help with paperwork, such as filling out forms, settling financial or legal matters." All

SHARE variables about formal and informal care received that are used in this chapter are based on these questions.

The SOEP is a longitudinal data set collected every year since 1984, covering a representative sample of German households. It includes an individual questionnaire for the inhabitants of surveyed households and, therefore, offers a rich set of household and individual specific information. For the following analysis, wave 36 is used, containing information from 1984 until 2019. SOEP only covers private households, therefore excluding individuals living in institutions. An exception to this are individuals who were already part of the SOEP and subsequently moved into an institution. These individuals initially remain part of the SOEP but the sample size is negligible and sample attrition very high. Therefore, only information from individuals living in private households was used. In the second part, some statistics are derived from the health ministry and/or the national institute for statistics. These tables and figures use a different definition of long-term care, which corresponds most of the time to all help financed by the social services, public insurance, and private insurance. For these statistics, notes will systematically clarify the definition of long-term care.

Limitations in ADLs and IADLs increase strongly with age. As shown in table 4.1, more than two-thirds of the population aged 65 and older report no limitations in ADLs or IDALs. Only about 10 percent of those individuals report difficulties in at least two ADLs, and about 6 percent have difficulties with three and more. These numbers nearly triple for individuals aged 85 and older, highlighting the increased dependence on support from others with an increasing age. For this age group, only 40 percent report no limitations in ADLs or IADLs.

With respect to IADL, limitations are most frequent in categories like "work in the garden," "leave the house," and "shop for groceries" (table 4.2). Conditional on having one or more IADLs, these shares increase strongly. With respect to ADLs, limitations in "get dressed" or "take a bath" are most frequent. Conditional in having at least one limitation in ADLs, the share of people reporting difficulties in these categories increases to between 60 and 78 percent.

4.2.2 Well-Being

In table 4.3 we report different measures of well-being by age and number of limitations. Generally, well-being is significantly lower for people with three and more limitations: Individuals aged 65 and older as well as those aged 85 and older have about 10 percentage points higher risk of poverty if they have more than three limitations as compared to the average poverty risk in their age group. As expected, self-reported health deteriorates with age and is drastically worse among individuals who report three or more limitations. The measures of life satisfaction, loneliness, and depression point in the same direction. Interestingly, individuals with more than three

Table 4.2 **Distribution of limitations with specific ADLs/IADLs**

	65+ All	65+ Conditional	85+ All	85+ Conditional
	Panel 1: IADLs			
IADL—Use a phone	0.029	0.124	0.104	0.185
IADL—Manage money	0.057	0.247	0.201	0.358
IADL—Take meds as prescr.	0.044	0.193	0.160	0.285
IADL—Shop for groceries	0.112	0.486	0.377	0.670
IADL—Prepare a meal	0.066	0.287	0.232	0.412
IADL—Use a map	0.082	0.355	0.241	0.429
IADL—Work in garden	0.174	0.752	0.425	0.757
IADL—Leave the house	0.114	0.495	0.372	0.662
IADL—Do laundry	0.087	0.376	0.309	0.550
Observations	*4.623*	*891*	*367*	*199*
	Panel 2: ADLs			
ADL—Use the toilet	0.044	0.239	0.114	0.280
ADL—Get dressed	0.133	0.724	0.315	0.772
ADL—Take a bath	0.110	0.599	0.318	0.779
ADL—Walk across a room	0.035	0.192	0.107	0.261
ADL—Eat	0.041	0.224	0.131	0.321
ADL—Get in/out of bed	0.047	0.258	0.122	0.300
Observations	*4,623*	*707*	*367*	*140*

Note: Pooled data from SHARE waves 6 & 7. Weighted data. Column 1 shows the share of the sample that report having difficulty with each activity, while Column 2 shows the share of people with at least 1 IADL (panel 1) or at least 1 ADL (panel 2) who report having difficulty with each activity.

Source: SHARE (doi: 10.6103/SHARE.w6.800 & doi:10.6103/SHARE.w7.800)

limitations who are aged 85 and older report a better health status than the comparison group of individuals aged 65 and older who also have more than three limitations.

In table 4.4 we focus on the distribution of available income and wealth by age. This is indicative of the distributional implications of the health status of individuals. Available income is weighted using the modified OCED equivalence scale while wealth data from SOEP are collected on the individual level.

The data show that income of the lower 10 percent of the sample does not differ between age groups. A possible explanation is that these households rely more strongly on means-tested government programs with that minimum income. In the upper income percentiles, the income of age group 85+ is lower. For example, the median is almost 3 percent lower and the 95th percentile almost 15 percent lower. One reason for this difference in income is a higher share of single women (often widows) in the older age group. Compared to other OECD countries, income inequality is roughly

Table 4.3 **Well-being for those 65+ and 85+ by ADL limitations**

	65+	65+ with 3+ lim.	85+	85+ with 3+ lim.
Poverty risk	0.167	0.281	0.237	0.334
Self-report of health— Good/Very good/excellent	0.488	0.096	0.311	0.137
Life satisfaction (0–10)	7.83	6.94	7.71	7.31
Depression (Euro-D scale > 4)	0.252	0.558	0.368	0.594
CASP	38.8	33.1	36.9	33.5
Loneliness (3–9)	3.83	4.55	4.08	4.39

Note: Pooled data from SHARE waves 6 & 7. Weighted statistics. ADLs include walking across room, dressing, bathing, eating, going to bed, and using the toilet. IADLs include using a map to figure out how to get around in a strange place, preparing a hot meal, shopping for groceries, making telephone calls, taking medications, doing work around the house or garden, managing money, such as paying bills, keeping track of expenses, leaving the house independently and accessing transportation services, doing personal laundry. Poverty risk is measured using the square root of household size. Euro-D scale measures depression, from 0 "not depressed" to 12 "very depressed"; the attainment of a scale score of 4 or higher is categorized as "case of depression" and a scale score below 4 as "not depressed." CASP is a measure of quality of life. The resulting score is the sum of 12 items, and ranges from 12 to 48. A high score indicates high quality of life. The Three-Item Loneliness Scale (Hughes et al. 2004) is a short version of the R-UCLA Loneliness Scale (Russel et al. 1978). It measures indirect loneliness. The three items companionship, left out, and isolated are answered on a three-point Likert scale ("often," "some of the time," "hardly ever or never"). The minimum of the resulting score is 3 ("not lonely") and the maximum is 9 ("very lonely"). The literature does not provide an indication of a threshold which categorizes "lonely" and "not lonely." For more details on these scales and operationalization in SHARE, see Mehrbrodt et al. (2019). The number of observations varies across items, the lowest number is 71 for the item "Loneliness (3–9)" and people aged 85+ with three and more limitations in ADLs. Most cells have well more than 100 observations.

Source: SHARE (doi: 10.6103/SHARE.w6.800 & doi:10.6103/SHARE.w7.800)

at the mean level of inequality (OECD 2019, p. 190f). The percentile ratio P90/P10 is at 3.3 (65+) and 2.9 (85+). The percentile ratio P50/P10 is at 1.8 (65+) and 1.7 (85+).

The wealth distribution shows similar differences between both age groups. The lower 10 percent have zero wealth, whereas median wealth is at 72,283 euros for the age group 65+ and nearly 50,000 for people aged 85 and over. Wealth levels are between 6 percent and 32 percent lower in the percentiles of the older age group. In line with the literature, wealth is more unequally distributed than income, with 10 percent of individuals in both age groups reporting no wealth at all.[1]

Table 4.5 reports the income distribution for those aged 65 and older as a

1. Using SOEP data from 2012, Geyer (2015) finds similar result: Households with a care dependent member have similarly high household incomes as households in which no person in need of care lives. However, the income share of public transfers is higher in households with a care dependent member. In addition, their wealth is significantly lower than that of households without members in need of care.

Table 4.4 **Income and wealth distribution, 2019/2017**

	Available equivalized income (in euro per year)		Wealth (in euro)	
	65+	85+	65+	85+
5th Percentile	10,060	10,060	0	0
10th Percentile	12,182	12,201	0	0
25th Percentile	16,403	15,893	5,164	4,627
50th Percentile	21,475	20,853	72,283	49,370
75th Percentile	29,196	27,517	198,442	187,845
90th Percentile	39,710	34,840	368,240	320,827
95th Percentile	47,519	40,471	565,478	493,696
Mean	24,747	23,027	165,120	139,385
Observations	5,362	391	5,785	442

Note: Equivalized net household income (OECD modified scale); without imputed rent. Income data from 2019. Only private households. Respondent weights are included in all calculations. SOEP collects wealth data on the individual level. Wealth data from 2017; adjusted to 2019 euros. Respondent weights are included in all calculations.
Source: SOEPv37

Table 4.5 **Income and wealth distribution by limitations for 65+ population**

	0 ADLs & 0 IADLs	0 ADLs & 1+ IADLs	1 ADL	2 ADLs	3+ ADLs	Total
			Panel 1: Income			
<50% Median HH Income	0.072	0.082	0.120	0.205	0.225	0.092
50–100% Median HH Income	0.446	0.524	0.557	0.641	0.498	0.472
100–150% Median HH Income	0.307	0.258	0.214	0.080	0.181	0.278
150–200% Median HH Income	0.100	0.072	0.064	0.024	0.076	0.090
200%+ Median HH Income	0.076	0.065	0.044	0.050	0.020	0.068
Total	0.746	0.062	0.090	0.041	0.061	1.000
Number of Observations	3,432	257	348	141	209	4,387
			Panel 2: Wealth			
Below Median HH Wealth	0.459	0.483	0.621	0.758	0.690	0.501
100–200% Median HH Wealth	0.184	0.198	0.112	0.115	0.085	0.170
200%+ Median HH Wealth	0.357	0.320	0.267	0.127	0.224	0.329
Total	0.740	0.069	0.091	0.037	0.063	1.000
Observations	1,712	142	175	65	107	2,201

Notes: Pooled data from SHARE waves 6 & 7. Weighted statistics. ADLs and IADLs include the items shown in table 4.2. The median is roughly 21,780 euros per year for (equivalized) net income and 69,974 euros for per capita wealth when adjusted to 2019 euros. Weighted income using square root of household size. Wealth data are from wave 6.
Source: SHARE (doi: 10.6103/SHARE.w6.800 & doi:10.6103/SHARE.w7.800)

percentage of within-sample median income of individuals by the number of ADLs with which they report having difficulties. Note that the number of observations declines with age and number of limitations in ADLs, thus reducing statistical precision. Nonetheless, individuals in the lower income bracket show higher shares of limitations in ADLs. Therefore, wealth and income are both highly unequally distributed in Germany, with the inequality growing even stronger by the health status of individuals.[2]

In the next section we provide a brief overview of the German long-term care system and describe ways how public insurance supports care recipients and caregivers, as well as the types of services it offers. This part will rely strongly on public statistics on labor, health, and social care provided by the German administration.

4.3 LTC system in Germany

Administrative data from public long-term care insurance include a specific definition of LTC that differs from general LTC measures commonly used in surveys such as SHARE or SOEP. Obviously, there is an overlap, since eligibility for public care benefits requires—among other things—substantial limitations in ADL and IADL. However administrative statistics do not include data on people who are not eligible for benefits from public insurance but only those eligible who claim benefits. Moreover, these data cover the population living in nursing homes, which are often not sampled representatively in surveys. Some statistics cover the whole cost of care, with a broad definition; some others are specific to costs included in the care insurance benefit, which is the main system to help elderly with disability. This section also provides information about private long-term care insurance, even if it represents only a small share of the population coverage against disability risk.

4.3.1 Financing and Benefits

Since 1970, spending on long-term care relative to GDP has been constantly increasing, as illustrated in figure 4.3. However, before Germany introduced its public long-term care insurance in the beginning of the 1990s, expenditures remained below 0.5 percent of the German GDP until 1992.[3] The share of expenditures increased strongly since then, reaching more than 2.5 percent of the GDP in 2020. Part of this increase in expenditures is explained by demographic aging and, in particular, by a growing share of the population aged 80 and over (cf. figure 4.1 and figure 4.2). Other important

2. Geyer et al. (2021) show that long-term care risk is negatively correlated with income and higher occupational status.

3. Long-term care insurance was introduced in 1995. Expenditures already began to increase in 1992 since the government started to increase benefits for long-term care via public health insurance.

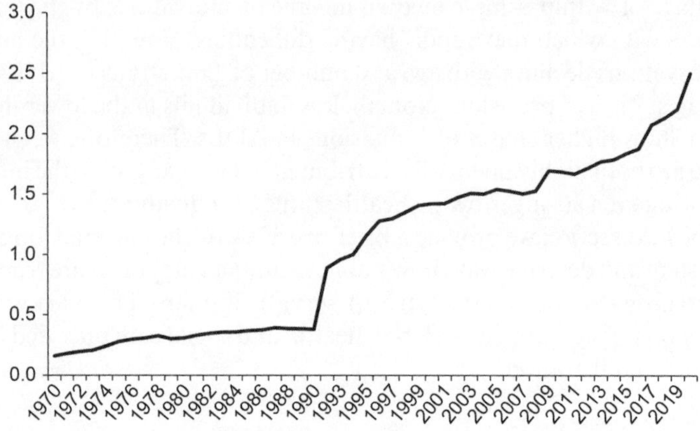

Fig. 4.3 Share of GDP spent on long-term care (1970—2020)

Note: Data come from the system of health accounts. Total LTC expenditure is the sum of health LTC (HC.3—HC stands for Healthcare Functions) and social LTC (HCR.1—Health Care Related Functions). Health LTC (HC.3) comprises inpatient LTC (HC.3.1), day LTC (HC.3.2), outpatient LTC (HC.3.3), and home-based LTC (HC.3.4).

Sources: OECD (https://stats.oecd.org/)

drivers of expenditures were larger expansions of public long-term care insurance, e.g. in 1995, 2008, and 2017. Note that the expenditures include spending for younger people as well. In 2020, about 20 percent of recipients of long-term care benefits are younger than 65. Per capita spending does not differ much across age.

The structure of the financing is explained by the institutional organization of long-term care in Germany, as illustrated by figure 4.4.[4] The major share of the financing is public: 63 percent` originates from the public long-term care insurance. The compulsory private insurance (2 percent) and other governmental schemes (7 percent) are financially less important. About a quarter (24 percent) represent out-of-pocket costs. In contrast, additional private long-term care insurance only plays a minor role, with around 4 percent of the total financing.

The long-term care insurance (LTCI) in Germany is organized in two independent branches, the social (public) LTCI and the private LTCI. Both are designed as compulsory insurances with identical benefits. About 88 percent of the population is insured through the social LTCI and 12 percent through private LTCI. This group mainly consists of civil servants, self-employed, and high-income earners who can choose between public and private insur-

4. Data come from the System of Health Accounts from the OECD (OECD 2017). HC.3 (HC stands for "Healthcare Functions") comprises expenditures for long-term care (health) and is composed of medical or nursing care and personal care services (help with ADLs). We do not include expenditures from HCR.1 (long-term care [social]) which relates to other assistance services. For more details, see Mueller et al. (2020).

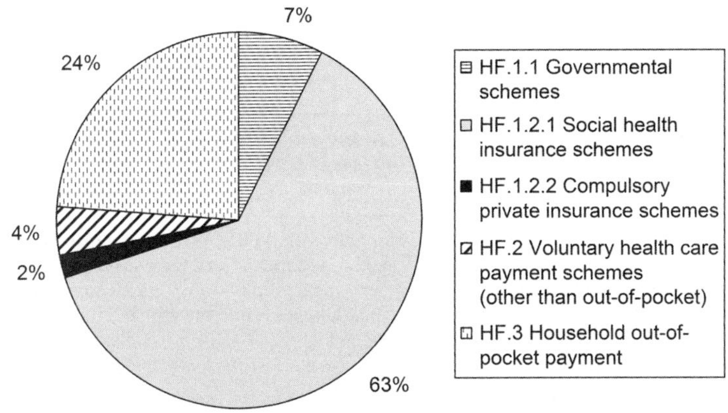

Fig. 4.4 Percent of LTC financing by source (2019)

Note: In this figure, long-term care includes total spending on home health care, nursing care facilities, and continuing care retirement communities. Data come from the system of health accounts. HF stands for "Financing Agents."

Source: System of Health Accounts (2019) (https://www.gbe-bund.de/gbe/)

ance.[5] The social LTCI is funded by social security contributions, with a contribution rate of 3.05 percent in 2022 and an additional 0.35 percent for people without children. The private LTCI is financed by a funded scheme with age-specific contribution rates. Both mandatory schemes offer the same set of services. Households who are eligible for means-tested social assistance receive LTCI that is financed by taxes and administered on the regional level.[6]

Individuals eligible for benefits from the LTCI are classified into one of five care levels. The care levels do not directly correspond to IADLs and ADLs but use similar criteria. Since 2017, care levels reflect the ability to live independently without the help of others. The assessment includes six[7] modules that refer to different areas of life:

1. "mobility" (10 percent);
2. "mental and communication-related abilities" and "behavior and psychological issues" (15 percent);
3. "self-care" (40 percent);
4. "independent handling of requirements and challenges associated with illness or therapy—and their management" (20 percent);
5. "everyday life and social contacts" (15 percent).

5. Individuals with earnings above a certain earnings threshold (64,350 euro per year in 2022) can choose between the social and private insurance.

6. The LTCI includes co-payments for care services and other costs, in particular in nursing homes. If people are eligible for benefits but cannot afford paying these co-payments, social assistance chips in.

7. Module 2 includes two areas of life.

Table 4.6 **Care insurance benefits depending on care level, 2022**

Payments per month in € for care levels.	Level 1	Level 2	Level 3	Level 4	Level 5
Cash benefits	—	316€	545€	728€	901€
Benefits in kind	—	724€	1363€	1693€	2095€
Nursing home benefits	—	770€	1262€	1775€	2005€

Note: This payment is made to cover needs for help with ADL/IADL. Benefits in kind can be chosen if the care recipient prefers professional home care services. Care services include, e.g., bathing, toileting, dressing, grooming, eating and meal preparations, and medication reminders. The care provider is directly reimbursed. Cash benefits and benefits in kind can be combined.

Source: §§36—43 SGB XI

The modules include different items to assess the independence in each area of life. Results are aggregated on a point scale that runs from 0 ("no help needed") to 100 ("completely dependent on others"). Care levels correspond to certain point value intervals on this scale. For more information on this assessment, see Geyer et al. (2016); Rothgang and Kalwitzki (2016); Nadash et al. (2018). Both psychological and physical limitations are integrated in the assessment, which is carried out by the medical advisory service of the statutory health insurance funds. The first care level applies to people not yet in need of more intensive support and only comprises consulting services or changes to the individual's residential environment.

Recipients can choose among different benefits: cash benefits, benefits in kind, and benefits for nursing homes. The level differs between benefits and across care levels (table 4.6). The lowest benefits are cash benefits that are direct cash transfers. The cash benefit is free to spend. Benefits in kind refer to the monthly payments for a professional home health care agency that can help with all ADLs and IADLs, including cleaning the house, help with meal preparation, and help with bathing. Individuals can choose to receive a mixture of both cash benefits and benefits in kind (see table 4.7 for the distribution of care recipients for benefit types). Note that the service provider is directly reimbursed by the LTCI. The nursing home benefit only covers care-related expenses. Co-payments, such as food, lodging, and investment costs for the facility, are not covered and must be borne by the individual. Patients must contribute an additional facility-specific co-payment that is the same for all patients in the same facility independent of their care level. These payments can be substantial and show great variation across German states.[8] Former East German states have the lowest co-payments, such as Saxony-Anhalt, with an average of €1,218 per month that divides into €338 for additional care expenses, €549 for lodging, and €286 for investment costs

8. As table 4.7 shows, LTCI benefits vary by level of care. This was also the case for co-payments in nursing homes until 2017. A reform in 2017 unified co-payments at the facility level.

Table 4.7 **Benefit types by care levels for social care insurance, 2021**

	Care recipients by care level					
Benefit type	Level 1	Level 2	Level 3	Level 4	Level 5	Total
Cash benefits	0.0	28.6	15.8	5.2	1.7	51.3
Benefits in kind	0.0	1.8	1.2	0.7	0.4	4.1
Mixture of cash benefits and benefits in kind	0.0	6.0	4.9	1.8	0.7	13.4
Nursing home benefits	0.1	3.0	6.2	5.6	3.1	18.0
Other*	0.0	5.1	4.6	2.4	0.9	13.0
Total	0.1	44.5	32.7	15.7	6.8	100.0

Note: *Other entails: day & night care, home care when the caregiver is unable to attend, short-term care, prevention care, stationary care for the disabled.
Source: Federal Ministry of Health

in January 2019. Monthly co-payments in North Rhine-Westphalia, at the other extreme, were more than €1,000 higher with €2,252 that divides into €717 for additional care, €996 for lodging, and €539 for investment costs. To reduce this burden, the co-payment for additional care expenses is partially covered since January 1, 2022, onwards, depending on the length of stay. In the first 12 months, 5 percent is covered, which increases to 25 percent for months 12 through 23, then 45 percent for months 24 through 35, followed by a maximum of 70 percent for a stay longer than 36 months. Lodging and investments costs still have to be borne solely by the care recipient. If households pass a means-test and wealth test, the co-payments are covered by social assistance.[9] In 2020, for about 400,000 individuals, the costs were covered by social assistance. This is close to 10 percent of all individuals in need of care. When focusing only on individuals in nursing homes, the relative effect is considerably higher and increases to close to 50 percent.

Additionally, there exist multiple schemes designed to relieve relatives who provide care. For example, recipients of home health care with any care level are entitled to an additional monthly payment of €125 that is meant to be used to relieve caring relatives or allow the recipient to live a more independent life. If a caring relative cannot provide care for a limited time of up to six weeks per year, for example due to vacation, increased cash benefits

9. The income limit is not a fixed sum but is calculated as follows: It is twice the standard benefit level of social assistance ("*Regelbedarfsstufe I*"; 449€ in 2022). In addition, reasonable costs for accommodation, excluding heating costs, are reimbursed. The exact rate varies regionally. In addition, there is a family supplement of 70 percent of the standard benefit rate for the non-separated spouse and dependents. Income above this threshold is withdrawn. However, the specifics are determined at an individual level with the social assistance agency. With respect to wealth, there is an allowance of €5,000 (2022) and a few exceptions, for example for owner-occupied housing. For people living in a nursing home, who cannot afford the services, social assistance covers all costs. Moreover, the individual gets a monetary transfer for personal needs of 27 percent of the standard benefit rate.

are available to compensate someone for this interim time. Furthermore, caring relatives are supported if their care work impacts their employment. The pay of up to 10 workdays can be compensated if someone cannot not work due to the (unforeseeable and sudden) need to take care of a relative. Relatives caring for someone more than 10 hours per week on at least two days are entitled to payments into their social security insurance (for more details, see Schulz [2010] and Nadash et al. [2018]). Moreover, there are two types of unpaid care leave for up to 24 months. Eligibility depends on firm size, and take-up is rather limited.

As mentioned above, the role of supplementary private insurance plans in Germany is limited, even by international standards. For example, in the United States, private insurance plans contribute 8 percent to the overall financing and, thus, are two times more important than in Germany. Since the public LTCI is designed as a partially comprehensive insurance, there is room for private complementary insurance. For example, as mentioned above, in 2019 co-payments for a place in a nursing home amount to nearly 2,000 euros per month (national average). There are two different types of supplementary insurances. The most important type of contract, which makes up about 95 percent of the market, is an insurance that provides fixed benefits ("Pflegetagegeldversicherung") in case LTC services are needed. Depending on the care level, the insurance pays a fixed amount that is not earmarked, and, therefore, the spending is not monitored. Since 2013, there is a public subsidy for these contracts—if they fulfill certain criteria.[10] The subsidy amounts to 5 euros per month and has not been changed since 2013. In 2020, there were about 2.6 million contracts with fixed benefits without subsidy and about 900,000 with subsidies (table 4.8).

There is also another type of contract that provides benefits in case of need for LTC ("relative benefits"). The benefits are directly linked to care. This means that the insurance only pays costs directly related to care—such as outpatient care service. The expenses must be proven with receipts. There are two tariff options for long-term care insurance. The services can either be agreed, such that they are covered up to a maximum amount per year. The other variant is that the long-term care insurance increases the benefits of the statutory long-term care insurance by a certain percentage.

There is a third type of contract, the care pension insurance, that works like life insurance and pays an annuity in case LTC is needed. As illustrated in table 4.8, the market is relatively small. Added together, about four million people own a private LTCI in 2020. Contributions amount to 1.7 billion.

According to SOEP data, about 9 percent of individuals older than 65 who are living in private households have a private insurance plan. As represented in table 4.9, the number is lower for individuals older than 85, with

10. These criteria include, among other things, the exclusion of health tests, no risk rating, a minimum contribution of 10 euros per month, and a cost cap.

Table 4.8 **Market for private long-term care insurance, 2010/2020**

Private long-term care insurance		
	2010	2020
Private LTCI (in 1000s)	1,700	2,854
Fixed benefits	1,506	2,644
Relative benefits	290	367
Contributions (Mio. EUR)	439	1,385
Payments (Mio. EUR)	35	325
Subsidized private LTCI with fixed benefits (since 2013)		
No. of insurances (in 1000s)		921
Contributions (Mio. EUR)		342
Payments (Mio. EUR)		54
Total private LTCI		3,775
Care pension insurance (in 1000s)		244
Contributions (Mio. EUR)		172

Note: Care pension insurances are not included in the total number of private LTCIs.
Source: German Insurance Association (GDV)

Table 4.9 **Population with LTC insurance, 2018**

	65+	85+
Population with private LTC Insurance	1,569,513	89,465
Share of Population	(0.087)	(0.05)
Observations	5,387	396

Note: Only private households.
Source: SOEPv36

only around 5 percent of individuals having private insurance. There exists a positive income and wealth gradient. Households with a private long-term care insurance plan have higher income and hold more wealth. The health situation differs between households with and without private insurance, however the number of observations is too low to draw strong conclusions (table 4.10).

4.3.2 Long-Term Care Receipt

The demand for long-term care increases with age. In the following, we focus on the distribution of long-term care receipt by age and health status. SHARE data provide self-reported information about whether the individual receives (or not) help when performing IADLs and ADLs due to a health problem. If the respondent receives help, SHARE ascertains the frequency (about daily; weekly; monthly; less often).

Overall, there exists a strong age gradient, as highlighted in table 4.11:

Table 4.10 **Characteristics by LTC insurance, 2017/2018**

	65+ Insured	65+ Uninsured	85+ Insured	85+ Uninsured
Total Household Wealth—Mean	354,519	147,251	356,611	144,792
Total Household Wealth—Median	175,000	68,000	255,000	50,000
Total Household Income—Mean	33,226	21,884	29,095	19,883
Total Household Income—Median	29,240	19,395	27,075	18,537
Live with Spouse or Partner	0.651	0.569	0.315	0.307
Formal Help with ADL/IADLs	0.016	0.029	0.169	0.131
Informal Help with ADL/IADLs	0.029	0.054	0.185	0.180
Observations	545	4,842	19	377

Notes: Net household income weighted by household size (OECD modified scale). Income from all household members. Wealth data from 2017; income data, asked in 2018, refer to 2017. Only private households. A part of the population receiving care does not answer the personal questionnaire, therefore, we do not have information about private insurance of this group.

Source: SOEPv36

Table 4.11 **Shares of elderly who received care by age and ADL limitation, 2015/17**

	65+	85+
Any Care—All	0.483	0.800
Any Care—0 ADLs & 0 IADLs	0.277	0.473
Any Care—0 ADL & 1+ IADLs	0.857	0.942
Any Care—1 ADLs	0.777	0.959
Any Care—2 ADLs	0.927	0.968
Any Care—3+ ADLs	0.949	1.000
Observations	2,841	271

Notes: Pooled data from SHARE waves 6 & 7. Respondent weights are used for all calculations. The care variable is defined as either living in a nursing home or having received either formal or informal home help from outside the household.

Source: SHARE (doi: 10.6103/SHARE.w6.800 & doi:10.6103/SHARE.w7.800)

While close to 50 percent of all individuals older than 65 receive some care, the share increases to 80 percent for the group of individuals older than 85. The age gradient persists when focusing on individuals with limitations in one ADL. However, among individuals with two or more limitations in ADLs, the share of individuals receiving care is above 90 percent irrespective of age.

Waves 1 and 2 of SHARE also include questions about the number of hours of help/care received. We use this information to calculate the distribution of the combined weekly hours of care received both from informal and formal sources and for help with both ADLs and IADLs. Table 4.12 highlights the unequal distribution in received care hours. While the median for those aged 65 and more is 8 hours per week, this number rises steeply to

Table 4.12 **Distribution of weekly hours of formal and informal care received by age**

	65+	85+
5th Percentile	1	1
10th Percentile	1	2
25th Percentile	3	7
50th Percentile	8	19
75th Percentile	21	35
90th Percentile	45	86
95th Percentile	112	196
Mean	22	35
Observations	276	63

Note: SHARE waves 1 and 2. Respondent weights are used for all population estimate calculations. Nursing home residents are automatically excluded from all calculations. Hours include care received from helpers who assist with ADLs or IADLs because of a health problem. Hours of help from each helper are limited to 16 hours per day to allow for eight hours of rest. Respondents could provide the number of days either overall in the last month, per week, or as every day. In the first case, the days per month was divided by 4.35 (365/7 * 12). In the second case, it is the stated number of hours; in case of daily help, the number was multiplied by 7. If it was less than monthly, we divide by 8.7 assuming that the frequency is—on average—bi-monthly. The hours include formal and informal care.

Source: SHARE (doi: 10.6103/SHARE.w1.800 & doi: 10.6103/SHARE.w2.800)

45 hours for the 90th percentile. We also observe an increased care supply for individuals older than 85. The average care hours received by this group is 13 hours higher than for individuals 65 and older. The results should be interpreted with caution due to a small sample size in the older age group. We can also distinguish provided care hours by formal and informal care (table 4.13). Again, we find a strong age gradient. This holds across the full distribution. At the median, older individuals receive—with 14 hours—about twice as many hours of informal care per week as individuals of the age groups 65 and older. The differences for formal care are very similar.

Similarly, the type of care strongly varies with age, as shown in figure 4.5. Informal care inside or outside the household is—at 54 percent—most common for individuals older than 65, with only 7 percent living in a nursing home.[11] At the age of 85 or older, about 17 percent of the care-dependent individuals reside in a nursing home while the share of informal care (as the only type of care) is reduced to 21 percent. The type of care also strongly depends on the health status and the number of limitations in IADLs and ADLs, as illustrated in figure 4.6. The pattern is similar for the two age groups we consider: Informal care is most common when the care recipient has fewer than two ADLs. For individuals with more ADLs, the share with formal care and in nursing homes is strongly increasing.

11. We adjust survey weights accounting for underrepresentation of the population living in nursing homes.

Table 4.13 Distribution of hours (per week) received by type

	65+		85+	
	Formal	Informal	Formal	Informal
5th Percentile	1	1	1	1
10th Percentile	1	2	1	2
25th Percentile	2	3	7	4
50th Percentile	7	6	14	14
75th Percentile	21	16	35	21
90th Percentile	37	45	84	80
95th Percentile	84	80	112	112
Mean	17	17	28	23
Observations	234	107	48	38

Notes: SHARE waves 1 and 2. Weighted statistics. Formal care includes paid help by a non-relative. Informal care includes help by a relative, whether paid or not. Individuals living in nursing home are excluded. Formal and informal care include only those associated with limitations for ADLs or IADLs, including managing money. The hours of help by caregiver cannot exceed 16 hours per day taking into account 8 hours of rest. The number of hours is declared either by month, by week or per day. If declared by month, the number of hours was divided by 4.35.

Source: SHARE (doi: 10.6103/SHARE.w1.800 & doi: 10.6103/SHARE.w2.800)

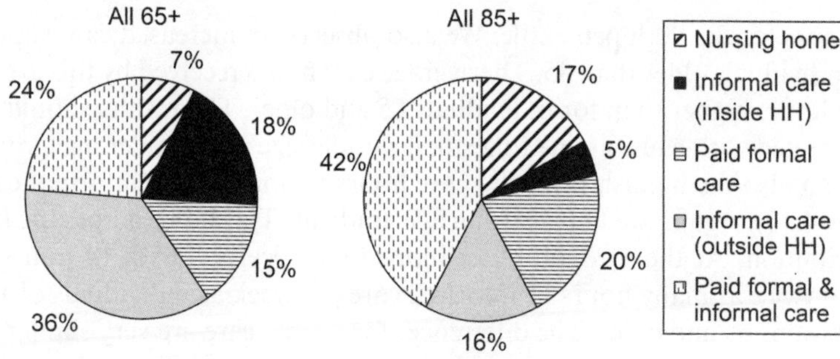

Fig. 4.5 Type of care received by age, Germany, 2015/2017

Notes: Pooled data from SHARE waves 6 & 7. Weighted statistics. Formal and informal care include only those associated with limitations for ADLs or IADLs, including managing money. Weights were adjusted accounting for underrepresentation of population living in nursing homes.

Source: SHARE (doi: 10.6103/SHARE.w6.800 & doi:10.6103/SHARE.w7.800)

Home care is the dominant form of long-term care in Germany and family members are the main care provider. Although Germany introduced a public long-term care insurance in 1995 (see above), it still relies heavily on informal care. In 2021, Germany had about 4.5 million beneficiaries of statutory long-term care insurance. Of those, about 84 percent received care at home. Most of them (~66 percent) did not receive formal care services but relied

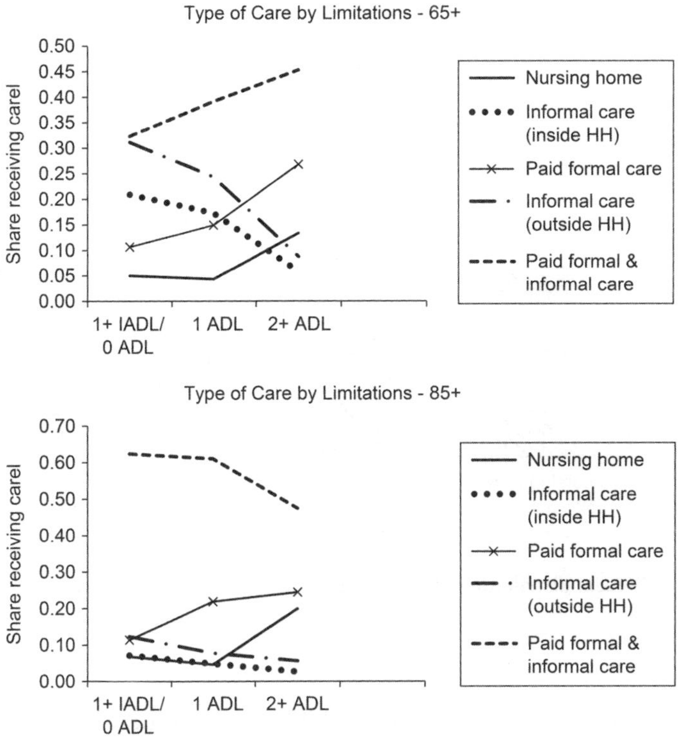

Fig. 4.6 Type of care received by age and limitations, Germany, 2015/2017

Notes: Pooled data from SHARE waves 6 & 7. Weighted statistics. Help can be with ADLs, IADLs, or managing money due to a health problem. Low number of observations for age group 85+.

Source: SHARE (doi: 10.6103/SHARE.w6.800 & doi:10.6103/SHARE.w7.800)

on self-organized informal care. According to different polls, this reflects preferences of caregivers and recipients, i.e. on average, Germans prefer informal home care over formal home care services (Schupp and Künemund 2004).

Stationary nursing care is less preferred by care recipients. Most people prefer aging in place and staying in their familiar surroundings as long as possible (Rudel et al. 2017; Lehnert et al. 2018). Moreover, nursing home beds require substantial co-payments (see next section), which constitutes another reason why they are not very popular. Often people move to a nursing home if care needs are extensive and/or if their social network is small.

Given the importance of informal care in Germany, it raises the question if and how informal caregivers are able to reconcile caregiving and working. People with a lower socioeconomic status have a higher risk of becoming care dependent but also fewer resources to pay for care services. Since the

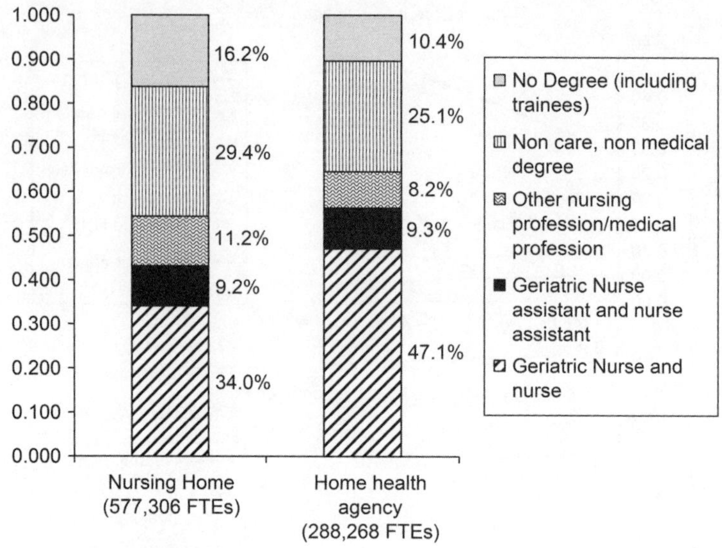

Fig. 4.7 Percent distribution of nurses, aides, and social workers at care facilities, 2019

Source: Pflegestatistik (2019)

care network is usually the spouse or children, the socioeconomic status of care recipients and caregivers is highly correlated.

4.3.3 Long-Term Care Supply

Formal caregivers work either in home health agencies, to help older individuals at home, or in nursing homes. In Germany, more than two-thirds of these workers were employed in nursing homes in 2019, representing 570,000 full time equivalents (FTE) in nursing homes and 290,000 FTEs in home health agencies (figure 4.7).

Formal caregivers are either with no qualifications, mostly for housekeeping, shopping, and preparing meals; or qualified caregivers. Qualification leads to four types of qualified caregivers: assistant-nurse, nurse, assistant-geriatric nurse, and geriatric nurse; each with differing responsibilities, tasks, training, and wages. A geriatric nurse is a nurse who specializes in the care of older adults. They typically care for frail and elderly patients with long-term, chronic medical conditions that are not related to an acute illness or injury. Prior to 2020, Germany had three different vocational tracks for nurses: nurses, geriatric nurses, and pediatric nurses. A reform in 2020 integrated the vocational tracks into one track that allows for specialization after two years. Nurse assistants require less training (see table 4.14). Care assistants support geriatric nurses in all activities related to the care and nursing of elderly people. They take on nursing tasks such as helping with personal hygiene and eating. They also support older people in coping with their everyday lives. The vast majority of formal care providers have some qualification. The share of trained nurses in ambulatory care is close to 50 percent, but lower (35 percent) in nursing homes. In nursing homes, workers without degree or with non-care related degrees are more common, which is related to, for example, cleaning or food provision.

The minimum training requirements varies by states between one and two years. The largest share of the population 65 or older resides in states with a minimum requirement of one year (table 4.14).

The pay structure in nursing facilities and in ambulatory care strongly depends on qualification and region (table 4.15). Geriatric nurses and gen-

Table 4.14 **Training requirements for long-term care workers, 2021**

Minimum training time required by state	Population aged 65+ living in states with corresponding minimum training time	Share of GER population aged 65+	# states
1 year	13,703,058	0.75	10
1.5 years	1,122,090	0.06	2
2 years	3,446,488	0.19	4

Source: Federal Employment Agency, https://berufenet.arbeitsagentur.de/berufenet/faces/index?path=null/kurzbeschreibung/ausbildungsdauerabschluss&dkz=9063, Population Data from Federal Statistical Office https://www-genesis.destatis.de/genesis/online

Table 4.15 **Pay for full-time care workers at nursing facilities and in home health care, 2019**

		Median monthly wage (full time employee) in € 2020		
		All	West Germany	East Germany
Nursing Home	(1) Geriatric nurse	3,099	3,160	2,776
	(2) Nurse	2,914	2,981	2,713
	(3) Geriatric aide/assistant	2,182	2,227	2,000
	(4) Nurse aide/assistant	2,526	2,609	2,085
Home Health Care	(1) Geriatric nurse	2,721	2,805	2,518
	(2) Nurse	2,776	2,859	2,573
	(3) Geriatric aide/assistant	2,039	2,138	1,949
	(4) Nurse aide/assistant	2,111	2,223	1,967
All Industries	All workers	3,401	3,526	2,827
	Without vocational degree	2,513	2,558	2,106
	Vocational degree	3,280	3,429	2,643
	Academic degree	5,235	5,438	4,488

Source: Carstensen et al. (2021): Entgelte von Pflegekräften 2020 (link); Bundesagentur für Arbeit (2021): Sozialversicherungspflichtige Bruttomonatsentgelte (Jahreszahlen) (Federal employment office)

Table 4.16 Minimum wage, June, 2022

	Nursing home and home care agency as employer		Household as employer	
	Hourly wage	Monthly wage	Hourly wage	Monthly wage
Care aide	12.55	2,175	9.82	1,701
Care aide with 1 year of training	13.20	2,288	9.82	1,701
Nurse	15.40	2,669	9.82	1,701

Source: Vierte Verordnung über zwingende Arbeitsbedingungen in der Pflegebranche (2020) (BAnz AT 28.04.2020 V2)

eral nurses receive the highest wages, while the wages of assistance are considerably lower. This is true for West and East Germany, which after more than 30 years after reunification still has a lower wage level. In West Germany, the median wage of a full-time employed nurse is below the median of all workers and similar for workers with a vocational degree—at least in nursing homes. In the East, this picture is mixed. Median full-time wages in nursing homes are above wages of all workers, but this is not true for workers in ambulatory care. Germany introduced a specific minimum wage for workers in the long-term care sector in 2011 that is higher than the general minimum wage (table 4.16). In 2022, it is €12.55 per hour for non-medical care and €15.40 per hour for a nurse.

In table 4.17, we describe the structure in nursing homes in Germany. In 2019, a total of 15,380 nursing homes hosted the elderly in Germany, with 796,489 employees, 886,654 beds and 82,899 day/night care. It means that 40 percent of elderly aged 85+ can get access to nursing homes. The occupancy rate is not saturated for beds, but it is for day/night care, showing an increasing demand for staying at home with a flexible supply of long-term care. The occupancy rate and the number of beds varies between states (table 4.18). The minimum rate amounts to 85 in Rhineland-Palatinate, the highest rate is with 94.2 in Mecklenburg-Vorpommern. The number of beds relative to the population is quite similar between the states.

Informal care is also a large part of the LTC supply. The elderly aged 65+ (resp. 85+) declare 2.32 times (resp. 1.8) more informal caregivers than formal caregivers for help with ADL and IADL (see table 4.19). It represents 1.6 million Germans who help their elderly relatives. Note that this number is probably a lower bound because these statistics rely on declarative surveys, which suffer from bias of under-declaration of helpers (in particular the help of spouses and children, which is sometimes not perceived as help but as normal contribution, especially for administrative tasks and cleaning).

Table 4.17 **Absolute number of nursing homes, beds, and occupancy rate, 2019**

	Type	
Supply		
Nursing homes		15,380
Employees	All	796,489
Beds		969,553
	Long-term nursing care	886,654
	Day/Night care	*82,899*
Occupancy		
Nursing home residents		957,536
	Long-term nursing care	818,317
	Day/Night care	*139,219*
Occupancy rate		98.76%
	Long-term nursing care	92.29%
	Day/Night care	*167.94%*
Ratio Supply Over Population		
Pop 65+		18,090,682
Beds per pop 65+		5.36%
Pop 85+		2,386,854
Beds per pop 85+		40.62%

Note: Nursing homes often offer day care services in addition to long-term nursing care. Occupancy rates can be more than 100 percent, since these beds can be used by different people over a range of time.

Source: Data on nursing homes are from Pflegestatistik (2019); population data from Federal Statistical Office, https://www-genesis.destatis.de/genesis/online

4.3.4 Who Are Caregivers?

Data from the long-term care insurance inform us about formal home care workers characteristics (figure 4.8). In 2019, the LTCI counted 421,550 people working in the home care sector. A relatively large share (77 percent) of these workers works part-time.[12] As in many countries, formal caregivers are mostly women (87 percent). The qualification level is comparably high: 44 percent are trained nurses, 8 percent have another nursing degree, and 9 percent are nurse assistants. That is, the majority of these workers have a vocational degree related to nursing care. Only about 12 percent of the workforce have no degree (including trainees). The composition by age is relatively homogenous, without any age range over-represented: 14 percent under 30 years old; 46 percent between 30 and 50; 40 percent over 50. The age composition does not differ much from the age composition of the general workforce.

12. About 17 percent work in so-called marginal employment ("Mini job") with a maximum monthly income of 450 euros (2019). The employee does not have to pay social security contributions or taxes.

Table 4.18 **Distribution of nursing homes occupancy rate and beds across states, 2019**

State	Occupancy rate (%)	Nursing home beds per one hundred 65+
Rhineland-Palatinate	85.4	4.7
Hamburg	87.5	5.3
Bremen	87.7	4.7
Bavaria	87.9	4.8
Lower Saxony	88.5	6.0
Hesse	89.4	4.7
Schleswig-Holstein	89.4	5.7
Saarland	89.9	5.3
Berlin	90.6	4.5
Baden-Württemberg	91.5	4.4
Saxony-Anhalt	92.7	5.2
Brandenburg	92.8	4.2
Thuringia	93.3	4.8
North Rhine-Westphalia	93.4	4.6
Saxony	93.9	5.0
Mecklenburg-Vorpommern	94.2	5.0
Min	85.4	4.2
Max	94.2	6.0

Note: Occupancy rate is defined as the percentage of beds occupied in nursing homes.
Source: Pflegestatistik 2019. https://www.destatis.de/DE/Themen/Gesellschaft-Umwelt/Gesundheit/Pflege/Publikationen/Downloads-Pflege/laender-pflegeheime-5224102199004.html. population data from Federal Statistical Office, https://www-genesis.destatis.de/genesis/online

Table 4.19 **Informal care provision—population est.**

	65 Plus	85 Plus
Formal Helpers—ADL/IADLs	676,483	343,059
Relative to 65+/85+ Population	0.035	0.150
Relative to 18–64 Population	0.013	0.007
Informal Helpers—ADL/IADLs	1,572,575	619,502
Relative to 65+/85+ Population	0.081	0.270
Relative to 18–64 Population	0.031	0.012
All Helpers—ADL/IADLs	2,249,058	962,562
Relative to 65+/85+ Population	0.116	0.420
Relative to 18–64 Population	0.045	0.019
Observations	428	146

Notes: Respondent weights are used for all population estimate calculations. Only private households. Note that this information is from the SOEP household questionnaire which includes a filter question whether someone in the household has a health problem that requires a permanent personal or professional assistance. Moreover, we don't know whether the person received help from several people in a certain category of helpers. This leads to a lower estimate of the number of helpers compared to, for example, SHARE or in the personal SOEP questionnaire.
Source: SOEPv36

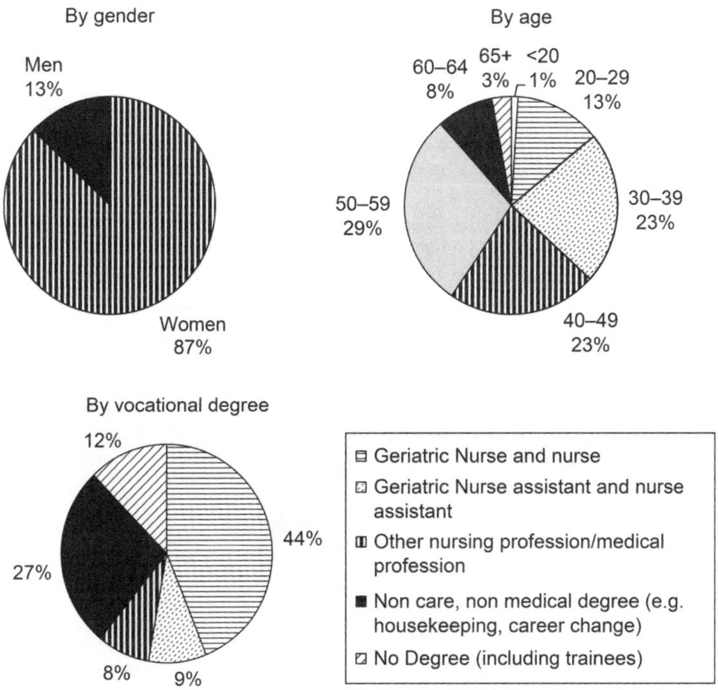

Fig. 4.8 Demographic composition of formal home care workers, 2019

Note: All employees in ambulatory care service sector. We report head-count ratios. Therefore, the shares differ compared to fig. 7, where we report FTE with respect to the composition by vocational degree.

Source: Federal Statistical Office (Pflegestatistik)

In many countries, the share of migrant workers among home care workers is relatively high. This is not the case in Germany. Although we cannot distinguish between workers in nursing homes and home care workers, the share of foreign nationals in 2021 was only about 13 percent in the long-term care sector. This is about the average across all industries in Germany. Interestingly, the share used to be much lower: in 2016 it was at about 7 percent. That is, within five years their share has nearly doubled. The increase was due to two main related factors: first, movement of labor within the European Union was liberalized for new member states, and, second, Germany increased its efforts to hire care workers abroad due to shortages in this sector (Bundesagentur für Arbeit 2022).

Figure 4.9 shows the composition of informal caregivers in Germany. As described above, most are relatives of the care recipient, often spouses or children, which explains in part their demographic composition. For comparison, we also show unconditional statistics for the population aged 50+. Informal caregivers are also mostly women (60 percent), however the share is

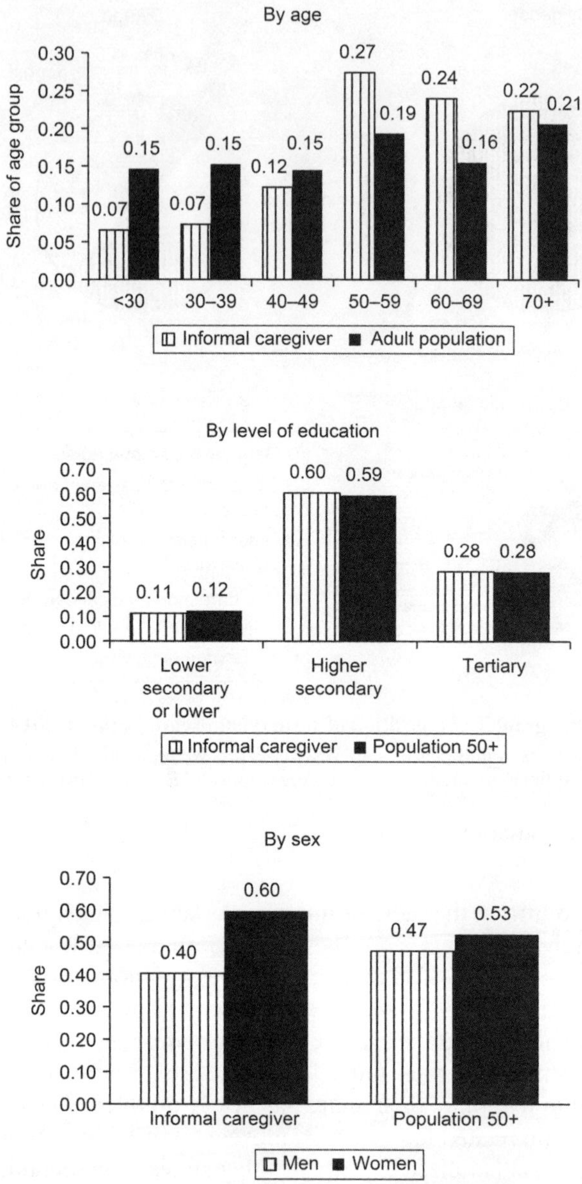

Fig. 4.9 Demographic composition of informal caregivers in comparison to adult population and population 50+, 2019
Note: SOEPv36.

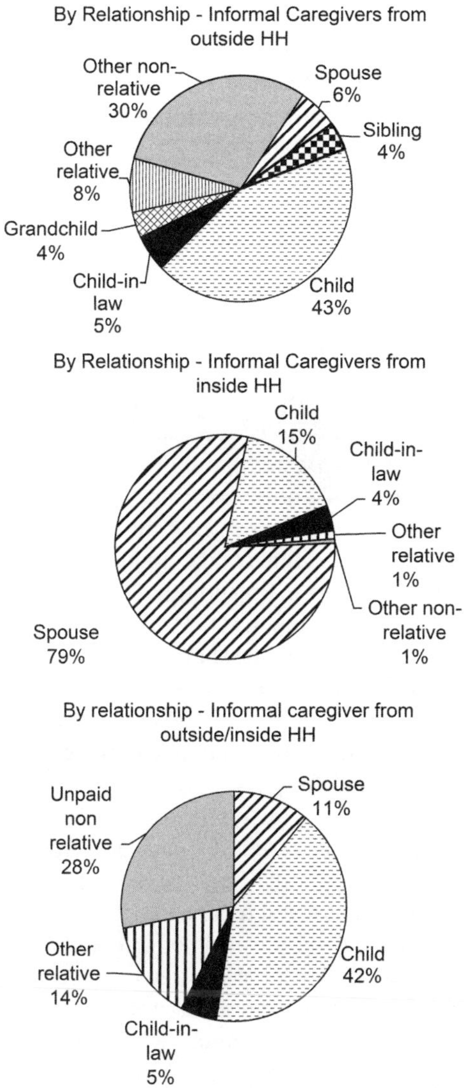

Fig. 4.10 Relationship between informal caregivers and the elderly
Source: SHARE (doi: 10.6103/SHARE.w6.800 & doi:10.6103/SHARE.w7.800)

lower than in the formal workforce. One important factor are male spouses who care for their care-dependent partner. Moreover, data come from a survey question about care provision without specifying exactly the type of care activity. Caregivers are often over the age of 50 (73 percent). While about 45 percent of the adult population is below the age of 50, it is only 26 percent of the informal caregivers. Among informal caregivers, 11 percent have low education and 28 percent have higher education. This is very similar to the education levels of the general population aged 50+.

Care provided within the household and from sources outside the household comes from different sources. Looking at caregivers from outside the household (figure 4.10, upper panel), about 43 percent comes from own children and 30 percent from other non-relatives. In other words, about 70 percent comes from relatives. Care within the household (figure 4.10, lower panel) comes almost exclusively from relatives (99 percent), most often from spouses (79 percent).

4.4 Total Cost and Spending

The cost of long-term care for the elderly (65+), including both cost of nursing home and home health agency, reached 61 billion euros in 2019 (table 4.20). Nursing homes are comparably expensive: Half of the spending is for nursing homes, while only about 22.5 percent of beneficiaries use these institutions. Out-of-pocket spending differs greatly between modes of care. Out-of-pocket expenditures make up only about 7 percent of total expenditures for home care. In nursing homes, 41 percent of expenditures are out-of-pocket payment (see figure 4.11). Most of the expenditures are covered by long-term care insurance. The share of other governmental schemes in expenditures for inpatient care is relatively high. This is explained by a relatively high rate of benefit recipients who cannot afford co-payments for nursing homes: about one-third of all nursing home residents receive means- and wealth-tested social assistance.

Since 2000, LTCI spending on institutional care has been gradually replaced by spending on home-based care and support for informal caregivers (figure 4.12). Thus, while about 46 percent of spending went to inpatient care in 2000, by 2020 this share fell to 31 percent.

In our next step, we focus on the costs of informal care. These costs are more difficult to quantify since a large share of care is unpaid and care provision is unregistered. Two main approaches are used for the quantification: opportunity cost method and HHA (home help assistant) cost method. The opportunity cost method estimates the opportunity cost of time of caregivers, while the HHA cost method uses the average cost of (comparable)

Table 4.20 **Formal care costs, annual, Germany, 2019**

Types	Number of users (65+)	Total spending (billion euro)
Nursing home	689,698	31
Home health agency	2,379,039	30

Source: Number of users for formal care come from BMG 2019. Total spending was adjusted for spending for people aged 65 and older. Expenditures from system of health accounts https://www.gbe-bund.de.

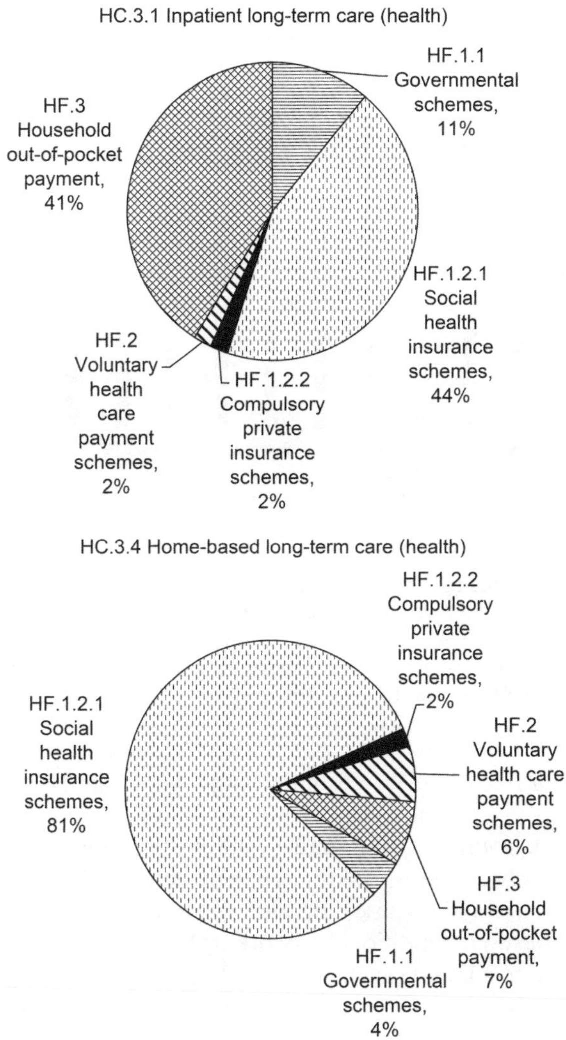

Fig. 4.11 Percent spent on home health care and nursing care facilities, by source of funds, 2019

Notes: Data come from the system of health accounts. HC denotes "Health care functions" and HF stands for "Financing Agents."

Source: System of Health Accounts (2019) (https://www.gbe-bund.de/gbe/)

formal caregiver to obtain an estimate of informal caregiver cost. These are the costs to pay for a professionnal instead of an informal caregiver. We use two approaches to give a lower and an upper bound for HHA estimates. HHA (1) uses the minimum wage for a home help assistant while HHA (2) uses the average wage of a trained home care nurse.

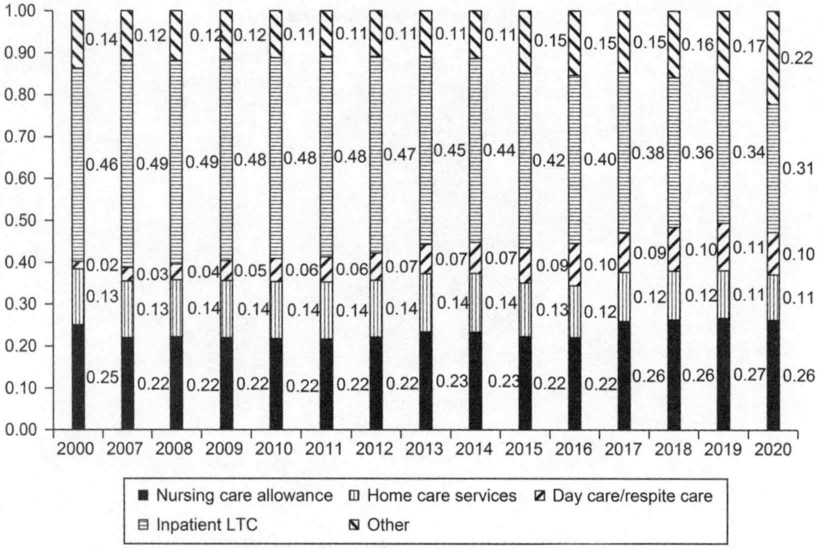

Fig. 4.12 LTCI spending on institutional care has been gradually replaced by spending on home-based care and support for informal caregiver, 2000–2020

Note: The category "other" includes, e.g., pension contributions for informal caregiver (5 percent) and a contribution to a provident fund to support future expenditures.

Source: Federal Ministry of Health

We use data from SOEP to estimate employment and wage equations based on a set of characteristics of caregivers (age, sex, education, region, migration background, marital status, working experience, unemployment experience, number of kids, health, and if the person in need of care lives in the same household). These data allow us to predict the probability of working and the wage conditional on working for each caregiver. Two methods are applied to compute such numbers. The first one is the "opportunity cost" method. It consists in multiplying each caregiver's hours provided by their predicted wage times and their probability of working. Using this method, the average caregiver wage would be 18.60 euros per hour if they were to work, but only about 60 percent of all caregivers would work if they did not provide care. The unconditional hourly wage is at 10.9 euros. The second method is the "HHA." In this method, we add the informal care hours multiplied by the probability of not working and multiplied by (1) the minimum wage of a home help assistant (12.50 euro/hour) and (2) at the average wage of a nurse working for a home health agency (16.90 euro/hour). Finally, we multiply the cost estimates by 0.76, which is the fraction of home care recipients who are over age 65.

As a result of these methods, the total cost of informal care ranges from 29 to 47.4 billion euros per year (table 4.21).

Table 4.21 **Informal care valuation**

	Estimation approach		
	opportunity cost	HHA (1)	HHA (2)
Total Valuation (LTC recipients 65+, in billion euros per year)	29	42.6	47.4
Total Valuation (in billion euros per year)	38.2	56.1	62.4
Total Hours Informal Help (billion hours per year)	3.5	3.5	3.5
E(Work)	0.59	0.59	0.59
E(Work) ∗ E(Wage)	10.9		
Hours of Working Caregiver (billion per year)	1.4	1.4	1.4
Hours of Non-Working Caregiver (billion per year)	2.1	2.1	2.1
E(Wage | employed)	18.6		
Minimum wage home care worker		12.5	
Average wage home care nurse			16.9

Notes: Opportunity costs with wage estimation based on SOEP (data from 2019); we value hours of working and non-working caregivers with predicted wage times probability of working. HHA (1) adds informal care hours multiplied by the minimum wage for a home care worker without experience multiplied by the probability of not working. In the HHA (2) approach we use the average wage of home care nurses (see table 4.15) multiplied by the probability of not working.

Source: SOEPv36

Finally, by combining results of tables 4.20 and 4.21 (column HHA 1), we can compute the total cost of both formal and informal care and disentangle between cost publicly and privately supported (table 4.22). It shows that the cost of a nursing home is largely publicly financed (60 percent) while the cost of home care is mostly publicly financed (83 percent). This changes if we add opportunity costs of informal care. Here we assume the HHA (1) approach and value provided hours using the minimum wage of a home help assistant. This results in an estimate of about 60 billion euros per year, i.e., about 41 percent of total expenditures. All in all, the majority of long-term care cost is privately funded (58 percent of all costs). If we apply the opportunity cost approach, the estimation would be slightly smaller. If we assume a higher hourly wage rate as in HHA (2), the estimated share of private financing would be even higher. We also show expenditures relative to GDP. Total expenditures amount to between 2.6 percent and 3 percent of GDP if we include cost of informal care, which amounts to between 0.8 percent and 1.2 percent of GDP depending on the valuation approach.

4.5 Conclusion

The population in Germany is among the oldest in the world, and it is expected to continue increasing, resulting in a strong increase in the share of people aged 85 and older. This has severe consequences for the organization and the financing of long-term care. To better understand the challenges for the long-term care system in the next decades, this chapter provides

Table 4.22 Total costs in billion euro by type of care and source, 2019

		Opportunity cost			
Care Type	Source	Cost (billio euros)	% of GDP	HHA (1)	% of GDP
Nursing Home	Public	18,3	0,53	18,3	0,53
	Private	12,7	0,37	12,7	0,37
	All	31	0,90	31	0,90
Home Care	Public	25	0,73	25	0,73
	Private	5	0,15	5	0,15
	All	30	0,87	30	0,87
Informal Care	Private	29	0,84	42,6	1,24
Total	Public	43,3	1,26	43,3	1,26
	Private	46,7	1,36	60,3	1,75
	All	90	2,62	103,6	3,02

Source: Own calculations based on table 4.21 (opportunity cost approach and HHA (1)) and System of Health Accounts (2019) (https://www.gbe-bund.de/gbe/). Germany's GDP amounted to 3,436 billion euros in 2019. Total spending was adjusted for spending for people aged 65 and older.

an overview of the current state of long-term care and the long-term care system in Germany.

About 60 percent of the population aged 85 or older report having limitations in ADLs and/or IADLs; more than 15 percent report three or more limitations in ADLs. We show that financial resources are distributed very unequally within this age group. We observe no or relatively low levels of wealth for the lower half of the income distribution. The data also suggest that individuals with lower incomes are more likely to have limitations in ADLs. This corresponds to a higher poverty risk, which is about 10 percentage points higher for individuals with more than three limitations as compared to the average poverty risk in their age group. We find also evidence of a higher risk to suffer from depression. For those aged 85 and over, the average prevalence is 37 percent, which is 10 percentage points higher than for the 65+ population. It increases to 59 percent for those individuals who have more than three limitations. These general patterns are further supported by measures of quality of life and loneliness where life quality decreases with age and limitations and loneliness increases with age and limitations.

Nearly 50 percent of all individuals older than 65 receive some type of care. Their share increases to 80 percent for the group of individuals older than 85. The age gradient persists when focusing on individuals with one ADL. Among those with two or more ADLs, the share of individuals receiving care is above 90 percent, irrespective of age. Unpaid informal care inside or outside the household is at 54 percent, most common for individuals older than 65. Only 7 percent live in a nursing home. At the age of 85 or older, about 17 percent of those individuals who need care reside in a nursing home while the share of informal care as the only source of care is reduced to 21 percent. The type of care also strongly depends on the health status and the number of limitations in IADLs and ADLs.

Formal care is provided either in nursing homes or as ambulatory care through home health agencies. Since 1990, spending on long-term care relative to GDP has been constantly increasing from about 1 percent to 2 percent in 2019, when the total cost of nursing home and home health agency for the 65+ reached 60 billion euros. Half of this amount is for nursing homes, while it covers only 22.5 percent of elderly using these institutions. Formal care is mostly financed by compulsory public long-term care insurance, which was introduced in 1995 and has been extended since, while private long-term care insurance only plays a minor role in financing the long-term care system. In addition, co-payments for nursing homes are required and a large part of care services is provided informally by family members. Out-of-pocket spending differs greatly between modes of care. Out-of-pocket expenditures make up only about 7 percent of total expenditures for home care. In nursing homes, 41 percent of expenditures are out-of-pocket payments.

Individuals eligible for benefits from the public long-term care insurance are classified into one of five care levels. Both psychological and physical limitations are integrated in the assessment, which is carried out by the medical advisory service of the statutory health insurance funds. Recipients can choose among different benefits: cash benefits, benefits in kind, and benefits for nursing homes. Additionally, multiple schemes have been designated to relieve relatives who provide care.

Most formal care providers have some formal qualification. The share of trained nurses in ambulatory care is close to 50 percent and lower (35 percent) in nursing homes. In 2019, Germany had 15,380 nursing homes. This capacity is sufficient for roughly 40 percent of the population aged 85+. There is no large regional variation in occupancy rates or number of beds.

Informal care is also a large part of the LTC supply. The elderly aged 65+ (resp. 85+) declare 2.32 times (resp. 1.8) more informal than formal caregivers for help with ADLs and IADLs.

According to our results, nearly 60 percent of the cost of nursing home care is publicly financed, while more than 80 percent of the cost of home care is publicly financed. In addition, we estimate total expenditures for formal and informal care by estimating a price for provided informal care. If included in the calculation, informal care amounts to about 40 percent of total expenditures. According to this calculation, the value of informal care amounts to about 1 percent of GDP. That is, the majority of long-term care spending, about 60 percent of all costs, is private. Given that part of the expenditures on home care consists of the long-term care allowance, one could argue that this aims to cover the cost of informal care. According to our estimates, the value of informal care ranges between 29 and 47 billion euros per year. The expenditures on the nursing care allowance amounted to about 12 billion in 2019. In addition, the long-term care insurance paid about 2.4 billion euros on pension contributions for caregivers. Even this rough comparison shows that, by and large, informal care is provided without or with low financial compensation.

Rising demand for long-term care raises challenges for public policy. One option is to further increase public spending via financing through social security contributions or the tax system. These are, however, already high in an aging Germany. Since private long-term care insurance in Germany is still of minor importance, as documented in this chapter, there may be greater opportunities to expand it than public insurance. This is recommended by the Council of Advisors to the German Economics Ministry. The introduction of a compulsory private long-term care insurance program would increase the financial stability of the German social security system but may have negative distributional effects. Direct subsidies might be needed if the goal is to make sure that households with low incomes can afford to buy private insurance plans.

There may also be calls for government programs to increase the supply of long-term care providers. Given that the work force is aging and that a shortage of labor is already a concern in many sectors, this is a big challenge for formal care provision. It is likely that the importance of informal care will further increase. Government policies could support such care by allowing for combining informal care provision with full- or part-time employment.

References

Börsch-Supan, Axel, Martina Brandt, Christian Hunkler, Thorsten Kneip, Julie Korbmacher, Frederic Malter, Barbara Schaan, Stephanie Stuck, Sabrina Zuber, on behalf of the SHARE Central Coordination Team, Data Resource Profile. 2013. "The Survey of Health, Ageing and Retirement in Europe (SHARE)." *International Journal of Epidemiology* 42 (4): 992–1001. https://doi.org/10.1093/ije/dyt088.

BMG. 2019. "Bundesministerium für Gesundheit, Pflegeversicherung, Zahlen und Fakten" https://www.bundesgesundheitsministerium.de/themen/pflege/pflegeversicherung-zahlen-und-fakten.html.

Bundesagentur für Arbeit. 2022. "Statistik Der Bundesagentur Für Arbeit. Berichte: Blickpunkt Arbeitsmarkt—Arbeitsmarktsituation Im Pflegebereich." Nürnberg. https://statistik.arbeitsagentur.de/DE/Statischer-Content/Statistiken/Themen-im-Fokus/Berufe/Generische-Publikationen/Altenpflege.pdf?__blob=publicationFile.

Carstensen, Jeanette, Holger Seibert, and Doris Wiethölter. 2019. "Entgelte von Pflegekräften 2020." IAB Aktuelle Daten und Indikatoren. http://doku.iab.de/arbeitsmarktdaten/Entgelte_von_Pflegekraeften_2019.pdf.

Destatis. 2019. "Bevölkerung: Deutschland, Stichtag, Altersjahre," Tabelle 12411–0005, https://www.destatis.de/DE/Home/_inhalt.html.

Geyer, Johannes. 2015. "Einkommen und Vermögen der Pflegehaushalte in Deutschland." *DIW Wochenbericht* 82 (14/15): 323–28. Available online: https://www.diw.de/documents/publikationen/73/diw_01.c.499956.de/15–14–1.pdf.

Geyer, Johannes, Peter Haan, Hannes Kröger, and Maximilian Schaller. 2021. "Need for Long-Term Care Depends on Social Standing." *DIW Weekly Report* 44/45: 339–46. Available online: https://www.diw.de/documents/publikationen/73/diw_01.c.827855.de/dwr-21–44–1.pdf.

Geyer, Johannes, Thorben Korfhage, and Erika Schulz. 2016. "Andere Länder, andere Wege: Pflege im internationalen Vergleich." *Gesundheits- Und Sozialpolitik* 70 (1): 52–58. https://doi.org/10.5771/1611–5821–2016–1–52.

Goebel, Jan, Markus M. Grabka, Stefan Liebig, Martin Kroh, David Richter, Carsten Schröder, and Jürgen Schupp. 2019. "The German Socio-Economic Panel (SOEP)." *Jahrbücher für Nationalökonomie und Statistik* 239 (2): 345–60. https://doi.org/10.1515/jbnst-2018–0022.

Hughes, Mary Elizabeth, Linda J. Waite, Louise C. Hawkley, and John T. Cacioppo. 2004. "A Short Scale for Measuring Loneliness in Large Surveys: Results from Two Population-Based Studies." *Research on Aging* 26 (6): 655–72. https://doi.org/10.1177/0164027504268574.

Lehnert, T., O. H. Günther, A. Hajek, S. G. Riedel-Heller, and H. H. König. 2018. "Preferences for Home- and Community-Based Long-Term Care Services in Germany: A Discrete Choice Experiment." *European Journal of Health Economics* 19 (9): 1213–23. https://doi.org/10.1007/s10198–018–0968–0.

Mehrbrodt, Tabea, Stefan Gruber, and Melanie Wagner. 2019. "Scales and Multi-Item Indicators in the Survey of Health, Ageing and Retirement in Europe." SHARE Working Paper Series 45–2019. 2019. Available online: http://www.share-project.org/uploads/tx_sharepublications/WP_Series_45_2019_Scales_and_Multi-Item_Indicators.pdf.

Mueller, M., E. Bourke, and D. Morgan. 2020. "Assessing the Comparability of Long-Term Care Spending Estimates under the Joint Health Accounts Questionnaire." Paris: OECD.

Nadash, Pamela, Pamela Doty, and Matthias von Schwanenflügel. 2018. "The German Long-Term Care Insurance Program: Evolution and Recent Developments." *Gerontologist* 58 (3): 588–97. https://doi.org/10.1093/geront/gnx018.

OECD. 2017. *A System of Health Accounts 2011 Revised Edition: Revised Edition*. OECD publishing.

OECD. 2019. "Old-Age Income Inequality." In *Pensions at a Glance 2019: OECD and G20 Indicators*. Paris: OECD Publishing. DOI: https://doi.org/10.1787/b00d8f0e-en.

OECD/Eurostat/WHO. 2017. *A System of Health Accounts 2011*, Revised edition. Paris: OECD Publishing. https://doi.org/10.1787/9789264270985-en.

Rothgang, Heinz, and Thomas Kalwitzki. 2016. "Auswirkungen des neuen Pflegebedürftigkeitsbegriffs." *Das Gesundheitswesen* 78 (8/9): A143. https://doi.org/10.1055/s-0036–1586653.

Rudel, Miriam, Martin Abraham, and Edmund Görtler. 2017. "Pflegepräferenzen und regionale Mobilität." *Zeitschrift für Gerontologie und Geriatrie* 50 (3): 200–209. https://doi.org/10.1007/s00391–015–0991-z.

Russell, D., Peplau, L. A., and Ferguson, M. L. 1978. "Developing a Measure of Loneliness." *Journal of Personality Assessment* 42(3), 290–294. https://doi.org/10.1207/s15327752jpa4203_11.

Schulz, Erika. 2010. "The Long-Term Care System in Germany." Discussion Papers

of DIW Berlin 1039. Available online: http://ideas.repec.org/p/diw/diwwpp/dp1039.html.
Schupp, Jürgen, and Harald Künemund. 2004. "Private Versorgung Und Betreuung von Pflegebedürftigen in Deutschland: Überraschend Hohes Pflegeengagement Älterer Männer." *Wochenbericht* 71 (20): 289–94.
System of Health Accounts. 2019. https://www.gbe-bund.de/gbe/.

5 Long-Term Care in Italy

Agar Brugiavini, Ludovico Carrino, and Giacomo Pasini

5.1 Introduction

The provision of long-term care (LTC) for the Italian older population is at the center of the recent policy debate. Italy has witnessed a spectacular increase in the share of people aged 65 and over, and in particular, of people aged 80 and over, especially women, which could translate into large increases in the number of people in need of care. At the same time, the

Agar Brugiavini is a professor of economics at Ca' Foscari University of Venice.

Ludovico Carrino is an associate professor of public economics at the University of Trieste and a visiting professor at King's College London.

Giacomo Pasini is a professor of econometrics and head of the economics department at Ca' Foscari University of Venice, and a research fellow at NETSPAR.

The authors are grateful to Rinaldo Naci (Ca' Foscari University of Venezia) for the support in data analysis and text revision. This paper uses data from SHARE Waves 1, 2, 3, 4, 5, 6, 7, 8 and 9 (DOIs: 10.6103/SHARE.w1.800, 10.6103/SHARE.w2.800, 10.6103/SHARE.w3.800, 10.6103/SHARE.w4.800, 10.6103/SHARE.w5.800, 10.6103/SHARE.w6.800, 10.6103/SHARE.w7.800, 10.6103/SHARE.w8.800, 10.6103/SHARE.w8ca.800, 10.6103/SHARE.w9ca800). See Börsch-Supan et al. (2013) for methodological details. The SHARE data collection has been funded by the European Commission, DG RTD through FP5 (QLK6-CT-2001–00360), FP6 (SHARE-I3: RII-CT-2006–062193, COMPARE: CIT5-CT-2005–028857, SHARELIFE: CIT4-CT-2006–028812), FP7 (SHARE-PREP: GA N°211909, SHARE-LEAP: GA N°227822, SHARE M4: GA N°261982, DASISH: GA N°283646) and Horizon 2020 (SHARE-DEV3: GA N°676536, SHARE-COHESION: GA N°870628, SERISS: GA N°654221, SSHOC: GA N°823782, SHARE-COVID19: GA N°101015924) and by DG Employment, Social Affairs & Inclusion through VS 2015/0195, VS 2016/0135, VS 2018/0285, VS 2019/0332, and VS 2020/0313. Additional funding from the German Ministry of Education and Research, the Max Planck Society for the Advancement of Science, the US National Institute on Aging (U01_AG09740–13S2, P01_AG005842, P01_AG08291, P30_AG12815, R21_AG025169, Y1-AG-4553–01, IAG_BSR06–11, OGHA_04–064, HHSN271201300071C, RAG052527A) and from various national funding sources is gratefully acknowledged (see www.share-project.org). For acknowledgments, sources of research support, and disclosure of the authors' material financial relationships, if any, please see https://www.nber.org/books-and-chapters/long-term-care-around-world/long-term-care-italy.

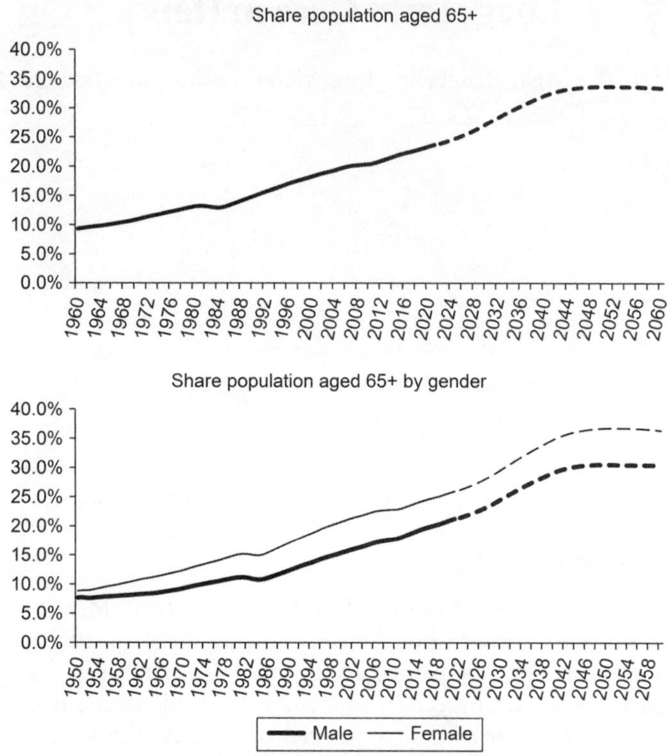

Fig. 5.1 Percentage of population aged 65 or older, Italy, 1950–2060

Source: OECD Stat, https://stats.oecd.org/Index.aspx?DataSetCode=POPPROJ. Graphs based on the historical population data and population projections of the OECD.

Italian long-term care framework is highly relying on the informal support of families, and especially women, and characterized by a substantial underground economy of unskilled carers. The public formal care system is mostly decentralized at regional level, so that both funding and eligibility rules to access care vary greatly across regions, while the private market for LTC insurance is still very limited (European Commission 2021).

The demographic transition is exemplified by figure 5.1: the trends for the prevalence (percentage) of individuals aged 65 and over as a whole or by sex (estimated by the OECD 2022 Population Prospects) increase from less than 10 percent in the 1950s to more than 20 percent in 2019, with an expectation of reaching at least 30 percent (for men) and 36 percent (for women) in 2060. Such transition will also see a large increase in the population of oldest old (85+): figure 5.2 shows that the prevalence of people aged 85 and over (as a percentage of the population 65+) will grow from the current value of 13 percent to 24 percent in 2060 for men, and from 19 percent to 32 percent for women.

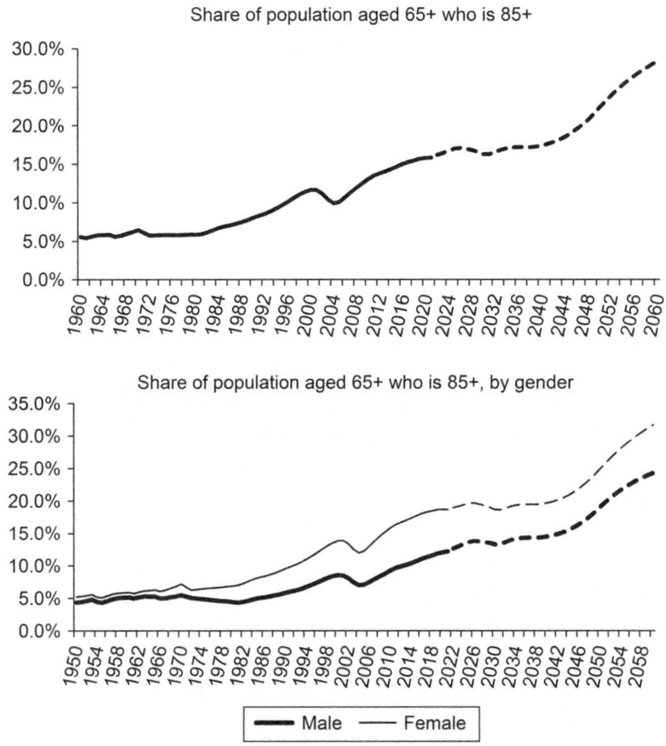

Fig. 5.2 Percentage of 65+ population aged 85 or older, Italy, 1950–2060
Source: OECD Stat, https://stats.oecd.org/Index.aspx?DataSetCode=POPPROJ. Graphs based on the historical population data and population projections of the OECD.

Several studies attempted to estimate how many years for the "gained" lifetime translate into time spent in good health, rather than into years of increased loss of autonomy and diseases. Among advanced economies, time spent in disability and with loss of autonomy is narrowing with population aging, while years with chronic diseases are increasing (Chatterji et al. 2015). Crucially for this paper, the picture for Italy is more worrisome, as recent studies have shown evidence of expansion of morbidity both in terms of loss of autonomy (among the main determinants of LTC use) and of chronic diseases supporting the expansion of morbidity hypothesis (Atella et al. 2018; Chatterji et al. 2015). Nonetheless, the aforementioned predictions offer only a partial perspective, as the future paths of morbidity will also depend on the success of promoting and implementing active aging policies (Barbabella et al. 2020; Kaeberlein et al. 2015; Rechel et al. 2013).

Such aging dynamics suggest that actual and potential demand for long-term care services in Italy will increase due to increasing prevalence of ill health and functional limitations with activities of daily living (ADL) and instrumental ADL (IADL) (European Commission 2021). However, documenting whether the supply of LTC can keep up with the increase in demand is more challenging. As we already stated, the public provision of LTC is highly decentralized, as the governance of the health care system is run on a regional basis. The services range from in-kind provisions to cash transfers following patterns that may vary even at the municipality level. Older individuals who need care often rely on professional caregivers who offer home services or even reside with the beneficiary paid out of pocket, but there is also a large "informal" long-term care component. It is often the case that older people make use of a mixture of public and private provision, plus informal care offered by relatives in order to meet their care needs (Gori and Fernandez 2015; Hashiguchi and Llena-Nozal 2020). The debate over the effectiveness and the sustainability of the Italian LTC is exemplified by a legislative discussion which has led to a new Enabling Law (Legge Delega n.33/23rd March 2023), that will potentially lead to a full restructuring of the public LTC setting.

In this chapter we present a novel description of the long-term care system in Italy. We rely on data from the Italian sample of the Survey of Health, Ageing and Retirement in Europe (SHARE), and, to a minor extent, on aggregate statistics from the United Nations, Eurostat, and the Italian Office for National Statistics (ISTAT).

Three major findings emerge from our study. First, frail older people have little financial means to pay out of pocket for their care, which is concerning given the prospects of an increase in demand for care in the future. Second, we document how publicly provided care is highly fragmented with stark differences in terms of coverage and generosity across Italian regions. Third, the largest fraction of long-term care is supplied informally, both in terms of quantity of services provided and in terms of (imputed) costs. Our findings highlight important lessons that can be drawn from the Italian case study, which are particularly relevant for policymakers and public health experts in both mature and developing economies.

5.2 Aging, Disability, and Well-Being

5.2.1 Data and Definitions

The primary source of data for our analysis is the Survey of Health, Ageing and Retirement in Europe (SHARE). This is a research infrastructure for studying the effects of health and socio-economic policies over the life course of European citizens, designed to be comparable with the US sister survey Health and Retirement Study (HRS) and the English Longitudinal Study of Ageing (ELSA). The SHARE survey, which is still ongoing, provides information on demographics and family structure, activities, income and wealth, health and long-term care needs. Since its first wave (2004), and up to wave 8 (2020), 616,000 in-depth interviews were performed with 160,000 people aged 50 or older from 28 European countries plus Israel, including Italy. In this chapter, we use data from SHARE wave 6 (which ran in Italy in 2015) and wave 7 (run in 2017). When focusing on "LTC beneficiaries," we refer to a subsample of respondents aged 65 or older in 2015.

Our baseline data sample includes 3,102 individuals, and we use the SHARE cross-sectional survey weights to compute our calculations and estimate the population correctly. However, those weights are designed to make the SHARE sample representative of the Italian population aged 50 and over, without taking into account the subgroup of older individuals who are living permanently in a nursing home. Although individuals who were previous respondents in SHARE are still interviewed even if they start to be residents of nursing homes, the survey under-represents this particular group.[1] This is a common issue in the HRS-family surveys. In the appendix, we provide details on the adjusted cross-sectional weights to reduce this problem. The procedure we follow is conceptually the same as it is done for England in chapter 3.

The key measures of health used in our analysis are based on self-reported limitations in ADL and IADL. ADL includes tasks such as walking across room, dressing, bathing, eating, going to bed, and using the toilet. IADL includes using a map to move around in an unknown place, preparing hot meals, shopping for groceries, making telephone calls, taking medications, doing work around the house or garden, managing money, doing personal laundry, and other unspecified difficulties. The respondent can select any of these 15 items if they report difficulties due to a physical, mental, emotional, or memory problem that they expect to last for more than three months. Although SHARE does not ask the precise extent to which a respondent is limited with the selected task, we consider the respondents to be significantly impaired for the activities that they reported to have difficulty with.

Table 5.1 presents the distribution of the number of limitations by age groups: overall, 18.7 percent of sample has at least one limitation in ADL, but important differences in the prevalence of limitations emerge when looking at the different age groups. Most individuals aged 65 and over have no limitations, while 10.6 percent report no ADL limitations but at least one IADL limitation. Among individuals aged 85 and over, 36.2 percent report no limitations, 14.1 percent report difficulties in IADLs but not in ADLs, and as many as 49.7 percent have at least one ADL deficit.

Table 5.2 reports the distribution of the specific types of ADL or IADL limitations for the age groups 65 and over, and 85 and over. We also report the distribution of ADL and IADL limitations, conditional on reporting

1. The probability of being in a nursing home conditional on age 65+ computed SHARE wave 6 data using cross-sectional weights is 0.0125, while if we take the same statistic computed on the Italian population by ISTAT, the percentage rises to 0.0218.

Table 5.1 **Percentage of 65+ and 85 population with difficulties in ADLs and IADL, Italy, 2015**

# of ADLs	65+, percent	85+, percent
0 ADLs & 0 IADLs	0.707	0.362
0 ADLs & 1+ IADLs	0.106	0.141
1 ADL	0.069	0.147
2 ADLs	0.037	0.071
3 ADLs	0.018	0.050
4 ADLs	0.017	0.056
5 ADLs	0.023	0.085
6 ADLs	0.025	0.089
Any ADLs	0.187	0.497
Any IADLs	0.260	0.603
Obs	3,102	265

Source: Data are from the SHARE Wave 6 (2015). ADLs include walking across room, dressing, bathing, eating, going to bed, and using the toilet. IADLs include using a map in a strange place, preparing a hot meal, shopping for groceries, telephone calls, taking medications, doing work around the house or garden, managing money, doing personal laundry, and unspecified difficulties. Weights used are adjusted to match national aggregates of the nursing home residents (see appendix).

Table 5.2 **Percentage of 65+ and 85+ population with difficulties in ADLs and IADLs, Italy, 2015**

	65+ All	65+ Conditional	85+ All	85+ Conditional
		Panel 1: IADLs		
Preparing hot meal	0.089	0.342	0.313	0.520
Shopping for groceries	0.134	0.516	0.378	0.627
Telephone calls	0.065	0.249	0.237	0.393
Taking medications	0.072	0.275	0.252	0.417
Managing money	0.093	0.357	0.316	0.524
Obs	3092	667	265	150
		Panel 2: ADLs		
Dressing	0.131	0.699	0.338	0.680
Walking across room	0.061	0.327	0.171	0.344
Bathing	0.138	0.737	0.452	0.909
Eating	0.051	0.271	0.175	0.351
Getting in/out of bed	0.083	0.442	0.270	0.543
Using the toilet	0.061	0.327	0.215	0.433
Obs	3,092	467	265	126

Source: Data are from the SHARE Wave 6 (2015). Column 1 shows the share of the sample that report having difficulty with each activity, while Column 2 shows the share of people with at least 1 IADL (panel 1) or at least 1 ADL (panel 2) who report having difficulty with each activity. Weights used are adjusted to match national aggregates of nursing home residents (see appendix).

Table 5.3 **Well-being for those 65+ and 85+ by ADL limitations (percentage), Italy, 2015**

	65+	65+ with 3+ Lims	85+	85+ with 3+ Lims
Income below poverty line	0.170	0.205	0.239	0.258
Self-report of health—good or better	0.451	0.060	0.221	0.066
Depressed during the last month	0.380	0.777	0.549	0.750
Observations	3,102	301	265	94

Source: Data are from the SHARE Wave 6 (2015). Our Limitations Index runs from 0–12 and is the number of ADLs/IADLs that are either difficult or not done for eating, bathing, dressing, using the toilet, walking across a room, and getting in/out of bed (ADLs) + using a telephone, managing money, taking medications as prescribed, shopping for groceries, and cooking a hot meal (IADLs). Poverty line is fixed at 50 percent of the median income. The depression variable used is the generated EURO-D by SHARE, which is based on a set of 16 variables that collect information on mental health in the last month before the interview; for this we identify as "Depressed" an individual with EURO-D>3. Weights used are adjusted to match national aggregates of nursing home residents (see appendix).

at least one limitation. The most frequent ADL limitations relate to ability to bathe and dress for both age groups. Respondents aged 65 or older are most likely to report problems with shopping for groceries. When we restrict the analysis to the group 85 or older, respondents are most likely to report difficulties with preparing hot meals and managing their money.

5.2.2 Well-Being

In order to understand the patterns of provision and utilization of long-term care for older people in Italy, it is important to provide a contextual analysis of the economic well-being of the population that might be in need of care. The relationship between health and economic well-being is an important research area *per se*, but it is of particular relevance when looking at older people, as it can determine major differences across groups, including inequalities in access to care (Floridi et al. 2021).

Hence, to properly describe these mechanisms, we first present a general overview of the socioeconomic situation of older people and their households in Italy by the number and type of limitations. Table 5.3 presents the association between the presence of three or more limitations in ADL (or IADL) and economic well-being. The first row of the table compares the poverty rate in the full sample and among respondents with at least three functional limitations (ADL or IADL): overall 17 percent of the older people have incomes below the poverty line, while 20.5 percent of individuals who report at least three difficulties are "poor." In the second and third rows of table 5.3 we report the association between physical and emotional/cognitive health status of the respondent by age group and degree of limitations. There is a clear negative gradient of health by age, as the percentage of individuals who report a "good or better physical health status" drops from

Table 5.4 **Income and wealth distribution, Italy 2015**

	Income 65+	Income 85+	Wealth 65+	Wealth 85+
5th Percentile	263	263	0	0
10th Percentile	3,383	1,664	2,058	0
25th Percentile	7,656	6,174	56,235	12,942
50th Percentile	11,936	10,290	112,504	174,930
75th Percentile	16,226	14,200	205,800	316,932
90th Percentile	22,912	18,385	324,478	411,600
95th Percentile	28,126	22,226	445,214	411,600
Observations	3,102	265	3,102	265

Source: Data are from the SHARE Wave 6 (2015). Both income and wealth are at household level and post-tax. Mean income for 65+ (85+) €13,164 (€10,686) and Mean Wealth €152,230 (€13,3417). Weights used are adjusted to match national aggregates of the nursing home residents (see appendix). All values are adjusted to 2019 euros.

45.1 percent in the full sample to 22.1 percent among the older group (85+). The same pattern emerges with respect to the prevalence of depression, which is substantially higher among people 85+ than in the overall sample.

A more focused analysis is presented in table 5.4 and table 5.5, where we look at income distribution and wealth distribution. The income measure and wealth measure are obtained as "generated variables" in SHARE, i.e. these are, for each respondent, the result of the aggregation of the different income (wealth) items, and, at the household level, the sum of all incomes (wealth) of all household members. In particular, total household income is obtained by aggregating all individuals' net income components, while household net worth is generated by aggregating household real assets and household net financial assets. We normalize each measure using the OECD equivalence scale.[2]

Table 5.4 shows the unconditional distribution of income and wealth, by age groups, for older individuals: these are slightly skewed distributions, quite similar to what was observed for the Italian population at large. For example, for the age group 65+, the mean value of income is €13,164, which is slightly higher than the median value of €11,936. When we turn to table 5.5, we observe large disparities in the income and wealth distribution by number of limitations. Each column of the table sums to 100 and shows the distribution of income (wealth) in each limitation category. Both income and wealth of individuals with no limitations appear as "evenly" distributed. The percentage of individuals falling in the two poorest categories (i.e., less than 50 percent of median income/wealth; and between 50 percent and 100 percent of the median income/wealth) is slightly higher than 45 percent in both distributions. However, when focusing on individuals affected by

2. We use the "OECD-modified equivalence scale." This scale assigns a value of 1 to the household head, 0.5 to each additional adult member, and 0.3 to each child.

Table 5.5 **Income and wealth distribution by limitations for 65+ (percentage), Italy, 2015**

	0 ADLs & 0 IADLs	0 ADLs & 1+ IADLs	1 ADL	2 ADLs	3+ ADLs	Total
	Panel 1: Income					
<50% median income	0.147	0.201	0.282	0.199	0.227	0.170
50%–100% median income	0.308	0.449	0.407	0.306	0.304	0.329
100–150% median income	0.311	0.242	0.193	0.356	0.300	0.296
150–200% median income	0.128	0.060	0.081	0.090	0.116	0.115
200%+ median income	0.106	0.049	0.037	0.049	0.053	0.089
Total	0.707	0.106	0.069	0.037	0.083	
Obs	2,327	305	184	95	191	
	Panel 2: Wealth					
<50% median wealth	0.206	0.3107	0.391	0.407	0.473	0.259
50%–100% median wealth	0.246	0.2796	0.233	0.192	0.223	0.245
100–150% median wealth	0.182	0.2267	0.131	0.176	0.117	0.178
150–200% median wealth	0.147	0.0602	0.074	0.095	0.055	0.123
200%+ median wealth	0.219	0.1228	0.171	0.131	0.131	0.195
Total	0.707	0.106	0.069	0.037	0.083	
Obs	2,327	305	184	95	191	

Source: Data are from the SHARE Wave 6 (2015). Each cell reports the share of respondents in the respective ADL/IADLs category who are in that row's income group. The median household income, based on the sample distribution, is €11,936, while median household wealth is €112,504. Weights used are adjusted to match national aggregates of nursing home residents (see appendix). All values are adjusted to 2019 euros.

any number of limitations, income and wealth distributions are more concentrated in the poorest groups. For example, in the group reporting more than three limitations in ADL, around 53 percent are in the poorest income groups, and 69.6 percent are in the poorest wealth groups.

5.3 Long-Term Care System in Italy

As shown in section 5.2, Italy faces a significant challenge in supplying adequate long-term care to an increasing fraction of older individuals. In this section we provide an overview of the main pillars of social protection for vulnerable older people in Italy, ranging from public interventions to substantial family provisions, and to limited private markets.

By using the SHARE data we can investigate the use of formal versus informal help or care. In particular, formal help/care includes personal care services (e.g., getting in and out of bed, dressing, bathing and showering), help with domestic tasks (e.g., cleaning, ironing, cooking), meals-on-wheels (i.e., ready-made meals provided by a municipality or a private provider), and help with other activities (e.g., filling a drug dispenser). Informal help/

Table 5.6 Distribution of hours of help received per week, Italy, 2015

	65+	85+
5th Percentile	<1	<1
10th Percentile	<1	<1
25th Percentile	2	6
50th Percentile	8	24
75th Percentile	40	40
90th Percentile	40	46
95th Percentile	46	64
Mean	19	28
1 Hour per Day or Less	0.173	0.105
5 Hour per Day or More	0.631	0.757
Observations	725	134

Source: SHARE wave 6. Respondent weights are used for all population estimate calculations. Nursing home residents are excluded. Formal help hours are imputed using data from W1 and 2 to an individual who reported to have used formal help in wave 6. Received informal help inside the household is imputed with ISTAT information and informal help outside the household is converted from the frequency: daily help as 40 hours per week, weekly help as 8 hours per week, monthly help as 2 hours per week and less often as half an hour per week.

care similarly includes personal care or services for domestic tasks; this can be further differentiated into: informal help or care received from individuals living outside the household, or personal care provided by people living in the same household (for the latter only personal care).

Table 5.6 shows the distribution of weekly hours of care received for both formal and informal care, conditional on receiving any type of care. The median number of hours of care per week received in the full sample is 8, but the mean is 19 hours and 25 percent of the population receives at least 40 hours of help per week. The data suggest that the care needs are higher for the oldest old: the median number of weekly hours of care for this group is 24, the mean is 28, and the top 5 percent of the distribution receives 64 or more hours of care per week.

In this section we focus on the public expenditure on long-term care (LTC): the overall amounts are in line with the European average, but differ from other countries in that formal cash-support comes in most cases, and for a large share of the overall benefits, from a national cash benefit (*Indennità di Accompagnamento*). The coverage of publicly subsidized home care and residential care is limited, with large differences across regions and municipalities in formal care availability and access criteria. The Italian LTC system is strongly based on informal family support and migrant care workers, often with irregular contracts (European Commission 2021; Jessoula et al. 2018).

In figure 5.3, we report the share of GDP spent on long-term care in Italy as computed by the national accounting office (*Ragioneria Generale dello*

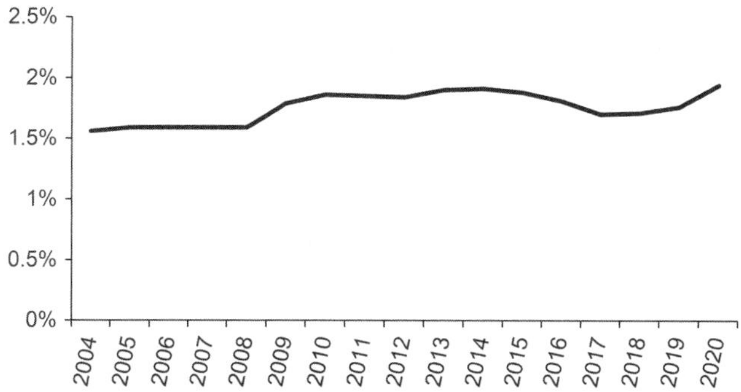

Fig. 5.3a Share of GDP spent on long-term care, Italy
Source: MEF (Ministry of Economy and Finance), https://www.rgs.mef.gov.it/VERSIONE-I/attivita_istituzionali/monitoraggio/spesa_pensionistica/, state general accounting department: mid/long-term trends for the pension, health and long-term care systems reports

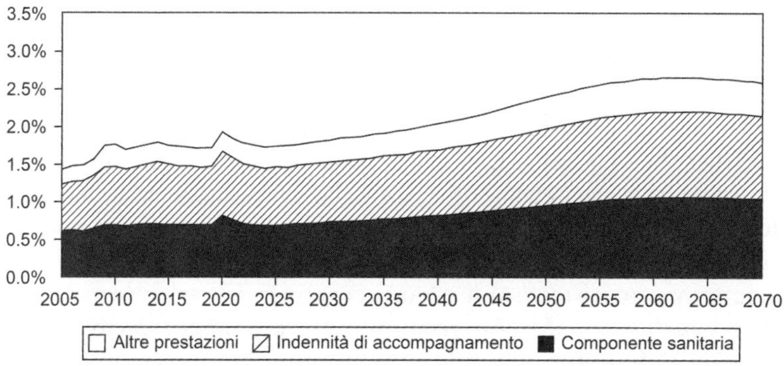

Fig. 5.3b Share of GDP spent on long-term care, Italy national baseline prospect
Source: MEF (Ministry of Economy and Finance), https://www.rgs.mef.gov.it/VERSIONE-I/attivita_istituzionali/monitoraggio/spesa_pensionistica/, state general accounting department: mid/long-term trends for the pension, health and long-term care systems reports

Stato) of the Ministry of Economics and Finance, available from 2004 to 2020. The overall aggregate includes expenditure on the health care component of long-term care, the national attendance allowance, a cash-benefit program called *Indennità di Accompagnamento*, and expenditure for other LTC provisions.[3]

Overall, the public expenditure on LTC lies between 1.5 percent of GDP in 2004 and 2 percent in 2020, with a notable increase in the years of the financial and economic crisis following the Great Recession at the end of

3. In particular, the *Indennità di Accompagnamento* is a non-means-tested cash benefit paid to dependent people. "Other LTC provisions" include heterogeneous benefits, largely in kind, provided at local level by municipalities. These are generally means-tested.

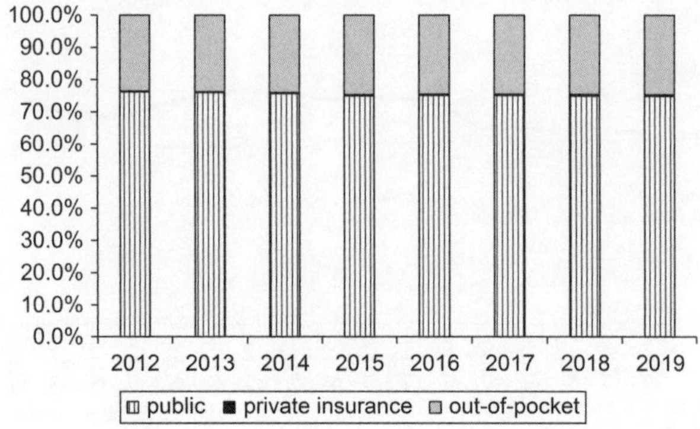

Fig. 5.4 Composition of LTC financing by source (in percentages)
Source: ISTAT—System of Health Accounts, http://dati.istat.it/index.aspx?lang=en&SubSessionId=796c45f4–7f70–43be-a3b3-eb77fef0cd9a. It provides statistics on health care expenditure and financing on the country's health system.

the 2010s. It is worth noting that this expenditure figures are higher than the those reported by the widely used OECD reports (OECD 2019), as the OECD figures only include health care–related long-term care costs. Figure 5.3a further shows how the LTC expenditure is split between its three components (health; cash benefit; other), and how it is predicted to increase in the following decades, based on simulations by the Ministry of Economics and Finance (MEF).

Long-term care is a form of insurance covering costs, which can be potentially very high, particularly in relation to the resources available to older households. In Italy, very few individuals hold private long-term care insurance, as people mostly rely on the public provisions or on out-of-pocket financing. Figure 5.4 shows the relevance of the various financing sources from 2012 to 2019. The share of expenditure covered by private insurance is basically negligible: more than 70 percent of the expenditure is financed by the government, while the remaining share is paid out of pocket by the user.[4]

Figure 5.5 shows how long-term care spending can be disentangled by type of expenditure. Long-term care expenditure in Italy is classified both according to the type of health care received and to the facilities that provide such care. The central statistical office, ISTAT, in particular the system of health accounts, provides a split of LTC expenditure into four groups: inpatient long-term care, day long-term care, outpatient long-term care, and home-based long-term care.

To back up these figures we look at the facilities that provide such long-

4. The reported statistics by the System of Health Accounts includes the final consumption expenditure of resident units on health care goods and services, including the health care goods and services provided directly to individual persons as well as collective health care services.

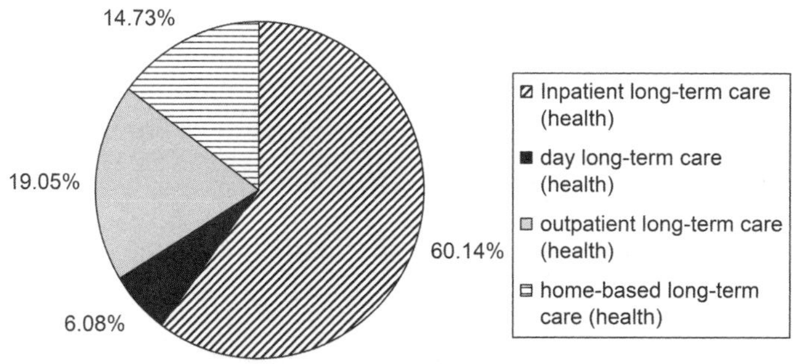

Fig. 5.5 Composition of LTC by type of long-term patient (in percentages)

Source: ISTAT—System of Health Accounts, http://dati.istat.it/index.aspx?lang=en&SubSessionId=4b1103ef-e51b-4a24–83a2-b1e7dc786251. It provides statistics on health care expenditure and financing on the country's health system.

Reproduced with permission from Fu, R., Noguchi, H. "Moral hazard under zero price policy: evidence from Japanese long-term care claims data." *Eur J Health Econ*, Volume 20, 785–99 (2019), Springer Nature.

term care services: the expenditure for inpatient long-term care (health) refers to hospitals[5] and residential long-term care facilities,[6] while for the other three types of care it refers to providers of ambulatory health care.[7] Figure 5.6 shows again the composition by type of expenditure, split between formal home care versus nursing home care, where the two categories are derived from the facilities that provide the service. The costs for care provided in nursing homes are financed by the government for 63.28 percent, while it is paid out-of-pocked for the remaining 36.39 percent. However, in the case of home-based care (nursing-care), the contribution of public funds to the total costs increases up to 92.77 percent.

5.3.1 Eligibility for Public LTC Programs

The Italian LTC in-kind or in-cash programs are mostly regulated at the regional level; the system exhibits high variability across regions in terms of

5. Hospitals (HP1): means licensed establishments that are primarily engaged in providing medical, diagnostic, and treatment services that include physician, nursing, and other health services to inpatients and the specialized accommodation services required by inpatients and which may also provide daycare, outpatient, and home health care services.

6. Residential long-term care facilities (HP2): means establishments that are primarily engaged in providing residential long-term care that combines nursing, supervisory, or other types of care as required by the residents, where a significant part of the production process and the care provided is a mix of health and social services with the health services being largely at the level of nursing care in combination with personal care services.

7. Providers of ambulatory health care (HP3): means establishments that are primarily engaged in providing health care services directly to outpatients who do not require inpatient services, including both offices of general medical practitioners and medical specialists and establishments specializing in the treatment of day cases and in the delivery of home care services.

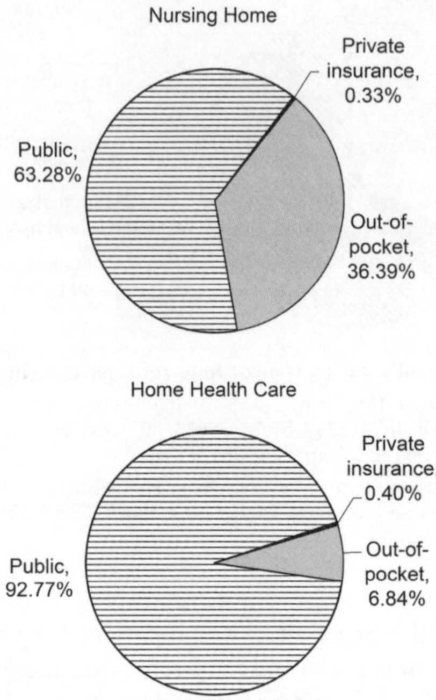

Fig. 5.6 Composition of home health care expenditure and nursing care facilities expenditure, by source of funds, Italy, 2015

Sources: ISTAT System of Health Accounts, http://dati.istat.it/index.aspx?lang=en&SubSessionId=4b1103ef-e51b-4a24-83a2-b1e7dc786251. It provides statistics on health care expenditure and financing on the country's health system. Given the categories defined by ISTAT, we include in nursing home the aggregation of HP1 and HP2, while we aggregate the other categories in home health care.

both the services provided and target population (i.e., the eligibility rules). A thorough review can be found in Brugiavini et al. (2017).

5.3.1.1 National Cash Benefit

A national cash benefit, called *Indennità di Accompagnamento* (IA), is available to individuals who are assessed as *invalid*. The definition of invalidity itself is somewhat fuzzy, as it refers to individuals who are (i) blind, (ii) physically/mentally disabled, (iii) unable to walk without continuous help, or (iv) need permanent assistance with ADL (Brugiavini et al. 2017). The assessment is performed by a health district level commission of the National Social Insurance Agency (INPS) and is initiated by the patient's general practitioner. In 2021, the IA amounted to a monthly cash benefit of €522.10 (see https://www.inps.it/prestazioni-servizi/indennita-di-accompagnamento-agli-invalidi-civili). The cash allowance is not subject to a stringent ex post monitoring, as recipients are free to choose how to spend it. This is part of a larger concern over the general lack of an established and homogeneous regulation of quality checks in the LTC governance in Italy (European Commission 2021).

5.3.1.2 Regional Programs

Most Italian regions offer specific programs of care to guarantee the minimum level of support for basic needs (*livelli essenziali di assistenza*), either in-kind or in-cash, targeting both domiciliary care and, to a lower extent, residential care. Regions obtain national funding to implement such policies, through the National Fund for the Loss of Autonomy (FNNA, *Fondo Nazionale Non Autosufficienza*) established in 2006 (Law 296/2006), complemented with region-specific funding from the Regional Funding for the Loss of Autonomy (FRNA, *Fondo Regionale per la Non Autosufficienza*) (Brugiavini et al. 2017).

The programs financed by FNNA or FRNA have two target populations: individuals with (i) extreme disabilities (*disabilità gravissima*) or (ii) with severe disabilities (*disabilità grave*). The former group includes individuals who are eligible for the IA benefit, and further have at least one additional severe condition, e.g., being minimally conscious or in intensive care, being heavily affected by dementia, living with extreme physical impairment (Brugiavini et al. 2017).

The definition of *severe* disability, which represents the minimum conditions for accessing public LTC support, is defined at regional level. Brugiavini et al. (2017) document a large variation across regions in the definition of the eligibility rules for LTC support, partially due to the absence of a unique definition of disability in the clinical literature, and to the different budget allocations which local authorities have at their disposal to fund LTC. Indeed, regions differ on the health items included in the eligibility evaluation, in the definition of an entry-level need-of-care condition, and in the unit of measurement of the need-of-care index. An example of such variation comes from the eleven regions which had set up a clear-cut definition of eligibility (Bolzano, Campania, Emilia-Romagna, Friuli–Venezia Giulia, Liguria, Lombardia, Piemonte, Sicilia, Toscana, Veneto), which are summarized in table 5.7. The table reports the main features of the assessment procedures, such as whether ADL and IADL difficulties are accounted for; whether availability of informal support is included in the evaluation; the definition of the minimum eligibility threshold; and what functional limitations carry the largest weight in the assessment. The table emphasizes that while all regions include ADL in their assessment, the role of IADL limitations, as well as of informal support, changes significantly across areas. Similarly, the working definition of eligibility is so different across regions that a comparison at face value is almost impossible.

Why should these differences matter for older people? The answer lies in the emerging literature in health economics showing that being eligible for public LTC can significantly increase the likelihood of receiving care, above

Table 5.7 **Summary of Italian LTC legislations: definition of "severe need," 2017**

Region	Program	ADL	IADL	Others	Informal support	Eligibility threshold
Bolzano	Assegno di cura (VITA)	✓	✓	C		2h die
Campania	Assegno di cura (SVaMA)	✓		C,	p	Barthel score 55
Em. Rom.	Assegno di Cura (BINA)	✓		C, M	✓	230 points
Friuli V.G.	CAF/APA (KATZ)	✓		C, M		2 ADL / cognition
Liguria	ADC (AGED PLUS)	✓	p	C		Invalidity & 3 ADL / Cognition / Behavior
Lombardia	Misura B2 (Triage + ADL + iADL)	✓	✓		✓	Invalidity + triage score 3 + 3 ADL + 4 iADL
Piemonte	Assegno di cura, bonus famiglia (cartella geriatrica)	p	✓	C, B		5 points
Sicilia	Buono sociosanit. (SVaMA)	✓	p	M	✓	Invalidity & Living with family
Toscana	PAC (MDS-HC)	✓*		C, B		2 ADL + cognition + behaviour
Veneto	ICD (SVaMA)	✓		C, M, B	✓	—

C = cognitive limitations; M=means tested; p = included partially i = Incontinence not included

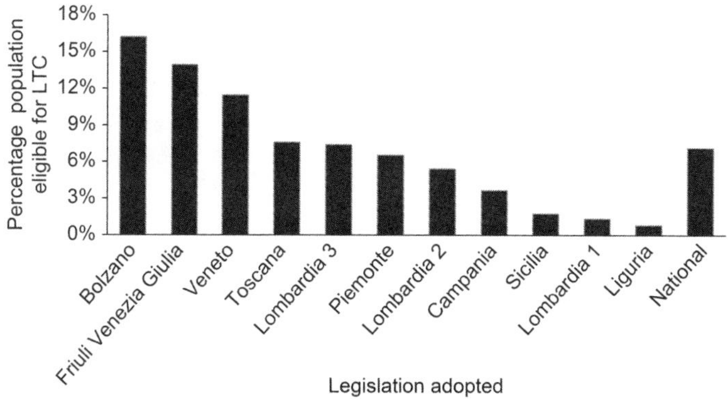

Fig. 5.7 Share of 65+ Italian population potentially eligible for LTC benefits under different rules

Source: SHARE wave 6 (2015), age 65+. Respondent weights are used for all population estimate calculations. Nursing home residents are excluded.

and beyond the role played by health limitations in determining the demand for care (Bakx et al. 2014; Carrino et al. 2018). In other words, eligibility rules are a major driver of care utilization rates, because they define the target population that has potential access to (and is *potentially covered by*) LTC support. Brugiavini et al. (2017) define the "potential coverage" rate of LTC rules as the ratio of the population aged 65+ that fulfills the requirements defined by a specific country-rule for LTC benefits. They show, by virtue of "direct-adjustment" standardization, that the proportion of older Europeans that would be covered by LTC changes substantially depending on the definition of need-of-care used. In figure 5.7, we adopt the same methodology and compute the proportion of older Italians who would be considered eligible to receive public LTC benefits, depending on the eligibility rule used. This is tantamount to asking, If we applied the eligibility rules of each region to the whole older population in Italy, what proportion of that population would be potentially covered by LTC services? A higher percentage tells us that a system is more comprehensive in its coverage than a lower percentage by virtue of its eligibility rules, as we keep health constant by focusing on the sample underlying population. Coverage is expressed as a percentage of the sample aged 65+ in Italy from the SHARE survey. We also report the predicted share of population that would be eligible to the national LTC program (*Indennità di Accompagnamento*). The results show striking differences in the potential coverage for LTC, depending on the adopted definition of needs. Some rules evidently focus only on a population of highly disabled older people (e.g., Liguria, Sicilia, and some of the health districts in Lombardia), while other areas (the northern regions of Bolzano, Friuli Venezia Giulia and Veneto) aim at covering a broader population which includes pre-frail individuals and lower degrees of loss of autonomy.

Table 5.8 **Population with LTC insurance, Italy, 2015**

	65+
Population with LTC Insurance	553,879
Share of Population	0.0419
Observations	3,092

Source: SHARE wave 6. Weights used are adjusted to match national aggregates of the nursing home residents (see appendix).

Table 5.9 **Characteristics of the population by LTC insurance, Italy, 2015**

	65+ Insured	65+ Uninsured
Total Household Wealth—Mean	236,360	148,199
Total Household Wealth—Median	164,640	109,847
Total Household Income—Mean	18,534	12,966
Total Household Income—Median	13,859	11,747
In Nursing Home (%)	0.051	0.025
Live with Spouse or Partner (%)	0.537	0.581
Formal Home Help (%)	0.170	0.132
Informal Home Help (%)	0.312	0.258
Observations	126	2,963

Source: SHARE wave 6. Weights used are adjusted to match national aggregates of nursing home residents (see appendix). Nursing home residents include both those who are living in a nursing home or stayed at one during the last year. All variables (income, wealth, types of help) are defined as they were in previous tables. All values are normalized, and they are in 2019 euros.

5.3.2 Private Insurance

The market for private LTC insurance in Italy is extremely thin. Moreover, most of the contracts are bundled with supplementary health insurance. As shown in table 5.8, in the Italian sample of SHARE the prevalence of respondents aged 65+ holding private LTC insurance is estimated to be 4.19 percent. The characteristics of private insurance holders are shown in table 5.9, and compared to the characteristics of non-holders. Within the group aged 65+, insured individuals seem to have a higher probability of living in a nursing home, are more likely to receive formal home help, and have higher wealth and income compared to the uninsured sample.

5.3.3 Long-Term Care Utilization

In table 5.10 we illustrate the joint percentage distribution of people receiving care by age and by different degrees of loss of autonomy.[8] Among

8. In order to increase the sample of individual over 85 years old we combined SHARE waves 6 and 7. We adjust the calibrated weights of waves 6 and 7 to take into account the under-representation of the nursing home population as explained in the appendix.

Table 5.10 Individuals receiving care by age and number of ADL, Italy, 2015

# of ADLs	65+, percent	85+, percent
Full Sample	0.265	0.578
0 ADLs & 1+ IADLs	0.441	0.598
1 ADL	0.534	0.690
2 ADLs	0.693	0.777
3+ ADLs	0.757	0.792
Observations	6,033	563

Source: The data are from the combining of SHARE waves 6 and 7. The care variable is defined as either formal or informal care received or both. Formal help includes help with personal care, domestic tasks, meals-on-wheels, other activities and nursing home, while informal help includes help received both from outside and inside the household, with personal care, practical household help, and help with paperwork. We adjusted the longitudinal calibrated weights, provided by SHARE for the combining data set of waves 6 and 7, so that individuals in nursing homes match national aggregates.

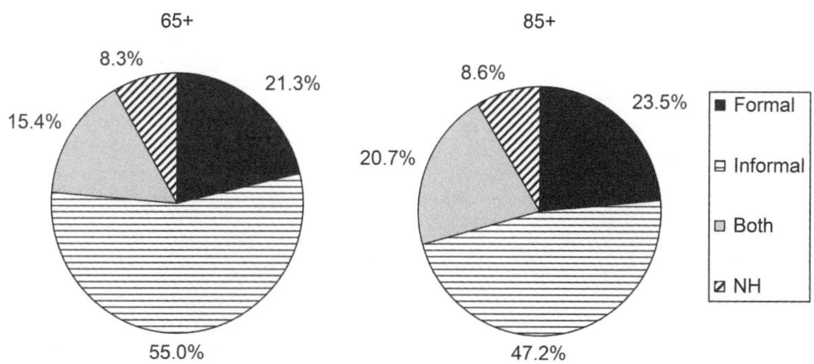

Fig. 5.8 Type of care received by age, Italy, 2015

Source: Data are from SHARE waves 6 and 7.The variables are defined as they were in previous tables. The individuals in nursing homes are those who have reported to have stayed in one of them permanently in the last 12 months. We adjusted the calibrated weights, provided by SHARE, so that individuals in nursing homes match national aggregates.

the full sample (which includes people with no ADL/IADL limitations), 26.5 percent are receiving some kind of help between formal and informal, domiciliary (i.e., home-based) and institutional (i.e., nursing home or residential care). A stark difference by age emerges: 57.8 percent of the individuals aged 85+ receive some form of help. However, once we condition on the presence and number of limitations, as a measure of need-of-care, the difference across number of limitations and between age groups decreases: 53.4 percent of people 65+ with one ADL limitations receives help, as opposed to 69 percent of those 85+. For people with three or more limitations, comparable figures are more similar—75.7 percent and 79.2 percent.

Figure 5.8 considers the types of care received among the sub-population of care users. We consider four types of care: formal home-based care only,

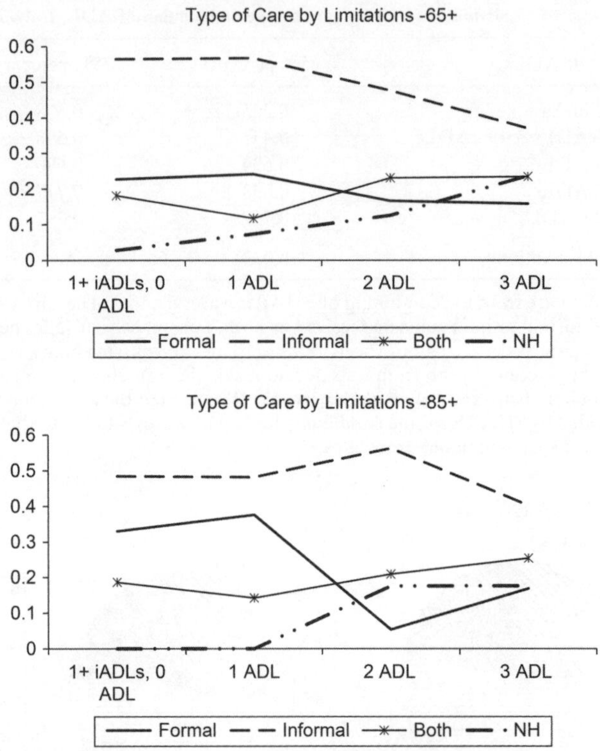

Fig. 5.9 Type of care received by age and limitations, Italy, 2015

Source: Data are from SHARE waves 6 and 7.The variables are defined as they were in previous tables. The individuals in nursing homes are those who have reported to have stayed in one of them permanently in the last 12 months. We adjusted the calibrated weights, provided by SHARE, so that individuals in nursing homes match national aggregates.

informal home-based care only, both formal and informal home-based care (mixed care), and institutional care. The majority of care recipients, 55 percent (47.2 percent among the 85+), receive only informal home-based care, while only 21.3 percent (23.5 percent) receive only formal home-based care. The share of respondents receiving mixed care is at 15.4 percent in the 65+ sample, and 20.7 percent for the 85+ sample. Finally, the share of people receiving institutional care is slightly more than 8 percent for both age groups.

Figure 5.9 presents the pattern of the types of care received with respect to the ADL/IADLs groups (as usual distinguishing also two age groups in the top panel and bottom panel). The X-axis reports the number of limitations, while the Y-axis shows the percentage of individuals receiving care: as the number of limitations increases, the percentage of individuals receiving only informal help decreases. As predicted by theoretical and empirical

Table 5.11 **Distribution of weekly hours of care received by type, for the sample of care recipients, Italy, 2015**

	Informal Help		Formal Help	
Percentiles	65+	85+	65+	85+
5th Percentile	<1	<1	1	2
10th Percentile	<1	<1	1	2
25th Percentile	2	8	2	2
50th Percentile	8	40	4	5
75th Percentile	40	40	11	16
90th Percentile	40	46	28	50
95th Percentile	46	46	56	80
Mean	17	25	13	18
Observations	556	107	282	60

Source: SHARE wave 6, subsample of Italian respondents receiving care. Respondent weights are used for all population estimate calculations. Nursing home residents are excluded. Formal help hours are imputed using data from W1 and W2 to the individuals who reported to have used formal help in wave 6. Received informal help inside the household is imputed with ISTAT information and informal help outside the household is converted from the frequency: daily help as 40 hours per week, weekly help as 8 hours per week, monthly help as 2 hours per week, and less often as half an hour per week.

evidence (Floridi et al. 2021), the percentage of people receiving mixed care increases with the number of ADL limitations, and this pattern is similar across age groups.

Table 5.11 shows the distribution of formal and informal hours of care per week, by respondent's age, among care recipients. As already noted, the distribution of hours of care for both formal and informal care is right skewed: the median number of weekly hours of formal care is 4 (that is, 50 percent of the care recipients receive less than 4 hours of care per week), while the mean is 13 hours per week. If we look at informal care, median and average care hours per week are 8 and 17, respectively. Individuals aged 85 years or older receive more informal care than younger respondents: median hours of help is 40, while 10 percent of oldest old receive at least 46 hours of help per week (to give a sense of the relevance of the care intensity for the oldest old, the comparable percentage of people receiving 46 or more hours of care per week in the full sample amounts to 5 percent). An even larger difference by age emerges when looking at the utilization of formal home-based care: people in the top 10 percent of the distribution of care hours among the oldest old receive 35 hours of weekly formal home-based care more with respect to the top 10 percent of care users among the population aged 65+.

5.3.4 Formal Long-Term Care Supply

There are over 12,000 nursing homes in Italy, endowed with almost 300 thousand beds (table 5.12). With more than 13 million individuals aged

Table 5.12 Absolute number of nursing homes, beds, and occupancy rate, Italy, 2018

	Italy 2018
Nursing homes	12,857
Nursing home residents aged 65+	282,385
Long-term care beds in nursing and residential care facilities	297,970
Occupancy rate	94.8%
Pop 65+	13,391,566
Beds per pop. 65+	0.022
Pop 85+	2,009,441
Beds per pop. 85+	0.148
Workers in nursing homes	413,706

Source: For beds in nursing homes (*posti letto in residenze comunitarie*), number of nursing home residents (*anziani per tipo di residenzialità*), and for number of nursing homes (*presidi residenziali socio-assistenziali e socio-sanitari*) *ISTAT*, http://dati.istat.it/Index.aspx?QueryId=21996. The total number of workers reported here includes paid and voluntary staff; in table 5A.2 we show their details by professional qualification. For population data, OECD Stat, https://stats.oecd.org/Index.aspx?DataSetCode=POPPROJ.

Table 5.13 Distribution of nursing homes occupancy rate and beds across regions, Italy, 2018

	Occupancy rate	Beds per pop 65+
5%	0.862	0.008
10%	0.894	0.011
25%	0.929	0.013
50%	0.940	0.020
75%	0.947	0.033
90%	0.961	0.039
95%	0.976	0.042

Source: ISTAT, http://dati.istat.it/Index.aspx?QueryId=21996, database on nursing home care facilities (*Presidi residenziali socio-assistenziali e socio-sanitari: Personale*)

65 or older, that amounts to 2 beds per 100 older persons and about 15 beds per 100 persons ages 85 or older. Approximately 95 percent of these beds are occupied at any point in time.

Table 5.13 shows a significant variation in nursing home capacity across the country: the number of beds per 100 older residents varies from 0.8 to 4.2, while the occupancy rate shows a relatively lower heterogeneity, as it ranges from 86.2 percent to 97.6 percent across regions.

Recent estimates report that in 2016 there were around 260,000 regular LTC workers in Italy, mostly females, which amounted to 1.9 per 100 people aged 65 and over, up from a ratio of 1.4 in 2011 (European Commission 2021). These figures, however, do not account for a vast population of irregular LTC workers, sometimes referred to as *badanti* (mostly migrants), whose numbers have been estimated around 800,000 (European Commission 2021).

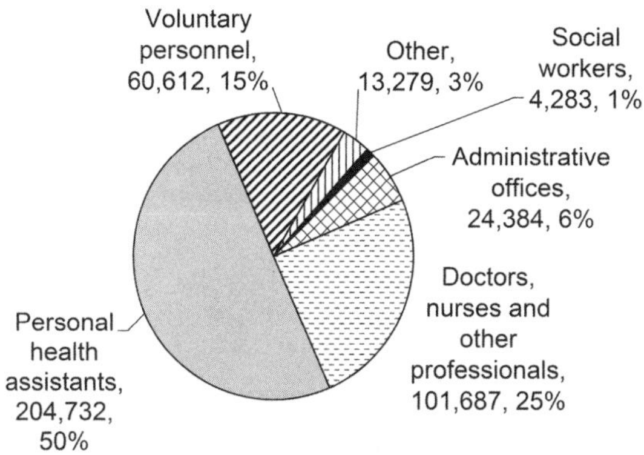

Fig. 5.10 Number and percent distribution of workers at care facilities, Italy, 2018
Source: Data from the ISTAT database on nursing home care facilities (Presidi residenziali socio-assistenziali e socio-sanitari: Personale)

Data on the care workforce is very limited in Italy, especially with respect to home-based care. The National Institute of Statistics (ISTAT) provides figures on the care workforce in care facilities (nursing homes), which we summarize in figure 5.10. Most workers in nursing homes are personal health assistants, followed by doctors, nurses, and other professionals, with a large residual share of voluntary personnel.

There are two main profiles of professional care workers in Italy who can work in both nursing homes and home-care settings: social-assistance operator (*Operatore Socio Assistenziale*, OSA), and medical-assistance operator (*Operatore Socio Sanitario*, OSS). The OSA is an auxiliary health care figure, officially recognized, trained, and prepared to directly assist people in carrying out daily activities, to help maintain and recover autonomy, to offer support for the psychological and physical well-being of the patient, and to reduce and avoid social isolation and social exclusion. The OSS has, unlike the OSA, health-related training and preparation, which also allows them to act as an assistant to nursing staff in the operating theater, besides working in the emergency room, and in nursing homes.

There is no comprehensive framework for quality checks on either residential LTC services or home-based services. Quality is monitored through authorization and accreditation processes, staff/users ratios, legislation on mistreatments, and training requirements for care workers (European Commission 2021).

Table 5.14 summarizes the training requirements for both OSA and OSS care workers. The OSA training lasts approximately 800 hours with compulsory attendance, in addition to the internship at an accredited facility. The OSS training is longer (about 1,000–1,200 hours).

The lower-skilled profile of *badante* requires no mandatory training or requirement to perform the job. However, since 2020, in order to incentivize

Table 5.14 Training requirements for formal home care workers, Italy

	Minimum training requirement
Assistant social worker (OSA)	800 hours
Health Social Worker (OSS)	1000 hours
Home Aide (Badanti)	Between 0 and 500 hours

Source: OSA, https://www.lab.care/operatore-socio-assistenziale-osa/, OSS https://www.lab.care/come-diventare-oss/, and *Badanti*, https://www.accredia.it/2020/06/24/colf-babysitter-badanti-la-certificazione-accreditata-sostiene-le-famiglie/. For the latter group, the minimum training requirement is not mandatory, and it is a professional certificate.

the training programs and increase the quality of the supplied care, *badanti* can be awarded a professional certificate if they complete at least 64 hours of no-cost training and pass a final examination, provided they have at least one year of experience providing care. Such a certificate allows workers to receive a higher hourly wage, which can reach a total of 8 to 10 euros per hour.[9]

Table 5.15 shows the earnings of workers in the health and social sector reported by the Italian Statistical Bureau, ISTAT, based on a two-digit NACE-code classification. The average hourly wage for workers in residential care activities is below the average salary for both part-time and full-time workers, with respect to the average hourly wage of workers in the industrial sector. Moreover, this average is also below the hourly wage of workers with less than a high school degree.

Unfortunately, we cannot retrieve information on the specific wages for the subset of jobs related to long-term care activities. On the basis of the distribution of workers presented in the third panel of table 5.15, also classified on a three-digit NACE code, we assume that most residential care and social work activities (without accommodation) are related to long-term care services.

5.4 Who Are the Caregivers?

This section of the study is of particular relevance, as we present, for the first time, robust estimates of the size of "informal help" in Italy, and the results are quite striking. Table 5.16 shows our estimates of the Italian population receiving help, with respect to the type of help and age groups. Informal help is almost *twice as large as* formal help: 34.7 percent of individuals (37.1 percent of the oldest old, 85+) receiving help report formal help, while this percentage is 83.8 percent (88.5 percent) for the reported informal help.

9. Further details available at the Italian National Office for Professional Accreditation website (ACCREDIA, https://www.accredia.it/2020/06/24/colf-babysitter-badanti-la-certificazione-accreditata-sostiene-le-famiglie/).

Table 5.15 **Pay for care workers at residential facilities and in health care, Italy 2015**

	Mean hourly wage			Median hourly wage		
	Full Time	Part Time	Total	Full Time	Part Time	Total
Panel 1: Human health and social work activities						
86: Human Health Activities	14.76	11.66	13.30	12.77	10.26	11.22
87: Residential Care Activities	11.55	10.86	11.17	10.43	9.84	10.15
88: Social Work Activities without Accomm.	11.27	10.63	10.79	10.18	9.65	9.78
Panel 2: All Industry						
All Workers	15.39	12.02	14.97	12.86	10.26	12.54
No High School Degree			13.17			11.99
No College Degree			15.63			13.25
College Degree or More			23.06			17.16
Panel 3: Distribution of employees in human health and social work activities						
86: Human Health Activities						239,028
861: Hospital Activities						37%
862: Medical and Dental Practice Activities						41%
869: Other Human Health Activities						22%
87: Residential Care Activities						152,440
871: Residential Nursing Care Activities						13%
872: Residential Care Activities for Mental Retardation, Mental Health and Substance Abuse						10%
873: Residential Care Activities for the Elderly and Disabled						51%
879: Other Residential Care Activities						26%
88: Social Work Activities Without Accommodation						148,247
881: Social Work Activities Without Accommodation for the Elderly and Disabled						55%
889: Other Social Work Activities Without Accommodation						45%

Source: ISTAT—http://dati.istat.it/Index.aspx?QueryId=33485&lang=en. Labor and wages. All euro amounts are in 2019 euros.

In a comparative perspective, the ratio of caregivers for the Italian population is not much higher than for other European countries: what characterizes Italian caregivers is the higher level of intensity of their commitment *vis-à-vis* the European average (European Commission 2021).

Figure 5.11 shows the demographic characteristics of informal and formal caregivers:[10] more than 85 percent of the formal home care workers are women, while women providing informal care amount to 61.8 percent of the total number of caregivers. However, it should be added that, in

10. Data source INPS, https://www.inps.it/osservatoristatistici/12/o/350. We are reporting information for the formal home worker (i.e., Colf/Badanti) in Italy 2015. *Colf* (Collaboratori Familiari) are helpers who perform a variety of household tasks, while *Badanti* are caregivers who provide personal assistance to older, disabled, or ill individuals.

Table 5.16 Population receiving help, Italy, 2015

	Recipient of Help 65+	Recipient of Help 85+
Any Help	4,160,961	1,230,817
Formal	1,444,410	456,938
Informal	3,485,136	1,088,875
Observation	3,102	265

Source: SHARE wave 6. Respondent weights are used for all population estimate calculations. Nursing home residents are excluded. Formal help includes help with personal care, domestic tasks, meals-on-wheels, and other activities, while informal help includes help with personal care, practical household help, and help with paperwork.

line with recent evidence from the Share-Corona Survey, some degree of gender-specialization emerges for informal caregivers, as women tend to provide personal care, which is a more demanding and intense activity, while men provide help with financial issues and shopping (Bassoli and Brugiavini 2023).

Our results are also very interesting when looking at the age and education composition of caregivers. Formal home care workers are of typical working age, but more than 85 percent of informal caregivers are older than 50; the majority of caregivers (55.7 percent) have less than a high school diploma or a high school diploma (32.7 percent); and very few have a college degree or more.

Finally, figure 5.12 provides details on the relationship between informal caregivers and care recipients: spouses and children amount to around 50 percent of the caregiver population. It emerges that daughters are twice as likely to provide care if compared to sons; 20 percent is the share of in-laws, while the remaining share is made up of other relatives (13.8 percent) or friends (15.9 percent).

5.5 The Cost of Long-Term Care

As discussed in previous sections, Italian long-term care expenditure is mostly financed with public funds. Table 5.17 reviews these total costs. In 2015, the total spending in nursing homes amounted to 7 billion euros, for a total of 288 thousand residents in nursing homes, while the reported total spending in the home-based care (home health services) is 4.63 billion euros with an estimated number of users of approximately 1.5 million.[11] Spending on nursing home care is 50 percent larger than home health agency, despite there being more than five times as many users in the latter case.

However, because most of the home care is provided informally, typically by relatives, a proper accounting of the total cost of long-term care in the

11. Based on table 5.16.

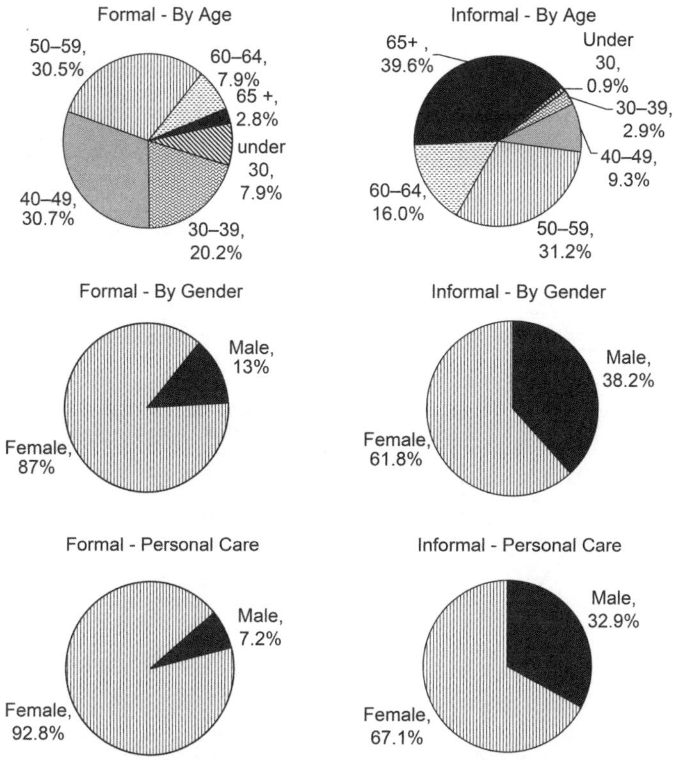

Fig. 5.11 Demographic composition of caregivers, Italy, 2015

Source: Formal caregiver data are from Home Worker data set of INPS. Informal care data come from SHARE w6. For each respondent who reported receiving help from a spouse or child, we were able to link them (spouse/child) to their general information (age, gender, education) provided by the respondent. For the respondents and their partners we classified as less than HS education those individual who have an ISCED 97 value lower than 3, with HS those that have a value between of 3 and 4, while the remaining two categories (college/ college plus) are for those with an ISCED 97 value of 5 or 6. For children the education is obtained from the reported level of education and degree they achieved. Respondent weights are used for all calculations. Nursing home residents are excluded.

economy should include the opportunity cost of their time as well. Valuing the opportunity cost of informal caregivers raises several issues and requires several assumptions. In the simplest model, with perfectly competitive labor markets and market wages equal to the value of leisure, the value of time spent in informal care would be the forgone wage. If high potential wage individuals choose to provide informal care rather than buy it, it is either because they get sufficient utility from the provision of care, or because the care they provide is of sufficiently higher quality to justify the "cost."

In such a model, even those who are not employed in the labor market would have an opportunity cost of time—that being the wage that they

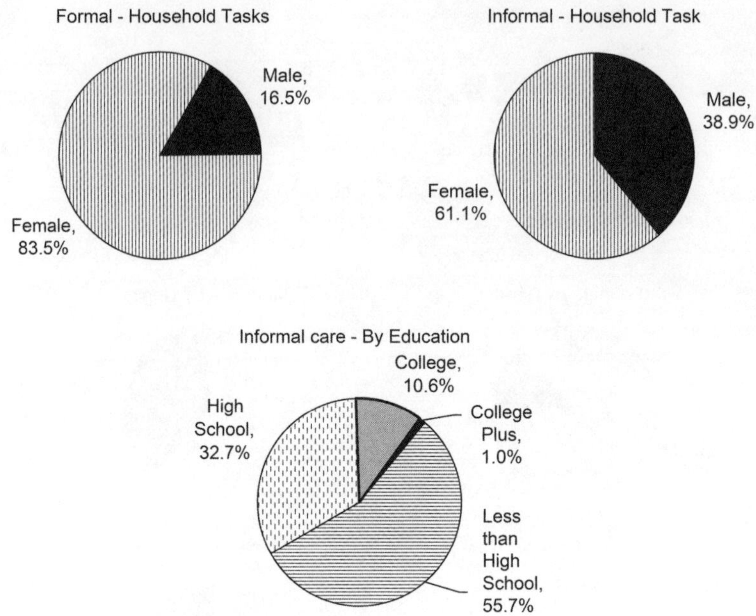

Fig. 5.11 (cont.)

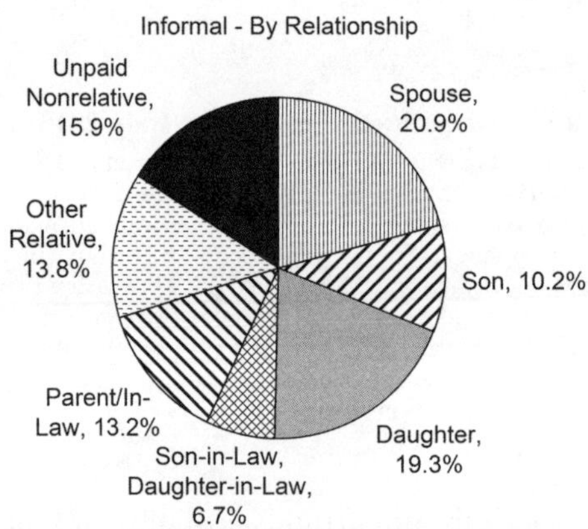

Fig. 5.12 Informal caregivers by relationship to care recipient, Italy, 2015
Source: Data from SHARE w6. Respondent weights are used for all estimate calculations. Nursing home residents are excluded.

would earn if they were to enter the labor market. In practice, however, retired individuals often do not have work opportunities that are equal to their value of leisure. It is also hard to value the potential wage for workers who are very old and/or have been retired for many years.

We therefore consider two options for valuing hours of informal care. In

Table 5.17 **Formal care costs, annual, Italy 2015**

	Number of users	Total spending (billion €)
Nursing home	288,000	7.00
Home health services (Formal)	1,444,410	4.63

Notes: Total spending data come from ISTAT System of Health Accounts. In particular, we report for nursing home the spending done in hospital and residential long-term care facilities while we aggregate the other categories in home health agency. We multiply the spending by the proportion of the elderly residential care receiver aged 65 and over (75%, https://www.istat.it/en/archivio/215525). The number of users for HHS is estimated from SHARE w6, excluding nursing home residents. Respondent weights are used for all population estimate calculations. All euro amounts are in 2019 euros.

both cases, if informal care is delivered by those who are working, the care is valued at their predicated wage. In one case, for those who are not working, we value their time at zero ("low valuation"). In the other case ("high valuation"), we value the time of those who are not working at the replacement cost of home care. It is not easy to obtain reliable information on actual wages for care workers in Italy. For the scope of our analysis, we first focus on the legislative minimum hourly wage for formal care workers, *badanti*: the minimum average wage for *badanti* is €5.43 per hour, which corresponds to the average between the minimum wage for the lowest contractual category and the highest contractual category as reported in the national collective bargaining employment contract for "Badanti & Colf." Second, we rely on estimates from the Economic Research Institute (www.erieri.com), which reports an average actual wage for formal caregivers in Italy of €11 per hour (https://www.erieri.com/salary/job/caregiver/italy).

Moreover, quantifying the hours of informal home care requires overcoming further challenges related to data limitation. In the SHARE data, respondents can give details only for the informal care they provided to people living outside the household; conversely, when they provide informal help inside the household, no information on intensity is reported. Total hours of informal help are therefore built based on the self-reported help given to recipients outside the household, by a respondent in the SHARE w6 (age50+), which we complement with an imputed measure of informal help intensity given to people living inside the household. The latter value is imputed based on data from the ISTAT-Multipurpose survey on households (Time Use [ISTAT-*Indagine Multiscopo sulle Famiglie: Uso del tempo*]). The ISTAT survey provides an average amount of care hours provided by caregivers differentiated by sex and age class, based on self-reported information provided through a "daily diary," and including activities such as help with household tasks and help with personal care.

In order to predict the potential wage, we need to account for the fact that in our sample, most respondents are retired, due to the sample selection of SHARE (people over 50 years of age at baseline) and due to the longitudinal nature of the survey. We therefore build an imputed measure of respondents'

Table 5.18 **Valuation of informal home care, Italy, 2015**

	I	II	III
Valuation	11.2	17.31	22.91
Total Hours Informal Help	2.6	2.6	2.6
E(Work)	0.39	0.39	0.39
E(Work) * E(Wage|Work) (unconditional expected wage)	4.05		
E(Wage|Work)	10.38		
Hours—Helper Working	1.21	1.21	1.21
Hours—Helper Not Working	1.69	1.69	1.69
Home Health Aide Wage		5.43	11

Notes: Column I values predicted working hours at the predicted wage, and non-working hours at zero wage. Column II values the hours of not working informal caregiver at the replacement cost based on the average home health aide wage of €5.43 computed taking the average minimum wage of professional home care between the lowest category and highest one reported in the national collective bargaining employment contract for "Badanti & Colf." Column 3 uses the average hourly wage for caregiver from ERI, https://www.erieri.com/salary/job/caregiver/Italy. Valuations are done at the helper level, with predicted wages and probabilities of work imputed from SHARE w6 using data for education, age and age square, sex, marital status and children in the household. Valuation and hours are reported in billions, and they are in 2019 euros.

hourly wage as well as their employment probability. We use a multiple imputation regression logit model based on the observable characteristics such as age, age-squared, years of education, sex, marital status, and number of children. The predicted average wage for respondents who are working at the time of the interview is €10.38 per hour, while the average probability to be in paid work is 39 percent.

The "low valuation" estimate of the economic value of informal caregiving is computed by multiplying the number of each caregiver's care hours provided in one year by the caregiver's predicted wage, by the probability of being in paid work. Conversely, the "high valuation" estimate is computed by adding to the low valuation estimation the product between caregiving hours provided by the home-based health aide wage, by (1-probability of being in paid-work). As previously explained, we use two alternative values for the wage for the home-based formal care substitute: the minimum wage of *badanti*, and the actual average wage of formal care workers in Italy. The resulting estimates of the economic value of informal care are reported in table 5.18: the yearly value of informal care in Italy ranges from 11.2 to 22.91 billion euros. In terms of the composition of total long-term care expenditure, we have shown in the previous section that this has three parts: the actual health care component, the cost for other LTC provisions, and the national attendance cash allowance. It should be stressed that while the first two can vary at regional level or even local level and are earmarked to long-term care services, the latter is a pure cash benefit granted to individuals aged 65 and over who qualify based on citizenship. There are basically very little constraints on the way this allowance is spent by the beneficiary

Table 5.19 **Total costs by type of care and source**

		Cost I		Cost II		Cost III	
Care Type	Source	€	% GDP	€	% GDP	€	% GDP
Nursing home	Private	2.57	0.15%	2.57	0.15%	2.57	0.15%
	Public	4.43	0.26%	4.43	0.26%	4.43	0.26%
	All	7	0.42%	7	0.42%	7	0.42%
Home health agency	Private	0.34	0.02%	0.34	0.02%	0.34	0.02%
	Public	4.29	0.25%	4.29	0.25%	4.29	0.25%
	All	4.63	0.28%	4.63	0.28%	4.63	0.28%
Informal Care	Private	11.2	0.67%	17.31	1.03%	22.91	1.36%
Total	Private	14.11	0.84%	20.22	1.20%	25.82	1.53%
	Public	8.72	0.52%	8.72	0.52%	8.72	0.52%
	All	22.83	1.36%	28.94	1.72%	34.54	2.05%

Notes: from ISTAT System of Health Accounts (http://dati.istat.it/index.aspx?lang=en&SubSessionId=4b1103ef-e51b-4a24–83a2-b1e7dc786251) and SHARE w6. The value of the formal and informal care cost is from tables 5.16–17. Italy's GDP for 2015 was €1683 billion. All euro amounts are in 2019 euros.

and her/his relatives, so that in fact it may not be covering just long-term care services but more general expenditure items as well. The cash benefit accounts for 0.64 percent of GDP: this implies that, for the year 2015, the public expenditure was 10.8 billion euros,[12] less than our lowest estimated cost for informal care.

We can combine this result with the previous data on long-term care spending to estimate the distribution of long-term care costs across public and private sources. We have shown in figure 5.6 that 63.28 percent of the cost of nursing home care and 92.77 percent of the cost of home health care are publicly financed while the remaining part is privately financed, out of pocket or with private insurance. On the other hand, the full cost of informal care is just privately financed.

In table 5.19, we show the expenditure in the nursing home and home health agencies financed by public and private funds. In addition, we include the estimated evaluation of informal care. We find that the majority of long-term care spending is privately financed when informal care is considered. Based on the "lower valuation" estimation of the economic value of informal care, private expenditure is €22.83 billion, which is equivalent to 1.36 percent of Italian GDP; while based on the "higher valuation," the economic value of informal care can be estimated in the range between €28.94 billion and €34.54 billion, both equivalent to 1.72 percent and 2.05 percent of the Italian GDP.

12. Italy's GDP for 2015 was €1,683 billion (2019 euros).

5.6 Conclusions

In this chapter we summarized the main features of the demand and supply of long-term care in Italy.

As per the demand side, we show that older people in need of care are generally poorer than healthier or younger individuals. Moreover, a large fraction of frail older people receives a substantial amount of care, from informal sources and/or from formal providers. This evidence, coupled with the aging trend of the Italian population, should alert policymakers to a clear rising demand for long-term care in Italy in coming decades.

On the supply side, Italy is characterized by a two-tier system, consisting of a publicly provided LTC, which is very regionally fragmented, and of informal care. Finally, private insurance for LTC services is negligible. The public programs of long-term care include a national cash benefit, complemented by local programs of in-kind and in-cash support in each of the twenty Italian regions. Generosity and eligibility rules vary widely across regions, creating disparities and unequal coverage. Informal long-term care is largely borne by daughters and by daughters-in-law, typically with a low education level. This informal care provision is complemented by a large irregular market for care workers, mainly immigrant women (*badanti*).

Our analysis also aimed at estimating the overall costs of long-term care provision. In this respect, our main finding is that the vast majority of LTC costs in Italy are financed privately, either out of pocket or through forgone working opportunities for family caregivers. This is due to the large role played by informal care in the provision of long-term care, and even when adopting a conservative approach to impute the economic value of informal care. From a prospective point of view, it is important to note that with Italy being a low-fertility country, such figures will hardly be reversed in the coming decades. This finding has important policy implications: policymakers should be aware that the expected increase in demand for care will hardly be met without a larger role of publicly provided LTC or quick development of a private insurance market. In absence of a substantial contribution through public provision, unmet needs in Italy could therefore increase and lead to lower welfare for older people and society as a whole.

Appendix

In this appendix we describe how we adjusted the cross-sectional weights present in SHARE to consider the attrition problems that arise for individuals in nursing homes. We can easily see that the probability of living in a nursing home conditional on age 65+ is 0.0125 based on the wave 6 sample

Table 5A.1

		Whole 65+ Population		
	Share of	All	Male	Female
In Nursing Home	65–79	0.005	0.001	0.004
	80+	0.017	0.004	0.012
Not in Nursing Home	65–79	0.693	0.321	0.373
	80+	0.285	0.103	0.182

Table 5A.2 Staff in residential social and health care facilities, Italy, 2018

Professional qualification	Paid Staff
Directors And Coordinators	10,301
Employee	14,083
General Practitioners	6,753
Specialized Doctors	3,355
Psychologists	6,227
Sociologists	269
Social Workers	4,283
Teachers	339
Professional Youth Workers	25,457
Activity Leaders	4,768
Cultural Mediators	614
Nurses	41,002
Physiotherapists	10,884
Rehabilitation Physiotherapists	1,001
Speech Therapists	1,018
Health And Social Workers	116,308
Other Staff Providing Personal Care	41,836
Staff Involved in the Preparation and Distribution Food	14,691
Other General Service Staff	31,897
Civilian Service	3,982
Parent Figures	747
Other Personnel	13,279
Total	353,094

Source: ISTAT, http://dati.istat.it/Index.aspx?QueryId=21996. Residential social and health care facilities (*Presidi residenziali socio-assistenziali e socio-sanitari*). In addition to the paid staff there were 60,612 voluntary staff that helped in the residential facilities, but for them ISTAT does not report the specific qualification.

and using cross-section weights; moreover, this probability falls to 0.0079 when we tried to add wave 7 data and adjust for longitudinal weights. On the other hand, looking at national statistics, such as the ISTAT, this probability is 0.0218.

Since SHARE does not create sample weights for those in a nursing home, we adjust SHARE weights to match the reported percentage in the national statistics for individuals living in nursing homes and those not. The procedure we adopt is essentially the same as it is done to adjust weights from the English Longitudinal Study of Ageing (ELSA).

National statistics provided by ISTAT allow us to retrieve the population of individuals 65+ in a nursing home, the percentage of females, and the percentage of those 80+. We use this information to compute the proportion of population in eight categories as illustrated in the table and to recalibrate the weights based on gender and age. In the following tables, we show the imputed proportion:

References

Atella, V., F. Belotti, C. A. Cricelli, D. Dankova, J. Kopinska, A. Palma, and A. Piano Mortari. 2018. "The 'Double Expansion of Morbidity' Hypothesis: Evidence from Italy." CEIS Research Paper, 396/2017.

Bakx, P., C. Meijer, F. Schut, and E. van Doorslaer. 2014. "Going Formal or Informal, Who Cares? The Influence of Public Long-Term Care Insurance." *Health Economics* 24 (6): 631–43. doi: 10.1002/hec.3050.

Barbabella, F., P. Checcucci, M. L. Aversa, G. Scarpetti, R. Fefè, M. Socci, C. Di Matteo, E. Cela, G. Damiano, M. Villa, D. Amari, S. R. Montagnino, L. D'Agostino, V. Iadevaia, A. Ferrante, G. Lamura, and A. Principi. 2020. "Le politiche per l'invecchiamento attivo in Italia." Rapporto sullo stato dell'arte. Dipartimento per le Politiche della Famiglia-IRCCS INRCA. http://famiglia.governo.it/media/2132/le-politiche-per-l-invecchiamento-attivo-in-italia.pdf.

Bassoli, E., and A. Brugiavini. 2023. "Unequal Care Provision: Evidence from the Share-Corona Survey." Research Paper Series No. 05/WP/2023. University Ca' Foscari of Venice, Dept. of Economics.

Börsch-Supan, A., M. Brandt, C. Hunkler, T. Kneip, J. Korbmacher, F. Malter, B. Schaan, S. Stuck, and S. Zuber, on behalf of the SHARE Central Coordination Team. 2013. "The Survey of Health, Ageing and Retirement in Europe (SHARE)." *International Journal of Epidemiology* 42(4), 992–1001.

Brugiavini, A., L. Carrino, C. E. Orso, and G. Pasini. 2017. *Vulnerability and Long-Term Care in Europe: An Economic Perspective*. London: Palgrave MacMillan.

Carrino, L., C. E. Orso, and G. Pasini. 2018. "Demand of Long-Term Care and Benefit Eligibility across European Countries." *Health Economics* 27 (8): 1175–188. doi:10.1002/hec.3665.

Chatterji, S., J. Byles, D. Cutler, T. Seeman, and E. Verdes. 2015. "Health, Functioning, and Disability in Older Adults—Present Status and Future Implications." *Lancet*, 385 (9967): 563–75.

European Commission. 2021. *The 2021 Ageing Report: Economic & Budgetary Projections for the EU Member States (2019–2070)*. Publications Office.

Floridi, G., L. Carrino, and K. Glaser. 2021. "Socioeconomic Inequalities in Home-Care Use across Regional Long-Term Care Systems in Europe." *Journals of Gerontology: Series B*, 76 (1): 121–32.

Gori, C., J. Fernandez, and R. Wittenberg. 2015. *Long-Term Care Reforms in OECD Countries: Successes and failures*. Bristol, UK: Policy Press.

Hashiguchi, T. C. O., and A. Llena-Nozal. 2020. "The Effectiveness of Social Protection for Long-Term Care in Old Age: Is Social Protection Reducing the Risk of Poverty Associated with Care Needs?" *OECD Health Working Papers*, No. 117. Paris: OECD Publishing. https://doi.org/10.1787/2592f06e-en.

Jessoula, M., E. Pavolini, M. Raitano, and M. Natili. 2018. ESPN Thematic Report on Challenges in Long-Term Care. Italy, Brussels.

Kaeberlein, M., P. S. Rabinovitch, and G. M. Martin. 2015. "Healthy Aging: The Ultimate Preventative Medicine." *Science* 350 (6265): 1191–193.

OECD. 2019. Health at a Glance 2019.

OECD. 2022. Historical population data and population projections. OECD Statistics, Paris.

Rechel, B., E. Grundy, J.-M. Robine, J. Cylus, J. P. Mackenbach, C. Knai, and M. McKee. 2013. "Ageing in the European Union." *Lancet* 381 (9874): 1312–1322.

6

Long-Term Care in Japan

Rong Fu, Toshiaki Iizuka, and Haruko Noguchi

Populations in developed countries are aging increasingly, with Japan aging the fastest. As shown in figure 6.1, in 1990, approximately 12 percent of Japanese people were 65 years or above (65+), nearly the same as in the United States but far lower than the other developed countries such as the United Kingdom (Tamiya et al. 2011). However, with reduced birth rates and improved life expectancy, the percentage of the 65+ population has increased to 28.4 percent in 2019 and is expected to rise to 37.7 percent by 2050 (Cabinet Office 2020a). Furthermore, as shown in figure 6.2, the fastest-growing segment of the older population in Japan is the oldest-old (i.e., people aged 85 years or above [85+]). In 1990, fewer than 8 percent of the 65+ population was aged 85+; this figure is predicted to increase to more

Rong Fu is an associate professor of health economics at Waseda University.

Toshiaki Iizuka is a professor at the Graduate School of Economics at the University of Tokyo.

Haruko Noguchi is a professor on the Faculty of Political Science and Economics at Waseda University.

We wish to extend our gratitude for the support rendered to this research project. Partial funding has been generously provided by the Ministry of Education, Culture, Sports, Science, and Technology in Japan (Grant No.: 22H00067; PI; Haruko Noguchi). We also acknowledge the Ministry of Health, Labour and Welfare (MHLW) for granting authorization to utilize data identified as 1124–3, effective as of November 24, 2022. Additionally, our study draws upon the resources of the Japanese Study of Aging and Retirement (JSTAR), a collaborative effort between the Research Institute of Economy, Trade and Industry (RIETI), Hitotsubashi University, and the University of Tokyo. The RIETI has granted us permission to access data categorized under JSTAR No.353, with effect from August 9, 2022. Our research adheres to the ethical guidelines outlined by the Waseda University Ethics Review Committee. In accordance with their determination, this study has been deemed exempt from ethical review (Approval No.: 2022-HN025; Date of Approval: August 3, 2022). For acknowledgments, sources of research support, and disclosure of the authors' material financial relationships, if any, please see https://www.nber.org/books-and-chapters/long-term-care-around-world/long-term-care-japan.

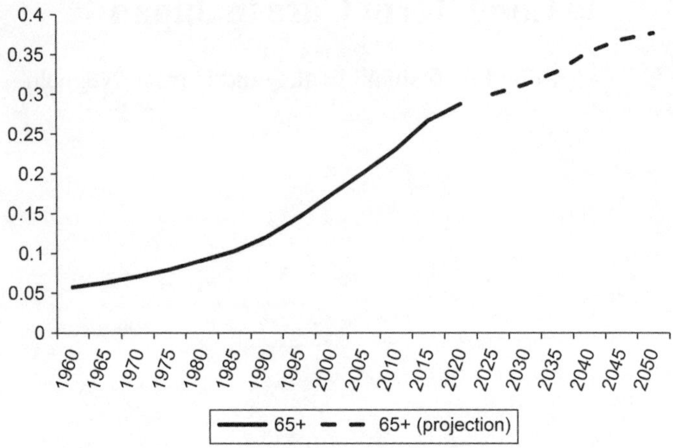

Fig. 6.1 Percentage of the population ages 65 or older, Japan, 1960–2050
Source: OECD Stat. https://stats.oecd.org/Index.aspx?DataSetCode=POPPROJ#

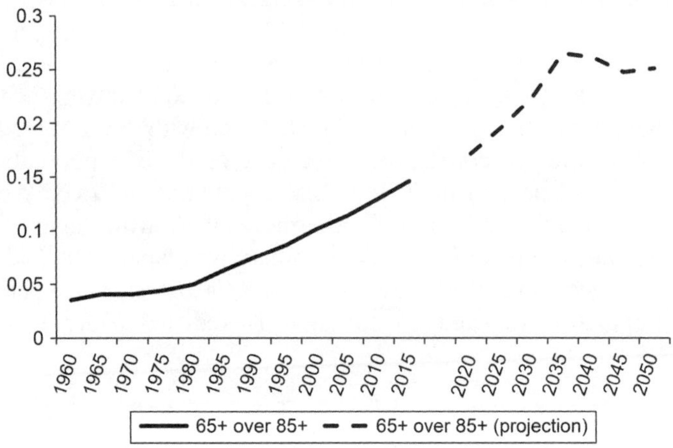

Fig. 6.2 Percentage of 65+ population that is age 85 or older, Japan, 1960–2050
Source: OECD Stat. https://stats.oecd.org/Index.aspx?DataSetCode=POPPROJ#

than 25 percent by 2050. Because of its demographic position, Japan's experience with social security systems provides critical lessons for policymakers in other societies that may soon confront comparable difficulties.

A particular concern of growth in the older population is the increased need for long-term care. Family members account for the majority of caregivers of older people in Japan (Ministry of Health, Labour and Welfare (MHLW) 2014). However, informal care has been declining because of demographic trends, such as smaller family sizes, lower fertility rates, increased mobility of younger generations, and a higher proportion of labor force participation among women, considered primary family caregivers earlier. Therefore, for a long time, concern for older people with long-term care needs has been at the center of welfare policy initiatives in Japan. In 1963, the government began providing limited long-term care services coverage. The economic boom of the 1970s enabled the government to make bold policy decisions: eliminating co-payments for all health care–related services for the elderly. The zero-price policy immediately caused a societal problem known as "social hospitalization." To avoid paying for long-term care after discharge, older people chose to stay (live) in hospitals, regardless of whether they had relevant medical care needs. Apart from soaring public health spending, one serious socioeconomic consequence of social hospitalization is the inability to accept urgent medical care demands owing to a scarcity of hospital beds, which has a knock-on impact on emergency medical services, resulting in "emergency refugees." To alleviate these issues, the government expanded the senior welfare plan for long-term care in the late 1980s to double institutional beds and provide more extensive home care services. However, given the post-crisis economic stagnation of the 1990s, such a generous plan created significant issues, the two primary ones being increasing public long-term care spending, and unclear eligibility and coverage standards (Tamiya et al. 2011). To address these issues in the 1990s, the government finally proposed a stand-alone social insurance framework for long-term care, known as public long-term care insurance (LTCI).

With the implementation of LTCI in 2000, Japan was one of the first countries to develop public insurance schemes for long-term care. LTCI is mandatory insurance that offers universal coverage for institutional care (i.e., public nursing homes) and home or community-based care, with clear eligibility standards for each type of care. Since the official purpose of LTCI is to help older people in need of long-term care to "maintain dignity and an independent daily life routine according to each person's level of abilities" (Ministry of Justice 1997), its emphasis is on home-and community-based care rather than institutional care. The LTCI was deemed successful in supporting older people's independent lives with dignity and relieving family caregivers of care duties (Tamiya et al. 2011). However, the LTCI did not successfully restrict relevant public spending, because it is a pay-as-you-go program. Indeed, a surge in demand for long-term care has imposed significant financial strain on the system. During the first five years of LTCI, public spending increased far faster than predicted, from 3.6 to 6.4 trillion JPY (Fu et al. 2017). Consequently, several reforms have been proposed to limit public long-term care costs since 2006 (Fu et al. 2017). The reforms were generally toward a lower level of coverage based on the need for care or the affordability by older people.

This paper presents an overview of long-term care in Japan. Most of the statistics are calculated using the Comprehensive Survey of Living Conditions (CSLC), a nationally representative repeated cross-sectional survey of Japan's non-institutionalized population. It includes four questionnaires that collect detailed information on a respondent's health status, household structure, income level, and long-term care utilization. If necessary, we supplement the CSLC with additional data sources, such as the Japanese Study of Aging and Retirement (JSTAR).

As in the other chapters, we begin by exploring the correlation between functional limitations and financial well-being in the older Japanese population. Functional limitations are assessed using limitations of activities of daily living (ADLs) and instrumental ADLs (IADLs). We then discuss the supply and finance of the long-term care system in Japan, emphasizing LTCI. Furthermore, we compare the incidence of formal vs. informal care and institutional vs. home care among the elderly based on their age and number of limitations and characterize the workforce in Japan's long-term care industry. Finally, we estimate the total cost of formal and informal long-term care in Japan.

6.1 Aging, Disability, and Well-Being

6.1.1 Sample and Definitions

The core data for this paper are from the CSLC. Since 1986, the MHLW has performed the CSLC every three years. Each survey year, 600 thousand to 800 thousand people, selected at random, are surveyed with health and household questionnaires. The income questionnaire randomly selects 10 percent of the whole sample to gather income information, while the long-term care questionnaire targets 5,000 to 6,000 individuals with care requirements from the whole sample to obtain information on long-term care use. We use data from the 2016 CSLC and limit our analyses to respondents aged 65+.

In the CSLC, we can identify primary informal caregivers for the 65+ respondents who receive care from co-residing family members. This feature of the CSLC enables us to obtain precise information on informal caregivers' health and socioeconomic status. However, the CSLC has some limitations. First, since the CSLC exclusively covers non-institutionalized populations, our statistics do not include information on older people who live in nursing homes. Furthermore, to reduce the load on interviewers and respondents, households selected for the income questionnaire are not sampled for the LTC questionnaire and vice versa. Therefore, there is no overlap between the samples of income and LTC questionnaires, and we cannot measure the income and LTC information of a single respondent. Finally, the definition of ADL in the CSLC is not perfectly comparable to that in other countries because it includes limitations with IADLs. The ADL index ranges from 0 to 5 and represents the number of limitations with (1) daily activities (dressing, bathing, eating, going to bed); (2) going outside; (3) working; (4) sports; and (5) others, where (2)–(5) correspond to IADLs. Due to this data limitation, the number of limitations with ADLs in Japan, the critical measure of older people's health in the analyses, may also reflect limitations with IADLs.

We also use the 2009 JSTAR to improve the comparability of ADLs and IADLs across countries.[1] The ADL and IADL indices in the JSTAR are strictly comparable to those in other countries. The ADL index includes 6 categories: walking across the room, dressing, bathing, eating, going to bed, and using the toilet. The IADL index includes 11 categories: going out alone by bus or train; shopping for groceries; boiling water with a kettle; managing money; filling out pension forms; reading newspapers, books, or magazines; being interested in articles and programs about health; visiting friends or sick persons; communicating with young people; using a telephone; and taking medications. Despite its strict comparability, the 2009 JSTAR has two key issues that prevent it from being referred to as core data. First, since all 2009 JSTAR respondents are under 85, statistics for the 85+ group are unavailable. Second, the JSTAR does not represent Japan's population because it includes only seven of its 1,718 municipalities. In the rest of the chapter, we supplement the CSLC statistics with JSTAR whenever possible and focus on the CSLC statistics unless otherwise specified.

Table 6.1 depicts the distribution of limitations with ADLs and IADLs according to age. More than 75 percent of the 65+ population in Japan has no limitations with ADLs or IADLs; about 13 percent of the sample has no limitations with ADLs but at least one limitation with IADLs; and approximately 11 percent of the sample has at least one limitation with ADLs. The oldest-old are less healthy: around 56 percent have no limitations with ADLs or IADLs, approximately 16 percent have no ADL limitations but one or more IADL limitations, and about 30 percent have one or more ADL limitations. It is essential to emphasize that the statistics from CSLC and JSTAR are comparable, lending credibility to international comparisons based on the definitions of limitations in the CSLC.

6.1.2 Well-Being

Table 6.2 further shows the relationship between the degree of limitations and physical/mental health among older people in Japan. A good or better self-reported health status is used to measure physical health. An indicator of being satisfied or very satisfied with life among retired people and Kessler 6 (K6) scores (Kessler et al. 2003) are used to measure mental health.[2] A higher K6 score indicates poor mental health. Around 26 percent of the 65+

1. The 2009 JSTAR is the most recent survey year that collects information on ADLs and IADLs.

2. K6 involves six questions about a person's emotional state during the past 30 days: (1) About how often did you feel nervous? (2) About how often did you feel hopeless? (3) About how often did you feel restless or fidgety? (4) About how often did you feel so depressed that nothing could cheer you up? (5) About how often did you feel that everything was an effort? (6) About how often did you feel worthless? Each question is scored from 0 (None of the time) to 4 (All of the time). Scores of the six questions are then summed, yielding a minimum score of 0 and a maximum score of 24. The higher the score, the poorer the mental health.

Table 6.1 Share with ADLs by age, Japan, 2016

	65+		85+
	CSLC	JSTAR (appendix)	CSLC
0 ADLs & 0 IADLs	0.757	0.787	0.556
0 ADLs & 1+ IADLs	0.132	0.183	0.156
1 ADL	0.043	0.010	0.109
2 ADLs	0.027	0.006	0.072
3 ADLs	0.019	0.005	0.045
4 ADLs	0.019	0.002	0.049
5 ADLs	0.003	0.005	0.010
6 ADLs		0.003	
Observations	*169,273*	*2,070*	*23,399*

Notes: Data were from the Comprehensive Survey of Living Conditions (CSLC 2016) and the 2009 Japanese Study of Aging and Retirement (JSTAR 2009). Individuals in nursing homes were not sampled. Respondent weights are used for all calculations. In the CSLC, the definition of ADL differs from that in other countries, which includes limitations from IADLs. The ADL index runs from 0 to 5 and is the number of limitations from (1) daily activities (dressing, bathing, eating, going to bed), (2) going outside, (3) working, (4) sports, and (5) others. IADLs include limitations (2) to (5). Owing to this data limitation, IADLs were included when calculating the proportion of 2+ ADLs. In JSTAR, individuals are aged between 52 and 79 years, and those in nursing homes were not sampled. Because all individuals in the 2009 JSTAR were younger than 85 years old, statistics for the 85+ cohort were not available. Respondent weights are used for all calculations. It is worth noting that the 2009 JSTAR is not a representative population because it covers only 7 of Japan's 1,718 municipalities. ADLs included walking across the room, dressing, bathing, eating, going to bed, and using the toilet. IADLs include going out alone by bus or train; shopping for groceries; boiling water with a kettle; managing money; filling out pension forms; reading newspapers, books, or magazines; being interested in articles and programs about health; visiting friends or sick persons; communicating with young people; using a telephone; and taking medications.

population reports good or better health. For the oldest-old, the share drops to 16 percent. For those with three or more limitations,[3] the share notably declines to 5–6 percent. The proportion of good or better health in Japan is significantly lower than in other countries. In fact, Japanese individuals may be reluctant to express positive opinions, which may result in an underestimation of their health. A study reveals that despite Japanese people having better population health than their Korean counterparts, their self-reported health is inferior (Park and Lee 2013). Regardless of age or degree of limitations, the share of older people who are satisfied with life after retirement remains stable at around 4–6 percent, which is significantly lower than in

3. Given that the definition of ADL/IADL in the CSLC differs from that in other countries, we select the number of ADLs that corresponds most precisely to 3+ limitations in JSTAR. In particular, we determine the proportion of the JSTAR sample with 3+ limitations (approximately 9 percent) and use it as a cutoff in the CSLC to represent the closest proportion of the elderly population. Due to the fact that JSTAR has no respondents aged 85+, we utilize the 9 percent cutoff for both the 65+ and 85+ groups in the CSLC. Notable is that this cutoff for the 85+ age group may underestimate the real proportion of the oldest-old with 3+ limitations.

Table 6.2 **Well-being for those 65+ and 85+ by ADL limitations, Japan, 2016**

	65+	65+ with 3+ Lims	85+	85+ with 3+ Lims
Self-Report of Health—Good or better*	0.26	0.05	0.16	0.06
Life Satisfaction—satisfied or very satisfied**	0.04	0.05	0.06	0.06
Kessler 6 Scores (0–24)*	2.97	6.12	3.89	6.03
*Observations**	*156,626*	*17,841*	*19,678*	*5,140*
*Observations***	*20,038*	*2,144*	*2,703*	*594*

Notes: Data are from the Comprehensive Survey of Living Conditions (CSLC 2016), health questionnaire (*), and income questionnaire (**). Individuals in nursing homes were not sampled. Respondent weights are used for all calculations. Given that the definition of ADL/IADL in the CSLC differs from that in other countries, we select the number of ADLs that corresponds most precisely to 3+ limitations in JSTAR. In particular, we determine the proportion of the JSTAR sample with 3+ limitations (approximately 9 percent) and use it as a cutoff in the CSLC to represent the closest proportion of the elderly population. Due to the fact that JSTAR has no respondents aged 85+, we utilize the 9 percent cutoff for both the 65+ and 85+ groups in the CSLC. This cutoff for the 85+ age group may underestimate the proportion of the oldest-old with 3+ limitations. Self-reported health is a five-category indicator that ranges from very bad, bad, neutral, good, and very good (*). We focus on the 65+ population who are not working or looking for employment to assess retirement satisfaction, and we utilize a life satisfaction indicator with five categories: very unsatisfied, unsatisfied, neutral, satisfied, and very satisfied (**). We utilize the Kessler Psychological Distress Scale (K6) (Kessler et al. 2003) (*). The K6 involves six questions about a person's emotional state during the past 30 days: (1) How often did you feel nervous? (2) How often did you feel hopeless? (3) How often did you feel restless or fidgety? (4) How often did you feel so depressed that nothing could cheer you up? (5) How often did you feel everything was an effort? and (6) How often did you feel worthless? Each question was scored from 0 (none of the time) to 4 (all of the time). The scores of the six questions were then summed, yielding a minimum score of 0 and a maximum score of 24. The higher the score, the poorer the mental health, and a score greater than 5 indicates stress.

other countries. The average K6 score for older people is around 3 points, lower than the 5-point cutoff for depressive symptoms (Kessler et al. 2003). The score increases to around 6 points for those with three or more limitations, indicating that limitations associate negatively with mental health.

We then examine how the financial status of the older population changes as the number of limitations with ADLs/IADLs increases. Table 6.3 shows the distribution of income and wealth in the older population. We use the post-tax household income and wealth recorded in the CSLC's income questionnaire, which is normalized to the measures based on the OECD equivalent scale.

The income distribution is skewed, with the mean value being higher than the median. The wealth distribution is far more skewed than the income distribution, with the mean wealth being twice as high as the median. Skewness is generally more noticeable in the oldest-old people. Interestingly, the oldest-old are, on average, more affluent than the overall 65+ population, possibly indicating a selection for more affluent older people who survive to age 85. Table 6.4 depicts the distributions based on the number of limitations with ADLs and IADLs.

Table 6.3 Income and wealth distribution, Japan, 2016

	Income		Wealth	
	65+	85+	65+	85+
5th Percentile	80	71	0	0
10th Percentile	112	102	0	0
25th Percentile	195	184	80	102
50th Percentile	309	310	510	510
75th Percentile	488	511	1529	1835
90th Percentile	751	824	3187	3752
95th Percentile	987	1121	5098	5108
Mean	408	426	1206	1335
Observations	*20,038*	*2,073*	*18,961*	*2,554*

Notes: The percentiles of income and wealth were calculated using the Comprehensive Survey of Living Conditions income questionnaire (CSLC 2016). Individuals in nursing homes were not sampled. Respondent weights are used for all calculations. Income and wealth are post-tax adjusted according to the OECD-modified scale and aggregated at the household level. Wealth is aggregated at the household level. All estimates were reported at 10,000 JPY in 2019.

In contrast to countries such as the United States, the relationship between older people's ADL/IADL limitations and their financial situation in Japan is moderate and not obviously negative. The income distribution is relatively stable across the degree of limitations. For example, approximately 17 percent of older adults free of limitations have less than the median income. This proportion rises to 24 and 21 percent for those with one and two ADL limitations, respectively, which then reduces to 19 percent for those with more than three ADL limitations. The share of older people in the top income category remains stable at around 11–16 percent, regardless of the number of limitations. Similarly, the wealth distribution also changes little with the degree of limitation.

The lack of changes may be driven by a trend in Japan in which frail older people are more likely to live with their families. Although the proportion of older people living with a child has decreased over the last several decades, co-residence with children is still higher in Japan than in other developed countries (Cabinet Office 2020b).[4] Some studies discovered that poor or fragile health caused by a variety of factors would trigger a shift in living arrangements among older Japanese people from single or couple households to living with families, especially children (Brown et al. 2002; Johar et al. 2015;

4. Since 1980, this survey has been conducted every five years by the Cabinet Office in Japan for people aged 60 and over living in Japan and other developed countries. The survey in 2020 was conducted in four countries: Japan, the United States, Germany, and Sweden. In each country, approximately 2,500 persons 60+ were randomly selected, and in each country, approximately 1,000 persons responded. According to this survey, the proportion of co-residence with children in Japan is 36.2 percent, while it is 12.2 percent, 8.1 percent, and 2.9 percent for the United States, Germany and Sweden, respectively. See "Chapter 2, Summary of Survey Results" (in Japanese), https://www8.cao.go.jp/kourei/ishiki/r02/gaiyo/pdf/s2–1.pdf (accessed September 30, 2020).

Table 6.4 **Income and wealth distribution by limitations for 65+ population, Japan, 2016**

	0 ADLs & 0 IADLs	0 ADLs & 1+ IADLs	1 ADL	2 ADLs	3+ ADLs	Fraction of full Sample
		Panel 1: Income				
<50% Median HH Income	0.170	0.181	0.240	0.210	0.188	0.177
50–100% Median HH Income	0.320	0.338	0.319	0.344	0.333	0.323
100–150% Median HH Income	0.230	0.224	0.190	0.236	0.218	0.227
150–200% Median HH Income	0.122	0.110	0.099	0.099	0.122	0.118
200%+ Median HH Income	0.159	0.148	0.152	0.112	0.139	0.155
Fraction of full Sample	0.757	0.134	0.045	0.029	0.036	
Observations	*15,099*	*2,698*	*905*	*598*	*738*	*20,038*
		Panel 2: Wealth				
<50% Median HH Wealth	0.364	0.346	0.418	0.357	0.348	0.363
50–100% Median HH Wealth	0.099	0.097	0.114	0.091	0.100	0.099
100–150% Median HH Wealth	0.115	0.116	0.122	0.106	0.127	0.115
150–200% Median HH Wealth	0.041	0.054	0.040	0.053	0.047	0.043
200%+ Median HH Wealth	0.381	0.388	0.307	0.395	0.379	0.379
Fraction of full Sample	0.755	0.135	0.046	0.029	0.036	
Observations	*15,099*	*2,698*	*905*	*598*	*738*	*20,038*

Notes: Data were obtained from the Comprehensive Survey of Living Conditions (CSLC 2016) health and income questionnaires. Individuals in nursing homes were not sampled. Respondent weights are used for all calculations. The definition of ADL in the CSLC differs from that in other countries, which includes limitations of IADLs. The ADL index runs from 0 to 5 and is the number of limitations from (1) daily activities (dressing, bathing, eating, going to bed), (2) going outside, (3) working, (4) sports, and (5) others. IDALs include limitations (2) to (5). Owing to this data limitation, IADLs were included when calculating the proportion of 2+ ADLs. Household income is the total family members' individual income, adjusted according to the OECD-modified scale. The sample's median household income was roughly 3.10 million JPY in 2019, and the median wealth was 500 million JPY in 2019.

Oshio and Kan 2018). Regarding the mechanism behind the high likelihood of living with children among older Japanese people, much research has been conducted from the perspectives of bequest motivations and altruism, albeit the results have not yet proven conclusive (Johar 2010; Niimi 2016; Horioka 2021). Regardless of the mechanism, consequently, the weak relationship between limitations with ADLs and household income (wealth) may be attributable to such changes in living arrangements among older people, which may safeguard older people from suffering serious financial difficulties.

Furthermore, the LTCI reimburses high-cost long-term care expenses when the recipient's total monthly payment exceeds the maximum amount to be borne.[5] The CSLC included the amounts of such reimbursement to

5. The maximum amount depends on the household's annual income. The maximum amount a user is required to pay is 14,100 JPY, 93,000 JPY, and 44,400 JPY per month for annual household income of more than 11.6 million JPY, 7.7–11.6 million JPY, and less than 7.7 million JPY, respectively. If all household members are exempt from local government tax, the cap is set between 15,000–24,500 JPY, and 15,000 JPY for households receiving public assistance.

respondents as a part of income, alongside social security benefits (i.e., public assistance, support benefits for pensioners, and maternity and child allowances). Therefore, the generous coverage of LTCI could be a factor in the moderate correlation between ADL limitations and income (wealth). Finally, the moderate-income gradient might result from selection bias, as the CSLC does not sample institutionalized individuals. This selection might lessen the income gradient if institutionalized seniors tend to have lower incomes than their community-dwelling peers. A few studies examine the difference in income between elderly people living in nursing homes and receiving care at home, utilizing small samples collected from specific municipalities (Izumida 2008; Akiyama et al. 2015). According to these studies, a smaller proportion of people with high income utilize institutional care than those with low income.[6] However, the studies utilize administrative data from rural and small-population cities, which unfortunately do not necessarily give nationally representative evidence. For instance, the number of private nursing homes has been rapidly increasing in Japan,[7] and approximately 43 percent of them are located in metropolitan areas like *Kanto* (suburbs of Tokyo) and *Kansai* (suburbs of Osaka) (MHLW 2022b).

Furthermore, the admission fees vary widely across private nursing homes; some are opulent and prohibitively expensive, allowing only the wealthy to reside there. To gain an accurate picture of the characteristics of the older population residing in nursing homes, it is necessary to undertake a nationally representative survey of this population.

In summary, older Japanese people have a relatively low degree of limitations that do not significantly correlate with financial difficulties. This moderate correlation may be due to Japan's universal coverage of its public long-term care system. Section 6.2 introduces the system in depth.

6.2 Long-Term Care System in Japan

Total long-term care spending in Japan has risen over the last two decades, from around 0.7 percent of the GDP in 2000 to more than 2 percent in 2019 (figure 6.3). Compared to concurrent health care spending, long-term care

6. For example, using long-term care claims data for 4,099 individuals aged 65 and above in a municipality in the Hokkaido prefecture in 2007–2009, Akiyama et al. (2015) found that 2.8 percent of those in high-income brackets with 2 million JPY or more per year (n = 1,606) are institutionalized, whereas 4.6 percent of those in low-income brackets with 0.8 million JPY or less per year (n=1,601) are in a nursing home. Likewise, Izumida (2008) discovered that 12.3 percent of high-income persons (n=261) are in a nursing home, whereas 22.9 percent of low-income people (n=395) are institutionalized, based on comparable data from 7,312 individuals in a municipality in the western region of Japan in 2005. Despite the fact that the definitions of income groups and institutionalization rates vary across municipalities, we observed that older individuals with greater incomes are less likely to reside in nursing homes based on these past studies.

7. According to Morioka (2020), the number of private nursing homes increased from 949 in 2000, when the LTCI was introduced, to 14,118 in 2019. Consequently, the number of old persons living in private nursing home increased from 66,495 in 2000 to 539,995 in 2019.

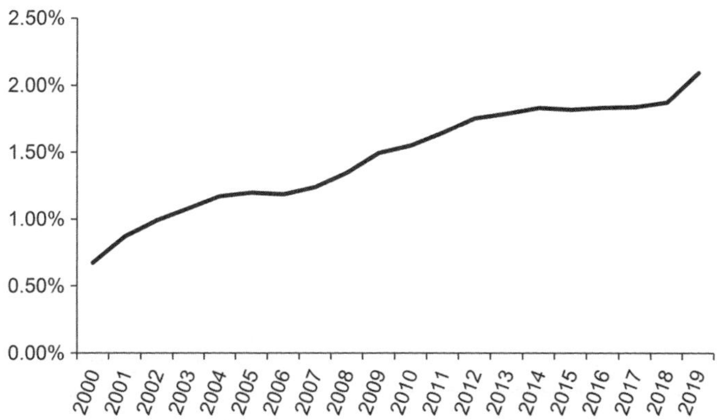

Fig. 6.3 Share of GDP spent on long-term care, Japan, 2000–2019

Source: Long-term care spending is taken from the MHLW (2019) White book. https://www.mhlw.go.jp/wp/hakusyo/kousei/19–2/dl/10.pdf. The GDP is taken from the Cabinet Office (2020a) National Accounts for 2019. https://www.esri.cao.go.jp/jp/sna/data/data_list/kakuhou/files/2019/2019_kaku_top.html.

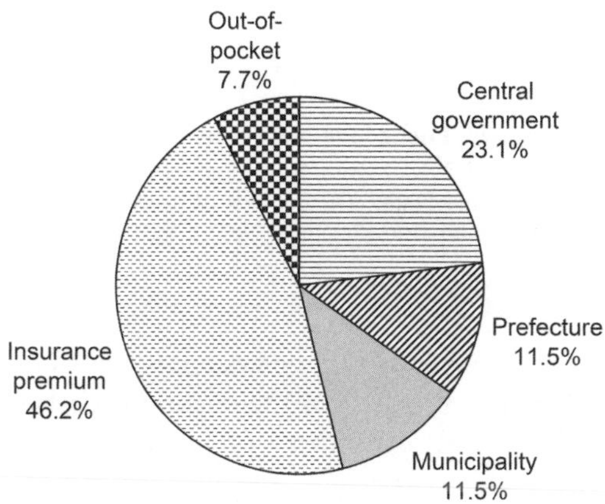

Fig. 6.4 Percent of LTC financing by source, Japan, 2019

Source: Cabinet Office, 2019. https://www5.cao.go.jp/keizai-shimon/kaigi/special/reform/wg1/310328/shiryou2–2.pdf Although the co-payment rate for formal services is 10 percent, it may not indicate the actual out-of-pocket payment due to the stop loss setting. We thus use the 7.7 percent of the "real" co-payment rate in 2016 that the MHLW reports determining the private costs of nursing homes, community-based care, and home care, respectively. (https://www.mhlw.go.jp/file/05-Shingikai-12601000-Seisakutoukatsukan-Sanjikanshitsu_Shakaihoshoutantou/0000140158.pdf, accessed November 2, 2022).

spending has increased from negligible in 2000 to approximately one-third of total health care spending in 2019 (MHLW 2019). Indeed, the long-term care system has become essential to Japan's social security system. Figure 6.4 shows the financial methods of the long-term care system. Out-of-pocket payments fund approximately 7.7 percent of the costs. The remainder is

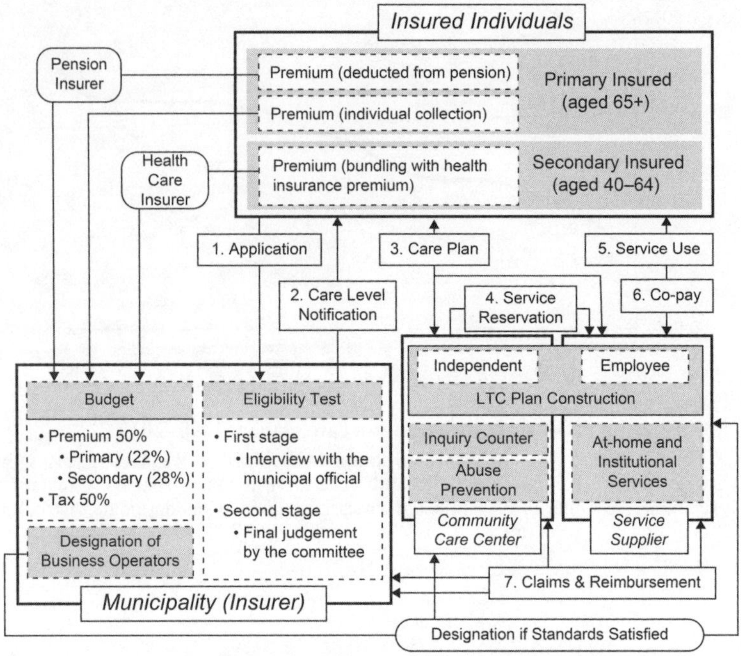

Fig. 6.5. Structure of Japan's public long-term care insurance.

Source: Fu, R., and H. Noguchi. 2019. "Moral Hazard under Zero Price Policy: Evidence from Japanese Long-Term Care Claims Data." *The European Journal of Health Economics* 20: 785–99. Reproduced with permission from Springer Nature. https://link.springer.com/journal/10198.

funded with public resources. Since the system is run as public insurance, the insurance premium covers half of the remaining costs (46.2 percent of the total costs). The central government, prefecture, and municipality each contribute 23.1 percent, 11.5 percent, and 11.5 percent of the total costs. Given that the long-term care system is designed and managed solely by the government and that the private long-term care market is insignificant in Japan, the following two sections will focus on LTCI details.

6.2.1 Public Long-Term Care Insurance

When LTCI was introduced in 2000, it was viewed as a solution to the dramatic increase in the number of older people in need of long-term care. As of January 2015, it has provided services to over five million people aged 65+, about 17 percent of this population. Figure 6.5 shows the overall structure of LTCI. The LTCI is mandatory insurance: all Japanese citizens aged 40 and over (40+) are required to enroll and are classified as either primary (aged 65+) or secondary insureds (aged 40–64). They pay their municipal monthly premiums through deductions or individual collections. Municipalities, as insurers, are responsible for managing LTCI budgets, administering demand-based eligibility tests, and appointing long-term care business operators (Fu and Noguchi 2019).

When primary insureds are aware of their care requirements, they should apply for long-term care eligibility by taking an eligibility test administered by the municipality of residence (Step 1 in figure 6.5). Secondary insureds can apply for the test if they require care due to aging-related diagnoses.[8] This test is divided into two parts: an interview based on a 74-item questionnaire on physical and mental functions and a final decision by the Long-Term Care Needs Certification Committee. In the first stage, an investigator (a municipality official specializing in the eligibility test) organizes an interview with an applicant who self-reports needing care. This interview is commonly held at the applicant's residence and conducted in the presence of a relative. The interview is based on a questionnaire in which all items are designed to measure one of five health-related functions: (1) physical function, (2) living function, (3) cognitive function, (4) behavioral disorders, and (5) the ability to adapt to social life. Notably, the interview does not include a means test. Table 6.5 summarizes the items of each of the functions. Each item is a multiple-choice question. The investigator circles the answer closest to the status quo.

After all the items are checked, a software package generates a hypothetical care time the applicant needs (table 6.6). The hypothetical care time is derived by statistical analyses using a sample of 3,500 randomly selected older people who are institutionalized, for which the types of service and corresponding service times are thoroughly documented over 48 hours. By aggregating hypothetical care times across all categories, the package provides a standardized care time (table 6.7) for the applicant, which is used to assign the applicant to a care level.

There are seven care levels. Each care level indicates the degree of limitation with ADLs/IADLs. Specifically, Support-required Level (SL) 1 applies to recipients living independently but requiring help with IADL, and SL2 denotes those requiring more assistance than SL1 recipients who might deteriorate to Care-required Level (CL) 1. CL1 recipients need more assistance in terms of IADL than SL recipients need. CL2 recipients have additional needs with ADL above CL1 recipients. CL3 recipients require more services than those in CL2 and, thus, need total care. CL4 recipients fulfill all the

8. Aging-related diagnoses are cancer (limited to those that physicians have determined, based on generally accepted medical knowledge, to have led to a condition from which recovery is unlikely), rheumatoid arthritis, amyotrophic lateral sclerosis, ossification of posterior longitudinal ligament, osteoporosis with fracture, dementia in primary age, progressive supranuclear palsy, basal ganglia degeneration, Parkinson's disease-related disorders, spinocerebellar degeneration, spinal canal stenosis, progeria, multiple system atrophy, diabetic neuropathy, diabetic nephropathy and diabetic retinopathy, cerebrovascular disease, arteriosclerosis obliterans chronic obstructive pulmonary disease, and osteoarthritis with significant deformity of bilateral knee or hip joints.

Table 6.5 **Contents of the first-stage eligibility test**

Function	Item
Physical Function	Q1–1 Experiencing paralysis Q1–2 Experiencing contracture Q1–3 Able to roll over Q1–4 Able to rise from bed Q1–5 Able to keep seated Q1–6 Able to keep an upright position on both feet Q1–7 Able to walk Q1–8 Able to stand up Q1–9 Able to keep an upright position on one foot Q1–10 Able to wash one's body Q1–11 Able to cut nails Q1–12 Vision level Q1–13 Hearing level
Living Function	Q2–1 Able to travel using devices Q2–2 Able to move from one place to another Q2–3 Able to swallow Q2–4 Able to eat a meal Q2–5 Able to urinate Q2–6 Able to defecate Q2–7 Able to perform oral hygiene Q2–8 Able to wash face Q2–9 Able to comb Q2–10 Able to wear clothes Q2–11 Able to wear pants Q2–12 Frequency of going outdoors
Cognitive Function	Q3–1 Communication level Q3–2 Understanding of daily routines Q3–3 Remembers birthdate Q3–4 Remembers a short-term memory Q3–5 Remembers his/her own name Q3–6 Is aware of the current season Q3–7 Is aware of the current location Q3–8 Loitering around Q3–9 Not able to return home after going out
Behavioral Disorders	Q4–1 Persecution complex Q4–2 Keeps talking Q4–3 Emotionally unstable Q4–4 Unable to distinguish daytime and nighttime Q4–5 Talks about the same topic repeatedly Q4–6 Shouts Q4–7 Resists care Q4–8 Has anxiety
Ability to Adapt to Social Life	Q5–1 Able to take medicine Q5–2 Able to manage money Q5–3 Able to make decisions in daily life Q5–4 Unable to get involved in the community Q5–5 Able to go shopping Q5–6 Able to cook

Notes: Edited from Fu and Noguchi (2019)

Table 6.6 Hypothetical care times regarding categories of assistance

Category of Assistance	Hypothetical Care Time Range (Minutes)
Eating	1.1–71.4
Mobility	0.4–21.4
Toilet	0.2–28.0
Hygiene	1.2–24.3
Housework	0.4–11.3
Dementia	5.8–21.2re
Exercise	0.5–15.4
Medical care	1.0–37.2
Standardized Care Time	**10.6–230.6**

Notes: Edited from Fu and Noguchi (2019)

Table 6.7 Care levels corresponding to standardized care times

Care Level	Standardized Care Time (Minutes)
Support required level 1 (SL1)	25.0–31.9
Support required level 2 (SL2)	32.0–49.9
Care level 1 (CL1)	32.0–49.9
Care level 2 (CL2)	50.0–69.9
Care level 3 (CL3)	70.0–89.9
Care level 4 (CL4)	90.0–109.9
Care level 5 (CL5)	110.0–

Note: Edited from Fu and Noguchi (2019). The standardized care times for support required level 2 and care level 1 are identical, although those certified to care level 1 have worse cognitive functions.

requirements mentioned above and function poorly in terms of ADL. CL5 recipients find it impossible to live without care and have more substantial ADL needs than CL4 recipients. Each care level is set with a monthly cap up to which the eligible insured can use services.[9]

This preliminary assigned care level is then checked by committee members using a protocol issued by the central government. With careful judgment, the committee officially assigns a care level to the insured individual and notifies him (Step 2 in figure 6.5). The care level is not permanent; it is assigned a valid period (commonly 6 to 24 months). Eligible insured individuals should renew their eligibility based on their expiration date. Based on their care levels, eligible insured individuals should make plans to use long-term care services (Step 3 in figure 6.5). They may construct these plans on their own or with the help of their families, but care managers are more

9. The monthly caps are 50,320 JPY (SL1), 105,310 JPY (SL2), 167,650 JPY (CL1), 197,050 JPY (CL2), 270,480 JPY (CL3), 309,380 JPY (CL4), and 362,170 JPY (CL5).

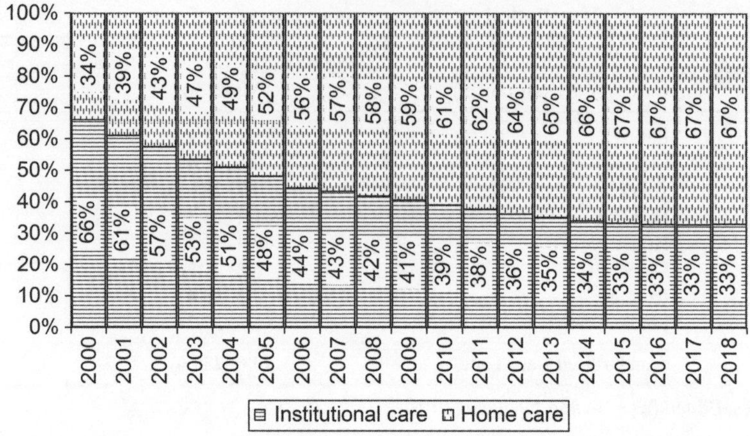

Fig. 6.6 Public spending on institutional care has been gradually replaced by spending on community-based care, Japan, 2000–2018

Source: Ministry of Health, Labour and Welfare (2000–2019) Long-term Care Insurance Status Report. https://www.e-stat.go.jp/stat-search/files?page=1&toukei=00450351&tstat=000001031648&cycle=8. The shares were calculated by annual public spending on home and institutional care. *Home care* is defined as either at-home or community-based care and includes home-visit services, daycare services, short-stay services, group-home services, and small-scale multi-function care services.

likely to assist them in deciding on a care plan. Some care managers work for municipally designated community care centers, while others work for nonprofit or for-profit service providers. Care managers should provide detailed information on long-term care services while making plans with the eligible insured individual and, if necessary, make reservations for services (Step 4 in figure 6.5). Based on the care plans, insured individuals can contract with any service suppliers to use the services.[10] Although eligible insured individuals can choose home care or institutional care, they are encouraged to use home care services until they reach a high level of care. Furthermore, only in-kind services are available to eligible insureds; a cash allowance is not allowed. As illustrated in figure 6.6, the share of home care–related spending has steadily increased since the LTCI's outset, accounting for 67 percent of the total long-term care spending in 2018.

Eligible insured individuals should co-pay 10 percent of their services (Steps 5–6 in figure 6.5). Two co-insurance rate reforms were implemented to cope with the rapidly rising public spending on long-term care services. Since August 2015, eligible insured individuals should co-pay 20 percent of the

10. The majority of services are offered to primary insureds. According to a 2016 MHLW report on LTCI, the care expenditures for secondary insureds represented only 2 percent of overall costs.

long-term care services if their incomes are comparable to the current workforce. Since August 2018, those with annual incomes greater than 4.63 million JPY (3.4 million JPY for a single household) should co-pay 30 percent of services used among insured individuals with 20 percent co-insurance.

6.2.2 Private Insurance

In Japan, several for-profit insurance companies provide private long-term care insurance.[11] In contrast to the public LTCI, payments for private insurance are made in cash. The services covered by private insurance plans vary among the insurance companies and the specific contracts, with potential co-payments, transportation costs for medical visits, and additional expenses like diapers, meals, and utilities while institutionalized, and housekeeping services not covered by the public LTCI. According to the National Survey on Life Insurance,[12] approximately 16.7 percent of Japanese households have private insurance for long-term care services (Life Insurance Culture Foundation 2021). However, the role of private long-term care insurance is small and only covers approximately 0.1 percent of the overall long-term care spending (Yong and Saito 2011). The reasons behind this discrepancy are multifold. Firstly, it is surprising to see that households with relatively young heads (aged 30–64) are more likely to opt for private insurance than those with older heads (aged 65 and above), with 20 percent of the former group enrolled compared to just 9 percent of the latter group (Life Insurance Culture Foundation 2021). This low demand for private insurance among older people may be due to insurance companies limiting enrollment to certain age groups or charging high premiums for those over 70 who are at higher risk of needing long-term care. Secondly, the percentage of users surpassing the maximum amount of LTCI benefits that may be reimbursed in cash by private insurance is 2.3 percent on average, and even for CL5 users, who have the greatest need for long-term care, the rate is only approximately 5 percent (MHLW 2017). In conclusion, the large disparity between the share of spending that comes from private insurance and the enrollment rate can be attributed to the mismatch between the age of the currently insured and their needs for services, as well as the higher maximum amounts of LTCI benefits than those needed to meet the demand for essential care.

11. As of 2010, 22 insurance companies out of 47 members of the Life Insurance Association of Japan and 25 members of the General Insurance Association of Japan offer long-term care insurance, and only 9 companies sell long-term care insurance as a stand-alone product (Matsuyoshi 2010).

12. The National Survey on Life Insurance is conducted by the Life Insurance Culture Foundation every three years, starting in 1965. The survey selects households with two or more family members using a stratified two-stage random sampling method from 400 locations across Japan, with a sample size of approximately 4,000 households (Life Insurance Culture Foundation 2021).

Table 6.8 Home care by age and ADL, Japan, 2016

	65+	85+
All	0.106	0.363
0 ADLs, 1+ IADL	0.148	0.363
1 ADL	0.410	0.641
2 ADL	0.474	0.682
3+ ADL	0.539	0.680
Observations	*169,273*	*23,399*

Notes: Data are from the Comprehensive Survey of Living Conditions (CSLC 2016), Health and Household Questionnaires. Individuals in nursing homes were not sampled. Respondent weights are used for all calculations. In the CSLC, the definition of ADL differs from that in other countries, which includes limitations from IADLs. The ADL index runs from 0 to 5 and is the number of limitations from (1) daily activities (dressing, bathing, eating, going to bed), (2) going outside, (3) working, (4) sports, and (5) others. IADLs include limitations (2) to (5). Owing to this data limitation, IADLs were included when calculating the proportion of 2+ ADLs. The indicator of any care takes the value of one if home-dwelling elderly people in need of care receive assistance from either family members or formal care providers. Respondent weights are used for all calculations.

6.2.3 Long-Term Care Receipt

Table 6.8 shows the proportion of the older population who receives home care based on the number of limitations with ADLs or IADLs. This table focuses on home care (both formal and informal) because individual-level data containing ADL information for institutional care are unavailable. Approximately 11 percent of the 65+ population receive formal or informal home care. For the oldest-old, the proportion is more than three times (around 36 percent). As the limitations increase, so does share. Approximately 54 percent of those aged 65+ with three or more limitations receive care, and 68 percent of the oldest-old do. It is worth noting that the proportion of elderly Japanese receiving care is generally lower compared to the United States and Europe, which may be due to differences in the measurement of limitations, with the CSLC scale less indicative of severe disability compared to the HRS/SHARE scale.

Figure 6.7 shows the proportion of the population according to the type of care they received. The populations in public nursing homes are calculated based on a governmental report summary of the 2016 Survey of Long-Term Care Service Facilities (MHLW 2016).[13, 14] The populations receiving home help are calculated based on the CSLC household questionnaire. "Formal home care" denotes respondents who use formal home care services; "infor-

13. According to the report, there were 886,000 people of age 65+ and 573,000 people of age 85+ living in public nursing homes.

14. Please note that the data presented in figure 6.7 only pertain to residents of public nursing homes and do not include residents of private nursing homes. As a result, the total number of nursing home residents is likely underestimated.

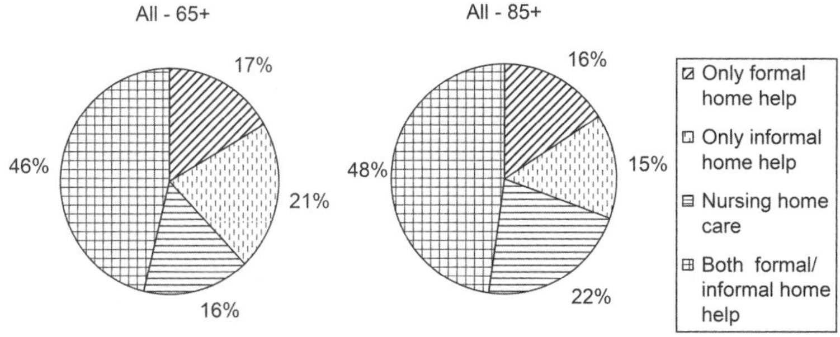

Fig. 6.7 Type of care received by age, Japan, 2016

Notes: Populations in nursing homes were calculated from the Summary of the 2016 Survey of Long-Term Care Service Facilities, https://www.mhlw.go.jp/toukei/saikin/hw/kaigo/service16. The populations receiving home help were calculated based on the Comprehensive Survey of Living Conditions (CSLC 2016) household questionnaire. Individuals in nursing homes were not sampled. Respondent weights are used for calculations using the CSLC. "Formal care" denotes respondents who are eligible to use formal care services; "informal care" denotes respondents receiving informal care from family members; "both from formal and informal care" denotes respondents receiving both formal and informal care.

mal care" denotes respondents receiving informal care from family members; and "both formal and informal care" denotes respondents receiving both formal and informal care. Seventeen percent and 21 percent of the 65+ population receive only formal and informal home care, respectively, and the majority (46 percent) receives both formal and informal home care. Approximately 16 percent of the population resides in nursing homes. For the oldest-old, the share receiving only informal care reduces to 15 percent, and the share living in nursing homes increases to 22 percent.

Figure 6.8 further shows how the type of care received varies by the degree of limitations. This figure again focuses on home care because individual-level data containing ADL information for institutional care are unavailable. The use of informal and formal home care increases with the degree of limitations in older people, with a substantial increase at one or more ADL limitations. The pattern is consistent among the oldest-old. Given Japan's universal long-term care coverage, it is natural for older people to seek assistance from both their families and formal long-term care workers as their limitations increase.

The distribution of the daily care hours received by the type of care is presented in table 6.9. In the CSLC long-term care questionnaire, care hours are the hours of home care that a needy older person receives from his or her primary caregiver. Primary caregivers can be either formal care workers or informal caregivers, and thus, the care they provide can be either formal home care or informal care, assisting with either ADL or IADL limitations or both. Formal home care is either at-home or community-based and includes home visits, daycare, short-stay services, group-home services, and

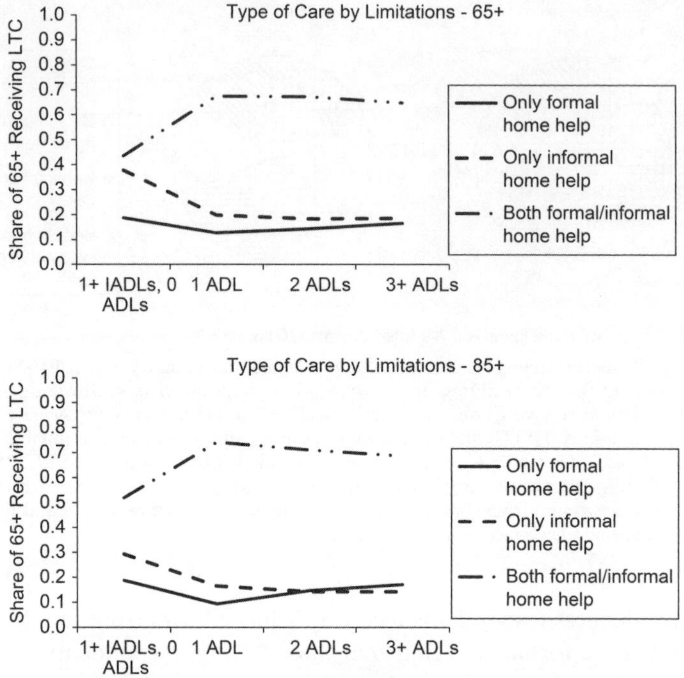

Fig. 6.8 Type of care received by age and limitations, Japan, 2016

Notes: Data were obtained from the Comprehensive Survey of Living Conditions (CSLC 2016) household questionnaire. Individuals in nursing homes were not sampled. Respondent weights are used for all calculations. "Formal care" denotes respondents who are eligible to use formal care services; "informal care" denotes respondents receiving informal care from family members; "both from formal and informal care" denotes respondents receiving both formal and informal care. The definition of ADL in the CSLC differs from that in other countries, which includes limitations of IADLs. The ADL index runs from 0 to 5 and is the number of limitations from (1) daily activities (dressing, bathing, eating, going to bed), (2) going outside, (3) working, (4) sports, and (5) others. IADLs include limitations (2) to (5). Owing to this data limitation, IADLs were included when calculating the proportion of 2+ ADLs.

small-scale multi-function care. The daily hours of care are measured by a categorical variable, ranging from "receiving care only when needed" to "receiving full-day care." Around 20 percent of older people, regardless of age, receive care all day long, and approximately 40 percent receive care only when needed. Distribution varies depending on the type of care received. Older people are most likely to receive informal care only when needed (44 percent for 65+ and 42 percent for 85+). In comparison, they are most likely to receive full-day formal care (28 percent for 65+ and 36 percent for 85+). Furthermore, more than 40 percent of older people report "others" for the number of hours of formal care received. This finding suggests that measuring the *daily* hours (or intensity) of formal care received is difficult.

Table 6.9 **Distribution of hours received by type**

	65+			85+		
	All	Formal	Informal	All	Formal	Informal
Full day	0.20	0.28	0.21	0.21	0.36	0.19
Half day	0.10	0.06	0.11	0.11	0.07	0.13
2–3 hours	0.11	0.10	0.12	0.14	0.10	0.15
Only when needed	0.39	0.14	0.44	0.38	0.13	0.42
Others	0.19	0.41	0.12	0.16	0.35	0.11
Observations	*6,052*	*649*	*4,644*	*3,032*	*290*	*2,385*

Notes: Data were obtained from the Comprehensive Survey of Living Conditions (CSLC 2016) LTC questionnaire. Individuals in nursing homes were not sampled. Respondent weights are used for all calculations. Care hours were home care received. Home care is defined as either at-home or community-based care and includes home-visit services, daycare services, short-stay services, group-home services, and small-scale multi-function care services. Formal care is defined as receiving formal long-term care from service providers, and informal care is defined as receiving care from family members. Daily hours of care are measured by a categorical variable ranging from "receiving care only when needed" to "receiving care during the full day."

6.2.4 Formal Long-Term Care Supply

Formal long-term care consists of institutional care and home care. Institutional care includes both public and private nursing homes. Public nursing homes are run by not-for-profit organizations, including social welfare corporations and municipalities, and the government regulates the fees and types of services provided. Private companies, including for-profit corporations, run private nursing homes, and the services and fees vary among nursing homes. LTCI covers long-term care services, rent, and food for daily living in public nursing homes. On the other hand, daily living expenses in private nursing homes, such as rent, management fees, meals, and utilities, are not covered by LTCI and must be paid out of pocket by the residents. However, the long-term care provided in both types of facilities is covered by the LTCI and is referred to as formal *home* care.

There are three types of public nursing homes in Japan: nursing homes for the elderly ("*Tokuyo*" in Japanese), geriatric health services facilities ("*Roken*" in Japanese), and sanatoriums for medical and nursing care ("*Kaigo-Ryoyou*" in Japanese). *Tokuyo* provides physical care and daily living assistance; residents often have intense care needs and are expected to stay for the rest of their lives once enrolled. The average length of stay was 1,405 days in 2016 (Japan Association of Geriatric Health Services Facilities 2016). *Roken* is designed to serve as a transitional facility between hospitals and homes to reintegrate seniors into their communities. The standard period of stay is three months; however, it can be extended if required. The average length of hospital stay in 2016 was 311 days. *Kaigo-Ryoyou* provides comprehensive medical treatment and long-term care. *Kaigo-Ryoyou* is intended to avoid "social hospitalization." The average length of stay in *Kaigo-Ryoyou* in 2016 was 483 days. *Kaigo-Ryoyou* was abolished at the end of fiscal year 2017 (i.e., March 2018), replaced by *Kaigo-Iryoin, which* was launched in April 2018. *Kaigo-Iryoin* provides physical and daily living assistance for old persons requiring long-term medical care, such as routine medical management, end-of-life care, and terminal care. The features of *Kaigo-Iryoin* are well-staffed with medical personnel like physicians and nurses, the provision of a wide range of medical care, and the authorization of long-term institutionalization.

Private nursing homes are classified into two types based on the way they provide long-term care services. One type is assisted living condominiums, which are operated with on-site medical care and long-term care specialists and thus provide long-term care within the facility. The other is retirement homes for independent older people or those with relatively minor care needs, of which the main purpose is to support residents' daily lives.[15] Because we lack relevant data or statistics, particularly on private nursing home residents and workers, we concentrate on formal care in public nursing homes throughout this section.

Table 6.10 shows the number of nursing homes, beds, and occupancy rates for public and private nursing homes. There are over 12 thousand public nursing homes, with a total capacity of approximately 884 thousand beds. There are approximately 830 thousand residents in public nursing homes, accounting for nearly 94 percent of the capacity. The number of public beds per person aged 65+ is 0.026. The number of private nursing homes is roughly equal to that of public nursing homes; however, the capacity of private nursing homes is significantly lower. Accordingly, there are only 0.013 private beds per person aged 65+.

Table 6.11 shows the geographical variations in public nursing home occupancies for the three types of public homes. The occupancy rate of nursing homes for the elderly varies slightly across prefectures, ranging from 95 percent to 99 percent. Enrollment in any public nursing home in Japan seems highly competitive. The most significant variation is in sanatoriums for medical and nursing care, where occupancy rates range from 64 percent to 99 percent. The number of beds per 100 people aged 65+ also varies across prefectures, ranging from 2.1 to 4.5.

As previously stated, formal home care can be either at-home or

15. Except for a few facilities called "certified facilities" which meet the standards of the Long-Term Care Insurance Law (standards for personnel, equipment, and operation) by the MHLW, private nursing homes are under the jurisdiction of the Ministry of Land, Infrastructure and Transport (MLIT), rather than the MHLW. Furthermore, the assisted living condominiums provide the long-term care service fee in the usage fee, whereas the retirement homes outsource long-term care services to an outside provider, incurring an additional fee for the residents.

Table 6.10 **Absolute number of nursing homes, beds, and occupancy rate, Japan, 2016**

	Japan, 2016	
	Public	Private
Nursing homes	12,235	11,739
Beds	883,845	457,918
Nursing home residents	829,387	—
Occupancy rate	93.84%	—
Pop 65+	34,590,611	34,590,611
Beds per pop 65+	0.026	0.013
Pop 85+	5,201,991	5,201,991
Beds per pop 85+	0.170	0.088

Source: Data on nursing homes are from the Report on the State of Nursing Homes in Japan by the Ministry of Health, Labour and Welfare (2017), https://www.mhlw.go.jp/toukei/saikin/hw/kaigo/service16/index.html. The number of public nursing homes is the aggregate of special nursing homes for the elderly ("*Tokuyo*" in Japanese), geriatric health services facilities ("*Roken*" in Japanese), and sanatoriums for medical and nursing care ("*Kaigo-Ryoyou*" in Japanese). The numbers of 65+ and 85+ populations were obtained from the Population Projection by the Statistics Bureau of Japan, https://www.stat.go.jp/data/jinsui/2016np/index.html.

Table 6.11 **Distribution of public nursing homes occupancy rate and beds across prefectures, Japan, 2015 and 2011**

	Occupancy rate (%), 2015			Nursing home beds per one hundred 65+, 2008	
Percentile	Nursing home for the elderly	Geriatric health services facility	Sanatoriums for medical and nursing care	Total	
5%	95.9	83.9	68.1	92.3	2.44
10%	96.5	85.4	72.5	92.5	2.64
20%	96.8	87.0	78.0	93.0	2.90
30%	97.2	88.1	83.5	93.5	3.10
40%	97.3	88.6	85.7	94.0	3.19
50%	97.5	89.5	87.5	94.2	3.25
60%	97.9	90.1	88.5	94.4	3.33
70%	98.1	90.8	89.8	94.6	3.52
80%	98.3	92.1	91.9	94.8	3.63
90%	98.5	92.5	93.6	95.6	3.85
95%	98.6	93.1	94.4	96.0	3.95
Min	95.0	82.0	64.1	91.5	2.16
Max	98.9	94.0	98.8	97.2	4.41

Notes: Data on the occupancy rate are from the Survey of Institutions and Establishments for Long-term Care by the Ministry of Health, Labour and Welfare (2015), https://www.e-stat.go.jp/stat-search/files?page=1&toukei=00450042. The percentiles are calculated using facility-level information on the quota and number of recipients in the facilities. Nursing home bed data were obtained from the same survey conducted in 2011.

community-based, including home visits, daycare, short-stay, group-home, and small-scale multi-function care. For both at-home and community-based care, two types of care are provided: long-term care benefit services for older persons with serious care needs and preventive care for those with relatively minor care needs.[16] There were approximately 247 thousand formal home care providers in 2020; around 30 percent were run by nonprofit organizations such as social welfare corporations or medical corporations, and the remainder were run by for-profit companies (MHLW 2020a). Providers are free to enter and exit the long-term care market to some extent,[17] and similar to medical care, the prices for long-term care services are controlled by the government under the LTCI and are reviewed every three years. Conclusively, this "*decentralized yet centralized*" system would lead to disparities in the provision and capacity of formal home care across regions (Shimizutani 2014).

The Japanese government just started a full-scale discussion on evaluating the quality of care. Although the LTC law requires facilities and care providers to report accidents to municipalities, they are not obligated to publicize the number of accidents. Therefore, the MHLW does not have a complete picture of accidents involving long-term care services. For example, of the 276 long-term care accidents reported by the Consumer Affairs Agency to the MHLW in 2014–2017, the most common type of accident is falls, tumbles, and slips (181 cases, 65.6 percent), followed by aspiration, ingestion, and engulfment (36 cases, 13 percent). In terms of the type of at-home care, daycare services account for 20 cases (7.2 percent of the total) and short-stay services for 254 cases (92 percent) (Care Work Foundation 2018). This is likely to be the tip of the iceberg.

Figure 6.9 depicts the staffing divisions by different skill levels at the three types of public nursing homes based on qualifications. They are classified as registered nurses, vocational nurses, care workers, social workers, and aids.[18] Aids are likely to be the least skilled workers, while registered nurses and care workers are the most skilled. We do not have data on formal home-care workers. Registered nurses make up 4 percent of nursing home workers, care workers make up 34 percent, and aids make up 57 percent. The proportion of registered nurses increases fourfold to approximately 19 percent in sanatoriums for medical and nursing care, where both comprehensive medical treatments and long-term care are provided, while the percentages of care

16. For independent old persons or those with relatively minor care needs, comprehensive services are provided, such as health promotion and senior citizen salons run by residents for the purpose of prevention. In principle, comprehensive services ("*Sogo-Jigyo*") are also partially covered by the LTCI, but they are initiated by the municipality.

17. The term "to some extent" refers to the fact that providers must meet personnel, equipment, and operational standards and be certified by the local government (prefectures or municipalities) in order for long-term care services to be covered by LTCI.

18. As postgraduate training, aides are employed in nursing homes without the national certification for formal care workers.

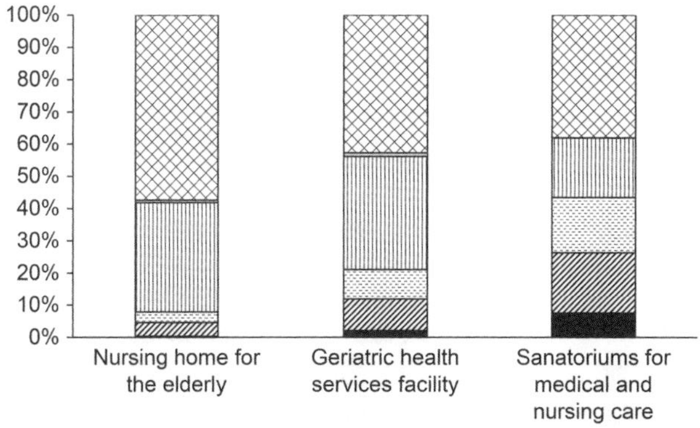

	Nursing home for the elderly	Geriatric health services facility	Sanatoriums for medical and nursing care
Aides	57.4%	42.7%	38.1%
Social workers	0.8%	1.1%	0.0%
Care workers	34.0%	35.1%	18.5%
Vocational nurses	3.3%	9.2%	17.1%
Registered nurses	4.2%	9.8%	18.8%
Physicians	0.4%	2.1%	7.6%

Fig. 6.9 Percent distribution of nurses, aides, and social workers at care facilities, Japan, 2016

Source: MHLW (2016) Summary of Survey of Institutions and Establishments for Long-term Care. https://www.mhlw.go.jp/toukei/saikin/hw/kaigo/service16/dl/kekka-gaiyou_06.pdf. The three types of care facilities belong to a public nursing home.

workers and aids decrease to about 19 percent and 38 percent, respectively. Figure 6.10 shows the procedures for obtaining certificates for formal care workers in Japan. A care worker's license can be obtained using one of three methods. All participants must pass both practical training and written tests.

Formal care workers' wages and salaries are largely unchanged by their qualifications (see table 6.12). Registered nurses in nursing homes earn 1,432 JPY per hour and 268 thousand JPY per month. Nursing home aids earn a comparable hourly wage of 1,001 JPY and a monthly salary of 212 thousand JPY. Registered nurses and aids for home care services earn slightly lower wages and salaries than those in nursing homes. Formal care workers earn less than the average hourly and monthly salaries across occupations and industries. Indeed, the hourly wage for care workers is slightly higher than the minimum wage of 901 JPY per hour and roughly equal to the average income for high school graduates.

6.2.5 Who Are the Caregivers?

Informal caregivers also perform a significant portion of care duties in addition to formal care workers. Table 6.13 shows the numbers of formal and informal caregivers in Japan. The number of formal caregivers is derived from the Summary of Survey of Institutions and Establishments for

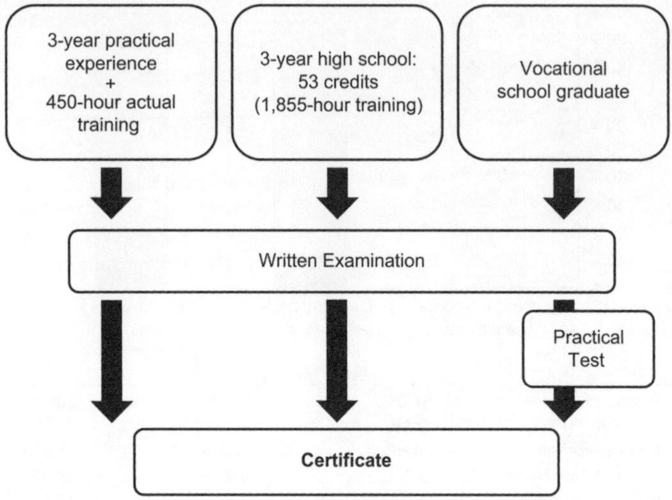

Fig. 6.10 Training requirements for formal care workers, Japan
Source: created by the authors based on a report from Kaigobatake, "How to become a care worker? Explanation of how to obtain qualifications, exams, job content, and salary," Published April 13, 2018, updated November 29, 2023. https://kaigobatake.jp/column/kaigofukushishi.php.

Long-Term Care (MHLW 2016). Kawagoe (2021) estimated the number of informal caregivers. In 2016, there were approximately one million formal care workers, accounting for 2.9 people out of 100 aged 65+. There were approximately seven million informal caregivers, seven times as many formal caregivers, accounting for 20 people per 100 people aged 65+.

Figure 6.11 shows the gender, age, and education distribution of formal and informal caregivers in Japan. As in other countries, formal care workers are overwhelmingly female (84 percent). Informal caregivers have a similar but less significant gender skew, with 67 percent female. Formal care workers are mostly in their working years, with 75 percent under 60 years of age. On the other hand, informal caregivers are often older than 60 years (64 percent). Given Japan's super-aged society, it is common for older people to receive care from other older family members. This situation is known as "*Rou-Rou Kaigo*" in Japanese. Most formal care workers have a high school diploma or equivalent, with 23 percent having some college education and 14 percent having a college degree or higher. Only 3 percent do not have a high school diploma. Formal care workers appear to have a higher degree of education than the general Japanese female population.[19] As an illustration, in 2010, approximately 9 percent of Japanese women did not have a

19. We compare the education level of formal care workers to that of the female population because women make up the large majority of care workers.

Table 6.12 **Pay for full-time care workers at nursing facilities and in-home health care, Japan, 2019**

Industry	Occupation titles	Mean hourly wage	Monthly mean wage
Nursing Care Facilities	(1) Registered nurses	1,432	267,553
	(2) Nursing aids, orderlies, and psychiatric aides	1,001	212,455
	(3) Medical and health services managers	1,291	246,373
	All occupations in nursing care facilities industry	1,185	231,135
Home Health Care Services	(1) Registered nurses	1,431	257,612
	(2) Nursing aids, orderlies, and psychiatric aides	990	204,468
	(3) Medical and health services managers	1,184	224,613
	All occupations in home health care services industry	1,111	221,239
All industries and occupations		1,272	307,700
National minimum wages		901	
High school degree			267,600
Junior college degree			283,200
College degree			372,600

Notes: Data were obtained from the Survey of Nursing Care Work Conditions (2020). The information on care workers at nursing home facilities is from the "2019 Nursing Care Labor Survey, Survey on nursing care work at business establishments" http://www.kaigo-center.or.jp/report/pdf/2020r02_chousa_jigyousho_chousahyou.pdf by the Public Interest Incorporated Foundation Care Work Stabilization Center.

The information on home care workers is from the "2019 Nursing Care Labor Survey, Survey on the actual employment status and work awareness of care workers," http://www.kaigo-center.or.jp/report/pdf/2020r02_chousa_roudousha_chousahyou.pdf by the Public Interest Incorporated Foundation Care Work Stabilization Center.

The information on average monthly and hourly salary for all industries and occupations is from https://www.mhlw.go.jp/toukei/itiran/roudou/chingin/kouzou/z2019/dl/01.pdf and https://www.mhlw.go.jp/content/000685358.pdf from the Ministry of Health, Labour and Welfare.

The information on national minimum wages is from "Minimum wage revision status by region in FY2020," https://www.mhlw.go.jp/stf/seisakunitsuite/bunya/koyou_roudou/roudoukijun/minimumichiran/ from the Ministry of Health, Labour and Welfare.

The information on monthly salary by education is from https://www.mhlw.go.jp/toukei/itiran/roudou/chingin/kouzou/z2019/index.html from the Ministry of Health, Labour and Welfare. All values are in 2019 JPY.

high school diploma, which was three times the rate of formal care workers (Statistics Bureau of Japan 2010).

The high level of education among formal care workers might be due to the requirements by care service providers and local governments. Providers typically prefer to hire workers with higher levels of education and training, since providing care for the elderly and disabled can be demanding and requires specialized knowledge and skills. This trend might also reflect the growing importance of human resources development in the long-term care

Table 6.13 Care provision by formal and informal caregivers

	Japan, 2016
Formal care workers	1,012,082
Relative to 65+ Population	0.029
Relative to 18–64 Population	0.014
Informal caregivers	6,990,000
Relative to 65+ Population	0.202
Relative to 18–64 Population	0.096
All caregivers	8,002,082
Relative to 65+ Population	0.231
Relative to 18–64 Population	0.110

Notes: The number of formal helpers is from the Summary of Survey of Institutions and Establishments for Long-term Care by the Ministry of Health, Labour and Welfare (2016), https://www.mhlw.go.jp/toukei/saikin/hw/kaigo/service19/dl/kekka-gaiyou_2.pdf. The number of informal caregivers is from a report "about informal caregiving" by Masahiro Kawagoe at Saitama Prefectural University Research and Development Center, Community Care Management Support Division https://www.spu.ac.jp/Portals/0/News%20file/sangaku/kenkyu/マネジメント支援部門/第4回_20211201_家族介護の現状.pdf. The statistics are aggregated at the population level; therefore, we cannot provide numbers separately for the 65+ and 85+ populations.

sector, as Japan faces an aging population and a shortage of care workers. Additionally, higher education levels among care workers might be related to the increasing professionalization of care work as Japan moves toward a more formal, regulated, and structured long-term care system. Despite their generally strong educational backgrounds, formal care workers tend to be underpaid (see table 6.12). The less-educated population usually provides informal care. One-fifth of the informal caregivers do not have a high school diploma. Less educated family members in Japan seem more inclined to provide informal care (Tokunaga and Hashimoto 2017; Kumagai 2017).

Figure 6.12 details the relationship between informal caregivers and their care recipients. Spouses provide 32 percent of informal care, followed by daughters (21 percent) and sons (17 percent). Compared to other countries, recipients' parents provide a notably larger proportion of informal care (11 percent).[20]

6.3 The Cost of Long-Term Care

Figure 6.3 shows that total spending on long-term care has grown steadily over the past two decades. Table 6.14 provides more details on spending on institutional and home-care services. In 2016, there were approximately 1.25 million nursing home residents, costing 3,275 billion JPY. Home care spending can be divided into community-based and at-home care. In 2016,

20. The distribution of the caregiver-recipient relationship may deviate from the true distribution because the sample contains only co-residing caregivers.

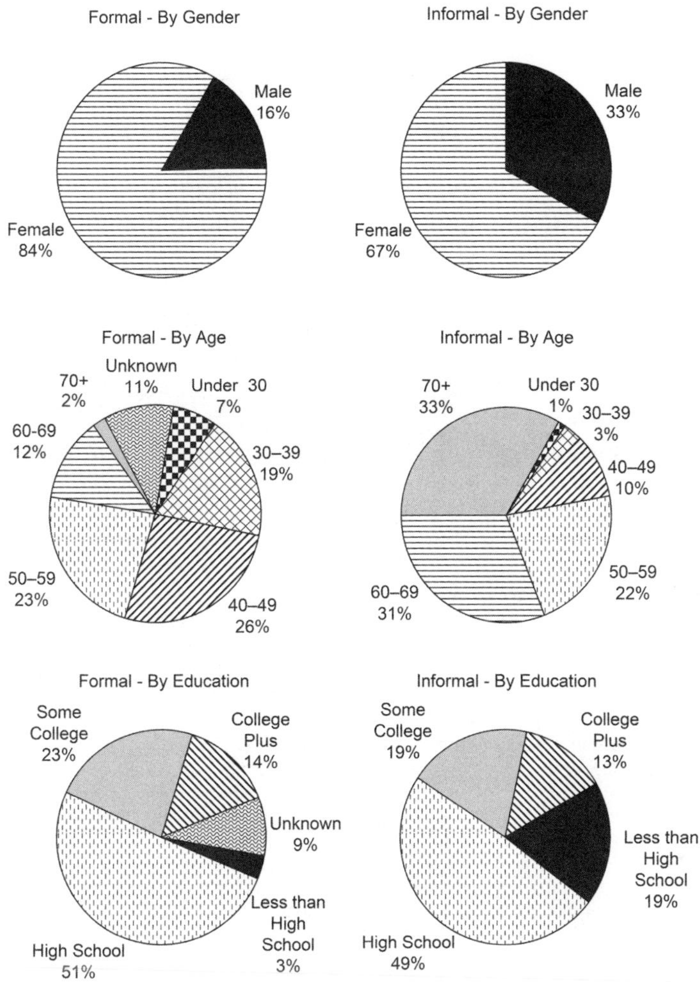

Fig. 6.11 Demographic composition of home care workers, Japan, 2019

Notes: Data on formal care workers are from the Report on the Results of the 2019 Survey on Employment Status and Attitudes of Nursing Care Workers. http://www.kaigo-center.or.jp/report/pdf/2020r02_chousa_roudousha_chousahyou.pdf. Data on informal caregivers are from the Comprehensive Survey of Living Conditions (CSLC 2016). An informal caregiver is defined as a family member who is the main caregiver of a co-residing care-needy elderly person.

around 1.1 million and 3.7 million people received community-based and at-home care, respectively, with total spending of 1,596 and 4,100 billion JPY. As shown in figure 6.6, spending on home care services is twice that of institutional care, reflecting the government's intention to keep care-needy older people at home rather than institutionalizing them.

However, focusing on the total spending of formal care overlooks the

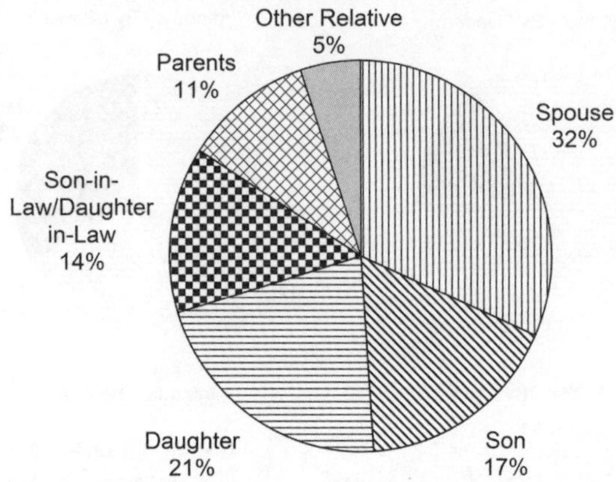

Fig. 6.12 Informal caregivers by relationship to care recipient, Japan, 2016

Notes: Data are from the Comprehensive Survey of Living Conditions (CSLC 2016). An informal caregiver is defined as a family member who is the main caregiver of a co-residing care-needy elderly person.

Table 6.14 Formal care costs, annual, Japan, 2016

Types	Number of users	Total spending (billion JPY)
Institutional care: nursing homes	1,250,700	3,275
Home care: community-based care	1,119,300	1,596
Home care: at-home care	3,735,200	4,100

Notes: The number of users and spending on formal care are from the Long-Term Care Insurance Status Report by the Ministry of Health, Labour and Welfare 2016. Number of users: https://www.mhlw.go.jp/toukei/saikin/hw/kaigo/kyufu/16/dl/02.pdf. Total spending and spending per user: https://www.mhlw.go.jp/toukei/saikin/hw/kaigo/kyufu/16/dl/03.pdf. The total spending was reported in billion JPY in 2019.

significance of the informal care provided by family members. As shown in table 6.13, the number of informal caregivers in Japan is approximately seven times that of formal caregivers. Ignoring the hidden costs of informal caregiving can lead to erroneous policy decisions. In this section, we use models from the United States chapter to assess the value of informal caregiving in Japan (table 6.15). Using the 2016 CSLC, we estimate the cost of care provided by informal caregivers based on two methods. Method I considers the price of informal care to be a caregiver's predicted wage if he or she is working and zero otherwise. Method II substitutes the wage of nursing aid for home care services (990 JPY) for the price of informal care provided by non-working caregivers (see table 6.12).

Specifically, we use the income questionnaire of the CSLC and calculate the caregiver's probability of working and the wage conditional on work

Table 6.15 Informal care valuation, Japan, 2016

	I	II
Valuation (billions of JPY)	2,935	6,646
Total Hours Informal Help (billions)	8.24	8.24
Probability of Working	0.458	0.458
Predicted Wage * Probability of Working	516	
Predicted Wage if Working (JPY)	1635	
Observations	*2,638*	*2,638*

Notes: Data are from the Comprehensive Survey of Living Conditions (CSLC 2016) and household and income questionnaires. Individuals in nursing homes were not sampled. Respondent weights are used for all calculations. Informal caregivers were identified using a question to each recipient in the household questionnaire, "Please report the household-member identification number of your main caregiver living with you," and cross-referenced the number to that of all household members of this recipient to identify the caregiver. The income of informal caregivers was obtained from the income questionnaire. Column I values predicted working hours at the predicted wage and non-working hours at 0. Column II values predicted working hours at the predicted wage. They predicted non-working hours at the mean hourly wage for home-care nursing assistants, orderlies, and psychiatric aides (990 JPY, see table 6.9). Valuations are made at the caregiver level, with predicted wages and probabilities of work calculated based on nine regions, six age groups, four education groups, sex, and marital status. Hourly wages were top-coded at 10,000 JPY. Valuations and hours are in billions, with all JPY amounts to 2019 JPY.

for each of the caregiver groups identified by caregivers' residence (regional level),[21] age (10-year-band), education, gender, and marital status (married, single, divorced, widowed). The valuation based on Method I is calculated by multiplying the probability of working (45.8 percent) by the predicted wage (1,635 JPY) and by the annual hours of informal care provided (8.24 billion hours). The annual hours of informal care were calculated based on the LTC questionnaire of the CLSC, which records daily hours of care received (see table 6.9). We recoded the categories care hours as follows: 16 hours for "full day" care, 8 hours for "half day," 2.5 hours for "2–3 hours," and 0.5 hours for "only when needed" or "others." The annual hours of care were then calculated by multiplying the daily hours by 365. Since the LTC and income questionnaires cover two distinct respondent groups, we cannot determine the care hours provided by caregivers who responded to the income questionnaire. Alternatively, we first calculate a mean hour of care for each caregiver group in the LTC questionnaire identified by the same set of characteristics listed above and then assign the mean hours to the caregivers in the income questionnaires with the same characteristics. Furthermore, we scale up the value of care and the hours of care by 10 to account for the fact that the income questionnaire covers around 10 percent of the entire CSLC sample.

21. There are nine regions in Japan: Hokkaido, Tohoku, Kanto, Chubu, Kinki/Kansai, Chugoku, Shikoku, Kyushu (including Okinawa).

Method I values informal caregiving at 2,935 billion JPY per year. Alternatively, the Method II valuation is derived by adding Method I valuation and the product of annual caregiving hours (8.24 billion hours), the probability of not working (54.2 percent = 100%—45.8 percent), and nursing aid salary (990 JPY). Method II values informal caregiving at 6,646 billion JPY per year.

Table 6.16 combines informal caregiving values with the total spending on

Table 6.16 Total costs by type of care and source, Japan, 2016

Care Type	Source	Cost I (billion, JPY)	Cost II (billion, JPY)
Nursing Home	Public	3,023	3,023
	Private	252	252
	All	3,275	3,275
Community-Based Care	Public	1,473	1,473
	Private	123	123
	All	1,596	1,596
Home Care	Public	3,785	3,785
	Private	316	316
	All	4,100	4,100
Informal Care	Private	2,935	6,646
Total	Public	8,280	8,280
	Private	3,626	7,337
	All	11,906	15,617

Japan, 2016 (% GDP)

Care Type	Source	Cost I (%GDP)	Cost II (%GDP)
Nursing Home	Public	0.54%	0.54%
	Private	0.05%	0.05%
	All	0.59%	0.59%
Community-Based Care	Public	0.27%	0.27%
	Private	0.02%	0.02%
	All	0.29%	0.29%
Home Care	Public	0.68%	0.68%
	Private	0.06%	0.06%
	All	0.74%	0.74%
Informal Care	Private	0.53%	1.20%
Total	Public	1.49%	1.49%
	Private	0.65%	1.32%
	All	2.15%	2.81%

Notes: Total spending on formal care (nursing home, community-based care, and home care) is taken from the Long-Term Care Insurance Status Report by the Ministry of Health, Labour and Welfare 2016 https://www.mhlw.go.jp/toukei/saikin/hw/kaigo/kyufu/16/dl/03.pdf. Although the co-payment rate for formal services is 10 percent, it may not indicate the out-of-pocket payment due to the stop loss setting. We thus use the 7.7 percent of the "real" co-payment rate in 2016 that the MHLW reports determining the private costs of nursing homes, community-based care, and home care, respectively (https://www.mhlw.go.jp/file/05-Shingikai-12601000-Seisakutoukatsukan-Sanjikanshitsu_Shakaihoshoutantou/0000140158.pdf. Accessed November 2, 2022). The informal care costs are from table 6.15. The costs are billions, with all JPY amounts in 2019 JPY. The GDP in 2016 was 544,365 billion JPY.

formal care (see table 6.14). We further split the spending on formal care into public and private sources (i.e., out-of-pocket payments).[22] With Method I, around 30 percent of Japan's overall long-term care expenditures are borne by private sources; with Method II, this proportion rises to 47 percent.[23] In either case, however, long-term care in Japan relies more on public spending.

6.4 Conclusions

This paper provides an overview of long-term care in Japan, including a detailed description of the characteristics of elderly individuals with care needs, a comprehensive introduction to the public LTCI, and an estimate of the cost of long-term care in Japan.

The elderly population in Japan, as in other countries, is continuously growing, with a sharp rise in those aged 85 and older. This demographic shift highlights increased limitations in ADLs and IADLs, leading to a growing demand for long-term care. However, compared to other countries, the elderly population in Japan with care needs has some unique characteristics. For instance, there appears to be no clear correlation between the economic well-being of the elderly population and the limitations reported. Specifically, the proportions of low/high income categories do not increase/decrease monotonically with the number of limitations. Meanwhile, the psychological well-being of the elderly population in Japan appears to be notably worse than in other countries, regardless of the limitations reported.

To cope with the demographic shift and the rising need for long-term care, a public LTCI system in Japan was established in 2000 as a mandatory social insurance program for people aged 40 and older. The program provides a comprehensive range of long-term care services for elderly individuals who need assistance with ADLs. The services can be provided in the home, community-based facilities, or institutional care settings. The program is funded through taxes and premiums that individuals and their employers pay. Eligible individuals receive benefits based on their assessed care needs and are assigned a care level with associated co-payments for services. The program aims to ensure that elderly individuals can age in place and receive necessary care as the official purpose was to assist old persons who need care

22. Although the co-payment rate for formal services is 10 percent, it may not indicate the actual out-of-pocket payment due to the stop loss setting. We thus use the 7.7 percent of the "real" co-payment rate in 2016 that the MHLW reports to determine the private costs of nursing homes, community-based care, and home care, respectively. See "User Burden" (in Japanese). October 19, 2016, Social Security Council Nursing Care Insurance Subcommittee (67th), https://www.mhlw.go.jp/file/05-Shingikai-12601000-Seisakutoukatsukan-Sanjikanshitsu_Shakaihoshoutantou/0000140158.pdf. Accessed November 2, 2022.

23. Based on Method I, out of the total costs of 11,906 billion JPY, 3,626 billion JPY was covered by private sources, which roughly corresponds to 30 percent. Based on Method II, out of the total costs of 15,617 billion JPY, 7,337 billion JPY was covered by private sources, which roughly corresponds to 47 percent.

"to maintain dignity and an independent daily life routine according to each person's own level of abilities" (Ministry of Justice 1997). However, two of the other significant goals of the system are to separate long-term care needs from medical care needs and contain medical care spending by moving older people who stay in the hospital for a long time to long-term care facilities or homes (Campbell 2002). The program also helps informal caregivers relieve family caregivers' burdens and prevent them from quitting their jobs due to care responsibilities (Tsutsui and Muramatsu 2007).

However, this generous system confronts the fundamental challenge of sustainability both financially and in terms of human resources. Given the ever-increasing cost of long-term care as the population ages and the stagnating public resources that may be used to fund LTCI, there are substantial pressures to form a financially balanced system. Various discussions are ongoing in the Social Security Council and others, with the majority concentrating on changing to services that can be provided at relatively low cost, increasing the co-payments for receiving long-term care services, and raising co-insurance premium rates, among specific cohorts of recipients (e.g., affluent and low-care-need cohorts). Specifically, for those with minor care needs, the LTCI program shifts to a service provider focused on prevention by utilizing volunteers and other resources in the community; in 2018, the co-payment ratio for receiving long-term care was raised from 10 percent to 30 percent for elderly persons with incomes equal to people in working age (MHLW 2022c). Then, the Social Security Council is finally considering a long-postponed debate to raise LTCI premiums for the elderly with high incomes (Social Security Council/Long-Term Care Subcommittee 2022).

On the other hand, some argue that the eligible age for LTCI should be lowered to under 40 (e.g., 20) years old, but there is strong opposition to this view. With the working-age population expected to decline rapidly and the number of social security beneficiaries tapering off, careful discussion is needed on requiring young people with relatively low wages to bear additional premium burdens. In Japan, welfare services for the disabled and the elderly are differentiated by age, with those between the ages of 18 and 65 being covered by the Act on Providing Comprehensive Support for the Daily Life and Life in Society of Persons with Disabilities, and those aged 65 and older requiring long-term care being treated by the LTCI Act (MHLW, 2022a). If the eligible age for LTCI were to be lowered to 20 years old, there would be a contradiction in the LTCI system's requirement of "aging-related diagnoses." In addition, while the LTCI is, in principle, based on social insurance and requires beneficiaries to pay out of pocket for the welfare services for the disabled, which is funded by general taxes, support groups for the disabled are vehemently opposed to any increase in co-payment for services provided. In other words, lowering the eligibility age for insurance premiums of LTCI would require the harmonization of these two acts, which have different financial structures.

The shortage of social security bearers and human resources to support needy care is another major issue of LTCI, given the consistent decline in working-age individuals and socioeconomic disparities among regions. Promoting labor force participation and innovation can help to safeguard human resources and boost productivity in the long-term care industry. The importance of compensating formal care workers, adopting robotics, obtaining and training human resources ranging from young people to energetic older people, admitting foreign care workers, and lowering administrative duties has been emphasized in various discussions. For example, Eggleston et al. (2021) find that robot adoption reduces care workers' and nurses' burden of care in nursing homes in Japan. Further, efforts are underway to apply artificial intelligence and deep learning methods to long-term care plans for older people, which are expected to reduce the administrative workload of care managers (Saint-Care Holding Corporation 2017). Furthermore, as of 2021, the LTCI claims data of all service users are merged with the Long-Term Care Information System For Evidence (LIFE) to construct a system with both the physical and cognitive functions and the content of the care the users received. Once such a comprehensive information system is established, it will be possible to implement "evidence-based long-term care" based on cost-effectiveness analysis (MHLW 2020b).

Japan's LTCI is continuously striving to improve solutions to the problems faced. The procedure can be a good lesson to countries seeking to develop a public insurance system for long-term care and those experiencing similar challenges in their public insurance systems.

References

Akiyama, N., T. Shiroiwa, T. Fukuda, S. Murashima. 2015. "About Factors Relating to the Admission of the Elderly with Nursing Care Needs Certification—Utilization of the Receipt Data from Medical Care and Nursing Care (in Japanese). *Journal of the Japan Society for Healthcare Administration* 52 (2): 79–86. https://doi.org/10.11303/jsha.52.79.

Brown, J. W., J. Liang, N. Krause, H. Akiyama, H. Sugisawa, T. Fukaya. 2002. "Transitions in Living Arrangements Among Elders in Japan: Does Health Make a Difference?" *Journals of Gerontology: Series B*, 57B (4): S209–S220. https://doi.org/10.1093/geronb/57.4.S209.

Cabinet Office. 2020a. *2020 White Book of the Ageing Society*. Accessed September 30, 2022. https://www8.cao.go.jp/kourei/whitepaper/w-2020/html/zenbun/s1_1_1.html.

Cabinet Office. 2020b. The 9th International Comparative Survey on the Lives and Attitudes of the Elderly in 2020. Executive Summary, in Japanese. https://www8.cao.go.jp/kourei/ishiki/r02/gaiyo/pdf_indexg.html. Accessed September 30, 2022.

Care Work Foundation. 2018. Survey on the Prevention of Accidents related to the

Use of Long-Term Care Services—FY2021 Research Grant for Health Promotion Program for the Elderly by the MHLW. In Japanese. http://www.kaigo-center.or.jp/report/pdf/h30_kaigojiko_houkoku_20180402.pdf. Accessed September 30, 2022.

Campbell, J. C. 2002. "How Policies Differ: Long-Term Care Insurance in Japan and Germany." In *Aging and Social Policy: A German-Japanese Comparison*, edited by R. Luetzeler and H. Conrad. Munich: Iudicium.

Eggleston, K., Y. S. Lee, and T. Iizuka. 2021. "Robots and Labor in the Service Sector: Evidence from Nursing Homes." NBER Working Paper No. 28322. Cambridge, MA: National Bureau of Economic Research. http://www.nber.org/papers/w28322. Accessed September 30, 2022.

Fu, R., H. Noguchi, A. Kawamura, H. Takahashi, and N. Tamiya. 2017. "Spillover Effect of Japanese Long-Term Care Insurance as an Employment Promotion Policy for Family Caregivers." *Journal of Health Economics* 56: 103–12. https://doi.org/10.1016/j.jhealeco.2017.09.011.

Fu, R., and H. Noguchi. 2019. "Moral Hazard under Zero Price Policy: Evidence from Japanese Long-Term Care Claims Data." *European Journal of Health Economics* 20 (6): 785–99.

Horioka, C. Y. 2021. "Is the Selfish Life-Cycle Model More Applicable in Japan and, If So, Why? A Literature Survey." *Review of Economics of the Household* 19: 157–87. https://link.springer.com/article/10.1007/s11150-020-09511-0.

Izumida, N. 2008. "Effect of Income Difference to the Use of the Long-Term Care Services." In Japanese. *Journal of Social Security Research/National Institute of Population and Social Security Research* 43 (4): 327–42.

Japan Association of Geriatric Health Services Facilities. 2016. Long-Term Care Insurance and Nursing Homes. https://www.roken.or.jp/about_roken/kaigo. Accessed September 11, 2022.

Johar, M., S. Maruyama, S. Nakamura. 2010. "Transition to Parent-Child Coresidence: Parental Needs and the Strategic Bequest Motive." Australian School of Business Research Paper No. 2010 ECON 05. https://papers.ssrn.com/sol3/papers.cfm?abstract_id=1549550. Accessed September 30, 2022.

Johar, M., S. Maruyama, S. Nakamura. 2015. "Reciprocity in the Formation of Intergenerational Coresidence." *Journal of Family and Economic Issues* 36: 192–209. https://link.springer.com/article/10.1007/s10834-013-9387-7.

Kawagoe, M. 2021. "Facts about Informal Caregiving." Accessed September 13, 2022. https://www.spu.ac.jp/Portals/0/News%20file/sangaku/kenkyu/マネジメント支援部門/第4回_20211201_家族介護の現状.pdf.

Kessler, R. C., P. R. Barker, L. J. Colpe, J. F. Epstein, J. C. Gfroerer, E. Hiripi, M. J. Howes, S.-L. T. Normand, R. W. Manderscheid, E. E. Walters, and A. M. Zaslavsky. 2003. "Screening for Serious Mental Illness in the General Population." *Archives of General Psychiatry* 60 (2): 184–89.

Kumagai, N. 2017. "Distinct Impacts of High Intensity Caregiving on Caregivers' Mental Health and Continuation of Caregiving." *Health Economics Review* 7, Article number 15. https://doi.org/10.1186/s13561-017-0151-9.

Life Insurance Culture Foundation. 2021. "The National Survey on Life Insurance." In Japanese. Accessed January 24, 2023. https://www.jili.or.jp/research/report/8361.html.

Matsuyoshi, N. 2010. "Current Status of Private Long-Term Care Insurance." In Japanese. Kyosai Soken Report, No 112. https://www.jkri.or.jp/PDF/2010/Rep112kyosai2.pdf. Accessed January 24, 2023.

Ministry of Justice. 1997. Long-Term Care Insurance Act (Kaigo hoken hō) 1997.

https://www.japaneselawtranslation.go.jp/ja/laws/view/3807. Accessed September 30, 2022.
Ministry of Health, Labour and Welfare (MHLW). 2014. Results of the Comprehensive Survey of Living Conditions FY 2013. https://www.mhlw.go.jp/toukei/saikin/hw/k-tyosa/k-tyosa13/index.html. Accessed September 12, 2022.
Ministry of Health, Labour and Welfare (MHLW). 2015. The Survey of Institutions and Establishments for Long-Term Care. https://www.e-stat.go.jp/stat-search/files?page=1&toukei=00450042. Accessed January 24, 2023.
Ministry of Health, Labour and Welfare (MHLW). 2016. Overview of the 2016 Survey of Long-Term Care Service Facilities and Establishments. https://www.mhlw.go.jp/toukei/saikin/hw/kaigo/service16/index.html. Accessed September 12, 2022.
Ministry of Health, Labour and Welfare (MHLW). 2017. Long-Term Care Claims Data. https://www.mhlw.go.jp/file/05-Shingikai-12601000-Seisakutoukatsukan-Sanjikanshitsu_Shakaihoshoutantou/0000175118.pdf. Accessed January 25, 2023.
Ministry of Health, Labour and Welfare (MHLW). 2019. About the Healthcare Spending in 2019. https://www.mhlw.go.jp/toukei/saikin/hw/k-iryohi/19/dl/data.pdf. Accessed September 11, 2022.
Ministry of Health, Labour and Welfare (MHLW). 2020a. Overview of the 2020 Survey of Long-Term Care Service Facilities and Establishments. https://www.mhlw.go.jp/toukei/saikin/hw/kaigo/service20/index.html. Accessed September 12, 2022.
Ministry of Health, Labour and Welfare (MHLW). 2020b. 10th Expert Committee on Provision of Information on Certification of Needs for Long-Term Care and Receipts for Long-Term Care—(Ref.3) Future Schedule for Consolidation of Medical and Long-Term Care Data, etc. In Japanese. https://www.mhlw.go.jp/content/12301000/000670766.pdf. Accessed September 30, 2022.
Ministry of Health, Labour and Welfare (MHLW). 2022a. Overview of Disability Welfare Services. https://www.mhlw.go.jp/stf/seisakunitsuite/bunya/hukushi_kaigo/shougaishahukushi/service/naiyou.html. Accessed November 4, 2022.
Ministry of Health, Labour and Welfare (MHLW). 2022b. Survey of Social Welfare Institutions, Table # H01K. https://www.e-stat.go.jp. Accessed January 24, 2023.
Ministry of Health, Labour and Welfare (MHLW). 2022c. About the Long-Term Care System in Japan. https://www.mhlw.go.jp/stf/seisakunitsuite/bunya/hukushi_kaigo/kaigo_koureisha/gaiyo/index.html. Accessed July 20, 2023.
Morioka, N. 2020. "Future Direction of Housing for Old People and Role of Referral Agencies." In Japanese. Mimeo for the seminar for elderly housing placement agencies. https://www.yurokyo.or.jp/contents/pdf/3026–1. Accessed January 23, 2023.
Niimi, Y. 2016. "The 'Costs' of Informal Care: An Analysis of the Impact of Elderly Care on Caregivers' Subjective Well-Being in Japan." *Review of Economics of the Household* 14: 779–810. https://link.springer.com/article/10.1007/s11150–016–9333–1.
Oshio, T., and M. Kan. 2018. "Impact of Parents' Need for Care on Middle-Aged Women's Lifestyle and Psychological Distress: Evidence from a Nationwide Longitudinal Survey in Japan." *Health and Quality of Life Outcomes* 16, Article number 63. https://link.springer.com/article/10.1186/s12955–018–0890–2.
Park, J. H., and K. S. Lee. 2013. "Self-Rated Health and Its Determinants in Japan and South Korea." *Public Health* 127 (9): 834–43.
Saint-Care Holding Corporation. 2017. Research on the Possibilities and Chal-

lenges of Introducing Artificial Intelligence in the Formulation of Care Plans to Promote Independence Support-FY2017 Research Grant for Health Promotion Program for the Elderly by the MHLW. In Japanese. https://www.mhlw.go.jp/file/06-Seisakujouhou-12300000-Roukenkyoku/7_senntokea_2.pdf. Accessed September 30, 2022.

Shimizutani, S. 2014. "The Future of Long-Term Care in Japan." *Asia-Pacific Review* 21 (1): 88–119. https://doi.org/10.1080/13439006.2014.925199.

Social Security Council/Long-Term Care Subcommittee. 2022. "Benefits and Burden." In Japanese. https://www.mhlw.go.jp/stf/newpage_28740.html.

Statistics Bureau of Japan. 2010. Summary of 2010 Census. In Japanese. Accessed January 13, 2023. https://www.e-stat.go.jp/stat-search/files?page=1&layout=datalist&toukei=00200521&tstat=000001039448&cycle=0&tclass1=000001059198&tclass2=000001062444&stat_infid=000023595642&tclass3val=0.

Tamiya, N., H. Noguchi, A. Nishi, M. R. Reich, N. Ikegami, H. Hashimoto, K. Shibuya, I. Kawachi, and J. C. Campbell. 2011. "Population Ageing and Well-Being: Lessons from Japan's Long-Term Care Insurance Policy." *Lancet* 378 (9797): 1183–192. https://doi.org/10.1016/S0140–6736(11)61176–8.

Tokunaga, M., and H. Hashimoto. 2017. "The Socioeconomic Within-Gender Gap in Informal Caregiving among Middle-Aged Women: Evidence from a Japanese Nationwide Survey." *Social Science & Medicine* 173: 48–53. https://doi.org/10.1016/j.socscimed.2016.11.037.

Tsutsui, T., and N. Muramatsu. 2007. "Japan's Universal Long Term Care System Reform of 2005: Containing Costs and Realizing a Long-Term Vision." *Journal of American Geriatrics Society* 55: 1458–63. https://doi.org/10.1111/j.1532–415.2007.01281.x.

Yong, V., and Y. Saito. 2011. "National Long-Term Care Insurance Policy in Japan a Decade after Implementation: Some Lessons for Aging Countries." *Ageing International* 37 (3): 271–84. https://doi.org/10.1007/S12126–011–9109–0.

7 Long-Term Care in the Netherlands

Pieter Bakx, Eddy Van Doorslaer, and Bram Wouterse

7.1 Introduction

The Dutch population is aging rapidly (figure 7.1). The share of the population over age 65 has grown from 12 percent in 1990 to 22 percent in 2020 and is expected to be around 25 percent by 2050. This trend is similar to trends in other European countries, including Germany and Denmark, and to the trend in the United States (Gruber and McGarry 2025; Geyer et al. 2025; Gørtz et al. 2025). The share of the oldest old has increased from about 1.5 percent in 1990 to currently about 2.5 percent and is expected to rise to nearly 6 percent by 2050, which is a fourfold increase in just 60 years. Consequently, among the over 65, the share of over 85 is expected to rise from 9 percent in 1990 to around 22 percent in 2050 (figure 7.2). The growing share of the oldest part of the population is, together with other—related—trends, likely to generate a rapid rise in the need for assistance and care (De Meijer et al. 2013).

Pieter Bakx is an associate professor affiliated with the Health Economics group at the Erasmus School for Health Policy and Management at Erasmus University Rotterdam.

Eddy Van Doorslaer holds a joint appointment as Professor of Health Economics at the Erasmus School of Health Policy and Management and at the Department of Applied Economics of the Erasmus School of Economics, both at Erasmus University Rotterdam.

Bram Wouterse is an associate professor in health economics at the Erasmus School of Health Policy and Management at Erasmus University Rotterdam.

Results based on calculations by Erasmus University using non-public microdata from Statistics Netherlands. We thank the Community Health Services, Statistics Netherlands & National Institute for Public Health and the Environment for access to survey data from the Public Health Monitor (Gezondheidsmonitor). Furthermore, we thank SCP Netherlands Institute for Social Research for access to the SCP informal care survey and Mirjam de Klerk for providing advice on using these data. For acknowledgments, sources of research support, and disclosure of the authors' material financial relationships, if any, please see https://www.nber.org/books-and-chapters/long-term-care-around-world/long-term-care-netherlands.

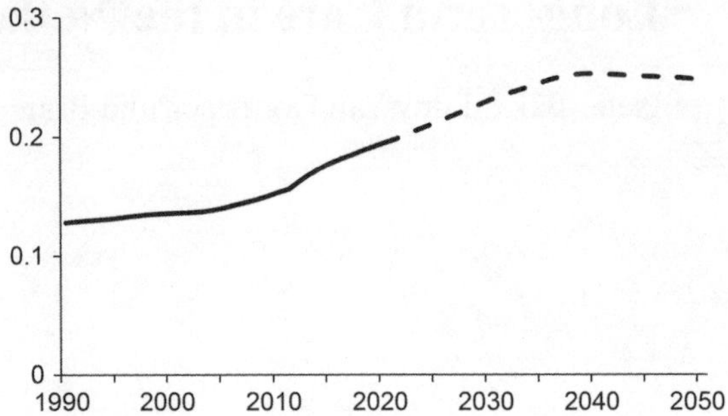

Fig. 7.1 Share of population age 65 or older
Source: CBS 2020a, 2021

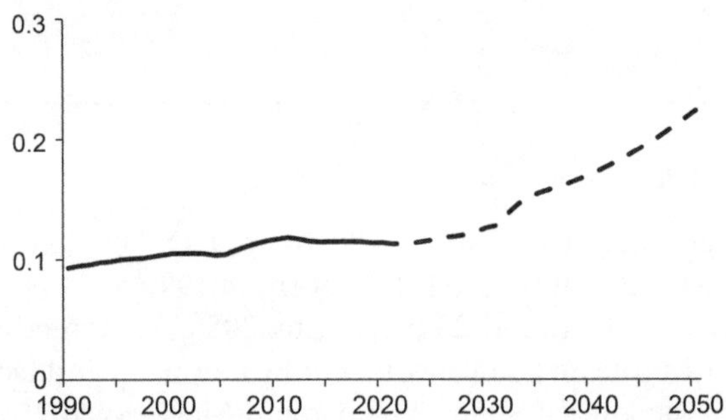

Fig. 7.2 Share of 65+ population that is age 85 or older
Source: CBS 2020a, 2021

Will the public programs be able to keep funding most of the care for those increased needs when the share of the working population is declining at the same time? The current public long-term care insurance system in the Netherlands is more generous than in most other countries. The Netherlands provides universal public long-term care insurance to its population, which is more comprehensive than in many other OECD countries. This means broad access to good-quality home care and nursing home care (Tenand et al. 2020, 2020a), while out-of-pocket costs are relatively low (Bakx et al. 2015), and relatives may be better shielded against the burden of informal caregiving than in other countries (Rellstab et al. 2020). But it also comes at the cost of having the highest public expenditures on long-term care of all countries when expressed as the share of the gross domestic product (OECD 2022).

In this paper, we provide an overview of the long-term care use in the Netherlands and highlight differences and similarities with other countries. We go beyond the care provided by professionals and consider informal care provided by relatives, friends, and others. While long-term care in the Netherlands is available for everyone with chronic health problems who requires care or support, we focus on the 65+ population, which is the largest group of care recipients.

The remainder of this chapter is structured as follows. Section 7.2 discusses the care needs, well-being, and costs of care for the 65+ population. Section 7.3 discusses how long-term care is financed and organized in the Netherlands. Furthermore, section 7.4 discusses the total costs of long-term care for the 65+ population.

7.2 Aging, Disability, and Well-Being

7.2.1 Sample and Definitions

For this chapter, we use two sets of data. First, we use aggregate-level statistics when these were available. These aggregate-level statistics have been generated by the OECD and Statistics Netherlands (CBS), among others, and these sources are cited in the respective footnotes to the tables and figures in which they are used.

Second, we use linked administrative and survey data for the year 2016. We use administrative registers for the full Dutch population. These administrative registers are linked at the individual level and include demographic information, information on income and wealth, and long-term care eligibility and use. Where needed, we link these administrative records to data from the Public Health Monitor survey of the Community Health Services, Statistics Netherlands and the National Institute for Public Health and the Environment (Dutch Health Monitor 2016). From these survey data, we use information on informal care provision and use, functional limitations, and measures of well-being. Nursing home residents are under-sampled in the Public Health Monitor. To deal with this, we apply probability weights by gender and five-year age groups to the analyses in which these data are used. Appendix A contains a full list of all data sets used.

Long-term care use is defined as follows. Informal care receipt is measured over the 12-month period prior to the interview, while formal care use is measured during the calendar year that we study (i.e., 2016). Home care consists of two types. First, it consists of nursing and personal care organized and financed through the social health insurance scheme. Second, it includes domestic help, ADL or IADL assistance, transportation, home adaptations and use of medical devices financed through the Social Security Act. The data on this second set of formal care types only contain information on person-specific care (i.e., tailored to one's needs, or *maatwerkvoorzieningen*) for which the user was charged a co-payment; use of other types of care and support (*algemene voorzieningen*) is not included because of data limitations. Nursing home care includes care received in a nursing home or substitute care that is received elsewhere, e.g., at home or another private setting such as a private care home; persons choosing care vouchers (4 percent; Hussem et al. 2020) are excluded. While the latter type of nursing home–like care has been growing in recent years, the total share of users who lived in a regular nursing home was 84 percent in 2016 (Hussem et al. 2020), i.e., the year this chapter focuses on. For this type of care, we only include care use by persons who are eligible for elderly care (*Verpleging en verzorging*) rather than care for the disabled or long-term mental health care, unless indicated otherwise. We do not have information on fully private expenditures on long-term care, but these are negligible and hence this group of users is likely very small (Hussem et al. 2020).

In the Public Health Monitor survey data, functional limitations are measured using the OECD scale rather than the activities of daily living scale (ADL) and the instrumental activities of daily living (IADL) scales. Limitations defined as not being able to or having much difficulty with (1) listening to a conversation with three or more persons; (2) having a conversation with one person; (3) reading the small print of a newspaper; (4) recognizing someone's face at 4 meters distance; (5) carrying an item of 5 kg for 10 meters; (6) reaching for something on the ground; (7) walking for 400 meters without stopping. Using other Dutch survey data (Health Survey) that contain both scales, we compare scores on this scale to scores on the five-item versions of the ADL and IADL scales as used in the other chapters. Based on the comparison (see appendix A), we conclude that the median person with 0–1 limitations on the OECD scale does not report any limitation on the ADL or IADL scale; the median person with 2 limitations reports at least one IADL limitation, while the median person with 3 limitations on the OECD scale has an ADL score of 1; the median person with 4 limitations on the OECD scale has an ADL score of 2, with 5 limitations has 3 ADLs, etc. When grouping by the number of limitations, we group individuals accordingly, to enable a direct comparison of the limitation groups used here to those based on ADLs in the other chapters.

7.2.2 Prevalence of Functional Limitations

Aging comes with increased functional impairment: 12 percent of individuals aged 65+ report three or more limitations from the OECD list of functional limitations, and about 7 percent at least four (table 7.1). These shares rise steeply with age: for those 85+, 44 percent report having difficulty with at least three and 29 percent with at least four limitations. Hence, the expected rapid rise in the share of the population aged 85+ (figure 7.2)—and hence in the number of individuals with functional limitations—is likely to lead to a substantial growth in the demand for care in the next few decades.

Table 7.2 details which limitations are most frequently reported by 65+ and 85+ respondents, both overall and conditional on reporting any. As soon as at least one limitation is reported, the probability of reporting other limitations also increases. For both age groups, and both unconditional and

Table 7.1 Share with functional limitations, by age

# of limitations	65+	85+
0–1	.82	.43
2	.06	.12
3	.05	.15
4	.03	.12
5	.02	.08
6	.01	.05
7	.01	.05
Observations	225,653	18,203

Note: Functional limitations are measured using the OECD scale, see appendix A for an explanation and a mapping of the OECD scale and limitations based on the IADL and ADL lists.

Table 7.2 Distribution of each of the functional limitations, by age

	65+		85+	
	All	Conditional on any	All	Conditional on any
Listening to a conversation with three or more persons	.11	.37	.36	.50
Having a conversation with one person	.03	.12	.13	.18
Reading the small print of a newspaper	.08	.28	.24	.33
Recognizing someone's face at 4 meters distance	.04	.15	.16	.22
Carrying an item of 5 kg for 10 meters	.17	.58	.55	.77
Reaching for something on the ground	.13	.43	.42	.58
Walking for 400 meters without stopping	.16	.55	.51	.71
Observations	225,653	57,829	18,203	11,359

Note: Functional limitations are measured using the OECD scale. See appendix A for an explanation and a mapping of the OECD scale and limitations based on the IADL and ADL lists.

conditional on reporting any limitations, the most frequently reported activity with severe limitation is carrying an item of 5 kg for 10 meters, while the least reported limitation is having a conversation with one person.

7.2.3 Well-Being

7.2.3.1 Health Problems

Next, we consider the self-perceived physical and depression scores at older ages (table 7.3) by age of the respondent and by number of functional limitations. Self-perceived health of the 85+ is much lower than of those aged 65+; the 85+ subgroup is only half as likely to report that their health is good or better. Furthermore, in both age groups, only 5 percent of the respondents with 5+ functional limitations rate their health as good or better.

Table 7.3 Well-being for those 65+ and 85+ by functional limitations

	65+	65+ with 3+ functional limitations	85+	85+ with 3+ functional limitations
Self-Report of Health—Good or Better	.62	.10	.34	.10
Depression score: high	.06	.34	.17	.32
Depression score: moderate or high	.43	.88	.67	.88
Observations (unweighted)	219,683	16,787	17,294	5,078

Note: Functional limitations are measured using the OECD scale; see appendix A for an explanation and a mapping of the OECD scale and limitations based on the IADL and ADL lists.

Mental health also appears to fall with rising age and functional limitations. While only 6 percent of the respondents aged 65+ have a high score on the depression scale, this percentage rises to 17 percent for the 85+. Among the group reporting 3+ functional limitations, the fraction with a high depression score rises to around one-third in both groups. Furthermore, no less than 43 percent of the 65+ and 67 percent of the 85+ have a high or moderate depression score. The fraction with moderate or high depression scores is 88 percent for both the 65+ and the 85+ with 3+ functional limitations. These findings are confirmed by prior research (Bom et al. 2022) showing higher levels of loneliness and a perception of limited control over one's life among the oldest old, both among those living at home and those living in a nursing home, when compared to the middle-aged population.

In sum, the health, income, and wealth distributions show similar patterns as elsewhere; how these distributions are correlated is similar as well. Yet, income poverty rates and inequality among Dutch 65+ are much lower than in other OECD countries.

7.2.3.2 Financial Situation

One determinant of the well-being of the older population is their financial situation. Table 7.4 examines the distribution of standardized net household income and wealth for those aged 65 and older, and 85 and older. For this population, income is not always a very adequate measure of financial well-being: older individuals above the retirement age who hold substantial assets may also use these assets to finance consumption. Not surprisingly, the wealth distribution for the elderly shows greater inequality than the income distribution. For instance, the bottom 5 percent of the 65+ wealth distribution on average report close to zero wealth, while the top 5 percent hold around 644,000 euro on average. The wealth inequality is slightly lower for individuals aged 85 and older.

The share of older people who have a standardized household income

Table 7.4 **Income and wealth distribution**

	Income in 1000s		Wealth in 1000s	
	65+	85+	65+	85+
Percentile				
5	14	14	0	1
10	16	15	1	3
25	18	17	12	12
50	23	20	89	43
75	30	26	218	206
90	39	34	414	398
95	47	41	644	597
Mean	26	23	201	173
Observations	3,281,069	420,208	3,281,009	420,207

Notes: 2015 figures for the population on 1/1/2016. All figures converted to 2019 euros using consumer price index information for 2015–2019 (CBS 2022). Income refers to standardized disposable household income; wealth is standardized total household wealth. Standardized using the OECD equivalence scale.

below 50 percent of the median is low (table 7.5, panel A). This suggests that Dutch pensions protect the incomes of the older population well, also at the bottom of the income distribution, and succeeds in keeping income inequality among the elderly low. The Netherlands has the lowest poverty rate among all OECD countries included in the OECD Pensions at a Glance report (2021), with 3 percent of the 65+ population having an income below 50 percent of median equivalent household income. Furthermore, the poverty rate is lower than the poverty rate for the entire Dutch population, which is 8.5 percent. In addition, the ratio of the median income to the income at the 10th percentile is 1.4 for the 65+ population, which is the lowest among the OECD countries included in the analysis, suggesting that income inequality is lower than elsewhere (OECD 2021).

Despite this extensive income protection, incomes and limitations are inversely related: as the number of functional limitations rises, the share of the population in the lower income categories also tends to rise (table 7.5). For example, 39 percent of those with 0–1 functional limitations have an income between 50 percent and 100 percent of the median household income while this share rises to approximately two-thirds for those with 3 or more functional limitations. Yet, the negative relationship between income and number of functional limitations is much weaker than in the United States (Gruber and McGarry 2025). The picture looks very similar for the relationship between wealth and functional limitations in Panel B: the lower wealth groups are more likely to report more functional limitations than the groups with higher wealth.

Table 7.5 Income and wealth distribution by functional limitations for 65+ population

Panel A: Income

% of median standardized household income	Functional limitations 0–1	1	3	4	5+	Share of total in row
<50	.01	.01	.01	.01	.01	.01
50–100	.39	.60	.64	.67	.64	.43
100–150	.39	.29	.27	.24	.24	.37
150–200	.15	.07	.06	.06	.09	.13
200+	.07	.03	.02	.02	.02	.06
Share of total in column	.82	.06	.05	.03	.04	
Observations	184,328	13,607	12,225	6,348	8,846	

Panel B: wealth

% of median standardized household wealth	Functional limitations 0–1	1	3	4	5+	Share of total in row
<50	.30	.46	.53	.52	.53	.33
50–100	.10	.09	.09	.09	.09	.10
100–150	.11	.09	.07	.06	.05	.10
150–200	.11	.08	.07	.06	.07	.10
200+	.38	.27	.24	.26	.25	.36
Share of total in column	.82	.06	.05	.03	.04	
Observations	184,355	13,607	12,227	6,348	8,848	

Note: Shares displayed are shares within the column, unless indicated otherwise. Income refers to standardized disposable household income; wealth to standardized household wealth. Standardized using the OECD equivalence scale. Median income is median standardized household income for the 65+ population; median wealth is median standardized household wealth for the 65+ population. The share of people with above median income or wealth is not equal to 0.5 because of under-sampling of lower-income individuals in the Public Health Monitor data that is not corrected for through sample weights.

7.2.4 Care Received

Table 7.6 reports the distribution of nursing and personal care use (panel A) and of informal caregiving (panel B) expressed in hours per week. The numbers from the two panels are not directly comparable and hence no overall distribution of care hours is reported. Panel A reports the distribution based on annual (administrative) data; panel B is based on current users at the time of the survey. Because some individuals use care for only part of the year (e.g., after a hospital admission or illness), the number of hours reported in panel A underestimates the number of weekly hours used by users in the weeks that they use care. Furthermore, nursing and personal care do not represent total formal home care use; data on the number of hours of domestic help, guidance, and support are not available.

Table 7.6 **Distribution of weekly hours of home care received in last month by type**

	Panel A: Distribution of weekly hours of nursing and personal care, among users		*Panel B: Distribution of weekly hours of informal care, among informal care recipients*	
	65+	85+	65+	85+
Percentile				
5	0.0	0.1	1	2
10	0.1	0.1	2	2
25	0.3	0.5	4	4
50	1.0	1.6	9	8
75	2.9	3.7	21	15
90	5.5	6.4	80	40
95	7.7	8.7	168	105
Mean	2.1	2.7	25.5	19.7
Observations	443,366	161,767	17,340	5,291

Note: Panel A conditional on receiving any nursing or personal care at some point during the calendar year. Administrative registers report total expenditures on nursing and personal care. This is approximately 42 percent of all formal home care in terms of expenditures (Bakx et al. 2021). Annual expenditures are converted to weekly hours using the average price per hour reported by NZa (2019): 54.42 euro.

Panel B conditional on receiving any informal care in the period directly prior to the interview.

Among users of nursing and personal care, the distribution is highly skewed (panel A): while the median users aged 65 only uses 1 hour per week (1.6 for 85+), this rises to 7.7 hours for the 95th percentile (7.8 for 85+). Panel B highlights that the distribution of informal care among users is even more skewed, ranging from only 1 (for 65+) or 2 (85+) reported hours per week at the 5th percentile to 168 (65+) and 105 hours (85+).

Nursing home care is an alternative to formal or informal care at home. In the Netherlands, most nursing home admissions are the final stage of life and only few residents return to their homes after admission. Table 7.7 reports the lengths of stay for nursing home residents in 2016. The distribution is highly skewed: while the average resident lived in a nursing home for almost three years, the median is only about two years. At the tails, the 90th percentile is at six years, while the 10th percentile is at just over three months.

The total costs for home care would be a substantial share of a user's income or wealth if they had to pay these costs out of pocket: the amount of home care that users use on a weekly basis (table 7.6) valued at the going rate of one hour of home care comprises a substantial share of the income for many older people (table 7.4). For instance, one year of three hours of home care per week, which is close to the 75th percentile of the distribution in table 7.6, would cost close to 9,000 euros per year (2019 price level), and that would be almost half of the median income of the 85+ population (table 7.4). Furthermore, the cost of a two-year nursing home admission at

Table 7.7 Distribution of nursing home stay lengths

	65+
Days since admission	
Average	996
Median	731
10th percentile	103
90th percentile	2,470
Share in nursing home in 2+ years	.50
Observations	193,202

Note: All users of nursing home care in 2016. If users had multiple stays during 2016, the length of stay was added over all stays, thus mimicking survey data asking about the total length of stay during the year.

175 euros per day (dementia care, 2016 price level) would cost approximately 130,000 euros, and hence exceed the income and wealth of most older persons. Wouterse et al. (2022) estimate that a Dutch 65-year-old will use, on average, 75,000 euros of formal long-term care over their remaining lifetime, with the top 5 percent of biggest users using over 320,000 euros of care. In the Netherlands, most of these costs are covered through social insurance. Despite this extensive coverage, user fees for nursing home care pose a financial risk. The remainder of this chapter discusses the public long-term care system in the Netherlands and what it means for the distribution of the costs of long-term care.

7.3 Long-Term Care System

7.3.1 Public Financing

The Dutch health care system aims to provide affordable care of good quality to all its citizens. Universal health coverage has been in place in the Netherlands for decades and has included long-term care as early as 1968. There is no private long-term care insurance in the Netherlands.[1]

This universal health coverage is achieved through three complementary public financing schemes that each pay for specific types of care (table 7.8). First, social long-term care insurance pays for institutional care (including nursing homes and hospice care). Second, social health insurance pays for nursing and personal care provided at home. Third, the Social Support Act makes municipalities responsible for organizing and financing assistance and social support for elderly living in their community. Each of these public schemes pays for care for the full population.[2]

1. Hence, the section about private long-term care insurance that is included in other chapters is omitted.

2. In addition to elderly care, the three schemes also cover care for individuals with severe physical or sensory disabilities, and care for individuals with a long-term mental illness. For

Table 7.8 **Main characteristics of public long-term care financing**

Scheme	Social long-term care insurance	Social health insurance	Social Support act
Type of LTC covered	Nursing home care[a]	Nursing and personal care at home	Assistance and social support
How it is paid for	Income-related insurance premiums and general taxation, income-related co-payments	Insurance premiums (partially income-related), general taxation[b]	General taxation, deductible
Eligibility for coverage	Full population, mandatory or automatic enrollment		
How benefits are paid	In-kind provision, beneficiaries may opt for a cash benefit		
What is covered	Formal care, but cash benefits may also be used to pay informal caregivers (few % of expenditures)		

Notes: [a] Including intensive (around the clock) care in other settings; [b] Home care covered through public health insurance is exempted from the deductible. Source: adapted from Bakx et al. 2021.

Enrolment in the social insurance schemes is mandatory. The two social insurance schemes are primarily funded through earmarked insurance premiums, and the Social Support Act is fully financed through general taxation. Cost sharing is relatively low (figure 7.4).[3] Income-dependent co-payments amount to 7 percent of spending on institutional care, and a deductible on home care financed through the Social Support Act pays for 4 percent of the expenditures on home care (figure 7.6). There is no cost sharing for home care paid for through social health insurance. This financing mix implies substantial intrapersonal (across the life-cycle) and interpersonal (from the healthy to those with limitations) redistribution (Bakx et al. 2016).

7.3.1.1 Expenditures

This universal and comprehensive coverage of long-term care expenditures comes at a cost. The Netherlands spends 4.0 percent of its Gross Domestic Product on long-term care (figure 7.3), which is more than any other country in the world (OECD 2022). Although cost containment has been mentioned as a policy objective when announcing policy reforms, costs have kept increasing substantially over the past decades, both in absolute amounts and as a share of GDP.

The share of long-term care expenditures devoted to institutional care

this reason, this part reports expenditures for all types of long-term care for the full adult population. This is also what is reported in other international comparisons, e.g., those done by the OECD, and what is focused on in this part of the chapter. Section 7.4 reports expenditure calculations for the 65+ population.

3. As table 7.8 shows, eligibility for long-term care is not age-restricted. Figures 7.3 and 7.4 are for the full 18+ population; estimates for the 65+ population are available from cost-of-illness studies from RIVM (2022) and show a similar trend. Expenditure data for the 65+ population are presented in section 7.4 of this chapter.

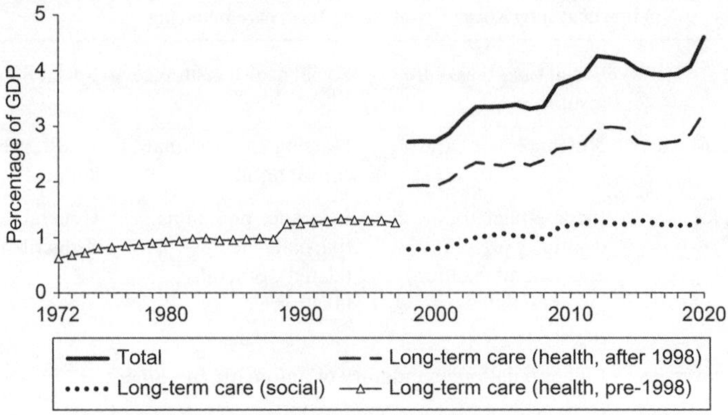

Fig. 7.3 Share of GDP spent on long-term care over time

Source: OECD 2022. Note: long-term care for the full 18+ population

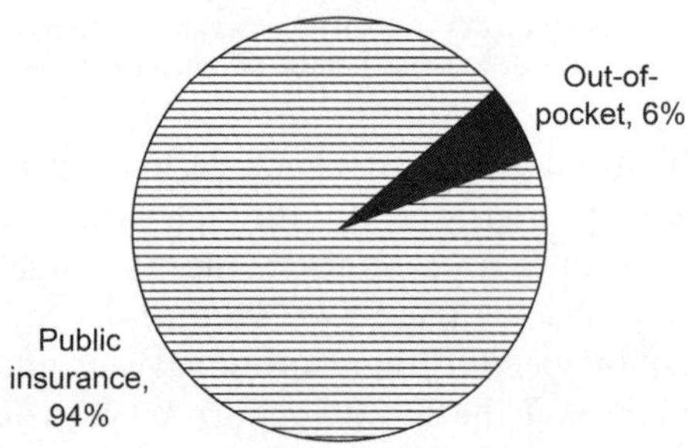

Fig. 7.4 Percent of long-term care financing by source

Note: Expenditures in million euros in 2020 for System of Health Accounts categories HC.3 (LTC Health) HCR.1 (LTC social) taken together. Public expenditures are category HF1; out-of-pocket expenditures are HF3, which equals HF3.2 (cost sharing) because HF3.1 (direct out-of-pocket payments) equals zero. Long-term care for the full 18+ population.

Source: CBS 2022a

versus home care has remained constant (figure 7.5), despite an increased number of the oldest old. Possibly this is in part because of policy measures promoting aging-in-place. Aging-in-place has been an explicit policy goal for at least three decades (De Meijer et al. 2015). This has led to a series of policy reforms, including increasing the availability of home care and stricter eligibility rules for institutional care. The share of long-term care expenditures devoted to institutional care is similar as in Germany (Geyer et al. 2025) but higher than in the United States (Gruber and McGarry 2025) and in Denmark (Gørtz et al. 2025).

7.3.1.2 Allocation and Contracting

Eligibility for benefits is assessed for each of the three schemes separately and is done by different organizations using different sets of rules (see Bakx

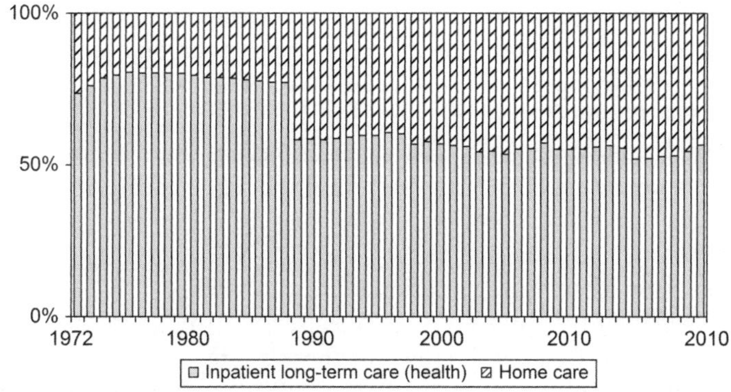

Fig. 7.5 Spending on institutional care versus home care, as a percentage of total expenditure

Notes: Definitions according to System of Health Accounts. Home care is defined as System of Health Accounts categories HC.3.2-HC.3.4 and HCR.1. Institutional care is defined as System of Health Accounts category HC.3.1. Definitions changed in 1998; the reason for the change in 1988 is unknown. Long-term care for the full 18+ population.

Source: OECD 2022

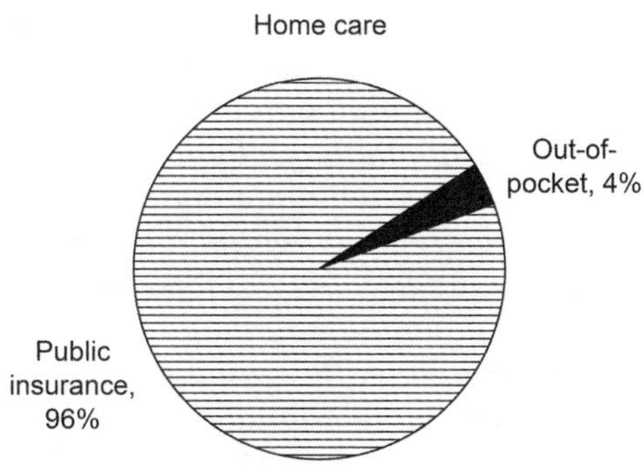

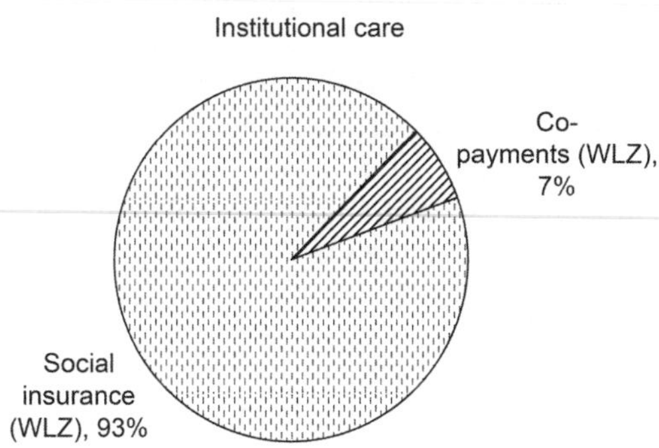

Fig. 7.6. Expenditures on home care and institutional care, by source of funds

Note: long-term care for the full 18+ population in 2020.

Source: CBS 2022b.

et al. 2021 for details). However, in all cases, eligibility is only based on need and not restricted to certain subgroups in the population according to, for example, income or age. A substantial share of all applications for eligibility to care financed through social long-term care insurance is rejected (Algemene Rekenkamer 2018). These rejections may have a number of reasons: for instance, applicants may not meet the requirements for eligibility; may end the application process; or they may be referred to care financed through another scheme. Tenand et al. (2020, 2020a) find that among the 65+ population, there is no variation in the probability of being eligible by income, age, and other non-need factors after controlling for differences in need studying data from 2012. However, there is some variation in long-term care use conditional on entitlements by socioeconomic and demographic characteristics.

Individuals who are eligible for long-term care may choose between care in-kind or a voucher (cash benefit) that they may use to contract a care provider themselves. In-kind benefits are provided by private organizations. These providers are contracted by a contracting party: municipalities contract providers of social support and assistance (Social Support Act); health insurers contract providers of nursing and personal care (social health insurance); and regional single-payers contract institutional care providers (social long-term care insurance). Providers negotiate an annual contract and are paid on a fee-for-service basis. In addition, contracts may include a budget ceiling. Home care providers may be for-profit or non-profit organizations, institutional care providers are all non-profit organizations. Vouchers may be used to contract non-professional caregivers, including family members. However, the share of informal caregivers that reports getting paid is merely 3 percent (SCP 2015).

In addition to the choice between care in-kind and a voucher, individuals who are eligible for institutional care may choose to receive care in-kind in an institutional setting or at home or another private setting.[4] The other housing options are all private initiatives, either set up by residents or by other private parties (for-profit or non-profit). These may include assisted living facilities, homes that may be fully adapted to the resident's functional limitations, and apartments that are built next to a nursing home and that enable people to use some facilities of the nursing home. Care that is received by people living in such housing arrangements is usually funded through the public system, and for this care the same eligibility criteria apply as for all other home care and institutional care. When care is used in an institutional setting, the costs of room and board are covered by the social insurance. In other settings, these costs are paid by the individual.

There is a growing niche market for high-end nursing home care with

4. Care at home or in another private setting may be provided by for-profit providers.

Table 7.9 Shares of elderly who received care, by age and functional limitations

	65+	85+
All	.24	.72
0–1 limitations	.12	.46
2 limitations	.56	.78
3 limitations	.78	.90
4 limitations	.87	.95
5+ limitations	.94	.98
Observations	225,653	18,203

Note: Functional limitations are measured using the OECD scale, see appendix A for an explanation and a mapping of the OECD scale and limitations based on the IADL and ADL lists. The grouping used in this table is closest to the grouping used in the other chapters.
Source: Own calculations based on linked survey and administrative data

about 300 high-end nursing homes that accounted for about 5,400 residents in 2019 (SCP 2019). Standard care is typically publicly funded, but these nursing homes allow topping up for additional services and require payments for room and board (Hussem et al. 2020).

7.3.2 Long-Term Care Receipt

Twenty-four percent of the 65+ population uses either formal or informal long-term care, while 72 percent of the 85+ population does (table 7.9). As expected, the probability of care use is strongly correlated with the number of functional limitations that are reported, and virtually all individuals with five or more limitations use some type of care. These shares are considerably higher than in the United States and Denmark, but substantially lower than in Germany (Gruber and McGarry 2025; Gørtz et al. 2025; Geyer et al. 2025).

Figures 7.7 and 7.8 zoom in on the mix of care types that is used. These figures highlight that a large share receives formal home care: 52 percent of the care recipients aged 65+ (46 percent for the 85+), while the share of care users who only receive informal care is only 19 percent, which is much smaller than in Denmark, the United States and Germany, where more than half of all care users are in the latter group (Gruber and McGarry 2025; Gørtz et al. 2025; Geyer et al. 2025). A large share of care users living at home reports using both formal home care and informal care. Approximately 44 percent of all formal home care users also receive informal care. Conversely, 55 percent of all informal care users also receive formal home care. Furthermore, the type of care that is used differs by age: the share using nursing home care is higher among those aged 85+ than among the total 65+ population (figure 7.7).

The type of care used also differs by the number of limitations (figure 7.8).

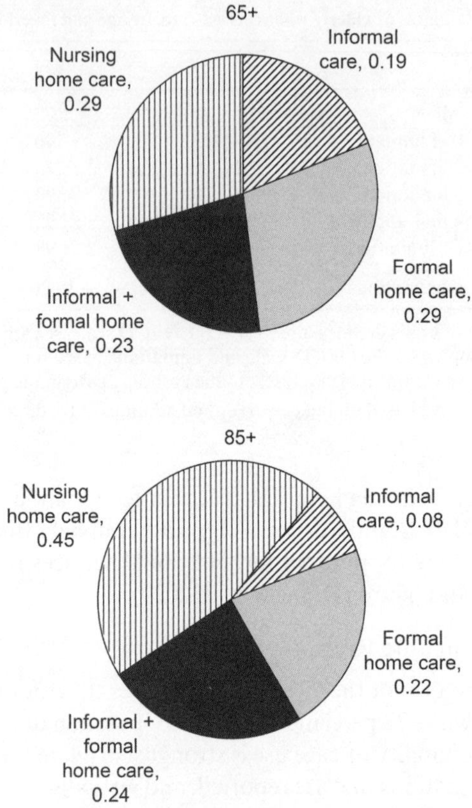

Fig. 7.7 Type of care received by age, conditional on using any care
Source: Own calculations based on linked administrative and survey data

Those with fewer functional limitations more often receive no care or care at home rather than in a nursing home. Furthermore, more than half of those with 4+ limitations who receive care at home receive a combination of formal home care and informal care instead of just one of these care types.

Nineteen percent of the care recipients aged 85 or older who report no or only one limitation receive nursing home care (figure 7.8; 65+: 0.10). A potential explanation is that because the functional limitations used in this analysis capture physical health problems requiring care or support, they are less likely to fully capture mental and cognitive limitations, which may also require care or support, and thus be a reason for long-term care use. Yet, this share is larger than the shares that are reported for the United States and Germany using similar measures (Gruber and McGarry 2025; Geyer et al. 2025).

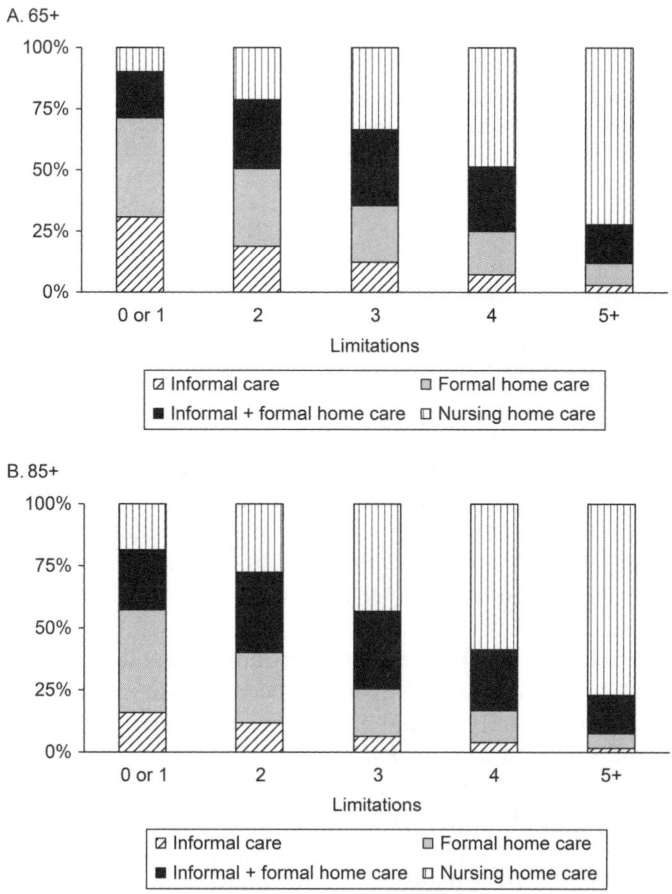

Fig. 7.8 Type of care by age and limitations, conditional on using any care

Note: Functional limitations are measured using the OECD scale. See appendix A for an explanation and a mapping of the OECD scale and limitations based on the IADL and ADL lists. The grouping used in this table is closest to the grouping used in the other chapters.

Source: Own calculations based on linked survey and administrative data

7.3.3 Formal Long-Term Care Supply

7.3.3.1 Nursing Homes

Table 7.10 reports that there are 1,922 nursing homes,[5] with 142 thousand beds, meaning that the average nursing home has 74 beds. In addition, 9,000 individuals received institutional care in another setting (TNO 2019). There is no publicly available information on occupancy rates by region,

5. Nursing homes may be part of a larger conglomerate.

Table 7.10 **Absolute number of nursing homes, beds, and occupancy rate**

Nursing homes	1,922 (2017 figure)
Nursing home beds in 1,000: theoretical	165 (2017)
Nursing home beds in 1,000: operational	152 (2018)
Nursing home beds in 1,000s contracted	142
Nursing home occupancy rate	.935 (2018)
Population size 65+	3,314,004
Beds per 1000 65+	43
Population size 85+	376,706
Beds per 1000 85+	377

Note: Figures for 2019 unless indicated otherwise.
Source: CBS (2020a), TNO (2019, 2020)

but information on waiting lists for nursing home care (ZN 2022) suggests that there is substantial variation in whether the supply of nursing homes is able to meet the demand: waiting lists are zero or very small in most regions but substantial in some regions. Compared to other countries, the number of beds in institutional settings (per 1,000 65+) is above the OECD average (OECD 2022).[6]

Nursing home care is provided in nursing homes that have been adapted to the needs of their residents. Nursing home residents typically live in one-person bedrooms. The types and amount of care that a resident receives depend on the type of care package that the resident is eligible for. Typically, nursing home residents receive between 11 and 29.5 hours of care and assistance per week (Bureau HHM 2010).[7]

To address concerns related to the quality of care in nursing homes, the government increased the budget by 2.1 billion per year in 2017 (Bakx et al. 2020), which is approximately 10 percent of the total budget. Organizations providing institutional care could apply for additional funding. The jump resulting from this increase in spending appear to be clearly visible in figure 7.3, though the effects on quality-of-care have not been reported so far, likely in part because data on nursing home quality are mostly limited to measures of the organization structure, processes, mortality, and hospitalizations (Bakx et al. 2020; Bär et al. 2022).

7.3.4 Long-Term Care Workers

Personal carers are the largest group of health care workers in nursing homes and in home care (figure 7.9). Doctors, registered nurses, and other registered workers make up for only one-tenth of all workers in long-term

6. OECD reports beds in all types of institutional care. Nursing home users make up 59 percent of all institutional care users (CBS 2022c).

7. Values for care packages 4–8. Care packages 1–3 have been phased out; package 9 is for rehabilitation and package 10 for hospice care.

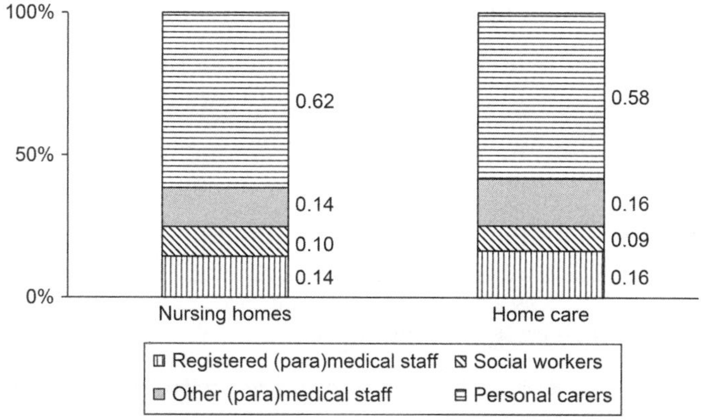

Fig. 7.9 Worker types in nursing homes and home care

Notes: 2021 estimates based on the CBS Health Care Workers Survey. The figure contains the number of workers rather than the fulltime equivalent (FTE). Registered medical and paramedical staff includes doctors, registered nurses and other medical or paramedical workers for which registration is mandatory (pharmacists, psychotherapists, physiotherapists, medical psychologists). Other paramedical and medical staff includes medical or paramedical staff for which registration is not mandatory such as practical nurses and medical assistants.

Source: CBS 2021a

care. The number of workers in nursing homes is twice as large as in home care (CBS 2022). This reflects the higher care needs of nursing home residents compared to home care users given that the number of home care users is three times as large as the number of nursing home residents (cf. section 7.4).[8]

Many workers do not have a full-time job; the mean full-time equivalent (FTE) per worker is 0.63 in nursing homes and 0.55 in home care in 2021 (CBS 2022d). As a full-time job in the long-term care sector is 36 hours a week, this means that on average these workers work 20–23 hours per week, which is lower than the overall mean hours worked (30 hours) reported for the Netherlands by Eurostat (2022). This is the case for all types of workers for which data are reported (CBS 2022e). Therefore, if expressed as the number of FTEs instead of the number of workers, the absolute number of workers would be much lower but the split across the types of workers may not change much.

There are only formal training requirements for medical and paramedical staff for which registration is mandatory, i.e., doctors, registered nurses and pharmacists, psychotherapists, physiotherapists, medical psychologists.

8. In addition to the categories listed in figure 7.9, nursing homes and home care providers also have support staff, including management and services jobs such as cleaning and cooking, and other staff. Support staff accounts for 19–25 percent (58,000 FTE in nursing homes; 34,000 FTE in home care); the other staff for 8 percent in nursing homes (25,000 FTE) and 7 percent in home care (9,000 FTE).

Table 7.11 **Pay for full-time care workers at nursing homes and in home care.**

	Annual pay per FTE in 1,000 euros	Hourly pay in euros
Total	44.4	23.6
Doctors	109.9	58.5
Registered nurses	53.4	28.4
Other registered medical or paramedical workers[a]	62.8	33.4
Other workers[b]	42.2	22.5

Notes: 2019 figures. All figures refer to gross payment, including overtime and other additional payments. Hourly pay is derived from annual pay (dividing by 156,5 hour per month times 12 months).

[a] For which registration is mandatory (pharmacists, psychotherapists, physiotherapists, medical psychologists).

[b] Including medical or paramedical staff for which registration is not mandatory such as logopedics, occupational therapists, exercise therapists.

Source: CBS 2022f

There are no formal requirements for other types of health care workers, yet providers need to ensure that their workers are sufficiently qualified for the tasks that they have been assigned; this is checked by the Healthcare Inspectorate.

Table 7.11 shows that hourly pay for formal care workers is 23.6 euros in 2019, which was close to the mean hourly pay in the Netherlands (23.1 euros—CBS 2021b). On average, working full-time yields an annual gross salary of 44 thousand euros, which is equal to the median income for all workers and close to the average income for the seventh decile of the overall income distribution (CBS 2021c). Wages are agreed upon at the sector level by employer's and employee's representatives and set in a collective labor agreement. An employee's wage depends on the type of job and the number of years worked in the current job.

7.3.5 Who Are the Caregivers?

Figure 7.10 reports the demographic characteristics of informal caregivers (left) and formal care workers (right). Compared to formal care workers, informal caregivers are older: the share of formal care workers aged 35 or under (0.30) is more than twice as large as the share of informal caregivers aged <30 (0.06) and aged 30–39 (0.08) combined. Furthermore, as in other countries (Gruber and McGarry 2025; Gørtz et al. 2025; Geyer et al. 2025), the vast majority (92 percent) of all formal care workers are female, while 61 percent of the informal caregivers are female. Finally, informal caregivers are less likely to have education level "middle" than formal care workers: informal care is relatively often provided by higher educated and lower educated persons compared to formal care. 79 percent of all caregivers provide

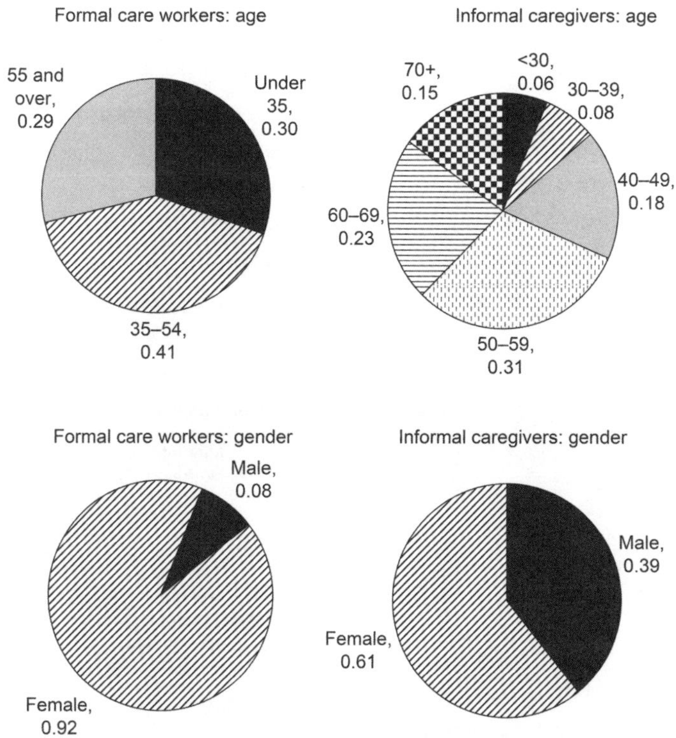

Fig. 7.10 Demographic composition of formal care workers and informal caregivers

Notes informal caregivers: The number of observations is 75,685. Education level categories "low" and "middle 1" were merged to best mimic the data available for formal caregivers. Informal caregivers provide care to care recipients of all ages; the data do not contain information about the age of the care recipient or the relationship between the caregiver and the care recipient. Figures for 2016. Notes formal caregivers: weighted average of nursing home workers and home care workers. Figures for 2021 quarter 4.

Sources: CBS 2020b, 2022g (formal care workers); own calculations based on Health Monitor data linked to administrative registers (informal caregivers)

care to another family member, roughly half to a parent and half to either a spouse or another family member; 21 percent provides care to a friend, neighbor or someone else (figure 7.11).

Taken together, the Dutch long-term care system is characterized by comprehensive, universal public programs in which eligibility is based on need. Hence, formal care is accessible for all who need it. Furthermore, user fees make up only a few percent of total expenditures. The workforce providing this formal care often works part-time and is predominantly female. Similarly, informal care is provided by a specific subgroup in the population.

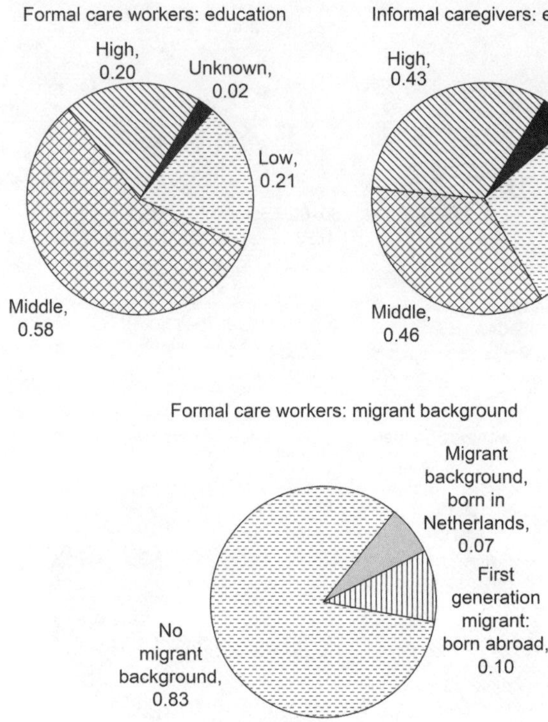

Fig. 7.10 (cont.)

7.4 The Cost of Long-Term Care

Private financing of long-term care is as good as absent in the Netherlands, which means that the costs of LTC are divided between publicly financed formal care and informal care. To calculate the costs of informal care, we apply the same approach as in the rest of this book, and use an estimate of opportunity costs based on wages.

We first report home care expenditures and nursing home care expenditures for the 65+ population. Subsequently, we measure the value of informal care. Finally, we combine the data on formal and informal care spending to derive estimates of total long-term care spending in the Netherlands.

7.4.1 Formal Care Costs

Table 7.12 reports the number of users, total spending, and average spending by user for formal home care and nursing home care for the 65+ population by source. 211 thousand individuals used institutional care in 2016, which is 6.4 percent of the Dutch 65+ population. Users aged 65 and over make up 67 percent of all institutional care users. Institutional care is fully financed by social long-term care insurance. In total, 13.4 billion euros are

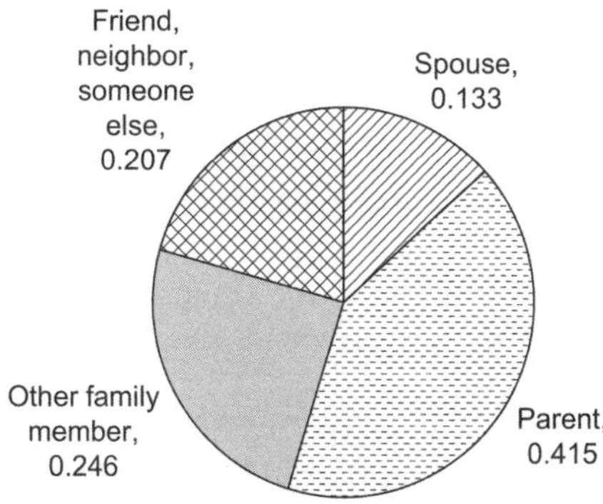

Fig. 7.11 Informal caregivers: for whom do they care?

Notes: 4,921 observations. Respondents are interviewed about the person they provide most care to. Parent category also includes parents-in-law and stepparents. See De Klerk et al. (2021) for details on the survey data.

Source: Own calculations based on SCP informal care survey 2019 (SCP and CBS 2020)

Table 7.12 Formal care costs for the 65+ population

Types	Number of users (in 1,000)	Total spending (in billion euros)	Spending per user (in 1,000 euros)
Institutional care	211	13.37	63.38
Home care—personal care and nursing	445	2.86	6.43
Home care—domestic help and assistance	367	4.10	11.17

Note: 2016 figures, expenditures adjusted to 2019 price level (CBS 2022). The total number of home care users aged 65+ is 614 thousand and hence mean spending is 11,335 euros.

Source: Own calculations based on administrative microdata and CBS (2022b), CBS (2022h), CBS (2022i), CBS (2022j), RIVM (2019)

spent on nursing home care for the 65+ population. Most of this care is provided in-kind in an institutional setting which includes room and board, but users can also opt to use care in-kind (excluding room and board) provided in a private setting or a cash transfer. Co-payments are income dependent and wealth dependent and equal 11 percent of total spending on institutional care (figure 7B.1).

About 445,000 65+ individuals use formal personal care and nursing, covered by public health insurance. For this type of care, users do not pay any cost sharing. Total spending on personal care and nursing is 2.8 billion euros. The rest of home care is domestic care and assistance financed by municipalities. Around 367 thousand individuals aged 65+ use this type of care. For the services that are person-specific, users pay a fixed monthly fee out of pocket, which amounts to 3 percent of the total spending on home health services.

There are large differences in expenditures per user across countries. Total costs per nursing home care users are 63 thousand euros in the Netherlands, which is very similar to expenditures per user in Denmark, yet almost 50 percent higher than in Germany, but half as much as in the United States (Gruber and McGarry 2025; Gørtz et al. 2025; Geyer et al. 2025). These differences may have many, potentially partially offsetting, causes, including differences in the case mix between these countries—the share of care users who are using nursing home care varies internationally—but also in the quality of care and other services provided, and which types of expenditures are included in these figures.

Combined expenditures on all types of home care (personal care, nursing, domestic help and assistance) are 11 thousand euros per user in the Netherlands, which is roughly similar to expenditures levels in Germany and Denmark and just over 50 percent of the expenditures per home care user in the United States (Gruber and McGarry 2025; Gørtz et al. 2025; Geyer et al. 2025). As with nursing home care, there may be large differences in the size and composition of the group using home care, but also in the types of care and the level of quality that are provided.

7.4.2 Informal Care Costs

We use the two approaches to estimating the opportunity costs of informal caregiving discussed in Gruber and McGarry (2022). First, we use a counterfactual (potential) wage for each caregiver based on the wage of individuals with the same characteristics in the general population (opportunity cost method). To estimate the counterfactual wage, we regress the probability of being employed and the estimated hourly gross wage of all employed respondents in the 2016 Public Health Monitor on age group indicators, gender, education, and household type. We then use the coefficients from these regressions to impute the potential wage for the respondents who provided informal care. The predicted average wage for those providing informal home care, and thus our estimate of the value of a caregiver's time, is 20.86 euros per hour (2019 price level).

Second, we combine the opportunity cost estimate with a market-based approach and value informal care using the average hourly wage of home care workers (proxy good method). Not everyone who provides informal care would otherwise be in paid work. Specifically, many informal caregivers are above the pension age (figure 7.10). The hourly wage for formal workers who do comparable tasks as informal caregivers was 11.70 euros on average in 2016 in the Netherlands (European Commission 2021). We use the opportunity cost method for those who work and the proxy good method for those who do not.

To estimate the number of hours of informal care that is provided to the 65+ population, we use the share of the 65+ sample of the 2016 Public Health Monitor who stated that they received informal care within the last

Table 7.13 Valuation of informal home care

	Opportunity cost method	Combined: opportunity cost and proxy good method
Valuation (billion euros)	9.51	10.65
Hours informal care received (million)[a]	456	456
Predicted probability of working	0.79	0.79
Predicted wage * probability of working	20.86	20.86
Predicted wage if working	26.45	26.45
Home Health Aide Wage		11.70

Note: 2016 figures, adjusted to 2019 price level (CBS 2022). [a]Hours are per week for respondents indicating that they currently received care. To get the number of hours, this conditional number of hours (20.5) is multiplied by the share of respondents indicating that they received care in the past 12 months (0.13), 52 weeks and the size of the 65+ population. Home health aide wage taken from European Commission (2021). Table 7B.2 contains the estimate using the proxy good method. The data do not allow us to distinguish between informal care recipients by age. In the SCP informal care survey (SCP and CBS 2020), the probability of working is 7 percentage points lower for informal caregivers to the 65+ population than in the overall sample of caregivers. This 7-percentage point lower probability to work would translate into a 1.8 billion euro lower (opportunity cost method) and 0.5 billion euro (combined method) lower valuation.

12 months (13 percent). The average number of hours of care received per week is based on the reported number of hours received in the last week, among those reporting currently receiving informal care (20.5 hours).

The results are shown in table 7.13. 456 million care hours per year are provided to the 65+ population in the Netherlands. Depending on the costing method used, the estimated costs of informal caregiving to the 65+ population are 9.51 billion euros per year (when using opportunity cost method) to 10.6 billion (when using the combined method).

7.4.3 Total Costs

Table 7.14 summarizes the estimates of expenditures on formal care and informal care costs to provide a national estimate of total long-term care spending. The total costs of long-term care for the 65+ population are 31 billion euros (4 percent of GDP). The costs of informal care account for around 34 percent of total costs (1.3 percent of GDP). Despite the extensive public formal care system, informal care costs are still substantial, both in absolute terms and as a percentage of total spending on long-term care for the 65+ population.

This 34 percent of total spending that is attributed to informal care is lower than the 50 percent reported for Germany by Geyer et al. (2025), which has traditionally relied less on formal care and more on informal care than the Netherlands. Estimates for the United States are similar to those for the Netherlands, while estimates of the share of informal care costs for

Table 7.14 Total costs by type of care, in billion euros and as a percentage of gross domestic product (GDP)

		Informal care valued at opportunity costs		Informal care valued using combination of opportunity cost method and proxy good method	
Care type	Source	Spending in billion euros	% of GDP	Spending in billion euros	% of GDP
Nursing home	Public	11.89	1.6%	11.89	1.6%
	Private	1.48	0.2%	1.48	0.2%
	Total	13.37	1.8%	13.37	1.8%
Home care	Public	6.78	0.9%	6.78	0.9%
	Private	0.19	0.0%	0.19	0.0%
	Total	6.96	0.9%	6.96	0.9%
Informal care	Private	9.51	1.3%	10.65	1.4%
Total	Public	18.67	2.5%	18.67	2.5%
	Private	11.18	1.5%	12.37	1.6%
	Total	29.84	4.0%	31.03	4.1%

Notes: 2016 figures, expenditures adjusted to 2019 price level (CBS 2022).

Source: Own calculations based on microdata and CBS (2022b), CBS (2022h), CBS (2022i), CBS (2022j), RIVM (2019). As explained in section 7.3, the number of informal caregivers who report that they get financial compensation is very small, meaning that the risk of double counting is limited.

Denmark are much lower than for the Netherlands (Gruber and McGarry 2025; Gørtz et al. 2025). Table 7.13 sheds light on some of the causes for these differences: they are caused not only by the number of informal care hours that is provided but also by the cost estimates per hour, which may differ by as much as a factor 2.5 across these four countries. These cost estimates per hour are in turn affected by who provides the informal care, the probability of working, the predicted wage if working. For instance, in the Netherlands 79 percent of the informal caregivers work, while 67 percent of the informal caregivers in Denmark work, 59 percent of the informal caregivers in Germany work, and 48 percent of the informal caregivers in the United States work (Gruber and McGarry 2025; Gørtz et al. 2025; Geyer et al. 2025). Strikingly, estimates of the hourly wage of home care workers are relatively small.

The share of formal home care costs in the total costs of long-term care are roughly equal to the share in the United States and in Germany (Gruber and McGarry 2025; Geyer et al. 2025) but lower than in Denmark (Gørtz et al. 2025). These differences possibly reflect differences in the relative focus of the long-term care system on nursing home care or home care as well as differences in costs per home care user and per nursing home care user that were described above.

7.5 Conclusions

This chapter provides an overview of long-term care use and the organization of long-term care in the Netherlands. We have documented the distribution of well-being and need for long-term care, the financing and organization of long-term care, the long-term care costs, and how they are paid for.

We arrive at four main conclusions. First, no other country spends more per capita on publicly financed formal care than the Netherlands, according to the System of Health Accounts of the OECD (OECD 2022). Although the Dutch definition of long-term care may be relatively broad in terms of services and population groups included, this chapter reconfirms that the Netherlands indeed has one of the most extensive and comprehensive public long-term care systems.

The frequent use of formal care is associated with a relatively limited reliance on informal care. The share of informal care costs in the total costs of long-term care is lower than in some countries. When considering the opportunity cost of informal care, the differences between the Netherlands and other countries in the total costs of long-term care become much smaller (cf. European Commission 2022). At the same time, the differences do not disappear entirely. For instance, while the share of GDP per capita spent on formal long-term care is three times larger in the Netherlands than in the United States, informal care costs as a percent of GDP are roughly twice as high in the Netherlands: 1.4% versus 0.7% (Gruber and McGarry 2023).

Second, accounting for informal care has a large impact not only on the estimated level of long-term care costs but also on the distribution of these costs. Formal care costs are paid for through public programs, and user payments make up for only a few percent of total revenues. Since the public programs are funded by income-dependent premiums and general taxation, the costs of these programs are by and large paid for according to ability to pay. By contrast, the opportunity costs of informal care—as well as the health costs (Bom et al. 2019; Bom and Stockel 2021)—are fully borne by informal caregivers, which is a selected and relatively small subpopulation. The findings presented in this chapter show that the average informal caregiver provides a substantial amount of care, meaning that these opportunity costs per caregiver may be substantial too. Furthermore, the demographic composition of the group of informal caregivers shows that some subpopulations, such as middle-aged or older women, are more likely to provide informal care than others and thus take on a greater burden, possibly despite being in a disadvantaged position for other reasons. Hence, factoring in the costs of informal care also changes the view on the extent to which overall long-term care costs are borne in an equitable way.

This conclusion also has implications for the consequences of future increases in long-term care use when population aging means that long-term care needs in the population will increase (De Meijer et al. 2013). Will the costs of this additional care be covered through public programs that increase expenditures when needs increase? Or by formal care users who pay greater user fees and by informal caregivers who step in if public expenditure rises do not keep up with increases in needs? Ultimately, how the costs of long-term care are allocated among three groups—society, users, and informal caregivers—is a political decision: to what extent is society willing and able to continue to take an increasing long-term care burden away from the other two groups (Bakx et al. 2020)?

Third, the threshold to receive formal care appears to be lower in the Netherlands than in other countries. That is, the probability of formal care use is already substantial at low or moderate levels of limitations. This is true for both home care and for nursing home care. Among the 85+ with 0–1 limitations, 44 percent receive formal care, of which 19 percent (i.e., 8 percent of the total population) receive nursing home care. These individuals may have other limitations (e.g., cognitive limitations) that are not captured by the measure that we use but that do cause a need for care. Yet, this percentage is twice the percentage reported in the chapters for other countries that used similar measures to report functional limitations (cf. Gruber and McGarry 2025).

Fourth, a relatively large share of formal long-term care workers in the Netherlands works part-time. This suggests that shortages in the labor market due to the increasing demand for formal care workers might be reduced if these workers can be persuaded to work more hours. Yet, persuading these workers may prove to be a major challenge because of increasing competing demands, including a rise in the demand for informal care. While informal care provision currently seems to have limited impact on the labor market outcomes of caregivers (Rellstab et al. 2020), this might change when demands for both formal and informal work increase.

Taken together, these findings highlight the importance of a complete view on long-term care use and costs when formulating responses to the expected increase in need for long-term care in the future. These findings are helpful in generating a better understanding of some of the trade-offs that policymakers will face when deciding about the future resource allocation in long-term care. The Netherlands is clearly on one extreme of the spectrum of policy choices, providing extensive and collectively financed social assistance, home care, and nursing home care to its population. As a result, care is highly accessible and the financial risks for older individuals are limited. At the same time, the extensive collective financing of care makes Dutch public finance relatively vulnerable to the pressure of population aging (Wouterse and Smid 2017). Dutch policymakers thus face the challenge of how to ensure fiscally sustainable growth of long-term care spending, which might entail limiting coverage or increasing private spending, while at the same time preserving access to care and financial protection for the most vulnerable groups.

Appendix A

Data

Tables 7A.2–7A.3 report the relation between limitations measured on the OECD and ADL scales. We use the Public Health Survey 2016, which includes both scales. We record the percentage of the 65+ respondents who report having IADLs and no ADLs, at most 1 ADL, at most 2 ADL, etc., by the number of OECD limitations reported. We use the smallest number of OECD limitations for which the share of reporting a particular number of ADLS is more than 50 percent as the cutoffs for our mapping from OECD limitations to ADLs in this chapter. Table 7A.3 shows the mapping that is used for table 7.5; table 7A.2 for all other tables and figures that contain information on functional limitations.

Table 7A.1 **Linked administrative registers and survey data**

Data source	Short description
Municipal registry	Address, demographics: age, gender
Central Administration Office Long-term care	Nursing home care use, co-payments, home care paid for through Social Support Act
Health survey	Functional limitations
Public Health Monitor	Functional limitations, informal care, employment information
Tax office	Tax office data: income, household wealth
Health insurance claims	Expenditures on nursing and personal care

Table 7A.2 **Comparison OECD- IADL/ADL limitation scales: ADL and IADL separate**

	≤ 1 IADL	≤ 1 ADL	≤ 2 ADL	≤ 3 ADL	≤ 4 ADL	≤ 5 ADL	Observations
0 OECD	.100	.040	*	*	*	*	942
1 OECD	.304	.178	.046	*	*	*	415
2 OECD	.541	.325	.192	.082	*	*	255
3 OECD	.746	.583	.408	.317	.208	.117	240
4 OECD	.848	.696	.518	.357	.241	.143	112
5 OECD	*	.821	.714	.607	.488	.321	84
6 OECD	*	*	*	.588	.500	.353	34

Note: * means fewer than 10 observations or more than the total minus 10.

Table 7A.3 **Comparison OECD-IADL/ADL limitation scales: ADL and IADL combined**

	Combined number of ADL and IADL						
	≤ 1	≤ 2	≤ 3	≤ 4	≤ 5	≤ 6	Observations
0 OECD	0.243	0.059	0.018	*	*	*	942
1 OECD	0.561	0.246	0.113	0.055	0.027	0.007	415
2 OECD	0.820	0.510	0.310	0.220	0.145	0.075	255
3 OECD	0.904	0.725	0.600	0.483	0.363	0.296	240
4 OECD	0.955	0.830	0.714	0.598	0.527	0.420	112
5 OECD	*	*	*	0.821	0.750	0.667	84
6 OECD	*	*	*	*	*	*	34

Note: * means fewer than 10 observations or more than the total minus 10. Shares not reported for 7–13 ADLs/IADLs.

Appendix B

Additional Results

Table 7B.1 **Demographic composition of formal home care workers.**

	Nursing homes	Home care
Gender		
Male	.09	.07
Female	.91	.93
Age		
Under 35	.32	.27
35–54	.40	.43
55 and over	.28	.30
Migrant background		
No migrant background	.83	.83
Migrant background	.17	.17
First generation migrant: born abroad	.10	.10
Education level		
Low	.21	.20
Middle	.60	.54
High	.19	.21
Unknown	.01	.05
Number of workers (in 1000s)	282.6	148.6

Note: figures for 2021 quarter 4.

Source: CBS 2022a, https://azwstatline.cbs.nl/#/AZW/nl/dataset/24025NED/table?dl=6909A; 2022b, https://azwstatline.cbs.nl/#/AZW/nl/dataset/24070NED/table?dl=690A1.

Table 7B.2 **Valuation of informal care using the proxy good (market wage) method**

Valuation (billion euros)	5.33
Hours informal care received (million)	456
Home Health Aide Wage	11.70

Note: 2016 figures, adjusted to 2019 price level (CBS 2022). Number of hours. Hours are per week for respondents indicating that they currently received care. This conditional number of hours (20.5) is multiplied by the share of respondents indicating that they received care in the past 12 months (0.13), 52 weeks and the size of the 65+ population. Home health aide wage taken from European Commission (2021).

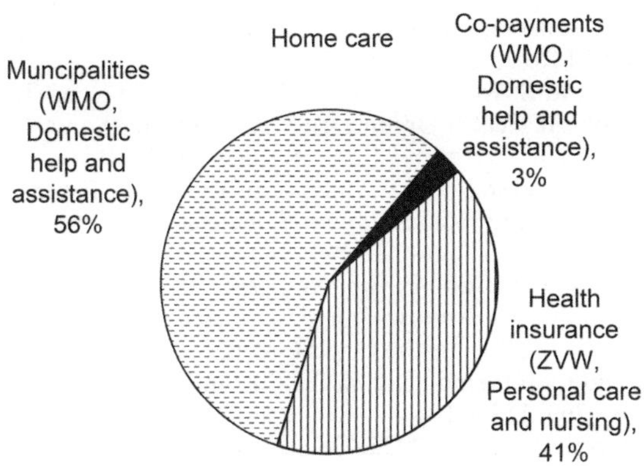

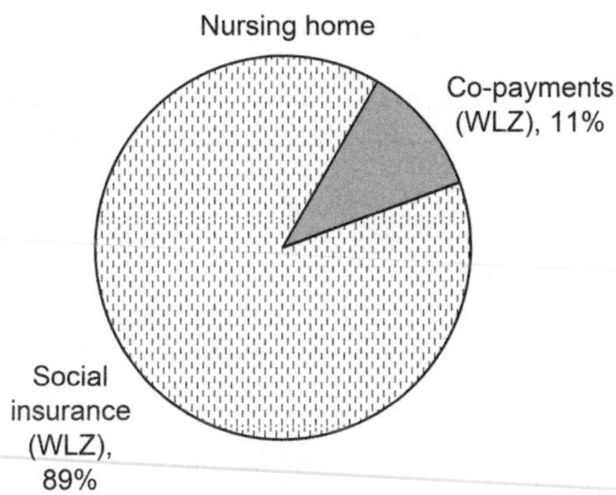

Fig. 7B.1 Formal care expenditures, 65+ population

Source: Own calculations based on administrative microdata and CBS (2022b), CBS (2022h), CBS (2022i), CBS (2022j), RIVM (2019)

References

Algemene Rekenkamer. 2018. Focus op Toegang tot de Wet langdurige zorg. https://www.rekenkamer.nl/publicaties/rapporten/2018/06/06/focus-op-toegang-tot-de-wet-langdurig-zorg.

Bakx, P., D, Chernichovsky, F. Paolucci, E. Schokkaert, M. Trottman, J. Wasem, F. T. Schut. 2015. "Demand-side Strategies to Deal with Moral Hazard in Public Insurance for Long-Term Care Insurance." *Journal of Health Services Research and Policy* 20 (3): 170–76.

Bakx, P., O. O'Donnell, and E. van Doorslaer. 2016. "Spending on Health Care in the Netherlands: Not Going So Dutch." *Fiscal Studies* 37 (3–4): 593–625.

Bakx, P., M. Bär, S. Rellstab, and B. Wouterse. 2020. Zicht op kwaliteit van verpleeghuiszorg? ESHPM Research report 2020.03.

Bakx, P., E. Schut, and B. Wouterse. 2021. "Price Setting in Long-Term Care in the Netherlands." World Health Organization Kobe Center Policy Series on Long-Term Care No. 6.

Bär, M., P. Bakx, B. Wouterse, and E. van Doorslaer. 2022. "Estimating the Health Value Added by Nursing Homes." *Journal of Economic Behavior and Organization* 203: 1–23.

Bom, J., P. Bakx, F. T. Schut, and E. van Doorslaer. 2019. "Health Effects of Caring for and about Parents and Spouses." *Journal of Economics of Ageing* 14: 100196.

Bom, J., and J. Stöckel. 2021. "Is the Grass Greener on the Other Side? The Health Impact of Providing Informal Care in the UK and the Netherlands." *Social Science & Medicine* 269: 113562.

Bom, J., S. Rellstab, and P. Bakx. 2022. "Well-being Right before and after a Permanent Nursing Home Admission." *Health Economics* 31 (12): 2558–2574.

Bureau HHM. 2010. Zorgzwaartepakketten Sector V&V Versie 2011.

CBS. 2020. Prognose bevolking; geslacht, leeftijd, achtergrond en generatie, 2021–2070. https://opendata.cbs.nl/statline/#/CBS/nl/dataset/84872NED/table?dl=6FAA7.

CBS. 2020a. "115 duizend mensen in verzorgings- of verpleeghuis." https://www.cbs.nl/nl-nl/achtergrond/2020/13/115-duizend-mensen-in-verzorgings-of-verpleeghuis.

CBS. 2020b. Werknemers met een baan in de zorg en welzijn; persoonskenmerken, 2010–2019. https://azwstatline.cbs.nl/#/AZW/nl/dataset/24025NED/table?dl=6909A&ts=1664437416075.

CBS. 2021. Bevolking; geslacht, leeftijd en burgerlijke staat, 1 januari. https://opendata.cbs.nl/statline/#/CBS/nl/dataset/7461bev/table?dl=6FAA5.

CBS. 2021a. Werknemers; beroep, regio. https://azwstatline.cbs.nl/#/AZW/nl/dataset/24094NED/table?dl=68FF7.

CBS. 2021b. Gemiddeld uurloon van werknemers in 2019. https://www.cbs.nl/nl-nl/longread/statistische-trends/2021/gemiddeld-uurloon-van-werknemers-in-2019.

CBS. 2021c. Inkomen van personen; inkomensklassen, persoonskenmerken. https://opendata.cbs.nl/statline/#/CBS/nl/dataset/83931NED/table?dl=697B1.

CBS. 2022. Consumentenprijzen; prijsindex 2015=100. https://opendata.cbs.nl/statline/#/CBS/nl/dataset/83131NED/table?dl=6096E.

CBS. 2022a. Zorguitgaven internationaal vergelijkbaar; functies en financiering. https://opendata.cbs.nl/statline/#/CBS/nl/dataset/84043NED/table?dl=5D7D1.

CBS. 2022b. Zorguitgaven internationaal vergelijkbaar; functies en financiering. https://opendata.cbs.nl/statline/#/CBS/nl/dataset/84043NED/table?dl=5D84A.

CBS. 2022c. Gebruik bijdrageplichtige Wlz-zorg; leveringsvorm, zzp, regio. https://mlzopendata.cbs.nl/#/MLZ/nl/dataset/40055NED/table?dl=6FB44.

CBS. 2022d. Werkgelegenheid in de zorg en welzijn; baankenmerken, regio. https://azwstatline.cbs.nl/#/AZW/nl/dataset/24017NED/table?dl=69096.

CBS. 2022e. Zorg; werkgelegenheid, beroepen in zorg en welzijn, zorgaanbieders. https://opendata.cbs.nl/statline/#/CBS/nl/dataset/83738NED/table?dl=52590.

CBS. 2022f. Zorg; werkgelegenheid, beroepen in zorg en welzijn, zorgaanbieders. https://opendata.cbs.nl/statline/#/CBS/nl/dataset/83738NED/table?dl=5DAB6.

CBS. 2022g. Werknemers; scholing en vaardigheden. https://azwstatline.cbs.nl/#/AZW/nl/dataset/24070NED/table?dl=690A1.

CBS. 2022h. Gebruik bijdrageplichtige Wmo-maatwerkvoorzieningen; type, vorm, regio. https://mlzopendata.cbs.nl/#/MLZ/nl/dataset/40060NED/table?dl=6FD0E.

CBS. 2022i. Wmo en Jeugdwet; gemeentelijke baten en lasten, regio. https://mlzopendata.cbs.nl/#/MLZ/nl/dataset/40050NED/table?dl=6EFFE.

CBS. 2022j. Zvw-wijkverpleging en -behandeling; declaraties. https://mlzopendata.cbs.nl/#/MLZ/nl/dataset/40042NED/table?dl=63CC5.

CBS. 2022k. Opbouw binnenlands product (bbp); nationale rekeningen. https://opendata.cbs.nl/statline/#/CBS/nl/dataset/84087NED/table?dl=783B6.

de Klerk, M., A. de Boer, and I. Plaisier. 2021. "Determinants of Informal Care-Giving in Various Social Relationships in the Netherlands." *Health and Social Care in the Community* 29: 1779–1788.

de Meijer, C., B. Wouterse, J. Polder, and M. Koopmanschap. 2013. "The Effect of Population Aging on Health Expenditure Growth: A Critical Review." *European Journal of Ageing* 10: 353–61.

de Meijer, C., P. Bakx, M. Koopmanschap, and E. van Doorslaer. 2015. "Explaining Declining Rates of Institutional LTC Use in the Netherlands: A Decomposition Approach." *Health Economics* 2015: S18–S31.

Dutch Health Monitor. 2016. Public Health Monitor 2016 of the Community Health Services. Statistics Netherlands and the National Institute for Public Health and the Environment.

European Commission. 2021. "Study on Exploring the Incidence and Costs of Informal Long-Term Care in the EU." Brussels: European Commission. https://op.europa.eu/en/publication-detail/-/publication/bafbb918-2197-11ec-bd8e-01aa75ed71a1/language-pl.

Eurostat. 2022. Average Number of Usual Weekly Hours of Work in Main job, by Sex, Age, Professional Status, Full-Time/Part-Time and Economic Activity (from 2008 onwards, NACE Rev. 2). Luxembourg: Eurostat. https://ec.europa.eu/eurostat/databrowser/view/lfsa_ewhun2/default/table?lang=en.

Geyer, J., A. Börsch-Supan, P. Haan, and E. Perdrix. 2025. "Long-Term Care in Germany." In *Long-Term Care around the World*, edited by Jonathan Gruber and Kathleen McGarry. Chicago, IL: University of Chicago Press. This volume.

Gørtz, M., B. Christensen, and N. Datta Gupta. 2025. "Long-Term Care in Denmark." In *Long-Term Care around the World*, edited by Jonathan Gruber and Kathleen McGarry. Chicago, IL: University of Chicago Press. This volume.

Gruber, J., and K. McGarry. 2025. "Long-Term Care in the United States." In *Long-Term Care around the World*, edited by Jonathan Gruber and Kathleen McGarry. Chicago, IL: University of Chicago Press. This volume.

Hussem, A., P. Bakx, and M. Tenand. 2020. "Publieke middelen voor particuliere ouderenzorg." Netspar Design Paper 143. Tilburg: Netspar.

OECD. 2021. Pensions at a Glance 2021: OECD and G20 Indicators. Paris: OECD. https://doi.org/10.1787/ca401ebd-en.

OECD. 2022. Stats.oecd.org. Paris: OECD.

NZa. 2019. Monitor contractering wijkverpleging 2019. https://puc.overheid.nl/nza/doc/PUC_274036_22/1/.

Rellstab, S., P. Bakx, P. García-Gómez, and E. van Doorslaer. 2020. "The Kids Are Alright—Labour Market Effects of Unexpected Parental Hospitalisations in the Netherlands." *Journal of Health Economics* 69: 102275.

RIVM. 2022. Kosten van ziekten 2017. https://statline.rivm.nl/#/RIVM/nl/dataset/50050NED/table?dl=6FD13.

SCP. 2015. Informele hulp: wie doet wat? The Hague: SCP.

SCP. 2019. Wonen met zorg. Verkenning van particuliere woonzorg voor ouderen met zorg. The Hague: SCP.

SCP and CBS. 2020. Informele Zorg—IZG 2019. DANS. https://doi.org/10.17026/dans-xzy-69n3.

Tenand, M., P. Bakx, and E. van Doorslaer. 2020. "Eligibility or Use? Disentangling the Sources of Horizontal Inequity in Home Care Receipt in the Netherlands." *Health Economics* 29 (10): 1161–179.

Tenand, M., P. Bakx, E. van Doorslaer. 2020a. "Equal Long-Term Care for Equal Needs with Universal and Comprehensive Coverage? An Assessment Using Dutch Administrative Data." *Health Economics* 29 (4): 435–51.

TNO. 2019. Prognose capaciteitsontwikkeling verpleeghuiszorg. Report, December 20. https://www.rijksoverheid.nl/documenten/rapporten/2019/12/20/prognose-capaciteitsontwikkeling-verpleeghuiszorg.

TNO. 2020. Prognose capaciteitsontwikkeling verpleeghuiszorg fase II. Report, July 28. https://www.rijksoverheid.nl/documenten/rapporten/2020/07/28/prognose-capaciteitsontwikkeling-verpleeghuiszorg-fase-ii.

Wouterse, B., and B. Smid. 2017. "How to Finance the Rising Costs of Long-Term Care: Four Alternatives for the Netherlands." *Fiscal Studies* 38 (3): 369–91.

Wouterse, B., A. Hussem, and A. Wong. 2022. "The Risk Protection and Redistribution Effects of Long-Term Care Co-payments." *Journal of Risk and Insurance* 89 (1): 161–86.

Zorgverzekeraars Nederland. 2022. Landelijke rapportage wachtlijsten Verpleging & Verzorging (Wlz) 4e kwartaal 2021. https://www.zn.nl/app/uploads/2023/02/Q4-2021-Rapport-landelijke-wachtlijsten-verpleegzorg.pdf.

8

Societal Aging and Its Impact on Singapore

Cynthia Chen, Julian Lim, Abhijit Visaria, and Angelique Chan

8.1 Introduction

Societal aging is arguably one of our most critical demographic challenges (World Bank 2016). Singapore is aging at a much faster rate compared to other countries. It will take only 27 years to transition from an "aging society" in 1999 (7 percent of the population aged 65+) to a "super-aged society" in 2026 (with 20 percent of its population aged 65+) (Tan Teck Boon 2015). Japan, China, Germany, and the United States took, or will take, 36, 32, 76, and 86 years respectively, to make that transition (East Asia Forum 2015).

Cynthia Chen is an assistant professor at the Saw Swee Hock School of Public Health at the National University of Singapore.

Julian Lim is a research assistant at the Saw Swee Hock School of Public Health at the National University of Singapore.

Abhijit Visaria is principal research scientist at the Centre for Ageing Research and Education at Duke-NUS Medical School in Singapore.

Angelique Chan is the executive director of the Centre for Ageing Research and Education at Duke-NUS Medical School, where she is also an associate professor in the Signature Programme in Health Services and Systems Research, and is an associate professor in the Department of Sociology at the National University of Singapore.

The authors acknowledge inputs and helpful comments from Nur Diyana Binte Azman, Yi Wen Tan, June May Ling Lee, Rahul Malhotra, and Wan Chen Kang Graham. THE SIGNS Study was supported by Singapore's Ministry of Health (MOH) under the agreement number MOH-NUS RL2015–053. TraCE was supported by the Singapore Ministry of Health's National Medical Research Council under its Health Services Research—Competitive Research Grant (NMRC/HSRG/0095/2018). The analysis work was supported by the Singapore Ministry of Health's National Medical Research Council under its Population Health Research Grant (PHRGOC22Jul-0020), and the Ministry of Education (MOE2018-T2–2-070). Views in the article do not represent the Singapore government and are of the researchers. For acknowledgments, sources of research support, and disclosure of the authors' material financial relationships, if any, please see https://www.nber.org/books-and-chapters/long-term-care-around-world/societal-aging-and-its-impact-singapore.

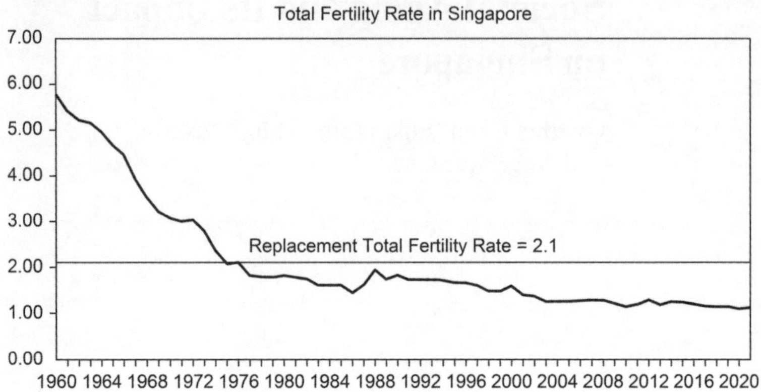

Fig. 8.1 Trends in total fertility rate, 1960–2021

Source: Department of Statistics, Singapore, https://tablebuilder.singstat.gov.sg/table/TS/M810091

The resident population (i.e., Singapore citizens and permanent residents) aged 65+ had doubled from 7 percent in 1999 to 15.2 percent in 2020 and is projected to increase further to 32 percent by 2060. The percentage of those aged 85+ among the 65+ population is projected to increase from 9.2 percent in 2020 to 26.8 percent in 2060 (Ministry of Manpower Singapore 2021b). As shown in figure 8.1, the total fertility rate in Singapore has fallen steadily from 5.76 children per woman in 1960 to 1.12 children per woman in 2021 (Department of Statistics Singapore 2021). Figure 8.2a shows the rising share of the population aged 65+, while figure 8.2b highlights the most rapid growth among those aged 85+ (OECD Stat 2022).

Singapore's Population White Paper published in 2013 warned of a rapidly aging population and shrinking labor force, projecting the old-age support ratio to fall from 5.9 in 2012 to 2.1 by 2030 (Prime Minister's Office Singapore 2013). Population aging could dampen business activity, cause job and employment opportunities to shrink, and negatively affect older adults and working populations if governments, policymakers, and societies do not recognize older adults' potential productivity and contributions to the community (United Nations 2017). Successful aging can be defined as older adults thriving in productive roles and having high levels of physical and mental well-being, social connectedness, and financial security (Chen et al. 2018). Previous research studies have typically focused on the association between physical health, e.g., delaying diseases, and its association with successful aging (Crimmins and Beltran-Sanchez 2011; Prince et al. 2015). The influence of social and economic factors on successful aging has recently been recognized, but the evidence for Asian countries is lacking.

Singapore has one of the world's highest life expectancies. However, health care expenditure has approximately doubled from S$8.5 billion in 2015 (Ministry of Health Singapore 2018) to S$15 billion in 2020 (Ministry

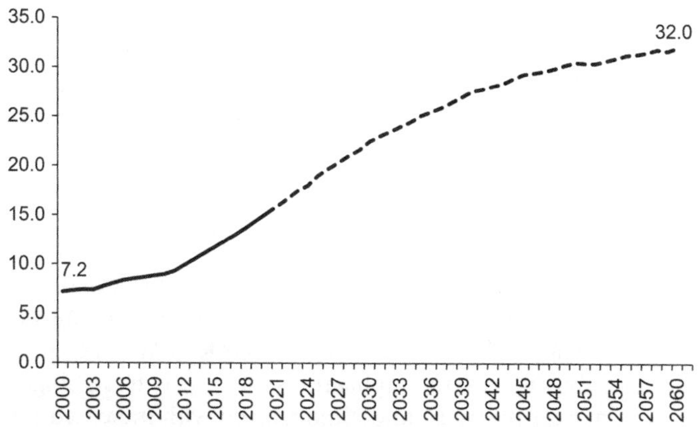

Fig. 8.2a Percentage of population ages 65 or older, 2020–2060
Source: OECD Stat. https://stats.oecd.org/Index.aspx?DataSetCode=POPPROJ

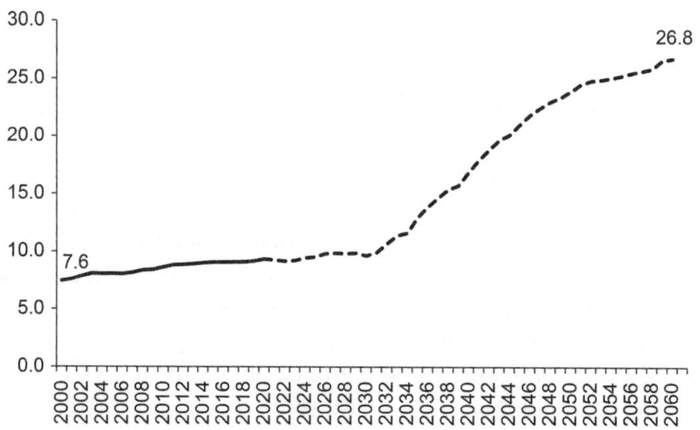

Fig. 8.2b Percentage of 65+ population that is age 85 or older, 2020–2060
Source: OECD Stat. https://stats.oecd.org/Index.aspx?DataSetCode=POPPROJ

of Health Singapore 2021). Previous research has found that the gains in life expectancy at birth in Singapore have outpaced gains in healthy life expectancy; while life expectancy increased by 8.7 years during 1990–2017, healthy life expectancy, defined as the number of years a person is expected to live in good health, excluding years lived with disability, poor health, or premature death, was comparatively smaller, rising by only 7.2 years over the same period (Epidemiology & Disease Control Division—Ministry of Health Singapore and Institute for Health Metrics and Evaluation 2019). This gap is attributable to the growing proportion of older adults aged 85+, i.e., the oldest old, in Singapore, and the greater likelihood of chronic diseases and disability at older ages compared to younger ages.

Chen et al. (2019) projected that among community-dwelling older persons, 1 in 6 older adults in Singapore would have at least one activity of daily living (ADL) disability, and 1 in 3 older adults would have at least one instrumental ADL (IADL) disability by 2050, an increase from 1 in 12 older adults with ADL disability and 1 in 5 older adults with IADL disability in 2014. The projected prevalence of ADL and IADL disability by 2050 among the oldest-old are 46 percent and 68 percent, respectively. The projected increase in disability prevalence is due to Singapore's population aging and rise in related comorbidities (Freedman et al. 2008; Lin et al. 2016; Yokota et al. 2016). In addition, the average family eldercare is also projected to increase by 41 percent from 29 to 41 hours per week, where informal family caregivers will disproportionately bear the caregiver burden (Ansah et al. 2013).

Population aging has several implications for caregiving in Singapore. A combination of later marriage and childbearing with increased longevity has resulted in a growing "sandwich generation" that simultaneously cares for children and older family members. Social norms related to filial piety and an emphasis in public policy to promote "aging-in-place" have meant that family caregivers (Mehta 2006) in Singapore are a primary caregiving source for older adults. The period of caregiving has also lengthened due to increasing longevity, resulting in caregivers' increased financial and emotional burden. Research from Singapore on caregiving experience typologies suggests that while a majority of family caregivers of older adults aged 75+ and with one at least one ADL limitation report a balanced or satisfied caregiving experience, a substantial proportion (nearly a quarter) report a dissatisfied or intensive caregiving experience (Sung et al. 2022). These caregivers also report a lower quality of life and a higher level of depressive symptoms than those who are satisfied (Sung et al. 2022).

This chapter provides an overview of the well-being and social care needs of older adults in Singapore. As mentioned above, formulating social and public policies that enhance the health span, extend productive life years (e.g., extending retirement age), support caregivers, and improve community health and social care services are crucial elements to help older adults age successfully.

We analyze how aging affects health, financial security, and well-being, exploring correlations between disability levels and these factors. We then discuss policies the Singapore government has implemented or will implement to help older adults age successfully. Lastly, we provide an overview of formal and informal care provided in Singapore, including assessing the overall cost of long-term care in Singapore.

8.1.1 Samples and Definitions of Data

Our primary data come from the Retirement and Health Study (RHS), a longitudinal survey panel established by the Singapore government to understand Singapore residents' retirement and health care needs over time. It comprises a nationally representative sample of 15,103 Singapore citizens and permanent residents aged 45 and older at baseline in 2014. The RHS has completed four waves of data collection every two years since then, and data collection for Wave 5 began in July 2022.

The sampling frame used for the RHS was the national registration database by the Singapore government. Stratified random sampling (without replacement) was used as the sampling method, based on sex and ethnicity, to ensure that every race was sufficiently represented. In addition, sampling weights for each respondent were calculated based on various demographics such as age, sex, and ethnicity to indicate the population units represented by each respondent.

Respondents were interviewed once every two years. Wave 2, i.e., the first follow-up survey, was conducted between June 2016 and April 2017 with 12,869 respondents, and Wave 3 was conducted between June 2018 and March 2019. We used data from 11,680 respondents in Wave 3 of the survey. Wave 3 did not survey individuals living in a nursing home, community hospital, or prison; thus, we could not conduct our analyses on institutionalized individuals. In addition, most of our analysis was among those aged 65+.

For some of the analysis in this chapter, we have used data from the first wave (conducted in 2016–2017) of the Transitions in Health, Employment, Social Engagement and Inter-generational Transfers in Singapore Study (THE SIGNS Study), a nationally representative survey of Singapore residents (citizens and permanent residents) aged 60 years and older. A representative sample of 9,736 Singapore residents was approached to participate in THE SIGNS Study. To recruit a sufficient number of minority subgroups, older adults aged 75 years and older and those in Malay and Indian ethnic groups were oversampled by a factor of two. A total of 4,549 older adults (or their proxy respondents in case the older adult was unable to respond himself or herself due to health-related reasons) were interviewed face-to-face using a structured questionnaire. Further information on THE SIGNS Study is available elsewhere (Chan et al. 2018).

We have also used data from Caregiving Transitions among Family Caregivers of Elderly (TraCE) (conducted in 2019–2020), an in-depth survey of 278 informal caregivers of Singapore citizens and permanent residents aged 75 years and older (Malhotra 2021). TraCE respondents were approached based on 1,086 older adults who had participated in two national surveys of older adults in Singapore: the third wave of the Panel on Health and Aging of Singaporean Elderly (PHASE) in 2015 (Chan et al. 2019) and the first wave of THE SIGNS Study in 2016–2017. In addition, a screener assessed older adults' current ADL and IADL status. If an older adult reported receiving human assistance for any ADL or IADL, the study attempted to identify and recruit his or her primary informal caregiver, defined as a family member or friend aged 21 years and older who was involved in at least two of three tasks: direct provision of care, ensuring the provision of care, and making care and treatment decisions for the older adult.

8.2 Health and Financial Security

8.2.1 Disability and Well-Being at Older Ages

As the Singapore population has aged, there is an increasing proportion of older adults with ADLs and IADLs limitations (Visaria et al. 2019). Our ADL measures included six tasks: taking a bath or shower, dressing, eating, standing up from a bed or chair, sitting on a chair, walking around the house, and using the sitting toilet. Respondents who stated they needed help with each of the respective ADLs are classified as having difficulty with the ADL. Individuals can claim long-term care insurance under Singapore's CareShield Life scheme (described later) if they cannot perform at least three of these six ADLs.

The IADL tasks assessed were using the telephone, shopping, preparing food, traveling, managing medication, and managing finances. Respondents were asked about their ability to do each of the respective IADLs. Only respondents who stated they were completely unable to complete the IADL task were classified as having difficulty with that particular IADL.

Most older adults aged 65+ (90 percent) were independent and did not need any help with ADLs or IADLs, while 4 percent needed help with IADLs only, and 6 percent needed help with at least 1 ADL (table 8.1). However, among the oldest-old group aged 85+, 46 percent needed help with ADLs or IADLs. Of these, 14 percent needed help with at least one IADL but did

Table 8.1 **Share of older adults with 0–6 difficulties in ADL, 65+ and 85+, 2018**

	65+	85+
0 ADLs & 0 IADLs	0.899	0.537
0 ADLs & 1+ IADLs	0.042	0.136
1 ADL	0.015	0.050
2 ADLs	0.007	0.050
3 ADLs	0.007	0.032
4 ADLs	0.006	0.036
5 ADLs	0.009	0.063
6 ADLs	0.015	0.096
1+ ADLs	0.059	0.327
1+ IADLs	0.086	0.424
Observations	5,187	284

Note: The six ADLs assessed were taking a bath or shower, dressing up, eating, standing up from a bed or chair, sitting on a chair, walking (around the house), and using the sitting toilet. The six IADLs assessed were using the telephone, shopping, preparing food, traveling, managing medication, and managing finances. Respondent weights were used for all calculations.
Source: Singapore Retirement and Health Study (RHS, Wave 3 in 2018)

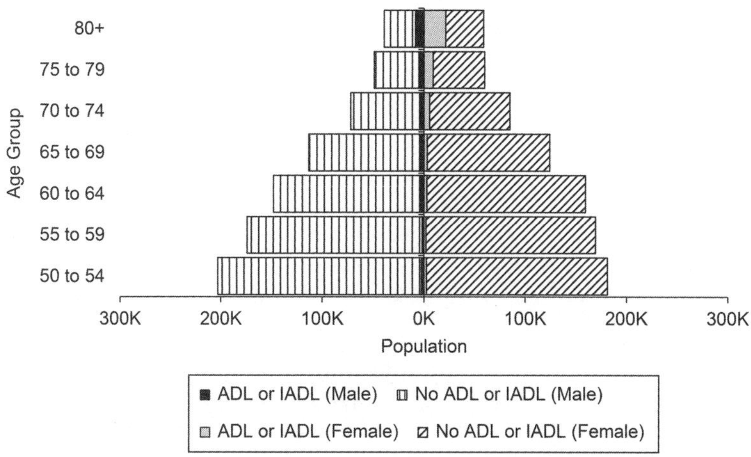

Fig. 8.3 Population pyramid of Singapore with ADL or IADL limitations, 50+, 2018

Note: The six ADLs assessed were taking a bath or shower, dressing, eating, standing up from a bed or chair, sitting on a chair, walking (around the house), and using the sitting toilet. The six IADLs assessed were using the telephone, shopping, preparing food, traveling, managing medication, and managing finances. Respondent weights were used for all calculations.

Source: Singapore Retirement and Health Study (RHS, Wave 3 in 2018)

not have any ADL limitations, and approximately 33 percent needed help with at least one ADL. In addition, 1 in 10 adults in the oldest-old 85+ group needed help with all six ADLs. It is estimated that about 60,000 older adults aged 65+ and 30,000 older adults aged 80+ needed help with either an ADL or IADL (figure 8.3). Among those who needed help with at least one ADL, 71.3 percent needed help walking around the house and 70.7 percent needed help taking a shower (table 8.2). Among those who needed help with at least one IADL, the highest proportion came from managing finances (68.4 percent), followed by managing medication (45.5 percent) for those aged 65+. Results were similar for those aged 85+, with a higher prevalence of needing help for most ADL or IADL tasks than those aged 65+.

Individuals with 3+ limitations in age groups 65+ and 85+ were more likely to have poorer self-reported health, worse cognition, and higher depression (table 8.3). Compared to the 65+ population, the proportion of older adults with 3+ limitations was less likely to report their health as good, very good, or excellent (17 percent vs. 55 percent), was also much less likely to have normal cognition (20 percent vs. 78 percent), and was 2.7 times more likely to report having depression (8 percent vs. 3 percent). Such differences were also seen among those aged 85+. However, the oldest-old were much less likely compared to the 65+ to report good or very good or excellent health (34 percent vs. 55 percent), were less likely to have normal cognition (33 percent vs. 78 percent), and were more likely to have depression

Table 8.2 Distribution of limitations with specific ADLs/IADLs, 2018

	65+ All	65+ Conditional	85+ All	85+ Conditional
	Panel 1: IADLs			
IADL—Using the telephone	0.032	0.371	0.209	0.493
IADL—Manage Finances	0.059	0.684	0.350	0.825
IADL—Managing Medication	0.039	0.455	0.268	0.631
IADL—Shopping	0.030	0.345	0.166	0.390
IADL—Preparing food	0.030	0.343	0.161	0.379
IADL—Traveling	0.007	0.080	0.039	0.093
Observations	5187	521	284	114
	Panel 2: ADLs			
ADL—Using the sitting Toilet	0.032	0.539	0.210	0.642
ADL—Dressing	0.039	0.669	0.241	0.737
ADL—Taking a bath or shower	0.042	0.707	0.273	0.834
ADL—Walking (around the house)	0.042	0.713	0.223	0.683
ADL—Eating	0.022	0.374	0.156	0.477
ADL—Standing up from a bed or chair; sitting down on a chair	0.030	0.514	0.177	0.541
Observations	5,187	347	284	86

Note: Column 1 shows the share of the sample that reported having difficulty with each activity, while column 2 shows the percentage of people with at least 1 IADL (panel 1) or at least 1 ADL (panel 2) who report having difficulty with each activity. Individuals that reported not doing these activities were also included as having difficulty with them. Respondent weights were used for all calculations.

Source: Singapore Retirement and Health Study (RHS, Wave 3 in 2018)

Table 8.3 Well-being for those 65+ and 85+ by ADL and IADL limitations, 2018

	65+	65+ with 3+ Limitations	85+	85+ with 3+ Limitations
Self-Report of Health—Good or Better	0.55	0.17	0.34	0.12
MMSE Score >= 24 (Normal cognition)	0.78	0.20	0.33	0.08
Self-Report Depression	0.03	0.08	0.06	0.08
Observations	5,187	332	284	91

Notes: The six ADLs assessed were taking a bath or shower, dressing, eating, standing up from a bed or chair, sitting on a chair, walking (around the house), and using the toilet. The six IADLs assessed were using the telephone, shopping, preparing food, traveling, managing medication, and managing finances. The limitations Index runs from 0–12 and was the number of both ADLs and IADLs that are either difficult or not done. Mini-Mental State Examination (MMSE) was a 30-point questionnaire used to measure cognitive impairment; a score of 24 or more indicated normal cognition, and scores below indicated cognitive impairment. Respondent weights were used for all calculations.

Sources: Singapore Retirement and Health Study (RHS, Wave 3 in 2018)

Table 8.4a **Distribution of monthly household income for those aged 18–64 and 65+**

Percentile of Income	Income Percentiles, 18–64	Income Percentiles, 65+
5% Percentile	600	90
10% Percentile	1,100	200
25% Percentile	2,200	500
50% Percentile	4,000	900
75% Percentile	6,800	1,800
90% Percentile	10,100	4,000
95% Percentile	11,400	7,700
Mean	5,400	2,100

Note: Household income from all sources in the HES refers to recurrent and regular income from work, and non-work sources, which include investment, rental, other sources such as pension and contributions from children, relatives, and friends, as well as regular government transfers received by individual members and transfers given at the household level.

Income data included employer Central Provident Fund (CPF) contributions.

Income values were normalized using the OECD equivalence scale, derived from the mean household size of 3.24 in 2018; thus, it was set at 2.4. Values were adjusted to 2019 Singapore dollars.

Exchange rate: USD 1 = SGD 1.39.

Source: Household Expenditure Survey (HES) 2017/2018, Department of Statistics Singapore

(6 percent vs. 3 percent). Similarly, the oldest-old group with 3+ limitations tends to have worse self-reported health.

Proactive interventions may aid in promoting functional adaptations among older adults (Mathieson et al. 2002). For example, initiatives to enhance independence with ADLs among older adults in Singapore include a scheme that subsidizes home modifications in government-built Housing and Development Board (HDB) flats. Under the Enhancement for Active Seniors (EASE) scheme, older residents can install grab bars, slip-resistant treatment to floor tiles in toilets, and ramps to navigate steps and different levels within homes (Housing & Development Board Singapore 2023).

8.2.2 Financial Security at Older Ages

Incomes were higher for the 18–64 population than for 65+ (table 8.4a). This was expected as the labor force participation rate decreased with age, from 91 percent among 30–34 years to 46.1 percent among those aged 65–69 and 17.6 percent among 70+ in 2018 (Ministry of Manpower Singapore 2020). The income ratio between those 65+ and those aged 18–64 increases as the income percentile increases. For instance, the income of the 50th percentile of those aged 18–64 was about four times that of those 65+, but the income of the 90th percentile of those aged 18–64 was only about two times that of those 65+. For seniors with low incomes during their working years, resulting in less retirement pension, the government introduced the Silver Support Scheme in 2016 (Silver Support Singapore 2022). This scheme is meant to support the bottom one-third of Singaporeans aged 65+ with quarterly cash supplements and was enhanced in 2021 to further support seniors with lesser means. Eligible seniors will receive support per quarter depending on household income and type of housing, ranging from S$180 to S$900 per quarter (Silver Support Singapore 2022). The quarterly cash supplements benefitted nearly 250,000 Singaporeans aged 65+, totaling S$2.2 billion since 2016. In addition, all Singaporeans aged 65 and above who are ComCare Long Term Assistance (LTA) recipients will receive support of $360 per quarter, regardless of their flat type. This Silver Support Scheme constitutes the fourth component of Singapore's social security system, complementing the first three components: CPF retirement income, home ownership, and health care coverage (discussed in the next section).

Older adults' income is less ideal as a measure of financial security since many would have retired. Although older adults no longer have a wage income, they may have assets in retirement savings plans, and these asset variables will be used to finance their consumption. Therefore, in table 8.4b, we report the distribution of wealth among older adults. Relative to the income measures, the wealth distribution for older adults was more skewed, with the wealth of the lowest 5 percent of the 65+ sample valued at SGD 11,700 and the highest 5 percent at least approximately SGD 2.3 million.

Table 8.4b **Distribution of wealth for elderly groups relative to the working-age population, 2018**

Percentile of Wealth	Wealth Percentiles, 45–64	Wealth Percentiles, 65+	Wealth Percentiles, 85+
5% Percentile	63,600	11,700	4,000
10% Percentile	131,900	30,500	9,100
25% Percentile	229,100	152,500	23,900
50% Percentile	381,700	281,100	181,200
75% Percentile	702,800	514,000	335,500
90% Percentile	1,392,400	1,265,500	838,300
95% Percentile	2,283,500	2,311,800	2,536,500
Observations	6,493	5,187	284
Mean	686,500	583,400	474,000

Note: The variable used to measure wealth is the addition of the respondent's net worth from property assets (Total apportioned housing asset + Value of commercial properties—Total apportioned housing loan—Commercial property loans) and the net worth from non-property assets in SGD (Total savings balance +Value of life insurance + Balance of Supplementary Retirement Scheme account + CPF net balances + Unused CPF LIFE premiums + Value of financial investments + Value of equity in business + Value of other assets—Credit card debts—Other liabilities). Respondent weights were used for all calculations. Values were adjusted to 2019 values.

Exchange rate: USD 1 = SGD 1.39.

Source: Authors' calculation based on Singapore Retirement and Health Study (RHS, Wave 3 in 2018)

Table 8.5 **Income distribution by limitations for 65+ population, 2018**

	0 ADLs & 0 IADLs	0 ADLs & 1+ IADLs	1 ADL	2 ADLs	3+ ADLs	Total
	Panel 1: Income					
Share <50% of Median HH Income	0.328	0.382	0.413	0.481	0.435	0.336
Share 50–100% of Median HH Income	0.159	0.235	0.244	0.161	0.156	0.164
Share 100–150% of Median HH Income	0.158	0.152	0.116	0.180	0.167	0.158
Share 150–200% of Median HH Income	0.107	0.126	0.067	0.045	0.108	0.107
Share 200%+ of Median HH Income	0.248	0.106	0.161	0.134	0.134	0.236
Total	0.899	0.042	0.015	0.007	0.037	
Number of Observations	4,579	261	88	37	222	5,187
	Panel 2: Wealth					
Share <50% of Median Wealth	0.210	0.483	0.391	0.289	0.336	0.230
Share 50–100% of Median Wealth	0.266	0.268	0.289	0.427	0.338	0.270
Share 100–150% of Median Wealth	0.188	0.147	0.141	0.164	0.110	0.182
Share 150–200% of Median Wealth	0.098	0.042	0.079	0.000	0.079	0.094
Share 200%+ of Median Wealth	0.238	0.061	0.100	0.120	0.137	0.224
Total	0.899	0.042	0.015	0.007	0.037	
Number of Observations	4,579	261	88	37	222	5,187

Notes: The six ADLs assessed were taking a bath or shower, dressing, eating, standing up from a bed or chair, sitting on a chair, walking (around the house), and using the toilet. The six IADLs assessed were using the telephone, shopping, preparing food, traveling, managing medication, and managing finances.

Median household income was the sum of respondent's and household members' gross monthly salaries (excluding bonuses and employer CPF contributions from all relevant current main jobs. It was calculated in the RHS Wave 3 and normalized using the OECD equivalence scale. It was set at approximately SGD 1,070.

We did not have information on the wealth of other household members; therefore, household wealth cannot be tabulated, as such personal wealth used for this section, with the definition similar to that of table 8.4b. Thus, median wealth was set at approximately SGD 280,000.

Respondent weights were used for all calculations, and values were adjusted to 2019 dollars.

(Exchange rate: USD 1 = SGD 1.39).

Source: Author's calculations based on Singapore Retirement and Health Study (RHS, Wave 3 in 2018)

Similarly, the lowest 5 percent of the 85+ sample had SGD 4,000 valued in wealth, and the highest 5 percent held at least approximately SGD 2.5 million in wealth.

In table 8.5, Panel 1 reports the household income from work as a percentage of the median household income by the number of ADLs, among the resident population aged 65+. Each column sums to 100 percent. Among those in worst health, i.e., with three or more ADL limitations, 44 percent had incomes less than 50 percent below the median, while 13 percent had incomes higher than twice the median income. Panel 2 reports the wealth as a percentage of the median wealth by the number of ADLs. Among those with three or more ADL limitations,

34 percent had incomes less than 50 percent below the median, while 14 percent had incomes higher than twice the median income. The proportion of those with incomes below the median household income indicated a clear negative gradient in the relationship between the extent of functional limitations and income. Individuals' financial security and access to care depend on their income, wealth, health status, and living arrangements.

8.3 Policy Approaches for Successful Aging in Singapore

8.3.1 Individual Responsibility

Singapore's stance on implementing policies for older adults, be it for financial security or health care, is individual responsibility for his/her finances in preparation for the challenges that come with old age without overburdening family members, the community, and the state (Ministry of Social and Family Development Singapore 1999). Various policies implemented throughout the years help older adults financially, especially during their retirement period, so they are not compelled to work at an old age to fund their living expenses. This also helps to reduce the reliance on their caregivers.

8.3.2 Central Provident Fund (CPF)

Singapore's pension system is based on defined contributions. Established in 1955, the Central Provident Fund (CPF) is a compulsory social security savings scheme and a crucial part of Singapore's social security system (Ministry of Manpower Singapore 2022). Singaporeans and their employers pay into the accounts under the CPF. These funds can be withdrawn at older ages or used to finance a home, pay for medical expenses, or other approved investments (Haskins 2011). Monthly, 20 percent of an employee's salary will be allocated to one's CPF account for employees aged 55 and below with a minimum monthly salary of $750. The employer contributes another 17 percent of the employee's salary into the employee's CPF account. The employee and employer's contribution rates will decrease as the employee's age increases. Monthly CPF contributions will go to an Ordinary Account (used for retirement, housing, insurance, and investment), Special Account (used for retirement), and MediSave Account (used for health care). A Retirement Account is also created for the employee when he or she turns 55. Older adults will receive monthly payouts from CPF savings when he or she turns 65 years old (Central Provident Fund Board 2022a). These monthly payouts will stop when savings run out. However, the earlier scheme has now been expanded to CPF LIFE, a national longevity insurance annuity scheme that provides individuals monthly payouts no matter how long they live. When one passes away, the CPF LIFE premium balance (if any) and any remaining CPF savings will be distributed to nominees (Central Provident Fund Board 2022b).

8.3.3 Home Ownership and Monetization

The home ownership scheme was introduced in 1964, providing grants and subsidies for most Singaporeans to own property. As a result, 89.3 percent of Singaporean households own their own houses, and 90.9 percent of those staying in public housing owned their flat in 2022 (Singapore Department of Statistics 2022b). In addition, most Singaporeans take up housing loans and can finish paying for their homes by the time they retire. As such, they need not worry about paying for rent post-retirement and can use their pension from their CPF account for daily expenses and medical bills. This was a critical public priority during the early years of post-independence nation-building, aimed at relocating the population from slums to decent housing. This policy created a nation of home owners and reduced the incidence of homelessness, where 81 percent of the population stayed in public housing; 79 percent of households owned their apartments, with only 2 percent renting from the government (Haskins 2011).

The Singapore government has also introduced various ways for older adults to monetize their public housing flats for retirement. Various schemes include the Silver Housing bonus, renting out flats or bedrooms, and the lease buyback scheme (Housing & Development Board Singapore 2022b). For the Silver Housing bonus, households can receive an additional maximum of 30 thousand SGD in cash provided they top up their proceeds from selling their old flat and buying a smaller flat into their CPF retirement account (Housing & Development Board Singapore 2022c). For the lease buyback scheme, older home owners can sell a portion of his or her flat's lease back to HDB while continuing to reside in the flat (Housing & Development Board Singapore 2022a). These measures alleviate older adults' concerns about paying rent for their houses during their retirement period and supplement the older adult's income, which they can use for living and medical expenses.

8.3.4 Health Care

In 2015, the government of Singapore launched an Action Plan for Successful Aging (Ministry of Health Singapore 2016), which outlined areas of focus for policymaking and program development: employability, lifelong learning, volunteerism, health and wellness, social engagement and inclusion, aged care services, housing transport, public spaces, and research on aging. Singapore's long-term care (LTC) landscape consists of nursing homes, inpatient hospice palliative care service (IHPCS), center-based care facilities, home care providers, and home palliative care providers. In addition, various services are provided under the intermediate and LTC frameworks. The Ministry of Health launched the Agency for Integrated Care in 2008 to enhance and integrate the LTC sector. It is currently Singapore's National Care Integrator and is responsible for discharge planning and assisting the movement of patients from inpatient facilities to the community (Agency for Integrated Care Singapore 2022). The agency aims to improve access to care and support patients and their caregivers while developing the primary and community care sectors. Much effort has been invested in developing a robust home- and community-care ecosystem that allows older adults to live in the community for as long as possible.

The government aims to ensure that excellent and affordable health care is available to all citizens through subsidies and schemes such as MediSave, MediShield Life, and MediFund. **Subsidies** are means-tested and can cover up to 80 percent of hospitalization charges in public hospitals, up to 80 percent for non-residential LTC, such as center-based and home care services, and up to 75 percent for residential LTC. **MediSave** is a national health care savings scheme established in 1984 to help individuals set aside a part of their income for their and their family members' health care expenditures and approved health insurance premiums, supplemented by employer contributions. In 1990, the government established **MediShield** to cover exceptionally high-cost hospital expenditures. The scheme was substantially enhanced in 2015 to form **MediShield Life**, which provides universal coverage for all Singaporeans, regardless of age or health condition. In addition, for those unable to afford their remaining subsidized medical bills, the government established a medical endowment fund in 1993, **MediFund**, to serve as a final safety net for needy Singaporeans (Tan et al. 2021).

In 2017, the operating expenditure of LTC was estimated to be around $580 million (Ministry of Health Singapore 2020), approximately 0.12 percent of Singapore's GDP. The Singapore government has taken steps to strengthen the LTC insurance system. As a result, many financing sources support LTC needs, including **ElderShield** (disability insurance), ElderShield Supplement plans, private disability insurance, private cash savings, central provident fund payouts, charity donations, and family support. Recent research, as shown in figure 8.4, suggested the following financing mix: out-of-pocket spending (40 percent), government spending and subsidies (42 percent), LTC insurance (9 percent), and charitable donations (9 percent).

8.3.5 Public Long-Term Care Insurance

CareShield Life was introduced in 2020, which provides enhanced coverage for LTC costs compared to ElderShield. CareShield Life payouts start at SGD600 per month and increase till age 67, or when one successfully claims, whichever is earlier. ElderShield is not a mandatory scheme. Although individuals were automatically enrolled at age 40, they could complete the opt-out form in the ElderShield package. The Interim Disability Assistance Scheme for the Elderly (IDAPE) assisted people who could not join Elder-

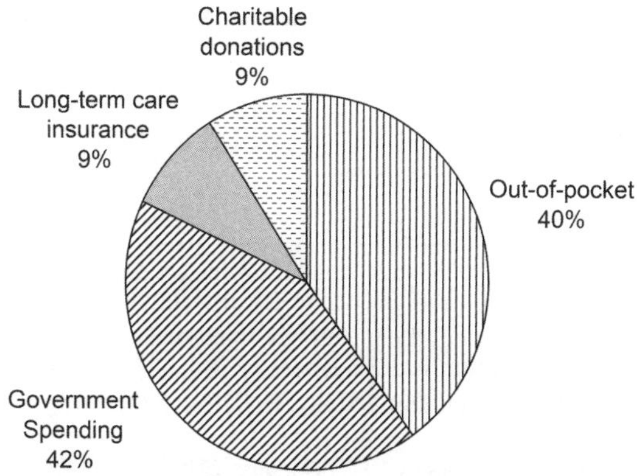

Fig. 8.4 Percentage of LTC financing by source, 2017

Source: Graham and Bilger (2017) Erratum in: Milbank Q. 2017 Sep;95(3):682. PMID: 28589606; PMCID: PMC5461396.

Shield, namely those who were too old or had existing disabilities as of September 30, 2002. IDAPE provides S$150 or S$250 monthly for up to 72 months, depending on household income. IDAPE payments assist with out-of-pocket expenses associated with medical bills and nursing costs or subsidize the costs of hiring a migrant domestic worker.

All Singapore citizens and permanent residents born in 1980 and after must have LTC insurance under CareShield Life. They were automatically enrolled into CareShield Life on October 1, 2020 or when they turn 30, whichever is later. Premiums can be fully payable by MediSave, a national health care savings scheme. In addition, premium subsidies are available for lower-income residents to ensure that no one loses coverage due to a genuine inability to pay premiums. Individuals receive CareShield Life payouts when they develop substantial limitations in their ability to perform at least three basic activities of daily living. Benefits are paid out in cash to maximize flexibility. For individuals in residential care, benefits can be paid directly to the residential care facility to help lower out-of-pocket expenses for the patient and their families. In addition, individuals could complement their basic CareShield Life plan with other benefits, such as higher monthly payout amounts, by purchasing additional coverage through supplement plans, which private insurers administer.

Table 8.6 presents estimates for the number and proportion of individuals with long-term care insurance. Approximately 65 percent of older adults had LTC Insurance. Table 8.7 reports descriptive characteristics for the insured and uninsured groups. Those with insurance tended to have higher incomes from work and wealth for both the 65+ group and the 85+ group. In addition, uninsured older adults were more likely to live with a spouse and receive informal help.

Table 8.6 **Population with LTC insurance, 2018**

	65+	85+
Population with LTC Insurance	353,000	31,000
Share of Population with Insurance	(0.645)	(0.632)
Observations	3,401	184

Note: LTC Insurance coverage refers to older adults being covered by ElderShield, which is a public long-term insurance scheme targeted at severe disability.

Respondent weights were used for all population estimate calculations. Population size was taken from the Department of Statistics Singapore.

Source: Singapore Retirement and Health Study (RHS, Wave 3 in 2018)

Table 8.7 **Characteristics by LTC insurance, 2018**

	65+ Insured	65+ Uninsured	85+ Insured	85+ Uninsured
Total Wealth—Mean	607,700	533,300	489,800	446,800
Total Wealth—Median	287,300	262,700	192,500	156,300
Total Household Income—Mean	4,200	3,800	3,300	4,400
Total Household Income—Median	2,500	2,100	1,400	1,200
Received Care	0.18	0.21	0.64	0.58
Live with Spouse or Partner	0.63	0.64	0.33	0.42
Formal Help with ADL/IADLs	0.06	0.07	0.33	0.34
Informal Help with ADL/IADLs	0.15	0.18	0.48	0.49
Observations	3,401	1,786	184	100

Note: LTC Insurance coverage refers to older adults being covered by ElderShield, which is a public long-term insurance scheme targeted at severe disability. The variable used to measure wealth was the addition of the respondent's net worth from property assets and the net worth from non-property assets in SGD, as elaborated in the notes in table 8.3a. Household income was the sum of respondent's and household members' gross monthly salaries (excluding bonuses and employer CPF contributions from all relevant current main jobs, which was similar to table 8.5's definition of household income; however, for this table, the household income was not equivalized. Respondent weights were used for all calculations, and values were adjusted to 2019 Singapore dollars.

Exchange rate: USD 1 = SGD 1.39.

Source: Author's calculation based on Singapore Retirement and Health Study (RHS, Wave 3 in 2018)

8.4 Formal and Informal Care in Singapore

8.4.1 Overview of Singapore's Care Landscape

Singapore's life expectancy at birth increased from 81.9 years in 2011 to 83.7 years in 2019 (Singapore Department of Statistics 2022a), much higher than the global life expectancy of 73.4 years in 2019 (World Health Organization 2023). Coupled with a low fertility rate that declined below replacement level in 1977 and has remained one of the lowest in the world, family sizes have rapidly decreased over time. While there have been many policies to promote successful aging (as described above), families are now facing a more significant care burden due to smaller family sizes (Ministry of Finance Singapore 2023). Many Singapore families simultaneously face the demands of childcare and eldercare, with the government's statement that "institutional care should remain as a last resort" (Ministry of Community Development and Sports Singapore 2001). As such, the government has been coordinating partnerships between community and family, playing the central role in providing necessary infrastructure and funding mechanisms for care within the community (Yeoh and Huang 2009).

At the individual level, older adults are personally responsible for keeping healthy and active through various programs such as the National Steps Challenge (Healthhub Singapore 2022). The government has also provided many other programs on preventive health to encourage older adults to keep "alert, active, and integrated" by maintaining their physical and mental well-being (Ministry of Community Development and Sports Singapore 2001). Frail older adults can also be cared for in their homes and tap into community services such as meal delivery, telephone hotline, befriender, and other supportive services (Mehta 2002). Nevertheless, anecdotal reports have raised the issue of disabled and frail older adults feeling trapped in their own homes, as they are unable to leave the house without assistance if they stay in units without direct lift access (The Straits Times Singapore 2006), which has been improved with the Housing and Development Board lift upgrading program and installation of ramps within the homes with the EASE program. In addition, nursing homes are also often perceived as contrary to Asian values and culture (Choong 2000). Thus, many middle-class and affluent families have turned to employing live-in domestic workers as surrogate caregivers to provide care for older adult(s) needing help with activities of daily living within the home (Yeoh and Huang 2009).

8.4.2 Institutional Care

Table 8.8 provides an overview of the long-term care facilities in Singapore. In 2020, there were 8,100 places for center-based services such as day rehabilitation, dementia daycare, and day activity centers; 10,000 for home-based services such as home medical, home nursing, and personal home care; and 16,221 nursing home beds. In addition, 3,100 clients may receive home-based palliative care anytime in the year. Finally, there were 2,069 community hospital beds (equivalent to skilled nursing facilities) where clients receive inpatient rehabilitation in preparation for returning to the community.

The overall nursing home bed occupancy rate has generally remained stable over the past five years, at around 90 percent, higher than other developed countries like the United States, with approximately 79.7 percent.

Table 8.8 Places in long-term care facilities, 2020

	2020
Nursing homes	77
Nursing homes beds	16,221
Nursing homes occupancy rate	90%
Population aged 65 and above	614,368
Population aged 85 and above	57,461
Nursing home beds per population aged 65 and above	0.026
Nursing home beds per population aged 85 and above	0.282
Places for center-based services	8,100
Places for home-based services	10,000
Places for home-based palliative care	3,100
Community hospital beds	2,069
Staff in ILTC sector	16,550

Notes: Data for the number of nursing homes were from Open Government Products, Government Technology Agency of Singapore, https://data.gov.sg/dataset/number-of-residential-long-term-care-facilities. Data for nursing home beds were from the Singapore Ministry of Health, https://www.moh.gov.sg/resources-statistics/singapore-health-facts/beds-in-inpatient-facilities-and-places-in-non-residential-long-term-care-facilities. Data for nursing homes' occupancy rate were from Lai (2021). Data for other long-term care facilities were from Singapore Ministry of Health, https://www.moh.gov.sg/resources-statistics/singapore-health-facts/beds-in-inpatient-facilities-and-places-in-non-residential-long-term-care-facilities. Data for number of staff in ILTC sector were taken from Singapore Ministry of Health, https://www.moh.gov.sg/news-highlights/details/the-number-of-staff-in-the-intermediate-and-long-term-care-sector/. Staff in the ILTC sector includes 6,490 registered professionals—doctors, nurses, dentists, physiotherapists, occupational therapists, speech-language therapists, diagnostic radiographers, radiation therapists, pharmacists, and 10,060 support care staff, administrative, ancillary staff. ILTC sector includes MOH-subvented community hospitals, nursing homes, center-based services, hospices, home care services, dialysis services, and others (e.g. psychiatric rehabilitation homes and diabetic education & care services).

However, our nursing home beds per 85+ population of 0.282 were similar to the United States, at 0.265. In addition, eight new nursing homes were set up between 2016–2020, adding 3,300 more nursing home beds (Lai 2021).

The primary input to LTC is labor supply. Table 8.8 also shows that there were 16,550 staff in the ILTC sector in 2020. Figure 8.5 shows the distribution of the workers employed in nursing homes and home health agencies. Most employers at care facilities consist of support staff, with health care professionals comprising only about 28 percent of residential and center-based care employees and 41 percent of home-based care employees. Table 8.9 shows the training requirements for formal health care assistants, consisting of 160 training hours for the health attendant or health care assistant and 218 training hours for the senior health care assistant.

Table 8.10 shows an estimated monthly wage in the long-term care center, from nursing facilities to home health care services, including health care professionals and administrative and ancillary staff. For comparison, we present several earnings metrics in the broader economy at the bottom. For example, some staff nurses and allied health workers earned less than

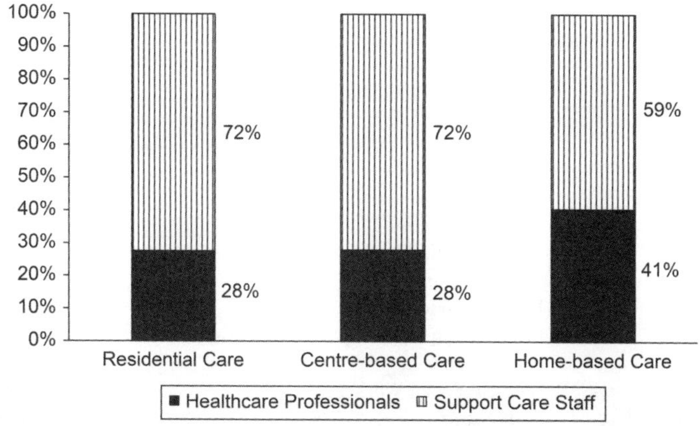

Fig.8.5 Percent distribution of employees at care facilities by job group, 2018

Note: Health care professionals refer to doctors, dentists, registered nurses, enrolled nurses, pharmacists, and Allied Health Professionals (AHPs), e.g., physiotherapists. Support care staff includes healthcare assistants, nursing, and therapy aides.

Residential Care refers to nursing homes and inpatient hospices. Center-based Care refers to senior care centers and day hospices. Home-based Care refers to personal home care, home medical, home nursing, home palliative, and home therapy services.

Manpower figures were based on Full-Time Equivalents (FTEs).

Source: Ministry of Health, Singapore https://www.moh.gov.sg/news-highlights/details/profile-of-healthcare-workers-providing-long-term-care-services-and-their-skill-and-manpower-gaps/

Table 8.9 **Minimum training requirements for formal health care assistants, 2022**

Occupation Title	Course Level	Training Hours
Health Attendant	Level 1 (Certificate)	160
Health Care Assistant	Level 2 (Higher Certificate)	160
Senior Health Care Assistant	Level 3 (Advanced Certificate)	218

Notes: These were the Singapore Workforce Skills Qualifications (WSQ) programs in 2022 for direct nursing care conducted by SkillsFutureSG, https://www.ssg.gov.sg/content/dam/ssg-wsg/wsq/ssg/documents/healthcaresupport/healthcare_support_wsq_cm_20140610_psd_v01draft.pdf.

the median wage of degree holders aged 25 to 29 years. In contrast, some nursing aides, therapy aides, and health care assistants earned less than the median wage of working adults who have only completed secondary school or post-secondary education aged 25 to 29 years.

8.4.3 Formal and Informal Home Care

Respondents of the Retirement and Health Study (RHS) were asked if they had received assistance with that particular ADL or IADL. Further questions included the relationship of the helpers, the number of hours each

Table 8.10 **Pay for full-time care workers at nursing facilities and in-home health care, 2022**

Industry	Occupation Title	Estimated Monthly Wage (SGD)
Nursing Homes	Staff Nurse	2500–4400
	Enrolled Nurse	1700–3200
	Nursing Aide/Therapy Aide	1600–2300
	Nursing Manager	4600–6300
	Locum In-House Doctor	3700–7400
	Physiotherapist/Occupational Therapist	2800–4600
	Housekeeper	1500–1800
	Medical Social Worker	2300–2800
Home Care Services	Staff Nurse	2800–4200
	Enrolled Nurse	2300–3200
	Health Care Assistant	1500–2200
All Industries	All Workers (Median)	3400
	Below Secondary (Median)	2100
	Secondary (Median)	2300
	Post Secondary (Non-Tertiary) (Median)	2400
	Diploma and Professional Qualification (Median)	2800
	Degree (Median)	4000

Notes: Data for the estimated monthly wages were taken from job openings in My Careers Future Singapore, https://www.mycareersfuture.gov.sg/, from various nursing homes and home care service providers listed on the Agency of Integrated Care careers page (https://www.aic.sg/resources/community-care-jobs?utm_source=aic-web&utm_medium=main-nav&utm_campaign=commcarejobs) in June 2022. Data for the median wage were the Median Gross Monthly Income from Work (Excluding Employer CPF) of Full-Time Employed Residents Aged 25 to 29 by Highest Qualification Attained taken from the Labour Force in Singapore 2021 (https://stats.mom.gov.sg/Pages/Labour-Force-in-Singapore-2021-Employment.aspx). Values were adjusted to 2019 Singapore dollars.

helper administered care to the recipient per week, and if the helper receive a cash allowance for the help administered. The relationship of caregivers to care recipients in Singapore mainly include paid migrant domestic workers, private nurses, or informal caregivers, who mainly consist of the respondent's spouse, children, or grandchildren.

Table 8.11 shows the proportion of older adults in Singapore receiving home care by age and the number of ADL or IADL limitations, where 19 percent of those 65+ received home help. The percentage of older adults who received care increased significantly with age and the number of ADLs limitations, with 62 percent of those 85+ receiving assistance. However, once we consider the disability level, the distribution across the number of limitations becomes more comparable by age: 94 percent of those 65+ with three or more ADL limitations received help. In comparison, 92 percent of those 85+ did.

Most long-term care in Singapore is provided by family, friends, and

Table 8.11 **Any home care by age and ADL, 2018**

	65 +	85 +
Full Sample	0.191	0.618
0 ADLs, 1+ IADLs	0.724	0.759
1 ADL	0.745	0.917
2 ADLs	0.982	1.000
3+ ADLs	0.935	0.915
Observations	5,187	284

Note: The six ADLs assessed were taking a bath or shower, dressing, eating, standing up from a bed or chair, sitting on a chair, walking (around the house), and using the toilet. The six IADLs assessed were using the telephone, shopping, preparing food, traveling, managing medication, and managing finances." Care received" refers to respondents who received home help with ADL or IADL difficulties. Respondent weights were used for all calculations.

Source: Singapore Retirement and Health Study (RHS, Wave 3 in 2018)

Table 8.12 **Distribution of weekly hours of home care received in a month by type, 2018**

Percentiles	65+	85+
5th Percentile	1	2
10th Percentile	2	3
25th Percentile	5	15
50th Percentile	20	48
75th Percentile	56	84
90th Percentile	84	112
95th Percentile	112	168
Mean	37	57
7 Hours per week or Less	0.33	0.19
40 Hours per week or More	0.35	0.55
Observations	962	146

Note: Home care consisted of formal help, informal help, and help from others. Respondent weights were used for all calculations.

Source: Singapore Retirement and Health Study (RHS, Wave 3 in 2018)

neighbors, where most caregivers are women, and most are between 45 and 59 years of age. Table 8.12 illustrates the weekly hours of care received, with a median of those aged 65+ at 20 hours, but the mean was 37 hours, and 10 percent of the population received care over 84 hours in the past month. The number of hours of care received was higher among the oldest old, where the median hours for those aged 85+ was 48, with an average of 57 hours. The top 10 percent of this age group received 112 or more hours of care.

Informal home care refers to care recipients receiving ADL or IADL assistance from family members or unpaid individuals. In contrast, formal home care refers to care recipients receiving ADL or IADL assistance from

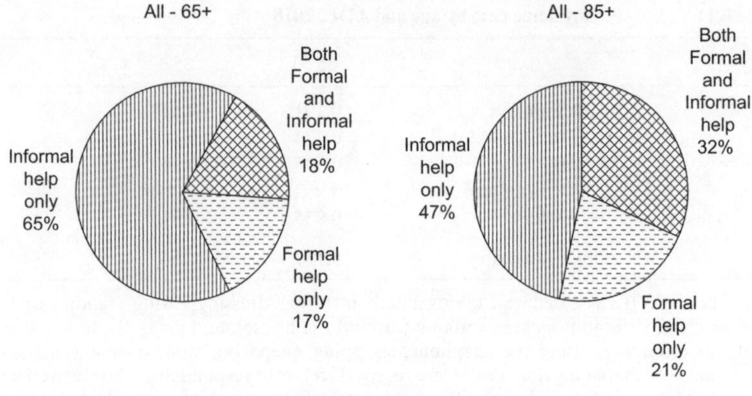

Fig. 8.6 Distribution of care type by age, 2018

Note: Informal help refers to receiving home help from family members or others who were unpaid. Formal help refers to receiving help from migrant domestic workers, private nurses, or others who were paid. Respondent weights were used for all calculations.

Source: Singapore Retirement and Health Study (RHS, Wave 3 in 2018)

migrant domestic workers, private nurses, or others who are paid. Of the care recipients aged 65+, 65 percent received only informal home care, 17 percent received only formal home care, and 18 percent received both formal and informal care (figure 8.6). Among the care recipients aged 85+, 47 percent received only informal home care, 21 percent received only formal home care, and 32 percent received both formal and informal care. The proportion of older adults using only informal care declined as the number of limitations increased (figure 8.7). About 21 percent received only informal care among those with three or more ADL limitations. Formal care and the use of both formal and informal care rose with the number of ADL limitations. The results were consistent among the 85+.

Families in Singapore frequently hire foreign female migrant domestic workers to assist in caregiving. As of December 2020, there were 247,400 migrant domestic workers in Singapore (Ministry of Manpower Singapore 2021a), or about one worker in every five households. In addition, approximately half of all families with disabled older members hire a migrant domestic worker to provide care. Furthermore, families can send their migrant domestic workers for short training courses on eldercare skills. Course fees are subsidized with a Caregivers' Training Grant.

It is difficult to parse out the amount of care that migrant domestic workers provide specifically to older adults since nearly all of them are full-time residents of the household in which they are employed. Their responsibilities relate to domestic chores, housekeeping, as well as caregiving. However, the TraCE study attempted to gather data on this and asked primary fam-

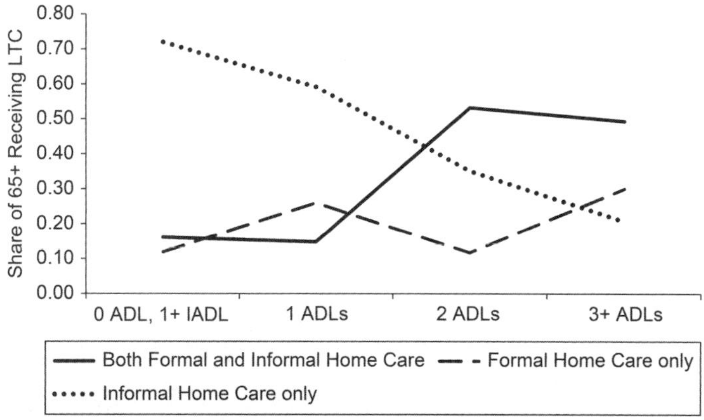

Fig. 8.7 Type of care received by age and limitations, 2018

Note: The six ADLs assessed were taking a bath or shower, dressing, eating, standing up from a bed or chair, sitting on a chair, walking (around the house), and using the toilet. The six IADLs assessed were using the telephone, shopping, preparing food, traveling, managing medication, and managing finances. Informal help refers to receiving home help from family members or others who were unpaid. Formal help refers to receiving home help from migrant domestic workers, private nurses, or others who were paid. Respondent weights were used for all calculations.

Source: Singapore Retirement and Health Study (RHS, Wave 3 in 2018)

ily caregivers about the number of hours of care that a migrant domestic worker provided older adults.

Table 8.13 illustrates the weekly hours of care for older adults receiving ADL care from informal caregivers and migrant domestic workers. Informal caregivers provided an average of 18.1 hours of ADL or IADL care per week. Not all 278 care recipients in the sample had a migrant domestic worker caring for them. Migrant domestic workers provided an average of 33.2 hours of ADL or IADL care per week to the 132 care recipients reported as receiving ADL or IADL care from a migrant domestic worker. We used a cap of 112 care hours per week, assuming at least 8 hours of rest per day for caregivers.

The annual cost of hiring a domestic helper in Singapore includes one-time costs such as maid agency costs and work permit costs, as well as monthly recurring costs such as salary, foreign worker levy, and daily living expenses. In another study, migrant domestic workers cared for older adults for an average of 14 hours daily (Association of Women for Action & Research and Humanitarian Organisation for Migration Economics 2020).

Home care for older adults can be provided by formal (paid) caregivers, informal (unpaid) caregivers, or both. Most formal care providers are not-for-profit social service agencies (SSAs) that receive financial support

Table 8.13 Distribution of hours of ADL or IADL care received by older adults, by type of caregiver, 2019

	Weekly hours of ADL or IADL Care received by Care Recipients 75+	
	From informal caregivers	From migrant domestic workers
Average (SD)	18.1 (22.6)	33.2 (27.5)
Observations	278	132

Notes: The maximum possible number of weekly hours of care received from each caregiver was capped at 112 hours, assuming at least 8 hours of rest per day per caregiver.
Source: The TraCE study conducted in 2019

from the government that offsets a portion of their operational expenses. In addition, social service agencies typically raise additional funds through philanthropic donations to augment their budgets. The Agency for Integrated Care (AIC) (Agency for Integrated Care Singapore 2021) manages all referrals to subsidized long-term care services. As Singapore is a small and densely populated city-state, access to services is typically supported by distance. Means-tested subsidies can reduce the out-of-pocket expenses for patients whose monthly per capita household income is S$2,800 and below. Households with higher monthly per capita household income typically face full, unsubsidized fees when using formal LTC (Ministry of Health Singapore 2022a).

Singapore has long emphasized families as the primary source of support for older adults (Malhotra et al. 2018). As such, the government is exploring ways to support caregivers. For example, the recent Home Caregiving Grant (2019) provides care recipients from qualifying households in the community with at least permanent moderate disability a monthly cash grant of SGD$200 to defray caregiving costs. The grant has been increased to up to $400 in 2023. In addition, most caregivers are female, and 25 percent were never married.

About 75 percent (120,000 out of 160,000) of those helping someone aged 65+ were informal caregivers, but that fraction fell to 67 percent (20,000 out of 30,000) when caring for those 85+ (table 8.14). In addition, more than half of these caregivers were 60 years and above, and 73 percent of the caregivers were female (figure 8.8). Majority of the caregivers who provided ADL care (figure 8.9, top) and IADL care (figure 8.9, bottom) were female, whereas 66 percent of the caregivers were children of the care recipients (figure 8.10) (Lim-Soh et al. 2023).

8.4.4 Cost of Care

LTC is financed through out-of-pocket (OOP) payments, government subsidies, and disability payouts such as LTC insurance and grants. Indi-

Table 8.14 **Informal care provision—population estimates, 2018**

	Recipient of Help 65+	Recipient of Help 85+
All Helpers—ADLs & IADLs	160,000	30,000
Relative to the 65+/85+ Population	0.293	0.634
Relative to the 20 to 64 Population	0.062	0.012
Formal Helpers—ADLs & IADLs	40,000	10,000
Relative to the 65+/85+ Population	0.074	0.296
Relative to the 20 to 64 Population	0.016	0.006
Informal Helpers—ADLs & IADLs	120,000	20,000
Relative to the 65+/85+ Population	0.219	0.338
Relative to the 20 to 64 Population	0.046	0.006
Observations	5,187	284

Source: Singapore Retirement and Health Study (RHS, Wave 3 in 2018). Respondent weights were used for all population estimate calculations. Population size was taken from the Department of Statistics Singapore.

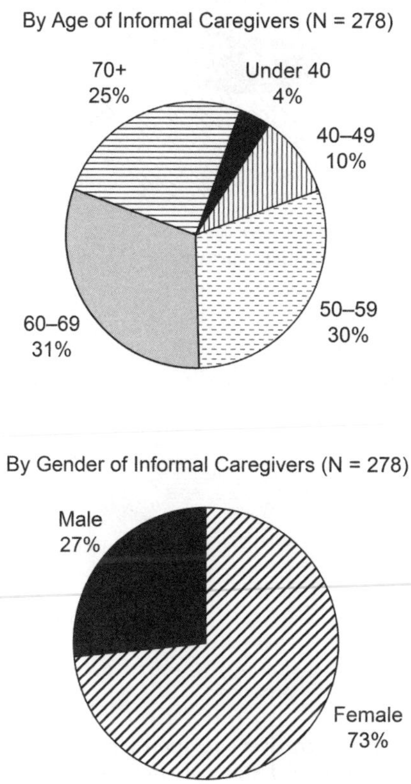

Fig. 8.8 Demographic composition by age group and gender of primary informal caregivers, 2019

Source: Lim-Soh et al. (2023)

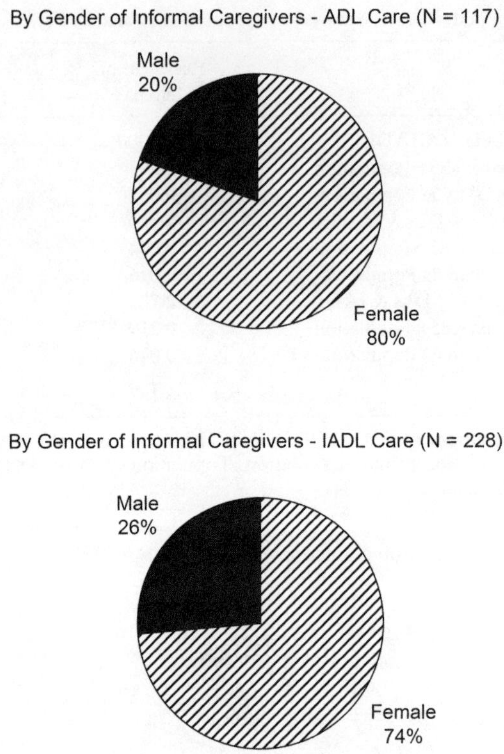

Fig. 8.9 Primary informal caregivers providing ADL and IADL care to the care recipients by gender, 2019
Source: Lim-Soh et al. (2023)

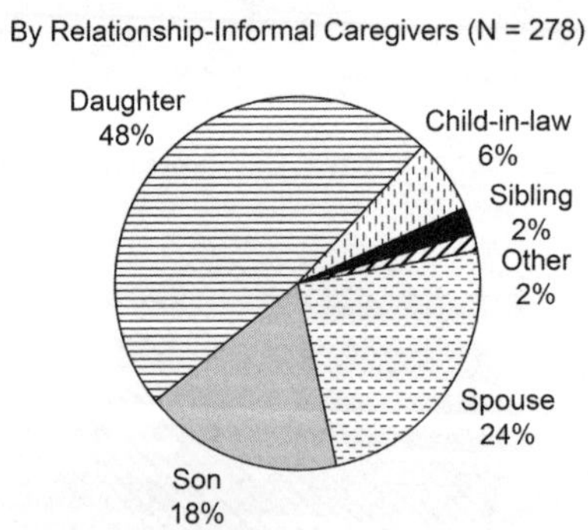

Fig. 8.10 Primary informal caregiver's relationship with the care recipient, for primary caregivers providing ADL or IADL care to the care recipient, 2019
Source: Lim-Soh et al. (2023)

viduals who pass the means-testing pay less OOP, as the government subsidies would cover a portion of the LTC expenses. The government centrally manages the means-testing and functional assessment processes that help determine eligibility for the various subsidy schemes. LTC insurance in Singapore has evolved from a voluntary financial instrument (ElderShield) to mandatory coverage (CareShield Life).

Singapore's morbidity patterns change from acute to chronic degenerative diseases and disabilities. Formal LTC service utilization in Singapore is lower than in western societies. Most families prefer to rely on migrant domestic workers to care for older family members. A migrant domestic worker can provide 24/7 care for an older adult and perform household chores. Recent research on Singaporeans' attitudes toward LTC shows that most concerns centered around financial accessibility, quality, and convenience (location of LTC services).

Data from 2017 show that the government's operating expenditure for long-term care services was about $580 million (table 8.15). About 60 percent of the expenditure was for residential long-term care. The remainder was for home and center-based care and other support schemes, such as active aging programs and the Seniors' Mobility and Enabling Fund. During this period, approximately 14,100 Singaporeans used nursing home services; 1,300 used inpatient hospice services; and 29,700 used home and center-based care services, where 90 percent were aged 60 and above. Private formal long-term care services are estimated to cost about $800 million (Table 8.15).

Before government subsidies, a nursing home care service could range from S$2,200 to S$4,200 monthly. Additional charges may include a one-time refundable deposit and administrative charges. Other expenses not covered by the essential cost may also be applied (Agency for Integrated Care Singapore 2021). Government subsidies for residential LTC are available only to Singapore citizens and permanent residents and range between

Table 8.15 **Formal care costs, annual, 2017**

Types	Number of users	Total spending (millions $)
Residential long-term care		
Public	15,400	348
Private		481
Home and center-based services		
Public	29,700	232
Private		320

Sources: Public formal care costs were taken from Ministry of Health Singapore, https://www.moh.gov.sg/news-highlights/details/government%27s-operating-expenditure-for-long-term-care-services. Private formal care costs were the author's calculations based on Graham and Bilger (2017). Erratum in: Milbank Q. 2017 Sep;95(3):682. PMID: 28589606; PMCID: PMC5461396. https://www.ncbi.nlm.nih.gov/pmc/articles/PMC5461396/.

10 percent and 75 percent, depending on income level. For individuals who can afford it, an unsubsidized private nursing home room costs S$4,000 to S$6,500 per month (Gusmano 2017). The payout from LTC insurance starts at S$600 per month in 2020. As such, out-of-pocket payments are critical because Singapore's health and long-term care systems emphasize "shared responsibility" and the need to minimize the moral hazard problem.

In June 2019, dementia daycare centers in Singapore had a daily capacity of 3,400 persons with dementia. As of August 2019, there were about 3100 (91.1 percent) active users (Ministry of Health Singapore 2019). However, there could have been more users as non-subsided users were excluded. Pre-subsidy costs of dementia daycare centers range between S$1,260 and S$1,575 (Agency for Integrated Care Singapore 2021).

To estimate the value of care provided by informal caregivers, we use two strategies. First, in a "potential wage" strategy, we value the time spent by informal caregivers using predicted wages, adjusting for the probability of working. The valuation is the predicted wages of informal caregivers * probability of working of informal caregivers * predicted hours of care for ADLs or IADLs received by older adults in Singapore from informal caregivers.

We used three sources of data for the analysis. The probability of working was first estimated using the Retirement and Health Survey, using a logistic regression model that regressed current work status (yes, no) on the age, sex, educational attainment (categorized as no formal education, primary only, and secondary and above), and housing type (1–2 room government-built housing, 3-room government-built, 4–5 government-built and private housing) of respondents. Additionally, we ran an ordinary least squares (OLS) regression model regressing the reported monthly wages of currently employed RHS respondents on the same set of characteristics. The coefficients from these models were used to estimate the predicted probability of work and the predicted wages for informal caregivers in the TraCE study (table 8.16). The average product of the probability of work and predicted wages was equivalent to caregivers' average "potential wage." The monthly wages were converted to hourly rates by annualizing (×12) and then converted to weekly amounts (/52) and further into hourly wage rates (/44), assuming a 44-hour work-week. We also used the TraCE data to predict the hours of care older adults receive for ADLs and IADLs. In TraCE, primary informal caregivers were asked to report on the number of hours of care for ADLs and IADLs that they or any other informal caregiver provided per week to the older adult, i.e., their care recipient. The relationship between informal caregivers that provided care to the older adult for ADLs and IADLs was primarily that of a child (60 percent), spouse (21 percent), or sibling (13 percent). We ran an OLS regression model regressing the total number of hours received by care recipients on care recipient characteristics: age, sex, living arrangement (categorized as whether living alone, with a spouse and a child, with a spouse and no child, with a child and no spouse, with others);

educational attainment and housing type (categorized as described above); number of self-reported ADL and IADL limitations; and number of self-reported chronic physical ailments. To arrive at a valuation of informal care that is representative of Singapore, the coefficients of this model were used to estimate the predicted hours of care received by the nationally representative sample of older adults in THE SIGNS Study—(table 8.16). We limited the prediction of hours of care to those older adults who reported that they had difficulty with any ADLs or IADLs and required human assistance. Our approach was thus based on the assumption that if older adults required human assistance with ADLs or IADLs, it was provided by informal caregivers. We used sampling weights to arrive at a nationally representative estimate. The annual average cost of informal care per individual estimated through this "potential wage" strategy was SGD 3683 (table 8.17), leading to a national valuation of SGD 463 million.

Table 8.16 Probability of work among caregivers and care received by older adults, 2018

1.E(Work) in TRaCE	0.51
2. E(Work) ∗ E(Monthly Wage from Work) in TRaCE	1126
3. E(Hours of informal care received per week) by older adults in THE SIGNS Study	10.82
4. Total Hours Informal Help (millions) in SIGNS	70.8

Note: Proportion of people who work in RHS was 58.7%. Once the wage prediction model from RHS (which is a slightly younger population) was applied to TRACE, the predicted wage was on average SGD 1800 per month. However, as TRACE was a much older population, the unconditional wages were SGD 1126 per month on average. Monetary values were adjusted to 2019 dollars.

Source: Author's calculations based on Singapore Retirement and Health Study (RHS, Wave 3 in 2018), the TraCE study (2019) and THE SIGNS Study—I (2016–2017)

Table 8.17 Annual costs of informal care receipt for all older adults needing human assistance with 1+ ADL or IADLs in Singapore, 2016–2020

		Potential wage strategy (I)		Market-based strategy (II)	
	Population	Average cost of care per individual	Total cost of care	Average cost of care per individual	Total cost of care
Number of older adults aged 60+ needing human assistance with 1+ ADL or IADL	125801	3683	463M	6366	800M

Note: The number of older adults needing human assistance with 1+ ADL or IADL was derived from the percentage of older adults aged 60+ in THE SIGNS Study—I (2016–2017) who reported difficulty with 1+ ADL or IADL and that they needed human assistance with any of them. These proportions were assumed to be constant until 2021 and applied to the resident population aged 60+ in 2021 (Singapore Residents By Single Year Of Age And Sex, At End June, Annual, published by Singapore Department of Statistics 2021). The valuations assumed that human assistance was provided by informal caregivers. The vast majority of informal caregivers reported (94 percent) were spouses, children (including a child-in-law), and siblings.

In an alternative "market-based" strategy, we value the time spent on caregiving as the potential wage valuation added to the predicted hours of care multiplied by the market wage of professionals who provide such care; that is, the hourly wage of the occupation listed in the Singapore Ministry of Manpower's data as "healthcare assistant and other personal care workers" multiplied by the probability of informal caregivers not working. (See the chapter on the United States in this volume on why the market-based strategy to valuation adds the potential wage valuation to the valuation of care provided by market-based substitutes.) We use S$9.30 as the hourly wage for this category of workers, based on the Ministry of Manpower's published median wage rates obtained originally as monthly gross values (i.e., inclusive of the mandatory contributory savings and pension plan for Singapore citizens and permanent residents). The annual average cost of informal care per individual per this "market-based" strategy is SGD 6366, leading to a national valuation of SGD 800 million (table 8.17).

We also estimated the value of the care provided to older persons for ADLs and IADLs by migrant domestic workers (MDWs). In the TraCE study, primary caregivers could also report if MDWs provided care to care recipients for ADLs and IADLs and, if so, how many hours of care they provided per week. Similar to the potential wage strategy, based on the OLS regression model of the number of MDW hours of care, we predicted the number of hours of care received from MDWs among the representative sample of older adults in THE SIGNS Study—I. We limited the estimation to older adults who reported requiring human assistance with ADLs or IADLs and had a cohabiting migrant domestic worker. The annual average cost of care provided by MDWs for ADLs and IADLs is SGD 3393, leading to a national valuation of SGD 156 million (table 8.18).

The overall cost of care is cumulated in table 8.19. In both valuation methods, most of the costs came from the private care sector, and the overall cost was approximately 0.5 percent of Singapore's total GDP.

Table 8.18 **Annual costs of receipt of care from migrant domestic workers among older adults needing human assistance with 1+ ADL or IADLs and who have a cohabiting migrant domestic worker in Singapore, 2016–2020**

	Population	Average cost of care per individual	Total cost of care
Number of older adults aged 60+ needing human assistance with 1+ ADL or IADL	46081	3393.0	156.3M

Note: Nationally representative estimates from THE SIGNS Study—I (2016–2017) indicated that approximately 36.63 percent of older adults who need human assistance with 1+ ADL or IADL had a cohabiting migrant domestic worker. This proportion was applied to the estimated resident population aged 60+ in 2021 (Singapore Residents By Single Year Of Age And Sex, At End June, Annual, published by Singapore Department of Statistics, 2021) with 1+ ADL or IADL limitations in the panel above.

Table 8.19 **Total costs by type of care and source in Singapore, 2016–2020**

Care Type	Source	Cost I (in millions)	% of GDP	Cost II (in millions)	% of GDP
Residential long-term care	Public	348	0.07	348	0.07
	Private	481	0.10	481	0.10
	All	829	0.17	829	0.17
Home and center-based services	Public	232	0.05	232	0.05
	Private	320	0.07	320	0.07
	All	552	0.12	552	0.12
Informal care	Private	463	0.10	800	0.17
Informal care from MDW	Private	156	0.03	156	0.03
Total	Public	580	0.12	580	0.12
	Private	1412	0.30	1757	0.37
	All	2000	0.42	2337	0.49

Note: GDP 2017 was used as a comparison, as tables 8.15, 8.17, and 8.18 consisted of 2017 data. Source of GDP was from Department of Statistics, Singapore, https://tablebuilder.singstat.gov.sg/table/TS/M015731. Costs were recorded in SGD millions.

8.5 Conclusions

Increases in life expectancy and sustained low fertility rates have transformed many countries, including Singapore, into aging societies. While the number of older adults is increasing in Singapore, the 85+ age group (oldest-old) is the fastest-growing segment. These older individuals are more likely to need formal and informal care to help with ADLs and IADLs limitations. At the same time, the need for formal care is increasing as the population of informal caregivers has decreased over time. This trend suggests that prices for formal care, such as wages, may increase to attract more care workers to this industry. The decrease in informal caregivers also suggests enhancing community-based health and social care services.

The government has recently introduced policies to improve availability and access to care in Singapore, including the rollout of mandatory long-term care insurance, known as CareShield Life; a means-tested monthly cash grant to defray the costs of caregiving expenses, known as Home Caregiving Grant, which will be further enhanced from 2023 onwards; and centers such as embedded Active Aging Centers and Active Aging Care Hubs that provide activities for older adults, including health and social care services. These measures are taken in the context of a health care system shifting its emphasis toward primary and community care. However, despite the various programs and policies, the cost of long-term care in Singapore is still not cheap, with a large portion of formal long-term care being financed by individuals (40 percent out of pocket) and government spending (42 percent) (Graham and Bilger 2017), as shown in figure 8.4. Moreover, subsidies for residential LTC services are only available to those with a monthly per capita household income of $2,800 and below (Ministry of Health Singapore 2022a). While individuals bear much of this cost out of pocket, the actual cost remains underestimated as most older Singaporeans do not use formal care. Thus, in addition to formal long-term care services, families often rely on informal support such as migrant domestic workers, especially if they have few or no ADL and IADL limitations. However, some families still struggle with finding or providing appropriate care, whether formal or informal care. This difficulty will likely escalate in the coming years as family support structure changes and the population ages.

The government has recently drawn attention to preventative care to improve Singaporeans' health spans as they age. Healthier SG, a recent government initiative, is intended to significantly reform Singapore's health care system by increasing the focus on preventative care provided through a decentralized network of family physicians. Healthier SG was developed in response to Singapore's aging population and the increased prevalence of various chronic diseases (Ministry of Health Singapore 2022b). The program includes providing free vaccination and screenings for chronic diseases such as high cholesterol and high blood pressure, increasing the number of programs that promote healthier lifestyles, and tasking general practitioners with drawing up preventative health and social care plans for individuals rather than focusing only on treatment and management of disease (Ministry of Health Singapore 2022b).

In recent years, Singapore has taken a particularly proactive approach to develop community-based health and social care services in response to population aging. The government has also launched the three assisted living developments whereby older Singaporeans can purchase "senior-friendly flats" that are outfitted with non-slip flooring, grab bars, adjustable countertops, etc., and receive health and social care services in their homes. One of these developments, Kampung Admiralty, has an intergenerational element embedded in the design. Playgrounds, nurseries, and spaces for older persons are co-located to encourage intergenerational contact and communication. The emphasis here is testing the social and psychological value of intergenerational living on older adults' well-being. As these developments are in nascent stages, proper evaluations of the impact of these typologies of living arrangements on successful aging have yet to be completed. Singapore presents an excellent test bed for evaluating an Asian response from older adults and family perspectives to assisted living and multigenerational co-location of care and services.

8.6 Other Information

8.6.1 Data Availability

Data on health and social status, health and long-term care utilization, and financing are available from the Ministry of Health, the Agency for

Integrated Care, and the Health Promotion Board. The Central Provident Fund Board leads the Retirement and Health Study in Singapore. In addition, longitudinal survey data was collected by universities. These include (1) the Transitions in Health, Employment, Social Engagement, and Intergenerational Transfers in Singapore Study (THE SIGNS Study) and (2) The Caregiving Transitions among Family Caregivers of Elderly Singaporeans (TraCE) study, both conducted by the Centre for Ageing Research and Education (CARE) at Duke-NUS Medical School.

References

Agency for Integrated Care Singapore. 2021. "Care Services." https://www.aic.sg/care-services.

Agency for Integrated Care Singapore. 2022. "About Us." https://www.aic.sg/about-us.

Ansah, J. P., D. B. Matchar, S. R. Love, R. Malhotra, Y. K. Do, A. Chan, and R. Eberlein. 2013. "Simulating the Impact of Long-Term Care Policy on Family Eldercare Hours." *Health Services Research* 48 (2, pt 2), 773–91. https://doi.org/10.1111/1475-6773.12030.

Association of Women for Action & Research and Humanitarian Organisation for Migration Economics. 2020. "Neither Family Nor Employee: the Caregiver Burden of Migrant Domestic Workers in Singapore." Report, November. https://www.aware.org.sg/wp-content/uploads/Neither-Family-Nor-Employee-AWARE-HOME-Report-Nov-2020.pdf.

Central Provident Fund Board. 2022a. "How CPF Works." https://www.cpf.gov.sg/member/cpf-overview.

Central Provident Fund Board. 2022b. "Receive lifelong monthly payouts with CPF LIFE." https://www.cpf.gov.sg/member/retirement-income/monthly-payouts/cpf-life.

Chan, A., R. Malhotra, N. B. Manap, Y. Y. Ting, A. Visaria, G. H.-L. Cheng, V. S. M. Goh, P. K. C. Tay, J. M. L. Lee, and A. Maulod. 2018. Transitions in Health, Employment, Social Engagement And Intergenerational Transfers In Singapore Study (THE SIGNS Study)—I: Descriptive Statistics and Analysis of Key Aspects of Successful Ageing. Singapore: Centre for Ageing Research and Education (CARE) and Duke-NUS Medical School.

Chan, A., Y. Saito, D. B. Matchar, T. Østbye, C. Malhotra, S. Ang, S. Ma, and R. Malhotra. 2019. "Cohort Profile: Panel on Health and Ageing of Singaporean Elderly (PHASE)." *International Journal of Epidemiology* 48 (6): 1750–1751f. https://doi.org/10.1093/ije/dyz172.

Chen, C., D. P. Goldman, J. Zissimopoulos, and J. W. Rowe. 2018. "Multidimensional Comparison of Countries' Adaptation to Societal Aging." *Proceedings of the National Academy of Sciences* 115 (37): 9169–9174. https://doi.org/10.1073/pnas.1806260115.

Chen C., J. T. Lim, N.C. Chia, L. Wang, B. Tysinger, et al. 2019. "The Long-Term Impact of Functional Disability on Hospitalization Spending in Singapore." *Journal of the Economics of Ageing* 14:100193. doi: 10.1016/j.jeoa.2019.02.002. Epub 2019 Feb 27. PMID: 31857943; PMCID: PMC6922027.

Choong, T. S. 2000. "A Caring System: Community-Based Schemes May Be the

Answer for a Graying Nation." *Medical Device and Diagnostic Industrial Magazine* 26: 29.

Crimmins, E. M., and H. Beltran-Sanchez. 2011. "Mortality and Morbidity Trends: Is There Compression of Morbidity?" *J Gerontol B Psychol Sci Soc Sci* 66 (1): 75–86. https://doi.org/10.1093/geronb/gbq088.

Department of Statistics Singapore. 2021. Births and Fertility. https://www.singstat.gov.sg/find-data/search-by-theme/population/births-and-fertility/latest-data.

East Asia Forum. 2015. "Can a Rapidly Aging Singapore Stave Off Economic Disaster?" Accessed January 21, 2022. http://www.economywatch.com/features/Can-a-Rapidly-Aging-Singapore-Stave-Off-Economic-Disaster1005.html.

Epidemiology & Disease Control Division, Ministry of Health Singapore, and Institute for Health Metrics and Evaluation. 2019. "The Burden of Disease in Singapore, 1990–2017: An overview of the Global Burden of Disease Study 2017 results." Seattle, WA: IHME.

Freedman, V. A., L. G. Martin, R. F. Schoeni, and J. C. Cornman. 2008. "Declines in Late-Life Disability: The Role of Early- and Mid-Life Factors." *Social Science & Medicine* 66 (7): 1588–1602. https://doi.org/https://doi.org/10.1016/j.socscimed.2007.11.037.

Graham, W. C. K., and M. Bilger. 2017. "Financing Long-Term Services and Supports: Ideas From Singapore." *Milbank Quarterly* 95 (2): 358–407. https://doi.org/10.1111/1468–0009.12264.

Gusmano, M. K. 2017. "Long-Term Care Delivery and Financing in Singapore." In *A Singapore Bioethics Casebook, 2 vols*. Singapore: National University of Singapore. http://www.bioethicscasebook.sg/backgrounder/long-term-care-financing/.

Haskins, R. 2011. "Social Policy in Singapore: A Crucible of Individual Responsibility." *ETHOS: Journal of the Society for Psychological Anthropology* 9 (June).

Healthhub Singapore. 2022. National Steps Challenge. https://www.healthhub.sg/programmes/37/nsc/.

Housing & Development Board Singapore. 2022a. Lease Buyback Scheme. Government of Singapore. https://www.hdb.gov.sg/cs/infoweb/residential/living-in-an-hdb-flat/for-our-seniors/monetising-your-flat-for-retirement/lease-buyback-scheme.

Housing & Development Board Singapore. 2022b. Monetising Your Flat For Retirement. Government of Singapore. https://www.hdb.gov.sg/residential/living-in-an-hdb-flat/for-our-seniors/monetising-your-flat-for-retirement.

Housing & Development Board Singapore. 2022c. Silver Housing Bonus. Government of Singapore. https://www.hdb.gov.sg/cs/infoweb/residential/living-in-an-hdb-flat/for-our-seniors/monetising-your-flat-for-retirement/silver-housing-bonus.

Housing & Development Board Singapore. 2023. Home Improvement Programme (HIP). Government of Singapore. https://www.hdb.gov.sg/residential/living-in-an-hdb-flat/sers-and-upgrading-programmes/upgrading-programmes/types/home-improvement-programme-hip.

Koh, G. "14 Hidden Costs You Should Know When Hiring a Domestic Helper." Singapore: Homage. https://www.homage.sg/resources/hidden-cost-domestic-helper/.

Lai, L. 2021. "8 nursing homes set up in past 5 years, but institutionalising elderly should be very last resort: Koh Poh Koon." *Straits Times*, August 3. https://www.straitstimes.com/singapore/politics/eight-nursing-homes-set-up-in-past-5-years-but-institutionalising-elderly-should.

Lim-Soh, J., N. D. B. Azman, H.-L. Quach, V. S. M. Goh, and R. Malhotra. 2023. "A Profile of Family Caregivers of Older Adults in Singapore." Research Brief Series no. 16. Singapore: Centre for Ageing Research and Education (CARE).
Lin, S.-F., A. N. Beck, and B. K. Finch. 2016. "The Dynamic Contribution of Chronic Conditions to Temporal Trends in Disability among U.S. Adults." *Disability and Health Journal* 9 (2): 332–40. https://doi.org/https://doi.org/10.1016/j.dhjo.2015.11.006.
Malhotra, R. 2021. "The Caregiving Transitions among Family Caregivers of Elderly Singaporeans (TraCE) Study—Rationale, Design and Participant Characteristics at Baseline." Presented at Centre for Ageing Research & Education (CARE) 2021 Symposium February 5, 2021.
Malhotra, R., M. A. C. Bautista, A. M. Müller, S. Aw, G. C. H. Koh, Y.-L. Theng, S. J. Hoskins, C. H. Wong, C. Miao, W.-S. Lim, C. Malhotra, and A. Chan. 2018. "The Aging of a Young Nation: Population Aging in Singapore." *Gerontologist* 59 (3): 401–10. https://doi.org/10.1093/geront/gny160.
Mathieson, K. M., J. J. Kronenfeld, and V. M. Keith. 2002. "Maintaining Functional Independence in Elderly Adults: The Roles of Health Status and Financial Resources in Predicting Home Modifications and Use of Mobility Equipment." *Gerontologist* 42 (1): 24–31. https://doi.org/10.1093/geront/42.1.24.
Mehta, K. 2002. "National Policies on Ageing and Long-term Care in Singapore: A Case of Cautious Wisdom?" Chapter 5 in *Ageing and Long-Term Care: National Policies in the Asia-Pacific*, edited by David R. Phillips and Alfred C. M. Chan, 150–80. Singapore: ISEAS Publishing. https://doi.org/10.1355/9789812307163–009.
Mehta, K. K. 2006. "A Critical Review of Singapore's Policies Aimed at Supporting Families Caring for Older Members." *Journal of Aging & Social Policy* 18 (3–4): 43–57. https://doi.org/10.1300/j031v18n03_04.
Ministry of Community Development and Sports Singapore. 2001. "Eldercare master plan (FY2001 to FY2005) http://www.mcys.gov.sg/mcdsfiles/Resource/Materials/MCDS_ElderCare_Masterplan.pdf.
Ministry of Finance Singapore. 2023. "Strengthening our Social Compact." Budget 2023: Budget Statement, Issue. https://www.mof.gov.sg/singaporebudget/budget-2023/budget-statement/e-strengthening-our-social-compact.
Ministry of Health Singapore. 2016. "I Feel Young in My Singapore! Action Plan for Successful Ageing." Singapore: Ministry of Health. https://www-moh-gov-sg-admin.cwp.sg/docs/librariesprovider3/action-plan/2015-action-plan.pdf.
Ministry of Health Singapore. 2018. Healthcare Financing.
Ministry of Health Singapore. 2021. Government health expenditure and healthcare financing (Excel file) https://www.moh.gov.sg/resources-statistics/singapore-health-facts/government-health-expenditure-and-healthcare-financing.
Ministry of Health Singapore. 2019. "Take-Up Rate for Dementia Day Care Services." Government of Singapore. November 4. https://www.moh.gov.sg/news-highlights/details/take-up-rate-for-dementia-day-care-services.
Ministry of Health Singapore. 2020. "Government's Operating Expenditure for Long Term Care Services." Government of Singapore. February 4. https://www.moh.gov.sg/news-highlights/details/government%27s-operating-expenditure-for-long-term-care-services.
Ministry of Health Singapore. 2021. "Government Health Expenditure and Healthcare Financing." Government of Singapore. https://www.moh.gov.sg/resources-statistics/singapore-health-facts/government-health-expenditure-and-healthcare-financing.
Ministry of Health Singapore. 2022a. "Subsidies for Residential Long-Term Care

Services." Government of Singapore. https://www.moh.gov.sg/cost-financing/healthcare-schemes-subsidies/subsidies-for-residential-long-term-care-services.

Ministry of Health Singapore. 2022b. "The White Paper on Healthier SG." September 21. https://www.healthiersg.gov.sg/resources/white-paper/.

Ministry of Manpower Singapore. 2020. *Labour Force in Singapore 2019*. Singapore: Manpower Research and Statistics Department, Ministry of Manpower. https://stats.mom.gov.sg/iMAS_PdfLibrary/mrsd_2019LabourForce.pdf.

Ministry of Manpower Singapore. 2021a. Foreign Workforce Numbers. Singapore: Ministry of Manpower. https://www.mom.gov.sg/documents-and-publications/foreign-workforce-numbers.

Ministry of Manpower Singapore. 2021b. Retirement and Re-Employment (Amendment) Bill 2021 and CPF (Amendment) Bill 2021. November 1. Singapore: Ministry of Manpower, Government of Singapore. https://www.mom.gov.sg/newsroom/press-releases/2021/1101-retirement-and-re-employment-amendment-bill-2021-and-cpf-amendment-bill-2021.

Ministry of Manpower Singapore. 2022. "What Is the Central Provident Fund (CPF)." Singapore: Ministry of Manpower. https://www.mom.gov.sg/employment-practices/central-provident-fund/what-is-cpf.

Ministry of Social and Family Development Singapore. 1999. Inter-Ministerial Committee (IMC) Report On The Ageing Population. https://www.nlb.gov.sg/main/book-detail?cmsuuid=64a126a3–8f72–4e65-aafe-b97626e3fb4d.

OECD Stat. 2022. Population Projections. https://stats.oecd.org/Index.aspx?DataSetCode=POPPROJ.

Prime Minister's Office Singapore. 2013. "Population White Paper: A Sustainable Population for a Dynamic Singapore." January 9. Government of Singapore. https://www.strategygroup.gov.sg/media-centre/population-white-paper-a-sustainable-population-for-a-dynamic-singapore.

Prince, M. J., F. Wu, Y. Guo, L. M. Gutierrez Robledo, M. O'Donnell, R. Sullivan, and S. Yusuf. 2015. "The Burden of Disease in Older People and Implications for Health Policy and Practice." *Lancet* 385 (9967): 549–62. https://doi.org/10.1016/S0140–6736(14)61347–7.

Silver Support Singapore. 2022. *Benefits*. https://www.cpf.gov.sg/member/retirement-income/government-support/silver-support-scheme.

Singapore Department of Statistics. 2022a. "Life Expectancy by Sex." https://tablebuilder.singstat.gov.sg/table/TS/M810501.

Singapore Department of Statistics. 2022b. "Resident Households By Tenancy." https://tablebuilder.singstat.gov.sg/table/TS/M810401.

Sung, P., V. S. Goh, N. D. Azman, A. Visaria, and R. Malhotra. 2022. "Types of Caregiving Experience and Their Association With Caregiver Depressive Symptoms and Quality of Life." *Journal of Aging and Health* 34 (4–5): 591–601. https://doi.org/10.1177/08982643211051568.

Tan, C. C., C. S. P. Lam, D. B. Matchar, Y. K. Zee, and J. E. L. Wong. 2021. "Singapore's Health-Care System: Key Features, Challenges, and Shifts." *Lancet* 398 (10305): 1091–1104. https://doi.org/10.1016/s0140–6736(21)00252-x.

Tan Teck Boon. 2015. "A Super-Aged Singapore: Policy Implications for a Smart Nation." *Today*, October 13. Accessed January 21, 2022. https://www.todayonline.com/singapore/super-aged-singapore-policy-implications-smart-nation.

The Straits Times Singapore. 2006. "More S'pore elderly being struck by disabilities." *Straits Times*, August 24.

United Nations. 2017. *Addressing the Challenges of Population Ageing in Asia and the Pacific*. Bangkok: United Nations Economic and Social Commission for

Asia and the Pacific. http://www.unescap.org/sites/default/files/publications/Addressing320the%20Challenges%20of%20Population%20Ageing%20in%20Asia%20and%20the%20Pacific.pdf.

Visaria, A., R. Malhotra, and A. Chan. 2019. "Changes in the Profile of Older Singaporeans: Snapshots from 2009 and 2016–2017." Centre for Ageing Research and Education (CARE), Special Issue 1. Singapore: CARE-Duke NUS Medical School.

World Bank. 2016. *Live Long and Prosper: Aging in East Asia and Pacific*. Regional report. Washington, DC: The World Bank. https://openknowledge.worldbank.org/bitstream/handle/10986/23133/9781464804694.pdf.

World Health Organization. 2023. "GHE: Life Expectancy and Healthy Life Expectancy." https://www.who.int/data/gho/data/themes/mortality-and-global-health-estimates/ghe-life-expectancy-and-healthy-life-expectancy.

Yeoh, B. S. A., and S. Huang. 2009. "Foreign Domestic Workers and Home-Based Care for Elders in Singapore." *Journal of Aging & Social Policy* 22 (1): 69–88. https://doi.org/10.1080/08959420903385635.

Yokota, R. T. d. C., W. J. Nusselder, J.-M. Robine, J. Tafforeau, P. Deboosere, and H. Van Oyen. 2016. "Contribution of Chronic Conditions to the Disability Burden across Smoking Categories in Middle-Aged Adults, Belgium." *PLOS ONE* 11 (4): e0153726. https://doi.org/10.1371/journal.pone.0153726.

9

Universalizing the Access to Long-Term Care
Evidence from Spain

Joan Costa-i-Font, Sergi Jiménez-Martín, Cristina Vilaplana Prieto, and Analía Viola

9.1 Introduction

Life expectancy in Europe is rising, particularly in Spain, putting pressure on countries to meet the growing demands for care and other needs of an aging population. According to OECD data in figure 9.1, the proportion of Spaniards over the age of 65 will rise from 19.9 percent today to 23.8 percent in 2030 and 30.3 percent in 2060. In 2060, slightly more than 27 percent of the population over 65 in Spain is projected to be 85 or older (10 percentage points higher than in 2021) as depicted in figure 9.2.

Individuals over the age of 65 may experience limitations in their activities of daily living (ADLs) at some point in their lives, and these limitations sharply increase as people age. Indeed, while 12.3 percent of those aged 65 and older have two or more ADL limitations, this figure rises to 34 percent among those aged 85 and older (according to data from SHARE for 2017). This includes relying on others to perform basic tasks such as bathing, eating, going to bed, or dressing. These figures suggest that there could be a high

Joan Costa-i-Font is a professor of health economics at the London School of Economics, a research fellow of IZA and of CESIfo.

Sergi Jiménez-Martín is a professor of economics at Universitat Pompeu Fabra, an affiliated professor of the Barcelona School of Economics, and an associate researcher at Fundación de Estudios de Economía Aplicada (FEDEA).

Cristina Vilaplana Prieto is a professor in the Faculty of Economics and Business at the University of Murcia.

Analía Viola is a Juan de la Cierva postdoctoral fellow at the Fundación de Estudios de Economía Aplicada (FEDEA).

Sergi Jiménez acknowledges financial help from the Spanish Research Agency project PID2020–114231RB-I00. For acknowledgments, sources of research support, and disclosure of the authors' material financial relationships, if any, please see https://www.nber.org/books-and-chapters/long-term-care-around-world/universalizing-access-long-term-care-evidence-spain.

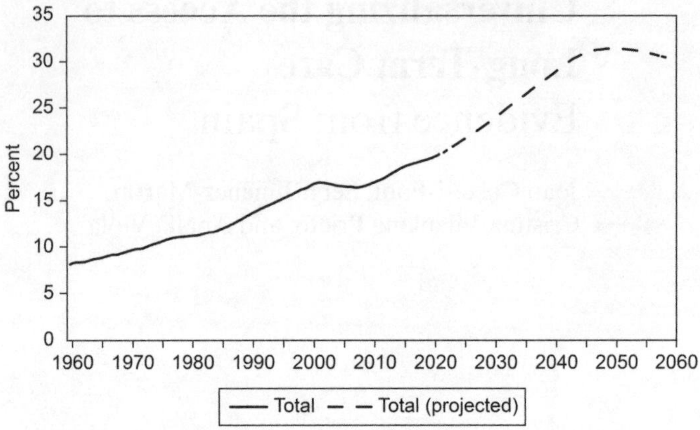

Fig. 9.1 Percentage of population age 65 or older, Spain, 1960–2060
Source: OECD stat, available at: https://stats.oecd.org/Index.aspx?DataSetCode=POPPROJ#, accessed on September 22, 2022

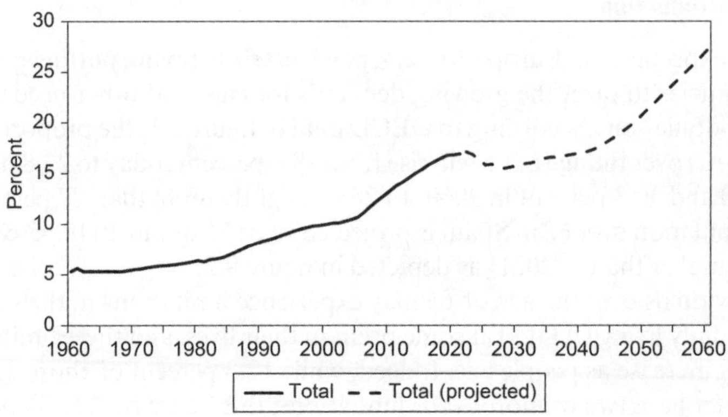

Fig. 9.2 Percentage of 65+ population that is age 85 or older, Spain, 1960–2060
Source: OECD stat, available at: https://stats.oecd.org/Index.aspx?DataSetCode=POPPROJ#, accessed on September 22, 2022

return to some planning to improve quality of life of people in a dependency situation (in terms of services, technology, and human capital) and more generally, in anticipating the effect on the demand for long-term care (LTC).

The purpose of this chapter is to explain how Spain's long-term care system is organized after the introduction of a reform in 2007 that universalised the access to LTC, which we refer under the Spanish acronym of SAAD (see Costa-Font et al. 2018 and 2022a for more recent description and effects of the reform). SAAD expanded the public funding of long-term care in Spain by introducing a universal benefit purely based on individual needs which overcame the means-tested access to publicly subsidized care before 2007. However, SAAD was subjected to austerity cuts in 2012, which reduced the generosity of economic and in-kind benefits and delayed access to the system for moderate dependent individuals.

Using a conservative cost method for the monetary valuation of informal care hours, long-term care costs are estimated to total 15,824 million euros per year (roughly 36 percent of public expenditure and 64 percent of private expenditure). However, using an alternative and more flexible estimation method for informal caregiving hours, the total long-term care estimates are much higher, at €21,204 million (roughly 27 percent of public and 73 percent of private expenditure). Long-term care spending in Spain amounts to between 1.27 percent (conservative estimates) and 1.70 percent (flexible estimation) of GDP (€1,245,513 million in 2019).

The structure of the paper is as follows. We begin with an overview of the institutional context of the LTC in Spain (section 9.2). Section 9.3 will examine nursing homes, formal home care, and informal home care in terms of sociodemographic characteristics and other relevant factors. Section 9.4 also covers financing and spending distribution. Section 9.5 examines the total cost of the LTC system (value of formal and informal care), and section 9.6 summarizes the findings.

9.2 Institutional Setting

9.2.1 Public Insurance Entitlement and Benefits

Long-term care in Spain is funded by a combination of national and regional tax revenues, as well as by individual co-payments. To date, the regional share of LTC funding has risen from 50 percent in 2007 to around 60 percent of total funding in 2019. The long-term care system's regulation and governance are regionally decentralized, with some coordination between regional and the central government.

The LTC system is grounded on the Act 39/2006, of December 14, on the Promotion of Personal Autonomy and Care for Dependent Persons (SAAD), which universalized access (not financing) to long-term care services and supports (LTCSS) and devised an effective expansion of public funding for all Spaniards, serving as the national framework regulation. Prior to the implementation of SAAD, subsidies were means-tested and funded by limited local government budgets (see figure 9.3 below). Disability allowances were only granted if the degree of disability of the claimant was greater than 65 percent and only under very strict income thresholds.

The implementation of SAAD led to an effective universalization of the LTC access (rather than the financing), regardless of age or other demographic characteristics. However, given that the implementation is regionally descentralized, cost-sharing arrangements were designed and implemented in a different way across regions. Although the system was initially intended to provide only home care services, the final design included a cash subsidy to assist households whose best care plan was to continue providing informal care. Following a needs test assessment, individuals were offered either a cash allowance or a number of hours of home care supports. In their needs assessment, all regions use the same ranking scale to evaluate about 47 tasks divided into ten activities.[1] Each task is usually assigned a different weight, and a different scale is used among people who have a mental disorder or a cognitive disability. Furthermore, the care evaluation considers the level of supervision required to complete each task. Evaluators conduct interviews with family members and consider broader social needs.

Following the needs assessment, individuals are classified as "non eligible," "moderate," "severe," or "major dependent." Those recognized as dependent receive an individual care plan, which identifies the type of supports and care that best meet their overall care and social needs (and includes a consultation with the family). The catalogue of services includes services for preventing dependency and promoting personal autonomy, telecare, home care, day and night center service, and nursing homes. Each regional authority establishes quality standards, and regional authorities accredit professional services. SAAD includes funding for day and night care centers, as well as residential care, in addition to home care assistance.[2]

When the competent administrations cannot provide these services, the dependent person is entitled to economic benefits: (1) service-linked financial benefit, only awarded when care is not possible through a public care service; (2) subsidies for personal assistance to facilitate the beneficiary's

1. The ranking scale evaluates 47 tasks grouped into the following ten activities of daily living: eating and drinking, control of physical needs, bathing and basic personal hygiene, other personal care, dressing and undressing, maintaining one's health, mobility, moving outside the home, and housework. Each activity of daily living is assigned a different weight, and there is a different scale for individuals with mental illness or cognitive disability. Additionally, the evaluation considers the degree of supervision required to perform each task. The final score is the sum of the weights of the activities of daily living for which the individual has difficulty, multiplied by the degree of supervision required. The degree of dependency is determined as the result of the sum: not eligible (less than 25 points), moderate dependency (25 to 49 points), severe dependency (50 to 74 points), and major dependency (above 74 points). Spain's Royal Decree 504/2007, of April 20, approved the dependency rating scale established by Act 39/2006, of December14, Promoción de la Autonomía Personal y Atención a las Personas en Situación de Dependencia.

2. It is important to mention that home help assistants are required to certify the professional qualification of Social and Health Care for People at Home, as established by Royal Decree 295/2004, dated February 20, which established certain professional qualifications that are included in the National Catalogue of Professional Qualifications, as well as their corresponding training modules that are incorporated into the Modular Catalogue of Vocational Training (Order SCB/429/2019, of April 1, amending Order SAS/2287/2010, of August 19, which regulates the requirements and procedure for the accreditation of the centers, services, and private entities, subsidized or not, that act in the field of personal autonomy and care for dependent persons in the cities of Ceuta and Melilla).

access to education and employment; and (3) cash subsidies for care in the family (to reward informal caregivers).

Focusing on the last type of economic benefit, it must be nuanced that receiving a cash subsidy is incompatible with any form of in-kind benefit, except for telecare. Cash subsidies to reward informal caregivers are designed for situations when the beneficiary is cared for by his or her family environment, and the dwelling meets the appropriate cohabitation and habitability conditions. Even though it was intended to be an exceptional benefit, it quickly became popular, with approximately 40–50 percent of SAAD beneficiaries receiving a cash subsidy.

Figure 9.3 depicts the changes in the availability and evolution of cash subsidies and home care supports. Caregiving subsidies for highly dependent individuals ranged from €390 to €487 per month in 2007 (nominal euros) and increased to €417 to €530 in 2011. However, the 2012 austerity measures slashed the amount to between €387 and €442 in 2013 (Rodríguez Cabrero et al., 2022). Cash subsidies were smaller when they referred to individuals with only severe dependency, ranging between €180 and €300 in 2011, but after the 2012 budget cuts, they were combined into one group that received between €236 and €268 in 2013. Subsidies have been designed to be always below the minimum wage and are unconditional (meaning that the funds are deposited directly into the care recipient's bank account, and no specific budget allocation is required).

At the onset of the SAAD, home care support intensity ranged from 70–90 hours/month for major dependency, level 1 (which was four times the average provision prior to the reform [16 hours/month]), to 55–70 hours/month for level 2. Between 2007 and 2011, the system was expanded to include severe and moderate dependency levels. Austerity cuts in 2012 reduced the number of hours of supports as well, in line with the reductions in cash allowances.

Government funding for the SAAD fell by 1,409 million euros between 2012 and 2014. Individuals with moderate care needs were added to the system in 2015, and social security contributions from caregivers were interrupted in 2013 but recovered in 2019 (Costa-Font and Vilaplana-Prieto 2022b).

The private sector is the main provider of residential care, with new nursing home centers opening in the aftermath of SAAD. However, most nursing home beds are still contracted out to the public sector. Municipalities typically manage public home care services, which are funded in part by tax revenues. To access both public and subsidized home care centers, individuals must need care and have a dependency level of 2 or 3. Applicants must apply through the region to be evaluated, and the individual care plan must specify the need for access to a nursing home. Individuals are placed on a waiting list once a care plan is issued until a vacancy becomes available. Finally, there are also home and community-based services, typically regu-

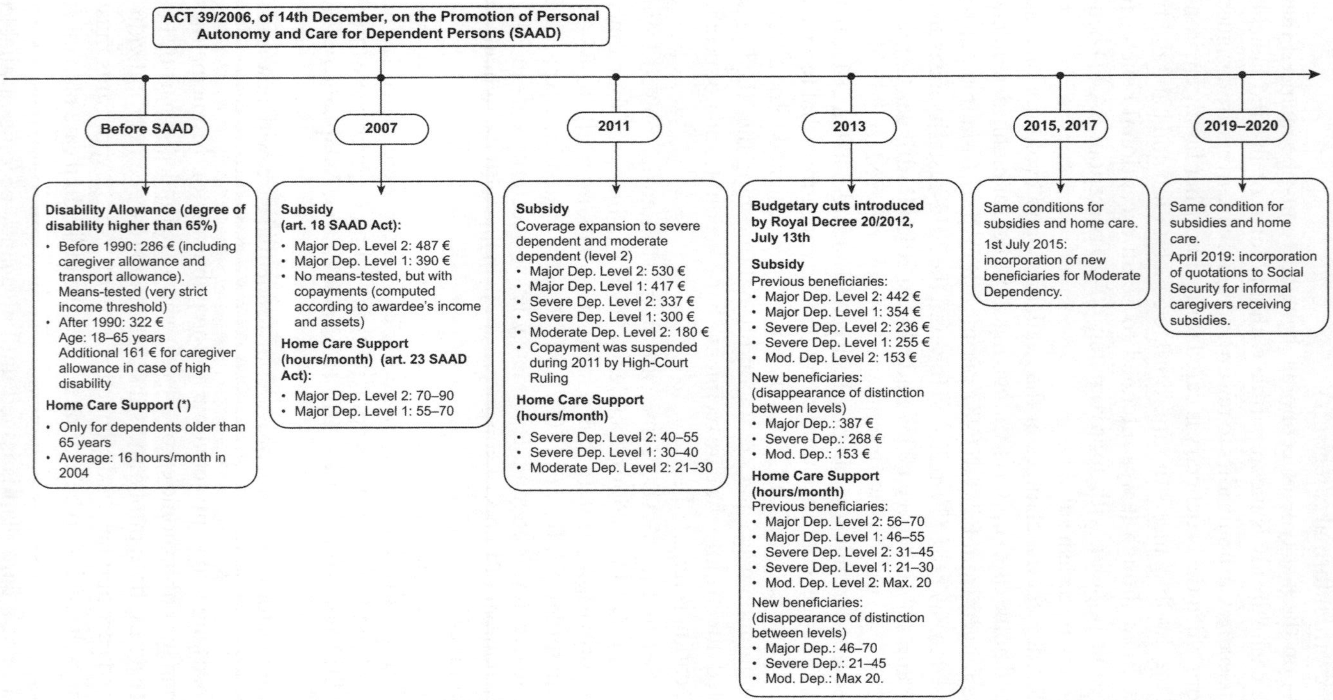

Fig. 9.3 The evolution of policy reforms after the Promotion of Personal Autonomy and Care for Dependent Persons (SAAD)

Source: Own work using information from Autonomía Personal y Dependencia—Instituto de Mayores y Servicios Sociales (https://imserso.es/autonomia-personal-dependencia)

lated and funded by the regional social service department, but provided by public or private centers and services that are subsidized and duly accredited. These services commonly include the following:

1. ***Services for the prevention care needs***, which refer to actions to promote healthy living conditions, specific preventive and rehabilitation programs aimed at the elderly and people with disabilities and those affected by complex hospitalization processes. Persons who have been awarded Grade I of moderate dependency will benefit from the following services for the promotion of personal autonomy:

- Habilitation and occupational therapy.
- Early intervention.
- Cognitive stimulation.
- Promotion, maintenance, and recovery of functional autonomy.
- Psychosocial training for people with mental illness or intellectual disability.
- Personal support and care in special accommodation (sheltered housing).

2. ***Telecare***, namely care using communication and information technologies (ICT), supported with human resources under special circumstances such as emergency, insecurity, loneliness, and isolation. It can either supplement or complement service to home help. This service is only provided to people who do not receive nursing home care.

3. ***Home Help*** is the most common home and community-based services (HCBS) delivered in Spain; it refers to supports in the care receiver's home to meet their daily care and is provided by accredited entities or companies. It includes support with: (i) domestic or household needs, such as cleaning, washing, cooking, or others; and (ii) personal care, which refers to services related to personal care to accomplish daily living activities.

4. Finally, the system considers ***day and night care***, both general and specialized.

9.2.2 Funding

The financing system is based on the existence of three levels of protection: minimum level, agreed level, and additional level. The financing of the minimum level of protection is funded by the central government. The allocation of regional budgets depends on the number of dependent persons entitled to care, based on the information that regions supply to the Information System of the System for Autonomy and Care for Dependency (ISSAAD). Next, the agreed level of protection is jointly funded by the central state and the regions, and is based on some criteria such as dependent population, beneficiaries with benefits, actual service benefits, regional investment in the SAAD, SAAD-related employment, ground area, dispersion, insularity, cost of services, economic capacity, administrative agility, persons pending resolution, or reduction of the waiting list. Finally, each region has discretion to top up their system.

Nonetheless, there have also been various exceptional financial allocations, such as the Special State Fund for the Dynamization of the Economy and Employment, where 400 million euros were distributed among the autonomous communities (regions) and cities for the improvement of the implementation of the SAAD. Likewise, central government has been financing the social security contributions associated with the special agreements that may be signed by non-professional caregivers of care receivers (informal caregivers), in such a way that they do not entail any expense for them.

9.2.3 Spending Cuts

The evolution of the long-term care budgets in Spain has been defined both by the spending cuts introduced in July 2012, as well as failure of the parliament to pass the general state budget bill for two consecutive years in 2019 and 2020, thus operating based on a budget extension of the year 2018 (Costa-Font et al. 2018, 2022a; Costa-Font and Vilaplana-Prieto 2022a, b, c).

Figure 9.4 depicts the evolution of the long-term care budget in Spain from 2008 to 2022. The budget for long-term care in 2008 accounted for

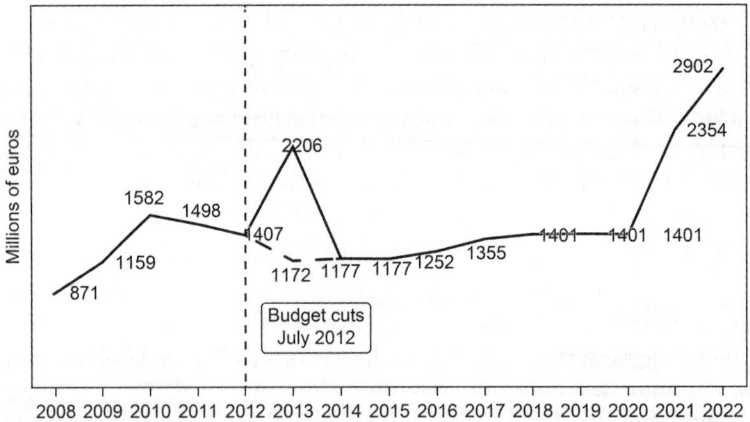

Fig. 9.4 Budget for long-term care (millions of euros), state's general budgets, 2008–2022, Spain

Note: It should be noted that 2013 was an atypical year because it was included the pending payment of obligations of social security contributions of non-professional caregivers, amounting to 1,034 million euros. The dotted line reports the budget taking away such payment.

Notes: 2019: 2018 extended and 2020: 2019 extended.

Source: Consolidated General State Budget Statistics

871 million euros, and in the two successive years it increased by 33 percent and 37 percent in 2009 and 2010, respectively. However, in 2012, severe budgetary restrictions were applied, representing a decrease in the budget of approximately 6 percent. It should be noted that 2013 was an atypical year because it was included the pending payment of obligations of social security contributions of non-professional caregivers, amounting to 1,034 million euros. That is why in 2013 the effects of the budget cuts introduced in July 2012 were not yet reflected.

Public LTC spending stagnated after the budget cuts from 2013 up to 2020. Finally, in 2021 and 2022, long-term care budget increased again to 2,902 million euros, 23.3 percent more than in 2021 and twice the amount registered in 2018 (see figure 9.4) (Jiménez-Martín and Viola 2022).

9.2.4 Waiting Lists

One of the consequences of the budget cuts has been the proliferation of waiting lists, often referred as the "dependency limbo"—the status that some individuals find themselves in when they are officially entitled to supports or subsidies but have not yet received any benefit—that is, people on a SAAD waiting list (WL), measured as the difference between the number of people entitled to benefits and the number of people with benefits.

Figure 9.5 depicts the evolution of the long-term care waiting lists from 2009 to date. We find that after the economic downturn in 2011 and the subsequent austerity reforms in 2012, some individuals with a moderate degree of care needs were entitled to SAAD in December 2015 rather than 2013 as scheduled (Jiménez-Martín and Viola 2022). Indeed, in Decem-

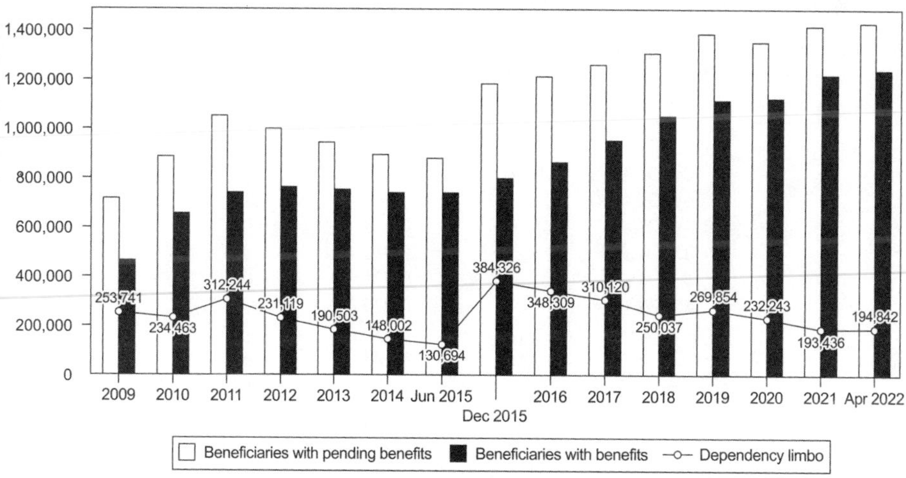

Fig. 9.5 Number of beneficiaries with benefits and pending benefits: dependency limbo, 2009–2022, Spain

Source: IMSERSO

ber 2015, around 385,000 people were pending receiving the benefit. Since then, the gap between people with and without benefits has been narrowing significantly (especially in the last two years), it currently stands at around 195,000 people.

9.3 Aging, Disability, and Well-Being

As individuals grow older, they may be susceptible to limitations in activities of daily living at some point in their lives. In other words, a person may need help or depend on another to carry out basic activities such as washing, eating, or dressing, for example. Indeed, population aging encompasses a rise in daily living activities, especially when people face serious limitations in their autonomy.

The percentage of Spanish people aged 65 and up who face limitations in their daily activities is displayed in table 9.1. Approximately 67.9 percent of the 65+ population report no limitations (neither ADL nor IADL), compared to about 31.7 percent of the 85+ population. Furthermore, 13.8 percent (65+) and 22.9 percent (85+) have no ADL limitations, but at least one IADL limitation. Focusing on the population with severe difficulties, 7.3 percent of the 65+ population and 22.5 percent of the 85+ population have four to six ADL limitations.

Aging is not always associated with care and health care needs (Costa-Font and Vilaplana-Prieto 2020), but as shown in table 9.1, the population aged 65 and over is a group that requires more care, especially in those groups with greater dependency, requiring constant attention and support for housework, personal care, and mobility. In this regard, table 9.2 depicts

Table 9.1 **Share with ADLs by age, Spain, 2017**

	65+	85+
0 ADLs & 0 IADLs	0.679	0.317
0 ADLs & 1+ IADLs	0.138	0.229
1 ADL	0.060	0.114
2 ADLs	0.028	0.064
3 ADLs	0.022	0.051
4 ADLs	0.022	0.061
5 ADLs	0.020	0.054
6 ADLs	0.031	0.110
Any ADL	0.183	0.454
Any IADL	0.302	0.665
Observations	3,280	590

Source: Data are from the Survey of Health, Ageing and Retirement in Europe (wave 7; 2017). ADLs include walking across room, dressing, bathing, eating, going to bed, and using the toilet. IADLs include using a telephone, managing money, taking medications as prescribed, shopping for groceries, and cooking a hot meal. Individuals who report not doing these activities are also included as having difficulty with them.

Table 9.2 **Distribution of limitations with Specific ADLs/IADLs, Spain, 2017**

	65+ All	65+ Conditional	85+ All	85+ Conditional
	Panel 1: IADLs			
IADL—Use a Phone	0.076	0.252	0.239	0.357
IADL—Manage Money	0.121	0.401	0.369	0.552
IADL—Take Meds as Prescribed	0.077	0.253	0.244	0.365
IADL—Shop for Groceries	0.143	0.473	0.381	0.570
IADL—Prepare a Meal	0.120	0.395	0.354	0.529
Observations	3,280	992	590	295
	Panel 2: ADLs			
ADL—Use the Toilet	0.080	0.437	0.251	0.552
ADL—Get Dressed	0.128	0.701	0.319	0.701
ADL—Take a Bath	0.141	0.773	0.393	0.866
ADL—Walk Across a Room	0.063	0.346	0.183	0.403
ADL—Eat	0.048	0.265	0.153	0.336
ADL—Get In/Out of Bed	0.094	0.513	0.273	0.601
Observations	3,280	599	590	268

Source: Data are from the Survey of Health, Ageing and Retirement in Europe (wave 7; 2017). Column 1 shows the share of the sample that report having difficulty with each activity, while column 2 shows the share of people with at least 1 IADL (panel 1) or at least 1 ADL (panel 2) who report having difficulty with each activity. Individuals who report not doing these activities are also included as having difficulty with them.

Table 9.3 **Well-being for those 65+ and 85+ by ADL limitations, Spain, 2017**

	65+	65+, 3+ Lims	85+	85+ 3+ Lims
Reports good or better health status	0.348	0.095	0.204	0.086
Very satisfied with life	0.648	0.404	0.553	0.441
Depressed much of time	0.290	0.354	0.353	0.348
Observations	3,307	662	598	309

Source: Data are from the Survey of Health, Ageing and Retirement in Europe (wave 7; 2017)

the distribution of limitations for the 65+ and 85+ populations based on the type of IADL or ADL. Shopping for groceries (14.3 percent for 65+ and 38.1 percent for 85+) and managing money (12.1 percent for 65+ and 36.9 percent for 85+) are the most reported problems for those with one or more IADLs. Furthermore, for those with one or more ADL limitations, the most common difficulties are taking a bath (14.1 percent for 65+ and 39.3 percent for 85+) and getting dressed (12.8 percent for 65+ and 31.9 percent for 85+).

Moreover, table 9.3 summarizes various measures of people's well-being. Individuals having multiple limitations (three or more) for daily life activities

Table 9.4 **Income and wealth distribution, Spain, 2017**

	Income		Wealth	
	65+	85+	65+	85+
5th Percentile	3,241.72	1,810.49	2,143.50	678.28
10th Percentile	4,783.08	3,884.75	8,498.29	3,294.03
25th Percentile	7,715.22	7,000.00	41,670.16	23,413.15
50th Percentile	14,943.25	13,730.50	113,333.30	79,161.04
75th Percentile	24,800.00	21,398.11	257,879.70	20,4004.10
90th Percentile	39,002.71	31,045.55	488,833.40	40,1828.60
95th Percentile	55,215.88	43,875.78	711,884.60	590,743.40
Mean	21,631.22	17,549.71	210,229.5	162,646.9
Observations	3,280	590	3,280	590

Source: Data are from the Survey of Health, Ageing and Retirement in Europe (wave 7; 2017). All income and wealth estimates are post-tax (2019 euros). Wealth includes bank accounts, bond, stock and mutual funds, savings for long-term investments, value of own business, value of home, value of cars and value of other real estate Income and wealth have been computed using the OECD scale.

(and at older ages) appear to exhibit, as expected, worse health. However, 9.5 percent of those 65 and older report good health, while 8.6 percent of those 85 and older report good health. Individuals who have no limitations, on the other hand, have a much higher percentage of people reporting good or very good health: 34.8 percent for those aged 65+, and 20.4 percent for those aged 85+. The percentage declaring themselves very satisfied with their life is 64.8 percent (65+) and 55.3 percent (85+), but decreases to 40.4 percent (65+) and 44.1 percent (85+) when we restrict to people with +3ADLs. Furthermore, the prevalence of depression is nearly identical between those who have no limitations and those who have three or more limitations for people aged 85+ (35.3 percent and 34.8 percent, respectively) (Costa-Font and Vilaplana-Prieto 2022b).

To conclude this section, we present table 9.4 and table 9.5, which show the distribution of household (HH) income and wealth by ADLs and IADLs limitations. First, table 9.4 depicts the percentile distribution of household income and wealth for those aged 65+, as well as those aged 85+ (using the OECD equivalence scale). Income and wealth rise along the income percentile distribution (with a slight increase at 90th percentile).

Our estimates document that the bottom 5 percent of the population 85+ has a wealth of €678, while the bottom 5 percent of those 65+ have a wealth of €2,143 (that is, more than three times higher). When we turn to the top 5 percent of those aged 85+, wealth amounts to €590,743; it is €711,884 for those aged 65+. Similar conclusions can be drawn when comparing income. Using the mean value as a guide, mean income (or wealth) for those 65+ is 1.23 (or 1.29) higher than for those 85+.

Next, table 9.5 relates income and wealth with ADLs and IADLs limita-

Table 9.5 **Income and wealth distribution by limitations for 65+ population, Spain, 2017**

	0 ADLs & 0 IADLs	0 ADLs & 1+ IADLs	1 ADL	2 ADLs	3+ ADLs	Total
		Panel 1: Income				
<50% Median HH Income	0.049	0.097	0.050	0.196	0.215	0.073
50–100% Median HH Income	0.376	0.520	0.496	0.490	0.463	0.409
100–150% Median HH Income	0.301	0.207	0.235	0.216	0.195	0.275
150–200% Median HH Income	0.124	0.066	0.118	0.039	0.044	0.108
200%+ Median HH Income	0.151	0.110	0.101	0.059	0.083	0.135
Total	0.679	0.138	0.060	0.022	0.073	—
Observations	2,228	453	198	91	332	3,302
		Panel 2: Wealth				
<50% Median HH Wealth	0.208	0.335	0.261	0.255	0.302	0.235
50–100% Median HH Wealth	0.256	0.273	0.277	0.314	0.302	0.265
100–150% Median HH Wealth	0.173	0.203	0.227	0.235	0.185	0.182
150–200% Median HH Wealth	0.109	0.066	0.042	0.059	0.117	0.101
200%+ Median HH Wealth	0.254	0.123	0.193	0.137	0.093	0.218
Total	0.679	0.138	0.060	0.022	0.073	—
Observations	2,228	453	198	91	332	3,302

Source: Data are from the Survey of Health, Ageing and Retirement in Europe (wave 7; 2017). Our ADL Index runs from 0–6 and is the number of ADLs that are either difficult or not done from eating, bathing, dressing, using the toilet, walking across a room, and getting in/out of bed. IADLs include using a telephone, managing money, taking medications as prescribed, shopping for groceries, and cooking a hot meal. Each cell reports the share of respondents in the respective ADL category who are in that row's income group. All income and wealth estimates are post-tax (2019 euros). Wealth includes bank accounts, bond, stock and mutual funds, savings for long-term investments, value of own business, value of home, value of cars and value of other real estate Income and wealth have been computed using the OECD scale.

tions. 21.5 percent of those with 3+ADLs are below 50 percent of median household income (compared to only 4.9 percent for those with neither ADLs nor ADLs). Thus, the percentage below half of median household income is four times higher among the elderly with +3ADLs. Conversely, the percentage whose income is between 1.5 and 2 times the median income is three times higher for those with no limitations than for those with +3ADLs. Finally, 15.1 percent of those with no limitations earn more than twice the median household income, compared to 5.9 percent of those with 2ADLs and 8.3 percent of those with +3ADLs.

With respect to wealth, the percentage with less than half the median wealth is 1.5 times higher for those with +3ADLs relative to those with no limitations. In contrast, the percentage with more than twice the median wealth is 2.7 times higher among those with no limitations relative to those with +3ADLs.

9.4 Long-Term Care System in Spain

9.4.1 LTC Financing

After a period of slowdown, spending on long-term care relative to GDP has been trending slightly upward since 2017 (figure 9.6). In fact, LTC spending as a percentage of GDP has risen from 0.5 percent in 2003 to nearly 0.9 percent today (data from 2019).

As mentioned in the institutional section, the LTC system in Spain is run by regional governments and the funding is regionally decentralized. Indeed, LTC funding is comprised of the general contribution of the central government (15 percent), contributions from autonomous communities (regions, 64 percent), and contributions from users (cost sharing, 21 percent) (see figure 9.7).

Regarding financing by type of care, figure 9.8 summarizes the share of public LTC expenditure aimed at institutional care, home care and day centers. The expenditure on institutional care accounts for 64 percent, although it has decreased 6 pp since 2003 (70 percent) and in consequence the share of public LTC expenditure devoted to home care and day centers has increased from 30 percent in 2003 to 36 percent in 2019.

The development of the private long-term care insurance market in Spain is very scarce. In 2017, only 2 percent of individuals aged 65 and older had subscribed and insurance contract (table 9.6).

9.4.2 LTC Recipients and Caregivers

Previously, we pointed out the limitations that face the elderly population in Spain in their daily life activities. Now we turn to analyze the number of

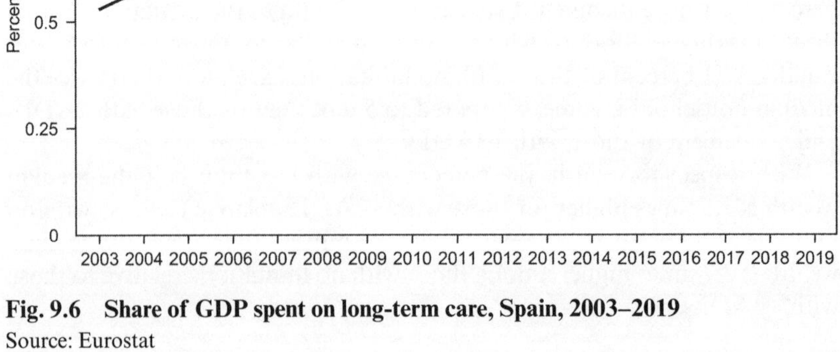

Fig. 9.6 Share of GDP spent on long-term care, Spain, 2003–2019
Source: Eurostat

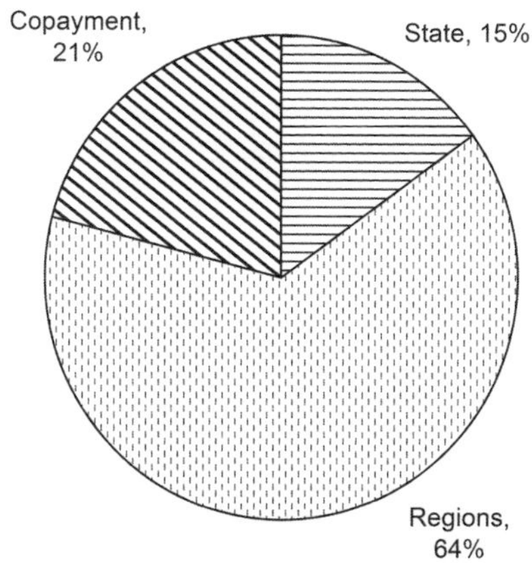

Fig. 9.7 Percent of LTC financing by source, Spain, 2019
Source: Asociación Estatal de Directores y Gerentes de Servicios Sociales de España, available at: https://directoressociales.com/wp-content/uploads/2021/01/INFO-GLOBAL-XX-DICTAMEN-3-3-20_compressed.pdf

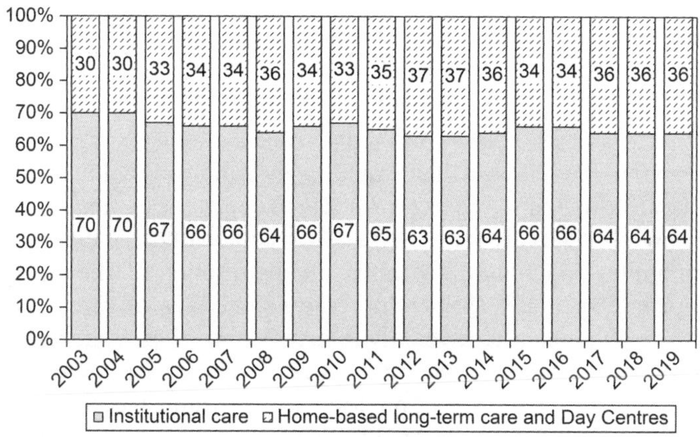

Fig. 9.8 Share of public LTC expenditure for institutional care and home care and day centers, Spain, 2003–2019
Source: Eurostat

recipients of the LTC system who ask for help to perform their daily routines, and afterwards, we will focus on another fundamental piece of the system, which are the ***caregivers***.

In Spain, 13.3 percent of people aged 65+ receive some form of care (22.2 percent for those aged 85+) (see table 9.7). As expected, the percentage of people who require care rises with the number of ADL limitations. In the population aged 65+, it ranges from 28.4 percent for those with no ADLs and only 1 ADL to almost 44 percent for those with at least 3 ADLs. This progression is also observed for the cohort aged 85+, although not as pronounced.

Table 9.6 **Population with LTC insurance, Spain, 2017**

	65 +
Population with LTC Insurance	176,386
Share of 65+/85+ Population	(0.020)
Observations	26

Source: Data are from the Survey of Health, Ageing and Retirement in Europe (wave 7)

Table 9.7 **Any care by age and ADL, Spain, 2017**

	65 Plus	85 Plus
Full Sample	0.133	0.222
0 ADLs, 1+ IADL	0.284	0.454
1 ADL	0.293	0.468
2 ADL	0.370	0.508
3+ ADL	0.437	0.499
Observations	3,280	590

Source: Data are from the Survey of Health, Ageing and Retirement in Europe (wave 7; 2017). Respondent weights are used for all calculations. The care variable is defined as either being in a nursing home for more than 100 days or having received either formal or informal home help with ADLs, IADLs. The nursing home population included in the Spanish sample has been considered.

LTC help comes either in its formal or informal way, though the latter plays a key role in Spain. Figures 9.9 and 9.10 depict the distinction between formal and informal care for each ADL category, namely one, two, or three or more limitations. Figure 9.9 shows the distribution of the type of care among people aged 65+ (85+) who receive some type of care. In the 65+ population, 49 percent receive only informal care, 27 percent receive only formal care, 10 percent receive both types of care, and 14 percent receive nursing home care. In the 85+ population, the percentage receiving informal care is a bit higher (51 percent), but the percentage receiving only formal care is smaller (19 percent), the percentage receiving both types of care increases until 14 percent, and 16 percent of the population receive nursing home care.

As for the distribution of type of care by number of ADLs (figure 9.10), in the population aged 65+, as the number of ADLs increases, there is an upward trend in the combined use of formal and informal care (from 12 percent to 19 percent), as well as nursing home care (from 2 percent to 14 percent). In the population aged 85+, there is an increasing profile of the probability of receiving only informal care as the number of ADLs increases. In contrast, the percentage receiving only formal care decreases from 28 percent to 15 percent as we move from 0 ADLs (+1 IADL) to 1 ADL. In the case of people with +3ADLs, we appreciate an increase in informal care and nursing home care.

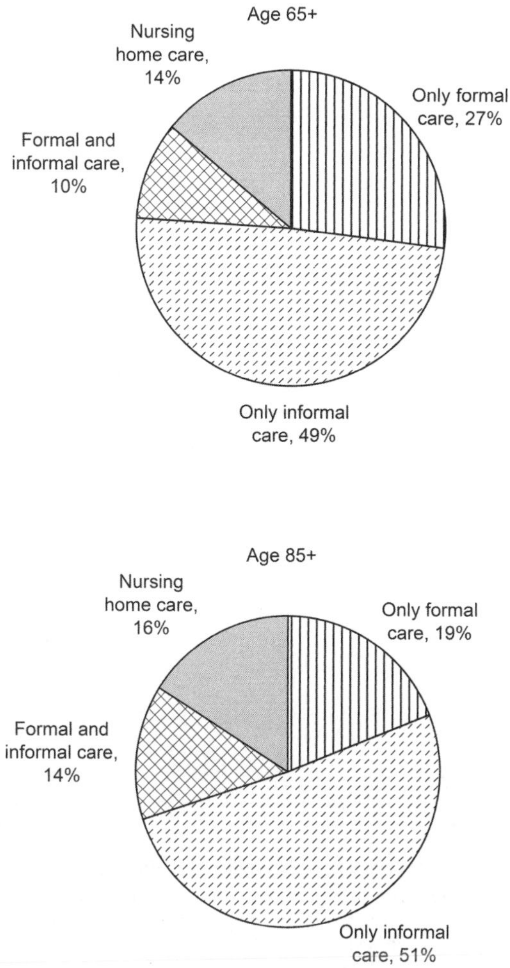

Fig. 9.9 Type of care received by age, Spain, 2017

Notes: Respondent weights are used for all calculations. The care variable is defined as either being in a nursing home for more than 100 days or having received either formal or informal home help with ADLs, IADLs. The nursing home population included in the Spanish sample has been considered.

Source: Data are from the Survey of Health, Ageing and Retirement in Europe (wave 7; 2017).

As for informal caregivers, table 9.8 reports estimates of the total number of individuals providing ADL/IADL-related help. In accordance with prior figures, the role of informal care providers is quite important: around 80 percent of people helping individuals aged 65+ were informal caregivers, from which 30 percent correspond to informal caregivers of dependents aged 85+. In general, most of the informal caregivers are daughters (40 per-

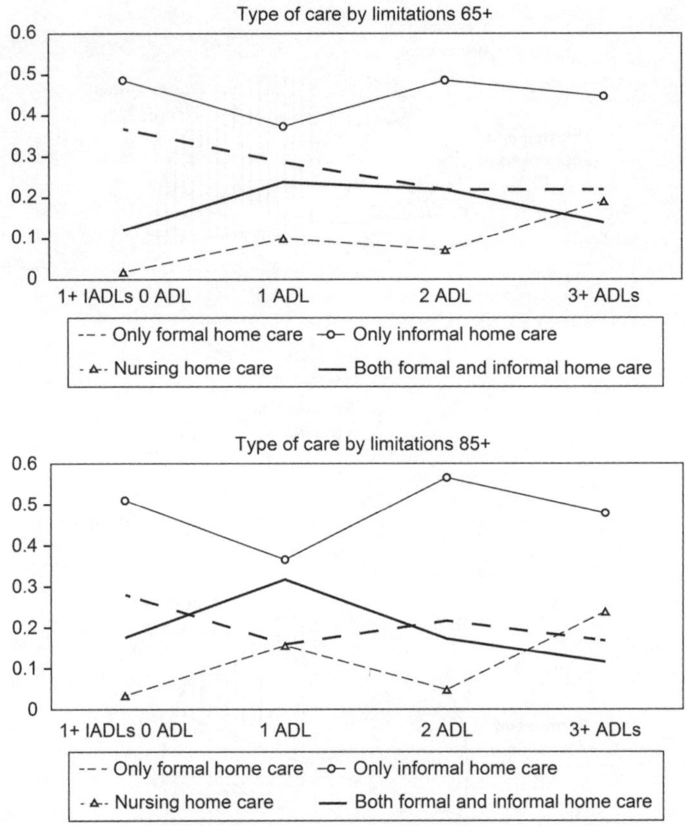

Fig. 9.10 Type of care received by age and limitations, Spain, 2017

Notes: Informal help is defined as help provided without pay or by a paid relative, while formal help is paid help by a non-relative. Help can be with ADLs, IADLs, or managing money due to a health problem. ADLs and IADLs are defined as before.

Source: Data are from the Survey of Health, Ageing and Retirement in Europe (using waves 6 and 7).

cent), spouses (30 percent), sons (19 percent), and other relatives (11 percent) (figure 9.11).

Caregivers' hours of care are typically capped at 16 hours per day to allow for 8 hours of rest, so the maximum number of hours per week should be 112 (95 percent of the time). Only 5 percent of caregivers devote less than 7 hours per week for people 65+ (or 14 hours per week for people 85+) (tables 9.9 and 9.10) (See Costa-Font et al. 2022a for a full analysis of the effect of SAAD on care use).

When it comes to sociodemographic characteristics, women make up most caregivers in both the formal (87 percent) and informal (58 percent) sectors (figure 9.12). Most caregivers in the formal sector are between the

Table 9.8 Home care provision—population estimates, Spain, 2017

	All	65 Plus	85 Plus
Formal Helpers—ADL/IADLs	503,433		
Relative to 65+/85+ Population	(0.058)		
	(0.41)		
Relative to 18–64 Population	(0.017)		
Informal Helpers—ADL/IADLs	2,082,579	1,446,502	636,077
Relative to 65+/85+ Population		(0.076)	(0.21)
Relative to 18–64 Population		(0.049)	(0.022)
All Helpers—ADL/IADLs	2,586,012		
Relative to 65+/85+ Population			
Relative to 18–64 Population			
Observations SLFS	1,812		
Observations SHARE	3,870	3,280	590

Source: Data are from the Survey of Health, Ageing and Retirement in Europe (wave 7) and Spanish Labour Force Survey (SLFS) for formal care. Respondent weights are used for all population estimate calculations. Those providing help to nursing home residents are automatically excluded from all calculations. ADLs and IADLs are defined as before. Informal help is defined as help provided without pay or by a paid relative, while formal help is paid help by a non-relative. For formal care, we cannot distinguish the population attended.

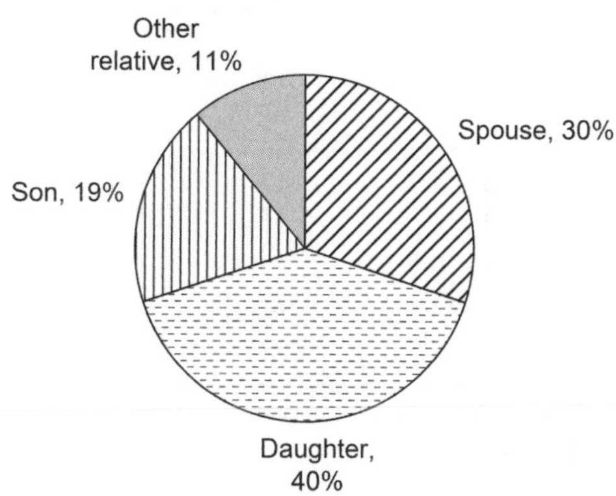

Fig. 9.11 Informal caregivers by relationship to care recipient, Spain, 2017
Source: Data are from the Survey of Health, Ageing and Retirement in Europe (wave 7)

ages of 40 and 59 (54 percent). Caregivers in the informal sector are older than those in the formal sector, those aged 50 to 69 accounting for 26 percent of caregivers and those aged 70 or older accounting for 56 percent of total caregivers. Furthermore, 53 percent of all formal care workers have a high school diploma (HS), with 42 percent having a college diploma or something comparable. The informal sector seems to be less qualified: 54 percent of informal workers attained less than a high school degree and only 19 percent have with some college degree. [In the comparison of the above figures, we

Table 9.9 **Distribution of hours of help received per week, Spain, 2021**

	65+	85+
5th Percentile	7	14
10th Percentile	14	21
25th Percentile	28	35
50th Percentile	77	91
75th Percentile	112	112
90th Percentile	112	112
95th Percentile	112	112
Mean	68	74
1 Hour per Day or Less	0.06	0.03
5 Hour per Day or More	0.68	0.77
Observations	*3,882*	*1,744*

Source: Survey of Disabilities, Dependency and Autonomy (2020). Interviews were conducted between April and August 2021.

Table 9.10 **Distribution of weekly hours received by type, Spain, 2021**

	65+		85+	
	Formal	Informal	Formal	Informal
5th Percentile	7	7	7	14
10th Percentile	7	14	7	14
25th Percentile	7	28	14	35
50th Percentile	14	70	14	84
75th Percentile	35	112	42	112
90th Percentile	84	112	98	112
95th Percentile	112	112	112	112
Mean	29	67	33	72
Observations	*863*	*3,739*	*445*	*1,683*

Source: Survey of Disabilities, Dependency and Autonomy (2020). Interviews were conducted between April and August 2021.

should note that while for informal caregiving, we do know that caregivers look after people aged 65 and over; however, in the case of formal caregivers, we ignore the age of the person they are caring for.]

Finally, another important aspect in the LTC sector are the working conditions. Table 9.11 analyzes the earnings distribution, hourly wages, and fraction of part time for formal care workers. A nursing facility worker (€1,437) earns on average quite the same per month as a home care worker (€1,424) and an average worker (€1,454.2). In terms of hourly wages,[3] the

3. The Social Security Working Histories do not report hours. In order to estimate hourly wages, we combine the information of part-time/full-time work from the Social Security files with the average hour's information from the Quarterly Survey of Labor Cost (INE 2018).

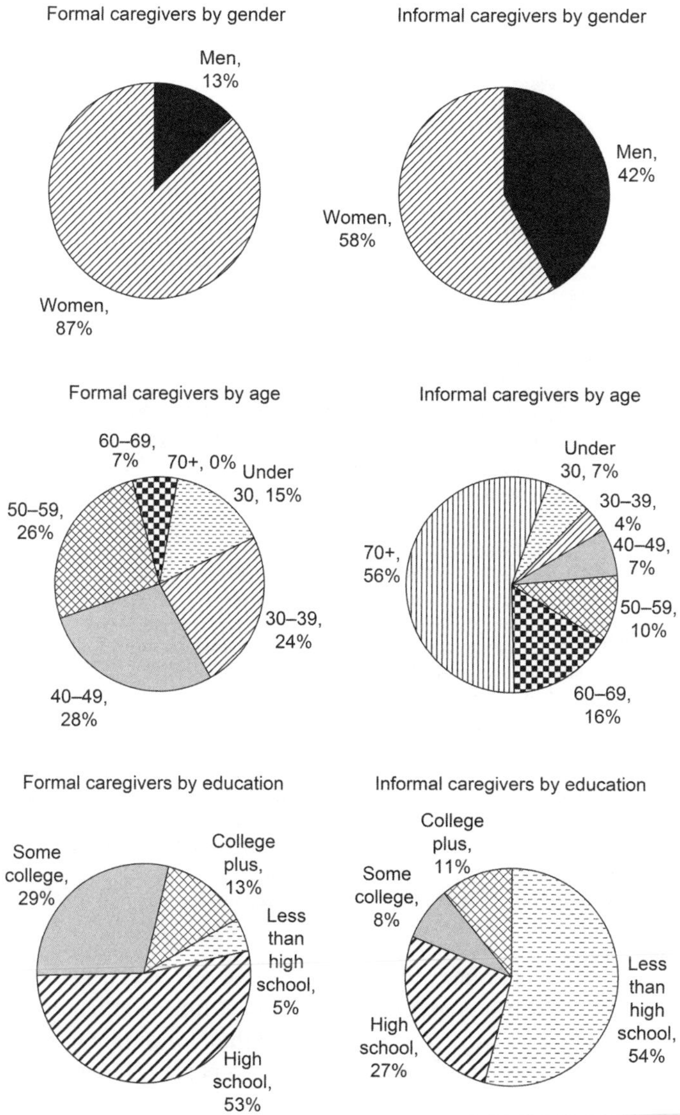

Fig. 9.12 Demographic composition of formal and informal caregivers, Spain, 2017

Source: Data are from the Survey of Health, Ageing and Retirement in Europe (wave 7) for informal care, and Spanish Labour Force Survey for formal care

Table 9.11 **Pay for full-time care workers at nursing facilities and in home health care, Spain, 2018**

Care Type	P10	P50	P90	Wage Euros/ month	Hourly wage	Part Time
Nursing facilities	877.9	1,305.7	2,078.3	1,437.4	10.92	0.229
Home care	625.6	1,207.6	2,541.6	1,424.3	11.29	0.362
All workers	747.72	1,296.9	2,355.47	1,454,2	11.22	0.284

Care Type	Skill	P10	P50	P90	Wage Euros/ month	Hourly wage	Part Time
Nursing facilities	Low skill	770.9	1,171.2	1,440.3	1,167.7	9.06	0.257
	Inter. skill	858.6	1,274.5	1,775.1	1,301.1	9.92	0.231
	High skill	1,067.8	1,732.2	2,974.8	1,871.6	14.11	0.213
Home care	Low skill	472.4	964.8	1,392.8	964.6	8.31	0.440
	Inter. skill	712.9	1,305.9	2,720.6	1,553.2	12.00	0.331
	High skill	822.3	1,722	3,108.2	1,846.6	14.37	0.316
All Workers	Low skill	567.6	1,100.9	1,558.1	1,088.2	8.90	0.362
	Inter. Skill	770.0	1,291.1	2,190.5	1,421.5	10.88	0.272
	High Skill	994.6	1,758.7	3,095.7	1,901.4	14.52	0.253

Note: High Skill: corresponds to contribution groups 1 to 4 which imply high education. Intermediate skill: contribution groups 5 to 7 which are administrative and clerical skills. Low skill: contribution groups 8 to 10.

Group 1: Engineers and Graduates. Group 2: Technical Engineers, experts and qualified assistants. Group 3: Administrative and Workshop Managers. Group 4: Assistants without official qualification. Group 5: Administrative Officers. Group 6: Juniors. Group 7: Administrative Assistants. Group 8: First and Second Category Officials. Group 9: Third Category Officials and Specialists. Group 10: General assistants without qualifications. Hourly wage has been obtained combining wages from the Continuous Sample of Working life and the Quarterly Survey of Labor Cost (INE 2018).

Source: Spanish Continuous Sample of Working Life (2018)

average for nursing facilities workers (10.92) is about 30 cents below that of home care and all workers. Apart from this, part time is much more prevalent among home care workers (36.2 percent) than for nursing care workers (22.9 percent). According to percentiles, the 10 percent of nursing facility workers (percentile 10) earn less than 878 euros per month and 626 euros in home care, while only 10 percent of nursing home workers (percentile 90) earn more than 2,078 euros per month and 2,542 euros in home care.

The second panel of table 9.11 allows us to extract several lessons about the earning distribution, hourly wages, and part time by skill. First, for all workers the wage distribution for low skill workers is much more compressed than for intermediate skill or high skill workers. Second, the ratio high skill vs low skill average wages (as well hourly wages) is much higher for home care workers (1.90) than for nursing care workers (1.60). Third, for all type of workers part time work is more prevalent among low skill workers.

Table 9.12 **Absolute number of nursing homes, beds, and occupancy rate, Spain, 2019**

	Spain, 2019
Nursing homes	5,542
Fraction public nursing homes	25.89%
Fraction private nursing homes	74.11%
Beds	399,417
Fraction public beds	61.90%
Fraction private beds	38.10%
Nursing home residents	250,708
Pop 65+	9,217,464
Occupancy rate	62.76%
Nursing home size	72.07
Coverage	4.33%
Beds per pop 65+	0.043

Source: IMSERSO

Occupancy rate is defined as the percentage of beds occupied in nursing homes. Nursing home size is defined as the number of beds per nursing home facility. Coverage is defined as the percentage of population 65+ who has a nursing home bed.

As mentioned before, expenditure on institutional care, most commonly nursing homes, accounts for 64 percent of total public expenditure on LTC. In Spain, there are 5,542 nursing homes, the majority of which are private (74.11 percent). On the contrary, the total number of registered beds in 2019 is 399,417 of which 61.9 percent are public (table 9.12). In these facilities, most workers are nursing aides (52 percent), followed by cleaning staff (9 percent) and finance and social science professionals (9 percent). Furthermore, nurses (5 percent) and administrative staff (5 percent) make up 10 percent of the total (figure 9.13).

The occupancy rate of nursing homes varies by region (table 9.13) expressed as the percentage of beds/places occupied in nursing homes. In Spain, the occupancy rate is around 63 percent. However, there are communities such as Castilla-La Mancha, Madrid, Murcia, Ceuta and Melilla where the occupancy level is well above the national average, reaching full capacity of the nursing homes (99–100 percent).

9.5 The Cost of Long-Term Care

In this section, we separate the analysis in two parts, one for the formal care and the other for the informal care sector. Afterwards, we sum them up to have the overall cost of LTC in Spain. The total costs in formal care are shown in table 9.14. Additionally, we distinguish between public and private costs for nursing homes and home care.

Public cost for nursing homes refers to public sector spending on residential places (direct provision and service-linked provision, when it is not pos-

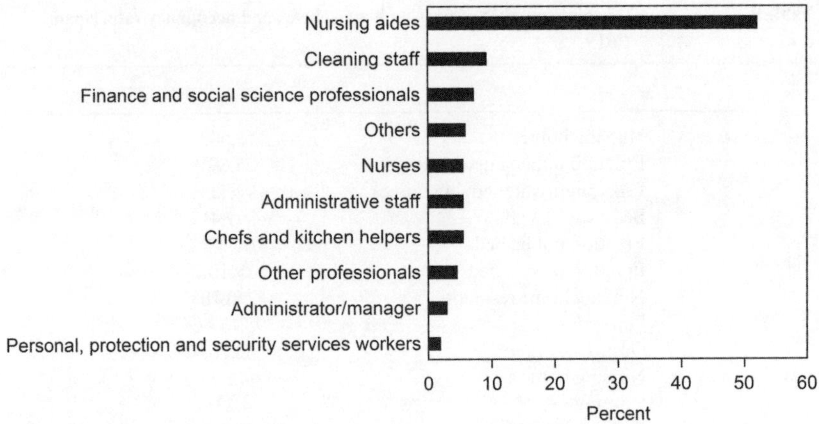

Fig. 9.13 Percent distribution of nurses, aides, and social workers at care facilities, Spain, 2019 (second quarter)

Notes: Administrative staff includes legal and social services support professionals. Nursing aides includes auxiliary technicians of pharmacy and health emergencies.

Source: Economically Active Population Survey—EPA

Table 9.13 **Distribution of nursing homes occupancy rate and beds across states; public and private nursing home places, Spain, 2019**

Region	NH places	NH users	Occupancy rate
Andalusia	45,543	21,919	48.1%
Aragon	19,318	6,817	35.3%
Asturias	15,204	5,987	39.4%
Balearic Islands	6,573	5,334	81.2%
Canary Islands	9,994	9,498	95.0%
Cantabria	6,444	4,401	68.3%
Castile and León	48,089	42,501	88.4%
Castilla-La Mancha	28,695	28,428	99.1%
Catalonia	65,379	44,746	68.4%
Valencia	27,248	16,657	61.1%
Extremadura	14,855	10,211	68.7%
Galicia	21,704	8,674	40.0%
Madrid	52,882	52,830	99.9%
Murcia	5,395	5,395	100.0%
Navarre	6,664	5,339	80.1%
Basque Country	21,765	14,819	68.1%
La Rioja	3,235	1,926	59.5%
Ceuta	199	199	100.0%
Melilla	231	227	98.3%
Spain	399,417	250,708	62.8%

Note NH users: Aragon, Canary Islands and Extremadura, data 2016. Galicia, data 2017.

Source: IMSERSO and Jimenez-Martin and Viola (2022)

Table 9.14 **Formal care costs, annual, Spain, 2019 (million €)**

Types	Number of users	Total spending (million €)
Nursing home (public)	155,439	3,979
Nursing home (private)	95,269	3,342
Home health (public)	296,927	1,742
Home health (private)	29,644	498
Public cash subsidies	426,938	1,277

Notes:

- Public nursing costs: calculated taking into consideration the number of people who receive the benefit directly in kind and those who receive it through the service-linked benefit (i.e., through a private provider because a public place is not available). In both cases, the average co-payment percentage borne by users has been deducted.
- Private nursing costs: includes (i) the co-payment borne by users who have a public place and (ii) the cost of the private place in the case of those who have resorted directly to a private nursing home. To estimate the cost of private residences, the number of users of private residences (inf_ssppmmesp2019.pdf (imserso.es)) was multiplied by the average price of a private residence (1,830 euros/month). (inforesidencias.com).
- Public home care costs: calculated considering the number of users who receive the benefit directly and those who receive it through the service-linked benefit (because there is no public provider available). The (average) number of hours was multiplied by the price and the (average) co-payment borne by the user was deducted.
- Private home care costs: includes two components: (i) the co-payment borne by those who receive the public service and (ii) the cost of private home care for those who opt for this type of care and pay 100 percent of the cost of the service.
- The cost of public cash subsidies has been estimated as the product of the amount of the benefit associated with the average distribution by degree of dependency (2019—Instituto de Mayores y Servicios Sociales (imserso.es)), discounting the co-payment (according to the economic capacity of the users). In addition, the cost associated with the payment of caregivers' social security contributions has been included.
- Average co-payment and average prices for public nursing home and public home care from: Servicios sociales dirigidos a personas mayores en España—Instituto de Mayores y Servicios Sociales (imserso.es).
- Average cost of private home care for those who opt for private home care has been estimated using SHARE (wave 7).
- Official data for number of recipients of home health and number of residents in nursing homes from 639265f6–27c5–4a86–6bfb-ab0a4a0b8c07 (imserso.es).
- The percentage of service-linked benefit recipients who have used it for home health is 18.62 percent (of total home health recipients), and the percentage of service-linked benefit recipients who have used it for nursing home is 45.89 percent (of total nursing home recipients). These percentages have been obtained from estudio_evaluacion_saad_completo.pdf (mdsocialesa2030.gob.es).

Source: IMSERSO, SHARE (wave 7) and Inforesidencias. Figures are expressed in 2019 euros.

sible to find a public provider), and discounting the co-payment borne by the user. Private cost for nursing homes includes the expenditure derived from people who opt for a place in a private nursing home (paying 100 percent of the cost of the service) plus the co-payment borne by users of public places.

Public cost for home care refers to public sector spending on home care (direct provision and service-linked provision, when it is not possible to find a public provider), and discounting the co-payment borne by the user. Private cost for home care incorporates the expenditure derived from people who choose to receive home care from a private company (paying 100 percent of the cost of the service) plus the co-payment borne by the users of public places.

We have also estimated the cost associated with public cash benefits. The cost of public cash subsidies has been estimated as the product of the amount of the benefit by the average distribution by degree of dependency, discounting the co-payment (according to the economic capacity of the users). In addition, the cost associated with the payment of caregivers' social security contributions has been included.

In 2019 and for public services, the total number of nursing home users was 250,708, with a total spending of 7,321 million euros. Spending on formal home care amounted to 1,742 million euros for 296,927 users.

In relation to the receipt of private services, it is estimated that there are 95,269 nursing home beneficiaries and 29,644 home care or health beneficiaries, which represents a cost to families of 3,342 and 498 million euros, respectively.

The cost associated with public cash benefits amounts to 1,277 million euros.

To obtain the valuation of informal care shown in table 9.15, we have proceeded in the following steps. In Cost I estimation, the Wage Structure Survey has been used to estimate a wage equation using as explanatory

Table 9.15 Informal care valuation, Spain, 2019

	I	II
Valuation (millions €)	5,096	11,642.81
Total Hours Informal Help (millions)	1,252.05	1,252.05
Probability of Working	0.37	0.37
Wage * Probability of Working	4.07	
Wage if Working	11	
Observations	3,280	3,280

Notes: Hours of informal caregiving per week from European Quality of Life Survey (2016). Average wage of working caregivers (€11/hour) from Wage Structure Survey, 2019).

Average wage of a formal caregiver: €8.31/hour (table 9.11).

Cost I: the Wage Structure Survey has been used to estimate a wage equation using as explanatory variables: age, sex, level of education, and region of residence. These same characteristics have been used to estimate the probability of being working, in this case, using the Labor Force Survey. These results were applied to SHARE to obtain the predicted probability of working and the predicted wage of the caregivers. Next, we obtained the average predicted unconditional wage of caregivers as the average of the predicted probability of work multiplied by the predicted wage conditional on working. Finally, the value of informal care is equal to the product of the predicted unconditional times the total hours of informal care.

Cost II: First, the complementary of the predicted probability of working for caregivers was multiplied by the wage of formal caregivers. Second, the predicted unconditional wage was added to this result, and finally, the sum was multiplied by the total hours of informal care.

variables: age, sex, level of education, and region of residence. The same characteristics have been used to estimate the probability of being working, in this case, using the Labor Force Survey. These results have been applied to SHARE to obtain the predicted probability of working and the predicted wage of the caregivers. Next, we have obtained the average predicted unconditional wage of caregivers as the average of the predicted probability of work multiplied by the predicted wage conditional on working. Finally, the value of informal care is equal to the product of the predicted unconditional wage multiplied by the total hours of informal care.

In estimation Cost II, first, we used the complementary of the predicted probability of working for caregivers multiplied by the wage of formal caregivers. Second, the predicted unconditional wage was added to this result, and finally, the sum was multiplied by the total hours of informal care.

The total number of informal caregiving hours in 2019 amounts to 1,252 million hours. The total cost (Cost I) amounts to 5,096 million euros (2019), which is 0.50 percent of GDP. For Cost II, the cost of informal care amounts to 11,643 million €, 0.93 percent of GDP.

Comparing this amount with the volume of spending on cash benefits (€1,277 million; 0.10 percent of GDP), it is clear that the cost of informal care is between five and nine times higher than the financial compensation that the Spanish public long-term care system allocates to caregivers.

In table 9.16, we have proceeded to obtain the total cost of LTC and also differentiating between public and private funding. We report figures in euros (top panel) and as a fraction of the Spanish GDP (bottom panel). The total cost of nursing home care amounts to 7,321 million euros (54 percent public and 46 percent private), which represent 0.59 percent of the Spanish GDP. The total cost of home care amounts to 2,240 million euros (77.27 percent public and 22.23 percent private) or 0.18 percent of the Spanish GDP. Adding the informal costs by both methods, we obtain a total cost of 15,824 million € (cost method I) and 21,204 million € (cost method II), which represents between 1.27 percent and 1.70 percent of GDP (1.245.513 million € in 2019).

The distribution between public and private costs is, according to method I, 36 percent (public) and 64 percent (private), and according to method II, 27 percent (public) and 73 percent (private). And the distribution by care type according to method I is 46 percent (nursing home), 14 percent (home care) and 40 percent (informal care), and according to method II, 35 percent (nursing home), 11 percent (home care), and 55 percent (informal care).

9.6 Conclusions

Spain's access to LTC is universal, though LTC funding can vary, depending on individuals' needs and means via cost sharing and regional budgets. Prior to the implementation of SAAD, caregiving benefits were restricted to

Table 9.16 Total costs by type of care and source, Spain, 2019

A. *Millions of euros*			
Care Type	Source	Cost I (Annual)	Cost II (Annual)
Nursing Home	Public	3,979	3,979
	Private	3,342	3,342
	All	7,321	7,321
Home Care	Public	1,742	1,742
	Private	498	498
	All	2,240	2,240
Informal Care	Private	5,096	11,643
Total	Public	5,721	5,721
	Private	10,103	15,483
	All	15,824	21,204

B. *In percentage of GDP (2019)*			
Care Type	Source	Cost I (Annual)	Cost II (Annual)
Nursing Home	Public	0.32	0.32
	Private	0.27	0.27
	All	0.59	0.59
Home Care	Public	0.14	0.14
	Private	0.04	0.04
	All	0.18	0.18
Informal Care	Private	0.50	0.93
Total	Public	0.46	0.46
	Private	0.81	1.24
	All	1.27	1.70

Notes: See notes for tables 9.14 and 9.15 for an explanation of formal and informal costs′ valuation.
For comparison purposes, public expenditure on cash subsidies amounts to €1,277 million (discounting co-payment). GDP (2019): 1,245,513 million euros. For comparison purposes, the percentage of cash subsidies with respect to GDP amounts to 0.10 percent.

means-tested allowances provided by underfunded local government budgets, as well as means-tested disability allowances granted only for a degree of disability greater than 65 percent.

The provision of care for older age adults in Spain has substantially developed after the introduction of SAAD in 2007, which has expanded care. We focus on the study of the relationship between age, disabilities, and well-being. We also try to analyze the characteristic of the workforce and the caregivers.

Based on the estimates reported in this chapter, we can reach the following conclusions:

- LTC expenditure as percent of GDP has increased from 0.5 percent (2003) to nearly 0.9 percent (2019), mostly due to the introduction and development of the SAAD.

- The Spanish dependency system has been largely based on a subsidization of informal caregivers. Spending on cash benefits (net of co-payments) represents 0.10 percent of GDP (€1,277 million) in 2019.
- Private insurance for long-term care plays a negligible role.
- LTC spending increases with need and with individual income, however, need explains mainly use of publicly funded care, while income drives privately funded care.
- The percentage of the population receiving some type of care represents 13.3 percent of the 65+ population and 22.2 percent of the 85+ population. In both groups, the percentage receiving care increases with the number of ADLs, reaching 43.7 percent (65+) and 49.9 percent (85+) for 3 or more ADLs.
- Having multiple limitations (three or more) for daily life activities (and at older ages) has an impact on having good health. However, 9.4 percent of those aged 65 and over report having good health, while 8.5 percent of those aged 85 and up report having good health. Individuals with no limitations, on the other hand, exhibit a much higher percentage of people reporting good or very good health: 34.3 percent for those 65+, and 20.1 percent for those 85+.
- In the 65+ age group, the prevalence of depression is five percentage points higher when comparing individuals with three or more limitations (35.4 percent) with respect to individuals without limitations (29 percent). For the 85+ age group, the percentage with depression among those with no limitations and those with three or more limitations is similar (35.3 percent and 34.8 percent, respectively).
- Finally, the estimated annual total cost using a conservative cost method is 15,824 million euros (with approximately 36 percent of public expenditure and 64 percent of private expenditure), and with a less conservative method it is much higher, 21,204 million euro (with approx. 27 percent of public and 73 percent of private expenditure).

Data Sources

SHARE Spain wave 7, 2017.
Labor Force Survey (EPA-INE), second quarter 2017 and 2019.
Muestra Continua de Vidas Laborales, 2018.
EDAD 2020, survey in 2021.
Institute for Older People and Social Services (IMSERSO), 2019.
National Health Survey 2020, survey 2019–2020.
Eurostat and OECDstat.
European Quality of Life Survey, 2016.
Quarterly Survey of Labor Cost (INE, 2018).

References

Costa-Font, J., and C. Vilaplana-Prieto. 2017. "Does the Expansion of Public Long-Term Care Funding Affect Saving Behavior?" *Fiscal Studies* 38 (3): 417–43.

Costa-Font, J., and C. Vilaplana-Prieto. 2022a. "Caregiving Subsidies and Spousal Early Retirement Intentions." *Journal of Pension Economics & Finance* 1–40.

Costa-Font, J., and C. Vilaplana-Prieto. 2022b. "Mental Health Effects of Caregivers Respite: Subsidies or Supports?" *Journal of the Economics of Ageing* 23: 100398.

Costa-Font, J., and C. Vilaplana-Prieto. 2022c. "'Investing' in Care for Old Age? An Examination of Long-Term Care Expenditure Dynamics and Its Spillovers." *Empirical Economics* 64: 1–30.

Costa-Font, J., S. Jiménez Martin, and A. Viola. 2021. "Fatal Underfunding? Explaining COVID-19 Mortality in Spanish Nursing Homes." *Journal of Aging and Health* 33 (7–8): 607–17.

Costa-Font, J., and C. Vilaplana-Prieto. 2020. "'More Than One Red Herring'? Heterogeneous Effects of Ageing on Health Care Utilization." *Health Economics* 29: 8–29.

Costa-Font, J., S. Jimenez-Martin, and C. Vilaplana-Prieto. 2018. "Does Long-Term Care Subsidization Reduce Hospital Admissions and Utilization?" *Journal of Health Economics* 58: 43–66.

Costa-Font, J., S. Jiménez-Martín, and C. Vilaplana-Prieto. 2022a. "Do Public Caregiving Subsidies and Supports Affect the Provision of Care and Transfers?" *Journal of Health Economics* 84: 102639.

IMSERSO. 2021. "Las personas mayores en España. Informe 2018." Instituto de Mayores y Servicios Sociales, Ministerio de Derechos Sociales y Agenda 2030.

Jiménez-Martín, S., and A. Viola. 2022. "Observatorio de dependencia. Cuarto Informe." Studies on the Spanish Economy, eee2022–16. Madrid: FEDEA.

Jiménez-Martín, S., and A. Viola. 2019. "La asistencia residencial en España y COVID-19." Estudios sobre la Economía Española—2020/20. Madrid: FEDEA.

Oliva-Moreno J., M. Trapero-Bertran, L. M. Peña-Longobardo, and R. Del Pozo-Rubio. 2017. "The Valuation of Informal Care in Cost-of-Illness Studies: A Systematic Review." *Pharmacoeconomics* 35 (3): 331–45.

Rodríguez Cabrero, G., V. Marbán Gallego, M. Aguilar Hendrickson, A. Huete García, A. Jiménez Lara, et al. 2022. "Informe de Evaluación del sistema de promoción de la autonomía personal y atención a las personas en situación de dependencia (SAAD)." Ministerio de Asuntos Sociales.

10

Long-Term Care in the United States

Jonathan Gruber and Kathleen McGarry

The population of the United States, as with the rest of the world, is aging rapidly. Although by most measures the United States is "younger" than many countries in this volume, it faces the highest per capita health care costs in the world (OECD 2022). Furthermore, the most rapid growth in the older population in the United States is among those ages 85 or older, the group for whom health care costs are the greatest and who are most likely in need of long-term care (CMS 2014). Figure 10.1 shows the rising share of the population ages 65 or older, while figure 10.2 highlights the fact that the most rapid growth is among those ages 85 or older. Seen another way, in 2020, in only 3 of the 51 US states (and District of Colombia) was more than one-fifth of the population above age 65. By 2050, the number of such states is projected to be 43.[1]

Population aging has a variety of implications for economic activity and for government finances, affecting issues ranging from labor force productiv-

Jonathan Gruber is the Ford Professor of Economics and head of the Economics Department at the Massachusetts Institute of Technology, and a research associate of the National Bureau of Economic Research.

Kathleen McGarry is a professor in and chair of the Department of Economics at Stony Brook University, a professor of economics at the University of California, Los Angeles, and a research associate of the National Bureau of Economic Research.

We thank Charlie Hanzel for excellent research assistance and Gopi Shah Goda and the other participants in the NBER's International Long-term Care project for helpful comments and suggestions. We also gratefully acknowledge support for this research from the National Institute on Aging of the National Institutes of Health under grant number P30-AG012810. For acknowledgments, sources of research support, and disclosure of the authors' material financial relationships, if any, please see https://www.nber.org/books-and-chapters/long-term-care-around-world/long-term-care-united-states.

1. Calculations derived by applying estimated national population growth by age group from Ortman et al. (2014) to population levels by age observed in the 2018 American Communities Survey.

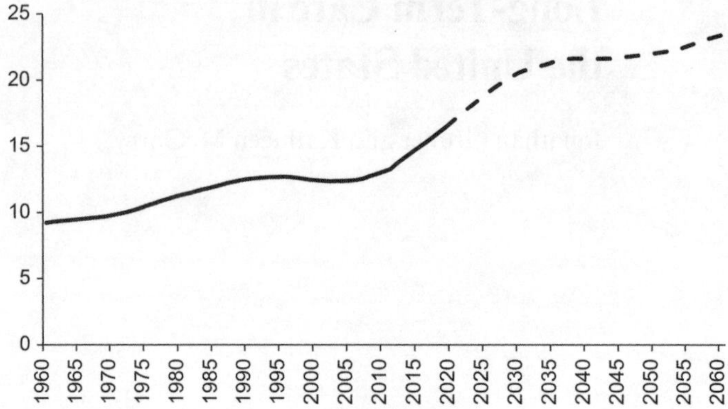

Fig. 10.1 Percentage of population ages 65 or older, United States, 1960–2060
Source: OECD Population Projections (2022)

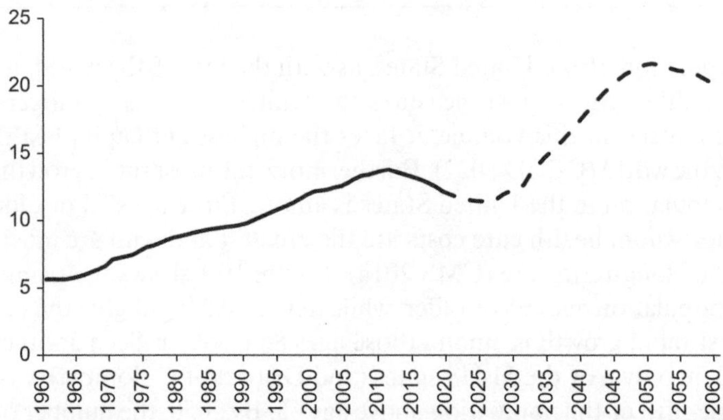

Fig. 10.2 Percentage of 65+ population that is age 85 or older, United States, 1960–2060
Source: OECD Population Projections (2022)

ity to public pensions to the costs of treating expensive acute disease. But one of the most important issues is the cost of long-term care: the costs of providing for those elderly who face limitations in caring for themselves. Nearly 30 percent of those ages 65 or older, and 60 percent of those age 85 or older, report at least some limitation in their ability to conduct daily activities. In the coming decades, as an increasing share of the population is above age 65 and the "oldest old" (those aged 85+) comprise a rising share of the elderly, the greater prevalence of limitations in daily activities will mean increased care needs for the population.

While the types of long-term care needed and associated expenses run the gamut, here we follow past practices and organize our discussion around two main categories of care: institutional care in nursing homes (or skilled nursing facilities) and home care. In 2018 spending for nursing homes totaled approximately $171 billion, while home care costs totaled $108 billion. As large as these expenditures are, they ignore an equally important cost of care, that being the implicit cost of informal care provided by millions of Americans to their elderly relatives and friends. A proper accounting of costs must include these costs as well.

In this chapter, we provide an overview of the long-term care system in the United States. The core data that we use for this exercise are drawn from the Health and Retirement Study (HRS). The HRS is a nationally representative panel study of individuals ages 50 or older and their spouses or partners. The survey collects detailed information on the health, economic well-being, and family structure of its respondents, making possible a thorough analysis of aging and long-term care in the United States.[2]

Our analysis proceeds in three steps. First, we explore the impact of functional limitations on the financial well-being of the elderly. In doing so we focus on the well-known measures of limitations, limitations with respect to activities of daily living (ADLs, activities such as toileting and bathing) as well as limitations with respect to instrumental activities of daily living (IADLs, activities such as cooking or shopping). We show that those who are older and in worse health have fewer financial resources as measured in several dimensions. We also show, unsurprisingly, that the intensity of care rises sharply with age and with the number of limitations. Finally, we document that the resources of most elderly in the United States are insufficient to finance these ongoing long-term care needs. It is clear that without public assistance, the elderly in the United States would be largely unable to finance the long-term care that they are now receiving.

We then turn to a discussion of how long-term care is provided in the United States. We document the division in financing between public and private sources, including the presence of a small private long-term care insurance market. We then show the distribution of care across types by age and degree of limitation, highlighting the growing use of both formal home care and nursing homes as individuals age and become more disabled. We discuss the workforce engaged in long-term care, focusing on their low level of pay.

Finally, we return to undertake a full calculation of the cost of long-term care for the elderly in the United States—including the costs of informal care. We use alternative methods of valuing the time spent in informal care to show that the costs of informal care are enormous, amounting to 27–40 percent of the total cost of long-term care in the United States. In total, spending on long-term care for the elderly amounts to almost 2 percent of US GDP when these informal care costs are incorporated.

2. At times we supplement these data with information obtained from other sources.

10.1 Aging, Disability, and Well-Being

10.1.1 Sample and Definitions

The primary data for our analyses come from the Health and Retirement Study. The first interview wave of the HRS was administered in 1992 to a sample of individuals born between 1931–1941 and their spouses or partners; interviews for this cohort have been repeated every two years. A second cohort of older Americans, those born before 1924 or earlier, was begun in 1993 with a follow-up survey administered in 1995. This second cohort was merged with the original sample in 1998 and two new cohorts were added at this time—one to fill in the missing interim birth years (1924–1930) and the second to refresh the sample with a younger cohort (1942–1947). Since 1998, new cohorts spanning ages 51–56 have been added every six years to keep the sample approximately population representative of the older US population ages 50 or older. The HRS collects information from respondents across a variety of topics, ranging from demographics and family structure to income and wealth to health and long-term care needs.

We use data from the 2018 survey and limit our analysis to those ages 65 or older in that year. Although the HRS does not include nursing home residents in its initial sampling frame, it does follow panel members who were previously living in the community into nursing homes. Our data thus do not include information on individuals who were living in a nursing home prior to the age at which they first entered the survey,[3] but such individuals constitute a very small fraction of nursing home residents. We are therefore able to conduct most of our analyses on all elderly individuals, both community-dwelling and in institutions.[4]

The key measures of health used in our analysis are based on reported functional limitations. These limitations include limitations related to activities of daily living (ADLs) and to instrumental activities of daily living (IADLs). We use six ADL measures: dressing, bathing, eating, toileting, getting in and out of bed, and walking across a room. We also use five IADL measures: using a telephone, cooking a hot meal, shopping for groceries, taking medications as prescribed, and managing money. For each of these 11 items, the survey asks respondents whether they have difficulty with the activity due to a health or memory problem that they expect to

3. Respondents in the oldest cohort were 70 years old or older when they entered the survey, so that cohort is missing many in that age range who were in a nursing home. However, because our analyses are based on data 25 years after that cohort was first interviewed, there are likely to be few such individuals in the sample.

4. We exclude the non-elderly in nursing homes. In 2018, only 16.9 percent of nursing home residents were under age 65 and almost half of these residents were short-stay residents, staying only temporarily for post-acute care and primarily residing in the community (Sengupta et al. 2022).

last more than three months. If they answer in the affirmative, we consider them impaired.

10.1.2 Aging, Disability, and Well-Being

Table 10.1 shows the distribution of limitations by age. The majority of those ages 65 or older have no limitations, while 9 percent of the sample has no ADL limitations but at least one IADL limitation, and 20 percent has a limitation with respect to at least one ADL. Among the oldest old (those ages 85 or older) 40 percent are free from any limitation, 18 percent have no ADL limitations but at least one IADL limitation, and just over 40 percent have at least one ADL limitation.

Table 10.2 illustrates the frequency of the various types of IADL and ADL limitations, both unconditionally and conditional on having difficulty with at least one such activity. For those with one or more IADLs, difficulty shopping for groceries is the most commonly reported problem, followed by managing money. For those with one or more ADL limitations, difficulty getting dressed is the most frequently reported, although taking a bath is the most common limitation among those aged 85+.

We further explore the relationship between limitations and well-being in table 10.3, which reports the emotional and physical health status of the respondents by age and degree of limitation. We include measures of subjective health status, retirement satisfaction, and self-reported feelings of being depressed. Among those 65 or older, 73 percent of the full sample report themselves to be in good or better physical health, while unsurprisingly, just 30 percent of those with three or more limitations do so. The differences are

Table 10.1 **Share with ADLs by age, United States, 2018**

	65+	85+
0 ADLs & 0 IADLs	0.710	0.399
0 ADLs & 1+ IADLs	0.089	0.176
1 ADL	0.083	0.144
2 ADLs	0.040	0.086
3 ADLs	0.028	0.058
4 ADLs	0.014	0.026
5 ADLs	0.016	0.043
6 ADLs	0.020	0.070
Any ADLs	0.201	0.425
Any IADLs	0.214	0.515
Observations	8,970	1,322

Source: Data are from the RAND-HRS (2018). Weights are used to include individuals in nursing homes. ADLs include walking across room, dressing, bathing, eating, going to bed, and using the toilet. IADLs include using a telephone, managing money, taking medications as prescribed, shopping for groceries, and cooking a hot meal. Individuals that report not doing these activities are also included as having difficulty with them.

Table 10.2 **Distribution of limitations with specific ADLs/IADLs, United States, 2018**

	65+ All	65+ Conditional	85+ All	85+ Conditional
		Panel 1: IADLs		
IADL—Use a Phone	0.062	0.288	0.205	0.398
IADL—Manage Money	0.110	0.513	0.314	0.609
IADL—Take Meds as Prescr.	0.044	0.205	0.135	0.262
IADL—Shop for Groceries	0.132	0.615	0.361	0.701
IADL—Prepare a Meal	0.116	0.544	0.348	0.676
Observations	8,970	2,195	1,322	662
		Panel 2: ADLs		
ADL—Use the Toilet	0.073	0.363	0.162	0.381
ADL—Get Dressed	0.116	0.578	0.238	0.560
ADL—Take a Bath	0.093	0.465	0.264	0.623
ADL—Walk Across a Room	0.095	0.472	0.250	0.588
ADL—Eat	0.047	0.236	0.146	0.345
ADL—Get In/Out of Bed	0.076	0.379	0.162	0.380
Observations	8,970	2,033	1322	557

Source: Data are from the RAND-HRS (2018). Weights are used to include individuals in nursing homes. Column 1 shows the share of the sample that report having difficulty with each activity, while column 2 shows the share of people with at least one IADL (panel 1) or at least one ADL (panel 2) who report having difficulty with each activity. Individuals who report not doing these activities are also included as having difficulty with them.

Table 10.3 **Well-being for those 65+ and 85+ by ADL limitations, United States, 2018**

	65+	65+, 3+ Lims	85+	85+ 3+ Lims
Reports good or better health status	0.73	0.30	0.63	0.41
Very satisfied with retirement	0.55	0.33	0.55	0.43
Depressed much of time	0.10	0.29	0.12	0.19
Observations	8,970	1,353	1,322	460

Notes: Data are from the RAND-HRS (2018). Our Limitations Index runs from 0–12 and is the number of ADLs/IADLs that are either difficult or not done from eating, bathing, dressing, using the toilet, walking across a room, and getting in/out of bed (ADLs) + using a telephone, managing money, taking medications as prescribed, shopping for groceries, and cooking a hot meal (IADLs). Because retirement satisfaction is only asked of those who are retired, the sample is restricted to those who are retired. The survey asks whether respondents have felt depressed much of the time over the last week. The poverty measure is produced by RAND to include income from all household members. Combined respondents/nursing home weights from RAND-HRS are used in all calculations.

Table 10.4 Income and wealth distribution, United States, 2018

	Income		Wealth	
	65+	85+	65+	85+
5th Percentile	9,000	7,000	0	0
10th Percentile	13,000	11,000	2,000	0
25th Percentile	21,000	17,000	57,000	37,000
50th Percentile	35,000	25,000	217,000	166,000
75th Percentile	58,000	43,000	618,000	535,000
90th Percentile	93,000	68,000	1,345,000	1,358,000
95th Percentile	130,000	93,000	2,204,000	2,109,000
Mean	52,000	42,000	612,000	615,000
Observations	8,971	1,323	8,971	1,323

Notes: Data are from the RAND-HRS and HRS Core (2018). Weights are used to include individuals in nursing homes. All income estimates are post-tax. We use the NBER's Taxsim program to estimate post-tax income based on family characteristics and each household's income sources. All values are adjusted to July 2019 dollars.

less stark for retirement satisfaction, but particularly strong with regard to feeling depressed, with just 10 percent of the elderly but 30 percent of those with three or more limitations reportedly feeling depressed much of the time. In every case, those who are older and more disabled are faring less well.

10.1.3 Financial Resources

To explore the potential financial implications of age and disability, tables 10.4 and 10.5 show the distribution of income and wealth by age category and the distribution of income by degree of limitation. We use the RAND-HRS imputed values for total household wealth and total household income, normalizing each measure using the OECD equivalence scale for comparison across other chapters in this volume.[5]

Both the income and wealth distributions are quite skewed with the mean values substantially higher than the medians. Because most of those in this age group are no longer working and thus have zero earnings, the distribution of income is less wide and less skewed than that for wealth. We also note slight differences by age, with lower income and wealth among the older cohort. The differences are less than one might imagine because of

5. A household is defined as the respondent and their spouse/partner (if any), so the equivalence scale simply involves dividing income and wealth of two-person households by 1.5. Total income consists of earnings, pension income, business income, government transfers (including Social Security), and an "other income" category. It does not include withdrawals from retirement accounts or cash transfers from family members. Total household wealth includes the value of a home and other real estate, retirement accounts, vehicles, financial wealth (including assets in defined contribution retirement plans, e.g., 401ks and IRAs), and an "other wealth" category, net of mortgages and other debt. It does not include estimated defined benefit pension wealth.

Table 10.5 **Income and wealth distribution by limitations for 65+ population, United States, 2018**

	0 ADLs & 0 IADLs	0 ADLs & 1+ IADLs	1 ADL	2 ADLs	3+ ADLs	Total
			Panel 1: Income			
<50% Median HH Income	0.142	0.204	0.256	0.353	0.404	0.186
50–100% Median HH Income	0.296	0.375	0.363	0.334	0.344	0.314
100–150% Median HH Income	0.221	0.185	0.204	0.127	0.127	0.205
150–200% Median HH Income	0.135	0.094	0.086	0.089	0.052	0.119
200%+ Median HH Income	0.206	0.142	0.090	0.098	0.073	0.176
Total	0.710	0.089	0.083	0.040	0.077	—
Observations	6,043	894	841	415	777	8,970
			Panel 2: Wealth			
<50% Median HH Wealth	0.287	0.414	0.461	0.555	0.625	0.349
50–100% Median HH Wealth	0.157	0.142	0.163	0.120	0.102	0.151
100–150% Median HH Wealth	0.094	0.104	0.104	0.075	0.055	0.092
150–200% Median HH Wealth	0.076	0.063	0.062	0.047	0.047	0.071
200%+ Median HH Wealth	0.386	0.277	0.210	0.204	0.171	0.338
Total	0.710	0.089	0.083	0.040	0.077	—
Observations	6,043	894	841	415	777	8,970

Notes: Data are from the RAND-HRS and HRS Core (2018). HRS household income estimates are post-tax, estimated using Taxsim based upon household characteristics and income components, and includes only respondent and spouse income. Our ADL Index runs from 0–6 and is the number of ADLs that are either difficult or not done from eating, bathing, dressing, using the toilet, walking across a room, and getting in/out of bed. IADLs include using a telephone, managing money, taking medications as prescribed, shopping for groceries, and cooking a hot meal. Each cell reports the share of respondents in the respective ADL category who are in that row's income group. Combined respondents/nursing home weights are used in all HRS Core calculations. The median household income and wealth are for the 65+ population, calculated in the HRS. The median is roughly $35,000 per year for income and $217,000 for wealth when adjusted to 2019 dollars.

selection in who among the 65 or older population survives to age 85. The similarity across the age bands is most pronounced at the upper portions of the distributions, and average wealth is actually higher for those aged 85 or older, wherein selection dominates cohort differences in lifetime earnings.

There are, however, enormous disparities in income by the degree of limitation. To illustrate the pattern, panel 1 of table 10.5 divides the sample by income and by number of limitations. Each column sums to 100 percent, showing the distribution of income among those with the corresponding number of limitations. For example, among those with three or more ADLs, 40 percent have incomes below the median, while only 7.3 percent have incomes greater than twice median income. There is a clear negative correlation between the degree of limitations and income. When looking at the lowest limitation category (those with no ADLs or IADLs), only 14 percent of the sample have incomes below 50 percent of the median, while 21 percent have incomes above twice the median. More generally, the share of people with less than 50 percent of the median income is rising consistently with the number of limitations, while the share whose incomes are in categories greater than the median is declining.

A similar pattern emerges in panel 2 of table 10.5, which examines the relationship between wealth and limitations. As before, limitations are negatively correlated with wealth—63 percent of those with three or more ADL limitations have wealth below 50 percent of median wealth, while only 17 percent have wealth greater than twice the median. In contrast, only 29 percent of those with no ADL or IADL limitations have wealth below 50 percent of the median, while 39 percent have wealth greater than twice the median. Thus, the need for care appears to be greatest among those least able to afford that care.

10.1.4 Care Received

With this understanding of the prevalence of long-term care need and its association with well-being and economic resources, we next examine the use of various types of long-term care. Because questions about the receipt of home care in the HRS are only asked if someone reports *difficulty* with at least one of the 11 ADL/IADLs, some forms of home care may be missed if they are not provided in conjunction with help with an ADL/IADL. This care could include, for example, care focused on monitoring vital signs, dispensing medications and injections, physical therapy or rehabilitation, and wound care, provided that the respondent can manage the listed ADLs and IADLs themselves. We expect that the majority of such care would be temporary in nature and not truly long-term care as such.

For each person who reports difficulty with an ADL or IADL in the survey, a follow-up question is asked about whether anyone ever helps them with that activity and if so, who helps them. After going through all 11 activities, the respondent is asked to report their relationship to each helper, whether the helper was paid, and the total number of hours of care this helper provided in the last month. Helpers can be professional caregivers or relatives or friends of the respondent such as a spouse or child. We provide summary figures here and explore the nature of long-term care received in more detail in section 10.2.

Table 10.6 shows the distribution of weekly hours of care received for both formal and informal care. The median number of hours of care received is 13, but the mean is 30 hours and 10 percent of the population receives well over 100 hours. Care needs are only somewhat higher for the oldest old, conditional on receiving home care. The median number of hours of care for this group is 14, the mean is 39 and the top 10 percent of the distribution receives 114 or more hours of care.

Much of this care is provided informally by family members. Just 2 percent of our sample receive some formal home care compared to 12 percent

Table 10.6 **Distribution of hours of help received per week, United States, 2018**

	65+	85+
5th Percentile	1	1
10th Percentile	1	1
25th Percentile	3	4
50th Percentile	13	14
75th Percentile	36	57
90th Percentile	107	114
95th Percentile	116	128
Mean	30	39
1 Hour per Day or Less	0.39	0.35
5 Hour per Day or More	0.26	0.33
Observations	1,410	389

Notes: Health and Retirement Study (HRS), 2018. Respondent weights are used for all calculations. Nursing home residents are automatically excluded from all calculations. Hours include both formal and informal care received from helpers who assist with ADLs, IADLs, and managing money because of a health problem. Hours of help from each helper are limited to 16 hours per day to allow for 8 hours of rest. Respondents could provide the number of days either overall in the last month, per week, or as every day. In the first case, the days per month was divided by 4.35 (365/7 ∗ 12).

who receive informal care. Formal care is expensive, with the median cost of home care workers at roughly $23 (Genworth 2019), while informal care can represent a substantial burden for caregivers, taking both an emotional and physical toll. We discuss these costs more below.

The primary alternative to home care is nursing home care. While nursing home residence is far less common than home care, and typically less preferred by the individual, it is often the only alternative—particularly when around-the-clock care is needed. Nursing homes are also very expensive. The median annual cost of a private nursing home room in 2019 was $102,000 (Genworth 2019), although in contrast to the measure of the cost of home care, the cost of nursing home care includes room and board, as well as any assistance with long-term care needs. While many nursing home stays are of short duration, data from 2018 indicate that 56 percent of nursing home residents had stays of over 100 days and the average length of stay was 485 days (Sengupta et al. 2022). With respect to the HRS sample, table 10.7 shows that just over 10 percent of those currently in nursing homes have been there for fewer than 100 days, with the average and median length of stay of over 450 days. (Note that these statistics are not completed stays, but rather stays in progress at the time of the 2018 HRS interview.)

As is clear, the cost of any type of care is sizeable, and this burden is readily apparent when comparing these costs to the financial resources of the elderly. The average recipient of formal home care receives 30 hours of care per week; over a full year, these costs would total over $35,000. This amount

Table 10.7 **Distribution of nursing home stay lengths, United States, 2018**

Average # Days since Entry	474
Median # Days since Entry	456
10th Percentile # Days since Entry	120
90th Percentile # Days since Entry	792
Share in N.H. 2+ Years	0.136
Observations	*155*

Notes: Health and Retirement Study (HRS) 2018. Respondent weights are used for all calculations. We use the RAND nursing home residence and duration variables but exclude those who report being in a nursing home but are given a respondent weight by the HRS rather than a nursing home resident weight, as these individuals were identified by the HRS as living in a different type of residential care setting.

is greater than the incomes of one-half of the individuals in our sample, and more than the net wealth of roughly one-fifth of respondents.

Nursing homes are even more unaffordable; the median annual cost of a private nursing home room is greater than the incomes of almost 90 percent of the elderly and greater than nearly 95 percent of those 85 or older. In fact, the median price of a nursing home is greater than the total wealth of approximately one-third of the elderly, and two years in a nursing home would exhaust the wealth of almost one-half of this population. While we expect the elderly to be spending down assets in retirement, even when drawing on wealth, few in the sample have the resources needed to support a long-term nursing home stay. Moreover, as we documented, those with the greatest need for long-term care in activities of daily living are also those with the most limited resources to purchase this care.

It is clear from this discussion that the current distribution of long-term care receipt, or anything like it, would be unaffordable if paid out of pocket. This leads naturally to the question of how long-term care is financed. We therefore turn next to an examination of the long-term care system in the United States, discussing the ways in which public programs and informal care may shield the elderly from bearing the full cost of care and quantifying the total cost of these supports and what those costs might amount to for the country as a whole.

10.2 Long-Term Care System in the United States

Formal long-term care costs comprise a rapidly growing portion of the US health care system, rising from less than 1 percent of GDP in 1990 to more than 1.5 percent by 2011 (figure 10.3). However, since that time, costs have been relatively flat in terms of percent of GDP as state and federal governments worked to find less costly pathways to care.

Despite the dramatic cost of long-term care, particularly relative to the resources of most elderly, few individuals have private long-term care insur-

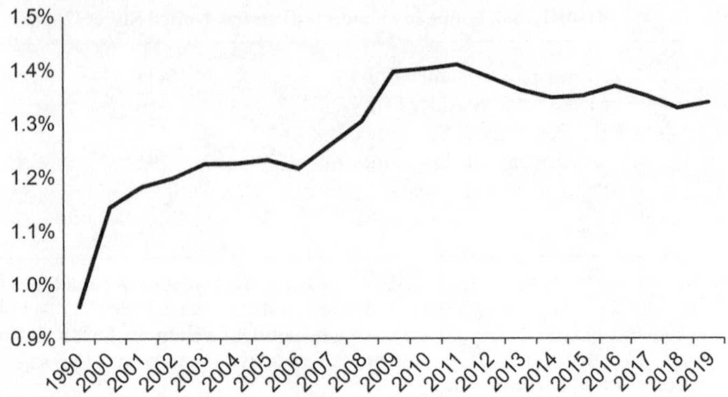

Fig. 10.3 Share of GDP spent on long-term care, United States, 1990–2019

Notes: In this figure, long-term care includes total spending on home health care,and nursing care facilities and continuing care retirement communities.

Sources: Centers for Medicare and Medicaid (CMS) National Health Expenditures data; St. Louis FRED Annual GDP data.

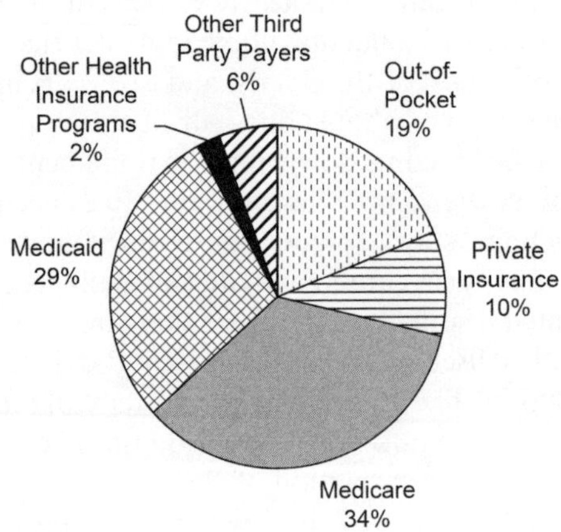

Fig. 10.4 Percent of LTC financing by source, United States, 2018

Notes: In this figure, long-term care includes total spending on home health care,and nursing care facilities and continuing care retirement communities. Spending is adjusted by the share of recipients who are under 65 from Sengupta et al. (2022), with the assumption that all of the under 65 recipients are receiving funding from sources other than Medicare, which is not adjusted.

Source: Data are for the year 2018. Centers for Medicare and Medicaid (CMS) National Health Expenditures data.

ance. Instead, much of the cost is borne by government programs. Figure 10.4 shows how this expense is shared across various financing sources. Even absent the existence of a true national long-term care insurance program, the public sector is the primary payer for long-term care. The two main public programs that cover such care are Medicare and Medicaid. Together these two programs pay for 63 percent of formal long-term care costs, while 19 percent of costs are paid for out of pocket and only 10 percent are paid for by private insurance.

10.2.1 Public Insurance: Medicare and Medicaid

Medicare is the universal health insurance program that covers both the elderly and disabled populations, with those aged 65 or older comprising 86 percent of the enrolled population and incurring 79 percent of the program costs (MedPAC 2021).[6] This federally administered program is financed by both a dedicated payroll tax and by general government funds. However, Medicare coverage of long-term care is limited to those needs that are deemed "medically necessary," rather than simple assistance with ADLs or custodial care; coverage of nursing home care is limited to 100 days, with individuals shouldering a substantial co-payment on the portion of the stay beyond 20 days.[7] Essentially, Medicare long-term care is targeted to acute care and not chronic illnesses; much of the spending, for example, is on post-hospital care.

The second public health insurance program, Medicaid, is targeted at low-income individuals and does provide assistance with limitations in daily living. The program provides coverage for eligible elderly individuals as well as for families with children and for the disabled, with again, the majority of benefits going to elderly enrollees. It is financed jointly by the federal and state governments but administered by the individual states. While the federal government specifies certain parameters of the program, eligibility criteria for long-term care—including income limits, asset limits, and care needs—vary by state. For single individuals, income limits in many states are currently just over $2,500 ($2,533) per month,[8] while asset limits are typically $2,000 (several important items—most notably, an owner-occupied home—are excluded from the valuation of assets). Elderly individuals who have incomes above the Medicaid limit may qualify for Medicaid coverage if they have sufficiently high medical expenses that they "spend down" their incomes below a "medically needy" level. The existence of medically needy programs and the eligibility guidelines vary significantly across states.

While Medicare coverage is limited in the number of days of care that can be covered and requires that care be medically necessary, Medicaid will provide indefinite coverage for a variety of needs, including custodial care. As with income and asset limits, states differ in the types of services they cover,

6. See "Medicare Beneficiary Demographics," section 2 of MedPac (2021), https://www.medpac.gov/wp-content/uploads/2021/10/July2021_MedPAC_DataBook_Sec2_SEC.pdf.

7. Because Medicare provides limited coverage of what we think of as long-term care (e.g., assistance with ADLs or IADLs) in the statistics below, we exclude these short-term stays in nursing homes.

8. See American Council on Aging (2021) for additional information on state income eligibility requirements.

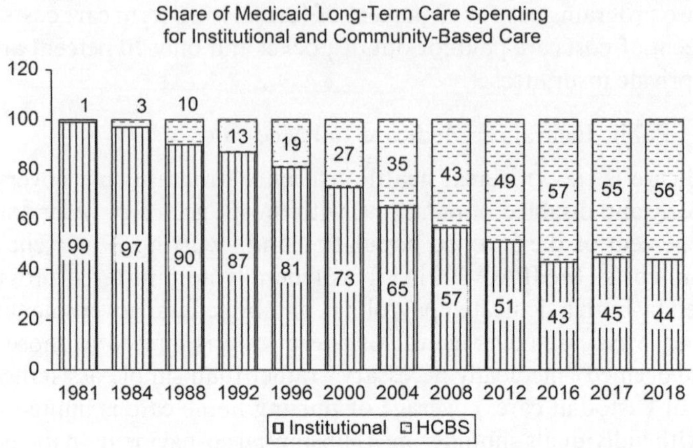

Fig. 10.5 Medicaid spending on institutional care has been gradually replaced by spending on community-based care, United States, 1981–2018

Sources: Eiken et al. (2018) for data from 2016 and before and Murray et al. (2021) for 2017–2018

particularly regarding home care. Although Medicaid guarantees nursing home care for those who qualify on health and income grounds, home care is not guaranteed, and there are often waiting lists for the receipt of such care. In recent decades, the federal government has allowed states to expand Medicaid coverage of home care, expansions that in many instances are authorized through "waiver" programs under which the state applies for coverage of additional services and the federal government shares in the cost. The goal of these programs is to provide services that can reduce institutionalization and allow elderly individuals to remain in the community. These services can include items such as adult day care or respite care, meals, or transportation assistance. Figure 10.5 shows the shift in Medicaid expenses from institutional to home care, with spending on home and community-based services now responsible for over half of Medicaid's long-term care spending.

Figure 10.6 illustrates the further division of financing by formal home care versus nursing home care. Medicare is by far the largest source of financing of home care, paying for almost half of the total costs of formal home care, while Medicaid covers approximately 30 percent. Individuals shoulder only a relatively small fraction of total costs at 10 percent. However, it is important to remember that much of the care covered by Medicare is short-term and associated with an acute event.

In contrast to home care, the cost of nursing home care is financed relatively equally by Medicare and Medicaid—each responsible for close to 30 percent of total costs. Private expenditures, either private insurance or individual out-of-pocket payments, are each responsible for less than one-

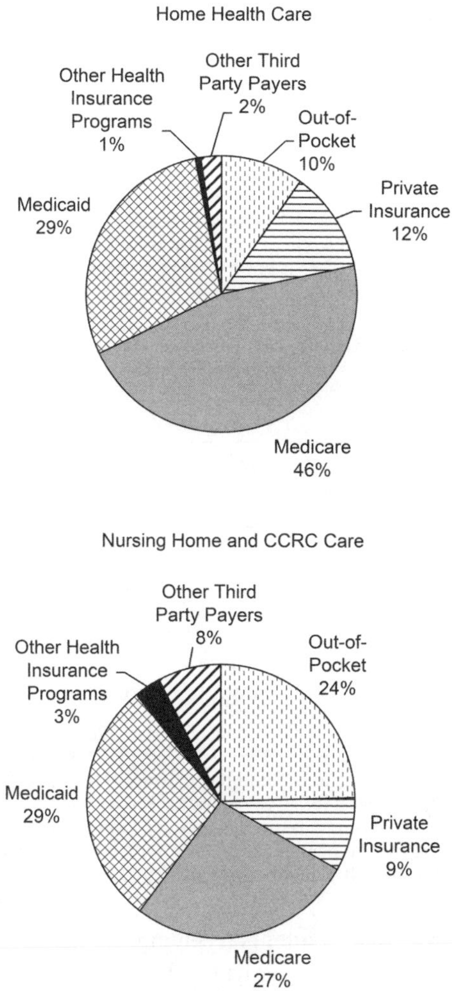

Fig. 10.6 Percent spent on home health care and nursing care facilities, by source of funds, United States, 2018

Note: Data are for the year 2018. Centers for Medicare and Medicaid (CMS) National Health Expenditures data. Nursing home care includes nursing home facilities and continuing care retirement communities (CCRC). Spending is adjusted by the share of recipients who are under 65, with the assumption that all of the under 65 recipients are receiving funding from sources other than Medicare, which is not adjusted.

eighth of the total. Although again, the coverage by Medicare is short-term while Medicaid covers a large proportion of truly long-term care. Consistent with that fact, the majority of nursing home residents have their costs covered by Medicaid rather than Medicare or are paying for their stays from private resources. A report from the Kaiser Family Foundation found that

Table 10.8 Population with LTC insurance, United States, 2018

	65 Plus	85 Plus
Population with LTC Insurance	7,700,000	900,000
Share of 65+/85+ Population	(0.146)	(0.141)
Observations	1,244	186

Notes: RAND-HRS and Health and Retirement Study (HRS), 2018. Combined nursing home/respondent weights from RAND are used for all calculations. All types of long-term care insurance, regardless of whether it covers home care, nursing home care, or both, are counted for the insured indicator.

Table 10.9 Characteristics by LTC insurance, United States, 2018

	65+ Insured	65+ Uninsured	85+ Insured	85+ Uninsured
Total Household Wealth—Mean	1,408,000	733,000	881,000	709,000
Total Household Wealth—Median	657,000	239,000	504,000	163,000
Total Household Income—Mean	72,000	49,000	52,000	40,000
Total Household Income—Median	49,000	33,000	37,000	24,000
In Nursing Home (> 100 days)	0.02	0.02	0.08	0.08
Any Home Care Last 2 Yrs	0.13	0.11	0.23	0.25
Live with Spouse or Partner	0.65	0.58	0.32	0.28
Formal Help with ADL/IADLs	0.01	0.02	0.03	0.07
Informal Help with ADL/IADLs	0.10	0.13	0.23	0.26
Observations	1,244	7,726	186	1,136

Notes: RAND-HRS and Health and Retirement Study (HRS), 2018. Combined nursing home/respondent weights are used for all calculations. All calculations are in 2019 dollars and income is post-tax, estimated using Taxsim. All types of long-term care insurance, regardless of whether it covers home care, nursing home care, or both, are counted for the insured indicator. All variables (income, wealth, types of help) are defined as they were in previous tables.

the share of nursing home residents receiving Medicaid coverage averaged 62 percent across states but ranged from a high of 80 percent in the District of Columbia, to a low of 48 percent in Iowa.[9] Medicaid thus plays a critical role, both in paying for long-term care among low-income and low-wealth elderly and in providing a safety net for those who exhaust their resources to purchase formal care.

10.2.2 Private Insurance

As noted above, there is a relatively small market for private long-term care insurance; 15 percent of the elderly have such private insurance (table 10.8), and only 12 percent of the cost of nursing home care is financed by such insurance. The characteristics of those holding private insurance are shown in table 10.9. Those with private insurance are wealthier and have higher

9. Kaiser Family Foundation (2017).

income than those without, but they do not appear to be in significantly worse health. As Finkelstein and McGarry (2006) document, this pattern arises from two offsetting forms of selection in the market. Those purchasing private insurance include both those who expect to use more care than average (adverse selection) and those who are particularly risk averse—the latter population is healthier on average, and thus "positively selected."

Some in the group without private insurance coverage may lack any sort of coverage and will need to cover such expenses with their own funds. However, others are likely to have sufficiently low income and assets that they are (or would likely become) eligible for Medicaid if they should need long-term care.

The lack of a more robust private insurance market has been attributed to numerous factors including a misunderstanding of Medicare coverage, suspicions regarding whether insurance companies will agree to pay for covered care if it is needed, the solvency of such companies, the high cost of policies, and the risk of future premium increases (Brown et al. 2012). Over time there has been considerable consolidation in the industry as many insurance providers have dropped out of the market and benefits from private plans often fall short of full insurance with a limited amount per day, a limited number of days/years, and little inflation protection.

In an effort to encourage the private market to develop further, state and federal governments have provided various tax incentives for the purchase of policies in general and for partnership plans which allow individuals to leverage public and private support. Premiums for "qualified" long-term care insurance policies are considered medical expenses and may be tax deductible.[10] Partnership plans are long-term care insurance plans that are tied to state Medicaid plans. Individuals who purchase such policies may qualify for Medicaid coverage despite having assets above the Medicaid limits. This practice allows individuals to preserve a certain amount of assets, typically equivalent to the amount paid for by the private long-term care insurance policy, and receive Medicaid funding of long-term care when (and if) long-term care costs exceed the policy limits.[11] The private coverage reduces the state's Medicaid spending because the initial costs of stays are paid for privately and allows individuals to retain resources should they exit long-term care or wish to reserve some funds for other purposes (for example, leaving an inheritance to children). Costa-Font and Raut (2021) find that these policies do increase the purchase of long-term care insurance and decrease Medicaid uptake.

10. Medical expenses are tax deductible from federal income tax if they total more than 7.5 percent of an individual's adjusted gross income, so such deductibility is unlikely to be helpful to relatively healthy individuals. States too may offer some deductibility of premiums.

11. States have set minimum coverage requirement. For example, New York State requires a minimum of three years of private coverage and a given amount of coverage per day, the latter of which increases with inflation.

Table 10.10 **Any care by age and ADL, United States, 2018**

	65 Plus	85 Plus
Full Sample	0.17	0.41
0 ADLs, 1+ IADL	0.45	0.50
1 ADL	0.39	0.54
2 ADL	0.64	0.78
3+ ADL	0.84	0.88
Observations	8,970	1,322

Notes: Health and Retirement Study (HRS), 2018. Respondent weights are used for all calculations. The care variable is defined as either being in a nursing home for more than 100 days or having received either formal or informal home help with ADLs, IADLs, or managing money because of a health condition in the last 30 days. We use the RAND nursing home residence and duration variables but exclude those who report being in a nursing home but are given a respondent weight by the HRS rather than a nursing home resident weight, as these individuals were identified by the HRS as living in a different type of residential care setting.

10.2.3 Long-Term Care Receipt

As noted earlier, the need for long-term care is pervasive among the elderly, yet such care is expensive. In table 10.10 we illustrate the fraction of elderly receiving care by age and health categories. Seventeen percent of all those in our full sample (including people with no ADL/IADL limitations) are receiving some sort of assistance, whether in a nursing home or at home, the latter including both formal and informal care. Here we see a stark difference by age, with 41 percent of the oldest old receiving assistance. However, once we condition on the number of limitations, the distributions are similar: 64 percent of those 65 or older with two ADL limitations receive help while 78 percent of those 85 or older do. Similarly, for those with three or more limitations, the comparable figures are 84 and 88 percent. These latter numbers also suggest that a significant fraction of those with a large number of limitations are not receiving assistance, though some of this may be due to underreporting of care and to differences in the severity of what constitutes a limitation.

Figure 10.7 considers the types of care received for those who do receive care. We consider four types of care: long-term nursing home care, formal home care only, informal home care only, and both formal and informal home care. We exclude from this figure those receiving 100 or fewer days of nursing home care. Short stays like these are typically covered by Medicare and are to enable an individual to leave a hospital more quickly after an acute event, and thus not what we generally think of as long-term care. We define formal home care as paid help with ADLs/IADLs from a non-relative or friend, and informal home care as either unpaid help with ADLs/IADLs or paid help with these activities from a relative.

The majority of elderly care recipients, 69 percent (57 percent among the oldest old) receive only informal home care, while just 5 percent receive only

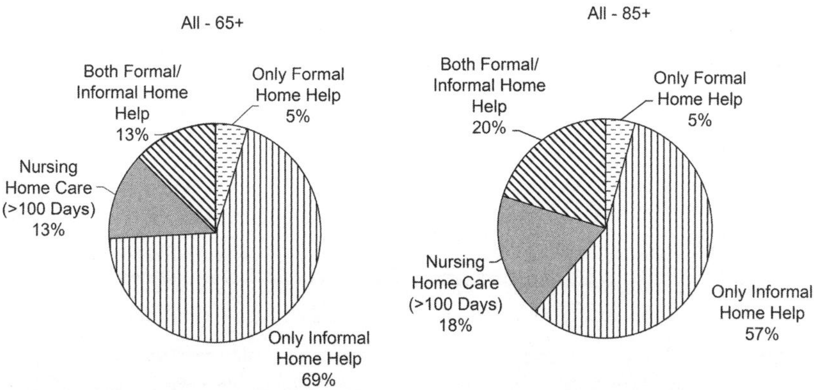

Fig. 10.7 Type of care received by age, United States, 2018

Notes: Health and Retirement Study (HRS), 2018. Respondent weights are used for all calculations. Some respondents do not report the type of at-home help they receive from some helpers. If this is the case for all of their helpers, they are omitted from these figures. We use the RAND nursing home residence and duration variables but exclude those who report being in a nursing home but are given a respondent weight by the HRS rather than a nursing home resident weight, as these individuals were identified by the HRS as living in a different type of residential care setting. Informal help is defined as help provided without pay or by a paid relative, while formal help is paid help by a non-relative. Help can be with ADLs, IADLs, or managing money due to a health problem.

formal home care. The share in a nursing home and the share receiving both formal and informal care are similar at 13 percent. Among the oldest old, the shares in a nursing home or receiving both formal and informal home care are each approximately 50 percent larger than for the entire 65 or older needy population.

Figure 10.8 presents a useful way to illustrate how the types of care received vary with health limitations, first for all elderly, then for the oldest old. The X-axis documents the number of limitations, while the Y-axis shows the percentage of individuals receiving each type of care. As the elderly become more limited in their health, the odds of using only informal care fall—dramatically so once elders have more than two ADLs. But even among those with three or more ADLs, roughly half the population receives only informal care, likely indicating a significant burden on family caregivers. Both nursing home care and the use of a mix of formal and informal care rise with the number of ADLs. As with figure 10.7, the results for the oldest old are similar. These figures illustrate the crucial role that informal care plays in the lives of the elderly in the United States—even among the oldest and most impaired individuals. In fact, the fraction of individuals receiving only informal care, regardless of age or the number of limitations, is consistently greater than that receiving all other types of care combined. We later return to what this care means to family members.

Table 10.11 shows the distribution of formal and informal hours of care

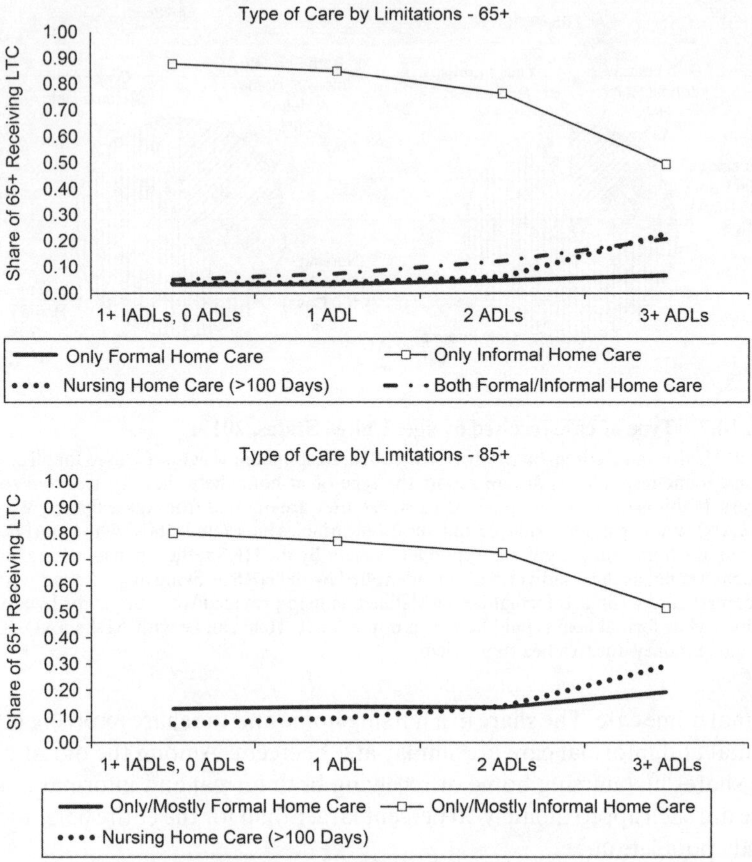

Fig. 10.8 Type of care received by age and limitations, United States, 2018

Notes: Health and Retirement Study (HRS), 2018. Respondent weights are used for all calculations. Some respondents do not report the type of at-home help they receive from some helpers. If this is the case for all of their helpers, they are omitted from these figures. We use the RAND nursing home residence and duration variables but exclude those who report being in a nursing home but are given a respondent weight by the HRS rather than a nursing home resident weight, as these individuals were identified by the HRS as living in a different type of residential care setting. Informal help is defined as help provided without pay or by a paid relative, while formal help is paid help by a non-relative. Help can be with ADLs, IADLs, or managing money due to a health problem. ADLs and IADLs are defined as before. Due to sample size restrictions, we report only/mostly formal and informal home care for the 85+ population, where people who receive both types are assigned to the type from which they receive the most hours.

by age. As noted earlier, the distributions of hours of care for both formal and informal care are relatively skewed—the median number of formal hours is 14 while the mean is 28. For informal care, these numbers are 9 and 26. Those who are 85 years old or older receive more of each type of care, with the difference between all elderly and the oldest more notable for formal than for informal care.

Table 10.11 Distribution of weekly hours received by type, United States, 2018

	65+		85+	
	Formal	Informal	Formal	Informal
5th Percentile	1	0	1	1
10th Percentile	1	1	2	1
25th Percentile	4	3	6	3
50th Percentile	14	9	26	11
75th Percentile	41	32	55	36
90th Percentile	83	86	110	110
95th Percentile	110	114	114	114
Mean	28	26	38	29
Observations	268	1,350	106	375

Notes: Health and Retirement Study (HRS), 2018. Respondent weights are used for all population estimate calculations. Nursing home residents are automatically excluded from all calculations. Hours include care received from helpers who assist with ADLs, IADLs, and managing money because of a health problem. Hours of help from each helper are limited to 16 hours per day to allow for 8 hours of rest. Respondents could provide the number of days either overall in the last month, per week, or as every day. In the first case, the days per month was divided by 4.35 (365/7 * 12). Informal help is defined as help provided without pay or by a paid relative, while formal help is paid help by a non-relative.

Overall, the receipt of long-term care is increasing substantially with both age and limitations. Moreover, the mode of care shifts from informal to formal care as limitations increase. We next turn to more detailed discussions of the formal and informal care sectors.

10.2.4 Formal Long-Term Care Supply

Formal long-term care in the United States is supplied by both nursing homes and formal home care workers. There are over 15,000 nursing homes in the United States, containing almost 1.7 million beds (table 10.12). With 50 million individuals ages 65 or older, that amounts to three beds per 100 elderly persons and about 25 beds per 100 persons ages 85 or older. Approximately 80 percent of these beds are occupied at any point in time. We mentioned previously the substantial shift that has occurred over the past few years from institutional-based care to home care years, and that shift is reflected in falling occupancy rates from over 90 percent in 1993 (DuNah et al. 1995) to under 80 percent in 2018 (table 10.12).

As shown in table 10.13, there is significant variation in nursing home occupancy and capacity across the United States, suggesting that the difficulty in finding appropriate care may also vary. The nursing home occupancy rates varies from 62 to 92 percent while the number of beds per 100 elderly residents similarly varies from 0.9 to 6.2.

In addition to cost concerns, a major criticism of the nursing home industry in the United States is the quality of care, and statistics back up these critiques. In 2016, nearly 45 percent of facilities were cited as deficient in

Table 10.12 Absolute number of nursing homes, beds, and occupancy rate, United States, 2018

	US, 2018
Nursing homes	15,600
Beds	1,655,400
Pop 65+	52,350,000
Beds per pop 65+	0.03
Pop 85+	6,540,000
Beds per pop 85+	0.25
Nursing home residents	1,320,000
Occupancy rate	79.8%
Nursing home employment	1,630,000

Source: Nursing home resident and bed data are from Sengupta et al. (2022), employment data are from the Census Bureau (2021), and the population data are from the OECD. Occupancy rate is defined as the number of residents divided by the number of beds. Nursing home residents are counted as a point in time estimate in the third quarter of 2018.

Table 10.13 Distribution of nursing homes occupancy rate and beds across states, United States, 2016 & 2019

Percentile	Occupancy rate (%)—2019	Nursing home beds per one hundred 65+—2016
5%	65	1.60
10%	68	1.97
20%	73	2.40
50%	82	3.41
80%	86	5.01
90%	88	5.50
95%	90	5.75
Min	62	0.89
Max	92	6.20

Source: Beds data comes from CDC NCHS (2017). Occupancy rate from Kaiser Family Foundation (2022).

infection control, 40 percent were lacking in food sanitation, 34 percent in the general quality of care, and 25 percent cited for the unnecessary use of drugs (Harrington et al. 2018). A variety of factors, ranging from payer mix to staffing levels, have been shown to be correlated with quality of care (Weech-Maldonado et al. 2019; Chen and Grabowski 2015). Of particular interest has been the relationship between the for-profit status of nursing homes and the quality of care. A recent influential study found that nursing home mortality is significantly higher for those institutions owned by large private companies while non-profit nursing homes typically fare better on this measure (Gupta et al. 2021; GAO 2020).

Formal home care is delivered both by agencies specializing in this business as well as by independent caregivers hired directly by care recipients.

Data on the latter form of care is limited, but in some states Medicaid waiver programs allow individuals to choose between personal care aides working for an agency or those working independently (Spetz et al. 2019). In 2017 almost 5 million people were cared for by home care workers from approximately 11,500 agencies. Over 80 percent of these agencies are for-profit, although many of their patients are covered by Medicare or Medicaid, which have strict limits on rates and the number and type of visits. As is consistent with the large number of agencies, most agencies are relatively small, with 43 percent providing care to fewer than 100 people per year. At the other end of the distribution, 33 percent of agencies provided care for 300 or more patients. The services provided in the formal home care sector vary widely and include nursing care (administering medication, monitoring vital signs), therapeutic services (rehabilitation after surgery), personal care (typically help with ADLs), and homemaking services (help with IADLs). However, there is considerable overlap in the provision of these services, with home health aides often providing more than one type of care.

Payment for these formal home care services depends upon patient characteristics and needs. As discussed earlier, Medicare covers skilled nursing care at home in both a post-acute and long-term context, but only for set periods of time after which the need for care is reassessed. Notably, it does not cover personal/custodial care unless such care is in conjunction with needed skilled care. Conversely, Medicaid will cover personal and custodial care as well as nursing care and household services and, as noted earlier, through recent waiver programs can provide additional services such as meals and transportation to help individuals remain in the community.

Both nursing homes and home health care agencies employ workers with varying levels of skills—with employees classified as aides, licensed practical nurses, registered nurses and social workers. (Absent from this discussion are non-patient facing employees like janitorial staff or office managers.) The least skilled workers are typically termed nurses' aides. This position requires no formal education and a minimal level of training, although requirements vary across states. Table 10.14 provides some descriptive information on the distribution of required training hours. Thirty-three states require just 75 hours of training for a nurses' aide (less than two weeks of full-time work)

Table 10.14 **Training requirements for formal home care workers, United States, 2016**

Minimum training hours required by state	# states	Population aged 65+ living in states with corresponding minimum training hours	Share of US population aged 65+
75 hours	33	35,288,595	72%
76–119 hours	11	5,114,669	10%
120+ hours	7	8,798,807	18%

Source: Paraprofessional Healthcare Institute (2016)

and 72 percent of the elderly population live in one of these states. Another 11 states require somewhere between 75 and 120 hours, and just 7 states require 120 hours or more.

Further up the skill ladder are licensed practical nurses (LPNs) and registered nurses (RNs). To be certified as an LPN one typically must have a full year of specialized schooling, while RNs are required to hold a four-year nursing degree. Finally, a small share of long-term care workers is licensed social workers; these workers are typically required to hold a graduate degree (a master's of social work, or MSW) in addition to four years of college. Licensed social workers do not directly provide care but help in the coordination of care.

As shown in figure 10.9, the prevalence of various types of workers differs substantially by type of long-term care. At home health agencies, the majority of the workers are highly skilled registered nurses, and roughly one-quarter are nurses' aides. But in nursing homes, almost two-thirds of workers are nursing aides, while only 12 percent are registered nurses.

These differences in skill levels are reflected in the amounts earned by long-term care workers (table 10.15). Wages for nursing assistants average only \$12 –\$13/hour, a figure below the average wage in the United States for those with less than a high school degree. Indeed, average earnings for a nurse's aide are not very far above the US poverty line for a family of four, and median earnings are below it. In contrast, registered nurses earn \$29 per hour on average, an amount approximately equal to the mean wage for all hourly workers in the United States, but well below the wages earned by those with a college degree or more. Earnings for LPNs lie between these nursing aids and registered nurses.

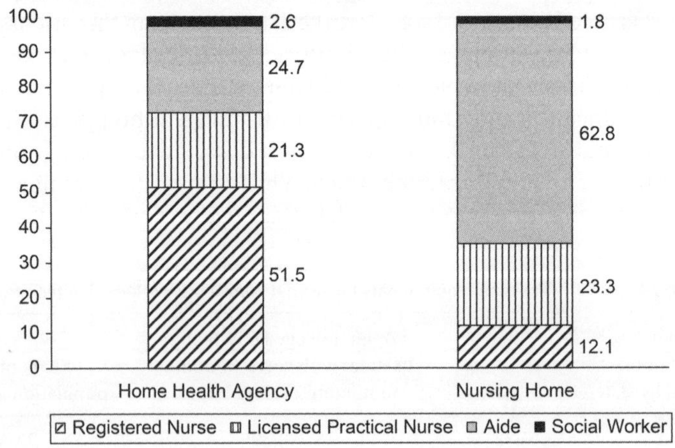

Fig. 10.9 Percent distribution of nurses, aides, and social workers at care facilities, United States, 2018

Source: Data are from Sengupta et al. (2022)

Table 10.15 **Pay for full-time care workers at nursing facilities and in home health care, United States, 2018**

Occupation titles	Mean hourly wage	Median hourly wage	Annual mean wage	Annual median wage
Panel 1: Nursing Home Industry				
Nursing Assistants	13.47	12.81	29,000	25,000
Licensed Practical Nurses	20.94	20.46	47,000	42,000
Registered Nurses	28.69	28.07	63,000	61,000
Panel 2: Home Health Care Industry				
Nursing Assistants & Home Health Aides	12.32	11.48	28,000	24,000
Licensed Practical Nurses	18.29	17.97	41,000	40,000
Registered Nurses	29.30	29.39	66,000	61,000
Panel 3: All Industries				
All Workers	28.74	21.29	64,000	46,000
No High School Degree	15.67	13.97	36,000	30,000
No College Degree	19.97	17.47	46,000	37,000
College Degree or More	37.80	31.61	93,000	70,000
Average Minimum Wage in 2018	8.89	8.40		
Poverty Line for a family of 4)			25,600	

Notes: All wage calculations are made using the 2018 ACS, but dollar denominated values are in 2019 dollars. The occupation and industry variables are used to identify those working as RNs, LPNs, and CNAs. Because the wage/salary income is reported annually, hourly wages are estimated by dividing the annual totals by the product of usual hours per week and weeks worked in the last year. Because this measure can be noisy for those working part-time, we restrict the sample to those working more than 30 hours per week and more than 40 weeks in the last year. Wages by for each group (row) are also winsorized at the 5th and 95th percentiles. In ACS person weights are used in all calculations. Minimum wage data for states was collected from the Department of Labor and are for 2018. Calculations are weighted by the 18–64-year-old populations of each state, estimated from the American Community Survey 2018.

10.2.5 Who Are the Caregivers?

As emphasized earlier, home care for the elderly can be provided either by formal (paid) caregivers or informal (unpaid) caregivers, or both. Table 10.16 shows the population of helpers of each type constructed from data from the HRS and using population weights to inflate the number to national totals. We estimate that there are 1.9 million people in the United States providing formal help with ADLs or IADLs to those ages 65 or older; 800,000 of these 1.9 million are providing help to those 85 years old or older. This amounts to 3.7 helpers per 100 persons ages 65 or older, and 12.6 per 100 persons ages 85 or older. A much larger population of individuals provide informal care. In 2018 approximately 10.6 million people were providing informal

Table 10.16 Home care provision—population estimates, United States, 2018

	65 Plus	85 Plus
Formal Helpers—ADL/IADLs	1,900,000	800,000
Relative to 65+/85+ Population	(0.037)	(0.126)
Relative to 18–64 Population	(0.010)	(0.004)
Informal Helpers—ADL/IADLs	10,600,000	3,100,000
Relative to 65+/85+ Population	(0.200)	(0.490)
Relative to 18–64 Population	(0.052)	(0.016)
All Helpers—ADL/IADLs	12,500,000	3,900,000
Relative to 65+/85+ Population	(0.237)	(0.618)
Relative to 18–64 Population	(0.062)	(0.020)
Observations	2,684	823

Notes: Health and Retirement Study (HRS) 2018. Respondent weights are used for all population estimate calculations. Those providing help to nursing home residents are automatically excluded from all calculations. ADLs and IADLs are defined as before. Informal help is defined as help provided without pay or by a paid relative, while formal help is paid help by a non-relative.

care to the elderly, and of these 30 percent were providing care to those 85 years old or older.

Figure 10.10 shows the demographic characteristics of formal and informal caregivers. Formal home care workers are overwhelmingly female; only 12 percent of paid home care work is delivered by men. Informal home care has a similar gender bias, but it is much less pronounced, with fully one-third of informal home care delivered by men (a figure that remains roughly the same when excluding care from spouses). The gender distribution in the provision of informal care differs by type of care with men more likely to help with IADLS than ADLs. With respect to the age of caregivers, formal home care is largely provided by working age individuals, with 85 percent of formal caregivers less than 60 years old and 60 percent younger than age 50. In contrast, informal home care is delivered primarily by older individuals; more than three-quarters of formal home care is delivered by those ages 50 or greater as one would expect, with adult children providing care for elderly parents who would likely be in their late seventies or eighties when they needed care, and spouses caring for each other.

Formal home care providers have little schooling, with almost one-fifth having no high school degree and only one-tenth having a college degree. In contrast, informal home care is provided by a much more highly educated population. Formal caregivers are also more racially diverse than informal caregivers, with approximately two-thirds being non-white (or Hispanic) compared to only one-third of informal caregivers. This distribution reflects that fact that informal caregivers are typically drawn from the ranks of those with sufficient resources to provide care—either those who have flexibility on

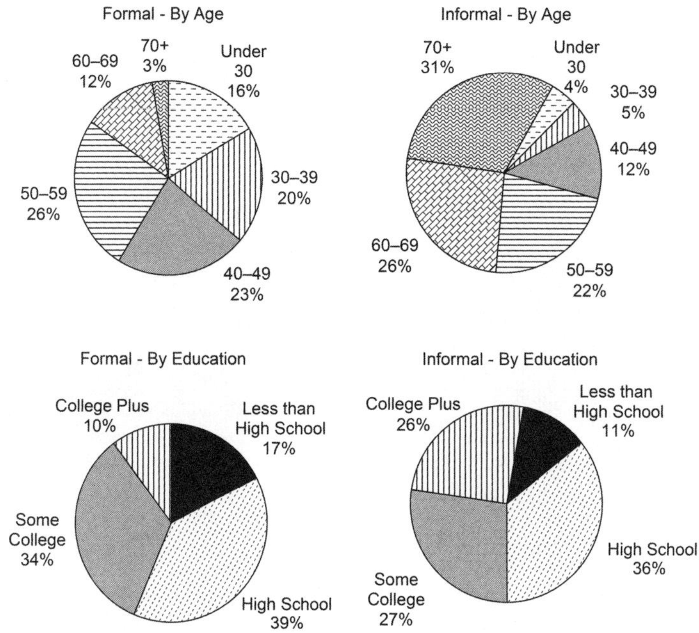

Fig. 10.10 Demographic composition of formal and informal caregivers, United States, 2018

Notes: Data on formal caregivers are from the 2018 American Community Survey, restricting to full-time home health, personal care, and nursing aides in the home care industry and using person weights in generating estimates. Informal care data comes from RAND-HRS and HRS Core Helper data, with respondent weights for the person being helped used in all calculations. Those recorded as helping individuals in nursing homes are excluded. Age and race are provided for spouse, children, and household member helpers. The RAND version of the HRS was used for spouses and the RAND family file for children and other household members. Education is provided for spouses and children helpers. The RAND version of the HRS was used for spouses and the RAND family file for children. Sex and relationship are provided for all helpers in the HRS Core Helper file. Data is for help in 2018, though some family file variables were collected in prior waves. All samples are restricted to informal helpers, defined as those providing unpaid help or paid help to a relative. Age, race, and education are restricted to the helpers for whom we have data.

their jobs, or the financial capacity to reduce labor market effort (Fahle and McGarry 2022). The formal caregiving workforce draws heavily on immigrants, with approximately one-third of formal caregivers being immigrants to the United States compared to only 14 percent of the overall population (Pew Research Center 2020).

Figure 10.11 shows the relationship of informal caregivers to the care recipient. Roughly one-third of informal care is delivered by spouses. The second most common relationship for caregivers is daughters, who provide more than one-quarter of informal care; sons provide only half as large a share.

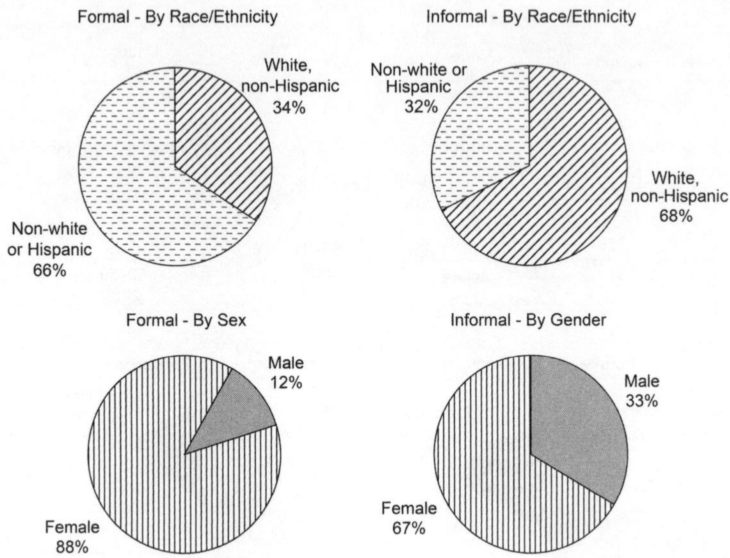

Fig. 10.10 (cont.)

10.3 The Cost of Long-Term Care

As noted earlier, expenditures on long-term care comprise a sizeable share of total health care spending in the United States. Table 10.17 summarizes these total costs. In 2019, total spending for the 1.1 million nursing home residents aged 65+ was approximately $142 billion. Spending on formal health home care is 60 percent as large, despite there being more than three times as many users. Note, however, that embedded in the figures for nursing home expenditures are the costs of room and board; absent this component, costs would be lower. Importantly, these figures do not include Medicaid spending on home-and-community-based services through waiver programs (HCBS), which we exclude because we focus on long-term care for the elderly and a large portion of HCBS recipients are under age 65. For example, only about 30 percent of Section 1915(c) waiver spending, which makes up approximately 60 percent of total Medicaid home care spending, is directed toward programs targeting the elderly and those with physical disabilities (Watts et al. 2020).

Because most home care is provided informally, typically by relatives, a proper accounting of the total cost of long-term care in the economy should include the opportunity cost of their time as well. Valuing the opportunity cost of informal caregivers raises a number of difficult issues and requires numerous assumptions. In the simplest model, with perfectly competitive labor markets and market wages equal to the value of leisure, the value of time spent in informal care would be the forgone wage. If high potential

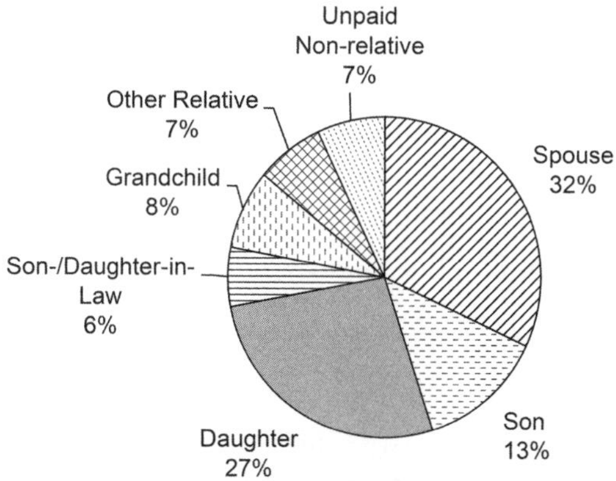

Fig. 10.11 Informal caregivers by relationship to care recipient, United States, 2018

Notes: Data on informal caregivers come from the HRS Core Helper file, with respondent weights for the person being helped used in all calculations. Those recorded as helping individuals in nursing homes are excluded. The helper relationship is provided for all helpers in the HRS Core Helper file. Data are for help in 2018. The sample is restricted to informal helpers, defined as those providing unpaid help or paid help to a relative.

Table 10.17 Formal care costs, annual, United States, 2018

Types	Number of users	Total spending (billion $)
Nursing home	1,100,000	142
Home health agency	4,100,000	89

Source: Number of users for formal care come from NCHS 2017–2018 Vital Health Statistics (Sengupta et al. 2022). Total spending on formal care come from CMS National Health Expenditure tables. Spending for nursing homes includes continuing care retirement communities, while number of users does not. Both the number of users and spending are multiplied by 1—proportion of users under age 65 (17 percent of both HHA and nursing home users are under 65, per Sengupta et al. 2022). Note that the number of users for nursing homes is a point in time estimate while home health agency users is for the full year in 2017.

wage individuals choose to provide informal care themselves rather than purchase such care, it is either because they receive sufficient utility from the provision of care, or because the care they provide is of sufficiently higher quality relative to what is available in the formal market to justify the "cost."

In such a model with the value of leisure equal to the forgone wage, the value of an hour of care provided by those who are not employed would be equal to the wage that they would receive if they were to enter the labor market, as it would be for those who are employed. In practice, however, retired individuals often do not have work opportunities that are equal to their value of leisure, which is why retirement is marked by a complete, rather than gradual, exit from work. It is also hard to value the potential wage for workers who are very old and/or have been retired for many years.

We therefore consider two options for valuing hours of informal care. In each case, we begin by estimating the probability the caregiver is working and by imputing an hourly wage. We then multiply the probability of working by the imputed wage, and then again by the number of hours of care provided. We add to that the product of the probability of not working, the imputed value of leisure hours, and the hours of care provided.

$$\begin{aligned} \textit{Value of care} &= (\textit{Prob of working}) \times (\textit{Imputed wage}) \times (\textit{hours of care}) \\ &\quad + (1 - \textit{Prob of working}) \times (\textit{value of leisure time}) \\ &\quad \times (\textit{hours of care}) \end{aligned}$$

The two options differ in how we value leisure time. In the first option ("low valuation") we value this non-labor market time zero meaning that the value of care is just: (Prob of working) x (Imputed wage) x (hours of care) as the second term in the equation has a value of zero. In the second option ("high valuation"), we value non-labor market hours as the replacement cost of care—that being the average wage for home care workers. Thus, the value of care is that from the "low valuation" + (1 – *Prob of working*) × ($25) × (*hours of care*).

We impute the probability of working and the wage rate as follows: For each caregiver, we have information on a set of characteristics including whether they are paid for care, their gender, and the census region in which the care recipient lives (presumed to be the same for the caregiver). For children, spouses, and other household members, we also know the caregiver's educational attainment, age, race/ethnicity, and marital status. Using data from the 2018 American Community Survey, we then use regression analyses to estimate the predicted probability of working and the predicted wage conditional on working for each caregiver using the set of characteristics that are available for the HRS caregivers.

The results of our estimations are shown in table 10.18 with the low valuation estimate being $86 billion and the high valuation being $151 billion. We note that these valuations differ from what has been frequently used in the literature in which all hours of care are valued at the median or mean wage rate for a caregiver. Were we to use this straightforward calculation with the mean wage rate of $12.32, our value for informal care would be just over $100 billion. We can combine this result with the previous data on formal long-term care spending for the elderly to estimate the distribution of long-term care costs across public and private sources. Two-thirds of the cost of nursing home care is publicly financed with the remainder being paid for from private sources (private insurance or out-of-pocket spending), while four-fifths of the cost of formal home care is publicly financed. In addition to this formal cost, we assume that the full cost of informal care is privately financed. The resulting distribution of spending is shown for both of our valuation methods in table 10.19. Even in the low valuation

Table 10.18 **Informal care valuation, United States, 2018**

	I	II
Valuation (billions of $s)	86.3	150.8
Total Hours Informal Help (billions)	8.35	8.35
Probability of Working	0.480	0.480
Predicted Wage * Probability of Working	10.34	
Predicted Wage if Working	25.47	
Observations	1,960	1,960

Notes: Column I values predicted working hours at the predicted wage, and predicted non-working hours at $0. Column II values predicted working hours at the predicted wage and predicted non-working hours at the average home health aide wage of $12.32 per hour from ACS 2018. Respondent weights from the HRS are used in all calculations. Valuations are done at the helper level, with predicted wages and probabilities of work calculated separately for the sample broken into 3 main groups: (1) Spouses, Children, and Household Members; (2) Household Members missing education data; and (3) other helpers. Group 1 valuations used ACS data for 4 education categories, 4 regions, 6 age groups, sex, marital status, and white vs non-white to separately predict the probability of work and the wage conditional on working. Group 2 valuations used ACS data for 9 Census Divisions, 6 age groups, sex, marital status, and white vs non-white to separately predict the probability of work and the wage conditional on working. Group 3 valuations used ACS data for 9 Census Divisions and sex to separately predict the probability of work and the wage conditional on working. Some individuals were missing one of the variables used for their group. Their probability of work and wages were predicted using ACS data that excluded the variable(s) they were missing. Hourly wages in the ACS were top-coded to $100. Nursing home residents were excluded from the analysis and only hours for those helping with ADLs were included. Informal care from paid relatives is also excluded, since this has already been compensated. Valuation and hours are in billions. All dollar amounts are in 2019 dollars.

Table 10.19 **Total costs by type of care and source, United States, 2018**

		Cost I		Cost II	
Care Type	Source	2019 $s	% GDP	2019 $s	% GDP
Nursing Home	Public	95	0.5%	95	0.5%
	Private	47	0.2%	47	0.2%
	All	142	0.7%	142	0.7%
Home Care	Public	70	0.3%	70	0.3%
	Private	19	0.1%	19	0.1%
	All	89	0.4%	89	0.4%
Informal Care	Private	86	0.4%	151	0.7%
Total	Public	165	0.8%	165	0.8%
	Private	152	0.8%	217	1.0%
	All	317	1.6%	382	1.8%

Notes: Total spending in 2018 on formal care come from CMS National Health Expenditure tables. Spending for nursing homes includes continuing care retirement communities, while number of users does not. Both the number of users and spending are multiplied by 1—proportion of users under age 65 (17% of both HHA and nursing home users are under 65, per Sengupta et al., 2022). The informal care costs correspond to columns I and 2 of Table 2.C.2. The NHE categories of other health insurance programs and other third party payers are included in the public category. All dollars are reported in 2019 terms.

method we find that almost half of long-term care "costs" are accounted for by private sources. At the higher valuation for informal care, we find that almost 60 percent of costs are informal or privately paid. Moreover, under the high valuation scenario, informal care costs are higher than the cost of either nursing home or formal home care, comprising approximately 40 percent of all costs.

10.4 Conclusions

To anyone with experience arranging care for an elderly family member, the dramatic costs of such care come as no surprise. The median cost of a year in a private nursing home room in the United States is over $108,000, and a year of formal home care can easily exceed $30,000 at just a total of four hours of care per day. While individuals bear much of this cost through out-of-pocket spending, the largest private cost is through the informal provision of home care for elderly relatives. And combining the two, we estimate national expenses on long-term care for the elderly in 2018 of $382 billion.

One dimension in which the United States differs from other countries is the mechanism for paying for the formal portion of this care. While many countries have specific public insurance programs for the provision of long-term care—programs that are typically paid for by dedicated taxes—the majority of long-term care in the United States is paid for by programs established to provide health care coverage more generally and extended to long-term care in only certain cases, either temporary care or through means-tested programs. Yet despite the lack of a specific long-term care program, the majority of formal long-term care in the United State is in fact financed by the government, with individuals shouldering about 19 percent out of pocket.

However, this fact can be deceiving in that the elderly often rely on informal support from family members, a burden that falls primarily on women. Our estimates suggest that the imputed costs of such care are far larger than those paid for either nursing home or formal home care. This burden exists not just in the United States but around the world as estimates in other chapters in this volume demonstrate.

As significant as these costs are, and as much as families struggle with finding or providing appropriate care, the difficulty is likely to increase in the coming years as the population continues to age. Not only is the number of elderly individuals growing rapidly but the greatest rate of increase is among the oldest old, ages at which care is typically the most intensive. While the demand for long-term care is increasing, the population of individuals able to provide that care is decreasing in relative terms due to lower fertility and increased labor force participation among women.

Dealing with these issues on not just a national but on a worldwide level is paramount. There is much to be learned by comparing the long-term care infrastructures across countries, and future advances in medical science and technology provide hope for improvements in the long-term care landscape. While the situation in the United States provides evidence on how private insurance systems might be structured and more recently, in understanding how non-medical forms of assistance might be used to reduce the reliance on institutional spending, the United States in turn can learn from other nations how a national public insurance system might best be employed and the advantages and pitfalls associated with such a mechanism.

References

American Council on Aging. 2021. State Specific Medicaid Eligibility Requirements. https://www.medicaidplanningassistance.org/state-specific-medicaid-eligibility/.

Brown, J. R., G. S. Goda, and K. McGarry. 2012. "Long-Term Care Insurance Demand Limited by Beliefs about Needs, Concerns about Insurers, and Care Available from Family." *Health Affairs* 31 (6): 1294–1302.

Budiman, A. 2020. "Key Findings about U.S. Immigrants." Pew Research Center. August 20. https://www.pewresearch.org/fact-tank/2020/08/20/key-findings-about-u-s-immigrants/.

Centers for Medicare and Medicaid Services. 2014. U.S. Personal Health Care Spending By Age and Gender. https://web.archive.org/web/20211104232912/https://www.cms.gov/Research-Statistics-Data-and-Systems/Statistics-Trends-and-Reports/NationalHealthExpendData/Downloads/AgeandGenderHighlights.pdf.

Centers for Medicare and Medicaid Services. 2021. National Health Expenditures by Type of Service and Source of Funds, CY 1960–2022. Baltimore, MD: Centers for Medicare and Medicaid Services. Zip file, https://www.cms.gov/data-research/statistics-trends-and-reports/national-health-expenditure-data/historical.

Chen, M. M., and D. C. Grabowski. 2015. "Intended and Unintended Consequences of Minimum Staffing Standards for Nursing Homes." *Health Economics* 24 (7): 822–39.

Costa-Font, J., and N. Raut. 2021. "Long-Term Care Partnership Effects on Medicaid and Private Insurance." IZA DP No. 14753. Bonn, Germany: IZA Institute of Labor Economics. https://www.iza.org/publications/dp/14753/long-term-care-partnership-effects-on-medicaid-and-private-insurance.

Department of Labor. 2022. Changes in Basic Minimum Wages in Non-Farm Employment Under State Law: Selected Years 1968 to 2021. https://web.archive.org/web/20220324012351/https://www.dol.gov/agencies/whd/state/minimum-wage/history.

DuNah Jr, R., C. Harrington, B. Bedney, and H. Carrillo. 1995. "Variations and Trends in State

Nursing Facility Capacity: 1978–93." *Health Care Financing Review* 17 (1): 183. https://pubmed.ncbi.nlm.nih.gov/10153471/.

Eiken, S., K. Sredl, B. Burwell, and A. Amos. 2018. *Medicaid Expenditures for Long-Term Services and Supports in FY 2016*. Report, May. Medicaid Innovation Accelerator Program & IBM Watson Health. http://www.advancingstates.org/sites/nasuad/files/ltssexpenditures2016.pdf.

Fahle, S., and K. McGarry. 2022. "How Caregiving for Parents Reduces Women's

Employment: Patterns across Sociodemographic Groups." In *Overtime: America's Aging Workforce and the Future of Working Longer*, edited by L. F. Berkman and B. C. Truesdale, 213–34. New York, NY: Oxford University Press.

Feenberg, D., and E. Coutts. 1993. "An Introduction to the TAXSIM Model." *Journal of Policy Analysis and Management* 12 (1): 189–94.

Finkelstein, A., and K. McGarry. 2006. "Multiple Dimensions of Private Information: Evidence from the Long-Term Care Insurance Market." *American Economic Review* 96 (4): 938–58.

Genworth. 2019. "Cost of Care Survey." https://web.archive.org/web/20200724144720/https://www.genworth.com/aging-and-you/finances/cost-of-care.html.

Gupta, A., S. T. Howell, C. Yannelis, and A. Gupta. 2021. "Does Private Equity Investment in Healthcare Benefit Patients? Evidence from Nursing Homes. NBER Working Paper No. 28474. Cambridge, MA: National Bureau of Economic Research.

Harrington, C., H. Carrillo, R. Garfield, and E. Squires. 2018. "Nursing Facilities, Staffing, Residents and Facility Deficiencies, 2009 Through 2016." Report, April 3. Washington, DC: Kaiser Family Foundation.

Health and Retirement Study (HRS Core) public use data set. 2022. Produced and distributed by the University of Michigan with funding from the National Institute on Aging (grant number NIA U01AG009740). Ann Arbor, MI: University of Michigan.

Kaiser Family Foundation. 2017. "Medicaid's Role in Nursing Home Care." Infographic, June 20. Washington, DC: Kaiser Family Foundation. https://www.kff.org/infographic/medicaids-role-in-nursing-home-care/.

Kaiser Family Foundation. 2022. Certified Nursing Facility Occupancy Rate. Table, State Health Facts. Washington, DC: Kaiser Family Foundation. https://www.kff.org/other/state-indicator/nursing-facility-occupancy-rates/?currentTimeframe=0&sortModel=%7B%22colId%22:%22Location%22,%22sort%22:%22asc%22%7D.

MedPAC. 2021. *Health Care Spending and the Medicare Program.* A Data Book, July. Washington, DC: MedPAC. https://www.medpac.gov/wp-content/uploads/import_data/scrape_files/docs/default-source/data-book/july2021_medpac_databook_sec.pdf.

Murray, C., A. Tourtellotte, D. Lipson, and A. Wysocki. 2021. "Medicaid Long Term Services and Supports Annual Expenditures Report: Federal Fiscal Years 2017 and 2018." January 7. Mathematica & Centers for Medicare and Medicaid Services. Chicago, IL: Mathematica. https://www.medicaid.gov/media/118231.

National Center for Health Statistics. 2017. Health, United States—Data Finder. Table 092: Nursing homes, beds, residents, and occupancy rates, by state: United States, selected years 1995–2016. Hyattsville, MD: National Center for Health Statistics. https://www.cdc.gov/nchs/hus/data-finder.htm?year=2017&table=Table%20092.

Organisation for Economic Co-operation and Development (2022). Healthcare Spending. Accessed 2022, reference year 2021. Paris: OECD. https://data.oecd.org/healthres/health-spending.htm.

Organisation for Economic Co-operation and Development (2022). Population Projections. Paris: OECD.Stat. https://stats.oecd.org/Index.aspx?DataSetCode=POPPROJ.

Ortman, J., V. Velkoff, and H. Hogan. 2014. "An Aging Nation: The Older Population in the United States." Report Number P25–1140, May. Washington, DC: US Census Bureau.

PHI. 2016. Nursing Assistant Training Requirements by State. Infographic. New York, NY: PHI (Paraprofessional Healthcare Institute). http://www.phinational.org/advocacy/nurse-aide-training-requirements-state-2016/.

RAND Corporation. 2022. "RAND HRS Longitudinal File 2018 (V2)." Document TL-A2097–1, August 9. https://doi.org/10.7249/TLA2097–1.

Ruggles, S., S. Flood, R. Goeken, M. Schouweiler, and M. Sobek. 2022. IPUMS USA: Version 12.0 [American Community Survey]. Minneapolis, MN: IPUMS.

Sengupta, M., J. P. Lendon, C. Caffrey, A. Melekin, and P. Singh. 2022. "Post-Acute and Long-Term Care Providers and Services Users in the United States, 2017–2018." *Vital Health Statistics Series 3* May (47): 1–93.

Spetz, J., R. I. Stone, S. A. Chapman, and N. Bryant. 2019. "Home and Community-Based Workforce for Patients with Serious Illness Requires Support to Meet Growing Needs." *Health Affairs* 38 (6): 902–9.

St. Louis Fed. 2022. Federal Reserve Economic Data. https://fred.stlouisfed.org/series/GDPA.

U.S. Government Accountability Office. 2020. Letter from John E. Dicken, director of Health Care, to Senator Ron Wyden, "Infection Control Deficiencies Were Widespread and Persistent in Nursing Homes Prior to COVID-19 Pandemic," May 20. https://www.gao.gov/assets/gao-20–576r.pdf.

U.S. Census. 2021. 2018 SUSB Annual Data Tables by Establishment Industry. May. Washington, DC: Census Bureau. https://www.census.gov/data/tables/2018/econ/susb/2018-susb-annual.html.

Watts, M. O., M. Musumeci, and P. Chidambaram. 2020. "Medicaid Home and Community-Based Services Enrollment and Spending." Executive Summary, February 4. Washington, DC: Kaiser Family Foundation. https://www.kff.org/medicaid/issue-brief/medicaid-home-and-community-based-services-enrollment-and-spending/.

Weech-Maldonado, R., R. Pradhan, N. Dayama, J. Lord, and S. Gupta. 2019. "Nursing Home

Quality and Financial Performance: Is There a Business Case for Quality?" *Inquiry* 56: 0046958018825191. https://doi.org/10.1177%2F0046958018825191.

Author Index

Subject Index

Note: Page numbers followed by *f* or *t* refer to figures or tables, respectively.